GORBACHEV

THE MAN AND THE SYSTEM

GORBACHEV

ILYA ZEMTSOV
JOHN FARRAR

Transaction Publishers
New Brunswick (U.S.A.) and London (U.K.)

First paperback printing 2008
Copyright © 1989 by Transaction Publishers, New Brunswick, New Jersey.

This book is printed on acid-free paper that meets the American National Standard for Permanence of Paper for Printed Library Materials.

Library of Congress Catalog Number: 87-30235
ISBN: 978-0-88738-222-2 (cloth); 978-1-4128-0717-3 (paper)
Printed in the United States of America

Library of Congress Cataloging-in-Publication Data

Zemtsov, Ilya
    Gorbachev, the man and the system / Ilya Zemtsov, John Farrar; edited by
  Yisrael Cohen.
      p. cm.
    Bibliography: p.
      1. Gorbachev, Mikhail Sergeevich, 1931- 2. Soviet Union—Politics
  and government—1982- 3. Soviet Union—Foreign relations—1975-
  I. Farrar, John. II. Cohen, Yisrael. III. Title.

DK288.Z46   1988
947.085'4'0924—dc19   87-30235

Contents

Acknowledgments

The authors particularly wish to express their thanks to, and acknowledge the invaluable assistance of, the many without whom this book would have been impossible. Particularly, we wish to express our gratitude for the invaluable research assistance provided over the entire period covered by this book by Professor Solomon Mogilevskiy and Mrs. Faina Perlova. Witold Jedlicki and Esther Rofe must be mentioned for their great contributions in checking data, names, and dates and in proofreading and offering editorial advice.

The largest debt of gratitude, however, goes to Dr. Yisrael Cohen, who edited, advised, and took care of all of the many administrative and technical details involved in preparing and publishing a book.

We, the authors, take complete responsibility for everything said in the book, but without the dedicated support of the aforementioned individuals we could not have completed our work.

Ilya Zemtsov
John Farrar

Prologue: Gorbachev's Dilemma

The seventy years that have passed since the Bolshevik Revolution in Russia are sufficient to allow a broad, retrospective evaluation, perhaps a reevaluation, of Soviet history. From such a perspective one readily discovers that within the framework of a single systemic continuum there has in reality been a succession of differing political models. Each has represented an attempt to reconcile the idealistic and humanistic goals of the ideology with the centralized and authoritarian elements of Leninism, responding to the particular demands of political and economic realities of the day.

Initially, there was an attempt to establish a sort of primitive communism based upon the principles of a classless society, a redistribution of wealth, equal pay for work, and a degree of self-management. This was forcefully imposed by impatient revolutionaries upon a vast, multinational empire that had been brought to a state near collapse and chaos. Under the pressures of establishing a functioning state, and in face of civil war and foreign intervention, the new rulers increasingly turned to arbitrary force. Greater reliance on the Cheka (the secret police) insured the ultimate triumph of the centralizing, authoritarian elements of Leninism over the ideals of the Revolution. This amorphous and self-contradictory political model was short-lived, lasting only until about 1920, less than three years after the Revolution.

It was succeeded by what might be called a naive communism that, in a more structured state, retained certain leanings toward a degree of liberalism and both cultural and economic diversity. These reached their peak with Lenin's New Economic Policy (NEP). The NEP was intended as a temporary, tactical step to salvage a crumbling economy, but by allowing elements of private property and a less than centralized economy, it produced a political-social model distinctly different from what soon followed. Its transformation began at the end of the 1920s when Stalin embarked upon forced industrialization and collectivization. Small and medium-sized private enterprises were done away with, and even the most mildly dissenting views ceased to be tolerated. The result was communist totalitarianism and an epoch of mass repressions and all-encompassing violence in which, inevitably, the totalitarianism of the senior elements of the Party oligarchy was transformed into the totalitarianism of the single dictator and his personal staff secretariat.

In essence, the totalitarian model lasted for many years, continuing through the periods of rule of Stalin, Khrushchev, Brezhnev, Andropov, and Chernenko. Each began his rule as the representative, or the first *among* equals, of a small collective Party leadership, and each set out to become the first *above* equals and then the supreme leader (or *vozhd*). Those who lived long enough after becoming general secretary succeeded in this intramural Party political struggle. They did so basically by two methods: one within the Party, and one aimed at the Party. Within the Party, they employed a combination of cadres policy and administrative reform both to build their own base of support within the hierarchy and to remove actual and potential rivals. When it was needed, they reached beyond the Party and temporarily employed the secret police and/or the armed forces against rivals within the Party.

Khrushchev allowed a temporary degree of controlled intellectual freedom and released large numbers of political prisoners, but did so for the most part to discredit Stalin and his Stalin-associated rivals. Khrushchev also did away with some of the arbitrary police terror applied to senior Party echelons and thus provided the Party oligarchy with a degree of personal security. His successors retained this important distinction from the latter part of Stalin's rule. Nevertheless, the basic economic and social model established by Stalin was unchanged, and the political model underwent only minor fluctuations in terms of the rights and security of the narrow senior Party elite and in the degree to which the Party leadership bought the passive or active support of its principal tools of control, the armed forces and the KGB, the only institutions that could, even theoretically, challenge the Partocracy.

With the death of the last of the old guard, Chernenko, the generation of participants in, and contemporaries of, the Revolution that had ruled the Kremlin for almost seven decades finally left the scene. A new, more pragmatic, and better educated (at least technically) generation led by Mikhail Gorbachev came to power. Like their predecessors, the leaders of this generation have had to be concerned with the consolidation and ensurance of personal power. Their own political socialization has also been in the context of communist totalitarianism, but faced with a stagnating and corrupt economy, they had to repair the system and make it viable for the future. The path that they have set out upon has marked a transition of the regime toward a system that is less totalitarian and more authoritarian. Under Gorbachev certain very restricted but definite whiffs of pluralism have appeared: a limited openness to criticism (*glasnost*), and elements of democracy that although directed and controlled from above, nonetheless appear to have greater content than the hollow and calculated misuse of democratic phraseology in which communist totalitarianism has cloaked its real nature.

Gorbachev has resorted to changing the system from above to forestall its disintegration under its own weight and from pressures for reform from below. The real questions are whether this change will prove permanent, and whether it will generate further changes that will fundamentally alter the system in ways that go far beyond the intentions of its implementors.

There are alternative interpretations of Gorbachev's policies. The first is in terms of universal human concepts. In this context the "reconstruction" that he has designed and has already begun implementing is only a palliative, a half-measure. New legislation is introduced, but old instructions retain their force. The people are promised the truth, but given only half the truth. Yet this half-truth contains what for many years was alluded to only in whispers: the existence of corruption, drunkenness, and drug addiction. So far, Gorbachev's half-measure amounts to an impressive-appearing but, in reality, only partially and largely ineffective policy of liberalization.

The other interpretation views Gorbachev's rule in the context of Soviet history. From this perspective it can be seen that Soviet society is undergoing a serious attempt at surgery to remove the malignancies of mature, even superannuated, socialism: political rigidity, intellectual petrification, and dogmatism. For decades the state has been increasingly afflicted by a spreading social paralysis. Gorbachev is attempting to reanimate the Soviet system by generating some dynamism and by teaching people to express their thoughts and take initiative, even if in an as yet clearly circumscribed manner controlled from above.

This process is unfolding slowly because after prolonged stagnation the social organism, like a human organism after serious illness, recovers gradually. The process is also rife with contradictions. Gorbachev's goal is not to change the system but to effect changes within it. He seeks not to transform the regime but merely to revitalize it, to inject some flexibility and dynamism into it. Still, in his "reconstruction" of society Gorbachev has already gone further and done more than any of his predecessors, including Khrushchev, who challenged Stalin's cult of personality only to raise a monument to himself in his own lifetime. Despite his attacks on Stalin, Khrushchev embodied in his person and manner of rule the most ominous features of communism: tyranny, lawlessness, and cruelty. His actions were directed against the subjective side of the system. Gorbachev's policies, in contrast, are directed against objective traits of the system, against its ability to generate new Stalins.

It is here that the contradictions between Gorbachev's motivations and his likely results become most pronounced. Subjectively, Gorbachev intends only to repair the system. He wants to modernize it, to inject some flexibility into it, and to make it capable of sustaining higher productivity. Objectively, however, Gorbachev is undermining the system, its political foundations, and its social structure. The contradiction between his subjective intentions and the objective consequences of his policies will impale him on the horns of a serious dilemma.

The dilemma will come when Gorbachev recognizes that his reforms entail serious dangers for the regime, for the rule of the Partocracy. At that point he will either have to halt his reforms or accept really revolutionary change as inevitable. In the former case he will engender a new wave of reaction. If he opts for fundamental systemic change, objectively it will no longer be appropriate to refer to him as a "communist leader" (although words being very malleable in the USSR, even an actually anticommunist path embarked upon by a Soviet leader would probably be cloaked in nominally communist terminology). The latter outcome does not seem likely as a scenario, but historical precedents in Hungary and Czechoslovakia do not entirely preclude such a possibility, even in the Soviet Union.

In any event, Gorbachev has recently been speaking increasingly of the "revolutionary" nature of his policies. In reality, there is little basis for assessing the changes he has made thus far as truly revolutionary. Rather, they are reformist in nature, for far from affecting the essence of the system, its foundations and principles, they affect only the modes of self-expression and the extent to which it is permissible to expose the ills of the society.

The entire social structure of the state and its basic culture—its morality, psychology, and philosophy—remain unchanged. The changes have been essentially cosmetic, barely touching the system itself. Its totalitarian and repressive character has been somewhat relaxed, but the machinery for repression has not been changed and at any time could be put into high gear. In other words, quantitative indicators may have changed; qualitative features of the system remain constant.

Regardless of the intentions of those who manage the system, the accumulation of changes in quantity can eventually produce a change in quality. If this occurs, it will conform to the laws of development as envisaged by Marxist dialectics. Said another way, Gorbachev's reforms may take on an impetus of their own that will sunder the rigid communist framework in which they are supposed to be contained. In effect, rifts may appear in the ostensibly monolithic foundation of the ideologized society, rifts that might well be all the more irreparable because of uncertainty as to when and where Gorbachev might stop or whether he would stop at all rather than carry his reconstruction to the point of objectively rejecting Soviet Marxism and its anachronistic and change-inhibiting character.

Changes in appearance should not be confused with changes in concept. Yet, concepts have their own dialectic. If Gorbachev calls for a revolution within the Revolution whose seventieth anniversary is now being celebrated, then does it not follow that his call embodies a counterrevolutionary character?

It is not by chance that a reassessment of the October Revolution is now taking place in the USSR. A reassessment is inevitable because of the generational change in the Soviet Union. The Kremlin has been taken over by completely new people, less narrow-minded, less concerned with ideology, and more cynical than their predecessors. These men advanced to positions of real power after the older Bolshevik generations had intellectually and physically exhausted themselves. Only when this had happened did it become possible to reconsider the ideas and ideals of the 1917 revolution. Nevertheless, that revolution, with the millions-strong army of Party apparatchiks it has produced, is entrenched firmly enough to challenge, in turn, Gorbachev and his programs. In the USSR the dead are often stronger than the living, and the past may take revenge on the present by repeating itself. There is precedent for this. Two major attempts at reform have ended in failure: the first in 1956 under Khrushchev, and the second in 1965 under Kosygin. There is, however, a critical difference between the reforms of Khrushchev and Kosygin and those of Gorbachev. The difference is that the previous attempts sought to transform Soviet society before it was socially and psychologically ready for a transformation, and at times when Soviet power was still apparently growing in comparison to its international rivals. Their timing was wrong because conditions were not ripe and the necessity of change not evident.

Gorbachev, in contrast, was propelled to power *by* the demand for major social and economic change. The necessity for change in the Soviet Union is inescapable. Change will take place anyway, with or without Gorbachev. Without change, this great country has no future; therefore, it follows that there is no real future for any individual or institution that stands in the way of change. The actual opposition to Gorbachev's policies could come *not* from the Party elite, desperately anxious to retain its perks and privileges, but from Gorbachev himself. To meet the challenge he will have to transcend his ingrained communist views, and he will have to neutralize the impact of the Soviet past upon his personality.

This is why a study of Gorbachev's personality and its interaction with the Soviet system yields major clues to understanding Soviet society, both in the present and in the future. It is possible that Gorbachev will discard communist orthodoxy. It is more problematic whether he will be able to discard totalitarianism.

Editor's Preface

Since 1977, the International Research Center for Contemporary Society (IRCCS), (formerly the Israel Research Institute for Contemporary Society) (IRICS), in Jerusalem, has produced a wide array of periodicals, special studies, and books dealing with Soviet affairs and international relations. Shortly after Mikhail Gorbachev was elected General Secretary of the Communist Party of the Soviet Union, the IRCCS began to publish a monthly newsletter and analysis of current Soviet developments, *USSR Overview*. As Gorbachev approached the end of his first crucial year in power, the idea was germinated to elaborate upon the data and findings previously published in *USSR Overview* in order to produce a timely assessment of the new Soviet leader's performance during his first year in power and of his probable future policies and prospects. This book, which became a wide ranging study of the interactions between Gorbachev in power and the Soviet system, rather than a capsule history, is the materialization of that idea.

The authors, Professor Ilya Zemtsov and Colonel John Farrar, bring a unique blend of complimentary expertise in, and experience with Soviet affairs to the task at hand. Professor Zemtsov lived most of his life in the Soviet Union, where he was a respected scholar, and a sociologist on the executive board of the Soviet Sociological Association. In those capacities he had direct personal contacts with some of the senior Soviet political elite, including Gaidar Aliev who is now a member of the Politburo. After emigration to the West, Professor Zemtsov founded the IRICS and has been its Director ever since. He is also a member of the American Academy of Political Science and has earned wide renown as the author of numerous articles and books including: *Lexicon of the Soviet Political Language, Soviet Sociology, Corruption in the USSR, The Private Life of the Soviet Elite*, and *Struggle for Power in the Kremlin: I—Andropov*. He has become particularly renowned for his penetrating insights into hidden factors behind Soviet social facades.

Colonel John Farrar, a US Army, retiree, spent over two thirds of his 30 year military career as a specialist in Soviet affairs. He observed the Soviet armed forces first hand as a liaison officer attached to the Group of Soviet

Forces in Germany. As a strategic intelligence officer assigned to the Department of the Army Staff and the Defense Intelligence Agency in Washington and to the International Military Staff at NATO Headquarters, Brussels, Colonel Farrar was directly involved in US and NATO official assessments of the Soviet military, of Soviet foreign policy directions, and of many aspects of the Soviet domestic scene. For four years (1978 to 1982) he had direct responsibility for all defense intelligence support to US arms control negotiations and in the national arms control policy-making arena. In this capacity he not only supervised and prepared political military intelligence inputs to the formation of the US arms control strategy, but also came into personal contact with Soviet negotiators. On his last military assignment, he was director of Soviet and East European studies and also taught arms control, US national security decisionmaking, strategy, intelligence capabilities, and other subjects at the US Army War College in Carlisle, Pennsylvania. From September, 1984, through June, 1987 Colonel Farrar was head of the Department of Strategic Studies at the IRCCS where he was also the managing editor and principal analyst (especially for foreign policy and military developments) for *USSR Overview*. In July, 1987 he returned to the United States. After years of confining his writing to the US classified arena, Colonel Farrar has recently begun to bring his insights to wider public and academic audiences.

In tandem, Professor Zemtsov and Colonel Farrar bring to their analysis almost two lifetimes of study and experience acquired under originally quite different circumstances. As the reader will have the occasion to see, this has allowed them to comprehensively cover virtually every aspect of Soviet reality.

The data and analysis presented in this book are primarily based on Soviet open source materials. These Russian language Soviet sources have been supplemented and compared with a wide range of Western press and academic studies. Only by systematically confronting the Soviet versions of affairs with Western critical commentary on the same issues was it possible to identify the factors shaping Gorbachev's personal identity, his aims, and his new team's achievements, errors, successes, and failures. In this way it was also possible to identify systemic barriers to change in the USSR, restrictions in the range of foreign policy options and the limitations posed by ideologically induced preconceptions. These factors set a limit to what Gorbachev can possibly achieve. Such considerations—backed by a multidisciplinary analysis—shape the book's projections of what the future is likely to bring. However the reader may evaluate particular interpretations of the authors, the insights and conclusions that their book presents need to be taken into account in any fundamental Western assessment of the Soviets and for any informed policy debate on appropriate Western responses.

Dr. Yisrael Cohen

1

A New Leadership for Old Problems and Future Challenges

> *Once more into the breach, dear lads, once more into the breach...*

On 10 March 1985 Konstantin Chernenko died after a prolonged illness, only one year after he replaced Yuri Andropov as general secretary of the Communist Party of the Soviet Union. On the very next day Mikhail Gorbachev was proclaimed as the new Soviet leader.

Thus, a generational change finally took place in the Kremlin leadership. In place of rulers who in one way or another were linked to, or associated with, the Communist Revolution in Russia, a leader came to the fore for whom the establishment of the new state was "ancient" history, not part of his experience or an active part of his consciousness, a person who suffered from neither ideological prejudices or complexes. On the eve of the seventieth anniversary of the Communist coup, there rose to the top of the Kremlin pyramid a figure who, in comparison with other Soviet leaders, was less tied to revolutionary dogmas and agendas. He was a pragmatist for whom the main, the supreme value of the regime was its effectiveness and usefulness, usefulness to the ruling class and to himself personally.

How and why did Gorbachev succeed in attaining top power? The answer to this question should be sought less in the biography of the new Soviet general secretary and more in an understanding of the essence of the system that produced him and adapted him to Communist realities. Furthermore, Gorbachev's life corresponds well to the history of the Soviet state, stems from it, and is quite explicable in its context. He is the first general secretary to have been socially and intellectually formed when the class struggle had almost completely ended and socialism had been achieved in the form in which it had beckoned to the creators of the Russian Revolution (although, as it turned out, not unalterably so).

Gorbachev was born in 1931 in the Northern Caucasus into a peasant family that was one of the first in the region to join a collective farm. He was still young when his father perished during World War II. This unfortunate circumstance had a major effect upon his life: to earn money to help feed his family, deprived of its primary breadwinner, Gorbachev was forced to go to work when he was still in his teens, first as a field worker and subsequently as a combine driver. The determined, diligent, and obviously intelligent youth came to the attention of the regional authorities and received a commendation for his good work. After his completion of secondary school in 1950, the commendation gained him admittance to the most prestigious institution of higher learning in the USSR: Moscow University. As was the case with other such institutions, Moscow University reserved a set number of places for outstanding industrial or agricultural workers. Gorbachev was one.

The student milieu in which young Mikhail found himself was typical of the early postwar years. It contained many demobilized officers who had been admitted to the university outside the normal entrance procedures and often without an examination: people no longer young, tested in battle, but who had not had the opportunity to receive a systematic education or who during the long years of war had forgotten what they once knew. Gorbachev, who had graduated from only a mediocre rural school, excelled to such a degree that he had enough time for sociopolitical activities while his older classmates had to spend hours in the library cramming or, in the little time between classes and sleep, in earning their way through school. Gorbachev's comparatively high stipend from his *kolkhoz* allowed him the freedom for involvement and advancement in Komsomol work. He began making a name for himself there due not only to his free time and his proletarian-peasant origin but also his undoubtedly good mind, which quickly recognized that Komsomol work, more than knowledge, would ensure a successful career. Hence, he entered the Party, and before he reached twenty-one he became a secretary of his faculty's Komsomol organization and thereby a member of the Komsomol committee of the university. Although this was not yet a job, it was still a *nomenklatura* position of regional import.

At this point a hitch occurred in Gorbachev's career. He should have remained in Moscow because top officials of the Komsomol central committee and instructors of the Party's regional committees were drawn from the ranks of activists to which he belonged. Yet, Gorbachev was instead sent, or more precisely ejected, to provincial Stavropol, hardly a plum among Komsomol postings. Considering his education and Party experience at the university, this was an obvious slight that could have had various causes. It may have been that at the university he had blocked the path of the son of some influential person. It may have been that his dynamism and self-esteem were not to the taste of some Komsomol authority. Further, it may have been due to his lack of roots and appropriate connections in the capital. In any event, he was compelled to return to his native region to work off his scholarship. Whatever the reasons for his presence in Stavropol, Gorbachev was one of the few, if not the sole, law graduate of Moscow University in the Komsomol organization there. This, together with the Moscow polish he had acquired, facilitated his rapid advancement in the Party. Within a year he was first secretary of the city Komsomol organization; within another two years, the second and then the first secretary of the Stavropol territorial committee.

How does one explain the ascendant career after Gorbachev's inauspicious departure from Moscow? Among the flood of rumors and explanations surrounding Gorbachev's personality, there is one worthy of consideration and belief: his style of work. He apparently never, at any party forums, meetings, or conferences (at least until his recent assumption of the post of general secretary), took the lead. Rather, he would patiently listen to the views of those around him and then always support the majority view. This usually coincided with the views of the higher-ups. In those rare cases when some Party secretary remained in the minority or even in isolation, which could happen in debates on minor problems or when his downfall was imminent, Gorbachev inobtrusively and under cover of his colleagues joined the majority opposition. Thus, no one had reason to find fault with him: the leadership knew it could count on him at least to the degree it could count on the others, and Party figures around him knew that Gorbachev would neither oppose nor withhold his support from a decision that had a good chance of being taken.

In the territorial (Kray) apparat the feeling grew and soon became a conviction that Gorbachev was a dependable person: someone who could be counted upon, who was distinguished by his knowledge and understanding of how to stay in tune with the Party line. Moreover, he was not a dyed-in-the-wool conservative but could also be found among those who quickly and sensitively reacted to the slightest, as yet barely detectable changes in the policies of the central authorities—and he did this while firmly cleaving to the majority. There was evidently no greater supporter of Stalin when he was being hailed as a genius; nor could one find a more passionate anti-Stalinist than Gorbachev when the Politburo ordered the former idol and "wise teacher" cast from his pedestal and denounced.

What was particularly valued in Gorbachev was his sincerity. He totally identified himself with directives from above. He believed in, and submitted to, the cult of personality as long as the Party did so, and was perturbed by it and criticized it when the Party's attitude changed. These characteristics attracted the attention of Fedor Kulakov, who in 1960 was appointed first secretary of the Stavropol territorial committee of the Party. Kulakov suddenly appeared in the high ranks of the Party. He had evidently been noticed by Khrushchev, who was involved in his latest scheme for reorganizing the government structure and who felt he could make good use of Kulakov's organizational talents, outstanding personality, and appreciation of the value of change. Kulakov was a self-taught agronomist; he graduated from an institute only after he had already attained the rank of deputy minister of the RSFSR. He had worked many years on a state farm (*sovkhoz*) and then at a sugar-processing plant. With such experience, he was intimately acquainted with the problems of Soviet agriculture. He rose to influence on the wave of postwar personnel reshufflings and purges, becoming chairman of the Penza Province Soviet (council). There he attempted, without success, to change the system by which farmers were paid for their work. He proposed to substitute a guaranteed wage for payment in kind (grain and vegetables), calculated on the basis of collective farm workdays. Later Kulakov tried again, in the late 1950s, when he was deputy minister of agriculture of the RSFSR, and this time, with the support of Khrushchev, he succeeded in introducing the change.

To understand and appreciate the significance of Kulakov's reform, one should be acquainted with at least the outlines of the life of Soviet peasantry in the 1940s and 1950s. The peasants' lives were hard, miserable, and discouraging. Their homes were pitiful clay-walled huts, tilted with age, and usually with skimpy roofs made of a mixture of hay and manure. The dwellings were shared with chickens, pigs, and cows, if the peasants were fortunate enough to have them. The interiors were cold, damp, and dark. The stove provided some heat, but smoke filled the room because, to conserve heat, there was no chimney. Peasants performed very strenuous work in the fields or the pigsties, and each received in return a pittance: several dozen kilograms of grain, potatoes, or beets, annually when things went well. Other years they received practically nothing. Recompense in kind for their workdays was given once, after the harvest and calculation of its results. Because quite often the *kolkhoz* failed to furnish the requisite supply of grain, meat, or milk products and did not cover its debts to the state, the *kolkhozniks* would have to feed themselves exclusively from the tiny private plots they worked on the side.

Gorbachev showed himself to be a fervent follower of Kulakov. He did so in part by following his instincts, which instructed him to act as if the boss were always right. But this was not the only reason. An additional possible motivation could be that, having been born in the country and having begun his own work life there at a young age, he was well acquainted with the difficulties of the farmer. In any case, Gorbachev's loyalty was noted and rewarded; in 1962 he was transferred to Party work and to a responsible post, head of the agricultural division of the Party territorial committee. Gorbachev reacted with dispatch and calculation to the favor shown him by the secretary. He apparently resolved to ingratiate himself even further in the latter's favor, and did so by enrolling in the Stavropol agricultural institute instead of relying on the distinction of his Moscow University law diploma. Of course, he may also have been motivated in part by the perceived need to obtain credentials in the field upon which his career seemed now to rest. Nevertheless, the parallel with Kulakov's own education pattern is striking and cannot be dismissed. Although Gorbachev's studies as an external student could not have provided him with a systematic education, this did not prevent the Soviet press from describing him many years later when he became general secretary as a specialist in agronomy. In the meantime his efforts to enrich himself with knowledge of agriculture was appreciated by Kulakov, who viewed his protégé as a model Party worker, always studying, always endeavoring to improve himself.

Acquaintance with, and working alongside, Kulakov brought Gorbachev great advantages and his life was affected in many ways. He not only followed his mentor's instructions but tried to model himself on Kulakov in behavior, manner, and style. Nor did Kulakov disdain his disciple. When he was called to Moscow, where he eventually became a member of the Politburo and a secretary of the Central Committee, Kulakov pulled Gorbachev after him up the slopes of the Party Olympus: in 1966 Gorbachev was made first secretary of the Stavropol city committee of the Party; within a few years he was second and then first secretary of the territorial committee; in 1971 he was made a member of the Central Committee of the CPSU. Then the norms of the Brezhnev gerontocracy brought him a halt. At thirty-nine Gorbachev was the youngest head of a territory. (Gorbachev had always been the youngest in his level in the top *nomenklatura*: first in the society of white-haired professors on the Party committee at Moscow University, then among the members of the Stavropol city and territorial Party committees, and finally in the Central Committee, CPSU itself, where the rule was to allow entrance mainly to superannuated Party functionaries.) It was Gorbachev's youth that blocked his patron from the possibility of moving him into the apparat of the CC. But what Kulakov could not achieve when he was alive was brought about by his sudden and mystifying death, which resulted in Gorbachev's finding a place in Moscow.

In the mid-1970s there was much talk in the Soviet capital about Brezhnev's being seriously ill and the likelihood of his soon being pensioned off. One rumor was that he would receive the symbolic post of chairman of the Presidium of the Supreme Soviet. Then death snatched not Brezhnev but Kulakov; ironically in part because of his robust health coupled with his ambition and his too obvious desire to become Brezhnev's successor. Something quite unexpected, and shocking for the Kremlin veteran, had happened in the Politburo. Defying the rules of the *nomenklatura* game, Kulakov either had attempted, unsuccessfully, to organize a Party conspiracy together with Mazurov and with the support of Podgorny's men, or alone, desperate, and not wishing to take the blame for the failure of agriculture, he had opposed the policies of the general secretary. In either case his death proved the alternative to political disgrace. It was obvious that he could have expected harsh chastisement for his action when the Politburo chiefs Brezhnev, Kosygin, and Suslov were conspicuous by their absense at his funeral.

It is not really clear whether Kulakov committed suicide in despair, as rumor reported, or whether he had sudden heart failure because of his humiliation at the hands of Brezhnev, as the official medical report said. In either case he was the victim of the Politburo. But Brezhnev recovered from his long illness, brought his loyalist Chernenko into the Politburo, and resolved finally to push aside Kosygin and assure himself of a long period of recognition as the sole leader of Party and state.

With Kulakov's demise, the need arose for a new Central Committee secretary who could be blamed for agricultural failures. The choice, which fell on Gorbachev, reflected both cynicism and refined hypocrisy. Having gotten rid of the previous ruler of the agriculturally rich Stavropol territory, those in power gave its present ruler the "opportunity" to find a way out of his predecessor's failures. Contrary to expectations, Gorbachev ultimately succeeded both in avoiding the trap and in becoming general secretary rather than tragically perishing along the way as Kulakov had done. In 1978, however, no one in the Politburo foresaw such an eventuality.

Gorbachev was less a replacement for Kulakov (although this element did play some role, for it was convenient that a supporter and disciple succeeded a secretary who had died under rather mysterious circumstances so as to still some of the rumors disturbing Moscow) than an alternative to him. In contrast to his ambitious and uncompromising predecessor and to the aged Moscow leadership yearning for consensus and tranquility, Gorbachev appeared to be moderate and yielding, and likely to adopt whatever political coloration needed. He then seemed, and he remained, a man ready to meet all the expectations of the Politburo and the general secretary—or at least he did so as long as Brezhnev retained real power, until about 1982.

When the Politburo began to change, with a reshuffling of positions and factions—first with Brezhnev's illness, then with the death of Suslov who had strictly monitored the subordination of Party authorities, and finally with the fall of Kirilenko—Gorbachev dropped his ideological wishy-washiness and political conformity. He showed himself to be more resolute and consistent in meeting the demands that Andropov had begun to make on those whom he had gathered around him in his attempt to win the mantle of Brezhnev. At this point many in the Party were surprised to see a new Gorbachev, one who openly displayed ambition, firmness, and hardness.

It is not a simple matter to understand and assess this apparent change in Gorbachev. Did it represent yet another example of psychological mimicry in response to his new political status of being close to the Party throne occupied by Andropov, or did it represent at last disclosure of his real nature?

It is possible that for the long duration of his earlier political career Gorbachev had been playing roles scripted for him by various Party "directors," getting into the roles and projecting the social behavior that they required. As he approached the director's chair himself and then finally reached it, he may have cast off the old roles (the old masks). There is another possibility: his casting off of roles, both those scripted by others and those scripted by himself, is yet another role. If so, then he has been playing it with considerable success on the Soviet political stage for a respectable run, from 1982 to the present.

In joining Andropov when Brezhnev was ill but still might have recovered, Gorbachev made a daring move entailing definite risk. Moreover, he remained close to Andropov when soon after the latter's accession to power the balance of forces in the Politburo shifted in favor of Brezhnev's followers. Gorbachev did not join the Chernenko faction, as did Romanov, but stayed loyal to the political course pursued by Andropov. He remained an advocate of moderate reform and of the campaign against corruption. In doing so, he cast his lot with the group of younger, more pragmatic elements in the Party who saw the need for changes to make the system more successful at meeting its own goals. This position or principle aided Gorbachev in becoming Party leader, and in vanquishing Grishin and Romanov, and then their supporters and like-minded confederates. In the process the image of Gorbachev when he became the new general secretary took on some additional features without fundamentally changing. One could notice threads, limited to be sure, of liberalism, flexibility, and political acumen.

We are running ahead of ourselves. Let us return to 1978. That year, after the death of his erstwhile main patron, Kulakov, Gorbachev was brought to Moscow as Kulakov's replacement. It has been posited that he was obligated to Andropov for his transfer, and that this established an increasingly close link between the two. This sequence is based on the assumption that Andropov presented Gorbachev to Brezhnev. Supposedly, the fateful occasion occurred on 19 September 1978, when General Secretary Brezhnev made an "unforeseen" stop at Mineralnye Vody, a spa town, on his way to Baku. The alleged picture that emerges is tempting because it allows one to explain how, four years later, Gorbachev turned out to be one of Andropov's principal supporters, and it is also symbolic because it would show four general secretaries (one current, three prospective) meeting at a small Northern Caucasus station. On this early fall evening, Andropov, who was undergoing a health treatment in Kislovodsk, met Brezhnev and his fellow traveler, Chernenko. Gorbachev was not there by happenstance but in his capacity as Party boss of the Stavropol territory, which included the village of Mineralnye Vody. The conclusion to be drawn from this meeting of the famous four is that the future fate of Mikhail Gorbachev was decided in this short encounter. The picture is impressive, thought provoking, but undoubtedly false.

There was no need to introduce Gorbachev to Brezhnev; they had met on a number of occasions. The initial encounter was probably when Gorbachev's appointment as a territorial Party chief was confirmed and the two of them had a chance to converse. Numerous later occasions were provided by plenary meetings of the Central Committee. There were also opportunities for discussions in smaller groups in the Politburo and Central Committee Secretariat because the position of first secretary of a territorial committee has a status equivalent to that of the first secretary of a medium-sized union republic. (In the Soviet Union there are only a few Party territorial committees, *Kraykoms*, as opposed to many regional or provincial committees, *Obkoms*.)

In addition to the reasons already noted, Gorbachev's selection as a secretary of the Central Committee may be related to two other circumstances. In the mid-1970s, when Gorbachev was in charge of Stavropol, the territory achieved record grain harvest. This may well have encouraged the Politburo to hope that the newly appointed CC secretary might somehow be able to overcome the perennial crisis state of Soviet agriculture.

A second possible relevant factor was Mikhail Suslov, who had reason to support Gorbachev for the secretaryship. All of the republics, territories, and provinces of the Soviet Union are divided into spheres of influence among the members of the Secretariat. Stavropol was part of Suslov's turf because he had been Party chieftain there during the prewar and early postwar years. From time to time he would discover talent and bring his "finds" to serve at important posts in the Central Committee's ideological apparatus. Although Suslov was sufficiently powerful not to be worried by the formation in Moscow of a ruling clique recruited by Brezhnev (first from Dnepropetrovsk and later from Moldavia), he would still not have been likely to have been pleased to have yet another CC secretary, the one responsible for such a sensitive area as agriculture, chosen from the

Brezhnev "mafia." It was hard enough for Suslov to put up with the presence in the Politburo of Chernenko, whom he considered to be a political upstart who owed his political rise only to the favor of the general secretary.

In any event, Gorbachev was brought to Moscow as a Central Committee secretary, but he still had not fully penetrated to the real inner circle of the Kremlin elite. He was initially ensconced in a five-room apartment in a government building on Alexei Tolstoy Street. Only two years later, as a member of the Politburo, he both fully joined the inner elite and moved to luxurious quarters on Kutuzov Prospekt, where he was one of Brezhnev's neighbors.

When Gorbachev succeeded in making his way to the CC Secretariat and then to the Politburo, he undoubtedly brought with him some beliefs that had been shaped by his past in Stavropol. He had consistently achieved results far above the Soviet average, regardless of which managerial and organizational techniques he used. Such a man could be expected to be convinced that the system could be made to work through conscientious management, flexibility, attention to detail, motivation of subordinates, and hard work and discipline. When he became general secretary, these precepts were to be central hallmarks of his efforts to "reform" the ailing Soviet economy. Apparently, at this time he also acquired the belief that successful local Party and economic managers were better equipped to deal with real problems than those who mostly stayed in, and operated from, the center. When he was in a position to do so, first as a Party secretary dealing with cadre promotions and then later as general secretary, he demonstrated a strong preference for selecting such "local" people for advancement. Moreover, as general secretary faced with the imperative of ensuring the preeminence of the central apparat, he apparently is demanding that his close associates in the Politburo and Secretariat make frequent visits to Party and economic organizations and activities throughout the country. His formative experience presumably also convinced him that the central planning apparatus should give real attention, not just lip service, to regional inputs. Finally, he can be assumed to have, like any "self-made" man, a deep belief in the opportunities available to any loyal, hard-working, result-oriented citizen, as well as a strong self-confidence bordering on vanity.

At the national level Gorbachev's continued advancement could no longer be attributed to agricultural successes because Soviet agriculture remained chronically ill. Rather, his progress must have reflected his ability to please senior patrons and thread his way safely through the labyrinthine corridors of Soviet political intrigue. His main apparent patrons then were Suslov and Andropov, two of the most adroit practitioners of the Soviet art of *kto-kogo* (literally, who-whom), which, whatever its original Leninist meaning has come to epitomize the concept that what matters is whom one knows, whom one can influence, to whom one must accommodate, and whom one can take advantage of or do in—i.e., that relative power is what really matters. There can be little doubt that mastery of these skills is an integral part of Gorbachev's own personal political socialization.

Gorbachev's period as a part of the central leadership, as both CC secretary and Politburo member, coincided with the protracted period of aged, ill, and increasingly ineffective general secretaries, with only a short intermission before the dynamic Andropov also began to fail physically. During this time domestic economic and social problems and a series of foreign policy failures became increasingly evident. In such a climate secretaries and Politburo members staked out personal fiefdoms, usurped one another's and the general secretary's prerogatives, and intrigued against one another in shifting alliances to a degree that was abnormal even for the Soviet Union. The lessons for Gorbachev were that the general secretary needs full control, a competent and loyal but not too independent and ambitious leadership team, and that constant attention must always be paid to power play within the leadership. The lessons were now of no lesser importance to him than the precepts he had internalized earlier. Once Gorbachev became general secretary, he would have to consolidate his own power and put his own team in place both at the center and throughout the *nomenklatura*. Then he would have to guarantee somehow that his supporters did not turn into his rivals. This obvious iron law of Soviet central politics would apply regardless of whether he indeed wanted to make significant changes in the system or whether he wished merely to ensure his own longevity at the top. Either motive would be sufficient to explain the speed and thoroughness with which he would later move to reshuffle personnel at every level.

When Andropov became general secretary, Gorbachev's career took off. With Andropov's patronage and apparent sharing of many of his goals and beliefs, Gorbachev became for the first time a serious future contender for the very top position. However, Andropov's reign was short, and his increasing incapacitation soon allowed the system to sink back into the mire of uncertainty, ineffectiveness, and intrigue from which it had just begun to free itself. By the time of Andropov's death, Gorbachev was no more than one of several contenders for the Party throne, and one who was viewed as a threat to the entrenched old men who owed their positions to Brezhnev cronyism more than to demonstrated ability and performance.

In February 1984 the tired old guard reasserted itself, and Brezhnev's colorless sycophant, Chernenko, was given the position that Gorbachev and several others so earnestly desired. Under Chernenko's ineffective and increasingly incapacitated leadership, the individual barons of the Politburo and Secretariat further infringed on the authority of the general secretary and pursued their shifting intrigues, with Gorbachev right in the thick of them.

Late 1984 and the beginning of 1985 was a crucial period for Gorbachev. His pride, deeply wounded when he had failed to win the contest for succession fought over Andropov's grave, soon received considerable uplift when Chernenko fell seriously ill. From being the "second general secretary," as he was referred to by the editor-in-chief of *Pravda*, Afanasyev, Gorbachev rose to be de facto first, even though he was not yet the only general secretary.

The Party could not afford to make national politics dependent on the vicissitudes of Chernenko's health during his terminal medical treatment. Such a situation had occurred with Brezhnev, when an incapacitated general secretary well suited a Politburo filled by lethargic elders, anxious only to avoid all political or social change. The main interest of both Brezhnev and his superannuated colleagues was to live out their days without undue stress or upset, in precious comforts attached to their positions, until they would find their last resting place by the Kremlin wall—and, if fortunate enough, in Soviet history as well. The unresolved problems, which tended to pile up in the long years of Brezhnev's term of office, were for the most part left for a succeeding generation. But when Brezhnev died and a new generation came to power, it soon turned out that it was hardly newer or younger than the preceding one. Brezhnev's milieu continued to serve as its pool of recruitment and its leader, Andropov, although dynamic, proved to be seriously ill. This not only paralyzed the regime but also threatened its very existence. Because the Soviet mind is habituated to equate the system with the person of the general secretary, a noticeable weakness of the latter is liable to suggest the frailty of the former.

Soviet history reverted to the past. Andropov was replaced by Chernenko, who ushered the country into a pale and indistinct replica of the stagnation of the last years of Brezhnev's rule. The Party apparat was not dissatisfied with Chernenko; after all, he did his best to halt the slide of the Brezhnev generation from power, and made it possible for the old men to enjoy their privileges for a little while longer. This is why the Politburo preferred Chernenko to Gorbachev, who was expected to complete the reshuffling of the Politburo initiated by Andropov.

Under Chernenko the very functioning of the regime became erratic. Its global position and its prestige in the eyes of the Soviet populace were slipping rapidly. This explains the decision to undertake some generational changes after—and even a very few before—the death of Chernenko. To preserve continuity, members of the Politburo would be phased out gradually, gently, with all the honors due to deserving pensioners. Gorbachev was selected in advance for leadership, apparently conditional upon his assent to these terms. He assented, whereupon he was allowed to journey to England for the sake of gaining the requisite international experience, reputation, and polish behooving a future leader.

The death of Marshal Ustinov changed the balance of forces. Gorbachev had lost an influential ally, prompting Romanov, who also aspired to the Party throne, to make his move. Romanov was despotic and power-hungry, yet under Andropov he had somehow managed to find a *modus vivendi* with Gorbachev. The two shared power as equals: Gorbachev was in charge of Party cadres; Romanov supervised military industry and the armed forces. Andropov intentionally pitted these two Central Committee secretaries against each other, for he assumed that he could rein them in if the ambitions of the unruly Romanov or of the relatively vain Gorbachev drove them too far. In the meantime both remained useful to Andropov as allies against Chernenko. But the outcome was different and sudden. Andropov was soon dead, and Romanov and Gorbachev stood pitted against each other in a major political rivalry. Yet Romanov, who had supported Chernenko against Gorbachev, failed to become second secretary of the Central Committee. He was a lone wolf in the Politburo, lacked a solid base in Moscow and firm support in the Secretariat. The post of second secretary went to Gorbachev. Romanov had to console himself with third place in the Party hierarchy, as one of the three secretaries of the Central Committee who were full members of the Politburo. He had to build up his own power base, and felt his time had come with the death of Ustinov.

Gorbachev seemed to have a slim majority of the Politburo on his side. He was evidently firmly backed by Andrei Gromyko, Solomentsev, and Vorotnikov, but the support of the other Politburo members was less certain. Because Tikhonov, Shcherbitsky, and Kunaev had risen to power under Brezhnev, Gorbachev's selection as general secretary meant that they would sooner or later be retired. Aliev had compromised his propsects by his closeness to Chernenko; originally raised to power by Andropov, he quickly switched factional sides in favor of Chernenko. Thus, he had no reason to expect favors from Gorbachev, unless the latter would have found it useful to exploit his opportunism for some purpose of his own.

There remained Grishin, who observed Gorbachev's rise with amazement and envy, and who was convinced that due to seniority he, rather than Gorbachev, should become the general secretary. Romanov—realizing that he had no chance to win enough Politburo support for his own candidacy for general secretary—attempted to take advantage of Grishin's aspirations and began pushing the latter's candidacy. At first he did so indirectly, as when he proposed that this "worthy" Party functionary preside at Politburo sessions. Then upon the death of Chernenko, during the few hours between the session of the Politburo and the plenum of the Central Committee, he did so openly and with desperation.

Romanov calculated that a majority of Central Committee members who had been raised to their positions in Brezhnev's time would prefer the cautious Grishin to Gorbachev because as general secretary, Gorbachev could be expected to push for major changes in the leadership. Romanov had miscalculated. First at the Politburo session and subsequently at the plenum of the Central Committee the majority supported Gorbachev. Romanov and Grishin then knew that they would eventually pay dearly for their abortive maneuver. Their wait was not long. First, however, Gorbachev had to set the stage by establishing a set of major policy requirements that would justify wholesale personnel changes and begin the process of bringing his own loyalists into the Politburo and Secretariat and curtailing the excessively independent power bases of those who had helped bring him into power.

At the same time the new general secretary found himself president over an empire beset by accumulated problems. The economy was increasingly stagnant, inefficient, out of balance, unable to match the West in applying and utilizing advanced technology, except perhaps in the defense field. It was facing a period when the old labor and capital-intensive growth strategy had somehow to be replaced with one of productivity and rationality. Corruption was a way of life permeating every level of society, including even the Party hierarchy from the top to the bottom. The population was cynical and apathetic, yet yearned for a better life. Alcoholism had reached levels unparalleled anywhere else in the world. Agricultural production was chronically incapable of meeting the needs of the population. Grain imports were a constant drain on the limited reserves of hard currency, eating up earnings from exports of oil, gas, arms, and occasionally gold—virtually the only significant sources of hard currency—that were desperately needed to finance industrial modernization and to import the consumer goods the populace demanded. Continued earnings from oil and gas were increasingly dependent upon exploitation of deposits in remote and inaccessible regions of inhospitable Siberia, something that itself would require considerable investment of financial resources and either dramatic improvement in Soviet technology or access to that of the West. Arms exports, which in some years in the early 1980s had accounted for a quarter of Soviet hard currency earnings, had probably reached their limit. Consumer goods were shoddy and scarce, and even those that were produced were distributed highly unequally in both geographic and social terms. Furthermore, basic economic resources were maldistributed: the educated and technically skilled work force was concentrated largely in the West; the natural resources were concentrated in underdeveloped, inhospitable, and largely unpopulated regions of Siberia that lacked adequate infrastructure; and the largest and growing, population pool for the future work force was in the less educated, less trusted masses of still largely Islamic Central Asia. The centralized system of economic management and, indeed, even of Party direction of society and the economy had become intensely bureaucratic, ossified, and inflexible—out of touch with problems arising outside Moscow, Leningrad, and a few other major cities.

On top of all this was the burden of a massive defense complex that every year ate up anywhere from 14 percent to well over 20 percent of the entire gross national product (depending on whose analysis one believes) and siphoned off the best technicians and the lion's share of many critical industrial products. The absorption of resources by the miliary posed a major dilemma. Relative military power, more than anything else combined, was the underpinning of Soviet influence in a world perceived as "objectively" characterized by conflict and struggle—the internal reality of *kto-kogo* writ large on the global stage. Military power could not be weakened in relative terms without jeopardizing all of the USSR's so doggedly pursued international achievements. Moreover, it was the basis for one of the most important and powerful internal political constituencies, encompassing not only the armed forces but also a substantial portion of the Party and industrial bureaucracies.

Soviet foreign policy was in a lengthy period of similar stagnation. Under President Ronald Reagan the United States had become much more assertive and successful in limiting further gains for the USSR in the international arena. It was a process greatly helped by growing foreign perceptions, especially in the Third World, that the USSR had little to offer except military assistance with strings attached and of questionable relative quality and effectiveness. The latter was strongly implied by the succession of regional conflicts in which Soviet-equipped clients were badly beaten by U.S.- and Western-equipped opponents. U.S. military modernization threatened the gains achieved in the long struggle to obtain at first strategic parity and then superiority. It also confronted the USSR with the potential need to increase greatly its own already huge military economic burden, with the possibility that stepped-up Soviet efforts would still be incapable of keeping up technologically even if the burdensome sacrifices were made. Moreover, Soviet diplomacy had abysmally failed to stem this trend. Threats, arms control stonewalling, and attempts to marshal Western neutralism, anti-Americanism, and fears of nuclear war had succeeded in creating waves but did not halt the deployment of U.S. intermediate-range nuclear weapons systems (Pershing 2s and the ground-launched cruise missiles) or stop NATO conventional force improvements, even if they materialized in fits and starts. Nor was the USSR making any apparent headway in undermining support for French nuclear military modernization, and precious little in regard to that of the British.

Throughout Europe governments were swinging toward the right. In the Third World even some Soviet clients were increasingly seeking closer economic relations with the West at the expense of fidelity to the Soviet model and susceptibility to Soviet influence. Eastern Europe was an economic burden on the already flagging Soviet economy, and social unrest, such as in Poland in the early 1980s, was an ever-present specter. The People's Republic of China was modernizing, still intractably opposed to much of Soviet foreign policy, and more and more engaged in political, economic, and even military cooperation with the West. Major Soviet clients, such as Angola, Vietnam, and to a lesser extent Ethiopia, were enmeshed in protracted civil or regional conflict. The USSR itself was bogged down in the ever more costly and apparently endless Afghanistan war. Soviet influence in the Middle East was becoming limited to such partially isolated and imperfectly controllable states as Syria and Libya; Iraq, under the pressures of its war with Iran, was drawing closer to anti-Soviet regimes; and the Palestinians were in disarray. Perhaps even more important, the combination of all these developments had brought the economic and technical benefits of detente to a trickle precisely when the Soviet economy most urgently needed them.

The daunting challenges that these protracted domestic and foreign policy failures presented were compounded by the fact that the long period of ineffective and incapacitated general secretaries had fractured the total centralized control and power upon which the ideological and systemic foundations of the Soviet structure were based. The Party-state defense bureaucracy under Ustinov had become almost a separate fiefdom, a condition only partially rectified by the shunting aside of the dynamic, highly competent, and ambitious Marshal Ogarkov and the subsequent exclusion of Ustinov's colorless successor from the Politburo. The influence of the police security establishment, especially the KGB, had grown. Western analysts who foresaw a KGB influence exceeding that of the Party apparatus were undoubtedly mistaken; nevertheless, the KGB had clearly re-emerged as a serious, semi-independent influence group. The foreign policy establishment, traditionally no more than an implementing arm of Politburo decision making, had under Gromyko almost become another independent fiefdom, split between the formal Gromyko organization in the Ministry of Foreign Affairs and that of the dogmatic, independently minded, and autocratic Boris Ponomarev, the head of the International Department of the Central Committee. Moreover, at home centrifugal "regionalism" was rampant at the expense of the central leadership's ability to manage the economy and society.

On the other hand, the empire over which Gorbachev assumed leadership had several real strengths. The rigid, partially fractured leadership and means of control retained great capabilities to respond to effective central direction. If the economy was inefficient and stagnant, it still commanded the third-largest GNP in the world; in addition, the huge and diverse natural resources of the USSR have made it potentially an economically self-sufficient nation. Even in its doldrums, the economic growth rate was equivalent to that of most Soviet rivals. If there were serious problems in applying modern technology, Soviet pure science had many strengths and accomplishments to its credit. If the population was apathetic, it remained that resilient, highly patriotic, and usually docile mass so evident in Russian history. Although the defense establishment had become a burden and was in danger of not being able to keep pace with the current Western modernization, it was still the major source of Soviet global influence, the basis of Soviet superpower status, and a major tool of the CPSU's monopoly of power. Even if the USSR and many of its clients were enmeshed in protracted and conceivably unwinnable conflicts, few of the client states were in real danger of being overthrown, victories were still quite possible, and in actuality the United States was not doing that much better. Third World economic and political problems and the legacy of colonialism and the global economic imbalance still provided fertile fields for Soviet policies to exploit. In the West there were still very strong popular peace and antinuclear movements, there was still a strong desire for more open economic relations with the USSR, there were still many real and enduring differences of perception among Western governments, and there was a historically demonstrated tendency for Western governments and particularly that of the United States to change course on a periodic basis rather than sticking to long, costly programs of military growth, economic barriers, and confrontation.

Since assuming the post of general secretary, Gorbachev has moved quickly to deal with all of the issues facing him, in some ways more quickly than any Soviet leader since Lenin. He has done so in ways that clearly reflect the lessons he learned in Stavropol and in the corridors of power in Moscow. The evidence suggests that he is perhaps as firm a believer in the promises of the Soviet system as was Khrushchev, but he is simultaneously more flexible than any general secretary since Lenin. He seems to possess a determination to wield Stalin's iron control sheathed in the velvet glove of Andropov. He appears to fully match, if not exceed, the healthy Brezhnev's ability to manipulate personnel and the Party apparatus. Gorbachev has brought a dramatic flair and personal style to leadership that are reminiscent of those of Khrushchev but far more sophisticated and polished. Moreover, he is a strongly determined, immensely self-confident man who is oriented more toward results than appearances, a man who seeks to win in whatever he tries—whether at home or abroad. In short, he may well be the most capable Soviet leader since Lenin. Nevertheless, he faces an array of fundamental, and in some cases apparently intractable problems; it may yet turn out that there is less to Gorbachev than meets the eye. In the remaining chapters of this book, we will examine and evaluate what he has done and will attempt to project where he and the Soviet Union are likely to go in the future.

Part I
Internal Politics

Oh wad some power the giftie gie us
To see oursels as others see us!

—Robert Burns
"To a Louse"

Selected Chronology of Significant Internal Developments and Events March 1985 through June 1987

1985

10 March   General Secretary Konstantin Chernenko died after a protracted illness. Announcement was made nineteen hours later on 11 March.

11 March   Mikhail Gorbachev was elected general secretary, CPSU.

22 March   Communique of first Politburo meeting since Gorbachev's election, presumably held 21 March. As in the majority of all subsequent reports of Politburo meetings, the lead item on the agenda dealt with mobilization of Party and state organizations to deal with economic and social problems and programs. (A complete listing of reported Politburo meetings and agendas is included in Appendix II.)

First reported retirement or transfer of a regular Party first secretary (Kirov Obkom) after Gorbachev's election. During Gorbachev's first two and one quarter years some 2/3 of the 150 city, regional (Obkom and Kraikom), and autonomous republic Party committee first secretaries would be replaced, with the majority reflecting retirements or demotions, not promotional shifts. Most would occur prior to the XXVII CPSU Congress, but by late summer of 1986 the incidence of by-name criticism of regional first secretaries would greatly increase, suggesting heavy future turnover.

24 March   First announced retirement or transfer of a government minister or chairman of a state committee since Gorbachev's election. By June 1987 over two thirds of all members of the Council of Ministers would be Gorbachev appointees. (See also Appendix I.)

5 April   Communique of Politburo meeting reported that the issue of alcoholism was addressed. A formal decree of major measures to combat alcoholism would not be announced until May.

16–17 April   Gorbachev met and mixed with factory workers and officials in Moscow in the first of what would be several highly publicized events around the country, providing an opportunity to demonstrate a new, "accessible" style, obtain firsthand impressions, and make major exhortations for improved performance.

23 April	Plenum of the Central Committee. Three new full members were elected to the Politburo (KGB Chairman Chebrikov from candidate member; CC Secretaries Ligachev and Ryzhkov); one new CC secretary was elected (Nikonov); and one new candidate Politburo member was elected (minister of defense, Marshal Sokolov). Numerous economic and social problems and tasks were defined, with Gorbachev's speech focusing heavily on economic development.
15–18 May	Gorbachev visited Leningrad, again meeting and mixing with ordinary people. He made a dramatic speech at the Smolny Institute (headquarters for the Bolshevik takeover of the city in 1917) demanding new, improved forms of Party work. The speech was later broadcast on national television in prime time.
17 May	Central Committee, Council of Ministers, and Supreme Soviet decree on overcoming drunkenness and alcoholism was published. Severe rules and penalties were set.
11–12 June	Meeting of Central Committee, Council of Ministers, and other top and middle leadership. Gorbachev made a major speech outlining program to restructure and improve the economy. (For Central Committee meetings, agendas, and decrees, see also Appendix II.)
25–26 June	Gorbachev visited Kiev and Dnepropetrovsk in another publicized public contact and exhortation "event."
1 July	Plenum meeting of Central Committee. Romanov was "retired" from the Politburo and Secretariat; Shevardnadze was advanced from candidate to full member of the Politburo; and Yeltsin and Zaykov were elected CC secretaries.
1–2 July	Meeting of the Supreme Soviet. Gromyko was elected chairman of the Presidium of the Supreme Soviet and replaced as foreign minister by Shevardnadze. Election on 2 July selected Politburo member and CC Secretary Ligachev as chairman of the Foreign Affairs Commission of the Supreme Soviet, a position once held by Suslov and traditionally occupied by the Party's ideological watchdog. This in effect made him the number-two man in the Party leadership.
10–11 July	Gorbachev made another contact-and-exposure visit, to Minsk. He also held a reportedly significant meeting there with military leaders but details were not published.
1 August	A Soviet Party official (deputy head of the International Department of the CC, Zamyatin) confirmed that Gorbachev was automatically chairman of the Defense Council by virtue of being Party general secretary.
4 August	A Central Committee and Council of Ministers joint decree was announced on new methods of economic management.
4–7 September	Gorbachev made another contact-and-exhortation trip to locations in the Tyumen Region, where he made a major

	speech on oil and energy industry tasks and problems, and to Tselinograd, where he made a speech on agriculture.
20 September	Gorbachev addressed an assembly of Stakhanovite veterans. The tenor of the speech underlined that discipline and extra work are an integral part of economic improvement program.
27 September	Special meeting of Presidium of Supreme Soviet. Tikhonov was retired as chairman of Council of Ministers and replaced by Ryzhkov (who thereupon ceased to be a CC secretary).
9 October	"Complex Program" for the production of consumer goods to the year 2000 was published in the Soviet press. It promised great results but was weak on details of how they would be achieved.
14 October	GOSPLAN Chairman Baybakov was replaced by Nikolay Talyzin, who was additionally appointed as a first deputy chairman, Council of Ministers (Baybakov had been only a deputy chairman) and candidate member of the Politburo. Western speculation was that Baybakov's and Tikhonov's replacements were indicative of opposition to intended real systemic economic reform, a conclusion not supported by any announced concrete measures until possibly around and after the Party Congress in 1986.
15 October	Gorbachev made a major economic speech at a Central Committee plenum in which he stressed the errors of the past quarter-century and the need for flexibility and realism.
26 October	Draft of the new Party Program was published. The domestic emphasis was on economic revitalization and improving Party methods.
2 November	Draft of the new Party Regulations was published.
9 November	Text of "Basic Direction of Economic and Social Development in the USSR for 1986–1990 and for the Period to the Year 2000" was published. The emphasis was on the introduction and utilization of new technology, discipline, and managerial reform to achieve greater efficiency; however, the content of any real "reforms" was mostly left unclear.
23 November	Announcement made of Central Committee and Council of Ministers decree establishing a new "super ministry," the USSR State Agro-Industrial Committee, GOS-AGROPROM, to revitalize Soviet agriculture. Five previous ministries and one existing state committee were subsumed into this one organization.
26–27 November	Session of the Supreme Soviet. GOSPLAN Chairman Talyzin reported on results so far of the 1985 economic plan. He emphasized both successes and some notable cases of failing to meet goals, and described the 1986 plan goals.
24 December	Gorbachev participated in a Moscow city Party plenum that retired Politburo member Grishin as first secretary of the city Party committee and replaced him with CC Secre-

	tary Yeltsin. Grishin's formal removal from the Politburo and Yeltsin's from the Secretariat were not confirmed until February 1986.
1986	
18 February	Plenum meeting of the Central Committee confirmed Grishin's retirement from the Politburo and formally relieved Yeltsin as CC Secretary, a step required due to his election as Moscow city Party 1st secretary, and named him candidate member of the Politburo. Rusakov was retired from the CC Secretariat.
25 February–6 March	*XXVII Congress of the CPSU.* The congress retired CC secretary and candidate Politburo member Ponomarev, although he, like some other notable earlier retirees (Tikhonov, Baybakov, Admiral Gorshkov), was retained as a Central Committee member. CC Secretary Zaykov became a Politburo member, making him arguably the number-three man in the Party. Five new CC secretaries were elected: ambassador to the United States Dobrynin, A. P. Biryukova (the first woman since Khrushchev's days), V. A. Medvedev, G. P. Razumovsky, and A. N. Yakovlev. Two new candidate members were named to the Politburo: Yu. F. Solov'ev (the first secretary of the Leningrad Party organization, a position traditionally included in the central leadership) and N. N. Slyunkov.
	The new Party Program and Regulations were adopted with very minor changes from the earlier draft versions. The major emphasis was on reiteration, with little new added in the way of concrete implementing details, of earlier announced economic "reforms" and on foreign policy (particularly in Gorbachev's speech), with major emphasis on arms control.
23 March	The creation of the State Committee for Computer Technology and Information Science was announced. Designation of its chairman was not made until early April.
7–9 April	Gorbachev traveled to the Kuibyshev Region, where he mixed with workers at automotive plants and made a strong economic speech combining exhortation, criticism, and reiteration of his economic programs.
20 April	The Soviet press published the "results" of the first quarter of 1986 of the state plan. Although successes and improvements were featured, the list of areas in which goals were still not being met was similar to the previous year's reporting.
26 April	Nuclear accident at Chernobyl. The first, very brief, notices appeared in the central Soviet press on 29 April and continued that way until well into May, when more complete coverage finally began. Full reports of the causes and assessing fault appeared only in late summer.
6 May	The Soviet press published a Central Committee and Council of Ministers decree on improving light industry and con-

sumer goods production that would introduce possibly significant pricing and planning reforms on 1 January 1987.

15 May Gorbachev appeared on Soviet television to make his first public address on the Chernobyl nuclear accident. Much of the speech was turned into a forum for nuclear test ban appeals. He and other Soviet spokesmen stated that the extensive nuclear energy program would continue unabated.

22 May Gorbachev addressed a combined Central Committee and state ministerial meeting on improvements needed in the machine-building industry.

28 May Central Committee and Council of Ministers decree to "step up the struggle against unearned income." This campaign clearly threatened a number of reforms previously announced in regard to agriculture, light industry, and services because it promised to undermine the illegal but necessary "second economy" on which parts of these sectors depended. Reports in the press in late summer confirmed this predicted outcome.

31 May A new program to restructure and improve higher and middle specialized education was published.

16 June Plenum of the Central Committee. Gorbachev made a blistering speech in which he criticized failures to adopt new measures and meet demands in the economic sphere. Ryzhkov made a similar, only slightly less critical speech. For the rest of the period covered, the emphasis in the press and in major speeches was on overcoming such "immobilism" at all levels and on imposing discipline on those who did not switch to new methods. In July and August several Party Control Committee reports assigned punishments, including both Party expulsions and reprimands, for such delinquent individuals.

18 June Meeting of the Supreme Soviet. Several senior personnel changes were announced in the Presidium, including the reassignment of Demichev from minister of culture to first deputy chairman of the Presidium.

20 July The press published the official statistics of economic performance for the first six months of 1986. Except for oil, production indexes were generally up, as was labor productivity. However, most of the improvement was concentrated in the first few months of the period covered (with relative downturns in May and June), and most of the ministries, sectors, and regions that previously had been repeatedly criticized were again listed as problem areas.

21 July The first sacking of a Gorbachev-appointed state minister (G. P. Voronovsky, minister of electrotechnical industry) was announced. This should be seen as a pointed warning that performance, not patronage, was what matters. During the summer months of 1986 a number of ministries (including Voronovsky's) headed by Gorbachev appointees were expressly criticized.

21 July	The All-Union Ministry of Nuclear Energy was formed, undoubtedly in large measure to deal with safety issues raised by the Chernobyl accident. At the same time, the existing State Committee for the Utilization of Nuclear Energy apparently continued to operate.
25–31 July	Gorbachev made another personal appearance trip, this time to the Soviet Far East. Besides mixing with citizens and officials, he made major speeches at Vladivostok and Khabarovsk that affected both foreign affairs and internal policies.
30 July	Central Committee, Council of Ministers, and Supreme Soviet decree was published on "measures to further strengthen the role and accountability of Soviets [legislative councils] in social and economic development." The same day a Central Committee communique addressed measures to enhance and strengthen the role of CPSU members in guiding these Soviets.
20 August	Supreme Soviet decree was published reorganizing the national management of construction activities in a manner similar to the October 1985 reorganization of agriculture. The existing State Committee for Construction Affairs was redesignated a union-republic committee, and three new regionally oriented ministries of construction were added to the existing Ministry of Construction in the Far East and Transbaikal. The heads of three sector-oriented construction ministries were appointed as the ministers in charge of the new regional ministries, and their ministries evidently were subsumed into the new ones. The somewhat expanded decree by the Central Committee and Council of Ministers followed in mid-September.
17–19 September	Gorbachev traveled to Krasnodar and the Stavropol Region, where he again mixed with ordinary people and Party workers and made major speeches. Although similar to his earlier such public events, this one was notable for the degree to which he defended his policy lines from unnamed opponents and "foot-draggers."
1 October	Gorbachev made an important speech at an All-Union Conference of the Directors of Faculties of Social Sciences, stressing, among other things, "responsible" glasnost and social-economic reconstruction.
22 October	Gorbachev met with a large group of first secretaries of Union Republic Parties and Oblast Party Committees, "laying down the law" and demanding improvements in the way construction is implemented.
23 October	CC met and discussed "the unsatisfactory implementation of CC CPSU resolutions on eliminating whitewashing (ochkovtiratelstvo) and fake reporting of achievements (pripiski)."
8 November	Gorbachev used his speech at the reception in the Kremlin in honor of the sixty-ninth anniversary of the Revolution to further promote his domestic and foreign policies.

16 November	Gorbachev's speech at a CC conference honoring awardees of state prizes for production criticized inadequacies in quality of products.
1 December	Meeting was held in Moscow of representatives of collective farm councils to discuss the tasks of the agro-industrial complex.
2 December	The fourth session of the Supreme Soviet of the RSFSR discussed improving the social and economic sectors.
3 December	Gorbachev met with leading artists and directors of theatrical arts organization and exhorted them to use glasnost in a way that would support the goals of reconstruction.
12 December	Plenum of the Supreme Court of the U.S.S.R. discussed judicial independence and the subordination of judges to the law as stipulated in the Soviet Constitution.
15 December	The CC and Council of Ministers discussed the follow up in dealing with the effects of the Chernobyl disaster—salvaging the damaged energy block, evacuating population from endangered areas, material aid to victims, cleaning up areas affected by radioactivity, etc.
17 December	The communique of the results of the Supreme Soviet preparatory commission for reconstruction measures criticized managers of heavy industry for not abandoning "administrative" (by fiat) methods of management.
24 December	Gorbachev presided over a meeting at the CC with heads of union ministries and offices addressing their results thus far in 1986 and the tasks ahead. The tenor of the meeting was critical.
1987	
17 January	The Central Statistical Directorate published the economic results for 1986. Predictably, the main figures showed improvements over 1985 in almost every sector and total industrial production was 5% higher and agricultural was up by 9%. However, closer examination and subsequent speeches and articles showed continuing problems and shortfalls in many of the sub-sectors which were most important to the achievement of the goals of the economic reconstruction. In fact, many of the same problem areas identified in April of 1985 and in every subsequent quarterly report were again singled out for criticism. Throughout January, there were numerous meetings in ministries and in the CC which singled out particular sectors and ministries for continuing problems in Health, Higher and Intermediate Education, regional preparations for winter, social and living conditions of workers, Communications, and Agriculture.
23 January	Gorbachev made a major speech on agriculture and its continuing problems at a meeting of most of the central leadership and officials connected with agriculture held in the CC.
27 January	The press published a 13 January decree on rules for the

	establishment and operation of Joint Ventures (JVs) with foreign firms. Although aimed ostensibly at foreign economic and political relationships, such JVs could profoundly affect internal Soviet economic patterns.
27–28 January	The Central Committee met in Plenum, reportedly after delays caused by difficulty in obtaining advance agreement for proposals and actions to be taken. Gorbachev made a very major and dramatic speech in which he demanded acceleration of the social and economic reconstruction and called for increases in democracy via allowing multiple candidates and secret ballots at Party levels up to Union-Republic and in many state offices. In the speech he alleged that the central leadership and the people were fully in support of his reforms, but that there was major passive resistance entrenched in intermediate layers of the bureaucracy.
	At the Plenum, DA Kunaev, the deposed head of the Kazakh CP, was formally removed from the Politburo, and CC Secretary Yakovlev was made a Candidate Politburo Member. Two new CC Secretaries, Slyunkov, who was already a Candidate Politburo Member, and Lukyanov, were appointed; and Zimyanin was retired from the Secretariat leaving only two Party Secretaries, Ligachev and Dolgikh, who were not directly appointed by Gorbachev.
8 February	The draft of a new law on state enterprises and trusts was published for public consideration and comment. The law, which predictably would later be passed virtually as drafted in all major aspects, greatly expanded the number of activities which would have to operate on a self-financing, cost accountability basis while ostensibly increasing the independence of local managers from central ministries. etc.
17–21 February	Gorbachev traveled and spoke in Latvia and Estonia promoting his programs.
13 February	Gorbachev made a major speech at a meeting in the CC of heads of organs of mass information and propaganda. In the speech he promoted glasnost, but emphasized that its main task was to help the people understand the reconstruction and support it.
24–28 February	Twenty-eighth Congress of the national trade union organization. Gorbachev made a major policy speech exhorting support to his reconstruction programs.
14–16 March	At the Sixth Congress of the Union of Soviet Journalists, Ligachev reminded all that glasnost did not mean overemphasizing the errors of the past, but had to also glorify the "reality" that the revolution and Soviet history had brought great success in all fields.
March	Many members of the central leadership traveled and spoke in outlying regions, emulating Gorbachev in what was apparently a concerted effort to drum up greater support for policies. Among those traveling in this way were: Ryzhkov,

	Gromyko, Dolgikh, Lukyanov, Aliev, Vorotnikov, Zaikov and Solovyev.
15-18 April	Twentieth KOMSOMOL Congress, Gorbachev made another impassioned speech defending his programs and exhorting support, First Secretary Mironenko was reelected but there were many other personnel changes.
24 April	The economic results for the first quarter of 1987 were published. The same problem areas were identified as reported every quarter since April, 1985. Industrial production growth was below the target for the quarter. Throughout the month, CC meetings and special assemblages of sector personnel were told by representatives of the central leadership that progress was too slow and more must be done.
April	Other members of the central leadership continued to travel and meet with local representatives and populace to exhort greater effort. Among those doing this were: Vorotnikov, Shcherbitskiy, Nikonov, and Yakovlev.
11-13 May	Gorbachev, accompanied by almost the entire senior leaders of the military-industrial complex, Marshal Sokolov the Minister of Defense, Zaikov the Politburo Member and CC Secretary overseeing defense industries, Maslyukov the Council of Ministers Deputy in charge of defense industries, Cherebrikov the head of the KGB and Marchuk the President of the Academy of Sciences, made a major speech praising the capabilities of Soviet science to meet space defense needs.
22 May	A conference was held in the CC on failures to meet consumer goods needs and goals. Ligachev and Biryukova made hard hitting speeches basically arguing that everything needed was in place to do so, but that discipline and application were lacking. Other such meetings during May attacked the performance in agriculture, environmental protection, etc; while Zaikov, Dolgikh, and Vorotnikov continued the practice of central leadership traveling the provinces to defend the reconstruction and exhort the masses a la Gorbachev.
30 May	An extraordinary meeting of the Politburo was held following the incident in which a West German youth flew a light aircraft into the U.S.S.R. and landed in Red Square. Defense Minister Sokolov was sacked and replaced by a junior Deputy Defense Minister, General Yazov. The CinC of PVO Strany (National Air Defense forces), Deputy Defense Minister Marshal Koldunov was also sacked.
8-9 June	CC discusses radical reconstruction of the administration of the economy. CC Secretary Slyunkov delivered a report.
22 June	Elections took place for deputies to local councils and for judges of peoples' courts.
25-26 June	Plenum of the Central Committee. Several dramatic personnel changes were announced including elevation of

three CC Secretaries, all Gorbachev proteges, to Full Member, Politburo (Slyunkov, Yakovlev and Nikonov—the latter without even having been a candidate Politburo member) bring the total of CC Secretaries who were simultaneously full Politburo members to a virtually unprecedented number. The new Defense Minister, General Yazov, was also made a Candidate Politburo Member. Gorbachev's speech at the plenum claimed many successes in creating the conditions for social and economic reconstruction and revitalization; but was noteworthy for the number of continuing problems identified and the admission that changes were not being achieved at lower levels or in the methods of work of many ministries. The Plenum also approved a program for the future "radical reform" of the economy, mostly reiterating and expanding the application of previously announced reforms, and agreed to the convocation of an All-Union CPSU Conference for the first time in a great many years. Both of these measures were announced in the press on the 27th. The CPSU Conference would allow Gorbachev to do the same kinds of things in terms of policy and personnel changes that normally have to await a CPSU Congress.

29–30 June The Seventh Session of the Eleventh Supreme Soviet. Ryzhkov's speech reiterated and expanded in great critical detail on Gorbachev's at the Party Plenum. Three new Members of the Presidium were announced and other state personnel changes during 1987 confirmed.

2

New Wine in Old (?) Bottles: Leadership and Personnel Changes

The main problem confronting the new general secretary of the Central Committee (CC) of the Communist Party of the Soviet Union (CPSU) was that of real, assured power. Being chosen general secretary was only the prelude to ruling. To become a real ruler, Gorbachev had to consolidate and ensure his position in the Politburo and the CC Secretariat. The dialectics of the Soviet system require that a new general secretary free himself both from his political rivals, because they may prevent the realization of his ambitions, and from those who supported his rise to power, because they may limit his independence of action. Indeed, this is how Gorbachev began: he rid himself of dependence on both enemies and friends. Only by eliminating this double dependence can a general secretary proceed to the implementation of his political, social, and economic goals.

For Gorbachev, the transitional period lasted only one year, and was really accomplished at the national level in a much shorter time. This was a record. But he owed the accomplishment not only to his talents but also to an auspicious configuration of forces in the Kremlin. The death of three successive general secretaries in the course of two and a half years had undermined political alliances within the Politburo.

Throughout Gorbachev's time as Soviet leader, all of his actions, including foreign policy initiatives, administrative reorganizations, the shakeup of the bureaucracy, and the various social campaigns, can be best understood in the context of his struggle for the consolidation and retention of power. The decisions a new general secretary makes and the policies he embarks upon can be linked to his need of advancing "his" people to higher positions of power. Everything else he does is of secondary importance.

The period of genuine policy-making on Gorbachev's part could not really begin until the apparatus to carry out his policies in exact conformity with his political preferences and personal ambitions was in place.

Gorbachev first needed two things: a set of issues to justify wholesale changes at the top and all through the system, and a safe working majority in the central leadership. The issues were ready-made in the economic, social, and foreign policy drift of recent years. Gorbachev had already, in December 1984, associated himself with a policy aimed at "an intensive, highly developed economy." A campaign against corruption had been used by Andropov and given lip service by Chernenko as a vehicle for shaking up the bureaucracy, and a campaign against alcoholism was a handy tool for promoting social change. Moreover, because these involved real issues facing the USSR, if Gorbachev wanted eventually to introduce any radical or fundamental changes in order to solve them, he had to first ensure his absolute power base.

Before Gorbachev could move concretely on any issue, he had to shore up a very slim majority in the Politburo. He did this in April when he brought the Andropov-appointed CC secretaries, Ligachev and Ryzhkov, to full Politburo membership without their even having been candidate members. At the same time he reensured the support of the KGB by elevating Andropov's man, Chebrikov, from candidate to full member. He mollified the defense establishment for his intended sacking of Romanov by making Defense Minister Sokolov a Politburo candidate member. Ligachev and Ryzhkov were excellent illustrations of his preference for promoting men who had demonstrated great success in regional work; Ryzhkov, in fact, had his primary professional working background in industry as an engineer, manager, and planner rather than in Party work.

All of these Politburo appointments, except that of Sokolov, were made from among men whom Andropov had brought to central leadership prominence. Gorbachev was not yet in a position to bring his own people into the central leadership in any numbers. For that, he was in too early a stage in the struggle for power; he was completing the consolidation of power by the Andropov group, but was doing so in a way that would make some of them fully *his* protégés and so that he could later isolate others. The only exception at this time, April 1985, was the appointment of the new CC secretary in charge of agriculture, Nikonov, a career agricultural specialist who had long, close ties to Gorbachev.

With his Politburo majority shored up, Gorbachev was in a position to be much more openly critical of the economic failures of the old guard. More important, he was now in a position both to axe his principal former rival and to move to isolate supporters who had accumulated too much independent power. The convening of the Supreme Soviet at the beginning of July and the concurrent plenum meeting of the Central Committee provided the opportunity.

Grigori Romanov, who had only recently collided with Gorbachev in the struggle to succeed Chernenko, was ousted from his positions in the Politburo and Secretariat, and pensioned off. In a very different manner, Gorbachev's ideologically compatible friend and supporter in his bid for power, Gromyko, was removed from active political life. The new leader was beginning to distance himself from those to whom he was indebted. Gromyko relinquished his post as foreign minister and was promoted to chairman of the Supreme Soviet. Although according to the Soviet Constitution this post entails significant responsibilities, in fact it is largely ceremonial. By this move, Gorbachev opened up the foreign policy field for himself.

From then on Gorbachev would both set priorities in Soviet foreign policy and determine the means for their realization. He needed, however, to find a nominal head for the foreign policy establishment and there was no appropriate candidate, i.e., one who would be totally subservient and dependent upon Gorbachev, in the Moscow political deck. Therefore, he settled upon a member of the republic *nomenklatura*, the first secretary of the Georgian republic Central Committee, Eduard Shevardnadze, and promoted him to full membership in the Politburo. Shevardnadze was chosen for several obvious reasons. First, he was dynamic, comparatively young, fairly well educated, and experienced as an administrator. In Georgia he had risen to prominence rapidly. In the 1950s he was secretary of the Central Committee of the Komsomol; from the mid-1960s he was republic minister of internal affairs; and from 1972, first secretary of the republic Central Committee. During his career he had gained a reputation for his uncompromising fight against corruption. This provided a second reason for his promotion, for evidently Gorbachev had decided to conduct a thoroughgoing purge of personnel in the Ministry of Foreign Affairs under the pretext of rooting out corruption in the diplomatic milieu. A third possible reason could have been Gorbachev's desire to make a positive impression on Western public opinion by giving the appearance that Soviet policy is made not just by Russians but also by members of the other nationalities. This goal could be achieved if the West did not realize that Shevardnadze's functions would be confined to executing policy, not making it.

At the same time, the CC Plenum "elected" two new members of the Secretariat. Lev Zaykov had succeeded Romanov as Leningrad first secretary when the latter moved to Moscow and was reportedly on very good personal terms with Gorbachev. Now Gorbachev made him Romanov's replacement as the CC secretary supervising defense. It was a very adroit move, for it appeased the powerful Leningrad regional Party organization

while allowing Gorbachev to put his own man there, and it also contributed to the expansion of Gorbachev's team in the central leadership. Significantly, Zaykov later—at the XXVII CPSU Congress in 1986—became
virtually the number-three man in the Party, behind Gorbachev and
Ligachev. At the same time Gorbachev brought Boris Yeltsin to Moscow as
the CC secretary in charge of construction. Yeltsin was another member of
Kirilenko's old entourage, which had been so effectively coopted by Andropov in his defeat of Chernenko. As it turned out, Yeltsin's appointment
to the Secretariat was only an interim step in the replacement of another of
Gorbachev's former rivals, Grishin. With these changes, Gorbachev had
assured an absolute majority of supporters in both the Politburo and the
CC Secretariat.

Following these moves to restructure the central Party leadership, the
Gorbachev team began to move more virorously to bring new blood into
government ministries and into regional Party first-secretary posts. In addition to Shevardnadze, five new ministers were appointed in July, bringing
the total to nine since Gorbachev became general secretary. Meanwhile,
through the summer the total of new regional first secretaries replaced
since Gorbachev had succeeded Chernenko rose to at least twenty-two. To
this list of regional satraps selected or approved by Gorbachev should be
added an even larger number appointed before his rise to the supreme
leadership, when he was Party secretary for cadres, i.e. in charge of personnel appointments.

Also in July two major personnel changes in the armed forces leadership
were announced. This was done "through the back door," i.e. via answers
to questions at press conferences, as befits the tradition of Soviet uncom-
municativeness in direct official, publicized announcements about senior
military command changes. A new commander in chief of the strategic
rocket forces and a new head of the main political administration of the
armed forces were installed. In diplomatic scuttlebutt this was widely reported to have been due to the incumbents' opposition to Gorbachev's
plans for wide-ranging arms control proposals. Such a version cannot be
precluded, but the more important of these changes in such a regard, the
retirement of Marshal Yepishev, the army's political watchdog, was officially attributed to health and, in fact, he died only two months later.
Moreover, as will be discussed in subsequent chapters, neither the extent of
Gorbachev's arms control proposals nor any real indications of military
disapproval had at this time reached the proportions that they did later.

The Gorbachev team was at this stage in a position to speak with increasing openness about past failures, to begin to propose new reforms, and to
emphasize new foreign policy lines. These proceeded mostly in generalities
whose real content would remain unclear into the fall. Then in September

the axe fell on the most senior remaining member of the Brezhnev-Chernenko team, the eighty-year-old chairman of the Council of Ministers (the official Soviet "premier") Nikolai Tikhonov. Tikhonov was replaced by Gorbachev's man Nikolai Ryzhkov, who epitomized the type of officials favored by the new general secretary: those who had demonstrated technical competence in a successful regional post, were loyal to him, and were likely to be willing to undertake innovative approaches to "get the job done." If one assumes that Tikhonov's departure was not mainly, or at least not only, due to age and illness, it appears to have three possible explanations. First, it may have been simply part of the consolidation of Gorbachev's personal power, although this could have awaited a more fitting time, such as at or just before the Party congress. Second, and most likely, it was related to economic plans, with the young (only fifty-six years old) and dynamic Ryzhkov's being appointed to carry through economic reforms that Gorbachev hoped to pursue. Even if major changes were not intended, Ryzhkov's appointment contributed to the appearance of the new vigor necessary for psychological impact if the program for reform was to be mostly only window dressing and a combination of exhortation and discipline. A third reason for the timing may have been to show the West, on the eve of Gorbachev's visit to France, that the new leader was firmly in control, with the struggle-for-power stage already behind him.

The economic explanation became more compelling when Tikhonov's replacement was followed in early October by the sudden resignation of a key economic planner, the chairman of the State Planning Committee (GOSPLAN) and deputy chairman of the Council of Ministers, N. K. Baybakov, who had held this key post almost twenty years! Moreover, Baybakov's replacement, Nikolai Talyzin, was made a first deputy chairman of the Council of Ministers and a candidate member of the Politburo, positions his predecessor had never held.

In the same vein, the rest of the year saw a turnover in the state apparatus that was virtually unprecented in both scale and rapidity. In the last three months of 1985 Gorbachev removed five of the then eight deputy chairmen of the Council of Ministers, appointed two new first deputy chairmen (out of then four), and removed twenty-two USSR ministers or chairmen of state committees. Of the latter, fourteen were directly replaced, including two who were simultaneously deputy chairmen of the Council of Ministers; the other eight were heads of ministries or state committees that were abolished as separate entities and subsumed into two new larger ones. In January primarily, and also in February, prior to the Party Congress, this pace continued with nine more such changes being announced.

The Gorbachev axe also fell on more of the old guard in the Politburo and Secretariat. Erstwhile rival Grishin was sacked as first secretary of the

Moscow city Party organization in December. In February the formality of removing him from the Politburo was completed when Gorbachev's protégé Yeltsin moved from the Secretariat to become a candidate member of the Politburo as well as, from December, first secretary of the Moscow organization. At the same time another Brezhnev era CC secretary, Rusakov, was retired.

During these months leading up to the Party Congress, the Gorbachev machine was also busy restaffing the regional Party organizations. Four more republic Party first secretaries were named (a replacement for Shevardnadze in Georgia had been announced after the former had become full Politburo member and minister of foreign affairs), and at least another 24 regional (*Obkom*) first secretaries were appointed. In fact, just before the Congress a senior Party figure was quoted as stating that some 23 percent of the heads of the 430,000 primary Party organizations, or some 100,000 functionaries, had been replaced. Meanwhile, prior to the Congress some nine heads of the key CC departments had also been replaced.

The winter of 1985-86 also saw another key change in the top military leadership. Fleet Admiral Gorshkov, who had led the Soviet navy for almost thirty years, was unceremoniously retired and replaced by his deputy, Admiral Chernavin. Gorshkov could well have been retired primarily due to age; however it cannot be discounted that as with the military leadership changes in July, there *may* have been other factors involved. If the military was slated to lose some of its traditional priority claim on Soviet resources—an assumption that is still not fully confirmed—the influential and combative Gorshkov may have had to be replaced because unlike the other leaders in the Ministry of Defense, he was less willing to accept cutbacks docilely. It may also be significant that in addition to the two service commanders in chief (Gorshkov and Tolubko, the former commander in chief of the strategic rocket forces) and the head of the military political administration (Yepishev), there appears to have been an unusually high turnover of major operational commanders in the Soviet armed forces under Gorbachev. Moreover, this turnover again reached the level of deputy, and even first deputy minister of defense in late summer 1986, when a few other, more persuasive indications of concern with military ranks over the directions of Gorbachev's economic and arms control policies began appearing. Finally, in mid-1987, Gorbachev installed his "own" new minister of defense. (These changes will be discussed in greater detail in chapter 12.)

At the Congress itself the process of Gorbachevization of the leadership continued in a dramatic fashion. Zaykov, a Gorbachev appointment to the Secretariat, became the third individual to be simultaneously a full Politburo member and a Party secretary. Five new Party secretaries were "elected": A. P. Biryukova from the trade union organization, the first woman since Khrushchev's time; A. F. Dobrynin, the long-time ambassador to the United States; V. A. Medvedev, the head of the Science Department of the Central Committee; G. P. Razumovskiy, an Obkom first secretary; and A. N. Yakovlev, a Gorbachev adviser who earlier was ambassador to Canada. At the same time Boris Poñomarev, the longtime head of the key International Department of the CC, was removed from both the Secretariat and from candidate membership in the Politburo. Two new candidate Politburo members were also appoined: Yu. F. Solov'ev, the first secretary of the Leningrad Obkom; and N. N. Slyunkov, the first secretary of the Byelorussian Party. Similarly, 147 (i.e., almost half) of the Central Committee full members were new.

As a result of these changes, five of the twelve full Politburo members were Gorbachev appointees, and either two or three more were staunch Gorbachev loyalists. (The third of these, Gromyko, was originally a full Gorbachev supporter, but in that he has increasingly been shunted into relative impotence, he could now conceivably be no longer as zealous a Gorbachev loyalist as before.) One more (Aliev) is a weathervane who can be counted upon to go with the prevailing winds. The remaining two— Shcherbitskiy and Kunaev—were Brezhnev-era holdovers. They were both regional leaders often away from Moscow and the day-to-day decisionmaking, and both came increasingly under heavy clouds for corruption and inefficiency in their home bases. In fact, at the end of 1986 the axe fell on the more vulnerable of these two old Brezhnev cronies. Kunaev was ousted as first secretary of the Kazakh Party and replaced not by another Kazakh but by a Russian. His removal from the central leadership was then only a formality. In January 1987 he was stripped of his Politburo membership and in June of Central Committee membership. Shcherbitskiy held on through 1986 and the first half of 1987, but he was obviously under fire. He walked a more careful line, but the Ukraine with its long history of nationalism and its vital position in the Soviet economy was a much stronger base of localism (*mestnichestvo*) than Kazakhstan in the overall all-Union scheme of things.

To return to spring of 1986, after the Party Congress five of the candidate Politburo members and seven of the CC secretaries were then Gorbachev appointees; an additional secretary, although not appointed by Gorbachev, was, after all, Gorbachev's number-two associate and close colleague, Ligachev. With such majorities, and with at least half of all ministries and state committees—including a majority of the most important ones— headed by his appointees, along with an absolute majority of his men in the Presidium of the Council of Ministers, there was then nothing to prevent Gorbachev from introducing almost any reforms or new directions that he wished. By spring of 1986, one short year after his election as general secretary, Gorbachev had essentially ensured his control over the senior echelons of both the Party and state.

He had also appointed at least half of the city, regional (*oblast*) and territorial (*krai*) Party committee first secretaryships. But here he evidently still faced problems, problems not so much of conscious or organized opposition but of immobilism and unwillingness or inability to adapt to the new ways he was preaching. As discussed in the next chapter, throughout the period after the XXVII Party Congress the main themes of the Gorbachev leadership and of the Soviet press turned to the need to root out entrenched resistance to change.

Throughout the rest of 1986 these themes became even more shrilly expounded, and direct by-name or by-position criticism of ministers, enterprise managers, and regional and local Party officials became common features in speeches and press reporting. Even more significant, the criticism began to be addressed to individuals whom Gorbachev himself had earlier appointed, as well as to holdovers from the past. Concurrently, from July there was a new spate of ministerial-level personnel changes, including one Gorbachev appointee. Although these were not accompanied by the appointment of many new regional Party secretaries, the high number of such individuals who were heavily castigated for failures indicated that there could be little doubt that the future would eventually see another sizeable turnover of these officials.

If Gorbachev had insured his personal control at the top by spring of 1986, what did the further flurry of personnel changes in late summer and fall of that year suggest? Certainly, to some degree it could be considered simply the further consolidation of the general secretary's power. In view of the ages of many of the remaining holdovers, some changes must be evaluated as part of the normal turnover of any government. But there seemed to be more to it than that.

Gorbachev's tentative and limited economic and social reforms were not producing the kinds of results anticipated. Resistance to new methods, the "immunological system" of the Soviet bureaucracy, was the norm rather than the exception. Gorbachev's foreign policy had so far failed to transform U.S.-Soviet relations or eliminate the challenge of the U.S. Strategic Defense Initiative and military modernization. Indications of concern and a potential basis for political opposition were appearing in the military establishment. Each hesitant and limited economic reform and each foreign policy initiative or arms control concession seemed only to require further, more controversial steps. Although this will be discussed in subsequent chapters, its implications for Gorbachev and for his personnel policies seem clear.

First, the "*Gorbachevishchina*" (Gorbachev purge) had to reach much more thoroughly down into the regional Party and state apparatus. Second, a new criterion—results—was beginning to complement and replace that of patronage, which had dominated the earlier consolidation of power at the top. This factor explains the tenor and pointed criticism that came to dominate the press and the leadership's speeches. It explains the fact that some of Gorbachev's own appointees were being criticized by name or position, and even sacked. The fact that the latter phenomenon originated with Gorbachev and his close cronies rather than elsewhere indicates that it did not yet reflect serious political opposition or any diminution of Gorbachev's authority.

Foreign policy also was now clearly in Gorbachev's hands, although this process, which began when Shevardnadze replaced Gromyko in the Ministry of Foreign Affairs, was not fully completed until after the Congress. Nevertheless, initially Gromyko's direct influence on foreign policy decision making undoubtedly continued, even though it was diminished. After all, when Gromyko left the Foreign Ministry, his coterie of loyalists still manned key positions there and filled ambassadorial posts around the world. More significant, until February 1986 Boris Ponomarev still headed the shadow foreign ministry, the International Department of the Central Committee, which many observers believe to have been the real locus of policy-making below the Politburo.

In the several months prior to the Congress, two new deputy foreign ministers were appointed, including a personnel reorganization man (Nikiforov), and there were twenty-five ambassadorial changes (twenty new ambassadors, three transfers and two double postings). After the Congress, through the end of 1986, forty-seven more ambassadorial appointments were announced (thirty-eight new ambassadors, seven transfers, and two more double postings). More important, two new first deputy and five more deputy foreign ministers were named, all but one in May 1986. The turnover pace resumed in March 1987 after a two-month hiatus, and by mid-1987 another nine ambassadorial appointments were announced.

Meanwhile, the most important former first deputy foreign minister, Kornienko, was transferred to a similar position in the CC International Department under new CC Secretary Dobrynin. In June the other older first deputy was reassigned as ambassador to Yugoslavia. These were all changes of scale and pace far higher than could normally be expected in a similar time frame.

The leaderships of the Ministry of Foreign Trade and of the State Committee for Foreign Economic Ties (GKES), two other ministries closely related to foreign policy, were also overhauled during Gorbachev's first year. Then in September of 1986 the entire management of foreign economic relations was restructured to operate under the Council of Ministers.

Gorbachev's personnel purges also affected the Council of Ministers dep-

40   Internal Politics

TABLE 2.1
Composition of the Top Leadership bodies
A: The CPSU

11 March 1985	30 June 1987

Politburo
Full Members

11 March 1985	30 June 1987
Gorbachev, 54 (1980)	* Gorbachev, 56 (1980)
Romanov, 62 (1976)	* Ligachev, 66 (1985)
Tikhonov, 80 (1979)	* Zaykov, 64 (1986)
Gromyko, 76 (1973)	Ryzhkov, 57 (1985)
Grishin, 70 (1971)	Gromyko, 78 (1973)
Aliev, 62 (1982)	Shevardnadze, 59 (1985)
Vorotnikov, 59 (1983)	Chebrikov, 64 (1985)
Solomentsev, 72 (1983)	Aliev, 64 (1982)
Shcherbitskiy, 67 (1971)	Vorotnikov, 61 (1983)
Kunaev, 73 (1971)	Solomentsev, 74 (1983)
	Shcherbitskiy, 69 (1971)
	** Yakovlev, 64 (1987)
	* Nikonov, 58 (1987)
	* Slyunkov, 58 (1987)
Average age: 67.5	Average age: 63.7
Average tenure: 9.7 years	Average tenure: 4.2 years

Candidate Members

11 March 1985	30 June 1987
Demichev, 67 (1964)	Demichev, 69 (1964)
Ponomarev, 80 (1972)	Dolgikh, 63 (1982)
Kuznetsov, 84 (1977)	Yazov, 64 (1987)
Shevardnadze, 57 (1978)	Talyzin, 58 (1985)
Dolgikh, 61 (1982)	Yeltsin, 56 (1986)
Chebrikov, 62 (1984)	Solovyev, 62 (1986)
Average age: 68.5	Average age: 62
Average tenure: 7.2 years	Average tenure: 5.3 years (1.8 excluding Demichev)

Secretariat

11 March 1985	30 June 1987
Gorbachev, 54 (1978)	General Secretary since March, 1985	* Gorbachev, 56 (1978)
Romanov, 62 (1983)	* Ligachev, 66 (1983)
Ponomarev, 80 (1961)	* Zaykov, 64 (1985)
Ryzhkov, 55 (1983)	Dolgikh, 63 (1982)
Ligachev, 64 (1983)	Dobrynin, 68 (1986)
Dolgikh, 61 (1972)	* Slyunkov, 58 (1987)
Zimyanin, 71 (1976)	** Yakovlev, 64 (1986)
Rusakov, 75 (1977)	* Nikonov, 58 (1985)
	Razumovskiy, 51 (1986)
	Medvedev, 58 (1986)
	Biryukova, 58 (1986)
	Lukyanov, 57 (1987)
Average age: 65.3	Average age: 60.1
Average tenure: 8.5 years	Average tenure: 1.8 years

Note: The number immediately following each name is the age the incumbent reached in the year in question. The year appears in parentheses.
* both Party secretary *and* full Politburo members.
** Yakovlev was also a candidate member from January 1987 to his promotion to full member in June.

TABLE 2.1 (Continued)
B: The State

11 March 1985	31 March 1987
Presidium, Council of Ministers	
Chairman	
Tikhonov***	Ryzhkov***
First Deputy Chairmen	
Aliev***	Aliev***
Arkhipov	Murakhovskiy
	Talyzin*
Deputy Chairmen	
Antonov	Antonov
Marchuk	Shcherbina
Shcherbina	Batalin
Bodyula	Gusev
Baybakov	Kamentsev
Dymshits	Maslyukov
Martynov	Silayev
Nuriyev	Vedernikov
Ryabov	Voronin
Smirnov	Tolstoy
Talyzin	

*** Also full member or candidate member of the Politburo.

uties who most frequently deal with foreign relations. Three of these were replaced. Deputy Chairman Ryabov was reassigned to become ambassador to France in June 1986. In October First Deputy Chairman Arkhipov was retired at age eighty, reportedly for reasons of health, and Deputy Chairman Marchuk, who was also chairman of the State Committee for Science and Technology, was moved from his positions to become the new president of the Soviet Academy of Science.

At the CPSU Congress itself the key CC departments for foreign policy were brought under the control of new Gorbachev men. The most important of these shifts was the retirement of Ponomarev. He was subsequently replaced by the new party secretary and former longtime ambassador to the United States, Dobrynin.

Dobrynin could be expected to be a fully loyal adviser who would see to it that the International Department faithfully carried out Gorbachev's policies. Moreover, throughout 1986 he appeared to have an expanded role in comparison with his predecessor. Whereas Ponomarev normally participated in meetings with foreign Party heads, the ostensible and traditional role of the International Department, Dobrynin was frequently reported in attendance at meetings of Gorbachev and the other top leadership with both visiting Party officials and those more purely from foreign *state* leaderships. At the same time Dobrynin's holdover first deputy in the International Department, Zagladin, was reported as the official most often meeting with the kind of foreign Party officials with whom Ponomarev had normally met. These patterns obviously would fit in with the hypothesis that Dobrynin had become the primary overall foreign policy adviser to Gorbachev.

Concurrently, the International Information Department was evidently subsumed into a new Information and Propaganda Department with an expanded role. Leonid Zamyatin, its longtime head, was subsequently appointed ambassador to Great Britain. His replacement was another of the new CC secretaries, Aleksander Yakovlev, a former ambassador to Canada and subsequently a close Gorbachev adviser. Then in late May 1986 Gorbachev evidently read the riot act to the assembled foreign policy establishment, including ambassadors recalled for the meeting. On this occasion he listed mistakes of the past and laid down guidelines for the future. Just before this meeting two more new deputy foreign ministers were named. It is noteworthy that Gromyko was not among the senior Politburo and Secretariat members participating.

Clearly, the process of Gorbachev's taking personal control of foreign policy and putting his own people in key positions to implement it was, like that for domestic economic policy, essentially completed by spring of 1986. Moreover, it appeared that the main locus of foreign policy decision-making input below the Politburo had become, in fact, the CC International Department.

This last judgment, about the centrality of the International Department, began to come into doubt during the first half of 1987. Yakovlev, the new head of the expanded successor to the International Information Department of the CC since the XXVII CPSU Congress, was promoted to candidate Politburo member in January 1987 and then to full Politburo membership in June. Meanwhile, he—and, to a lesser extent, CC Secretary Medvedev, who clearly had the East European Secretariat portfolio—increasingly accompanied Gorbachev on trips and in meetings with foreign visitors. At the same time, at least in press reporting, Dobrynin slipped into a more traditional International Department head's role except for his continuing special access with U.S. visitors who remembered him from his long years as ambassador in Washington.

Two conclusions seem warranted. By mid-1987 Gorbachev had succeeded in establishing a de facto committee of major foreign policy advisers with influence and responsibilities shared among a number of individuals in the Secretariat and with the Foreign Ministry safely returned to its traditional role as implementer rather than policymaker. Within that de facto committee, Yakovlev, not Dobrynin, evidently held the ascendent position. Besides the relevant CC secretaries, Ryzhkov and some of the other state officials (Aristov, Katushev, et al.) may have some policy-input roles in addition to executive functions. Of course, Cherebrikov, as KGB head and obviously a close Gorbachev ally, also has a foreign policy advice role. Meanwhile, the appointment of General Yazov, who owes his position solely to Gorbachev, ensured that the military voice will be very manageable. Gromyko is now undoubtedly merely symbolic.

The second conclusion is that as he has done in the central leadership as a whole, Gorbachev has diffused responsibility, and hence potential power, within foreign policy so as both to ensure that he himself has a firm grip and to prevent any further challengers from arising.

To return from our foreign policy personnel excursion to the overall picture, Gorbachev has demonstrated that he believes in results rather than in slogans and exhortations. He is attempting to make the system work without changing its nature or underlying principles. To do this, he needs people who can blend dynamism with pragmatism, and who will renounce the old working habits and get things done. This has given rise to Gorbachev's central problem: he has made the bureaucrats jittery about their own security and stability of their *nomenklatura* positions, which in Soviet parlance is called "concern for cadres." Gorbachev has subverted this cornerstone of Soviet personnel policy. Not so long ago Brezhnev could maintain himself in power for eighteen years because of his commitment to that policy and the elite support that his commitment generated.

In the fall of 1986 Gorbachev was in complete control of the situation, although prospects for the future were beclouded by two circumstances. The first was the already-mentioned fear and disillusionment of Party and government bureaucrats over the shakiness of their personal positions and privileges, which now were made dependent on how they perform in a system that tended to stymie achievement. The second circumstance had to do with the dynamics of Gorbachev's reforming thrust. As the first reforms failed to bring the desired results, Gorbachev was increasingly prompted to resort to more radical and comprehensive measures, entailing the growing risk of sparking radical and comprehensive social change. Each of these circumstances portended the eventual emergence of an opposition to the general secretary; together they magnified the potential for it.

The first period of Gorbachev's rule, which lasted from March 1985 through December 1986, was marked by purges on a scale and at a speed unseen since the 1930s. True, Gorbachev's methods were incomparably more humane than those of the Soviet history's most famous purger, Stalin. Apparently by mid-fall 1985, and undoubtedly by the end of 1986, opposition to Gorbachev was too weak to obstruct the progress of any reforms or innovative measures he wished to pursue. This shows that Gorbachev's consolidation of personal power was at least by the latter date already completed. However, his exact intentions still remained unclear. In particular, there was doubt as to whether Gorbachev really wanted to make fundamental changes in the system, and whether the system would permit him to effect radical transformations. Thus far the events of 1987 have done little to clear up this uncertainty. Personnel changes have continued, as expected, reaching high tide during two Central Committee plenums (in January and June). They also extended into the armed forces.

In January 1987 the Central Committee secretariat was expanded by the addition of two new members: Slyunkov, brought to Moscow from Byelorussia, where he headed that republic's Party organization; and Lukyanov, promoted from his post as head of a Central Committee department. At the same time another CC secretary, Yakovlev, clearly a protégé of Gorbachev, became a candidate member of the Politburo, and still another, Zimyanin, was pensioned off because of his closeness first to Brezhnev and subsequently to Chernenko.

The January CC plenum was "theoretically enriched" by a resolution dealing with "reconstruction," in particular with a review of Party cadre policy principles. The resolution stated that directors of enterprises would be elected, and that their selection and confirmation would be determined by competition. The practice of nomination of single candidates in elections to state and local governing organs and to the Supreme Soviet was to be discarded, with voters granted the right to select from several candidates. Further, the idea of secret ballots was espoused.

Both of these proposals were seized upon in the West as indicative of a fundamental liberalizing drive on Gorbachev's part. Such a conclusion seems premature. Whether to have multiple candidates is so far a question left to local levels to decide, and in the more significant examples quoted in the Soviet press during the first half of the year permitted candidates had to be expressly approved by the relevant Party committee and election board (the same thing). With Gorbachev himself reiterating the inviolability of "democratic centralism"—the primacy and unquestionability of the higher Party echelon discussion—choosing among several approved candidates rather than rubber-stamping one seems to have relatively little meaning. Only in some managerial positions in some enterprises and in the more symbolic and executive, as opposed to policy-making positions in local state councils (soviets) has there been any sign of surprise candidates among the multiple candidates reported. And it is as yet hardly certain that these were true surprises rather than staged events. For multiple candidates to signify anything even remotely approaching Western liberal values, they would have to include viable candidates put forth in opposition to the Party choices. This has not yet been in evidence. Similarly, secret ballots will not mean what Western optimists have attributed to them until it can be shown that they can lead to rejection of the Party choice or the proposal and election of a true, i.e. unapproved, write-in or nonsanctioned candidate. Again, this had not yet happened by mid-1987.

Moreover, secret ballots were called for only up to the union-republic level. Along with the specification that multiple candidates were a matter of local choice, not obligation, this may be a key to the real intentions of these highly touted reforms. Gorbachev's problems so far lie in the middle levels of the Party and state bureaucracies, not in the central leadership. Whatever else they may portend or be intended for, multiple candidacies and secret ballots at these levels are an ideal tactic to counter entrenched protectionism in the localized arena (*mestnichestvo*). Further, Soviet rubber-stamped elections with 99% or 100 percent votes for single candidates have long since lost credibility on the outside. As part of the campaign to convince a doubting world that *glasnost* is really meaningful, the admission of some opposing views and the occasional election of a second choice among centrally selected candidates is a small price to pay. Finally—and this also fits with what we can deduce about Gorbachev's priorities—such elections can provide the central leadership with a more reliable feedback on local opinion than was previously available under the rigid and sycophantic process previously in place.

Before we can join those who see these reforms as major indicators of true liberalization, we must examine the substance behind economic, social, and foreign policy reforms. This will be done in subsequent chapters.

The June CC plenum led to a new constellation of political forces in the Kremlin. Some officials were precipitously raised to the Party Olympus while the power of others was undermined. CC secretaries Slyunkov and Yakovlev were promoted from candidate members to full members of the Politburo, and Nikonov became a full member without having ever been a candidate member. These changes yielded six CC secretaries who were simultaneously Politburo members: Gorbachev himself, Ligachev, Zaykov, Nikonov, Yakovlev, and Slyunkov, a record in Soviet history. What was Gorbachev's purpose here? Probably, he most of all wanted thus to reduce this exalted status. From Stalin's time onward all general secretaries came from among this elite group of CC secretaries who were also Politburo members. There was a logic to this, for the usual two or three CC secretaries who were also members of the Politburo were by necessity bound to accumulate tremendous power, influence, and authority. But when Gorbachev enlarged the number of such aspirants to the top post to six, their power realms were bound to overlap, with the effect that none of them could claim unchallenged status. When half of the Politburo strove for a top position, not one of them could emerge from the field to overcome the others.

A strange situation developed in the Politburo. Several of its members who concurrently served as CC secretaries began to be responsible for the same sectors of Party activity. Yakovlev assumed authority over ideology, and Slyunkov over the Party apparat. Thus, Gorbachev signaled to Ligachev that the latter was no longer irreplaceable. In fact, Ligachev's authority was so circumscribed that his removal from the post of second secretary of the Central Committee became a distinct possibility, especially in the event he dared to oppose the policies or reforms of Gorbachev. Ligachev had recently begun to demonstrate his independence. Although indebted to Gorbachev for bringing him to Moscow and making him second man in the Party, he had begun to take the liberty of expressing views differing from those of the general secretary. As a result of this, the conservative Party bureaucrats who were frightened by the reforms of Gorbachev and concerned about where the general secretary's unbridled dynamism might lead began to gravitate toward and unite around Ligachev. Gorbachev therefore has reason to cut Ligachev down to size. It is now quite possible that Ligachev's turf will be taken away from him and split between Yakovlev and Slyunkov, with the former assuming responsibility for ideology, and thus becoming heir to Suslov, and the latter for industry. Agriculture has already been removed from Ligachev's control and become the responsibility of Nikonov. Under such circumstances, Ligachev could at best retain only the oversight of Party cadres.

The June plenum revealed the extent of Gorbachev's power, but it also revealed its limits. He did not succeed in removing from the Politburo his two main and most dangerous opponents, Aliev and Shcherbitsky, who might have been protected by Ligachev. Neither Aliev nor Shcherbitsky chose to oppose Gorbachev; rather, both found themselves in opposition to him by the force of circumstances. Shcherbitsky's "problem" was that he had been too close to Brezhnev. He would have no objection to getting close to Gorbachev, and indeed made efforts toward that end, but his past record damned him. Aliev's offense was of a more subjective nature. Being a clever and crafty courtier, he made a fatal political mistake after the death of Andropov by staking his future on a wrong "horse." He eagerly joined the camp of Chernenko without any premonition of the brevity of the latter's rule. Now both Shcherbitsky and Aliev faced the prospect of accounts being settled on Gorbachev's terms. They succeeded in retaining their Politburo posts in June 1987, but their position there is highly precarious and their careers are likely to be cut short at the upcoming Party Congress in 1988. (It should be noted that Party conferences are a tradition that Gorbachev has revived; they used to be convened in the prewar years in the USSR but later fell into disuse.)

The June CC plenum also marked Gorbachev's purge in the armed forces. Although careful plans had already been made, chance also played a role. Personnel changes in the Ministry of Defense were more cautious and narrower in scope than those in the Party and government bureaucracies. Like his predecessors, Gorbachev displayed tact and restraint in dealing with the armed forces, in obvious recognition of their potential influence and political leverage. Although in times of political stability the army may stay on the sidelines, it does gain political clout in crisis situations, particularly at watershed points in Soviet history. It suffices to recall that the support of the armed forces fundamentally affected the outcome of the struggle for succession in the Kremlin each time a new general secretary was to be chosen. This explains why Gorbachev could ill afford any risks in his dealings with the Ministry of Defense hierarchy. Consequently, his dismissals and personnel reassignments were carefully planned and carried through gradually. He attempted to retain the favor of the army not by recourse to the political fist but by a show of sensitivity to the army's importance and to its needs. One of his concrete actions was to waive income taxes for military personnel, but this was not enough to ensure his full control over their ranks. Minister of Defense Sokolov was not one of his men. Like many other top-ranking generals, Sokolov had been "inherited" from Brezhnev. There existed, of course, the proven way of winning the favor of the armed forces by raising their influence and prestige. Gorbachev was far from disdaining such methods. He made Sokolov a candidate member of the Politburo, even though he feared to promote him to full membership.

While Gorbachev was treading carefully through this minefield, fortune came to his aid. On 28 May, a nineteen-year-old West German youth, Mathias Rust, suddenly landed a single-engine light aircraft in Red Square. Rust flew across the Soviet border, which had been considered impermeable, traversed a thousand kilometers of Soviet territory guarded by the most modern radar system, remained untouched by the antiaircraft defenses on his route, and finally, to the Soviet leadership's utter dismay, landed in the very heart of Moscow, where he presented himself as an idealistic young man on a self-designated friendship mission. Two aspects of this affair are striking. The first was that Rust's plane was not brought down by the renowned Soviet air force. The second was that the Politburo convened specially to discuss Rust's flight and to deplore the "unacceptable negligence and indecision" of the commanders of the Soviet antiaircraft defenses.

Gorbachev's reaction was two-tracked. In relation to the West it was moderate, without the shrill accusations one might have expected on such an occasion. But in relation to the top army brass that had not shown itself capable of "intercepting the flight of an intruding aircraft" it was precipitous. In fact, the ouster of the commander of the antiaircraft defense,

Alexander Koldunov, was unconstitutional: by Politburo resolution. The removal of the minister of defense, however, was carried out in the formally correct manner: on the basis of a resolution of the Presidium of the Supreme Soviet, evidently at the request of the Politburo.

Gorbachev finally gained the opportunity fully to carry out a purge in the armed forces. He proceeded to do so: horizontally by hitting the commands of various types of forces (something already well under way; see chapter 12, "The Metal Eaters"); and vertically by hitting the central hierarchy of the Ministry of Defense, including the minister himself. Appointed as new minister was Dmitry Yazov, general of the army, who only shortly before had been appointed deputy minister of defense for cadres. Yazov was not a member of the Central Committee of the CPSU and did not have connections with the centers of power in Moscow. This was the first time in Soviet history that a man with so low a Party status was chosen as minister of defense, but this handicap was soon to be remedied. At the June 1987 plenum Yazov was coopted not only to the Central Committee but also to the Politburo as a candidate member. Thereupon all three traditional loci of high power were firmly in Gorbachev's hands: the Party apparatus, the organs of state security, and now the armed forces as well, all three subject to his political manipulations, according to the timeless device *divide et impera.*

Meanwhile, the *Gorbachevishchina* had continued steadily if unspectacularly through the state apparat and lower levels of the Party hierarchy in the first half of 1987. At the top in mid-1987, Gorbachev could count eight of thirteen other members of the fourteen-man Politburo as his appointees (two others, Vorotnikov and Solomentsev, were Andropov appointees who had supported him from the beginning, and Gromyko was increasingly symbolic). Similarly, four of six candidate Politburo members were his appointees, and nine of the eleven other Party secretaries were. Considering these figures and recognizing his adroit diffusion of responsibilities among them, it was clear that whatever else he might be, Gorbachev was a master of Kremlin internal politics.

3

To Build a Better Mousetrap: The Economy

There is an incisive Soviet joke of recent years that goes like this: It is winter, and across one of the wide Russian rivers is a gleaming new bridge. On the approach to the bridge is a large sign whose words indicate that the bridge, provided for the people of the USSR by the Soviet government and the CPSU, is a tribute to Soviet science and production. A peasant in a horse-drawn cart approaches the bridge, reads the sign, and then carefully leads the horse and cart down the bank of the river and cautiously crosses on the ice! On the other side he builds a small fire and warms his hands. A battered truck driven by a *kolkhoznik* (collective farmer) next approaches the bridge. He repeats the puzzling procedure and is soon warming his hands with the peasant. The next approaching vehicle is a shiny, black Chaika limousine. It speeds onto the bridge and when it is halfway across, the bridge collapses and the official car plunges through the ice. The peasant shakes his head sadly and says, "He didn't read the sign!"

Truly, there is much in the Soviet economy that does not work as it is supposed to, and awareness of this has been increasingly evident in recent years. The overriding emphasis of the new Gorbachev leadership has been on the economy and the need to revitalize it in every way possible. In fact, even the main themes of Gorbachev's avowed foreign policy and social programs can be largely traced to their potential contributions to his program of economic recovery.

In stark departure from normal Soviet political discourse, Gorbachev and his followers have been unusually candid in cataloguing past failures, ineffeciencies, and shortcomings. Moreover, a series of major programs and proclaimed reforms have been announced, first in general terms but then, especially after the 1986 Party Congress, in increasing detail. The key questions that we will attempt to answer in this chapter are these: What are the main elements of Gorbachev's economic program? Why have they

49

taken the form of presentation and content that they have? To what extent do they represent meaningful, fundamental systemic reform? In the process we will necessarily touch upon the question of what their intended or unintended short- and long-range outcomes are likely to be. However, a more extensive prediction of their likely long-range effects will have to await the final chapter of the book.

It has already been noted that accumulated economic problems provided Gorbachev with a very effective vehicle for consolidating his power by replacing the entrenched supporters of both past and potential future rivals—the main justification of the *Gorbachevshchina,* or Gorbachev purge, that has swept the USSR during the new leader's still-short reign. Given the realities of Soviet politics, power would seem to be a sufficient explanation for the entire push for economic change, yet this explanation is insufficient for several reasons. Some real management and organizational changes have taken place that seem unnecessary for merely bringing in the new leader's supporters. The amount of fairly sharp, if often convoluted and opaquely phrased, "criticism" that appeared in the press was quite out of the ordinary. Further, the most striking changes in Soviet economic practice have been announced after the XXVII Congress, when Gorbachev's power and position could have been presumed to be fully consolidated. Finally, and most relevant, is the fact that the economic problems were real and had to be addressed. Let us examine the chronology of the new programs and reforms and the way in which they have been presented. Then we will be better able to evaluate them.

A considerable number of sharply pointed criticisms of economic inefficiency and corrupt practices began to appear right at the beginning of Gorbachev's rule and they increased in frequency thereafter. The same holds true for academic-type discussions of problem areas and proposed solutions in the Soviet press. None of this was entirely new, but the frequency of such articles in the central press, as opposed to specialized journals, and especially the tone of the criticisms were rather different from normal practice. Organizations and individuals responsible for malpractices were often explicitly named. Regional Party conferences throughout the country addressed economic issues. The low level of industrial discipline was singled out for criticism, especially, although not exclusively, in the regional bases of the old Brezhnev-Chernenko leadership (Moldavia, the Ukraine, Kazakhstan, and so on). Management in various regions was repeatedly accused of "sham" efficiency, "pulling the wool over people's eyes," "words in place of action," "arrogance," "irresponsibility," "mental lethargy," and "sticking to outmoded methods." Notably however, these failures were attributed not to the system of centralized administration but rather to the negligence of certain top functionaries. Hence, they provided the rationale for the removal of various ministers and regional Party functionaries.

In his speech at the April 1985 plenum of the Central Committee, Gorbachev focused on the economic and social tasks facing the country. Although he provided virtually no details of how, in practical terms, they would be accomplished, he did identify the major goals that subsequent programmatic decrees and decisions were supposed to achieve. In effect this speech foreshadowed the rest of the year's actions in the economic, social, and foreign policy fields.

Gorbachev began with the theme that the Soviet Union's place and success in the world depended upon its economic performance. He set the following tasks before the nation and the Party: to increase the productivity of labor and the efficiency of management; to expand and perfect the introduction of modern science and technology into the production process; to integrate more effectively different aspects of the economy and, particularly, of its different branches (special emphasis was put on the agricultural-industrial complex); and to improve the range and quality of consumer goods and products. He also enumerated, albeit in very general terms, the prerequisites needed for achieving these goals: improvement of the effectiveness of central planning; a willingness to try new methods; greater local responsibility and accountability; greater discipline; more receptivity to criticism; and the full participation of central leaders and management in regional and industry conferences. The Party role, in particular, was emphasized. Finally, all was to be integrated into a "complex program" to be developed for 1986 to 1990 and then on to the year 2000.

The draconian May 1985 decree on combating alcoholism (see chapter 4) was largely couched in terms of its connection with labor discipline and productivity. Council for Economic Mutual Assistance (CEMA) meetings—in May of the executive council and in June at the heads-of-state level—emphasized the integration of the economies of the member states in ways both directly paralleling the emerging Soviet economic revitalization program and geared to the same long-term program. (Throughout this book we have used the acronym CEMA for this organization rather than the equally common Western usages of CMEA or COMECON. The Russian is Sovyet Ekonomicheskoy Vzaimopomoshchii [Council of Economic Mutual Assistance] and is abbreviated in Russian as SEV.)

Through most of the summer the economic program continued to be expressed in generalities that, although largely devoid of meaningful specific content, established the broad directions and priorities to be followed. Priorities were assigned to retooling the machine-building, construction, and resource-extraction and -processing industries; introduction of more modern technology; more efficient central planning and local management; and strengthening discipline and improving incentives for quality production. On 4 August 1985 a significant Party and government decree was published calling for new methods of economic management. It included a provision allowing enterprises to use government financing to support production for export in a way that would apparently reduce the traditional central monopoly of foreign trade. In this regard stress was placed on direct enterprise cooperation and contracts with foreign, mostly Eastern European, counterparts to supplement and replace traditional state-to-state agreements. The decree exhorted enterprises to take the initiative and make their own arrangements for retooling. This type of reconstruction modernization of management and capital inventory was to be given priority over expansion and new construction, the traditional method of Soviet economic growth. Enterprises producing better-quality goods were to retain higher percentages of their wholesale receipts for use as incentive bonuses. Simultaneously, the penalties for poor-quality products were to be increased. Along with this, local managers were to have greater discretion in distributing bonuses and even in firing inefficient workers.

The significance of the August decree, like the basic strategy that Gorbachev had outlined in April, lay not so much in any immediate application as in the directions toward which its contents pointed. Concrete measures to implement the new techniques still needed to be worked out in detail. At the same time senior planners and managers had to be either forced or persuaded to operate in different ways, or replacements had to be found who would do so.

Throughout the summer and early fall of 1985 the press carried a number of relatively straightforward articles on economic developments in the German Democratic Republic, the People's Republic of China, and Hungary, where rather diverse economic experiments had been producing some fairly dramatic results. Significantly, the achievements in the GDR, where the emphasis was on integration of separate branches of a broad general industrial field into complex associations, tended to be given the most favorable and complete treatment. The articles about the PRC, although giving some of the dramatic production growth figures achieved, tended to emphasize the social costs in corruption and the like while downplaying the actual extent of marketization. The articles on Hungary left out some key features, such as the fact that "worker-management" programs included real local elections of the worker-managers. Significantly, after the long-term program of economic development was announced in the fall, such articles decreased in frequency, although they did not disappear entirely. As we shall see, they again reappeared in greater frequency, especially those related to the PRC, in late summer of 1986, and election of managers in some state firms was called for in 1987.

In the autumn and winter of 1985 the pace of change stepped up. From mid-September, when Ryzhkov replaced Tikhonov, through January 1986 there was a considerable turnover in the Council of Ministers, the senior state apparatus; concrete economic goals were defined; and major organizational changes were introduced in parts of the economy.

On 9 October a "complex program" for improved consumer goods production and services was published. On 26 October the text of the draft of the new Party Program restated the already-set general economic goals and methods of achieving them; and on 9 November the text of "The Basic Directions of Economic and Social Developments in the USSR for 1986–1990 and to the year 2000" was published. All of these documents were impressive in their descriptions of goals and prospects for the future, but they were also emphatic in stressing the difficulties of the tasks ahead. They avoided repeating Khrushchev's overblown promises of surpassing the West and quickly achieving a paradise of Communist abundance. Rather, significant rewards were promised for succeeding generations, but the present one was called upon to bear sacrifices and subject itself to discipline in order to achieve benefits for the future. As before, there were few specific details on how this was to be accomplished.

In November, however, there was a major organizational change affecting the most blatantly and chronically unproductive sector of the Soviet economy: agriculture. Five ministries—agriculture, rural construction, the food industry, the meat and dairy industry, and the fruit and vegetable industry—were combined into one new institution, the State Committee for Agricultural Industry (GOSAGROPROM). The State Committee of Production and Services of Agricultural Technology was done away with. This allegedly "very far-reaching and newest" reconstruction of the economy was in fact neither "new" nor "far-reaching." First, similar reorganizational measures had been undertaken by Khrushchev; and second, the reform was not "far-reaching," for it did not transform the system and organization of agriculture, which remained centralized and collectivized. Moreover, the person who was named superminister heading GOS-AGROPROM was appointed at least as much for his personal loyalty and dependence as for any practical or organizational abilities. Previously, the fifty-nine-year-old Vsevolod Murakhovsky had worked alongside Gorbachev in Stavropol and had succeeded him as first secretary of the regional committee (*Kraykom*) when Gorbachev was called to Moscow to the Central Committee Secretariat.

On 1 November, Murakhovsky had been called to Moscow and announced as a first deputy chairman of the Council of Ministers. When the formation of GOSAGROPROM was announced, he was named its chairman.

Agriculture is the most dramatically troubled sector of the Soviet economy. Over the past five years alone, the USSR has had to import more than 30 million tons of grain annually. However, in the Soviet Union under Gorbachev it has not been acceptable to speak of a crisis in agriculture. At most, negligence on the part of collective farm chairmen and certain failures and irregularities have been noted. This, of course, can be attributed to the fact that in recent years Gorbachev himself supervised agriculture. To remind people that agricultural targets have not been met would be to undermine the prestige of the new leader; yet it is not possible to pass over the failures in silence. Hence, a formula that Gorbachev himself originated has appeared in the Soviet lexicon: allocations to agriculture have already reached "reasonable limits." This is why, at this stage, the Party decided to concentrate on "decisive sectors," as Gorbachev put it, for which it was deemed necessary to create a new economic facade: the Committee on Agriculture.

Gorbachev convened a special, extraordinary meeting of CEMA at the heads-of-state level in December. With Ryzhkov, he presented the Soviet demands, which had largely been worked out in a preceding series of mostly lower-level economic consultations. Formal commitment of all the CEMA states, with the apparent exception of Romania, was obtained for an integrated, long-term (to the year 2000) "complex program" of economic development heavily focused on development and introduction of new technologies. When one reads between the lines, one quickly understands that the Eastern Europeans are expected to bend their efforts to help the Soviet economy.

The XXVII Party Congress (25 February to 6 March 1986) also focused heavily on the economic program. As before, there were far more generalities than specific details. What was presented in some detail were the far from encouraging results of the previous, the eleventh, Five-Year Plan. Over the preceding five years national income rose, if official Soviet statistics can be trusted, by 17 percent instead of the planned 20 percent. There were admitted shortfalls of 145 million tons of coal, 35 million tons of rolled metal, and 50 million tons of oil. According to Gorbachev, these failures were attributable to "fake reporting, nonexistent achievements and palliative measures." In a real departure from time-honored custom, the blame was placed not on top Party functionaries but on ministries and ministers, most of whom had already been purged by Gorbachev.

It is noteworthy that this somewhat dismal accounting directly paralleled the report in January of the results of the 1985 plan and preceded another report, in April, that summarized the results of the first quarter of 1986. With few exceptions, the same industries and areas of the economy were singled out for shortfalls and continued inefficiencies. Moreover, the fact that the oil industry led the list of culprits in all of these accountings, as it had the previous autumn, was particularly discouraging, for the bulk of hard currency earnings, which the USSR needs to pay for grain and consumer goods imports and to finance modernization, has come from oil and gas exports. The revenues from these exports had already been sharply reduced because of the precipitous drop in their world prices.

Another notable, if predictable, characteristic of the economic discussion just preceding the Party Congress, and even more in its aftermath, was its tone. Explicit criticism of past failures became more muted and less specific. After the Congress emphasis shifted to unnamed, unidentified functionaries who were said still to be resisting adoption of new methods and to be stuck in dogmatic bureaucratic "immobilism." At the same time even the accountings of target failures in areas of the economy were increasingly presented via selective statistics designed to show that the latter months of 1985, when Gorbachev's programs were beginning to be instituted, were marked by fairly dramatic improvements over earlier performance. Moreover, concrete figures concerning agricultural production continued to be noteworthy primarily for their incompleteness and the absence of some of the most important indicators.

On the other hand, in press interviews at the Congress, in major press articles following the Congress, and in a Central Committee and Council of Ministers decree on improving light industry and consumer goods production published in early May, one could finally find some concrete guidelines on new operating methods and some substantial data on potentially significant reforms. Although the decree basically reiterated information available in the interviews and articles, it did include some distinctly new elements that if allowed to function as implied, would mark significant changes from the past.

The basic thrust of the decree was that light and consumer industry enterprises would have much more discretion both in determining what and how much to produce and in handling distribution and sales of their products. In large measure the decree reiterated the incentive and investment flexibilities announced the previous August; however, it also added elements novel for the USSR. Economic indexes, worked out largely on the basis of wholesale orders placed with these enterprises at biennial wholesale fairs, were to be stable for the duration of each five-year plan, and long-term contracts were to be made between associated branches and enterprises. Within the RSFSR (the Russian republic) in 1987, all contracts made between light industry and the trade enterprises were to be long term, evidently as an "experiment" for potential adoption nationwide. Enterprises were to be given the authority autonomously to develop their own plans for economic and social development. New associations of quality industries were to be formed to set standards and style for the main branches of light industry. Profits (bonuses) were no longer to be distributed within branches with the effect of covering the losses of less profitable elements at the expense of those that had been more successful. Long-term credit was to be available and to be the preference as a source of investment funding. Small-enterprise branches and "name"-product sales outlets for quality goods were to be allowed and encouraged. Potentially most significant, enterprises were to be allowed to set their own reduced prices for goods produced in excess of the state orders so as to sell them profitably at such sales outlets or to other trade organizations if the items did not sell within one month of their appearance on the market. These reforms and others in the package were to go into effect throughout light and consumer industries in January 1987, a transitional year.

In a similar fashion, a limited number of reforms had been proclaimed that would facilitate legal operation of some more private-enterprise-type activities (automotive repair shops, for example, as long as no employees were involved) and the peasants' markets, which had long provided a disproportionate share of the nation's fresh vegetables and fruits. However, at the end of May 1986 the Central Committee and the Council of Ministers issued decrees "to strengthen the struggle against unearned income," which, if anything, seemed to undercut these particular limited reforms legalizing small parts of the "second economy" and helping the peasant markets.

In June 1986 the proverbial substance hit the fan. Both Gorbachev's and Ryzhkov's speeches at the CPSU Plenum, but especially Gorbachev's, amounted to blistering condemnations of the economic bureaucracy and its immediate Communist Party supervisory committees. The revealing catchwords and phrases were "resistance to change"; "immobilism"; "failure to adopt new methods"; "unwillingness to adapt"; "paper shuffling"; "bureaucratic stifling of initiative"; "false reporting"; and the like—almost ad nauseam. These themes continued into the fall, were stepped up in the beginning of the next year, and still predominated at the time this analysis was written, late summer 1987. Initially, the criticisms mostly singled out second-level officials and local enterprise or regional managers and officials for identification. Ministers and chairmen of the state committees were charged by implication via harsh castigation of methods and results in entire industries or sectors. Then as the summer progressed, the latter aspect (critiques of whole ministries and sectors) increased and the ministers in charge were directly identified. Some were even reprimanded officially by the Party Control Committee and, in a September press report, were said to be the objects of legal action stemming from a procuracy investigation.

In July 1986, a new wave of personnel replacements began, mostly starting with ministers who had just been the subject of direct, by-name criticisms or whose ministries had been singled out for continuing problems. As noted in the previous chapter, one striking thing about this was that beginning in July there was both specific criticism and some firing of officials whom Gorbachev had appointed.

The statistical report on the economy for the first six months of the year was revealing both for what it said and what it left unsaid. As usual, the vast majority of the statistics showed improvements in both production and labor productivity over the same period of the previous year. They also indicated that almost every ministry and sector was ahead of its planned targets for production for the six months. However, in a very large number of cases they revealed that for all three of these indicators—percentage of plan fulfillment, and production and labor productivity compared to the same portion of the previous year—the six-months' figures were lower than those for the first three months of 1986. In other words, between April and June there was a relative economic downturn. This suggested that the predictable, initial benefits of new management, new encouragement, organizational streamlining and modest reforms had already reached, or were approaching, the limits of their abilities to help. If so, it was a strong indictment of their inadequacy for transforming the economy rather than simply and probably temporarily taking up some of the existing slack.

The text of the statistical report on the economy was also revealing. As before, there was a noticeable repetition of the same industries and sectors previously singled out for continued failings. What was new in its degree of emphasis was that industries were castigated for failure to introduce new technology, for not meeting quality targets even when they exceeded quantitative ones, and for generally mismanaging their research and technological support assets. Because introduction and utilization of advanced technology was to be perhaps the major criterion of success in revitalizing the Soviet economy and preparing it for the twenty-first century, there could hardly be a more discouraging indicator of the inadequacies thus far of Gorbachev's reforms.

As in the previous summaries published for earlier periods of Gorbachev's helmsmanship, those presented in July were notable for the incompleteness of data and the mostly favorable descriptions of agriculture. But as the summer progressed, the real picture was not hard to discern from the press. In the normal exhortations published as the fall harvest approached, one could sense an increasing urgency and worry. Articles referring to agricultural wastage proliferated. Republic Party plenums and regional meetings regularly scored shortcomings in agricultural management, and several republic branches of GOSAGROPROM were chastised. In pointed contrast, examples were cited of places where a good harvest was expected in spite of the extensive drought that had beset parts of the country. Finally, when grain figures were published, they showed a harvest slightly over 210 million metric tons. This was better than 1985 (190 million tons) and above Western estimates, which had ranged between 175 and 185 million tons, but it was far below the goal of 250 million. Once again, the USSR would have to import huge quantities of grain. Gorbachev's first major structural reorganization had been in agriculture when he created the superministry GOSAGROPROM. The first year's results stood in sorry contrast to the dramatic successes achieved by real structural agricultural reform in the PRC.

During much of the summer the emphasis continued to be on exhortation. A few more industries were directed to switch to a system of "full self-financing" (*khozraschet*) in 1987, and several relatively minor decrees were issued to fine tune parts of the economy, especially in the directions of greater accountability for output and of meeting sales contracts. Then in August and September more dramatic organizational and operating reforms were announced.

In a manner similar to the restructuring of agriculture under GOS-AGROPROM, the contruction industries were reorganized. The existing State Committee for Construction Affairs, which had been somewhat in limbo, was redesignated as a union-republic committee analogous to GOS-AGROPROM. A deputy chairman of the Council of Ministers, Yu P. Batalin, a Gorbachev appointee, was named its chairman, and one of his first deputy chairmen was designated a minister of the USSR and member of the Council of Ministers. These levels of appointments were reminiscent of almost identical steps in agriculture the previous fall. Three new ministries were created—apparently on the basis of the existing ministries of construction, of industrial construction, and of construction for enterprises of heavy industry, whose heads, all Gorbachev appointees, were designated as the ministers of the new organizations. More strikingly, the three new ministries were regional. Together with the redesignated previous Ministry for Construction in the Far East and Transbaikal, they divided the USSR into four parts for most construction. They and several other construction ministries would now all come directly under the new construction superministry (GOSSTROI), and other related ministries and state committees would coordinate and work closely with it. As with GOS-AGROPROM, this reorganization streamlined management, although it created a new centralized bureaucracy at the top, but of itself did little or nothing to change the basic features of the system.

Another August 1986 decree, on "perfecting planning, economic stimulation and management in state trade and consumers cooperatives," further refined earlier generalized reforms and the more specific spring decree on light industry and consumer goods. Probably the potentially most significant provision of this decree was that retail turnover, along with quality and assortment, was to be the main planning indicator and criterion for bonuses and so on for both the trade network and its product suppliers. The decree also called for greater use of credit in sales, as well as for the setting up of special high-fashion shops in major cities.

A third important August decree stopped the long-standing project to divert waters from north-flowing Siberian rivers to irrigate Central Asian regions. Although couched in terms of a need for more environmental-impact evaluation, the decision was more likely taken primarily for the purpose of saving a sizeable amount of near-term investment and construction costs. It also served as an example and object lesson in support of the ongoing campaign urging ministries, city and regional planners, and the like to review their current projects and eliminate those that do not meet current standards for intensive modernization and are not based on the most modern technology. A great deal of criticism was directed at scientific and research institutions, as well as production and construction organizations, for wasting time and money on already outmoded or irrelevant projects. In fact, a July evaluation published with considerable fanfare in the central press indicated that some 40 percent of all projects currently under way within institutions under the State Committee for Science and Technology fit these negative descriptions.

Yet another potentially very important reorganization and reform was announced in September 1986, this one affecting foreign trade. Although the USSR is uniquely rich in natural resources, foreign economic relations—long focused more on the goals of political influence than on economic needs—have become increasingly important in economic and social terms. As already noted, for many years now the USSR has had to import vast quantities of grain and other foodstuffs just to meet minimal population needs. Moreover, acquisition of advanced Western industrial goods and technology, already long important to Moscow, is now a central element in Gorbachev's economic revitalization program. To obtain sufficient quantities of goods and technology, the Soviets need many things. They need the kind of political detente that could reduce Western barriers to technology transfer and that could encourage greater access to credit and investment. They need adequate hard currency earnings to pay for Western goods, and they need to find ways in which better to deal with market economies whose representatives distrust Soviet state monopolies and find the Soviet political-economic bureaucracy difficult to do business with.

The search for political detente with the West will be addressed in part 2 of this book. Here it is sufficient to note that there is a major economic aspect to its rationale and that the other aspects of Gorbachev's foreign economic strategy, including the reforms and reorganizations, are also partly intended to provide the requisite atmosphere and "carrots" to encourage detente.

Obtaining the amount of hard currency needed to import Western products and grain is a major problem for Moscow. Few Soviet industrial products are competitive on the world market. Rather, Soviet hard currency earnings have basically come from the export of raw materials—primarily oil and natural gas, as well as gold, platinum, chromium, and diamonds—plus arms sales. Normally, about two-thirds of Soviet hard currency earnings have come from oil and gas sales, primarily to Western Europe. As prices dropped in 1985 and plummeted in early 1986, Moscow faced major problems. Even assuming that late-summer OPEC efforts to restore higher prices for petroleum continue in stabilizing world prices in the $15-$19-per-barrel range, the Soviets stand to lose some $10 to $13 billion in hard currency earnings compared to normal years.

In 1985 Moscow virtually doubled the amount of gold it sold compared with 1984, and 1986 sales were high in an attempt to recoup some of the losses in oil and gas sales. However, even if trade barriers to South Africa (Moscow's major rival as an exporter of gold, diamonds, platinum, and chromium) become much more effective than they have so far been, it is clear that a freer hand in the market for those commodities cannot make up the difference in petroleum and gas losses. Further, the arms market has little if any significant room for expansion, especially because the principal hard currency buyers are themselves suffering from dramatic drops in oil income and because the USSR faces intense competition from often superior, if more costly, Western military hardware exporters. Eventually, of course, most experts believe that the global oil market will once again become a sellers' paradise. Still, this is not projected before the 1990s, and even then is not entirely a certainty. In any event, Gorbachev needs remedies much earlier than that if his economic strategy is to work.

In part, the Soviets have turned to Eastern Europe for technology and industrial and consumer products. In fact, the main foreign trade reforms have been aimed first in that direction. This also has other purposes and is further addressed in the chapter on relations with Eastern Europe. Here, it is only necessary to note that Eastern Europe is unlikely to be able to satisfy Soviet needs. And in part, Moscow has turned to Western lending institutions, increasing the amounts it is borrowing. This not only has both limits and drawbacks but also appears unrealistic as an answer to the requirements of Gorbachev's modernization program. One very respected Western analysis (by Jan Vannous, as summarized in the *Washington Post*) has concluded that merely to match previous levels of machinery imports from the West, the Soviets would have to increase their gross foreign debt by some $25 billion over the next five years. But matching previous import levels would not satisfy the needs of the economic modernization upon which Gorbachev's long-term political legitimacy so heavily rests. This would probably require, in addition to all the other internal and external measures, an increase in gross foreign debt on the order of $50 billion during the same period. Even if this scale of lending can be obtained from the Western banks, which is hardly certain, it would probably be too much for Soviet political leaders to swallow. It appears that other solutions have to be found. The autumn 1986 reform of the foreign trade structure and methods was part of the attempt to do so.

The foreign trade reform was both organizational and procedural. Organizationally, it somewhat paralleled the model used for GOS-AGROPROM and GOSSTROI. The State Foreign Export Commission was created under the Council of Ministers to supervise and coordinate foreign export ministries and organizations, and its chairman (not initially designated) was to be on the same level as a deputy chairman, Council of Ministers. This is similar to the other aforementioned superministries but not quite the same. Such a commission is not truly a ministry or state committee, and the Ministry of Foreign Trade and the State Committee for Foreign Economic Ties (GKES) are not really subsumed by it but are apparently to be generally guided and coordinated by it while they control much of the export-import activities of ministries and enterprises and ensure that the state's needs are accounted for. Moreover, some exports will continue to be conducted by other ministries, as in the past.

The procedural reforms were much more significant. Over twenty ministries and some seventy large trusts and enterprises, under many ministries and state committees, were to be given the right to conduct their own direct export and import operations, similar in theory to Western firms, and to enter into joint investment and production enterprise operations with foreign firms both on Soviet soil and abroad. All of this, like most of the other 1986 announced reforms and changes, was to go into effect 1 January 1987. In this case these independent and joint operations were to be primarily focused initially on Eastern Europe and selected developing states with a socialist orientation. Nevertheless, similar activities were to be allowed with capitalist firms on mutually beneficial terms as long as they were conducted in accord with Soviet laws. Here, of course, is where these steps are envisioned as part of the strategy to obtain access to credit, investment, and technology and to provide potential answers to the hard-currency dilemma. Presumably, the products of joint enterprises constructed in the USSR with the assistance of Western funds and technology would be much more competitive as exports than purely Soviet products, at the same time serving to meet growing Soviet domestic needs.

Concurrently—and for much the same purposes—the Soviets expressed interest in joining the International Monetary Fund and the General Agreement on Trade and Tariffs (GATT), and the Soviet-dominated East Bloc economic union (CEMA) engaged in talks aimed at establishing formal working relationships with the European Economic Community (EEC). At the same time, for the first time ever, a Soviet bank joined with Western banks in underwriting a Eurocredit offer. In the West this was widely believed to be a trial prelude to Moscow's presenting its own Eurobond offerings to raise needed investment capital. Needless to say, these new departures, including the foreign trade reforms, were mutually complementary and supportive in their aims.

Another reform was announced later in the fall. It further extended and clarified earlier changes designed to legalize some small-business sales and service activities, such as appliance and automotive repairs, and so on. Like the earlier, limited moves in this direction, it was restricted: it did not allow the hiring of employees by such "private businesses," and its tight rules were designed to prevent its practitioners from utilizing state property, facilities, and time. More than anything, this move represented the leadership's grudging recognition of a long-extant fact of life, namely, that the "second," or "black," economy of the USSR was in many ways the essential leavening that permitted a modicum of products and services that the state system seemed incapable of supplying. However, regardless of its motivation, this action clearly cracked open the door to pressures for further reforms that could have more fundamental and systemic effects.

Finally, two other potentially very significant developments appeared to be under way in autumn 1986. Both carried possible major implications for the future. The first suggested the possibility of more far-reaching reforms to come. In September, First Deputy Chairman Talyzin of the Council of Ministers (and candidate Politburo member), the GOSPLAN chairman, led a senior economic ministry and foreign affairs delegation in a week-long trip to the PRC. Undoubtedly, the primary purposes of the trip related to Gorbachev's attempts to improve relations with Beijing. However, it is noteworthy that Soviet spokesmen told Western business people and press representatives that Talyzin would be carefully studying Chinese economic reforms and programs. Moreover, while there, the Soviet delegation not only held very protracted discussions with senior Chinese officials and academic theoreticians but also extensively toured both industrial and agricultural regions in which the Chinese reforms had been applied. At the same time the Soviet central press once again began to feature more frequent and relatively straightforward articles describing many of the features of the Chinese economy.

Along with the dramatic personnel and social changes announced in January, the year 1987 also started with a bang in the economic sector. In mid-January, the long-awaited law on joint ventures (JVs) with foreign firms was published, and in Feburary a new draft law on state enterprises was circulated for discussion and comment. Meanwhile, at the Party plenum Gorbachev encouraged greater worker control of enterprises and agricultural collectives through elections of managers by the workers and kolkhozniks. In February a new decree encouraging cooperative societies for food production was issued.

Ever since initial announcement of the intent to allow JVs there had been reports of many interested foreign firms, but the bottom line had been that too many details had yet to be revealed and the January law only partially met this need. Its basic provisions sounded good: JVs had freedom to decide on their own operating policies without interference from Soviet state planning organs; they had direct export and import rights; they had full self-financing; there were to be no taxes on profits for two years, followed by only a 30 percent tax thereafter; they were "legal persons" with right to redress in Soviet courts; and they had the right to raise investment funds through the sale of shares to third parties. However, many key concrete details were still unstated, and there were caveats that did not bode well for marketing and managerial freedom. Most of the contracting freedoms, fund-raising rights, and so on were expressly to be subject to approval by relevant Soviet state authorities—leaving a great many practical realities in question. At least 51 percent of each JV had to be Soviet-owned, and all of the Soviet "owners" would be enterprises, or their subsidiaries, fully integrated into and quite responsible to Soviet central planning. If profits were not initially to be taxed, property was. Moreover, JVs were to be required to sell some unspecified proportion of their products to the state (at state prices, naturally). And the real degree that other domestic prices would be subject to anything like market demand and costs was not at all clear. In addition, JVs were to be subject to all Soviet laws, calling into question their abilities to hire and fire freely or to institute other management procedures considered normal in the West.

The one area of JV operations for which the new law clearly indicated marketing freedom was in export of products and the import of needed tools, technology, and the like. Here, then, was evidently the key to Soviet intentions. JVs are primarily intended to help the Soviets earn hard currency through export and to facilitate the acquisition of modern technology. In fact, for non-CEMA firms, the profits that the foreign partner can take out of the country were expressly limited to those earned by foreign trade.

Such arrangements were presumably not quite what most Western capitalists could be expected to have in mind, for their main interest could be expected to be to gain access to a potentially large Soviet domestic market. In the following months (through midsummer), although there were continuing reports of great foreign interest, there were very few JVs announced with Western firms and less than half that were not production ventures but, rather, banking and investment or tourism JVs. Further, a significant percentage of the other Western firms that seemed the most interested and closest to completion of agreement were to be found among those that could gain by greater access to Soviet raw materials (petroleum, for example) for their own international marketing, while at the same time aiding the USSR in successfully exploiting those resources.

Nevertheless, the successful introduction of any sizeable number of Western joint-production ventures into the Soviet domestic economy holds the prospect of potentially forcing far more meaningful reforms and rationalities into the system than, perhaps, anything else that Gorbachev and company have done in the economic field—a point we will return to. Similarly, such ventures are potentially a very attractive means for the Soviets to alleviate some of their consumer goods inadequacies without having to shift significant investment of their own away from heavy industry and the military.

The February draft law on state enterprises and trusts, which was dutifully ratified with minor changes in June, incorporated most of the basic features of partial reforms introduced in more general terms earlier, e.g. the basic things that are supposed to make Soviet industry work effectively and to provide the stimulus for technological regeneration. Some of its more significant features included (1) self-management by workers' collectives; (2) one-person management (*yedinonachaliye*; not exactly workers' collective management, in an apparent partial contradiction) chosen by the collective in either secret or open balloting; (3) the right to operate their own branch and supporting activities (agriculture, construction, research, and so on); (4) self-financing to include salaries; (5) responsibility (read: accountability) for technical modernization; (6) competitive operations, including contracts with suppliers and the enterprise's own branches, and the like; and (7) provisions for closing down unsuccessful or unprofitable enterprises.

In theory, this should improve matters by introducing accountability, encouraging innovation, and adding flexibilities. In practice, it seems liable to fall far short of its goals. On the one hand, much was said about self-management and enterprise independence, but on the other, the principles of "Democratic Centralism," of strengthening the central economic planning organs, and of the continual close control by higher state and Party organs were stressed when the law was published and have been reiterated ever since. Candidates for election to management must be approved (read: selected or carefully screened) by the Party. As in the past, "self-management" is to be strictly within the context of close adherence to the state economic and social plan, state criteria and long-term goals, and all state laws. In the USSR these still add up to an incredibly detailed and restrictive body of rules and requirements that must be met *before* an enterprise can exercise any real independence. Both fundamentally and legally, the first task of every Soviet enterprise is to satisfy the interests of the state.

Perhaps the provisions for closing unsuccessful enterprises are the most intriguing aspect of the law. Although the law provides for workers in closed enterprises to be transferred to new jobs or given new-job training and paid for three months, closings inevitably raise the prospect of unemployment—something that traditionally is not supposed to exist in "socialist" systems. Moreover, although the enterprise law was less than fully explicit on this point, other announced "experimental" reforms had stressed the right to fire unsatisfactory or superfluous workers. Considering the extensive work-force padding and inefficiency in most Soviet industries, and the fact that the new law is very specific in requiring enterprises to give top priority to the introduction of modern high technology and automation, the possibilities of significant unemployment could be very real if such provisions are really allowed and enforced. In fact, a shutdown (of a Leningrad construction firm) was announced in March, and in the same month articles were published admitting to very sizeable unemployment in Uzbekistan and Azerbaijan (1 million and ¼ million, respectively). A long-standing sacred tenet of socialist propaganda appears to be in real jeopardy. Moreover, acceptance of unemployment would have to give any potential rivals some real ammunition to use against Gorbachev.

The decree on cooperatives for food-product production should be understood as another of the several efforts to harness the "second economy" and bring it under control and taxation. The decree encourages such activities by making them legal and allowing initial capitalization via state loans but also seeks to reduce the endemic illegal diversion of state assets (both material and in terms of time spent away from state jobs) both by its terms and by its admonition that such cooperatives are expressly envisioned to be formed by pensioners, students, housekeepers, and other people not in the work force, with others allowed to join only in their free time.

In part, the early 1987 reforms represented only slight additions and a "crossing of t's and dotting of i's" to earlier announced programs. In addition, however, they seemed to have been given greater impetus by the economic record so far. The figures for 1986 were published in January 1987, but their main aspects had to be known to the central leadership earlier—in time to convince the Gorbachev team that more had to be done.

Most of the gross 1986 figures did show improvement and progress. Overall volume of production, as well as labor productivity in almost every sector, ministry, or complex, was higher by several percentage points than in 1985 (although petroleum industry productivity was down). Similarly, the overall figures indicated plan fulfillment or overfulfillment, although by noticeably smaller percentages. Total industrial production grew by almost 5 percent, and agriculture by 9 percent. But, as usual, these happy figures were followed by long lists of areas and specific categories of production for which severe problems and shortfalls remained. Moreover, many of the problem areas were the same ones that had been noted in quarterly reports over the preceding two years, and they reflected disappointing results in precisely many of the higher-priority areas of Gorbachev's economic revitalization strategy, including machine construction, technical equipment, chemicals, mineral fertilizer, industrial synthetics, and capital construction (below plan targets in forty-two of forty-four listed ministries and under 70 percent of plan targets in six cases).

Foreign trade turnover dropped by 8 percent in 1986. This was attributed to the fall in oil prices, but the inescapable fact is that increased trade, focused on importing high technology, is a central component of the economic strategy.

Even more unsettling, it was admitted that product qualitative goals were not being met and that a main factor in the achieved growth had been the switchover to two or three shifts. The admission did not bode well for the future because such gains are a one-time boost that demands greater efforts now from workers whose rewards are only a promise of an uncertain future.

The April report of economic performance in the first quarter of 1987 was similar. Overall industrial production grew by 2.5 percent over the first quarter of 1986, but the target was a 3.3 percent growth. The same critical high technology and energy sectors were cited as problem areas, while in consumer goods the falling volume of production had not been overcome and quality was still below standard.

To make matters worse, the press in March published a scathing article by a leading economist of the Economic Institute of the Academy of Sciences, A. Sergeyev, who declared that padded statistics were inflating production estimates by at least 3 percent. If true, and his assertion conforms to what many outside observers have said for years, even the stated successes of Gorbachev's economic reforms may be largely chimerical.

Concurrent with, and especially following, the early 1987 reforms, there was a very strong emphasis on the theme that the problems all could be attributed to immobilism, foot-dragging, and resistance at intermediate and local levels. Gorbachev was especially harsh in his description of widespread bureaucratic but unorganized resistance to the new methods. He insisted on many occasions that all the necessary prerequisites for a successful economic program had been laid and that all that was needed was to implement them wholeheartedly at every level. Yet he also admitted that his reforms—he referred to them as the reforms of the unified central leadership—were breaking new ground and that future adjustments could be expected. In doing this, he both gave notice that he was prepared to go further if necessary and implied that if any details of his existing reforms proved unnecessary or counterproductive, they could be adjusted. This was an adroit way to reasssure any of his current supporters who might be becoming nervous over the extent of change. At the same time he was firm in insisting that there could be no turning back.

Meanwhile, Gorbachev mobilized much of the rest of the Politburo and Secretariat. From early February up to the June Party plenum large numbers of these individuals, including such lukewarm supporters of Gorbachev as Shcherbitskiy and Aliev, could be found frequently traveling in the provinces and emulating the general secretary's style of meeting with local officials and the general public to explain and espouse the new methods. Their message was the same as Gorbachev's: the problem is with implementation, not with the changes or the system. They reaffirmed their leader's claim that the necessary means were in place to achieve the desired results while making it equally clear that the individuals who continued to resist the new methods would be the ones who would suffer. In a particularly revealing speech at a consumer goods conference in May, CC Secretary Biryukova told the officials present that they would not receive more resources or investment but had to find the answers to their problems in effective and innovative management in the spirit of the reforms already in place.

At the June 1987 Party plenum Gorbachev continued in the same vein, emphasizing implementation of what was already in place and threatening those who failed to comply. Nevertheless, the massive injection of young loyalists from the Secretariat into the expanded Politburo clearly set the stage to facilitate new reforms in the future should Gorbachev deem them necessary.

All of this is not to say that real systemic reform, a modern NEP, is just around the corner or necessarily even being seriously contemplated. (New

Economic Policy, NEP, is the name given to Lenin's temporary flirtation, in the 1920s with a fairly wide-ranging private economy side by side with the state economy, which was to occupy the "commanding heights.") There are many real and perceptual barriers to such a development. Nevertheless, if Gorbachev's limited reforms continue to fail to produce their intended results, it is almost inescapable that he will be increasingly pushed in the direction of ever more radical changes in order to salvage his program and retain leadership legitimacy. Although the irrevocability and eternal devotion to the basic tried-and-true principles of the Socialist economic system and centralized planning are invariably reaffirmed, it is noteworthy that in a number of leadership speeches and major theoretical articles this formula has been accompanied by the statement that temporary adjustments are sometimes objectively required.

When one examines the events and developments related to the economy and to leadership and cadres' positions, one can detect five phases. Each phase represents a continuation and logical extension of the earlier ones, but each also is marked by distinctive features of its own. This pattern demonstrates an evolution in the processes Gorbachev and his companions have been imposing upon the USSR, and they point the way in which Gorbachev and the Soviet system appear to be moving.

The first period extended from Gorbachev's accession to the general secretaryship until mid-September 1985. It was characterized by the critical consolidation of power at the top of the Party structure and by a setting of broad, general economic themes and goals. The changes made in the Politburo and Party Secretariat in the spring and early summer effectively ensured Gorbachev's position as general secretary and allowed him to begin to impose more extensively his personnel choices in the state apparatus and in the lower Party echelons. The process began to gather steam in July, August, and early September with the appointments and personnel shifts noted in the previous chapter. The period also marked Gorbachev's first, at-the-pinnacle move to put foreign policy into his own hands: his replacement of Gromyko by Shevardnadze as foreign minister. Economically, this first period basically reflected the process of defining problems—particularly at the April 1985 Party plenum—and of outlining the broad fundamental strategy and tactics to solve them.

The second period extended from mid-September until the Party Congress in 1986. It was marked by the massive infusion of Gorbachev appointees into the senior state structure and an accelerated turnover at lower Party echelons, and it culminated with the thorough restaffing of the Secretariat and the major Politburo changes that accompanied it at the Congress. Economically, the period was marked by the fuller emergence of the organizational strategy of vertical cartelization (exemplified but not limited to the creation of GOSAGROPROM as a superministry for a particular problem area) and by the setting of more specific economic goals and strategies. Even accounting for Soviet hyperbole and the need to reinforce leadership legitimacy by demonstrating success at every step, this was undoubtedly a period of satisfaction and optimism for the Gorbachev leadership. Themes and goals had been set, at first very generally and then more specifically; personal leadership and power had apparently been consolidated; and the economic indicators seemed to show that the economy was beginning to move in the right directions. As we shall see, it was also a time when the central thrust of Gorbachev's main foreign policy program, East-West detente, was proceeding in desired ways. At the same time the new leadership's trial-and-error process of shaping its own Third World strategy had evidently led to basic decisions.

The third period extended from the Party Congress to the latter part of the summer of 1986, sometime around mid-July to early August. This might be called a period of disappointment and disillusionment. It was marked by the realization that consolidation of power at the top was not enough to move the ponderous Soviet bureaucracy smoothly into new ways, and by the dawning recognition that a few reorganizations and the defining of new goals, coupled with a few shifts in priorities and in the degree of emphasis upon managerial tools, might not be enough to effect a sustained revitalization of the economy. The period started with a focus on foreign policy: on restructuring the lower echelons of the foreign affairs apparatus and establishing new procedures within it. It signaled the following through on the process of completing the full transformation of the foreign policy structure into Gorbachev's own creature, necessary after the Gromyko-Shevardnadze and Ponomarev-Dobrynin replacements of the previous summer and at the Congress. But the most characteristic expression of the period was the June Party plenum. Here, in Gorbachev's and Ryzhkov's speeches, one can see the recognition that the system was simply not moving as had been hoped, that consolidation of power at the top and limited reform had not succeeded in overcoming the inertia of decades. This was reinforced by the unpleasant fact of a comparative economic downturn, revealed by the July figures on the economy for the first six months of the year. The initial visible response was exhortation and threat: the whole generalized reference to immobilism and those unnamed lower-level individuals who refused to adapt to the new ways. Behind the scenes, however, it was evidently a period of reexamination.

The fourth period extended through the rest of 1986 and the early part of 1987. It was marked by (1) a continuation of the exhortation and threats, but made more explicit; (2) a resumption of personnel turnover in the senior state bureaucracy and throughout the lower Party echelons (including Gorbachev appointees!); and (3) further economic reorganizations and reforms. The reorganizations in construction and foreign economic structure were simply the application of an earlier model to additional sectors of the economy. The reforms—foreign economic relations, new laws for State enterprises, legalization of additional portions of the "black economy," and so on—were also extensions, but in addition they included elements that potentially had much greater systemic impact. In foreign policy, the fourth period was highlighted by the very successful, from Gorbachev's viewpoint, Reykjavik summit with President Ronald Reagan (see chapter 8) and by an increasingly confident activism in other regions of the world.

The fifth period slightly overlapped the fourth, beginning in some ways with the January 1987 Party plenum. Major economic reform was again suspended after February, and a much increased emphasis was placed on galvanizing intermediate layers of the state and Party *nomenklatura* and overcoming and eradicating the largely passive resistance of the entrenched bureaucracy and the workers. In fact, it is very possible to understand most of Gorbachev's calls for multiple candidates, secret ballots, and election of managers by workers as a means to overcome entrenched localism and *protektsia* far more than as any nascent political liberalization. Meanwhile, at the January and June 1987 plenums Gorbachev moved to add to his dedicated supporters in the central leadership and weaken the position of those erstwhile ones who might be tempted by, or tempting to, the intermediate and lower-level Party bureaucrats who feared, or were incapable of, implementing his new methods. In foreign policy the motif was continued pressure on the United States to accede to arms control demands and on the entire West to liberalize trade and technology transfer to the USSR, and a continuing pursuit of carefully calibrated attempts to gain advantages in the Third World.

By the end of summer 1987 the fifth period seemed to be still on track. However, the senior personnel changes Gorbachev had made in the central leadership had left him in a position to expand his reforms if he felt it necessary, and the prospects looked good for another major foreign policy milestone involving a second U.S.-Soviet summit and an arms control agreement on intermediate nuclear weapons.

A pattern has just been posited. An assessment of its correctness as well as of its full meaning must await examination of social, foreign policy, and military developments under Gorbachev. However, at this point an examination of the content of the reforms introduced into the economy and the state structure can provide some clues as to what Gorbachev and company have really been trying to do, how far they intend to go, and what probably lies ahead.

Almost two and a half years after Gorbachev's election as general secretary, and almost as long since he set down the tasks and basic general means to achieve them at the April 1985 CC plenum, the economic results of all of this *sturm und drang* remained quite debatable. Evidently there have been increases in output and productivity in many branches of industry during the latter parts of 1985 and especially the beginning of 1986. Given the previous slack in the Soviet economy and its parlous state, this might or might not be attributable to any of the actual reforms. It could just as easily be the outcome of the psychological climate created by a new, dynamic leadership. If so, it will likely prove ephemeral. What is possibly more significant is that in June and July of 1987 the very same goals, the very same shortcomings, and roughly the same general methods of solving the same problems were being reiterated in the press. Given the multitude and scale of Soviet economic problems, the immobility and the corruption of the entire system, and the pervasive lethargy and cynicism, two and a half years is too short a time frame to effect the kinds of changes in attitude, behavior, and efficiency that Gorbachev had demanded or to judge his reforms on the basis of demonstrated results. Instead, one has to evaluate their content. This brings us to the question of whether Gorbachev yet deserves to be called a reformer, or whether he is rather a tinkerer whose main purpose has merely been to sustain the basic system while concentrating all power in his own hands.

In the first place, the overwhelming priority for investment was still in the heavy and extractive industries, along with badly needed infrastructure. In this sense, there had been no real change. The USSR's economic priorities were still primarily geared to those aspects of the economy that produce national power, and particularly military power. All that happened in this regard was a change in the current economic strategy for achieving heavy industrial growth. Instead of extensive growth through the building of new facilities, there was to be intensive growth on the basis of retooling existing ones and applying modern high technology, especially robotics, microelectronics, automation, new materials, and biotechnology. Of course, all such technologies are directly applicable to, and indeed prerequisites for, modern military strength. Moreover, this strategy shift follows a broader historical pattern. Twice before new technologies had generated major changes in military doctrine. The changes were both accompanied and followed by a period of economic retrenchment and reform; initiation of a basic foreign policy line predicated on "peaceful coexistence"; and a temporary scaling down of direct military growth while the economy was restructured and the armed forces cadres retrained to enable them to apply the new doctrines and technologies. As in each of these two previous periods (and only then), under Gorbachev there were indications that the share of the military in the economic pie was being reduced.

The implied conclusion that all of this is only a tactic for raising military power in the long run, however, may be premature. The same economic modernization strategy also makes sense as a necessary prelude to a wider economic reorientation. In the absence of an effective Soviet agricultural sector, extractive and processing industries, especially oil and gas, would have to be modernized and made more effective if they are to continue to provide the hard currency needed to pay for grain imports. In turn, major infrastructure improvements would be a prerequisite for exploitation of Siberian deposits. Moreover, such a strategy, whether intended to strengthen the sinews of military power or to achieve more benign purposes, would be greatly dependent upon access to foreign credits and technology. The latter would call for a policy of detente.

In addition heavy industry in the USSR constitutes the backbone of both the Party ل state bureaucracy, and its priority has been traditionally emphasized by the ideology. These considerations would argue for Gorbachev to proceed rather cautiously in introducing any radical transformation of the economy at the expense of these sectors, even when his personal power *is* absolute. If his power still does not extend fully down into the economic and Party bureaucracies, he would be even more advised to avoid becoming too involved in tampering with basic economic priorities and goals.

Given these conflicting realities and explanations, even a qualified answer to the question of Gorbachev's long-term intentions, whether he wants to restructure heavy industry to serve the overall economy better or whether he is merely employing a tactical approach to building national and military power, must await a closer examination of foreign and military policy and other aspects of the "radical reforms" proclaimed by Gorbachev. A definitive answer can be provided only by future developments. This applies particularly to the specific question of whether there has been or will be any real shift of defense industry assets to civil production. (We will look at this question and the defense industry more closely in chapter 12.) What can be said about Gorbachev's other reforms? About incentives; increased local authority; restructuring of agriculture and construction; the emphasis on multibranch enterprise conglomerates coordinating research and development, production and aspects of sales and distribution; and especially the new features in light industry, state enterprise operations, and foreign economic relations? How are they to be evaluated so far?

In fact, the restructuring of agriculture and construction management administration and the creation of complex, multifaceted conglomerates by themselves do nothing to alter the centralized system. Rather, they represent a very reasonable strategy to improve the system's efficiency by streamlining management and making it easier to coordinate the activities of different branches and of different sectors. Logically, they should allow reductions of redundant personnel. The early reports about GOS-AGROPROM suggest that this is what has happened in the agricultural bureaucracy. This alone could be expected to boost efficiency to a degree. Moreover, the East German experience with vertical cartelization suggests that real improvements in some sectors can be achieved this way. On the other hand, these kinds óf organizational reforms do nothing to address what most outside observers, except doctrinaire Marxists, assess as the fundamental problem for the Soviet economy, namely, the absence of a workable market mechanism capable of providing realistic costs and prices for planning and workable incentives for better performance—in other words, a mechanism prerequisite for economic rationality. Finally, the stultifying impact of the heavy-handed central and subordinate layers of bureaucracy seems to be only marginally reduced by the transition to a "two-links" (*dvukhzvenny*) management system whereby one intermediate layer is to be done away with. The effect is bound to be limited precisely because the Party organizations at every level have been called upon to be more thoroughly involved in ensuring that goals are met. Like the senior and local economic managers, the Party bureaucrats were given clear notice that they will be held more fully accountable for results. Predictably, they will find it difficult, if not impossible, to refrain from continued heavy-handed meddling.

This brings us to one of the major question marks about the ostensibly systemic reforms, i.e. those dealing with incentives, increased enterprise autonomy, very limited private enterprise, pricing rationality, and broader planning guidelines, including real attention being paid to inputs from the field and avoidance of detailed nuts-and-bolts meddling and overcontrol. If they are not to be mere "eyewash" (*ochkovtiratelstvo*—a common Soviet term), Gorbachev's announced programs of linked performance, linked bonuses, enterprise independence in allocation and distribution of investments and in the use of profits, and especially the very limited price-setting freedoms announced for light and consumer industries will clash with the ingrained systemic habits and traditional priorities. They will also bring the Soviet leadership face to face with some very predictable and uncomfortable results.

Insofar as ingrained habits and traditional priorities are concerned, the proof of the pudding can come only in the future. Thus far it has been made very clear that in the final analysis the central planners will still set production targets and prices for some level of production earmarked for sale to the state, and that they will still allocate a percentage of the investment funds granted to enterprises for directed purposes. Even the announced contractual arrangements between Soviet and Eastern European enterprises, supposedly direct enterprise-to-enterprise agreements, have been reported to have been negotiated with the full participation of ministers of the USSR. This kind of "independence" and freedom of decision making by enterprise managers and workers' collectives can be meaningful only if two conditions are met. First, there must be a substantial regular flow of sizeable discretionary investment grants and a realistic production capacity above the levels demanded for the state. Second, there must not be excessive informal pressure from either state or Party "supervisors" to dictate choices. Given ingrained Soviet habits of control, the stake of the central planners in achieving maximized and ever-improved results in the production of goods for the state, the high costs of significantly reducing some of the artificial prices of certain goods and products for various segments of the populace and for many of the prime industrial "contractors," and that the Soviet economy is primarily a *political* economy designed to serve the interests of thepolitical elite and the foreign policies of the state, there is good reason to doubt whether these reforms will turn out to be very meaningful.

Further, there are very real problems with significantly varying levels of bonuses and penalties, with the announced freedom for enterprise managers to get rid of redundant and inefficient work staff, and with closing inefficient or unprofitable enterprises. Such policies potentially strike at the very legitimacy of state authority and of the CPSU's monopoly of power. Punitive or even discriminatory measures against unprofitable enterprises have very real limits in the Soviet context. In the past Soviet ideology did not allow unprofitable enterprises to be closed down, and such action can be expected to still be very sensitive. Traditionally, Communism tolerates no unemployment. Even large-scale firing of inefficient workers traditionally, or of workers displaced by modern technology would be very unpalatable for the same reason. New industries and enterprise-operated brand-name retail outlets do not really solve this problem because success-oriented, upwardly mobile, career-conscious managers would be unlikely to entrust such operations to the people fired for inefficiency and poor performance. An equally unpalatable alternative would be to maintain a certain number of enterprises (in fact, a huge number of them), which would be unprofitable and economically inefficient but would absorb unproductive manpower. Paradoxically, again because of the strictures of Soviet ideology, which require at least the appearance of equality, there would be great pressure to raise wages in such inferior enterprises to roughly the same real level as those at the more profitable ones. Such action would have the effect of undermining the very incentives for better work that underlie the whole concept of Gorbachev's reforms.

Further still, Gorbachev's new program has called for central planners to take into consideration—in fact, to be guided by—the inputs from enterprise managers, which are to be based on wholesale market requirements and local judgment. For the most part, this simply reiterates the theory of the existing centralized planning system, which has always included this element *and has always ignored it*. Given human nature, the self-interest of the still powerful central planners and managers, and the Soviet meaning of "democratic centralism," those responsible for planning and supervision (the central authorities and the Party organizations at all levels) can be expected to operate under extremely powerful incentives to ensure that the "independent," "rational" inputs of the local enterprise managers are dictated from above. In fact, the entire formula of improving, and hence increasing, central management—a corollary of the monopoly of power in the hands of a Leninist Party—and simultaneously increasing the independence, authority, and accountability of local managers is self-contradictory. Its real-life results are most likely to be an increase in the accountability of the local managers and the creation of a pool of convenient scapegoats for future shortcomings.

It is also significant in this regard that the Gorbachev Soviet leadership has called for and passed decrees allowing, even demanding, that the local Soviets (councils) of Workers' Deputies (the facade of representative democracy and popular participation) take a greater role in and assume direct responsibility for improving the economy. But the Gorbachev leadership has simultaneously clearly expounded the demand that the equivalent Party echelons take a greater role and assume greater control in ensuring that the Soviets do this in prescribed ways. (See, for example, the Central Committee and Council of Ministers decree of 30 August 1986, and the Central Committee resolution of the same date.) Once again, this is nothing new. Khrushchev issued similar "reforms" expanding the role of the local Soviets, and just as predictably emasculated them of any real meaning by having them directed and supervised by Party *activs* at the same level. In fact, there is much in Gorbachev's approach to political mobilization of the masses that is reminiscent of the Khrushchev era, only updated and modified to fit different circumstances. This is hardly surprising, considering that Gorbachev was in part shaped by the events of the 1950s and early 1960s.

The foreign economic reforms could be very significant, but the question remains whether they will prove to be so in reality. As with the planning "reforms," of critical importance is the issue of who will really set the ground rules and specifics. The ministers and enterprise managers who are acquiring the right to conduct their own business affairs abroad remain state employees. More importantly, they still operate within a state plan set at the center and are still subordinate to other state and Party officials

TABLE 3.1
Selected Economic Performance Indexes
Part A

	January-September, 1985			All of 1985		
	% of Plan	Compared with 1984		% of Plan	Compared with 1984	
		Production	Labor Productivity		Production	Labor Productivity
Energy and electrification	100.7	104	102	101	104	102
Oil industry	96	97	94	96	97	94
Oil refining and petro-chemical industries	100.5	100.1	100	98	100.4	100.3
Gas industry	100.1	109	106	100.6	110	107
Coal industry	100.2	101	100.7	101	102	102
Ferrous metallurgy	99	100.4	100.3	99.3	102	102
Chemical industry	99.3	104	103	99.3	104	104
Mineral fertilizers	97	106	103	98	107	104
Heavy and transport machine construction	100.9	105	105	101	105	106
Instruments, means of automation and control systems	102	105	106	102	105	107
Wood, paper-cellulose, and wood products	98	102	103	99	103	104
Construction materials	99.6	101	101	99	103	104
Light industry	99.9	102	106	99.8	102	103
Food industry	101	102	103	100.3	103	102
Especially singled out in textual report for shortfalls and inefficiencies	Oil extraction, mineral fertilizer, finished rolled ferrous metal, chemical fibers, finnished wood products, industrial presses, paper-cellulose products, cement, television sets, light industry, electric motors, fruit products			Oil extraction, mineral fertilizer, finished rolled ferrous metal, chemical fibers, finished wood products, industrial presses, paper-cellulose products, cement, color television sets, light industry. For labor productivity: oil refining and petrochemicals, coal, chemical, ferrous metallurgy, construction materials and light industry.		

TABLE 3.1 (Continued)
Part B

	January-March 1986 % of Plan	Compared with 1985 Production	Compared with 1985 Labor Productivity	January-June 1986 % of Plan	Compared with 1985 Production	Compared with 1985 Labor Productivity
Energy and electrification	100.6	103	101	101	103	102
Oil industry	99.1	100.9	97	99.7	102	98
Oil refining and petro-chemical industries	100.9	105	105	101	103	103
Gas industry	103	110	107	103	109	107
Coal industry	103	107	106	104	105	105
Ferrous metallurgy	102	109	109	103	106	106
Chemical industry	102	112	112	101	108	109
Mineral fertilizers	103	116	114	102	111	110
Heavy and transport machine construction	102	109	108	102	107	107
Instruments, means of automation and control systems	103	112	111	103	110	109
Wood, paper-cellulose, and wood products	103	110	110	102	108	108
Construction materials	102	109	109	101	106	106
Light industry	101	104	106	100.6	103	105
Food industry	104	106	106	103	105	105

Especially singled out in textual report for shortfalls and inefficiencies

Oil extraction and sales; production of AC motors, sulphuric acid, color televisions, pipes, plastic pipe fittings, pneumatic looms, automated work stations; product sales of wood, paper-cellulose, finished wood products and light industry (quality problems). In general, faults were found with enterprises and branches more than whole industries.

Oil extraction and sales; mineral fertilizer; equipment for chemical industry; tools and instruments for automation and control systems; AC motors; color televisions; machines for transportation and building construction; wood. paper-cellulose, and wood products; ferrous metal products; light industry. In most cases problems were primarily in regard to quality of products, introduction of new technology, and science and technology planning.

Source: Based on official statistics published in *Pravda*, 20 October 1985, 20 January 1986, 20 April 1986, 20 July 1986.

TABLE 3.2
Selected Economic Performance Indicators
Part C
January—June, 1987

A. Performance in meeting contracts and in planned profits	% fulfilled contractual obligations for total sales	% of enterprises not doing so	% of plan in profits
Fuel-energy complex	99.0	34	107.2
Metallurgical complex	98.6	36	101.5
Machine construction complex	96.2	59	94.7
Chemical-wood complex	97.7	47	97.6
Agroindustrial complex	99.4	18	98.0
Social complex (Light industry)	98.6	27	96.5
Construction complex	98.5	29	100.5

B. Selected production figures	% of production plan	Compared with first half, 1986
Electroenergy (KW-hrs)	100.6	104
Oil (tons)	101	102
Gas (cubic meters)	102	106
Steel (tons)	100.4	100.3
Turbines (KW)	99.8	115
Generators (KW)	94	78
Metalcutting lathes (rubles)	93	99
Metal pressers (rubles)	85	93
Industrial robots (number)	104	97
Means of computer technology & spare parts (rubles)	99.7	107
Instruments, means of automatization & spare parts (rubles)	98	103
Chemical equipment & spare parts (rubles)	88	93
Technical equipment for light and food industry (rubles)	89	95

Tractors (number)	94	94
Mineral fertilizer (tons)	100.8	103
Sythetic resins and plastics (tons)	99	102
Capital construction (fuel-energy complex)	92	108
Capital construction (machinebuilding complex)	87	114

C. Singled out for problems in text: (in addition to repeating some of the above shortfalls)

The metallurgical complex for not producing the assortment demanded.

—The machinebuilding complex for not meeting plans for high quality, modern technology.

—Low quality in consumer goods and inadequate assortment of the same

—Half of all service industries below plan

In general, rather than listing items of production (as in previous years) which had problems, the text named industries, republics and even enterprises in some cases which were performing inadequately.

This part of the table is taken from *Izvestiya*, 19 July, 1987. Because the data was presented differently than previous years, the format is not the same as that in Table 3.1.

whose continued position and perquisites depend upon fully satisfying the demands of a centralized political economy. Their real independence—their freedom to control their own budgets and their planning inputs, and their ability to make decisions based upon rational economic rather than political goals—is likely to be quite emasculated. Further, the main arena in which these reforms are to take place first is in regard to Eastern Europe and the other states of the socialist community. As will be discussed later, this seems to be as much aimed at more effective economic integration and political control as toward economic rationality. All of this suggests that a—perhaps *the* major—underlying intent relates to access to Western credit, trade, and technology rather than true systemic reform.

The widening of legal rights for single individuals and families to conduct private enterprise operations, and the expansions of the rights and types of cooperatives in comparison with true state industries, basically reflect recognition of reality and the attempt to ensure a few more amenities for the population on the cheap. They have all the earmarks of being intended as a temporary palliative. They do not of themselves directly affect the basic system as it applies to the major parts of the economy. Nevertheless, they do somewhat widen the crack in the door to wider reform. It is clear that the leadership recognizes this because it has simultaneously attempted to hedge these modest liberalizations by a parallel and more restrictive emphasis on the struggle against unearned income.

The ever-expanding list of institutions and sectors that are to go over to full *khozraschet* (financial self-sufficiency) also gives the reform the appearance of being a major reform. But is it? The announced decrees often state that self-financing is to be total, but the rest of the texts of the same decrees makes it quite clear that this will in large measure be a bookkeeping exercise because much of allocated investments, required production, state sales, even salary bases, and so on will still be controlled centrally, from the top. For the proclaimed reform to be truly meaningful in liberalizing and rationalizing the economy, it would have to be applied almost universally. More important, it would have to be accompanied by adoption of a rational pricing mechanism based on true costs, demand, and the like.

In sum, then, what can we say about Gorbachev's economic reforms? First, one very fundamental rationale behind the whole program has undoubtedly been to provide the new general secretary with a vehicle with which to consolidate his personal position and absolute power. This was particularly and directly applicable to the limited measures undertaken during the first two periods we have identified. In fact, it might well be safe to conclude that this goal was dominant up until the Party Congress. The fact that the fourth period featured somewhat greater actual reforms and that the fourth and fifth periods were marked by a resumption of personnel purges suggests that either Gorbachev has decided that his consolidation of power was incomplete or that other criteria are beginning to play a greater role.

Second, we can say that given the severity of Soviet economic difficulties and Gorbachev's background as an adroit, flexible, and successful manager, it is quite reasonable to assume that he really does wish to galvanize the system. Moreover, his background and approach suggest that in the event of one reform's failure, he may well be likely to try another, even one that is more far-reaching. Significantly, he has chosen many key subordinates who could be expected to be compatible with this mode of operation. He could just as easily, and perhaps more safely, have chosen only pliable and totally subservient flunkies. Nevertheless, Gorbachev's background, the imperatives of CPSU control, and the evidence to date all strongly support the conclusion that his objective has been to keep the system basically intact, but to somehow make it work more effectively.

In fact, both Gorbachev and Ligachev are reliably reported to have told private audiences that there will be no adoption of a bourgeois market mechanism, no abandonment of the "proven paths" of Soviet socialism, nor any move towards even a Hungarian-style reform. In terms of their real content, Gorbachev's economic changes to date have to be assessed as only tinkering with the fringes of the system. The fundamentals of central control and of emphasis on heavy industry have remained fully intact, even if allegedly modified. The potentially significant reforms introduced so far in light industry and in legalizing parts of the "second economy" represent attempts to cut losses by introducing change in sectors not assigned high investment priority in the hope that some efficiencies will result. In effect, it has been an effort to reconcile as painlessly as possible the conflict between the perceived interests of the leadership in strengthening the country and the growing disaffection and lethargy of the population. In conjunction with enhanced discipline and Party control, the whole program to date has been aimed at a modicum of improvement without affecting the primacy of the centrally directed and controlled heavy industry that sustains the power of the USSR and the position of the CPSU.

The reforms in foreign economic policy seem basically to represent (1) a tactical facade to gain access to Western credit and technology and to improve hard currency balances, and (2) a means to increase integration and control within the Eastern bloc. They may also represent another tactic: potentially to satisfy demand for consumer goods better without having to shift Soviet investment priorities. Anyone who believes that the "independent" economic transactions of Soviet enterprises and ministries will be really independent or shaped by purely economic considerations has to be seen as naively optimistic until far more comprehensive changes take place throughout the Soviet system.

It remains conceivable, nonetheless, that Gorbachev personally is in fact amenable to systemic reform, or that he will be so in the future. A conjecture to this effect has been made by a number of analysts in the West, and is based on the supposition that Gorbachev is very much ahead of his compatriots but that he has as yet been severely constrained because he has failed to consolidate personal control and power to a degree sufficient to give him real freedom of action (and to ensure his retention of power no matter what he does). Part of the evidence usually cited in support of this conjecture is the circumspectly phrased articles with oppositionist overtones that appeared in the Soviet press during 1985 and, to a lesser extent, even after the Congress. Usually cited as evidence also is the fact that orthodox economic managers sacked by Gorbachev, such as Tikhonov and Baybakov, have retained their membership in the Central Committee; that some stalwarts of the old guard, such as Shcherbitsky, have remained on the Politburo; and that it took until the end of 1986 to remove Kunaev. In a similar vein, some outside observers have argued that the KGB has usurped a major part of the Party's power; they try to prove this assertion by counting the KGB officers on the Central Committee and even in the Politburo.

None of this is convincing. People like Tikhonov and Baybakov were allowed to retire gracefully while temporarily retaining some honors. According to the Moscow rumor mill, this was part of Gorbachev's preelection agreement as far back as 1984. Moreover, it fits the general historical pattern: Stalin's opponents were shot; Khrushchev's were exiled to minor posts in places like Mongolia; and Brezhnev's foes retained limited perquisites in relative anonymity. More fundamentally, except in very rare circumstances, such as when Khrushchev used the CC to defeat the "anti-Party" group in 1957, only some of the members of the CC have any real central leadership influence. With over 400 full CC members, many of them obvious token representatives of various industries, the general secretary needs no more than a comfortable working majority in this body. As for Kunaev and Shcherbitsky, as long as they servilely acquiesced in the new leadership team, they could be tolerated, particularly because their resident base away from Moscow precluded their regular involvement in day-to-day Politburo activities. Kunaev is, of course, gone, and Shcherbitsky's days are surely numbered in spite of his entrenched position in the Ukrainian *nomenklatura*. The number of Politburo and CC members with present or former KGB affiliation is indeed fairly high, but, if we consider only those currently with the KGB, it is still only a fairly modest seven. Moreover, their ranks include such former Party supervisors of the KGB, and hence not really secret police professionals, as Shevardnadze, who is clearly a Gorbachev man.

The continuing publication of economic articles implicitly critical of some aspects of Gorbachev's reforms is more meaningful evidence, but only to a degree. These are tolerated in the spirit of *glasnost,* or frank public criticism (see chapter 4), and mostly they represent the kind of immobilism that Gorbachev decries. As such they serve as safety valves. In addition, they provide useful propaganda facades for both domestic and foreign audiences. What they probably do indicate, however, is that although by spring 1986 Gorbachev's control of the central apparatus was virtually complete, such was not the case at lower levels.

Two other points are worth considering in discussing the question of whether Gorbachev, between 1985 and 1987, really intended to make fundamental systemic reforms. The first is the possibility that he might not have sufficiently consolidated personal power until the Party Congress. This point may well have some validity, but if it does, it would mean only that we should have seen some real systemic reforms at the Congress or just afterward. Yet, all that happened then was the light industry reform, which does not appear to have major systemic impact. The second point is that the lietmotiv of the four to five months following the Congress (our third period) was growing awareness of, and frustration over, the failure of earlier steps to make a sustained, meaningful difference. This further reinforces our earlier conclusions.

Consequently, the resumed purges and widened reforms of the fourth period seem to be explainable by the fact that the Gorbachev leadership found itself required to move further than initially intended in order to achieve the successes and results without which it would lose legitimacy and open the door to opportunistic political opposition. In effect, the modest tinkering at the edges of the system—tinkering that was designed to consolidate personal power and to make the existing system work a little better—may have put a result-oriented leadership on the path to a slippery slope leading to ever more extreme tinkering and possibly to real reform. That Gorbachev is well aware of the political dangers of this path is clear from the greatly increased attempts to justify his policy lines that can be seen in his subsequent speeches since the fall. Domestically, the reportage of his visits to Krasnodar and Stavropol harped much more heavily than before on the degree to which "the people" supported his policies and made many more references to those unnamed individuals who questioned them. In foreign policy the same phenomenon was manifest in almost unprecedented repetition of major speeches explaining the events of the Reykjavik summit (discussed more thoroughly later in this book). These self-justifications, especially the former, do not indicate that real (i.e., organized) political opposition has yet arisen to Gorbachev, but they do show that he is well aware that failure to achieve the results he has promised could create the basis for such opposition. They also indicate that Gorbachev, the Soviet pragmatist, is determined to achieve results even if he has to go farther than he ever intended in modifying the system.

Gorbachev has admitted that there is extensive passive opposition at intermediate and lower levels. This not only threatens to emasculate his reforms but holds the possibility of turning into organized political opposition at the top if potential rivals there think he has become vulnerable. Here, perhaps, is the best explanation of his calls for the option of secret ballots and multiple candidates at lower levels. These can give him another tool with which to circumvent *mestnichestvo* and the local political machines with their *protektsia*. This explanation reinforces the conclusion that he has no intent to fundamentally change the nature of the system but only to make it work and to ensure his own total power.

Finally, one must also recognize that if Gorbachev were interested in systemic reforms, he would have to proceed very gradually and be very wary of setbacks, for they would provide a pretext for his would-be rivals to mobilize support and outmanuever him. We will consider this problem more closely in our concluding chapter. In the meantime, however, in light of Gorbachev's performance in power, his biography, and the nature of the Soviet political system, the overwhelming evidence argues that he has no desire to change the system through any fundamental reform and that he is merely seeking ways of making the existing system work more effectively. Given the extent of Soviet economic problems and the systemic barriers to their effective resolution, the question becomes whether Gorbachev can in effect have his cake and eat it too, or whether he will have to choose between ever more radical reform, threatening the Party and current political elite, and presiding over the steady slide of the USSR into a second- or third-rate status.

4

Images versus Reality:
The Society and the Style

Once, long ago, there was a parade in Red Square on a particularly frosty day. An old marshal who shivered as he watched remembered that he had a flask of vodka in his back pocket, but his fingers were too numb and frozen to get it out. Spying a young boy, the old man requested assistance. The boy politely agreed, but then took out the flask, opened it, and poured its contents on the ground. Angrily, the marshal demanded the lad's name. "Mikhail Gorbachev, sir," was the reply.

—Apocryphal Soviet tale

On 4 April 1985, one month after Gorbachev became general secretary, the Politburo addressed the problem of endemic alcoholism in the USSR. Almost six weeks later the Central Committee, Council of Ministers, and Supreme Soviet together issued a draconian decree enunciating sharp measures designed to remove this scourge from Soviet society. Among the concrete measures listed were publication of the names of those who manufacture illegal alcoholic beverages, along with the loss of any awards they have received and of part of their salaries; similar penalties against workers and employees who are found drinking in public places; a ban on the sale of alcohol near enterprises, institutions, and construction sites; and increased medical treatment for alcoholism.

The rules struck at pervasive, ingrained, and tradition-honored patterns of conduct in the USSR, and in spite of the very heavy propaganda, an educational and public relations campaign that saturated the media in the succeeding months met with considerable resistance and mixed results. Subsequent reports revealed such determined resistance as that of workers digging tunnels to sales outlets in order to avoid being detected when they brought alcoholic beverages to their workplaces. Later up to four hundred

85

places in Moscow alone were permitted to resume the sale of alcohol, a development probably related to the fact that alcohol sales were a significant source of government revenue. Even though the amount of liquor sold remained lower than before, incidents of alcohol-related crime were reported to have dropped, and fruit juices replaced vodka at official functions including overseas embassy receptions, by the end of 1985 spirits were once again relatively accessible. The antidrinking campaign continued but became noticeably more muted as time went by.

In mid to late summer of 1986 the campaign apparently began to pick up again. The Politburo discussed it. Then articles about it began to increase. Finally, in September pointed criticisms were published condemning one union-republic bureaucracy (the Kirgiz Republic) and the Ministry of Trade for failing to deal with rampant alcoholism. Gorbachev's campaign against the abuse of alcohol continued in 1987, and included specific published condemnations of officials. Why had Gorbachev declared war against a deeply ingrained tradition that in the USSR is associated with hospitalty, proof of manliness, and escape from drudgery?

First of all, drunkenness and alcoholism had become recognized as a very real blight. The Soviet Union, alone among developed nations, has experienced declining male life expectancy and increasing infant mortality. Both have been attributed to the effects of prolonged, heavy drinking. Moreover, the economic costs have been extremely high, with massive absenteeism and drunkenness on the job a pervasive feature of Soviet life. Second, alcoholism had begun to permeate even the ranks of Party activists and senior officers in the armed forces. This could not be tolerated. Third, the dramatic decree of 1985 fit with the desire of the new leadership to create from the outset its own, more dynamic style even while it was still unprepared to proceed on more fundamental issues. The campaign against alcohol also complemented the more comprehensive campaign against corruption that Gorbachev had inherited from Andropov, and that served both general secretaries well as a rationale for personnel replacement. It is in this context, all the objective reasons for a campaign against alcoholism notwithstanding, that the antibooze saga begins to make particular sense.

In the preceding chapter we identified five periods of Gorbachev's rule to date. During the first two periods, consolidation of power via personnel purges predominated. The antialcohol campaign accompanied this process, at first vigorously, then tailing off a bit. During the third period there were very few personnel changes, other than in the Foreign Ministry, and relatively little was heard of the campaign. In the fourth period, when personnel replacements resumed on a larger scale, the stress on the social and economic costs of drinking and the castigation of those who failed to enforce the antialcohol decrees also resumed. This continued in the fifth period, with alcoholic abuse providing an additional useful rationale for the removal of lower-level officials who were unwilling to adopt the new methods with the enthusiasm being demanded.

To a degree, the antialcohol campaign probably reflects Gorbachev's own personal values and convictions, and it undoubtedly has some support from the rest of the top leadership if for no other reasons than the obvious necessity to rectify a very real problem. Nevertheless, the coincidence between the periods of greatest emphasis on it and the timing of heavier personnel purges is too striking to be dismissed. The conclusion has to be that its primary purpose—at least as it is sufficiently important to warrant direct, continuing attention—is to serve as a vehicle for cadres policy.

Whatever its motivations, the antialcohol campaign has made some progress, according to figures published in the beginning of 1987. For the first time in years, the birthrate (19.9 per 1,000 compared to 19.4 in 1985) and life expectancy (now 69) were up and the death rate was down (9.7 versus 10.7). Nevertheless, it remains clear that the campaign still has a long way to go and that it still meets significant opposition.

Another long-hidden or denied aspect of Soviet reality has also begun to be exposed to view: drug use. For a long time drug addiction was officially described as purely an ill of corrupt capitalism and backward societies. Now the Soviets are admitting that they too have a problem, although, by official statistics, one that is miniscule compared to the West's. An eradication campaign against drugs has also started, although without anything like the fanfare or emphasis of the antialcohol program. On balance, the publicity given to it seems as much or more a fallout of *glasnost* (see chapter 5) as anything else. Nevertheless, because most of the reported addiction is centered in Central Asia, it cannot be discounted that this too is designed to serve a purpose in facilitating the removal of local officials in Soviet union-republics with long traditions of *mestnichestvo*. It also may be a Soviet way of responding to and dealing with, the increased exposure to easily available drugs of their troops in Afghanistan. That circumstance is subject to much reporting and commentary in the West but seldom reflected in the Soviet press, except on the few occasions that the Soviets attempt to respond to Western reports of defections.

A more enduring feature of Gorbachev's rule is arguably the anticorruption campaign. His own background suggests that he has considerably less tolerance for major corruption than most Soviet officials. In spite of his obvious enjoyment of the good things in life, he is apparently relatively modest by Soviet-leader standards in his personal tastes, more concerned with achieving results than amassing perquisites. Further, he has clearly recognized the disastrous impact of pervasive corruption on efficiency in management. Moreover, although the anti-corruption drive has largely achieved its primary initial purpose as a vehicle to effect personnel changes, it still retains its utility for justifying further changes at lower levels of administration, and potentially for demoting or derailing prospective rivals from among his present coterie of loyal followers. These are the reasons the campaign against corrupt practices can be expected to continue. Yet, it will undoubtedly be applied with discretion because Gorbachev knows only too well that the corruption-fueled "second economy" remains a vital cog in the Soviet economic mechanism. Only if he ever succeeds in infusing efficient management into the Soviet economy can he risk doing more than attacking marginal and selected instances of the most flagrant and politically harmful corruption.

In fact, in his midautumn reform somewhat widening the private-market legality of individual and family enterprises and in the decree on cooperatives in February 1987, Gorbachev was almost certainly attempting to do more than simply recognize a fact of life and grease the economic wheel. This can also be seen as an additional step in his campaign to transform the whole attitudinal malaise that besets the USSR. It is a case of "if you can't beat 'em, join 'em." By legalizing needed practices, Gorbachev both "joined 'em" and filled a need. By combining newly legalized private operations with tighter enforcement of rules against using state time and property for these purposes he did two things at once. He moved to prevent the example from getting out of hand, and he retained a justification for individual crackdowns whenever desired. The trick will be to achieve a balance. This will not be easy. What is likely, as with most halfway steps, is that the result will not be a public willingness to stay within legal bounds. Rather, the small loosening of barriers will only whet the public appetite for more economic freedoms, and the constraints will prevent any real amelioration of the situation wherein violating the law is the only way to make the process work. Once again, a small, relatively innocuous step may be a further move onto a slippery slope.

Gorbachev is also attempting to revitalize the lower echelons of the CPSU. The new Party Program and especially the Party Regulations (*ustav*) are replete with demands for more constant and creative supervision of aspects of life, especially economic aspects, by Party committees and *activy* (cells). Furthermore, Party members themselves are enjoined to undertake numerous obligations. The new Regulations state that Party members are obliged to work to achieve greater production efficiency, increased labor productivity, the assimilation of science and technology into industry, and so on. Such statutes not only fit well with Gorbachev's apparent preferences and values but provide another convenient tool for controlling and replacing potential rivals within the Party. At the same time they could enhance the legitimacy of the Party's monopoly of power should reform inadvertently encourage the perception that the CPSU is redundant. Moreover, like a number of Gorbachev's programs, they have an eerie resemblance to many from the past.

Under Khrushchev there was a great outburst of rhetoric about the development of the ideal of the state of the whole people by means of expanding the role of the Soviets and of other mass organizations. Then as now, this was accompanied by the reality of increased CPSU control and direction of these structures. The idea is a recurrent and logical one. The CPSU needs the facade of popular institutions of government, but it cannot allow them to be more than a facade without jeopardizing its own position; real political participation can be only within the constraints of the Party. The whole approach to the Soviets is simply another part of Gorbachev's efforts to mobilize the full human resources of the Soviet Union while still retaining full control over those resources. But it may also carry potentially dangerous seeds. Any degree of successful and beneficial initiative on the part of the local Soviets may call into question the need for the Party. On the other hand, reinforcement of the perception that only through the Party and Party initiatives can anything be accomplished would only reinforce the cynicism of the people and the feeling that their ostensibly separate political institutions are a sham. Neither alternative serves the goal of mobilizing public enthusiasm and support. Moreover, the mainstream tendency of Party bureaucrats is basically to avoid such pitfalls. Khrushchev's stress on the Soviets and mass organizations was one of the first things that his successors relegated to its traditional position of pure lip-service. By itself, the call to widen the role of the Soviets and other mass organizations is not anything that would generate opposition to Gorbachev where it counts, in the Party hierarchy. But if other "reforms"—or more realistically, failures—lead to such opposition, it could add to their momentum. Meanwhile, however, as noted in the previous chapter, the attempt to increase Party supervision and accountability at local levels is likely to deprive of any real meaning the concurrent attempt to grant some autonomy to local enterprises.

From early in Gorbachev's general secretaryship there were persistent rumors that he intended to allow greater freedom of life-style choice for Soviet citizens in general and greater emigration rights for Jews and other similar groups in particular. Until relatively late in 1986 there was little positive action behind the smokescreen of rumor and reassuring words, although there were a few isolated cases of highly visible releases of well-known dissidents such as Anatoly Shcharansky. Moreover, it may not have been at all coincidental that these stepped up shortly before the Reykjavik summit. Meanwhile, Jewish activists continued to be harassed, reportedly more determinedly, and jailed through much of the year, and the KGB and other security leaders continued to stress the vital importance of vigilance and firmness against subversion and "espionage."

Then late in 1986 and continuing through mid-1987, there began to be some apparent substance to confirm the rumors. The process of measured liberalization began in December 1986, when Andrei Sakharov was freed from internal exile and allowed to return to Moscow and make contact with the West and internal audiences with no evident restrictions. By mid-1987 more than a hundred highly visible releases of well-known dissidents had taken place.

At the same time Jewish emigration began to increase to several hundred a month, and by late summer of 1987 many well-known "prisoners of Zion" had been freed and were apparently being given exit visas. The number of Jews allowed to emigrate in the first half of 1987 was not insignificant, but was still a very far cry from the peak periods in the mid-1970s. In fact, there was an ominous aspect to the whole exercise. In autumn of 1986 the Soviets announced a new emigration law that was to go into effect on 1 January 1987. Hailed as an enlightened liberalization, the new rules actually tightened the grip on any would-be emigrants who did not have immediate blood or marriage ties to persons already abroad. The suspicion had to be that Moscow was engaged in a calculated ploy to defuse foreign pressure by allowing the most visible refusniks to leave while intending to slam tight the door on the many thousands of others whose situation did not fit the new rules.

A limited number of short, carefully controlled (but in a very discreet manner by Soviet standards) demonstrations were permitted to be held by Jewish activists. Then late in summer of 1987 a much larger demonstration was allowed in the Baltic republics, one that had nationalist overtones because it recalled the harsh measures applied during Stalin's takeover on the eve of World War II.

It is possible that the tip of an iceberg of internal liberalization is beginning to surface. But until it really appears in much more meaningful forms and to a much greater extent, one must conclude that it is not an iceberg, or if it is, that it is an iceberg that Gorbachev does not intend to release fully but may not be able to control fully. When one looks at each of these indications of liberalization, one can detect deliberate limitations, obvious facades, and highly suspicious correlations in time with other goals and circumstances.

Freeing previously banned literary works for publication is part of the *glasnost* campaign, and will be treated in more detail and perspective in the next chapter. It has not yet reached the scale of Khrushchev's "thaw" in literature, which, although it had many ramifications both direct and subtle, hardly changed the essential human rights condition within the USSR very much—or very long for that matter.

Freeing a few prominent dissidents costs little in realty and always holds the possibility of deflecting Western criticism and thereby promoting Soviet foreign policy. Notably, such moves, unaccompanied by any action for the much larger numbers of less publicized dissidents, were more frequent before and after the Reykjavik summit (a point to which we will return later), as were visits by major Western leaders and public relations forums such as the antinuclear festival in February 1987. As a probable fall 1987 summit drew closer the releasing of dissidents seemed to be on the upswing again.

Even freeing a sizeable number of political prisoners would seem to cost little if it convinced foreign audiences that the USSR had changed and could be really trusted. If things threatened to get out of hand at home, it would be an easy matter to round them up again on one pretext or another. A few small, short demonstrations are also in the same category; even larger ones can be tolerated if they focus on wrongs committed by past leaders, not current policies.

Until much, much more is done—and confirmed and proven over time—one can only conclude that we are seeing a combination of a public relations ploy, more wrapping than content, and the desires of a confident general secretary who wants to acquire an attractive image at home and abroad and enlist greater support for his policies from Soviet intellectual circles. Whatever his personal preferences, Gorbachev is aware of the dangers of liberalizing the Soviet society in the full senses of Western definitions of human rights as applied to dissent or emigration. To do so would entail many risks in a society based on total centralized control and made up of many ethnic groups who might be tempted to assert themselves if the fetters were loosened. Also, the men in the Kremlin are sensitive to foreign criticism in this area. The carefully controlled, symbolic releases and the increased effort to redefine human rights in terms of full employment and the like confirm this conclusion. Their sensitivity is heightened during any period when detente is sought. The greater and the more consistent the pressure from the West on such issues, the more likely it is that Gorbachev will relax these bonds. Still, it would take a great deal of consistent pressure. Like terrorists trading hostages, the Kremlin has an almost inexhaustible supply of dissidents and would-be emigrants whom it can dole out at whatever pace the market demands.

In a related vein, late in the fall of 1986 the Soviets announced another ostensibly significant reform campaign, this one against illegal actions and brutality by the police. Suddenly there were pointed reports about citizens who were held for excessive periods without valid charges or who were beaten or otherwise mistreated by the police when they were innocent or before their guilt was established. Police corruption and susceptibility to bribery were also mentioned. Measures were laid out to correct these abuses of "socialist legality." A real elimination of such abuses, an elimination grounded upon independent authority, would be a significant change in Soviet reality. However, as has been the case every time this kind of thing has been publicly addressed in the past, it is the cat who is being set to watch the cream.

In May 1987 the minister of justice reported that in 1986 some 14 judges had been disbarred and 76 had been removed from their posts, presumably for aggravated illegalities, for he also stated that 837 had been found to be incompetent. One might of course wonder what the apparent retention of some 750 incompetent judges says about the hopes for a greater degree of impartial law in the USSR.

Again, the connection with the problem of passive resistance to change at lower levels may be more meaningful than any real move toward some rule of law. In any event, there seemed to be a clear pattern in which most of the announced cases of illegality by police and legal organs conveniently took place in regions or ministries under attack by the Gorbachev leadership or where *mestnichestvo* was the strongest. Moreover, it is quite significant that, with one exception, criticism of illegal actions was directed at parts of the police and security structure other than the KGB. The exception was the report made by KGB Chief Chebrikov himself in January 1987 of malfeasance in a KGB office in the Ukraine. Some in the West seized upon this as indicative that Gorbachev was now at odds with the KGB. Nothing supports this. What was involved was simply another attack by the Gorbachev team at the center against a local crony-and-mutual-protection network. The target was not the KGB but the Ukrainian hierarchy and Shcherbitsky.

Unless the future shows that there has been a real change—which seems very improbable—we can conclude only that legal and police reform, like so many other reforms, is all on the surface and has no real depth. It most likely seeks only to reduce excesses (by Soviet standards) while encouraging a better public attitude without really hindering the means of control.

The fact that these reforms apparently exclude the KGB may be significant for other reasons. Inherently, the KGB sees the other police and security organs as rivals. Part of the program may simply be institutional rivalry. The fact that a Gorbachev appointee runs the Ministry of Internal Affairs (MVD) does not mean that the KGB is moving against Gorbachev, even if the institutional rivalry thesis is valid. Gorbachev's entire reign has been a sort of love affair with the KGB. His purges and criticisms have not touched it, and it has consistently presented him and his policies in the most favorable light. In fact, like Andropov before him—and one must remember that Gorbachev came from Andropov's select group of political proteges—Gorbachev has used the KGB to expose "corruption" and malfeasance on the part of his rivals and those he wished to replace. And he clearly relies on the KGB as one of his main means to ensure that no one steps out of line, a means that could be particularly important if his economic or foreign policies were to generate any real opposition from within the military and wider defense industrial complex. The Soviets like to call the KGB, and the armed forces of which it is theoretically a part, the sword and shield of the Party. Everything to date indicates that the Chebrikov KGB is, in fact, the sword and shield, not a rival, of Gorbachev and his associates. Moreover, as so often in the past, such a condition allows the general secretary to use that sword and shield against his associates if he finds it necessary.

Like all previous Soviet leaders, Gorbachev and his associates pay lip service to Soviet ethnic diversity and to the rights of Soviet nationalities to their own cultural distinctiveness. Still, as has frequently been the case, the new leadership has reemphasized the common bond of all Soviet citizens while stressing the unique contribution of the Russian people. Concretely, Gorbachev reversed traditional practice in several instances by appointing Great Russian or other Slavs to local Party leadership positions in non-Slavic regions. Furthermore, for very sound economic and miliary planning reasons, full mastery of the Russian language by all non-Russians has been stressed. Whatever their practical rationale, these steps inevitably promote Russification. Finally, in the later months of Gorbachev's first year in power the press stepped up its campaign against what was called the growing influence of Islam in Central Asia. The dangers to Moscow of too nationalistic an approach, however, were demonstrated in December 1986 when there were riots by Kazakhs in Alma Ata over the replacing of Kunaev by a Great Russian as leader of the Kazakh Party. Like his predecessors, Gorbachev will probably have to peform a balancing act in regard to nationalities policy.

None of the above policies, except for the campaign against alcoholism and—if they were to be really broadly applied—the permitting of a few limited demonstrations and the campaign against police and security organ illegalities appears to represent anything new in Soviet society. Khrushchev released large numbers of political prisoners and permitted a literary thaw. Less extensive and less fiercely waged periodic campaigns against alcohol abuse have been waged in the past, including one under Andropov. And lip service has also periodically been given to correcting police excesses. Because none of the "new" programs is really new, what novelty, if any, has Gorbachev brought to Soviet society and political life?

The answer can be found in the flair and style of the new Soviet leader. Compared with previous general secretaries, Gorbachev has repeatedly demonstrated an ability to listen to others and to argue his positions in a firm but reasonable manner. His style of speaking is confident, often dramatic, and notably less pedantic than that of most of his predecessors. His attractive wife Raisa is the first Soviet "first lady" since Nadezhda Krupskaya, Lenin's wife, to be allowed a place in the limelight. Both the Gorbachevs have repeatedly demonstrated wit, charm, and interest in, and knowledge of, diverse cultural matters. Moreover, he has selected associates who are also adept at projecting a more sophisticated and reasonable image. Significantly, this has been most evident in regard to foreign policy. Shevardnadze is a relatively "smooth apple," harking back to the urbane Litvinov, and is a far more eloquent and charming spokesman than the dour Gromyko. Among the new CC secretaries, Dobrynin and Yakovlev, both concerned with foreign policy and the image of the USSR abroad, are noted for their charm and easy manner.

Gorbachev himself has shown a flair for using the foreign media to play on the susceptibility of Western publics, and leaders, to the deceptive lures of personal diplomacy. No Soviet leader since Lenin has so openly played this game. Khrushchev tried it on a lesser scale, but his crudities made him a minor-leaguer compared to Gorbachev. The record so far, however, is not entirely clear as to how successful this approach to public and person-to-person diplomacy has been. Certainly, Gorbachev has succeeded in impressing those segments of Western public opinion and officialdom that tend to see every new Soviet leader as the long-awaited moderate reformer, and even such hard-nosed anti-Communists as Margaret Thatcher found him "a man I can do business with." Still, in practical terms there have been few identifiable positive results. Western governments have continued to reject many of his arms control ploys, the United States-inspired restrictions on technology transfer have remained in force, and human rights campaigns targeted on the USSR have continued much as before.

One possible exception to the above judgment must be noted: Reykjavik—a prime example of a carefully prepared and orchestrated public and personal diplomacy ploy in the Gorbachev style. Opinions are mixed, but many in the West have evaluated Reykjavik as a victory for Gorbachev and a setback for Ronald Reagan. Only time will provide the final answer, but we shall examine Reykjavik and its significance in some detail when we look at arms control.

Domestically, Gorbachev has demonstrated a similar, relatively unusual public relations flair. The most characteristic aspects of this were his frequent flying trips to outlying regions, where he mixed, listened to, but mostly exhorted the locals, and his fairly regular use of Soviet national television to address the nation. This tactic may have partially backfired somewhat in May 1986, at least in foreign eyes, when he failed to address either the nation or the world on the Chernobyl accident until over two weeks after it occurred. The delay demonstrated that the polished new leader was apparently just as captive to Soviet insecurity, dissembling, and covering up as were his predecessors. A true sense of public relations timing, in regard to foreign audiences at least, would have demanded a much earlier public appearance to address Western concerns and/or an attempt to exploit the accident for other purposes, such as arms control, which Gorbachev eventually made.

Gorbachev's personal style undoubtedly reflects much that is authentic in the man, but there is also clearly a heavy dose of calculation in it. This is illustrated by several episodes at the CPSU Congress at the end of February 1986.

In the process of manufacturing for himself the image of a new type of leader at the Congress, Gorbachev did away with the traditional forms of leader adulation, such as "Long live Comrade Gorbachev." He did not permit, at least not then, references to himself as "the great continuator of the glorious traditions." Nor did the Congress accord him the usual "thunderous applause swelling into an ovation." The choice of attributes applied to him reflected better taste than that of his predecessors and also a certain intellectual bent. Ordinary workers and peasants among the Party delegates addressed him or spoke of him in a friendly and trusting manner, "dear Mikhail Sergeevich," so as to imply the love and esteem the popular masses have for their leader. His staid and stolid Party colleagues and the officially recognized servants of the muses expressed themselves with more restraint and sophistication, by stressing such qualities as his "truly scientific approach" and "revolutionary boldness." Others commended his "political acumen," his "new vision of the times," his "Bolshevik spirit," his "very profound realism," and the like.

It goes without saying that there was nothing spontaneous in this. Far from expressing the views of the delegates, all forms of address and commendation were prescribed by the proper administrative organs, perhaps by the Central Committee itself. An incident involving the movie director Kulidzhanov, who represented the film industry at the Congress, was instructive. When Kulidzhanov in a burst of zealotry exceeded the limits of adulation considered appropriate, Gorbachev immediately retorted, "Don't get carried away." The shrewd Kulidzhanov recovered his aplomb and replied, "That is an example to be emulated."

Kulidzhanov's was not the only such example. Some were fortunate, others less so. Among the former, one has to count the style of the ongoing "de-Brezhnevization": The person responsible for all of the social failures and economic disasters was never named directly, merely alluded to, as in the formulation, "There was evident and manifest conservatism in the leadership and a penchant for idle talk, complacency and irresponsibility." The tone of castigation of Brezhnev had been set and the parts assigned in advance. Some delegates, as a rule the higher-ranking ones, were assigned the role of delivering quite sharp denunciations. For balance, however, others were instructed to speak with moderation. This would emphasize the general principle that "on its historical path the Soviet people has attained great successes; it therefore serves no purpose to wax emotional to the point of losing perspective and denigrating the achievements."

In terms of its impact upon society, the criticism voiced before and at the Congress was not insignificant. First, the criticism underscored the contrast between the old and new Soviet leadership. Second, in the absence of more substantial means, it rather succeeded in achieving its intended purpose of drawing popular attention to, and eliciting popular support for, Gorbachev's policies.

In sum, Gorbachev has brought a new style and flair to the traditionally drab and secretive Kremlin leadership. Until such time as he succeeds in really revitalizing the Soviet economy, in introducing real structural reforms in the system, or in achieving a major and enduring foreign policy success, this may be his most noteworthy contribution and achievement. Much of his style is contrived, as carefully calculated a technique as Eisenhower's disingenuousness, or Stalin's "Uncle Joe" persona. Yet, much of it does reflect the man, with a velvet glove over his iron fist.

Gorbachev's new style should not be confused with a shift away from enduring patterns of Soviet behavior, nor taken as a sign that his goals are very much different from those of his predecessors. His style may in fact make him an unusually effective proponent of Soviet views on the world stage. At least thus far it has apparently generated a degree of new hope and enthusiasm in the Soviet population at home. There, however, his style could ultimately be his downfall, particularly if his policies founder on Soviet realities. Familiarity and the "common touch" can be useful political tools, but familiarity may also breed contempt, especially on the part of a people long habituated to, and apparently comfortable with, inaccessible father figures.

5

Is the Media the Message?
Glasnost and the Arts

"It's curiouser and curiouser," said Alice.

The Soviet arts have had a long up-and-down history, from the wildly intoxicating breath of innovativeness following the Revolution through the incredible dullness of Stalin's "Socialist Realism," and from the creative burst of Khruschev's thaw to the long slide back into mediocrity under Brezhnev only partially ameliorated by a final, grudging acceptance of such Western imports as modern pop rock music. Throughout, the content, style, and most of all the strictures imposed on the arts and the media have provided one very important indicator about the state of society, the goals and confidence of the leadership, and the degree of the people's identification with, and confidence in, their leaders.

Gorbachev began his leadership with vigorous condemnations of deception and lying by economic managers. He has repeatedly demanded that officials at every level listen to the "truth" from their subordinates, no matter how critical it might be. He has stressed the importance of honest Communist "self-criticism." In presenting the new Party Program, he has insisted that the mistakes of the past be honestly recognized and that overblown promises not be substituted for sober presentation of realistic prospects. All of this clearly served two purposes. It was a prerequisite for improving managerial efficiency and, even more, it was a useful adjunct to his campaign to discredit and replace the old guard.

Such a policy line, encapsulated in the term *glasnost* (open and frank discussion) could not fail to have an influence on the attitudes and behavior of artists and writers. This peaked in December 1985 but has continued sporadically ever since and began to build again in the fall of 1986. At the 1985 Congress of Writers of the RSFSR (the Russian Republic) the famous fifty-two-year-old poet, Yevgeny Yevtushenko, gave a speech that

97

impressed many observers for its radical nature and the extent of criticism it expressed. In fact, it completely fit in with the latest resolution and decisions of the new general secretary, and Yevtushenko made no effort to conceal this, saying that "the long-awaited changes in the life of our country are changes for the better and they are beginning to be implemented." The poet posed a question that is vitally important for the Soviet people: Will the changes affect the sphere of ideology? A closer look confirms that the answer to this question is clearly no.

Yevtushenko's speech was printed in *Literaturnaya gazeta* in a severely cut version that eliminated the sharpest and most direct cirticsm. It appeared in its entirety only in the West, which Yevtushenko had attacked harshly. The West was blamed for holding the atomic bomb over the world, for prisoners in Chilean prisons, and for the death rattles of the ruins of Beirut. Yevtushenko hardly came up with this rhetoric on his own; it evidently reflected the political directives of the new second man in the Kremlin, Yegor Ligachev, who called on the workers on the ideological front to completely politicize their "creative work." At the same time, however, within the framework of what is permitted, Yevtushenko also touched upon aspects of Soviet life that it has not been politic to address openly until quite recently. He called for a reevaluation of Soviet history, for an objective account of the period of "lack of legality," when masses of peasants were annihilated, when millions of people were forcibly uprooted or arrested, exiled, or executed—when they were eliminated "from participation in developing" the Soviet state. More significantly, the poet also called for exposing the failures of the present, not just those of the distant past.

The real surprise came in the concluding section of Yevtushenko's speech. There, the poet described the privileges enjoyed by the members of the Writers Union as "unjust." He even generalized from this to touch upon the special status of the entire ruling class, noting that any closed system of distribution of foodstuffs and goods was morally unacceptable, "and within such undeserved prerogatives I include the chit in the pockets of each of us which entitles bearer to obtain goods at the special kiosks set up at our Congress."

The obvious question is what in the poet's speech was inspired by his own desire to shock the audience and what was determined by Party fiat. It is clear that regardless of the answer to this question, the whole speech fully fit within the framework of the policy of public disclosure that was so prominently featured by Gorbachev. In this policy, it must be stressed, what was being exposed was *only* those social manifestations or people objectionable to the Gorbachev leadership. This point explains the slight opening of the curtain to reveal the lawlessness dominating Soviet commerce. Thus, the Soviet press had reported extensively on spoiled food and stale bread arriving at the table of the ordinary consumer due to negligence, price juggling, and corruption. Delicacies such as black caviar and smoked salmon were reported to be available at reasonable prices in other than stores reserved for the elite only when they had gone bad. The press scrupulously traced these "crimes" to sources in Bryansk, Stalingrad, Barnaul, Pskov, and Yaroslavl, clearly presaging that Gorbachev's purges would soon reach these locations. What was happening was that Gorbachev was establishing a justification to remove potential opponents and their supporters. This is in fact what happened to Grishin, whose removal followed a campaign of criticism of housing construction in Moscow.

The innovative ideas of Yevtushenko should be understood in this context. Their intent was clear: one should fully rely on Gorbachev, and then life will become better and people will be happier. So that there would be no doubt as to whom Gorbachev was following, Yevtushenko clearly identified the leader's model. It was none other than Lenin, who had no qualms about attacking bureaucrats when destruction and disaster threatened. The implicit conclusion was that the country should not fear the purges and changes going on.

The real content of *glasnost* in the arts was clarified later, in the spring, so that no one would develop any "wrong ideas" about it. On April 20 *Pravda* reported on a previous day's conference of theatrical workers, theater directors, playwrights, secretaries of Party organizations, and heads of artists unions held in the Central Committee. Member of the Politburo, CC secretary, and the appointed guardian of ideological purity, Gorbachev's number-two man Yegor Ligachev spoke at the conference, stating that the Party was calling on literature and art to depict "the truth and only the truth." He specified that "the whole truth," as pointed out in the political report to the XXVIIth Party Congress, "consists in the achievements of the people and the problems of development of society, in the heroism and the daily toiling reality, in victories and failures, that is, in life itself in all its multifacetedness, drama and grandeur." Going on to stress that the present period was transitional, requiring a heightened work rhythm and the full measure of effort from each citizen, Ligachev reminded his audience that during all periods, and particularly at transitional stages in the development of the society, Soviet literature and theater had "promoted the image of the fighter for the new against the outmoded." The duty of the theater was defined as "disclosing and revealing the sources of all types of deviations from socialist morality." Speaking about the tasks of the cultural policy of the Party, the Party's ideological spokesman emphasized that "it was imperative for the masters of literature and art to be more active in showing the Soviet way of life, and in demonstrating more initiative in the struggle against burgeois ideology."

The same themes with the same nuances were repeated later in the year by Gorbachev and others at the June Congress of Soviet Writers; at a plenum of the directors of the Union of Journalists and at a Central Committee meeting with writers and journalists the same month; at another meeting with theatrical officials in August; and again at a September plenum of the Union of Journalists. Even a Central Committee and Council of Ministers decree in September on the further development of fine and graphic arts was in a similar vein.

The same pattern of extolling *glasnost* and free expression, and then setting real limits to it, was continued in 1987 by Gorbachev, Ligachev, Yakovlev, and many others. In fact, Gorbachev, in a reprise of Ligachev's remarks the previous year, expressed it best at the February meeting of the CC with heads of the media and mass information and propaganda organs. Emphasizing the need for criticism, he said that "one thing is absolute—criticism must always be in line with the Party approach, based on truth, and this must depend upon the Party editors' Party spirit [*partiinost*]. . . . [The press] must actively assist those who struggle for reconstruction. . . . The press and criticism must unite all, not split." He added, "Today, the main task of journalists et al is to help people understand reconstruction and to support it." In sum, *glasnost* is great as long as it is aimed at those who oppose or resist Gorbachev's policies.

Compared to all this, the partial rehabilitation of such authors as Pasternak and the announced publication in the USSR of selected works (undoubtedly quite selected) by such emigres as Nabokov still cannot yet be viewed as more than the tiniest cracks in the doorway to cultural liberalization, a bone thrown for public effect.

Against this backdrop, the following quotation from *Literaturnaya gazeta* in March, 1986 from a speech by the first secretary of the Board of the Union of Writers of the USSR assumes the nature of an "economic assignment":

> The very psychological climate of speeding up the socioeconomic and intellectual development of the country causes the writers [also] to speed up. The issue is not speed accompanied by bustle, which merely causes damage; what is required is the intensification of creative labor, a resetting of the rhythm of the work of the writer.

> Certain of our classics have shown that speed does not mean poor quality. This experience of theirs was put to good use by Soviet writers during the Great Patriotic War when, in a short period of time, a literature of the highest ideological and artistic temper was created which has become a lasting model of writers' fulfilment of their patriotic duty.

Finally, in an amazing bit of unconscious irony, *Pravda* in the spring of 1986 sharply criticized Soviet television for its dullness and for its lack of objectivity both at home and, especially, in depicting life in the West! It was the pot calling the kettle black!

As this curious saga illustrates, in Gorbachev's USSR doublespeak remains alive and well, and woe betide the writer or artist who does not conform by producing the "objective truth" no matter how dull, repetitious or unbelievable it might be. Moreover, the artist, bending every effort to the cause, is somehow not only to try to sound more interesting but also to write and work faster. It appears that a modernized version of "Socialist Realism" will still reign in the USSR as it struggles to perfect socialism and enter the twenty-first century.

Part II
Foreign Policies

About 150 years ago Tocqueville predicted that eventually the United States and Russia would compete for world domination.

6

Happy Days Can Be Here Again: Relations with the United States and the Industrialized West

> *[The contemporary era] is the era of the transition from capitalism to socialism and communism, of the historic competition between two global social-political systems. . . .*
> *The citadel of international reaction is the imperialism of the USA.*
> *Three centers of intraimperialist competition have been formed: the United States of America, Western Europe, and Japan.*
> *The Communist Party of the Soviet Union firmly and consistently upholds the Leninist principle of peaceful coexistence.*
>
> —*Third Program of the Communist Party of the Soviet Union,* adopted 6 March 1986

Throughout Soviet history a fundamental element of the ideology of the leadership has been that of the "objectively inevitable" conflict of interests and struggle to the end between socialism (i.e. the USSR and the "socialist camp") and capitalism (i.e. the industrialized West). (The formulation "objectively inevitable" here is not considered to indicate a current or temporary condition. Rather, according to the Soviet ideology it represents a basic reality akin to a natural law such as the law of gravity. Consequently, any responsible leader must keep it in mind when determining policy or taking political action. The contest must be prepared for and conducted in every feasible way.) Before Khrushchev, it was a cardinal point of faith that this struggle would eventually lead to a final cataclysmic war between the two camps. Since Khrushchev, it has been held that the final war is no longer inevitable precisely, and only, because of the growing relative strength of the socialist camp. Before Khrushchev, "peaceful coexistence," a policy initiated by Lenin, was a means of temporarily managing the struggle while preparing for the inevitable war. Since Khrushchev, "peaceful consistence" (or "detente," a term the Soviets seldom use) has been a way to manage and win the struggle, if possible without the war. Moreover in continuity with pre-Soviet Russian history, the entire period of Soviet history has been marked by a mixed fascination with, and revulsion against, the West.

As long as the above beliefs hold sway, the West is inescapably the central and ultimate focus of Soviet foreign policy. Ever since World War II, with the United States the leader and far and away the most powerful state in the West, the United States has been the basic focus of Soviet foreign policy, the rival to be surpassed and displaced, as well as, paradoxically, in certain ways the model for how a superpower behaves.

Soviet foreign policy under Gorbachev has also been based upon these precepts, with one potentially important ostensible change. Formerly, the ultimate military confrontation, if it were to occur and even if it were nuclear, would nevertheless be won by the socialist camp. Under Gorbachev, the Soviets have declared that there would be no winners in a nuclear war and that the very survival of humanity would be threatened by a nuclear holocaust. Whether this critical distinction reflects the present genuine Soviet belief or merely an assessment of the current—not necessarily immutable—situation, or whether it constitutes no more than a self-serving propaganda formula is crucial in terms of understanding basic Soviet strategy for the present and the future. In any event the concept of war deterrence through relative superiorities, the relative "correlation of forces" in Soviet terminology, and the continuing possibility of war are sufficient to explain the continuing economic priority the Soviets assign to heavy industry, other quite logical and real rationales notwithstanding.

Gorbachev came to power faced with several undeniable facts and unavoidable considerations affecting Soviet relationships with the United States and the industrialized West; virtually all of these had negative implications for the USSR. Brezhnev's policies during the period of detente of the early and mid-1970s had resulted in a number of distinct gains for the Soviets. The USSR had been recognized as a superpower, ostensible coequal to the United States in world affairs. Arms control negotiations and agreements, the centerpiece of U.S.-Soviet detente, had permitted the Soviet Union to continue to amass military might and contributed to a slowing of Western military growth and modernization. The result was that the USSR was at least equal to, and possibly on the verge of achieving some superiorities over, the West in overall strategic nuclear capabilities. At the same time, the Soviet Union was widely judged to be superior in most categories of conventional military power, at least in Europe.

For the Soviets, detente had increased access to Western trade, credits, and technology, although nowhere near the extent hoped for. The United States had been first embroiled in, and then traumatized by, a losing war in Southeast Asia and, as a consequence, was reluctant to take any major direct action to reverse apparent Soviet gains in many parts of the Third World. This attitude was shared to an even greater degree but for somewhat different reasons by most of Western Europe. Although Soviet relations with the Western European Communist parties were burdened by various conflicts, for much of this period, socialist parties were on the ascendancy in Western Europe. Lured by better economic and human relations, the parties were particularly susceptible to making accommodations to Soviet interests, a susceptibility epitomized by West Germany's Ostpolitik. Japan posed no strategic threat, for it appeared content to concentrate on economic growth and showed no signs of a more than token willingness to contribute to Western military power.

Concurrently with all of this, Soviet influence in the Third World seemed to be producing many concrete gains at the expense of the West. Although relations were still very cold with the PRC and although there had been some disturbing rapprochement between the United States and Beijing, the Chinese challenge to Soviet "leadership" in the world's communist and revolutionary movements abated as Mao's successors turned inward to focus on domestic issues. Moreover, the capitalist economies were suffering far more from the explosion of oil prices than was the USSR, which was reaping the export benefits of being the world's largest producer of petroleum and natural gas. Truly, for the men in the Kremlin, the early 1970s had been "happy days."

In the late 1970s and particularly in the 1980s, right up to Gorbachev's accession to power, almost all of this framework had come unglued. The catalogue of domestic and foreign policy failures, drift, and stagnation has been summarized in the introductory chapter and need not be reiterated here. A few observations, however, are in order.

Much of the foreign policy drift was a direct result of, and was exacerbated by, Soviet domestic problems. Increasingly evident inadequacies in the structure and performance of the Soviet economy were robbing the USSR of much of its international appeal, both as a model and a market, and simultaneously depriving the Kremlin of adequate means to promote its global interests and foreign policy objectives. A rigid bureaucracy, heavy-handedness, and frequently empty promises to would-be and actual clients contributed to the reduction of Soviet influence. Failure to abide by the human rights provisions of the Helsinki accords alienated many in the West. Moreover, its obviously senescent and increasingly incompetent leadership added to the impression that except for the awesome nuclear power and the military hardware it could provide its chosen clients, the USSR was becoming increasingly irrelevant to the satisfaction of Third World aspirations as well as to the solution of pressing global issues. Client regimes were discovering that after the USSR had aided them in coming to power, their own and Soviet interests often differed and that Soviet aid and ties seemed to be of limited usefulness in regard to many of their domestic needs and foreign policy goals. Their dissatisfactions apparently fed into Soviet internal policy discussions about whether military and economic assistance provided the expected degrees of influence and, more important, control. As a result, in the late 1970s and early 1980s there was a surprisingly vigorous, if low-keyed and low-profile, debate in specialized Soviet journals about whether the USSR was getting its money's worth and whether it could afford the scale of global activism and commitment to Third World causes it had once undertaken.

A series of disastrous foreign policy miscalculations were also major factors. The Afghanistan involvement might have had, and may still have, a number of valid justifications in the minds of the men in the Kremlin, but its price has been high, particularly so in light of initial expectations of a relatively quick and painless victory. The shootdown of a Korean airliner and the way in which the matter was handled on the international stage gave the USSR another black eye. Bluster and stonewalling on the issue of the U.S. intermediate-range nuclear weapons in Europe had totally failed to achieve the successes achieved earlier in a similar campaign against enhanced radiation weapons, the so-called neutron bomb. The apparent decision to conduct, or to permit subordinates to conduct, field tests of mycotoxins ("yellow rain") further contributed to the tarnishing of the Soviet image. Finally, even though the evidence was inadequate to prove Soviet complicity, the attempted assassination of the pope, coming as it did on the heels of a serious challenge to Soviet rule in the pope's native Poland, led many to believe that beneath all the smoke there must have been some fire.

All these things would have been bad enough in themselves, but their effects were augmented through the sheer contrast with a reawakened, notably dynamic, and highly activist U.S. administration. Much as Reagan's policies might frighten and bring condemnation from some, they also were evidently convincing to even more. In particular, the contrast to the pre-Gorbachev leadership was devastating. More important, the prospects of a vigorous two-sided arms race and competition for economic influence, along with the increasingly effective barriers to the legal acquisition of Western technology, must have been terrifying at a time when Soviet economic problems and inability to adapt to the technologies of the postindustrial age were so clearly in evidence. In sum, the cumulative effects of domestic stagnation and foreign policy blunders were made synergistic by U.S. dynamism.

To Mikhail Gorbachev, and evidently to most of his associates, the remedy was obvious. Domestically, the creaking Soviet bureaucracy had to be galvanized and the economy rescued and rebuilt. Globally, this had to be accompanied by quieting the rivalry with the United States and particularly by avoiding a high-technology arms race that might well be unwinnable no matter how many precious resources and how much effort needed for other purposes would be poured into it. Although the failures of the Brezhnev regime were anathema to Gorbachev, the relative successes of the early detente period were not. Economic revitalization was not only desperately needed for domestic reasons but additionally prompted by foreign developments and challenges. Furthermore, economic revitalization would also probably require, or at least be significantly facilitated and speeded up by increased access to Western trade, investment credits, and technology—all of which were obtainable only through a detente.

Because of these considerations Gorbachev's foreign policy has been ultimately focused on the U.S.-Soviet equation, specifically on restoring detente and defusing the renewed U.S. challenge while preventing any major reversal of fortunes in the wider global competition. Almost every Soviet foreign policy action for the period should be viewed in light of those goals and of a search for less palatable fallback options should the primary objectives prove unachievable.

One important additional factor may also have been at play. Compared to his predecessors, Gorbachev is less directly influenced by World War II, and he made his early career in the domestic and "peaceful" sectors of public administration. This may be consistent with a receptivity on his part to the arguments of those who see the nuclear arms race as a highly costly dead-end road and nuclear war as unwinnable. Gorbachev can be expected at the very least to be impatient with the lion's share of investment, human resources, and effort being devoured by the military. In any event, he has made the futility of nuclear weapons competition a central theme of his public pronouncements. Whether this is more than a good propaganda stick with which to beat Washington about the head and shoulders can be judged only in connection with other policies and in light of future developments. Consequently, it will be assessed in our conclusions, after a discussion of concrete arms control policies and of developments in official military doctrine. Meanwhile, let us look at what the Soviet leader has done in regard to the West, beginning with his policies and actions toward the United States.

Even before Gorbachev was elected general secretary, U.S.-Soviet relations had shown some tentative signs of a thaw. In September 1984, contrary to the predictions of those who had expected the Soviets to refrain from doing anything that might help President Reagan win reelection, Gromyko came to Washington to meet with the president. This was followed over the next months by a series of mostly low-level contacts and discussions, which reversed the previous apparent determination not to seek any common ground with the United States. One such contact was the early 1985 joint discussions by relatively senior foreign policy officials on the problems of the Middle East. How much of a hand Gorbachev had in these attempts to shift policy toward the Reagan administration is not at all clear. Chernenko's debility was already evident in August 1984, if not earlier, and the presuccession maneuvering that made Gorbachev the "second secretary" was definitely under way. Still, Chernenko's prestige, however limited, was based on his long service as Brezhnev's toady, and he undoubtedly realized also that one of the high points of Brezhnev's rule was associated with the successes of detente in the early 1970s. Hence, Chernenko himself may have been involved in these initial attempts to reopen the possibilties of restoring detente-as-it-was.

Defense Minister Ustinov, too, seems likely to have played a role, with the sacking of Marshal Ogarkov in fall 1984 possibly being a reflection of differences between these two top defense policymakers on this issue. Detente had been the period of the greatest accumulation of influence and prestige by the defense establishment since World War II. Subsequent developments, such as Afghanistan and the Korean Airline incident, had called its competence into question. Further, the prospects of keeping up militarily with the United States at the same time that it found itself under pressure from those in the leadership who saw other urgent nondefense-related needs for the economy must have worried the defense establishment. Finally, Ustinov and his associates must have come to appreciate the degree to which their own defense planning was greatly simplified when detente and arms control bounded the parameters of the Western threat and response.

The role of Foreign Minister Gromyko, the other major Gorbachev supporter from among the old leadership, is less clear. Gromyko had long been seen as overwhelmingly preoccupied with U.S.-Soviet relations and as a leading exponent of the belief that U.S.-Soviet rivalry was fundamental to all Soviet foreign policy. During most of his career he was no more than a useful tool of the real Soviet foreign policy decision makers; he bent to the winds of others' decisions so completely that Khrushchev could publicly humiliate him by stating that if told to do so, he would "drop his trousers and sit on a block of ice." After his elevation to the Politburo, Gromyko did acquire some degree of policy influence, and during the years of leaderhsip turmoil and drift he was able to stake out a position of power of his own.

On the other hand, he was known as "Mr. Nyet" (Mr. No), and the most frosty period in U.S.-Soviet relations coincided with the period when his own power base and influence were greatest. But even Gromyko, who was described by his own daughter as being totally immersed in his job as foreign minister and completely isolated from the rest of the Soviet reality, could not escape an awareness of how serious the economic stagnation was and how detrimental were the foreign policy setbacks that an unyielding Soviet hard-line policy was producing.

Despite the likelihood that Gromyko himself favored a U.S.-oriented foreign policy predicated on competition and struggle rather than the search for rapprochement, it seems probable that he had no trouble in accepting the opening to the United States. Moreover, although every Soviet leadership—whose advisers included such presumed experts from academia as Arbatov, who was really more a propaganda hack than an adviser, and Dobrynin in the diplomatic corps—had repeatedly demonstrated a limited ability to understand and correctly predict U.S. developments, it was probably quite obvious to the Foreign Ministry that Reagan was going to win reelection no matter what the Soviets did. Finding a *modus vivendi* with his administration as quickly as possible seemed a far better option than four more years of largely sterile confrontation. In sum, Gromyko's subsequent easing out of real power is more than adequately explained by reasons previously discussed. There is no need to attribute his "reassignment" to his opposition to either the goals or modalities of Gorbachev's pursuit of detente with Washington, as some Western observers have done.

Once in power, Gorbachev built on the meager beginnings of late 1984 and early 1985, accelerating their dynamics with an almost single-minded devotion matched only by his desire to revitalize the economy and to consolidate his domestic power. Gorbachev's policies and actions in regard to the United States reveal three primary goals:

- derailing and reversing U.S. military modernization and expansion;
- increasing access to U.S. trade and technology; and
- preventing the newly reassertive United States from eroding Soviet positions and gains globally, in particular in the Third World.

Whatever his other motivations, the goals fully fit with the *kto-kogo* mentality and the relentless pursuit of the "historic struggle." Evidence also shows that Gorbachev and his team have emphasized four means of achieving the goals:

- arms control;
- mobilizing U.S. domestic and international pressure on Washington;

- public diplomacy and propaganda; and
- the lure of potential profits.

With some variations in emphasis, the three goals and four means have also dictated and shaped Soviet policies toward the rest of the industrialized West, particularly Western Europe and Japan. Each of the goals and the ways in which they may have been pursued require more detailed analysis in order to assess their variations in application toward different parts of the West and to predict Gorbachev's most probable future courses of action.

Halting Western, primarily U.S. military modernization has been without a doubt the central focus of Soviet foreign policy during all of Gorbachev's reign to date. Within this broad objective, the preeminent objective has been to stop the U.S. Strategic Defense Initiative (SDI, or "Star Wars"). In fact, Soviet efforts to forestall SDI can be described only as increasingly frantic through the years. As will be shown in the next chapter, every one of Gorbachev's many arms control proposals and maneuvers had stopping SDI either as a primary or as a corollary objective. It is a measure of how important this is to Gorbachev's policies that for virtually the first time in the long history of East-West arms control, the Soviets assumed the role of the supplicant, making one proposal and apparent concession after another while the U.S. administration has stood firm on its commitment to SDI. New arms control initiatives directed at the Western Europeans have all been designed with an eye for encouraging opposition to European participation in Star Wars and generating European pressure on Washington to make concessions on SDI and nuclear arms control in general.

Of course, European and regional objectives were also reflected in the Soviet proposals offered in Vienna and Stockholm, as well as in those calling for direct, separate-theater nuclear negotiations with France and the United Kingdom. French and British nuclear modernization plans concern Moscow because they affect the overall East-West strategic balance and jeopardize Soviet desires both to dominate Western Europe politically and, if need be, to successfully wage a conventional war in Europe without nuclear escalation. In the same regard it has long been recognized by Moscow that political domination of Western Europe requires the breakup of NATO. Such an achievement would be nullified, however, if out of the ashes of NATO a Western Europe emerged sufficiently strong to stand up against, rather than accommodate, the USSR.

More than any previous Soviet leader, Gorbachev has used public diplomacy and propaganda to advance his causes. Long personal interviews in Western journals, publicized responses to letters from various Western public figures, appearances on Western television, and personal meetings with Western leaders and politicians in and out of power, to say nothing of his summitry abroad with Mitterand and Reagan, by their frequency and scope are almost unprecedented departures from the customary behavior of a CPSU general secretary. In each of these events Gorbachev's principal theme has been nuclear arms control and the need to "prevent the militarization of space." Reportedly, almost every meeting with Third World leaders has emphasized this same issue. Expressions of Soviet support for a new international economic order and for almost any regional issue that happened to be dear to a given Third World leader's heart, as well as almost every promise to increase economic aid to Third World nations, have been tied to the need to stop SDI and the arms race so that resources can be freed to tackle economic problems. Even Gorbachev's reluctant television appearance after the Chernobyl disaster was turned into a plea for nuclear arms control. Similarly, the U.S. Challenger disaster and other Western space program accidents have been exploited by Gorbachev to argue that Star-Wars-related technology is inherently unreliable and unworkable. Moreover, virtually all of the many attempts to attract trade and technology from Western business people or state officials have been accompanied by the proviso that such profitable endeavors can reach their full potential only if SDI and Western nuclear modernization is stopped or slowed.

A clear, and perhaps even the most urgent, reason for putting SDI and Western military improvements at the top of Gorbachev's foreign policy priorities is economic. This applies irrespective of his long-term outlook in regard to the priorities to be assigned to Soviet defense industries and military power. The defense industry, in any case, needs major renovation and reorientation to retain its ability to satisfy the requirements of modern weapons, command and control, and mobility, The Soviets have increasingly, been forced to switch from relatively cheap and easily produceable, simple military technologies to much more costly systems based on complex advanced technology. Although Ogarkov may have fallen into relative disfavor, his impassioned 1983 and 1984 criticisms of the capabilities of Soviet industry and economy to meet the needs of the military did not fall on deaf ears; in fact, they have since been frequently reaffirmed by other military spokesmen, although more obliquely. Matching a vigorous and sustained U.S. SDI program—not an easy task in any event, and perhaps a hopeless one—would inevitably require a quantitative increase in the degree of militarization of the Soviet economy and would affect the approaches to technological modernization in ways that could have an adverse impact on programs to improve nondefense sectors. In addition, Gorbachev undoubtedly believes, and with good reason, that a detente based upon arms control would not only slow or halt U.S. military improvements but also tend to improve the terms of trade and facilitate access to Western technologies.

By and large such considerations probably were sufficiently persuasive to all major factions in the Soviet leadership and to the Soviet equivalent of interest groups, including the bulk of the defense establishment. This means that Gorbachev could enjoy a wide consensus for his policies. But the risk that he runs is that in the process he might be tempted to make unpalatable arms control concessions that would nevertheless fail to stop the U.S. programs. At that point his potential rivals would have plenty of ammunition for their own power games. Similarly, if he were to make too-far-reaching concessions in regard to human rights or the secrecy that undergirds the Soviet conception of state security without pocketing commensurate gains in favorable arms control terms or access to trade and technology, the same potential rivals could mobilize support within the KGB and other security organs.

A second reason for Gorbachev's preoccupation with SDI and nuclear arms control may be a conviction that nuclear weapons really are unusable, that SDI is indeed inherently a blind alley leading only to greater instability at great cost. If he indeed has any such "pacifist" bent, Gorbachev would be likely to have little support on this basis from the interlocking military and Party defense bureaucracies. Habits are hard to change. The military of any nuclear power does include many who are as terrified of the potential consequences of nuclear weapons as any other segment of public opinion—possibly even more so, for military personnel know how unpredictable and unmanageable nuclear war is bound to be. Nevertheless, the military mind is geared to finding ways to manage even the most terrifying weaponry, thinking in terms of security (the military's raison d'etre) as stemming from relative superiorities in any and all forms of military power, and has a vested interest in maintaining vigorous military programs. The Soviet defense establishment would thus be predisposed to object to any arms control policies perceived as leading to reductions involving permanent restrictions on its programs.

There is a third and most disturbing possible explanation for Gorbachev's frantic search for a way to stop Reagan's programs. It is the one most favored by so-called cold-warrior circles in the West. According to this explanation, detente and arms control have facilitated significant gains in Soviet military power and capabilities relative to the West, and those gains were—and may again be—translatable into more effective political pressure on Western governments and into greater Soviet freedom of action in the Third World. This hypothesis cannot be disregarded. Detente in the 1970s had precisely such results, although it is not entirely certain that arms control by itself was a major reason. The fact that Gorbachev's sweeping and lofty-sounding arms control proposals (see chapter 7) have apparently not yet been accompanied by either the concrete specifics or the wider policy changes capable of preventing this outcome reinforces such suspicions. What additionally reinforces such suspicions is the fact that the frenetic opposition to the U.S. SDI program is still accompanied by a vigorous and long extant Soviet research and development effort in similar technologies and capabilities. This strongly suggests that the Soviets are nowhere near as convinced as their rhetoric would indicate that strategic defenses cannot work sufficiently well to provide a significant military advantage. If such ideas indeed influence Gorbachev, they would complement rather than exclude the economic rationale behind his foreign policies. It could then be presumed that his policy line is supported by the defense and security establishments, hard-line ideologists, and significant elements of the foreign policy bureaucracy.

The second objective evident in Gorbachev's foreign policy pursuits has been greater access to Western trade, investment, and technology. Soviet needs in this regard are self-evident and have already been discussed. What is noteworthy is the way in which Gorbachev has pursued this goal. It can be described in terms of the choice of audiences. U.S. business people and economic managers have not been neglected for obvious reasons. First of all, U.S. investment potential and high technology, if they only can be tapped, are obviously the most attractive. Moreover, the United States is the driving force behind Western barriers to trade and technology (CO-COM). What better address could there be to try to marshal support for the repeal of these barriers than the U.S. business community? Second, U.S. business circles would be a potentially influential target audience for encouraging U.S. domestic opposition to the Reagan defense programs.

While U.S economic interests have not been neglected, those of Western Europe and Japan have clearly been more ardently courted. Premier Ryzhkov even addressed a group of Western European business people by two-way satellite linkup in early 1986. Judging from notices that appear in the Soviet press, far more Western European and Japanese than American business people have recently visited Moscow. Soviet government ministers of various branches of the economy have widely traveled to Western European nations and to Japan. Soviet parliamentary (Supreme Soviet) delegations have visited the industrially advanced allies of the United States frequently; for the United States itself, contacts of this type have mostly consisted of congressional delegations visiting Moscow. In all such interparliamentary contacts, potential economic relations have been one of the main subjects on the agenda. Bodies authorized to promote bilateral economic cooperation between the USSR and Western European nations have met regularly. Since becoming general secretary Gorbachev's one state visit to a Western nation other than the summits with the United States, was to France; most Western European prime ministers have visited Moscow.

Reasons for the emphasis on Western Europe are not hard to surmise. If grain is excluded from the count, Soviet trade volume with Western Europe is far higher than with the United States; even in grain, European agricultural sales to the USSR, buoyed by recent bumper crops and heavy state subsidies, are now competing for the U.S. share of the market. Western Europe is the main market for Soviet gas and oil, sales that are the principal source of Soviet hard currency earnings and potentially a means of Soviet pressure on Western governments when and if world oil demand rises again. Western Europe is more interested in better ties with Eastern Europe (whose troubled economies account, in turn, for their governments' strong interest in Western European trade and credits) than is the United States, its strong Eastern European emigré communities notwithstanding. A number of Western European states have very large and vigorous antinuclear, and usually anti-American, peace movements with considerable influence in major political parties. Some Western European governments, such as Papandreou's Greece, have a strongly anti-American, anti-NATO bent. Others, such as Sweden, have a traditional commitment to arms control. The heavy traffic of Soviet visits to Europe and Soviet hostings of European visitors reflect, therefore, both economic and political concerns. Of no minor importance, especially if Gorbachev fails to establish the kind of detente he wants with the United States, is the fact that Western Europe has both economic wealth *and* a very impressive technological capability.

Under Gorbachev, virtually no Western European state has been neglected, but the top priority was initially assigned to France, with West Germany probably second. Gorbachev, probably even more so than his predecessors, has swallowed Mitterand's strong support for NATO and U.S.-European defense improvements. It is true that France is a significant Soviet trading partner, and is officially not part of the integrated NATO military structure. But these two factors do not adequately explain the Soviet focus on France, especially because the trade is not that important per se and the degree of French military cooperation with NATO states is greater than generally realized. Moreover, Soviet military contingency planning undoubtedly takes it for granted that France would be involved on the NATO side in any major European war. The most likely explanation lies in the fact that Paris has generally opposed the U.S. SDI.

The reasons for assigning high priorities to relations with the FRG are even more readily understandable. After all, Bonn commands the mightiest Western European economy and probably the strongest technological base. It has sought better relations with the East more persistently than has any other Western European government. At the same time the present conservative government faces leftist opposition from a party whose leadership in recent years has been increasingly dominated by accommodationist, antinuclear, and somewhat anti-American elements.

Under Gorbachev the British were not neglected, but for a long time the overtures to London were less frequent and lower in profile than to the other two of Western Europe's "big three." However, as Prime Minister Margaret Thatcher's apparent troubles mounted, the Kremlin appeared to step up its approaches to the UK, especially toward the opposition parties with their antinuclear and anti-NATO platforms. Then in early autumn 1986 Shevardnadze and Murakhovskiy made formal visits to London, signed agreements, and even invited Thatcher to Moscow. Her visit took place in spring 1987. The Italians (as the number-four Western European power) and the Spanish (with their economic problems and popular ambivalence about NATO) appeared to stand next on the list for Soviet attention.

The Soviet search for closer ties with the Japanese has been definitely stepped up under Gorbachev. There have been visits by economic and cultural ministers and several parliamentary exchanges. But even more significant was the first trip to Tokyo in a long time by a Soviet foreign minister Shevardnadze, and the return visit to Moscow at the end of May 1986 by Japanese Foreign Minister Abe. The reasons for these contacts are similar to those that have shaped Soviet policy toward Western Europe. Economics has played a key role. Japan has by now outpaced the USSR as the second-largest national economy. Its technological capabilities are immensely attractive, and Tokyo is potentially a vital source of investment, trade, and technology for Moscow's plans to develop Siberia. Moreover, Moscow has traditionally been worried about the prospects of closer Japanese economic ties with the PRC, with which the Soviets still have some major unresolved political problems and where they seek to compete economically with the West. The recent Soviet focus on Tokyo is also intelligible in terms of Gorbachev's overriding concern with the U.S. SDI. Every effort was made to discourage Japan from participating in SDI. Soviet warnings on this score were even more strident and ominous in their wording than those addressed to the Europeans. Although more fundamentally aimed at the PRC, Gorbachev's sweeping proposals for Asian and Pacific security and economic development (in his Vladivostok speech at the end of July, 1986) were also clearly aimed at Tokyo.

To counter increased U.S. activism in the Third World and to maintain existing Soviet positions there, the Gorbachev regime has relied primarily on propaganda, but it has also dispensed military and economic aid to selected clients and undertaken a series of consultations with the United

States. The details will be discussed in chapter 11. Two aspects are worth mentioning here.

The first and the most arduously pursued approach was to exploit Third World issues and U.S. policies toward parts of the developing world for the sake of encouraging anti-Americanism and pacifism *in the industrialized West* in general and for the sake of building up a stronger U.S. domestic opposition to Reagan's policies in particular. Moscow seized every opportunity to exploit popular apprehensions and dissatisfaction about U.S. policies toward Nicaragua and South Africa. In both cases Gorbachev and his aides realized that they had effective propaganda weapons with which to galvanize not only left-wing elements in the West but also many moderates who feared a new U.S. military intervention in a Third World country or detested Pretoria's apartheid policies. U.S. ties to right-wing dictatorships in countries like Chile, Pakistan, the Philippines, or South Korea were also repeatedly highlighted in Soviet propaganda. Except in regard to the Pinochet regime in Santiago, this propaganda line was pursued with less fervor and was rather less effective in promoting Soviet purposes in Western public opinion. Other then the militant anti-American Left, the Western public is not overly concerned with excesses committed in Santiago or Asunción, and the positive response of the U.S. administration to the overthrow of the Marcoses in the Philippines robbed Moscow of an issue that was beginning to concern U.S. and Western moderates. Soviet involvement in Afghanistan served in large measure to deprive the issue of Pakistan's repressions of any utility except with the Western Left, and of course India. Even Chile was simply too remote an issue for most in the West, other than the anti-Reagan Left, which needed no prompting from Moscow.

Moscow also tried to utilize the U.S. air strikes against Libya in March and April of 1986 to weaken support for U.S. policies in general and to encourage Western public opinion to pressure Washington in the direction of greater receptivity to Soviet arms control proposals. The issue seemed ready-made, and Moscow's public declarations, in which strident condemnations were blended with a few ostensibly reasonable proposals (such as the withdrawal of superpower fleets from the Mediterranean), tried to increase fears of Reagan's bellicosity in the West while presenting Gorbachev as a potential peacemaker. The wide gap between Moscow's strong words and its much more moderate actions may have helped Gorbachev to build his "peace-loving" image.

The Libyan affair did not seem to be as effective in persuading Western publics as Moscow had hoped. In the United States itself, the Reagan actions against Gaddafi were quite popular with the majority of the public opinion from the start. In continental Europe—Britain being a special case—the initial strongly negative public and governmental reactions tended to dissipate considerably as the evidence linking Tripoli to direct support of international terror mounted and appeared to be increasingly persuasive in forcing the Western European governments themselves to take greater numbers of diplomatic and economic measures against Libya. True, the Libyan issue did reinforce the attitudes of anti-American militants, and it did seem to win some support for the political Left in the United Kingdom, but it did not appear to have served Gorbachev's goals as much as had initially seemed likely.

Ironically, given Western fears that Reagan's attacks on Libya or other similar targets were likely to trigger a global war, it was precisely Moscow's restraint and avoidance of confrontation with the United States over Libya that turned into a factor depriving the USSR of propaganda advantages that might otherwise have been detained. Nevertheless, the long-term effects of the Libyan incident on East-West relations and on European and U.S. public opinion remained unclear. The crisis, like other Third World issues that Gorbachev had been attempting to exploit, does not appear on balance to have added very much to the strength of Western disapproval of Washington's policies. The one possible exception to this generalization is that the European public's desire for some real progress in arms control has probably become firmer than ever. However, throughout 1987 public demands concerning this issue were increasingly directed toward both Washington *and* Moscow. The greatest impetus here was probably the Chernobyl nuclear reactor accident and initial Soviet dissembling about it. The Chernobyl disaster may even have indirectly increased Western appreciation for U.S. arguments about the importance of tight verification procedures.

The second significant aspect of Gorbachev's handling of Third World issues in regard to his relations with the United States, and by extension with the entire West, has been also largely one of style and form. By continuing the process begun in early 1985, before his election as general secretary, of periodic United State State Department-Soviet Foreign Ministry discussions on various regions of the world, Gorbachev attempted to shore up the perception that Washington and Moscow were global equals in every way. The apparent lack of any concrete results from such discussions has so far not helped this goal.

This brings us to the point where we can partially evaluate the success or failure of Gorbachev's policies toward the West. By mid-1987, after almost three years in power, Gorbachev had achieved precious little success in his bid to stop the U.S. SDI and general Western military modernization and force improvements. In spite of all his grandiose proposals and the sequence of apparent concessions in arms control, and in spite of all his exercises at using both the carrot and the stick to encourage Western public opposition to these programs, Western governments were one after another either formally signing up for participation in SDI or permitting their private businesses to do so. U.S. intermediate weapons deployments in Europe and the French and U.K. nuclear modernization were continuing on schedule. The possibility of thwarting the Reagan programs had less to do with Soviet actions and more to do with U.S. domestic opposition to them—opposition whose strength was largely unaffected by Soviet rhetoric—and with the implications of the U.S. budget deficit and the Gramm-Rudman-Hollings bill. Meanwhile, the Western Europeans were beginning to sound serious about a European Defense Initiative (EDI), which was only slightly less objectionable to Moscow than SDI, and Japan was moving to increase its defense programs, even if incrementally. The future of SDI and the other Western military expansion programs, however, remained yet uncertain.

For Gorbachev, the strategies that he was using could have serious future repercussions. If all his rhetoric and all his apparent concessions failed to stop these programs, his potential rivals would have an issue to use against him. In such a case he would badly need to neutralize his foreign policy failures by successes in other policy sectors, primarily the economy. But to prevent his foreign policies from total collapse, he would also need to avoid any major Third World setbacks as well as find an acceptable fallback position in regard to U.S.-Soviet and Western European-Soviet relations.

Gorbachev's attempts to increase Soviet access to Western trade, investments, and technology had some success, but concrete achievements were paltry. Trade agreements with Western governments and firms were generally reported to call for increases over the past but were noticeably short of concrete figures. When some overall figures appeared, they showed a decrease in imports from the West. The collapse of oil prices in the winter of 1986 was a serious setback for Gorbachev over which he had no control. It deprived the USSR of what was both its main source of hard currency and its main export to Western Europe just when hard currency capital was most urgently needed. Moscow had to turn more heavily to international credit markets and/or reduce its purchases from the West. In fact it did both and had some successes, obtaining increasing amounts of credit from banks in the United States and several other Western countries. Increased borrowing is nonetheless potentially a two-edged sword for Moscow. Meanwhile, Soviet efforts to persuade the West to ease its restrictions on transfer of strategic technology had not produced any significant results.

How Gorbachev will handle these problems relating to the industrialized world remains uncertain. The evidence to date supports three potential scenarios. The first, and for him the most desirable, would be to restore the kind of updated detente with the United States that he has so ardently pursued. Right up to the close of the period covered in this book, Gorbachev was still making new proposals and new concessions to influence the Americans. Moreover, his new foreign policy adviser team was heavily weighted with experts whose field of competence was the United States and North America. At the same time, rhetoric notwithstanding, Gorbachev seemed to be by no means anxious for provocations and confrontations in the Third World.

Gorbachev's approach has also featured actions that can be best understood both as preparing the groundwork for a fallback policy in the event of failure to achieve his goals with the United States and as part of a longer-range strategy toward the West. By placing greater emphasis on improving economic relations with Europe and Japan than with the United States, by stepping up the pace and scope of new Soviet offers in European arms control forums, and by frequently meeting with major European political figures (both in and out of power), Gorbachev was probably aiming for more than just increasing pressures on the United States. Because Soviet political theory sees the United States, Western Europe, and Japan as rival centers of world capitalism, the Soviets have a rationale for such a fallback policy, and consequently for paying more attention to U.S. allies than to the United States itself, at least for selected purposes. In this second scenario Gorbachev would give up on Washington and accelerate Soviet efforts to disrupt Western unity so as to obtain a selective detente with present U.S. allies. He would then focus on European arms control, and on trade and technology access by trying to sway the Europeans and Japanese away from COCOM coordination with the United States.

In midspring 1986 there were some indications that Gorbachev was contemplating just such a policy. Since his accession there had been occasional articles in the Soviet press dedicated to the theme that Europe was an entity and that the Western Europeans were working against their own real interests by deferring to Washington. Simultaneously, through most of Gorbachev's first year, ever since the Geneva summit had been announced, Reagan as a person was treated with respect in the Soviet media. All the evils of U.S. policies were attributed to unrepentant militarists and capitalists centered in the Pentagon and the "military-industrial complex."

In spring 1986 the attitude toward Reagan as a person and his administration began to change slightly, giving way to a tone of disillusionment and even indignation, and the references to "real interests" of Western Europeans increased in frequency. Throughout the summer this pattern continued. There was an increased focus on Western Europe, and then, at the end of July, on Japan and the Pacific. By and large the U.S. president was still treated with some respect, and problems with Washington were blamed on his associates and the defense, industrial, and other capitalist monopolists. Still, the occasional more pointed criticisms of Reagan himself, mostly in the military organ *Krasnaya Zvezda,* that had appeared in the spring were repeated from time to time. Similarly, the lure of the promised second summit in the United States was continuously dangled before, but never allowed to be seized by, the Americans.

Gorbachev again extended the Soviet nuclear test moratorium, in early August, and then at the end of the month appeared to spit directly in the eye of the United States by apparently authorizing the crude tit-for-tat seizure of U.S. journalist Nicholas Daniloff on trumped-up spy charges. At the same time Soviet public coverage of arms control discussions with the Americans took on an increasingly negative or noncommittal tone (discussed further in the next chapter).

The negative tone seemed to harden for most of September. Moreover, the tactic of special consultations and appeals to the Western Europeans was stepped up. At this point many Western commentators were suggesting that the Kremlin had abandoned hope of reaching a satisfactory *modus vivendi* with the Reagan administration. Moscow appeared to be either turning toward the fallback strategy suggested earlier or, at best, settling down to await the outcomes of the November 1986 U.S. congressional or, more likely, the 1988 presidential elections.

Then, after Shevardnadze had held four meetings with Secretary of State George Shultz and one with Reagan, the summit—which was not to be a true summit but rather a "preparatory, working meeting"—in Reykjavik was announced. At the same time Daniloff, who earlier had been released from jail to the custody of the U.S. Embassy in Moscow, was allowed to go home in an evident exchange for the Soviet spy Gennadi Zakharov, whom the United States had in custody. At that point it appeared that Gorbachev was ready to come to terms with Washington, and evidently the U.S. administration felt that this was so.

As it turned out, the Reykjavik summit proved a failure and U.S.-Soviet relations hit their lowest point since Gorbachev came to power. Two critical questions need be answered. The first is whether Gorbachev and company saw Reykjavik as a real opportunity or a trap for Reagan. The second is whether the meeting in Iceland marked a turning point in U.S.-Soviet relations and a shift from Gorbachev's preferred strategy of detente with the United States to his fallback of a separate detente with U.S. allies. We will look at Reykjavik in greater detail in our examination of arms control, but we can provide a firm answer to the second question on the basis of post-Reykjavik developments.

Following the Iceland summit, Gorbachev and the Soviet press heavily castigated the US, but in an adroit manner that was more sorrowful than aggressive. By the beginning of 1987 Gorbachev was ready to begin a new phase in his pursuit of an advantageous detente with the US. As noted earlier, a series of highly visible steps in regard to dissidents and human rights, the increase in Jewish emigration and, in fact, all the trappings of glasnost and ostensible liberalization were at least partially designed to influence Western opinion and facilitate Soviet foreign policy goals. The new law on Joint Ventures with foreign firms was announced and the publicity accompanying the program emphasized that, for Western firms to take maximum advantage of this opportunity, progress in nuclear arms control and a relaxation of COCOM barriers to trade and technology transfer would have to take place.

In January Gorbachev hosted a much publicized, gala "Conference for a Nuclear-Free World and the Survival of Mankind" in Moscow. Western public figures, businessmen (lots of them) and media and arts celebrities attended, were feted and exhorted as the Soviets stepped up the effort to enlist opinion molders to pressure Washington and other Western governments.

Meanwhile, Moscow had signalled its renewed determination to negotiate arms control with the US by appointing a first deputy foreign minister, Voronstov, as the new head of its strategic arms negotiating team and by continuing a wide range of arms negotiations and experts talks with Washington. Clearly, any cooling from Reykjavik was now to be put behind by Gorbachev's minions.

Subsequently, although the Soviets did resume nuclear testing, the Kremlin announced two more partial compromises in regard to the INF negotiations, but then stood essentially firm (as far as the public record shows) in arms control through the rest of the summer (see Chapter 8).

Meanwhile, economic inducements to the West, glasnost and the general impression of a definite, if ultimately uncertain, liberalization inside the USSR both served to encourage pressures on the US administration and to demonstrate that detente was still the current Soviet objective.

Clearly, then, Reykjavik did not mark a turning point in US-Soviet relations in the sense that it signalled Gorbachev's shift away from his preferred strategy of detente with America. In a very definite sense, Gorbachev's subsequent additional compromises notwithstanding, it is fair to say that the summit at Reykjavik marked a turning point of a different nature. Prior to Reykjavik, Gorbachev was basically the supplicant, continuously offering new compromises to bring Reagan and the US to agreement. The period up to Iceland justified the US administration's strategy of holding firm and building-up militarily in order to wring concessions from Moscow. Widespread public disappointment over Reykjavik, coupled with other, unrelated developments, gave Moscow the opportunity to change this equation. After the summit, Gorbachev needed only to decorate the frosting on his arms control cake a bit and let public pressure, budgetary difficulties, and the need to politically overcome the setbacks connected with Iran, the contras, etc., turn the US into the apparent suplicant again. By the onset of autumn, 1987 a major arms control treaty in intermediate and possibly short range nuclear missiles and a new Gorbachev-Reagan summit appeared to be very much in the offing. Moreover, by that time it was the US which appeared to be backing off on some of its earlier demands, such as in verification provisions (see the next two chapters on arms control).

Finally, it must be noted that a third strategy may exist for Gorbachev in his relations with the West. The third scenario, the second fallback policy line, could only be a head-on East-West confrontation. This has to be assessed as a disastrous course for Gorbachev, both in terms of Soviet international and domestic priorities and interests and in terms of preservation of his personal power. Gorbachev probably realizes this. Nevertheless, like any good strategist, he has apparently taken this worst-case scenario into account. Three circumstances provide the evidence for his thinking in such terms (and all three have the quality of serving Gorbachev's preferred policy goals and simultaneously preparing a salvage operation in the event that his primary hopes are frustrated. The first is his policy of strengthening the organs of internal security, particularly the KGB. The second is his policy of pressuring the Eastern European states to integrate more closely with the USSR and to reduce their economic dependence on the West. And the third, which is more circumstantial, is the way his "generous" and "well-intentioned" concession proposals—which are said to go to the point of taking calculated risks with Soviet security— are always accompanied by an "or-else" caveat. Extending a one-side nuclear test moratorium is a good illustration of this. The implications are clear: if all this goodwill and self-renunciation is nevertheless rejected by the "powers of reaction," the USSR will in the end have no choice but to take all the necessary measures to protect its own interests, of course reluctantly.

If Gorbachev cannot succeed in his main objective of reaching a workable detente with the United States, he may well jeopardize his chances of staying in power, unless he can somehow still achieve major successes in his economic revitalization program while steering clear of other major policy setbacks. Despite Soviet ideological preconceptions about the depth of the "objective" contradictions between the different centers of capitalism, a selective detente with Western Europe and/or Japan does not seem to be a promising means for Gorbachev to employ. First, as a help in curing the Soviet economy, a selective detente is not likely to suffice. Secondly, a selective detente is bound to increase rather than decrease the danger of confrontations with the United States in the Third World. The last-ditch fallback option, Socialist bloc autarky and a renewed cold war against the entire West, would entail for Gorbachev the need to emulate Stalin in his domestic policy in order to stay in power. It is not at all clear that the USSR and the CPSU of the 1980s would consent to that.

Thus far Gorbachev has shown considerable flair, tactical skill, and coherence of purpose in his policy toward the West, yet he faces daunting challenges. Some of the tactics he has used carry with them the risk of jeopardizing other foreign policy goals in other parts of the world or of undermining his domestic support and control. To assess how well Gorbachev will meet these challenges, we need to look at the rest of the interrelated and interdependent mosaic of domestic, foreign, and military considerations. But first we need to take a closer look at a central component of Gorbachev's policy toward the West: arms control.

Selected East-West Chronology

March 1985

11	Mikhail Gorbachev was elected general secretary, CPSU.
12	The first round of U.S.-Soviet strategic weapons negotiations opened on schedule in Geneva.

Note: Most chronological entries relating to arms control, including all remaining dates of regular negotiating rounds, will be found in the chronology to chapter 7; only selected highlights are repeated here.

13–14	Gorbachev held personal meetings with heads of state, or their representatives, who had come to the Chernenko funeral: President Mitterand, France; President Pertini, Italy; Prime Minister Thatcher, United Kingdom; Chancellor Kohl, FRG; President Koivisto, Finland; President Kirschlaeger, Austria; Prime Minister Gonzales, Spain; Prime Minister Mulrooney, Canada; Prime Minister Nakasone, Japan; and Vice President Bush, United States. Other Western state representatives from Turkey, Norway, Malta, Belgium had private meetings with either Tikhonov or Gromyko. Gorbachev also singled out heads of two Western Communist parties (from Italy and Japan) for personal meetings.
22	The first announcement of a change in ambassador to a Western government, the Netherlands. Through June 1987 thirteen new Soviet ambassadors to Western states would be announced. In addition, both UN ambassadors (in New York and in Geneva) would be changed, the former twice.

April 1985

30 March–7 April	Foreign Minister Clark of Canada visited the USSR, met with Gromyko and Vorotnikov.
4	Deputy Chairman Ryabov, Council of Ministers, met with President Mitterand in Paris. Ryabov was in France with a delegation to the XIX Meeting of the Soviet-French Commission for Scientific-Technical and Economic Cooperation. A protocol for scientific and cultural cooperation for 1985–86 was signed.

9–10	The Dutch foreign minister made an official visit and met with Foreign Minister Gromyko.
10	Gorbachev met with a U.S. House of Representatives delegation headed by Speaker of the House Thomas P. O'Neill.
18	The first reported Gorbachev meeting with a major Western businessman (director of the Deutsches Bank). Through June 1987 only a few selected business and banking leaders would be "honored" with individual personal meetings with the new general secretary during visits primarily involving discussions with government ministers and offices.

May 1985

5	Gorbachev met with the Chairman Schmidt of the Socialist Unity Party of West Berlin, in Moscow.
14–17	Politburo member and Minister of Foreign Affairs Gromyko was in Vienna for ceremonies commemorating the thirtieth anniversary of the Austrian peace treaty; met with several Western foreign ministers including U.S. Secretary of State Shultz.
20	Gorbachev met with U.S. Secretary of Commerce Baldridge, who was in Moscow as head of U.S. delegation to the first meeting of the U.S.-Soviet Joint Trade Commission since 1978.
20	Gorbachev met with a senior representative of the Italian Communist Party, Chervetti.
27	Gorbachev met with former West German Chancellor Brandt, in Moscow.
27 May–2 June	Politburo member Vorotnikov led a delegaton to Canada for an official visit; met with Prime Minister Mulrooney.
29	Gorbachev met with Italian Prime Minister Craxi and Foreign Minister Andreotti, who were in Moscow for a three-day official visit.
30	US Department of State and Soviet Foreign Ministry officials met in Paris to discuss Southern Africa. This was a continuation of regional affairs consultations begun earlier and such meetings would continue regularly thereafter.

June 1985

14	In Brussels, the Polish ambassador presented a CEMA proposal to the EC for formal regular contacts and consultations.
16	Austrian Foreign Minister Hieden visited and met with Gromyko.
17	President Koivisto of Finland met with Tikhonov and Aliev in Soviet Karelia.
17	The East-West conference on human rights (a follow-on to

CSCE) ended after six weeks of meeting in Ottawa with no agreement reached on a final report.

•The Soviets canceled the scheduled meeting in Washington to discuss measures to prevent dangerous incidents at sea. The cancellation was in protest over U.S. "changes" in the agenda because of the "unsatisfactory" Soviet reply over the earlier fatal shooting of a U.S. military liaison officer in East Germany.

July 1985

2	Eduard Shevardnadze was announced as new minister of foreign affairs.
3	Formal announcement was made of the scheduled November summit in Geneva with U.S. President Reagan, preceded by an early October summit with French President Mitterand in Paris.
5	Gorbachev met with former Canadian Prime Minister Trudeau, who had arrived in June.
25–26	British Government Minister for Foreign Affairs Rifkind visited and met with officials of the foreign and foreign trade ministries.
27	Gorbachev met with Portuguese Communist Party leader Cuñhal.
	Gorbachev made the opening speech to an international youth festival in Moscow, again demonstrating his adroit utilization of nontraditional forums to argue Soviet policy positions.
29	Gorbachev announced a Soviet unilateral moratorium on nuclear testing until end of year.
29 July–1 August	Politburo member and Foreign Minister Shevardnadze was in Helsinki for the CSCE anniversary meeting. He met with several counterparts, including U.S. Secretary of State Shultz and French Foreign Minister Dumas for general foreign policy discussions and preparations for fall summit meetings.

August 1985

17	The Soviet press published Foreign Minister Shevardnadze's letter to the UN secretary general proposing an international conference to develop a treaty banning militarization of space and to create a formal worldwide organization of cooperation in peaceful development of outer space.
28	Gorbachev gave a lengthy interview to *Time* magazine, which was published in September.

September 1985

2	Gorbachev met with French Communist Party leader Marchais, in Moscow.

3	Gorbachev met with group of U.S. senators, including Senate Minority Leader Byrd, who were in Moscow for a five-day official visit that began in August.
10	Gorbachev met with West German Socialist Democratic Party leader Rau, who was in Moscow for a four-day visit.
16	Gorbachev and Ponomarev met with a delegation from the Socialist Party of Japan.
18–27	Politburo member and Foreign Minister Shevardnadze was in New York for the UN General Assembly opening; he made major foreign policy speeches and met with many counterparts from allied, Western and Third World states.
19	Gorbachev met with President Koivisto of Finland, who was on a ten-day official visit to the USSR.
27	Foreign Minister Shevardnadze met with U.S. President Reagan in Washington.
30	Gorbachev appeared in a major interview on French television.

•There were large-scale expulsions of Soviet diplomats and business representative from the United Kingdom counterexpulsions from the U.S.S.R.

October 1985

2–5	Gorbachev, accompanied by Shevardnadze and economic officials, was in Paris for daily meetings with French President Mitterand and other officials. Gorbachev made a major arms control speech including an offer of separate negotiations with France and the United Kingdom.
24–26	Foreign Minister Shevardnadze was again in New York for the UN anniversary celebrations. He met with U.S. President Reagan, Secretary of State Shultz, and FRG Chancellor Kohl.
26	The new Draft Program of the CPSU was published; it called for peaceful coexistence and mutually beneficial relations with the West, denounced nuclear weapons, and called for comprehensive arms control.

November 1985

5	Gorbachev met with U.S. Secretary of State Schultz, who was in Moscow for a two-day official visit to prepare for the Geneva summit.
18–20	Gorbachev and Foreign Minister Shevardnadze, with a delegation, were in Geneva for the summit with U.S. President Reagan. Extensive one-on-one (other than translators) discussion resulted in a "positive" communique.
27	Gorbachev made a "major" foreign policy speech at the Supreme Soviet, reiterating standard themes and reporting optimistically on the summit with U.S. President Reagan.

•It was also reported that U.S. and Canadian banks had agreed to provide $400 million in new low-interest credits for grain purchases, bringing North American commercial credits to the USSR for 1985 to at least $600 million. A Western report in spring 1986 estimated total 1985 East Bloc commercial borrowing at $5.2 billion, mostly from the FRG and Japan.

December 1985

10	Gorbachev met with U.S. Secretary of Commerce Baldridge, who was in Moscow for the IX Meeting of the U.S.-Soviet Trade and Economic Council Forum 9–12 December. Representatives of over 250 U.S. firms reportedly participated.
12	Gorbachev met with Chairman Mermaz, of the National Assembly of France, who headed a parliamentary delegation for an official visit.

In addition, during 1985
(after Gorbachev's selection as General Secretary)

•Other major (recurring) economic forums were held with Australia, Austria, Canada, Finland (2), France, Greece, Italy, Ireland, Norway and Sweden.

•Other state ministers (or their equivalents) from Australia (2), Austria (4), Canada (4), Finland (2), the FRG, France, Italy (2), Iceland, Norway, Spain, Turkey and the US (3) visited the USSR, while those from the Soviet Union visited Finland, France and Japan.

•Senior foreign ministry (below minister level) delegations from the FRG, Italy, Japan and the US travelled to the USSR for consultations and similar Soviet foreign ministry representatives were reported visiting Denmark, France (2), Iceland, Italy (2), Japan (2), Norway, Sweden and the US.

•Western parliamentary/congressional delegations from Austria, Canada, the FRG (2), France, Italy, Japan (3), Luxemburg, Turkey, the UK, the US (4) and the European Parliament visited the USSR, while Supreme Soviet delegations travelled to Australia, Canada, Cyprus, Finland (2), the FRG (2), France (2), Japan, Portugal and Spain.

•Other senior defense or military officials from Finland (3) and Turkey (the Chief of Staff) visited the USSR and Soviet counterparts travelled to Finland.

•The Soviet press also reported naval port calls in the USSR by Greece and by Soviet combatants to Iceland.

•Senior Communist Party delegations from five Western states, as well as a West German Greens Party and a UK Labor Party delegation visited the USSR, while CPSU delegations were reported visiting nine Western states.

•The Soviet press highlighted visits by businessmen from eight Western states (Austria, the FRG (ten reports), Finland (two reports), France, Italy (three reports), Japan (three reports), the UK and the US (three reports)).

The following diplomatic or major commercial agreements were reported:

With Denmark: a protocol of agricultural cooperation;

With the FRG: a 1986–1990 tourism agreement;

With France: a television cooperation agreement, and

a 1985–1986 scientific and cultural cooperation protocol;
With Greece: an agreement to build an alumina factory there;
With the Netherlands: a television cooperation agreement;
With Spain: an agreement for economic-technical cooperation;
With Sweden: a television cooperation agreement;
With the UK: a 1985–1987 scientific, educational and cultural exchange agreement; and
With the US: an agricultural cooperation agreement.

January 1986

1
Gorbachev and U.S. President Reagan exchanged New Year's greetings to each other's nations on television. The texts were published in the Soviet press on 2 January.

15–19
Politburo member and Foreign Minister Shevardnadze made official visit to Japan; met with Prime Minister Nakasone and other officials

16
Gorbachev made his major speech proposing a plan to eliminate nuclear weapons by the year 2000.

27–28
Gorbachev met with Italian Communist Party leader Natta during both days of an official visit.

February 1986

5
Chairman Ryzhkov, Council of Ministers, addressed a Western European business conference in Davos, Switzerland, by direct two-way satellite linkup.

6
Gorbachev met with U.S. Senator Kennedy, who was in Moscow with a Senate group.

25
The XXVII Congress of the CPSU opened with delegations from 153 parties and movements from 113 states (including 21 delegations from Western socialist or social-democratic parties) in attendance. The foreign policy speeches by Gorbachev and Shevardnadze during the congress stressed the themes developed during the previous year.

March 1986

14–16
Politburo member and Chairman of the Council of Ministers Ryzhkov represented the USSR at the Palme funeral in Stockholm. While there he met with a number of Western and Third World leaders and representatives.

24
Gorbachev met with the outgoing French ambassador, who was the French foreign minister-designate.

24–25
U.S. strikes in Libya were made in response to armed reaction to U.S. presence in the waters of the Sidra Gulf claimed by Libya. The Soviet reaction was heavy on condemnation, included a Gorbachev "offer" for removal of

both superpower fleets from the Mediterranean, but was noticeably lacking in concrete actions.

25   Gorbachev met with the chairman of the Italian Chamber of Deputies, who led a parliamentary delegation visiting the USSR. The occasion was used to attack U.S. actions against Libya.

30   Gorbachev addressed the nation and the world on television, stating the need for the USSR to protect its own security if the United States would not join the nuclear test moratorium.

April 1986

2   Gorbachev met with Austrian Chancellor Sinovatz, who was in Moscow for an Austrian industrial exposition.

4   Gorbachev met with the chairman of the U.S. House Foreign Affairs Committee, Rep. Fascell, and another congressman who had been in the USSR since late March.

8-15   Politburo member and CC Secretary Zaykov led the Soviet delegation to the Italian Communist Party Congress; while there, he met with Italian Prime Minister Craxi.

14-15   U.S. strikes were made against Libya in response to Tripoli's involvement in international terrorism. The Soviet condemnation was shrill and protracted, and included cancellation of the planned Shultz-Shevardnadze meeting in May to discuss the next summit.

15   Gorbachev met with Swedish Prime Minister Carlson, who brought a foreign policy and economic delegation to Moscow for a four-day official visit.

May 1986

1-8   Candidate Politburo member Yeltsin led the delegation to the West German CP congress. While there he met with both government and SPD officials.

7   French President Mitterand, en route home from Tokyo, stopped over and met with Chairman Ryzhkov, Council of Ministers, in Novosibirsk.

15   Gorbachev used a speech on the Chernobyl accident to promote for his arms control policies.

19   Gorbachev met with Portuguese Communist Party leader Cuñhal, who was in Moscow for a short official visit.

20   Gorbachev met with Spanish Prime Minister Gonzales, who led an economic and foreign policy delegation for a four-day official visit to the USSR.

23-24   A major foreign policy review meting was held, including virtually the entire government and Party foreign policy establishment plus ambassadors recalled from abroad. Notably, Gromyko was not listed as in attendance, possibly confirming his separation from active foreign policy decision making. Gorbachev made a major speech reported in the press as analyzing conditions, criticizing past shortcomings, and setting future directions for improvement.

26	Gorbachev met with visiting U.K. palrliamentarians. Talks reportedly centered on arms control.
30	Gorbachev met with Japanese Foreign Minister Shintaro Abe, who was in Moscow for the first visit by a Japanese foreign minister in a long time. At the meeting Gorbachev said that he was "still open" to a summit in 1986 with U.S. President Reagan, but that it must take place in a constructive atmosphere with good prospects for productive results. The Japanese foreign minister also held two days of extensive consultations with Shevardnadze and signed a cultural agreement.

•After six weeks the CSCE-related human rights conference in Bern ended in a deadlock with no agreed communique because of U.S. insistence on stronger language over Soviet performance.

June 1986

12	The Soviet press published Chairman of the Council of Ministers Ryzhkov's formal letter to the UN secretary general proposing a program for the peaceful exploitation of space. This was essentially a reiteration of the program outlined by Shevardnadze in August 1985.
25	Gorbachev met with West German SPD leader Rau, who was in Moscow for an industrial and trade fair. Rau also met with much of the other senior leadership separately.

July 1986

1–6	First Deputy Chairman Murakhovskiy, Council of Ministers, made an official visit to the United Kingdom and signed an agreement in agriculture.
7–9	French President Mitterand, with a foreign affairs and (mostly) economic delegation, made an official visit. Gorbachev and Mitterand met on each of the three days for extensive discussions.
13–16	Politburo member and Foreign Minister Shevardnadze made an official visit to the United Kingdom. He met with Prime Minister Thatcher and other officials and signed three agreements.
18	Gorbachev met with former US President Nixon who was in Moscow on a private trip during which he also met with Gromyko and Dobrynin separately.
20–22	West German Foreign Minister Genscher visited the USSR

| | and met with Gorbachev on 21 July and with other senior officials on other days. |
| **27 July–1 August** | Prime Minister Ozal of Turkey made an official visit; met with Ryzhkov, Gromyko, and Shevardnadze, and signed several agreements. |

August 1986

11	Gorbachev met with the chairman of the Presidium of the Japanese Communist Party.
19	In another major television speech, Gorbachev again extended the unilateral nuclear test moratorium.
30	Soviet KGB agents arrested U.S. news correspondent N. Daniloff on trumped-up spy charges two days after a Soviet UN employee, Zakharov, had been arrested by the United States in New York City, triggering a diplomatic and major media incident.

•Also during August, the Soviet Foreign Trade Bank joined fifteen Western banks in underwriting a $97 million Eurobond offer.

September 1986

15–19	First Deputy Defense Minister and Chief of the General Staff, Marshal Akhromeev, made an official visit to Turkey, a NATO country.
16–30	Politburo member and Foreign Minister Shevardnadze was at the UNGA where he met with some forty counterparts or heads of state and made major speeches. Enroute to the UN he stopped over in Ireland and met foreign ministry officials.
17	The United States published a list of twenty-five Soviet UN employees who were required to leave the United States by 1 October.
19–20	Foreign Minister Shevardnadze made a trip from New York City to Washington, where he met with President Reagan and Secretary of State Shultz.
22–24	Representatives of CEMA and the EEC met in Geneva to discuss formal cooperation ties.
23	The CSCE Review Conference preparatory conference opened in Vienna.
26–29	IAEC Special Safety Session held in Vienna. On 29 September the regular general session of the IAEC opened. Considerations generated by Chernobyl remained the major focus, along with nuclear nonproliferation. At earlier experts' meetings in July and August the Soviets had begun presenting candid data on Chernobyl.
30	The United States and the USSR announced that President Reagan and General Secretary Gorbachev would meet in

October in Reykjavik in what was billed as a preparatory meeting, not a real "summit." It was also announced that Daniloff and Zakharov, along with Soviet human rights dissident Yurii Orlov, were being released.

October 1986

11–13	Gorbachev, with a very large political and military delegation (and his wife Raisa), traveled to Reykjavik, Iceland for a two-day summit with US President Reagan. Discussions on East-West relations and Soviet human rights behavior were on the agenda, but Gorbachev was able to keep the focus virtually confined to arms control. In successive speeches afterwards (his press conference on the 14th and Soviet TV appearances on the 16th and 24th) Gorbachev preached an increasingly "regretful" appraisal and account of the summit and US obstinacy.
21	Gorbachev met with the Prime Minister of Denmark who was in U.S.S.R. on an official visit.
31	Gorbachev met with a delegation of the World Federation of Trade Unions, using the occasion to emphasize and promote his policies.

November 1986

3	Gorbachev met with the General Secretary of the Communist Party of Greece.

December 1986

1	Chairman, Council of Ministers Ryzhkov met with and addressed V Round Table Conference (representatives of Soviet and Japanese society) on Pacific security and arms control—especially nuclear, and in regard to space.
7	Gorbachev met with the Prime Minister of Norway who was in the USSR on an official visit.
15	Gorbachev met with (then) US Presidential hopeful Gary Hart.
31	Gorbachev met with Portuguese Communist Party leader Cunhal.

In addition, during 1986

•Other major recurring economic forums were held with Australia, the Benelux Economic Union, Denmark, Finland (2), France (2), the FRG (2), Greece, Italy, Japan, the Netherlands and Sweden; and forums of jurists were held with Finland and the US.

•Other state ministers or their equivalents from Canada, Cyrpus, Finland, France, the FRG (2), New Zealand, Turkey, the UK, and the US visited the U.S.S.R. and those of the Soviet Union visited Finland (2), Japan, and Spain while Deputy Ministers of major economic ministries or state committees visited Belgium and Switzerland.

•Senior Foreign Ministry (below Minister level) delegations from France, Ireland, Italy (2), Japan (2), Sweden and the US (2) visited the U.S.S.R. for consultations and similar Soviet ministry representatives were reported visiting Austria, Cyprus, Denmark, Finland (4), France (3), Italy, Spain (2), Turkey, the UK (3), and the US (2). In addition US and Soviet representatives also met in Stockholm for regional foreign affairs discussions.

•Western parliamentary/Congressional delegations from Austria, Australia (2), Belgium, Canada, Cyprus, Denmark, Finland, France, the FRG, Japan (2), the Netherlands, Norway, the UK, and the US visited the U.S.S.R. and Supreme Soviet delegations traveled o Denmark, France, the FRG (2), Greece, Luxemburg, Portugal, Sweden, and Turkey.

•Other senior D. fense or Military officials from Finland (2 including the Chief of the General Sta... visited the U.S.S.R. and Soviet equivalents visited Finland (the Minister of Defense and the CinCs of the Air Force and the Navy).

•Senior Communist Party delegations from ten Western states, as well as from the Belgian Flemish Socialist Party, the FRG Greens, SPD (2), the FDP and the CDU, and the Norwegian Left Socialists visited the U.S.S.R. and CPSU delegations were reported visiting ten Western states.

•The Soviet press individually highlighted visits by businessmen from six Western states: Austria (2), the FRG (3), France, Netherlands, Sweden, and the US (4), plus claimed large numbers not individually identified at two major forums and reported large numbers of Soviet firm managers at trade fairs and conferences in Austria, France, and Japan.

The following diplomatic or major commercial agreements were reported:

With Belgium:	a protocol for annual meetings on ocean transportation;
With the Benelux states:	a 1986 program of cooperation in agriculture;
With Denmark:	a number of unidentified contracts between firms;
With Cyprus:	a cooperation agreement between TASS and the Cypriot counterpart a 1986–1990 trade agreement;
With Finland:	a contract for a Finnish firm to build twelve eye clinics in the USSR, and a number of unidentified other contracts between firms;
With France:	a 1988 joint space flight protocol;
With Italy:	a contract for an Italian firm to build a $5 million food packaging plant in the Kuban;
With Japan:	a cultural exchange agreement;
With Malta:	a 1987–1990 trade protocol;
With the Netherlands:	a shipping construction protocol;
With Spain:	a 1986–1987 sports exchange protocol;
With Turkey:	a cooperation agreement between state planning organs, a tourism cooperation agreement, an agreement whereby Turkey would pay costs of a pipeline extension from Bulgaria;
With the UK:	an agreement for cooperation in agriculture and food production,

an agreement to prevent incidents at sea,
a 1986–1990 program of economic and industrial cooperation,
a financial regulatory agreement (mutual compensation
claims, Tsarist bonds, etc.);

With the US: an agreement of cooperation and exchange between academies of science,
a protocol of cooperation in nuclear energy research,
an agreement on thirteen education and research exchange
programs.

January 1987

6–9 Chairman Ryzhkov, Council of Ministers, with Trade Minister Aristov and First Deputy Foreign Minister Kovalev,
visited Finland and signed several agreements.

15–16 A special foreign ministry representative visited Brussels
for negotiations on formal relations between CEMA and
the EEC.

27 The CSCE review conference, focussing on human rights
and economic, scientific and cultural relations, resumed in
Vienna after a break.

27 The Soviet press published decrees providing rules for Joint
Ventures between Soviet and foreign firms.

February 1987

3 The 43rd session of the UN commission on human rights
opened in Geneva. The byelorussian representative was
elected chairman.

4 A group of senior scholars and former government officials
from the US Council of Foreign Relations, including
Kissinger, Vance, Kirkpatrick, Brown and others, met with
Gorbachev. The group was there for a visit sponsored by the
Academy of Sciences and also met with Gromyko,
Dobrynin, Yakovlev and others either individually or in
groups.

14–16 A gala conference "For a Nuclear-Free World and the Survival of Mankind" was held in Moscow. Attendees included
present and former Western government officials, many
businessmen, media and arts "stars," etc. Although the
conference focus was on selling Soviet arms control positions, extensive business talks were also held.

26–27 Italian Foreign Minister Andreotti made an official visit
and met with Gorbachev on the 27th.

March 1987

1–3 Prime Minister Hermannsson, Iceland, visited and met
separately with both Gorbachev and Ryzhkov on the 2nd.

3–5	Foreign Minister Shevardnadze, on a major tour of SEAsian and Pacific nations, was in Australia where he met with the Prime Minister and the Foreign Minister.
8–15	CC Secretary and candidate Politburo member Yakovlev led a Supreme Soviet foreign affairs delegation to Spain where he met with the Prime Minister, the King and other officials.
16	Representatives of the US, Japan and the USSR met in Vienna and agreed on a program of cooperation in thermonuclear energy research.
21–1 April	British Prime Minister Thatcher made a state visit, holding extensive talks with Gorbachev and Ryzhkov and touring. Several agreements were signed. A notable aspect was the completeness in which the Soviet press printed Mrs. Thatcher's remarks, including statements not flattering of Soviet policies.

•Also in March, US-Soviet arms control prospects took a dramatic turn when the strategic weapons talks in Geneva were extended two days for new INF proposals and a special INF session was convened from the 10th to the 26th (see arms control).

April 1987

13–15	US Secretary of State Shultz, with a large entourage, made an official visit. He held extensive meetings with Gorbachev, Ryzhkov, Shevardnadze and others and signed a space agreement.

May 1987

3–4	Policies and goals were addressed at a widened meeting of foreign ministry officials and ambassadors. This year Shevardnadze, not Gorbachev as in 1986, was the principal speaker, indicating continuation of policies rather than new directions or a shakeup of methods.
4	Gorbachev met with French Communist party leader Marchais who had been on an extended visit since late April.
5	The first US-Soviet arms control related treaty agreement since Reagan and Gorbachev came to power was announced: to create and operate nuclear crisis centers (see arms control).
14–16	French Prime Minister Chirac, with a political and economic delegation, made a state visit, holding extensive talks with Gorbachev, Ryzhkov and others. As after the Thatcher visit, the Soviet press printed Chirac's uncomfortable remarks in full.
20	A major Gorbachev interview was published in the Italian

Communist newspaper "L'Unita." As in other such interviews, Gorbachev defended and promoted his policies.

June 1987

23   Gorbachev used a welcoming speech to an international
        women's Congress to promote his policies.
29   Gorbachev met with UN General Secretary Perez de-
        Cuellar, discussing arms control and regional conflicts.

In addition, during the first six months of 1987

•Other major recurring economic forums were held with Canada, Finland, France
(2), the FRG, Greece, Italy and Spain while a health conference was held with the
UK.
•Other state ministers or their equivalents from Canada, Finland (3 in two visits),
Greece, Italy, Japan, Luxemburg, Spain, Sweden, Turkey and the UK (2) visited the
USSR and those of the Soviet Union travelled to Austria, Finland, France, the FRG,
and the US (2).
•Senior Foreign Ministry (below Minister level) delegations from Finland, Italy,
Portugal, Spain, Sweden and the US visited the USSR for consultations and similar
Soviet representatives travelled to Canada, Cyprus (2), France (2), the FRG (2),
Iceland, Italy, Sweden and the UK (4).
•Western parliamentary/congressional delegations from Belgium, the European
Parliament (2), France, Japan, Portugal, Spain, Sweden and the US (2) visited the
USSR and other Supreme Soviet delegations travelled to Cyprus (enroute to Syria),
Denmark, Finland, Iceland, Norway, Sweden, Switzerland and the UK.
•Other senior Defense or Military officials from Finland (Defense Forces' CinC),
Greece (Commander of the Navy on a port call), Norway (Defense Minister) and
Turkey visited the USSR. The Commander of the Soviet Black Sea Fleet accom-
panied a naval port call in Turkey.
•Senior Communist Party delegations from seven Western states, as well as from the
French Left Radical Party, the West German SPD and Socialist Unity Party of
Berlin, the New Zealand Labor Party, the Spanish Socialist Worker's Party, the Swiss
Labor Party and the British Labor Party, visited the USSR, while CPSU delegations
were reported visiting twelve Western states.
•The Soviet press individually highlighted visits by businessmen from eight Western
states: Canada, France, the FRG (10), Italy (2 "groups"), Japan (6), Sweden (4), the
UK and the US (7 visits by 6) as well as larger forums with Italy. About half of these
individually reported visits may have been simply in conjunction with the gala anti-
nuclear festival in February since the reported meetings were either just before or
shortly afterwards. The Soviet press did not make it clear whether these reported
meetings were separate visits or not.
The following diplomatic or major commercial agreements were reported:
With Canada: a memorandum of future cooperation in agriculture, and a
                      $110 million contract for Lavalin, Inc. to develop a gas field
                      near the Caspian Sea;
With Finland: a trade sales protocol,
                      agreement to establish a tourism Joint Venture,

	an agreement on nuclear accident information sharing, and several unidentified enterprise agreements;
With France:	an environmental protection agreement, a Joint Venture banking and financial consultation agreement, a 1987–1990 protocol for financing sales of French machinery and equipment in the USSR, contracts for the engineering firm Technip to provide two production lines for a Rhone Pulenc fibers plant opening in Pinsk in 1990 and for participation in construction of a battery plant in Soviet Asia, and several sales and plant construction contracts with the agricultural corporation Interagra;
With the FRG:	an agrarian research and cooperation agreement, and a radio and TV cooperation agreement;
With Greece:	a protocol of cooperation in merchant shipping, and a contract for Soviet construction of an alumina plant in Greece (with the plant's initial output to be purchased by the Soviets);
With Italy:	a Joint Venture agreement with FATA to open a refrigerator and freezer factory in Volzhsk in 1989, and a Joint Venture with Ottogalli for food products;
With Japan:	an agreement for Japanese construction of a joint saw-timber enterprise in Irkutsk (with 75% of output to go to Japan), an agreement for fisheries cooperation and utilization of coastal resources, and "other" agreements for joint ventures in fishing, agriculture and forestry;
With the Netherlands:	a protocol for a Dutch firm to produce Soviet combines, a sales license for Soviet concrete-asphalt laying machines in Holland, and a supplementary airlines protocol;
With Spain:	a protocol of cooperation between ministries of culture, and a protocol of cooperation between TASS and the Spanish Information Agency;
With Sweden:	a 1,250,000 Kroner sales contract for Soviet petroleum;
With the UK:	an agreement for cooperation in peaceful space research, a cooperation agreement between the Prime Minister's office and the Kremlin, a memorandum of mutual assistance in culture, education and information, a 1987–1989 scientific, education and cultural cooperation agreement, contracts for English firms to construct a 250 million machine tool plant in Yereva and for 53 million for three firms to refurbish five Soviet textile plants along with a robotic paint spray project (by a fourth firm), and a supplementary airlines protocol;

With the US:	a sports cooperation agreement,
	a 1987–1991 historical archives research agreement,
	five grain purchasing sales totalling 3 million metric tons, and
	an agreement for cooperation in peaceful exploration of space;
With the US and Japan:	a program of cooperation in thermonuclear energy research.

(Almost without exception, this (and other) agreements listings represent those reported in the main Soviet press and consequently is not necessarily complete. Further, Western reporting indicates that many or most of the Joint Venture agreements reported in the Soviet press were not fully finalized as the Soviet reports would suggest)

7

Scorpions in a Bottle:
Arms Control Policy (Part One)

> *It is precisely this action-reaction phenomenon that fuels an arms race.*
>
> —U.S. Secretary of Defense Robert McNamara

> *As our defense budgets have risen, the Soviets have increased their defense budget. As our defense budgets have gone down, their defense budgets have increased again. As U.S. forces in Western Europe declined during the later part of the 1960s, Soviet deployments in Eastern Europe expanded. As U.S. theater nuclear forces stabilized, Soviet peripheral attack and theater nuclear forces increased. As the U.S. Navy went down in numbers, the Soviet Navy went up.*
>
> —U.S. Secretary of Defense Harold Brown
> (15 years later)

> *Nations don't distrust each other because they are armed; they are armed because they distrust each other.*
>
> —Salvador de Madariaga

The Negotiations

Gorbachev in power dramatically stepped up the U.S.S.R.'s arms control efforts. When he became general secretary, the United States and the U.S.S.R. were already scheduled to begin the first round of a new strategic arms negotiation, one that would combine three interlocking component negotiations: strategic offensive arms, intermediate theater nuclear weapons, and space defense arms. In addition, the two nations faced each other in three multilateral arms negotiations:

1. MBFR (Mutual and Balanced Force Reductions) in Vienna. A NATO-Warsaw Pact negotiation addressing troop reductions in Central Europe.
2. CSCBMDE (Conference on Security and Confidence Building Measures and Disarmament in Europe) in Stockholm. An outgrowth of the Helsinki process, involving all European states plus Canada and the United States; in the current phase, addressing confidence-building measures (troop movement and exercise notification, limits, and so on).
3. CD (Committee on Disarmament) in Geneva. A forty-nation forum under UN auspices addressing a grab bag of disarmament-related issues, including space, nuclear testing, chemical weapons, and the like.

Previously, there had been separate *bilateral* negotiations, which included:

- ASAT (antisatellite weapons). Discontinued by the United States but urged for resumption by Moscow.
- CW (chemical weapons). Discontinued by the United States; now in the CD but urged for resumption by Moscow.
- IO (Indian Ocean force limitations). Discontinued by the United States, apparently dead.
- INF (intermediate-range nuclear forces). Discontinued by the Soviets and now merged into the Geneva strategic talks.
- START (strategic arms reductions talks, the U.S. acronym). The outgrowth of SALT, discontinued by Moscow and now merged into the Geneva group of negotiations.
- CTB (comprehensive test ban). A trilateral negotiation, including the United Kingdom, on banning all nuclear weapons testing; discontinued by the United States, but urged for resumption by Moscow.

There had been also occasional, more peripheral negotiations on such things as measures to reduce the possibility of accidental nuclear war, and so on. And for many years the USSR had regularly sponsored proposals for various nuclear-free zones, no-first-use agreements on nuclear weapons, and negative security assurances (formal promises not to use nuclear weapons against a non-nuclear state as long as that state does not allow nuclear weapons to be stationed on its territory). The breaking off of each of the previous bilateral talks and the trilateral CTB negotiations had been given various justifications but were basically the result of the deep freeze in U.S.-Soviet relations. On Washington's part the justifications included Soviet international behavior (Afghanistan, Poland, "yellow rain," and so on), lack of progress on verification, or simply the belief that there was no foreseeable outcome to the talks that would serve Western security needs. Moscow had walked out of INF and START in protest over NATO's decision to go ahead with deployment of U.S. INF weapons—Pershing 2s (P2s) and the ground-launched cruise missiles (GLCMs)—in Europe. In fact, the only bilateral arms-related talks to have continued were the talks twice a year of the Standing Consultative Commission (SCC), which was really only a forum for addressing issues arising out of the SALT I/ABM Treaty rather than an arms control negotiation per se.

Gorbachev wasted no time in launching a propaganda campaign for arms control. He announced yet another moratorium on Soviet intermediate nuclear weapons (the SS-20) deployments. This was little more than a repeat version of similar moratoriums declared by his predecessors in their attempts to block the deployment of U.S. Pershing 2s and ground-launched cruise missiles. As was the case with the earlier moratoriums, there was a discrepancy between what Moscow had apparently promised and subsequent U.S. revelations documented by satellite photographs of increases in the number of operational SS-20s in the Soviet inventory, increases that could be explained only partially by the completion of previously started construction of SS-20 bases. Some of the increases evidently were due to new deployments, a clear violation of the moratorium. Gorbachev's spokesmen also continued to reiterate the formula that the existing theater nuclear balance was one of basic equality. The assertion had originally been made when there were no U.S. P2s and GLCMs and only 70 to 100 Soviet SS-20s in Europe, also when there were no P2s or GLCMs and some 243 SS-20s, and again when the initial P2s and GLCMs arrived and the SS-20s count had further risen. The only conceivable way that such a sequence of assertions could be logical would be with the assumption that the SS-20s, P2s and GLCMs were all irrelevant to the military balance.

At the first round of the newly resumed bilateral negotiations in Geneva, the Soviets apparently spoke only in generalities about possible deep cuts in strategic weapons. They concentrated their attention on the need for prior agreement on a treaty banning the U.S. SDI. This basic thrust of their strategic arms position was to continue throughout Gorbachev's first year, although it was subsequently supplemented by progressive "pot sweeteners" and carefully worded ambiguities concerning the kinds of strategic defense research that might be allowed. The guidelines for the Soviet delegation for the first round of the new Geneva talks had been formulated prior to Gorbachev's accession to the position of general secretary, but as "second secretary" and heir apparent, he presumably had a role in formulating them. In any event, once he was formally in charge, he set the subsequent pattern of these negotiations. As noted earlier, the pattern of

Gorbachev's arms control policies and proposals during the entire year was to make increasingly dramatic proposals and apparent concessions, all of them directly or indirectly aimed at stopping the U.S. SDI and derailing the Reagan nuclear modernization program. Several proposals also were specifically targeted at Europe with the objective of curtailing French and U.K. modernization programs, with the secondary goals of encouraging European pressure on Washington and providing a basis for Gorbachev's fallback policy of selective detente with U.S. allies in the event that Washington resisted a return to full-scale detente.

The Strategic and Theater Nuclear Issues and Approaches

To corroborate our analysis of Soviet aims, to assess the sincerity of Gorbachev's avowed policy regarding nuclear war and weapons in general, and to predict likely Soviet policy on arms control and military force issues, we must examine the basic points of contention and Soviet proposals and public statements in a number of the arms control arenas. In regard to the actual content of proposals, as opposed to public declarations, our analysis must rely on very partial information reported in U.S. and Soviet statements that themselves may have been subject to some purposeful slanting. The negotiations are conducted on the basis of confidentiality, but a careful reading and comparison of both U.S. and Soviet public statements, and especially U.S. leaks in Washington, usually allow the knowledgeable observer to identify much of the content of proposals and counterproposals by both sides—although their exact timing and sequence is not always as clear.

The strategic arms talks in Geneva are structured to bring under one umbrella three separate but interrelated negotiations: strategic offensive weapons, strategic defensive and space weapons, and intermediate (theater) nuclear weapons. The negotiations are generally perceived as the primary arms control forum. Any potential treaties to which they might lead would be widely accepted as the centerpiece of U.S.-Soviet detente. Therefore, we will discuss each aspect of the Geneva talks first and in somewhat greater detail than other negotiations.

Exhibit 7.1
The More Important Differences in Soviet and U.S. Positions at the Strategic Offensive Weapons Negotiations at the Start of Gorbachev's Rule
1. **Initial focus and phase-one reductions**
   U.S.:   Focus on ground-based intercontinental missiles (ICBMs) as the "most destabilizing" component of strategic offensive capabilities.

Soviet: Inclusion of all types of strategic offensive weapons and balanced reductions from the beginning.

2. **Definition of strategic offensive weapons**

U.S.: Those that have intercontinental delivery ranges.

Soviet: Any nuclear weapons system, wherever stationed, that can deliver a strike on the other side's homeland. If fully applied, this definition would equate U.S. long-range nuclear-capable tactical aircraft (including those based on carriers) and U.S. intermediate-range missiles stationed in Europe with Soviet intercontinental missiles and bombers. These are the forces referred to as forward-based systems (FBS).

3. **Unit of Measure for Reductions and Limitations**

U.S.: Warheads (and only later, bomb loads) plus aggregate throwweight.

Soviet: Launchers and bombers (as in SALT I and II).

4. **Extent and Emphasis of Reductions**

U.S.: Very deep reductions primarily focused on ICBMs.

Soviet: Significant but less drastic cuts, across the board in all weapons.

5. **Verification Measures**

U.S.: National technical means (NTM), generally understood as satellite reconnaisance platforms, supplemented by other means, including on-site inspection (OSI) *on demand* and *without delay*. A demand justified by Washington on the basis of claims of recurrent Soviet violations of both the spirit and letter of earlier treaties.

Soviet: NTM is basically adequate. Precedent for OSI in exceptional cases had been admitted by Moscow in other negotiations, but was always dependent on host-country agreement and control, never automatic or on demand.

6. **Sublimits for Different Categories of Weapons**

U.S.: Specific and low sublimits on "heavy" ICBMs. Only the Soviet SS-18 would be affected because the sole U.S. heavy ICBM, the Titan missile, was being phased out.

Soviet: No special limits on heavy ICBMs within sublimits on ICBMs in general or MIRVed systems (those with multiple independently targeted warheads; reentry vehicles) beyond a provision similar to that in SALT II for no increase in existing heavy ICBMs.

(Otherwise, both sides at various times had favored either specific sublimits on each major category of weapons or full freedom to mix systems within overall limits. SALT II, for example, resulted in a combination of these principles.)

7. **Limitations on New Weapons Systems**

U.S.: Strict and restrictive definitions to determine whether a new or upgraded development qualified as a "new" (therefore limited or banned) system or whether it would be considered a permissible modernization of an allowed existing one. Ship-launched cruise missiles (SLCMs) either allowed or outside this negotiation (relates back to the definition of *strategic*).

Soviet: Similar but less restrictive definitions of *modernized* versus *new* "strategic" cruise missiles, other than limited-range air-launched missiles (ALCMs, which already were included in the inventories) *banned.*

(In general, each side sought definitions that would block the other's planned new systems while protecting its own systems in the development stage.)

Moscow had taken the firm position that a strategic offensive weapons reduction treaty could be concluded and go into effect only when it was accompanied by satisfactory treaties on the other two components of the overall Geneva talks (INF, and space and defensive systems), and that no space and defensive systems treaty would be acceptable unless it would ban the U.S. SDI.

Over the following months, through September 1986, Soviet negotiators made one apparent concession after another in each of these areas of contention, with the key exception of the admissibility of the U.S. SDI. The United States, too, reportedly put forward some modifications in its positions, apparently less radical than the Soviet ones. But it just as adamantly insisted that SDI research should not be covered by any ban and that agreement on a space and defensive weapons treaty need not be a sine qua non for a strategic offensive weapons treaty. In fact, SDI and the extent and specifics of verification measures were still the most fundamental bones of contention, although there were increasing indications that the Soviets might bend a bit on the latter if they could succeed in blocking SDI. Other important differences remained, but their reconciliation through mutual compromise and adjustment was conceivable, provided the two fundamental differences were resolved first.

With some exceptions on the Soviet side, the exact content and nuance of each side's proposals, counterproposals, and concessions, as well as the precise time when they were put on the agenda in formal negotiations, are not critical to our discussion because we are examining Gorbachev's policies and actions rather than the respective merits of the proposals. What is germane to our analysis is the way Gorbachev continued to make concessions and the extent to which public declarations were matched by proposals brought to the table in the negotiations. In fact, the precise time, in which round of talks or when in the round, of the formal submission of new proposals is not always in the public record. What is known is that the first comprehensive new Soviet proposal was made with great fanfare in the fall of 1985 and somewhat fleshed out in June of 1986, after Gorbachev had announced on 16 January 1986 his comprehensive phased plan to eliminate nuclear weapons by the year 2000. These were the landmarks during the period we are examining in detail in this chapter. The Soviets brought forward another revised proposal in June, partially accommodating some of the U.S. concerns and slightly shifting the nuances of measures to stop SDI to strengthening and extending the ABM treaty. This was billed as yet another Soviet compromise.

It may also be significant, in connection with Gorbachev's personnel changes and his consolidation of power, that the first two rounds of talks, if we accept Western reports, basically consisted of regurgitation of "principles" and underlying arguments with little sign of any progress, except that by summer the Soviet negotiating team finally began to talk in terms of specific numbers and provisions that could possibly be included in a future agreement. The sequence of apparent Soviet concessions began in earnest only after Gorbachev had begun to pack the Politburo and Secretariat, eliminated Romanov, and placed Shevardnadze in the Foreign Ministry. There may not have been a direct cause-and-effect relationship here, but the sequence is suggestive of one. It is also interesting that in September, prior to the fall round of negotiations in which the Soviets presented their major concession for deep cuts, the Soviet central press reported that the negotiating delegation had met with Gorbachev, Gromyko, Chebrikov (KGB), Shevardnadze, and Sokolov (Defense) to receive final instructions. This disclosure of the identities of the actors in the Soviet arms control policy-making apparatus has apparently not been repeated. If such a disclosure were made today, one would see that Gromyko's name would have been dropped—although Zaykov's might appear in Gromyko's place—and that Sokolov's name would have been replaced by that of the new minister of defense, Yazov.

There are two basic sources of knowledge about the content, direction, and implications of new Soviet proposals and concessions: Soviet public statements and U.S. rejoinders and leaks about what was actually said or included in the formal negotiations. With due allowance for the fact that public statements by both sides are a part of negotiating tactics, and therefore that U.S. revelations may be biased, it is striking that the United States has consistently asserted that some major Soviet concessions given prominence in public pronouncements were not submitted in that same form at the negotiating table. (U.S. "statements," usually attributed to unnamed officials, appearing in the press also have to be evaluated with care for a reason beyond the fact that the official being quoted may be trying to influence Moscow or Congress. A lengthy statement is often excerpted and presented by the press in ways that paint significantly different pictures, according to the political bias of the journalist or editor.) Given the abundance of leaks from all sides of the political and policy spectrum in Washington, it is difficult to imagine that the official U.S. statements to this effect would not generally be true. Significantly, precisely when such an allegation was made in the spring of 1986 by the head of the U.S. negotiating team, Ambassador Max Kampelman, the Soviet press attacked it not so much on the grounds of its inaccuracy as because it had violated the rule of confidentiality. This divergence between apparent Soviet concessions as proclaimed to the world and as actually submitted in the negotiations is critical for assessing the extent of the sacrifices Gorbachev is genuinely willing to make in order to stop SDI or reduce nuclear arsenals. Obviously, it implies that he was merely trying to force the United States to abandon SDI and slow down its force improvements while retaining Soviet abilities to forge ahead in the future arms competition.

Soviet public statements have been numerous, well publicized, and presented at multiple levels—ranging from Gorbachev speeches and interviews, through frequent special press conferences, to press articles, broadcoasts, and lectures by Soviet academics abroad. Throughout there have been apparently deliberate ambiguities, generalities, and variations in the content and the potential modalities of many of the more significant concessions. For example, Gorbachev himself several times stated that where necessary for verification, on-site inspection measures can be negotiated as long as they do not open avenues for espionage. The caveats "where necessary," which is a quite subjective judgment, and concerning espionage can, of course, deprive such measures of any real utility—at least this is how the United States perceives them. To take another example, Gorbachev or other Soviet spokesmen on occasion have stated that the USSR envisions no barriers to pure research in technologies applicable to an SDI, but at other times have either insisted that "all" SDI research be banned or that no directed research or component testing and development could be included in authorized "pure" research. In sum, the frequency, high profile, and ambiguity of Soviet proclamations, in conjunction with the reported failure of Soviet negotiators to get down to the specifics of additional verification measures, or the definition of permissible research, development, and testing (in a manner analogous to previous treaties) suggested that the Soviets might have been more interested in appealing to audiences potentially capable of pressuring the United States than in finding reasonable intermediate compromises or in reaching arms control agreements acceptable to both sides. (In SALT I/ABM and SALT II all research and virtually all development up to even a limited number of full system tests were permitted for many types of new, treaty-controlled systems and technologies. Even other ostensibly prohibited systems were not totally banned. The ABM treaty, for example, included a gaping loophole in its prohibition of any missile system based on physical principles other than ground-launched antiballistic missile missiles by stating in effect that if such technologies were developed, the parties would consult on changes that might be required in the treaty. Moreover, in citing various passages to show that some of the potential components of the U.S. SDI are banned by the ABM treaty, critics conveniently ignore the fact that at the beginnning of the treaty text the ABM systems under discussion and to which treaty provisions apply are defined as antiballistic missile missiles.)

Nevertheless, Gorbachev did put forward a series of "pot sweetners" that were departures from previously held Soviet positions. If implemented, the concessions would have such wide-ranging impact on Soviet force structure and capabilities that they can be presumed to be acceptable to the Soviet political-military establishment only on the condition that they are balanced by very major gains in other arms control aspects, or possibly in corollary benefits from any detente that would accompany such a treaty. Thus, Gorbachev offered very deep cuts in force levels, including the mainstay of the Soviet capability and force structure, ICBMs. The cuts, although not going as far as the U.S. proposals, would also almost inevitably have to include some reductions in the formerly sacrosanct heavy ICBMs, a main U.S. target for deep cuts. In addition, Gorbachev backed off from the demand that an INF treaty would have to be accompanied by one banning SDI, and he apparently made concessions on other issues (e.g., long-range SLCM, on submarines). The Soviets seemingly agreed to accept limits on warheads and bombs as *one* valid counting measure. Throughout, however, Gorbachev stood by the demand that any offensive strategic weapons treaty, especially one containing any of these concessions, be conditional on the banning of SDI. Moreover, through September 1986 it was not at all clear that the Soviets were willing even to discuss their concessions in meaningful substantive detail prior to obtaining the U.S. consent to SDI.

The issues in the space and defensive weapons subnegotiation centered on SDI, verification, and the correct interpretation of the ABM treaty in regard to the definition of permitted research and development, that is, whether any SDI research program is indeed an ABM treaty violation. There was also the question of whether to resume or to include in these talks the ASAT negotiations. The negotiations had been broken off by the United States because of concern over a combination of external events (Afghanistan) and treaty-related issues, such as whether the U.S. space shuttle actually qualified as an antisatellite weapon because of its theoretical ability to capture a deployed satellite. Again, the entire Soviet position revolved around the SDI issue, its presentation being couched in terms of such catchy (especially in the West) phrases as "preventing the militarization of space." The rhetoric attempted to suggest that outer space—with all of the military satellites put up by both sides, with the heavy military recruiting base for astronauts and cosmonauts, with space as the medium through which ballistic missiles travel, and with anywhere from 60 percent to 80 percent of all Soviet space launches assessed by the West as having either a total or primary military application—is not already militarized. Moreover, proposals to resume ASAT negotiations were in part related to directly limiting potential SDI technologies. Aside from the fact that the USSR already had a limited ASAT capability in its crude but operational antisatellite system and in nuclear-tipped ABM missiles while the United States was still in the process of developing its own much advanced ASAT weapon, there are direct connections between ASAT weapons technologies and some of the SDI component systems under research. Finally, it must be noted that despite Soviet denials, U.S. intelligence continued to report that the Soviets were continuing their own long-extant and extensive research and development programs for advanced strategic defenses.

The intermediate-range weapons component of the Geneva negotiations was the outgrowth of earlier INF negotiations broken off by Gorbachev's predecessors when NATO proceeded to deploy the Pershing 2 and cruise missiles. The negotiations were crucially dependent on one of the fundamental issues dividing the United States and the U.S.S.R. in regard to strategic offensive weapons, namely, how to define a strategic weapon. Any estimation of what constitutes parity or, as the Soviets refer to it, "equal security," depends on that definition. At the same time these negotiations were essentially stalemated over a number of specific issues, some of which (for example, verification, whether to count launches, missiles or warheads; whether to include other intermediate-range nuclear delivery means; and the extent of reductions) were analogous to the main points of disagreement in START.

Two other key areas of fundamental disagreement also were evident. The first had to do with compensation for the Soviets for French and U.K. systems, a variation of the idea of "equal security." The second involved geographical applicability. Here the questions were whether limits and reductions would apply outside Europe (the U.S. position was yes; that of the Soviets, no) and whether Soviet systems reduced in Europe should be destroyed (U.S. position) or simply removed from the area (the Soviet position). As in regard to strategic offensive weapons, Gorbachev proceeded to offer concessions, e.g., the possibility of reductions to levels that would not require total elimination of the U.S. INF systems in Europe, destruction rather than removal of SS-20s from the European part of the USSR, and even modified proposals ostensibly not including full compensation for French and British forces. During his visit to France Gorbachev also suggested separate negotiations with London and Paris. The pattern was similar to that for strategic weapons. Public pronouncements were made that were more attractive than the concrete details apparently put on the table at the talks. In addition, U.S. and NATO intelligence denied Gorbachev's publicized claims that the U.S.S.R. had already begun some unilateral dismantling and destruction of SS-20 missiles.

Nevertheless, both the Soviets and the Americans did acknowledge some real progress toward a meeting of minds, more so than in the other talks. Prior to Reykjavik Gorbachev was apparently willing to make significant concessions in INF without the precondition of stopping SDI. (This was categorically stated publicly by several Soviet spokesmen, but it is not quite as clear whether this offer was also repeated formally in negotiations.) If so, he appeared to have had three main motives. First, a successful INF treaty would inevitably add impetus to the process of negotiating a strategic arms agreement, where the SDI remained the primary Soviet target. A second obvious motive was to encourage peace groups in both Europe and the United States to undermine public support for European and U.S. nuclear arms modernization programs and to step up pressure on Washington against SDI. A third motive could have been to exacerbate tensions between the United States and its European allies within NATO, with the prospect of weakening or splitting the alliance. This would be quite in line with both long-standing Soviet policies and the fallback policy for selective detente as described in chapter 6.

In August and September there were several developments in the superpower jockeying over this triad of "strategic" nuclear arms issues, developments that seemed to point to a hardening of positions by the Soviets. For example, in early August a high-level team of U.S. strategic arms control experts and policymakers went to Moscow for two days of talks with their counterparts. The Soviet press reported their planned arrival in advance, but thereafter ignored the talks. Soviet spokesmen addressing foreign correspondents in press conferences afterward painted a dismal picture of U.S. obstinacy, but this was not even mentioned in the domestic press. A similar trip by Soviet experts for talks in Washington in early September was barely mentioned in the Soviet press.

Issues and Approaches in Other Arms Control Talks

Relationships

There were fairly dramatic developments in other, non-"strategic" talks, developments that had some real significance for the central nuclear discussions. Although the public tends to look at the main nuclear arms control talks as the ones that really count, it must be recognized that all of the different arms control efforts and forums form an interrelated whole. For this reason, before further assessing the status of arms control at the end of this period—when the dramatic announcement was made on 30 September that Gorbachev and Reagan would meet in Iceland in less than two weeks—it is necessary to examine the rest of the arms control mosaic.

The purposes behind Soviet proposals and concessions in regard to nuclear testing, conventional arms reductions and limitations in Europe, and all the rest of the arms control zoo have been inextricably linked to those the Soviets have pursued in the strategic and theater nuclear talks. Western publics—and sometimes, it seems, governments—tend to treat these as distinct and separate issues. To do so is unrealistic. Moreover, the evidence that can be deduced from Soviet military doctrine, Leninist ideology and

Soviet, decision-making structure and practice all indicates that the Soviets labor under no such illusions. The reality is that all levels and types of military power and capabilities form a continuum, whether one is talking about actual war fighting, about deterrence, or about political pressure based upon perceptions of relative military power. The compartmentalization of, and distinctions between, conventional, chemical, or nuclear warfare, between strategic, theater, or tactical weapons, and even between offensive and defensive capabilities have become increasingly irrelevant. We live in an era of total war between entire societies rather than professional armies, and when weapons systems and force structures have become more and more multipurpose in nature. To a significant degree the compartmentalization reflects a combination of bureaucratic imperatives, reductionism (reducing a large problem into more manageable discrete components), catering to publics and political constituencies who are either unable or do not wish to see the connections, and downright wishful thinking. Only a partial listing of interrelationships need to be cited to illustrate this point.

So-called strategic nuclear weapons (those with intercontinental ranges) can just as easily be used for theater targets; in fact, it was long confidently assessed that many Soviet ICBMs were targeted against European sites. Even aside from the FBS issue and Soviet definitions of *strategic*, intermediate (i.e. theater)-range weapons can be used for many intercontinental targets, depending upon firing locations. The SS-20 can hit some North American targets with its normal three warheads, and it can hit many more if launched with only a single warhead. With aerial refueling many so-called tactical or theater bombers can be launched on intercontinental missions. "Tactical" weapons systems (those with ranges under 1,000 kms) are as much a part of full-scale theater nuclear balances as they are of any purely battlefield equation. Even short-range missiles (especially cruise missiles) and aircraft can be used for strategic targets when launched from aircraft or vessels at sea.

Although used for battlefield missions in the past, modern chemical weapons, to say nothing of biological weapons, can easily be envisioned for the same strategic uses as nuclear ones. In fact, they have many theoretical advantages over nuclear missiles for countervalue strikes (those against cities and other population and industrial targets rather than against weapons and purely military forces, or counterforce). Further, the same bomber, missile, or artillery shell that carries a nuclear warhead can be armed with either conventional explosives or chemical or biological agents, and in fact often are for shorter-range systems. Within an entire theater of military operations, such as Europe, the destruction by so-called tactical nuclear or chemical weapons would easily be as total as that from a massive exchange of strategic or intermediate weapons. And, increasingly, the destructive potential of modern conventional weapons employed on the scale of a major East-West war might be just as devastating. In fact, NATO strategy is expressly predicated upon the threat of staged nuclear escalation, and the ultimate linkage to U.S. strategic nuclear retaliation, to deter aggression by what is perceived as heavily and inherently superior Warsaw Pact conventional forces.

Finally, it is not possible to ignore the fact that a precedent in one arms control arena has direct implications for negotiations in all others. This has to be considered as especially applicable to Soviet positions, for by doctrine their definition of *strategic, operational*, or *tactical* is a function of employment and purpose, not such artificial criteria as range or weapons type. Soviet thinking defines the central determinant of the outcome of any contest, military or political, as the total correlation of forces: the amalgamation of all political, economic, morale, and military components of relative power. Moscow would not be true to its own concepts if it conducted one arms negotiation in a vacuum from another. Soviet policymakers may or may not always effectively integrate their tactics in different arms control forums, and they take positions in one that leads them to unforeseen situations in others, but it ill behooves the analyst not to look for conscious relationships between the policymakers' actions in one negotiation and their purposes in regard to another.

Nuclear Testing

The arms control arena obviously the most directly connected to the triad of nuclear weapons talks is that concerned with limiting or banning nuclear testing. Three existing treaties limited nuclear tests: the Limited Test Ban Treaty of 1963 (LTBT) banning nuclear weapons tests in the atmosphere, in outer space, and under water; the 1974 Threshold Test Ban Treaty (TTBT) prohibiting underground nuclear weapons tests in excess of 150 kilotons of TNT-equivalent explosive power; and the 1974 Peaceful Nuclear Explosions Treaty (PNET) defining and regulating non-weapons-related nuclear explosions. The LTBT was signed and ratified by the United States, the U.S.S.R., and the United Kingdom, and subsequently joined by many other nations (but notably not by France or the PRC, two other nuclear weapons states, or NWS). The other two treaties were between the United States and U.S.S.R. and in effect accepted by the United Kingdom, but were never ratified by the U.S. Senate. All three treaties essentially rely upon NTM for monitoring and verification, but protocols to the TTBT and PNET envisaged an extensive exchange of rather detailed seismographic, geographical, and test information, and in the case of the

PNET, very controlled and limited access to test sites. Because the TTBT and PNET were never ratified, the latter provisions were never instituted in practice. Over the years Western analytic methodologies based on seismographic data have suggested that varying numbers of Soviet weapons tests have exceeded the 150-kt limitation, leading to accusations of Soviet violations of treaty provisions.

During much of the 1970s the United States, the United Kingdom, and the U.S.S.R. engaged in trilateral negotiations toward a comprehensive test ban treaty (CTBT), but as noted earlier, these were broken off. During these talks, the sides had agreed on the principle, although not all the details or numbers, of national, remote, or automatically controlled seismographic monitoring stations on each other's territory. More important as a precedent, they had agreed to the principle of OSI to allay suspicions of violations. This was such an important "concession" by the Soviets that their chief negotiator characterized them as having reversed 200 years of Soviet and Russian history. The key drawback, however, was that the Soviets agreed to only a very limited OSI: after the fact, under very controlled and circumscribed parameters, and basically at the discretion of the inspected party. In the eyes of the West this left too much room for cover-ups or simple denials.

Other than almost *pro-forma* declarations, nothing much further was heard about either a nuclear test ban or permitting OSI in the forms the West demanded until the United States had announced SDI and Mikhail Gorbachev had come to power. Then, however, a test ban became a central motif of Soviet propaganda along with the argument that without new tests, nuclear weapons would be unable to expand in any improved ways. Of course, a total test ban would close off one of the main avenues of SDI development because, among other things, controlled nuclear explosions were an integral component of the power source for some of SDI's exotic weapons. At the same time Gorbachev and other Soviet spokesmen began to assert that the U.S.S.R. was prepared to agree to OSI in all sorts of arms control agreements. This apparent major concession was carefully hedged by the phrase "where necessary," and to the extent that it was actually put forth in concrete talks, in any formal negotiations rather than merely in public speeches—which is not at all certain—it was evidently not phrased in a way that would guarantee any timely, on-demand obligation to permit such inspections. The condition continued until late summer 1986, when there was a dramatic new development in a totally different arms control arena.

Meanwhile, throughout Gorbachev's period of rule, nothing so much epitomized the dramatic chain of his concessions as the whole series of announcements regarding the various extensions of the unilateral nuclear test moratorium first announced with great fanfare in late July 1985. Clearly, Moscow knew that this was a very appealing public relations ploy. The United States had long ago rejected a total test ban as unacceptable on the grounds that nuclear weapons remained a key component of Western security and deterrence strategy, and on the somewhat more questionable grounds of the ability to detect clandestine tests (verifiability). At present the ban would have the effect of stopping one part of U.S. SDI research in its tracks and seriously hampering U.S. missile modernization. But the Soviet military planners, too, cannot possibly be happy with their own protracted inability to test. Their long acquiescence to this sacrifice indicates how overriding is the priority of stopping SDI. It also seems to support the conclusion that Gorbachev is very firmly in control.

Conventional Arms Control in Europe

The second related arena in the overall arms control mosaic is that of conventional forces reductions, limitations, and controls in Europe. Here there have been two principal approaches and forums. One was the talks of mutual and balanced force reductions in Europe (MBFR), and the second was the Conference on Security and Confidence Building Measures and Disarmament in Europe (CSCBMDE). If for no other reason than the linkages in NATO strategy, these cannot be separated from the issues of the nuclear strategic and theater (intermediate) weapons reductions. More important, it was in the latter that a critical Soviet concession occurred, a concession with major implications for all arms control. Moreover, in the process, the only arms-control-related agreement of any consequence since SALT II was reached.

The CSCBMDE in Stockholm had been convened to develop new and expanded confidence-building measures (CBMs) that would add to those agreed to at Helsinki a decade earlier. Supposedly, there is to be a disarmament part of the conference later, a subsequent phase, after an agreed new CBM regimen has proven itself. Many months of talks had produced very little progress until the middle of 1986, when optimistic reports began to emerge and the differences began to narrow to a few critical ones. The differences, with unimportant exceptions, basically fell into two categories: those dealing with exercise notification and limitation modalities, and those related to monitoring and verification. Both categories were suddenly resolved in August and September of 1986 and a package of measures was agreed to, subject to ratification by governments.

Without going into details, it is fair to summarize the differences in the first category as boiling down to the following. The West basically sought notifications and limitations that would dramatically reduce the possibilities of a Warsaw Pact surprise attack while retaining maximum freedom of action for NATO to continue previous exercise patterns—such as the annual series of exercises relating to the reinforcement of Europe from North America, code named "Reforger"—and for the movement through Europe of forces, primarily U.S., intended for deployment in other regions. Preventing surprise attack, of course, was critical because the Warsaw Pact preponderances in conventional forces would be much more uncertain of bringing victory if NATO had warning and had taken full measures to prepare. The East had basically sought to maximize its control and limitations over such NATO activities while minimizing the impact on its own exercise patterns and, especially, the amount of useful information that it would have to provide to NATO.

The second category of disagreement, that of monitoring- and verification-related measures, had revolved around two issues, one major and one relatively minor. The lesser issue had to do with observers at previously notified exercises. The original CSCE CBMs had allowed for host nations to invite foreign observers to exercises above a threshold of 25,000 ground force participants. The West wanted to make this obligatory and applicable to all participatory states, not just the observers whom the host nation wished to invite. The major issue was again on-site inspection, particularly mandatory OSI that was not left to the discretion of the nation whose behavior was being challenged.

These negotiations also had the particular characteristic of not being conducted simply between the United States and the U.S.S.R. or between NATO and the Warsaw Pact. Like CSCE, they also included all of the neutral European states. This meant that even though the real negotiations were between the East and West, there was much less confidentiality and that both sides had to play much more to the sensibilities and desires of a wider audience.

Gradually through the spring and summer of 1986 East-West differences over the parameters of notification and limitation ceilings (the first category of differences) were resolved by a process of mutual accommodation. Neither side was left with what it had originally sought, although on balance the outcome was closer to Western positions than to that of Moscow. Suddenly, in August and September, the East agreed to provisions that resolved the outstanding problems related to verification.

First, the "minor" problem was resolved by Eastern acceptance of the principle that observers from all participatory states would be invited to exercises. When this concession proved insufficient, the Soviets made another, far more significant one. When the CSCBMDE reconvened for what was supposed to be the final session, the deputy minister of defense and chief of the general staff, Marshal Akhromeev, made an almost unprecedented visit to the talks. Suddenly, Moscow agreed to a program of obligatory, on-demand, on-site inspections. The agreement was severely constrained in terms of the number of inspections and the circumstance and parameters of implementation, and it required two extra full days of negotiation beyond the scheduled close of the round and some Western, primarily U.S., concessions on specifics to complete. (This unprecedented Soviet acceptance of OSI included not only ground but also aerial inspection; the final differences were over who would provide and pilot the aircraft.) Nevertheless, it represented a major breakthrough, one that could not help but impact the other, more substantive arms reductions and limitations arenas.

In one dramatic step Gorbachev had accomplished several purposes. First, he had demonstrated that the USSR was prepared to back up its declaratory rhetoric and ostensible concessions by reaching concrete agreements involving mutual give and take with the West. Second, he had demonstrated that East-West agreement was much more readily achieved with the full participation of U.S. allies in Europe, and by inference, that those allies were crucial to bringing the United States to agreement on other issues. Third, he had helped set the stage for Reykjavik. Finally, he had done this wholly within the context of a much more painless regime of confidence-building measures, not real weapons and force limitations; in real force reductions, OSI would have a much larger impact on any hidden plans or programs. Moreover, he had done so in a manner that still preserved the principle that the USSR could constrain any agreed-to OSI within acceptable parameters.

In Vienna at the long-stalled MBFR talks, which addressed real reductions and limitations, not just CBMs, there were two major issues plus a host of minor, technical disagreements essentially resolvable once the major issues could be agreed upon. By far the biggest block to an agreement had to do with verification provisions, with NATO's demanding that these be very intrusive, regularized on-site inspections and the East's rejecting this demand. The issue stemmed from what had been long described as the main stumbling block in MBFR: the large discrepancy between Western estimates and Eastern claims of the strength of Warsaw Pact forces in the so-called NATO Guidelines Area (Poland, the CSSR, the GDR, the FRG, and the Benelux countries). The West nevertheless made a major concession, dropping its demand for resolution of the data discrepancy prior to any agreement on reductions. As a result of this concession, the crucial importance of additional monitoring and verification was greatly enhanced in NATO eyes.

The other major issue had to do with the size of U.S. and Soviet reductions in the anticipated, first-phase agreement, with Soviet Warsaw Pact proposals calling for both smaller initial reductions and much less difference between the size of the forces removed by the two sides. Among the technical disagreements that appeared essentially resolvable, there was one that could possibly develop into a more intractable issue: the extent and form of restrictions or increases, within overall bloc ceilings, imposed on an individual state on the assumption that an ally of that state had reduced its forces in the area. Warsaw Pact proposals had over the years been obviously aimed at limiting West German forces (the Bundeswehr). Although the exact status of this controversy was not really clear in public well into 1986, there were indications that it was no longer a major obstacle to an agreement.

As usual, the Gorbachev regime accorded high publicity to its "new proposals" at the Vienna conference. Also as usual, Western spokesmen indicated that there was less to these proposals than met the eye. They were generally described as old goods in new wrappings. Yet, at the same time Gorbachev had made some concessions in the critical verification area. The problem with them, according to the West, was that they did not include the crucial verification aspect of obligatory on-site inspection to monitor residual troop strengths. Nor was the OSI concession at Stockholm liable to suffice to remove the problem entirely. In MBFR, which hit at the numerical heart of the European balance, the West was demanding a far more comprehensive, intrusive, and frequent OSI program.

Gorbachev's most stridently trumpeted European arms control proposal was made in mid-April 1986 when, at the East German Party Congress, he proposed major reductions in all types of ground and tactical aviation forces "from the Atlantic to the Urals." In the same speech he again alluded to the acceptability of on-site inspection, but (as always up until Stockholm) with the potentially very sticky escape clause "where needed." The dramatic proposal seemed to represent a major Soviet concession because it included reductions in the European parts of the USSR itself. On a closer look, however, it was not quite clear how meaningful the reductions would be, given the Soviet practice of maintaining partially manned units and stored equipment, and Gorbachev's stipulation that the equipment of the reduced forces could be stored on national territory. This would mean that Soviet force reductions both in the forward area and in the Western USSR could have equipment stockpiles for their reactivation as close as a few hundred miles (served by an extensive rail net) from the inter-German border, whereas the equipment for U.S. reduced forces would be located beyond more than 3,000 miles of ocean. Nor was it yet clear, as of the mid-autumn 1986, in which existing or new negotiating forum such a scheme could be examined in practical terms. (The most logical possibilities were either in Stockholm or a new Warsaw Pact-NATO forum, possibly an expanded version of MBFR.) Pending further clarifications, the proposal had to be assessed as no more than another propaganda maneuver resembling many other sweeping Soviet proposals of former years. Yet, it did imply one major departure from past Soviet practice, which if followed up, could have major implications domestically for the Soviet economy and particularly for the whole web of Gorbachev's relations with the Soviet military establishment. Moreover, in June some proposed reduction figures began to appear, 150,000 personnel on each side, that were both attractive to much of Western public opinion and had potential implications for the Soviet labor force and economy.

In other European arms control forums Gorbachev and his aides reiterated such traditional Soviet proposals as various European nuclear-free zones, chemical-weapons-free zones, and so on. These represented nothing new, although the chemical weapons proposals received increasing emphasis in an obvious attempt to prevent West European consent to U.S. binary-chemical weapons. Like Soviet proposals in Stockholm and Vienna and like Gorbachev's Berlin speech, they were part and parcel of Moscow's attempts to influence Western publics, complicate NATO force planning, emphasize the uniqueness and separateness of all-European considerations, and improve the atmosphere and the incentives for more important U.S.-Soviet strategic arms control talks.

Chemical Weapons and the Rest

Gorbachev's representatives were also active in Geneva at the Committee on Disarmament (CD). They used this forty-nation UN-affiliated forum to promote nuclear-test-ban agreements, the "demilitarization" of space, chemical arms control, and a host of other rather declarative agreements. Noticeable in all of this was the search for public persuasion effect, for precedents to encourage more important agreements with the United States, and in several instances for ways to block SDI. In addition, Gorbachev relied on the traditional Soviet ploy of using the CD as a forum to convince the Third World and European neutral participants that the United States was the main obstacle to peace and progress. The primary area where some further concessions were made by Gorbachev at the CD was in chemical weapons control. Both in the regular CD discussions and in U.S.-Soviet bilateral talks on elimination of chemical stockpiles and on nonproliferation of chemical weapons, Gorbachev's representatives somewhat eased traditional Soviet resistance to on-site inspections but did not go nearly as far as in CSCBMDE. In regard to chemical weapons this issue is critical because almost any peaceful chemical production facility can easily be utilized to produce lethal chemical weapons substances secretly (for example, the principal ingredients of nerve gas are very similar to those used for many insecticides).

Gorbachev also used the UN itself as a forum to advance his arms control aims at every opportunity. The most dramatic of the many Soviet initiatives at the UN was Shevardnadze's formal proposal in August of 1985, and Ryzhkov's reiteration the following June, for a new international treaty banning the militarization of space and establishing organizational and procedural frameworks for international cooperation in space. This proposal was referred to at every opportunity. The connection with SDI is obvious.

The Situation at the End of September

The preceding characterizations describe the basic thrust and much of the sequence of Gorbachev's arms control policies during the same eighteen months covered in this chapter. Then suddenly, on 30 September, after a rapid series of four separate meetings between Foreign Minister Shevardnadze and U.S. Secretary of State Shultz and one between Shevardnadze and President Reagan, it was announced that the U.S. president and the Soviet general secretary would meet in mid-October in Reykjavik, Iceland. It was not to be really a summit but rather a preliminary working meeting to iron out difficulties and set the stage for the long-awaited Gorbachev visit to the United States. We will return to Reykjavik in much greater detail in the next chapter. At this point it is useful to summarize briefly where arms control appeared to stand in the final weeks up to the announcement of the meeting in Iceland.

Basically, the two main parts of the nuclear arms triad (strategic offensive weapons, and strategic defenses and space) were at a virtual standstill. The Soviets had made some concessions to U.S. demands for deep cuts: first proposing a 50 percent reduction in all strategic weapons as they defined them, including FBS and bombers, and banning long-range SLCMs and ALCMs in fall of 1985; then modifying that to an initial roughly 33 percent reduction but allowing some ALCMs and some SLCMs on submarines. Moscow, however, had not moved beyond vague formulations of possibilities of OSI and, more important, was still adamantly insisting on linkages that would effectively terminate the U.S. SDI. Washington, for its part, had offered to defer any deployment but not development of SDI for several years—years in which, in fact, the published program did not envision deployment's commencing—and had (earlier) moved toward the Soviet demand that strategic bombers also be a part of the first-phase reductions and limitations. To make matters even more contentious, the time was drawing close when the Americans were due to exceed the SALT II weapons limits by deploying the one hundred thirty-first ALCM-equipped long-range bomber.

Things were a little better in the third part of the main Geneva negotiations, INF. Here, the Soviets had stopped demanding outcomes that totally removed all U.S. P2s and ALCMs. They had progressively modified their formula in regard to the French and British forces to the point that the linkages, while still there, were clearly less specific. In fact, there were enough hints, unofficial to be sure, to suggest to many observers that Moscow might be willing to forego the traditional demand to include all allied weapons in addition to those of the United States. More important, Soviet spokesmen had repeatedly indicated throughout the summer that an INF agreement was possible without any preconditions in regard to SDI. Still and all, these hopeful signs had appeared early in the summer and there had been no further apparent movement since.

Moscow was still using its again prolonged nuclear test moratorium (the latest extension occurring in August) as a propaganda stick with which to beat Washington. The United States was just as adamantly insisting that further testing had to continue as long as nuclear weapons of any sort remained a part of the arsenals of both sides.

A series of relatively senior- and middle-level U.S.-Soviet talks on such things as test monitoring, chemical weapons reductions, chemical non-proliferation, and nuclear crisis consultation centers had been held, but so far had produced only modest results. In any event, they were largely peripheral to the impasses in the major negotiations.

The only real sign of progress was in the European context at CSCBMDE, where Washington's allies played a direct role and where an agreement on confidence measures, not arms control, had been reached just eight days before the announcement about Reykjavik. Nevertheless—and even though the more basic European conventional arms control talks, MBFR, had still never really moved from dead center in the apparently endless minuet that had been played in Vienna since the early 1970s—the agreement in Stockholm was potentially very significant for two reasons. First, it had at long last established a limited precedent for mandatory OSI; and second, it appeared to reinforce the perception that the Europeans had a real role in bringing Moscow and Washington together.

The atmospherics in the several weeks prior to the Reykjavik announcement also greatly added to this mixed but overall negative picture. Increasingly throughout the months of 1986 the Soviet propaganda mill had been churning out accusations of bad faith and attacks on U.S. policy. Reagan was usually spared direct accusation, but even this was not always true. Moreover, relations seemed to have hit a new low with the Daniloff-

Zakharov arrests and the U.S. insistence on reductions in the Soviet UN staff. Finally, the entire panoply of U.S.-Soviet rivalries and mutual condemnations throughout the Third World showed no sign of change.

The overall situation was such that many Western observers were beginning to conclude that Gorbachev had given up on coming to terms with Reagan—at least until after the forthcoming congressional elections, when a revamped Congress might force the president to make the so-called historic compromise, trading SDI for a strategic arms control agreement, or might simply emasculate SDI and the whole Reagan strategic buildup, which would be even better from the Soviet point of view.

The preceding eighteen months of Gorbachev's rule in the Kremlin had revealed a fairly clear picture of his motivations. During this time the extent of his preoccupation with arms control was impressive. In fact, it was *the* central foreign policy preoccupation of the new Soviet leadership in regard to relations with the United States and the West. Its basic goals were to forge a new U.S.-Soviet detente and to stop the United States and West European military modernizations, especially SDI and its potential European counterpart, EDI. In the process Gorbachev had made a continuous series of concessions from traditional Soviet positions, putting the USSR for the first time into the position of supplicant at U.S.-Soviet arms control talks. The concessions had been part of a major public relations effort, pursued with greater intensity and far greater flexibility than almost any in the past. But because the concessions had not been backed up by more meaningful concrete details on verification, more than the limited opening given in Stockholm, and by iron safeguards against loopholes that would allow the USSR legally to circumvent the intent of any treaty more easily than the open and pluralistic Western societies possibly could, the real intent and implications of the concessions had to remain in question. They were far too open to the suspicion that they constituted nothing more than another in a long line of Soviet diplomatic and propaganda attempts to induce the West to make unilateral or imbalanced reductions in its defense programs. Also, many elements in Gorbachev's tactics and the content of his proposals meshed all too clearly with a conscious fallback strategy of selective detente in Europe.

Even more to the point, arms control could address only one major part of the symptoms of East-West rivalry. It could not deal with the causes of that rivalry and could alleviate only one of the many causes of the distrust that feeds it. Any Soviet profession of desire for arms control without a concurrent search for ways to alleviate other, more basic aspects of the rivalry had to be looked at askance.

This could not be the whole judgment on the concessions. After all, some had indeed been quite significant, or at least would be so if they were

to come to fruition in actual treaties that would include adequate verification provisions and exclude serious loopholes. Besides, there was an inescapable logic to the fact that arms control agreements that obviated the
need to match the United States in ever costlier and ever more technologically demanding efforts, and were thus capable of reducing overall
defense expenditure requirements, would greatly facilitate Gorbachev's domestic economy projects. Furthermore, even though significant defense
budget reductions would presumably be opposed by the defense establishment and therefore provide fodder for his potential rivals, Gorbachev
could have been anticipating that in the long run a reduced defense bureaucracy might be easier to manage. At the same time it was not at all
inconceivable that potential supporters for such reductions existed even
within the military and the civilian defense establishment. This could well
be true if the reductions could be managed so as to maintain or even
enhance relative Soviet advantages and security at lower cost and force
levels. It was perhaps not without significance that all Gorbachev's proposals contained formulations that could lead to these outcomes. For example, some combinations of Gorbachev's proposals could be seen as
leading to a world where nuclear weapons might not be perceived as a
counterbalance to Soviet conventional superiorities in Europe. In such a
case, the opportunities for Moscow to exert more effective political pressures on the West would be increased.

In sum, the evidence of Gorbachev's actions, and particularly the evidence that we have examined so far, mostly lead to the conclusion that he
had been trying to use arms control for temporary or strategic advantage.
Still, it also remained conceivable that he was engaged in trying progressively to move his Soviet associates to accept more truly equal arms reductions and a fundamentally different approach to war and peace, and the
"historic struggle," in the nuclear age. In either case Gorbachev would
obviously be risking a future challenge if he were to make too many concessions without commensurate gains. The fact that he nevertheless appeared to be still willing to incur this risk argues that his desire to reduce
military expenditure was genuine, that he would persist in this attempt in
the future, and that he truly believes nuclear superiority is a dangerous
illusion. Clearly, the sudden announcement that in spite of all the apparent
difficulties, or perhaps because of them, Gorbachev would meet Reagan in
Iceland had to impact on these judgments.

At the end of September when the meeting was announced, there were
widespread expectations in the West that even though Reykjavik was being
billed as only a preliminary working session, some fairly significant basic
arms agreement would come out of it. The expectations were reinforced by
the fact that since Geneva a year earlier, Gorbachev had been insisting that

any new summit had to lead to substantive results. The most commonly expected agreement was in INF, especially because Moscow seemed no longer to be making that negotiation dependent upon stopping SDI. Explanations of, and fears about, why the Soviets had suddenly proposed the meeting abounded in every part of the Western political spectrum. At one end it was confidently asserted that this was the natural outcome and move by a Soviet reformer who sincerely wanted to reduce arms and tensions. In some cases this explanation was buttressed by the argument that Gorbachev was faced with significant political opposition at home and had to move to preempt it and gain an arms control agreement quickly so as to contain the military and ideological hawks. Generally, at this end of the political spectrum there were many who hoped and some who expected that Reagan would trade SDI for a major arms reductions—the so-called historical compromise—but who feared that he would not. At the other end of the political spectrum it was asserted that U.S. firmness and a collapsing, overburdened Soviet economy had driven Gorbachev to come to Reykjavik hat in hand. The Soviets were expected to try first to trade a partial agreement for SDI, in effect to offer a "mess of pottage," but all the United States had to do was stand fast and Gorbachev would cave in—if not now, certainly later. Meanwhile, these observers hoped for and expected a partial agreement, again most likely in INF, that would bolster the Republicans in the coming congressional elections; their fears were opposite of those at the other end of the spectrum, namely, that Reagan would trade away SDI.

Then the Iceland summit, which had started with such optimism, ended with total disagreement and no apparent results except mutual recrimination. What had happened, who was to blame, and what did it all mean? The lead-up and the meeting itself resembled a detective thriller. The preceding eighteen months had provided strands of both direct and circumstantial evidence in each of the areas we have so far addressed. Clearly, one task for the detectives remained: to examine the "scene of the crime," Reykjavik, in detail and in light of the accumulated evidence, to discover the answers.

8

Arms Control Policy (Part Two) Reykjavik and Beyond: The Pendulum Swings

Make ye no truce with ... the bear that walks like a man!

—Rudyard Kipling

A well-chosen political moment can be compared to the precise timing of the launching of a space ship to another planet. A launch occurs when there is a celestial "window of opportunity," when the heavenly bodies are in the right positions and the rocket can reach its goal as planned. A "window of opportunity" in the political firmament occupied by the two superpowers appeared in October 1986. The United States was on the eve of congressional and state elections that were very important for President Reagan, who needed a Republican majority in the Senate during the final two years of his presidency to facilitate realization of his ambitious political and social plans. The circumstance obviously appeared to Moscow to be a rare chance to influence the immediate course of U.S. politics. To do so, the Soviets had to move quickly to convene a summit conference while the election campaign was in progress. Gorbachev's advisers evidently believed that they could trap the president. Presumably, Reagan would be compelled to make concessions to reach an agreement with Gorbachev, an agreement that at a different time and under different conditions he would resist.

For over a year the Soviets had been in the unusual position of being the supplicant in arms control. Now the time was seen to be ripe to change that. Reagan, the Soviets evidently thought, would be unable to face the electorate with empty hands lest he undermine public confidence in himself and his policies and thereby risk his party's defeat. Moreover, simply obtaining U.S. agreement to a quick summit would seem to guarantee some degree of success, for no U.S. president had ever allowed himself to return from a meeting with a Soviet general secretary without some politically positive results.

The problem boiled down to how to get the United States to agree to a spur-of-the-moment meeting within ten days of its being proposed. Moscow employed a clever tactic for this: the packaging of earlier, mostly U.S. arms control positions as if they were now the revised *Soviet* disarmament proposals. During the previous year and a half of negotiations in Geneva the two sides had gradually converged on most of the broad outlines of an agreement, although some critical differences remained on a few major issues and many more on vital details of implementation (sublimits, specific systems inclusions or exclusions, and so on). Now Gorbachev apparently used an indicated readiness to agree to almost all of the Americans' basic proposals as a lure to bring Reagan to a meeting for which the United States could not adequately prepare. (The exact full text of Gorbachev's proposals to hold the Reykjavik summit were not available when this analysis was written. The description here has been reconstructed from many bits and pieces, but particularly from Gorbachev's postsummit press conferences and speeches, especially the one appearing in the main Soviet press on 14 October. Unfortunately, it is not entirely clear how much of what he expressly stated to be his presummit proposals reflected the actual content of his letter proposing the meeting and how much reflected self-serving descriptions of concessions offered during the talks at Reykjavik.) Moscow suddenly appeared, for example, to accept the long-standing U.S. position of a zero-option in Europe for intermediate-range missiles, and evidently did so without demanding an unrealistic and one-sided inclusion of large numbers of U.S. long-range tactical aircraft. Gorbachev also borrowed the U.S. idea of retaining on both sides only 100 such missiles in Soviet Asia and in the continental United States. The Soviets had previously offered no more than a freeze on these forces. Further, all along Washington had rejected Soviet demands for some sort of formal or de facto inclusion of French and British forces in an INF agreement. The Soviets had proposed various formulas that ostensibly removed the allies' nuclear capabilities from the equation, but every time the wording was such that Moscow would obtain de facto compensation for these forces and for any modernization or expansion of them. Now suddenly Gorbachev appeared to be abandoning fully the linkages between a U.S.-Soviet INF zero-option in Europe and the status of French and British forces. Similarly, the basic U.S. positions regarding treaty verification and staged reductions were apparently also included in the new Soviet proposals.

The president was offered, then, a package that appeared to be generally the same as previous U.S. positions. It is therefore easily understandable how, after Reykjavik, Gorbachev and Reagan could each declare that the talks had been over his proposals. Gorbachev could claim authorship because the package had been presented to Washington before Reykjavik in the guise of Soviet proposals; Reagan had no less a basis to state that they were American in origin because they had at various previous times been put forth by U.S. negotiators at Geneva. In either case, the bottom line was that the president received a package of proposed agreements consisting of three sections. Gorbachev's accounts mostly imply that virtually all of the proposals outlined here were incorporated in his initial invitation and opening proposal. Some of his other statements suggest that elements were added during the talks. We have included full descriptions here because of the uncertainty and to encapsulate for the reader the scope of the agreements almost reached. Most likely, the broad outlines given here were included in the invitation, but some of the specific elements were added or clarified during the discussions.

The first section, on strategic offensive weapons, proposed a 50 percent cut in land- and submarine-based strategic missiles and strategic bombers. On the surface this was virtually what Washington had asked for all along. The Americans had started from a position that limited the first stage of such deep reductions to ballistic missiles, with bombers to follow, but this had evidently ceased to be a sticking point. The Soviets had proposed just such a 50 percent reduction a year earlier in Geneva but had included U.S. FBS (long-range tactical and theater forces in Europe) in the count. In June 1986 Moscow had shifted to only a 30 percent strategic weapons reduction with a freeze on U.S. FBS. The real problems in Geneva (other than the linkage to SDI) had not been the depth of the reductions but the sublimits (or other constraints, such as aggregate throwweight) on heavy ICBMs, mobile missiles, and MIRVed missiles, and the issue of whether to include cruise missiles in the strategic weapons count or even whether to ban some of them. Evidently, Gorbachev presented the U.S. leader with the possibility of reaching agreement on the basis of the general U.S.-proposed framework while leaving any residual details on sublimits and the like to the experts to be worked out—which he clearly implied the experts would not find difficult to do. More important, by apparently dropping the demands to limit FBS or to link the reductions to the decisions over most cruise missiles, he appeared to be making major concessions to Washington.

The second Soviet "initiative" related to INF. Moscow surprisingly withdrew all its previous versions of an INF agreement and offered to return to the U.S. proposal. In other words, as noted earlier, Gorbachev offered to eliminate all U.S. and Soviet INF missiles in Europe and to reduce those stationed in Asia to only 100, thereby avoiding the issue of whether the reductions would be via dismantling or merely geographical repositioning, which was unacceptable to Washington. Moreover, the new Soviet proposal no longer seemed to contain any linkage to French and British forces. Either in the presummit invitation or during the talks Gorbachev also indicated a willingness to compromise with the United States on the issue of tactical missiles (those with ranges under 1,000km in the U.S. lexicon) by freezing them until agreement could be reached about them.

Because Moscow had earlier indicated that an INF treaty could be achievable independent of the status of agreements about strategic "offensive" forces in space and defensive weapons, i.e. SDI, it is no wonder that the Americans agreed to such a quick summit and expressed so much optimism before the talks. With Moscow apparently now also adopting earlier U.S. INF positions, it had to have appeared to the United States that Reykjavik would be a major public success even if there were no agreement on strategic offensive or space and defensive issues. In fact, Western commentary right up to the sudden announcement of the summit's failure was confidently predicting an INF agreement, at least in principle if not in detail.

The third section of the package, treaty monitoring and verification, had long been a major sticking point. Now, to Washington's apparent amazement, Moscow suddenly came out in favor of measures that the United States had long advocated (real OSI), and did so in terms that went beyond the U.S. position of double controls by advocating a system of triple controls. Gorbachev later described his proposal as having affirmed Soviet willingness to accept any kind of verification controls. Again, it is not really certain how specifically and concretely Gorbachev presented this point, whether or not he still retained the ambiguous escape-hatch phrase "where necessary" in his proposal to accept OSI. However, it is likely that this fine-print qualification no longer seemed so important to Washington, given that just a short time earlier, in Stockholm, the Soviets had accepted (for the first time ever) some mandatory OSI.

According to Gorbachev's postsummit explanations, the Americans were presented in advance with only one condition: there had to be a guarantee that for the duration of any agreements neither side would strive to obtain "military superiority" over the other. In elaborating on the meaning of this, he spoke of not upsetting the mechanisms restraining the arms race and, first of all, the agreements relating to ABM defenses. Clearly, no one could object to agreeing not to seek military superiority, a very subjective term and a widely used political bromide. More important, such a relatively vague formulation in regard to the ABM treaty—and therefore the implications for what limits Moscow would demand on SDI in return for other agreements—must have been encouraging to Washington. Reagan and Gorbachev earlier had had an exchange of letters on this subject: the Soviets had asked for a fifteen-year guaranteed extension of the treaty accompanied by a tight definition of what kind of research and development was allowable; the United States had proposed a seven-year guarantee and much looser interpretation of the constraints against research and development activities. Also, Moscow had (in public statements at least; we are not certain of the exact formulations used in formal talks in Geneva) apparently moved from a demand to ban all directed SDI research and certainly any developmental testing to one that clearly allowed laboratory research and possibly some development outside the laboratory but not real-systems or major-component testing. Given this background (and the common belief in Washington that although Reagan might be more anxious to set a date for the promised summit in the United States, Gorbachev, for economic reasons, was even more anxious for an arms control agreement—a conclusion seemingly well demonstrated by the string of Soviet concessions over the past months), it is easily understandable that the United States could have expected that Moscow was finally ready to make an acceptable concession on SDI.

Later of course, in Iceland, Gorbachev sprang the trap. He had evidently all along intended to catch Reagan by demanding the effective killing of SDI in exchange for any agreements. But meanwhile, in addition to the ploy of suddenly offering the Americans what appeared to be the arms control outline that the United States had wanted, Gorbachev appealed to Reagan's pride and belief in his own powers of persuasion in direct negotiations. Again according to Gorbachev's postsummit statements, the presummit proposal transmitted by Shevardnadze in September had said, "My hopes for major changes in international relations after Geneva have not proved justified, Soviet-American negotiations have gotten nowhere and not without cause. Fifty or 100 different variants of proposals have been considered. . . . The world is in tumult and demands from the leaders of all countries, and first of all from those great powers led by the Soviet Union and the United States of America, political will, decisiveness, the capacity to put a halt to dangerous tendencies." Such words implied that Gorbachev was ready to bypass all the detailed differences by coming together on the broad outlines of the kinds of agreements Washington had been demanding. The words implied, too, that he was willing to be more forthcoming on a whole range of issues between the two countries, from human rights concerns to Third World tensions. The sudden impression of cooperation and hope was particularly attractive—a more effective lure—precisely because it came virtually "out of the blue" at a time when U.S.-Soviet relations appeared to have hit a two-year low. Soviet propaganda against the United States had increased, with even Reagan not being spared quite as consistently as previously. The Geneva talks had been stalemated, and the two discussions by high-level teams of experts in August and September had apparently fared no better, if not worse. And the Daniloff affair, in which Gorbachev pointedly eschewed any political cover by fully backing the Soviet action and rejecting Reagan's personal appeals, was in full swing.

Last, Gorbachev assuaged any misgivings that the Reagan team might have had about taking time out from a critical election campaign. The president was evidently assured that other matters need be put aside only for a day or two, and that a successful working meeting in Iceland would lead to the follow-up summit in Washington that Reagan so desired. Gorbachev, again after the Iceland summit, declared that his words had been, "We cannot allow, Mr. President, our meeting in Washington to fail."

Given all of this, it is hardly any wonder that Reagan consented to such a sudden and, in reality, unprepared summit. Whether he would have done so without the carefully laid inducements that Gorbachev so obviously orchestrated to bring him to Reykjavik is something that no one, except possibly Reagan, can answer. But given the circumstances of a tough election campaign, increasing congressional sentiment for budgetary cuts affecting his military buildup, and the undeniable political appeal of arms control, it seems likely that the president would have come around in any case. The Soviet lures were masterfully designed and executed, but they may not have been necessary to obtain the meeting.

In any event, the result was that the president and his advisers ended up with only a scant ten days to prepare for the meeting, a period that proved manifestly insufficient. These were days in which other issues, particularly the upcoming elections, competed for attention. By taking time out from the campaign, the president inevitably was put at a disadvantage because the circumstances made it all the more important that he bring success home from Iceland.

It is clear in retrospect that Gorbachev had prepared himself for a much longer period. The Shabanov article, which we discuss in detail in chapter 12, clearly presaged the shape of Gorbachev's newest "concessions" on strategic weapons reductions and INF. Its appearance in August indicates that Gorbachev's proposals had been prepared at least that far back. Furthermore, like his carefully orchestrated invitation to Reykjavik, Gorbachev made a number of statements and took a number of actions in August and September that can best be understood as part of the preparatory stages in the Reykjavik ploy, steps that were correctly calculated to give him the initiative and put him at the advantage when the meeting took place.

Rumors were circulated that a thaw in Soviet literature would include republication of the long-suppressed works of the poet Gumilev, who had been executed in the early years of the Revolution. Theaters were apparently to be given some leeway in setting their own repertoires. Pasternak was to be recognized, and Doctor Zhivago possibly published in the USSR. To this image of Gorbachev as the liberalizer was added the surprise release of the poetess Irina Ratushinskaya, and several Soviet emigrants were given permission to return to their homeland. Accompanying this, Moscow received a propaganda bonus (presumably unexpectedly, but who knows): an unemployed American physicist, Arnold Lokshin, suddenly defected to the USSR, giving the impression that the two societies were equivalent because defections "for freedom" have occurred in both directions.

Gorbachev meanwhile immediately informed Reagan when a Soviet submarine sank in the Atlantic—a totally uncharacteristic act for the Soviets—and he demonstrated his "magnanimity" by trading Daniloff for Zakharov and throwing in one of the USSR's inexhaustible supply of dissidents as a measure of "goodwill."

Throughout, the Soviet and Eastern European unofficial rumor mill churned out the stories that some in the West have always been so eager to believe, implying that Gorbachev was threatened by hard-liners in the Kremlin, the KGB, and the military. Such stories encouraged the belief that Gorbachev was coming to the summit in great need of success and would therefore have real concessions in his pocket if only the United States would meet him halfway. The picture conveniently ignores the facts: almost every other member of the top leadership had been appointed or promoted by Gorbachev; Gorbachev's criticisms of Soviet bureaucrats, ministries, or organizations had not touched the KGB, nor had any statements or disinformation releases attributable to the KGB touched Gorbachev except in a positive light; and senior Ministry of Defense spokesmen had consistently expressed full support for Gorbachev's policies, not only in their statements to foreign audiences but also in articles clearly intended to educate and reassure their subordinates.

Other than the Daniloff affair and the lost-submarine notification, these kinds of things had been going on for many months, but they definitely increased in August and September. Considered together in retrospect they seem too coincidental not to have been part of a careful buildup for the intended denouement at Reykjavik.

The foregoing is not to suggest that Reagan and his advisers were suddenly fooled into thinking that Gorbachev was a true liberal. In fact, in a speech before U.S. business people in October, Reagan specifically stated the contrary. Nevertheless, in the aggregate these themes, rumors, and actions certainly must have contributed to the beliefs that business could be done with Gorbachev and that Reykjavik would have a favorable outcome.

So the Reykjavik summit was set. Reagan evidently thought that it would be what it was billed: a working meeting that would pave the way for a Washington summit. He also had apparently good reasons to believe that it might well produce a major success on its own, one that would be finalized in Washington. He brought along all of his top experts and negotiators and left his wife at home. He arrived in fact about as one could expect for such a meeting: as if for a dress rehearsal without preliminary rehearsals, but still just a dress rehearsal.

In contrast, Gorbachev, who had planned the "dress rehearsal" as the real thing, came prepared to extract the maximum propaganda value out of the meeting no matter what the outcome. Kremlin watchers in the United States had long since noted the novel style and flair of the new Soviet general secretary; they should have anticipated that he would exert all of these skills and techniques at Reykjavik.

A veritable army of Soviet briefers, experts, and press representatives descended on Iceland ahead of the scheduled meeting. Then Gorbachev and his full entourage arrived. There may have been some observers who still expected to see a Soviet leader already corrupt with power, self-confident if not arrogant, who somewhat resembled Brezhnev in his earlier years but with more refined manners and better dressed. If so, they instead witnessed a carefully thought out and staged performance. Gorbachev, the very picture of a gentleman, beaming with optimism and energy, briskly descended from the plane with his charming, well-dressed wife preceding him—her appearance was the first of several surprises for the Americans. Then he gave an ostensibly impromptu speech, thanking the Icelanders and praising Reagan, and by implication himself, for bringing with him "an understanding of his responsibility before the nations of the world and the cause of peace."

Gorbachev's performance was marred by his being met by the Icelandic foreign minister and not the prime minister, as protocol should have demanded. The planned impact of his arrival and statement was thereby somewhat reduced, and the absence was apparently unexpected. (This follows from Gorbachev's fleeting show of annoyance and the fact that the Soviet ambassador was recalled to Moscow after the summit for what was evidently a dressing down for failing to check properly the schedule of the prime minister, who was busy at a session of the parliament when Gorbachev arrived. Late in November the ambassador was retired suddenly. Nevertheless, Gorbachev controlled his emotions and jocularly replied to the questions of the attending media representatives.)

Gorbachev and his advisory team (Dobrynin; the chief of the General Staff, Marshal Akhromeev; and others) were ensconced in *two* Soviet ocean liners brought to Reykjavik in advance for just this purpose. Here, away from prying eyes (in the normal Soviet atmosphere of strict order, subordination, and hierarchy), there was no need to play to an audience, and the experts and their many assistants could rehearse and examine each alternative tactic.

The rest of the small army the Soviets sent to Iceland operated from the Saga Hotel, gave press conferences, spoke on television, mixed with journalists, and so on. Compared to the past behaviors of such people, theirs was amazingly cordial, forthcoming, frank, and ostensibly reasonable in every way. At previous international gatherings Soviet spokesmen had often either walked out on, or responded angrily to, human rights questions, demonstrations, accusations, and demands as well as to similar questioning of Soviet activities in Afghanistan or elsewhere, all of which was in abundance at Reykjavik. This time their reactions were uniformly "civilized." They answered the accusations quietly and calmly, even offering to meet for quiet talks later; at those talks Soviet officials promised to look into the cases being raised! Meanwhile, the tenor of Soviet responses in public was always such as to stress that the first order of business was arms control, with the clear implication that all the rest could easily be worked out once agreement was reached on this overriding issue. The numbers of Soviets, their obvious preparation, and their totally uncharacteristic behavior when uncomfortable subjects were raised leave no possible doubt that this was a meticulously scripted performance played to the widest possible audience.

Raisa Gorbachev similarly played her role to the hilt. She appeared at functions and press conferences stylishly dressed, clearly supportive of her loving husband, and visited churches, tourist spots, and so on. Her modernity, charm, and understanding of the world were on display.

As far as can be determined, Gorbachev himself conducted his meetings with the US President in an extremely adroit manner—one that demonstrated a very coherent tactical game plan. (Unfortunately, we do not have at present a transcript of the discussions, nor is it likely that one will be a part of the public record in the near future. Our analysis of the private talks is therefore based upon a study of the public remarks of the two leaders. The problem is that Reagan's statements basically provide only a general picture with little specific detail. Gorbachev's remarks, not without obvious calculation, only partly pull back the curtain. Of course, Gorbachev presented the issues and sequence of discussion in the most favorable light he could for his purposes. Nevertheless, a juxtaposition of Gorbachev's remarks in his 12 October press conference and his television appearances on

14 and 24 October with U.S. statements and with Shevardnadze's 10 November press conference allow a more or less objective narrative to be reconstructed.)

The first meeting lasted from 10:30 A.M. to 12:30 P.M. Gorbachev immediately took the initiative and apparently never lost it. He proposed the creation of two working groups: one for disarmament issues, one for general concerns. He raised no objections to the inclusion of human rights on the agenda of the second working committee, and he quietly and patiently allowed Reagan to state his concerns in this regard. Still, each time after hearing out the president, Gorbachev switched the subject to disarmament. In this way he both demonstrated his mastery of the psychology of negotiating tactics and maintained control of the direction and focus of the discussions.

About an hour after the opening of the first meeting, as had been agreed beforehand, Secretary of State Shultz and Foreign Minister Shevardnadze joined the two leaders and their translators. At this point, according to Gorbachev, the character of the meeting changed from an unconstrained discussion of the general situation and definition of the issues to a more tense and businesslike exchange.

Gorbachev glanced at the outline of the papers Shevardnadze had brought to him and began to present his arms reductions proposals. When Reagan again attempted to bring the discussion back to broader international conditions and human rights, Gorbachev remained calm but insisted on addressing all questions in the context of a package in which disarmament was the central issue. Reagan acquiesced, thereby inevitably placing himself in the position of being basically the responder in a script prepared by the Soviets.

According to Gorbachev, he placed on the table a package of Soviet proposals that "would mark the beginning of new epoch in the life of humanity, the epoch without nuclear weapons." This idea of a complete ban on nuclear weapons would appear a number of times in Gorbachev's speeches and press conferences after Reykjavik; however, in the summit itself, it was evidently not raised in this fashion. What was certainly discussed was limiting and even eliminating certain delivery systems. Complete elimination of all nuclear weapons was never concretely broached. Rather, it was retrospectively injected into the discussions when the Soviet leader wished to blame the president for the failure of the talks.

In the Reykjavik talks Gorbachev evidently proposed that the two leaders direct their representatives to begin full-scale negotiations on banning nuclear explosions "in order to work out agreements on their total and final banning." This formula illustrates that in Iceland the emphasis was on halting testing and not production of weapons—no more and no less.

Subsequently, and in increasing scale as one Gorbachev account of the summit followed another, the picture was shifted from one in which the United States had prevented significant arms reductions and limitations by its "unrealistic" demand to continue SDI to one in which the Americans had blocked the opportunity to do away with the nuclear threat altogether.

At Reykjavik, according to one of Gorbachev's postsummit speeches, he proposed first to cut and later to ban strategic offensive weapons "on land, in the water and air in two stages, the first over five years and the second over a second five years." Somewhat in contradiction to this, he also alleged that "the president agreed, although without particular enthusiasm, to eliminate all—I stress—all, and not merely some particular strategic offensive weapons."

Could these seeming contradictions in Gorbachev's accounts be incidental? We suggest that they are not. Rather, the different remarks were addressed to two different audiences: to Western public opinion and to the U.S. president. In the former case it was necessary to show that if it had not been for the stubbornness of the Americans, the world would have been saved from the thermonuclear nightmare hanging over it, a particular Gorbachev concern. In the latter case the door to future negotiations should not be slammed shut. Gorbachev was preserving the opportunity to continue negotiating with the United States.

To return to the actual talks at the time they took place, Gorbachev had evidently decided well in advance to accept almost any compromise needed in regard to weapons reductions. As noted, this possibility had been clearly presaged in the Shabanov article as early as mid-August. When in the course of the talks problems arose in regard to strategic missiles, Gorbachev apparently instructed his aides in the working group not to include intermediate-range missiles or FBS in strategic cuts. In regard to INF, he not only directed them to agree to disregard the French and British forces but, to the surprise of the United States, endorsed the zero-option that had been official U.S. and NATO policy for so many years. Similarly, he seems to have directed his experts to far-reaching concessions in regard to other weapons issues.

The tactical idea was masterful. Almost the entire time was taken up in gaining agreements in these areas, agreements that by their nature could not help but excite the president and encourage him to respond in kind. This did several things. First, it kept the central focus fully on arms control, where Gorbachev wanted it, and not on human rights, regional conflicts, and so forth. Of course, there was a working group for these issues, but it was left in isolation while the two leaders spent their time as Gorbachev wanted and directed their attention toward the arms control committee of experts and advisers.

Second, focusing on offensive-arms reductions put off the real, in Soviet eyes, issue of SDI and defensive systems until the last minute. Then it could be suddenly raised as the prerequisite for all of the marvelously dramatic achievements to which Reagan would have so enthusiastically assented.

Third, it had another very important effect. Normally in the United States every arms control variation is excruciatingly vetted through multiple bureaucracies whose large numbers of experts on every possible aspect and implication examine it with care. Reagan had his principal experts with him, but they were not in a position to benefit from the advice of all their subordinates. More critically, the pace and nature of the proceedings meant that the U.S. experts were presumably being given the task of putting together the details of agreements already reached by Gorbachev and the president virtually alone rather than of examining them and searching for flaws. Because Gorbachev was apparently controlling the agenda and had obviously prepared himself well over weeks or months, not a mere ten days, the Soviets were not under such disadvantages. This aspect explains why the Americans at Reykjavik could actually agree to an INF zero-option. Whatever the option's real merits or demerits and despite the fact that it had all along been the declared U.S. and NATO position, the Americans' agreeing to it was subsequently greeted with total dismay by the West European governments and many U.S. strategic advisers. One can be sure that in the normal course of regular negotiations the objections later raised in these quarters would have been very carefully considered and taken into account.

Finally, at the very end of the talks, after reaching agreements of "breathtaking" scope, Gorbachev sprang the jaws of his trap. Everything—including even the INF agreement that the Soviets had for months indicated could be reached independently of other outcomes—was made dependent upon U.S. abandonment of SDI. Reagan tried to convince Gorbachev otherwise, and even repeated the earlier public offer to share the technology with the USSR. None of this worked, of course, for the Soviet intent all along had been to manipulate affairs so that either SDI would be killed or full blame for failure could be as convincingly as possible placed upon Reagan and his SDI.

Gorbachev evidently tried one more concession, offering to accept even stricter controls for verification, and reportedly an understanding was reached on such a program. But still the Soviet leader insisted on the whole package, including the effective termination of SDI. Under this condition it became senseless to continue the meeting. Reagan rose and collected his papers. The negotiations had come to an end. It was time for the mutual recriminations and Gorbachev's ever more one-sided descriptions of what had taken place to begin.

As well as can be reconstructed, this is what happened at Reykjavik. The questions remaining are why, what Reykjavik tells us about Gorbachev and his policies, and what Reykjavik implies for the future.

It appears that in planning this careful buildup, Gorbachev and his advisers had two scenarios in mind for the outcome. One had to be the success of the negotiations. Reagan might accept all of Gorbachev's arms reductions offers and trade SDI in return. Certainly, there was a great deal in the U.S. press, which is closely followed in Moscow, to suggest that faced with uncertain prospects for adequate financing from Congress and desirous of being remembered in history as the man who achieved real reductions in nuclear armaments, Reagan would make the so-called historic compromise. The Reagan administration had many times argued that U.S. firmness and the U.S. buildup would bring the Soviets to real arms control. Moreover, old Washington hands like Dobrynin and experts on U.S. politics like Arbatov were certainly attuned to the fact that there were many people, including members of the president's own party, who were advising him to do just that. Finally, there is a logic to Gorbachev's tactics at Geneva that is consistent with this scenario. Everything was conducted in a way so as to appear to give Reagan almost everything else he might want in arms control, and to imply that the other issues dividing the superpowers would then fall easily into line. Then, when these things had assumed almost irresistible proportions, would come the demand for termination of SDI.

A second scenario also fits the events. In it the Soviets either envisaged or expected the failure of the negotiations. Moscow had to enter the meeting in the best possible light, the talks had to come as close as possible to achieving the kind of results that so many people around the world fervently hoped for, and then all the blame for coming up short would be seen as accruing to the United States. In that event, a well-defined, multistage propaganda extravaganza would—and did—follow: Moscow would break one of the norms of negotiations and publicize aspects, all carefully selected and slanted for maximum effect, that had not been intended for publication. The goal here would be to influence decisively world and U.S. public opinion. This would both bring great pressure on the United States to cave in over SDI later and, even more desirable from the Soviet point of view, might well lead the U.S. Congress to effectively kill or at least hamstring SDI and the whole Reagan military buildup. A reading of the Soviet press in the weeks preceding Reykjavik reveals a heightened awareness of congressional tendencies in this direction.

The fact that the Reykjavik gambit was timed to occur just before the U.S. elections fits both scenarios. The timing ensured maximum pressure on the United States to accept the package, and offered the greatest chance of tilting electoral scales in favor of the Democrats, who were considerably less enthusiastic than Republicans about SDI and traditionally more prone to making concessions to the Soviets in arms control.

Our analysis of the separate aspects of Gorbachev's policies and of developments, especially during the months just preceding the Iceland summit, clearly indicates that either scenario outcome was acceptable to Moscow. What is less clear is which was preferred or expected. To judge this, we need to review our earlier evidence in the context of each scenario. At the same time we can see what Reykjavik demonstrated in regard to our earlier conclusions.

As documented throughout this book, Gorbachev had effectively consolidated his power, at least at the top. Nevertheless, he needs to ensure its continuation. His chosen vehicle for both of these tasks has been the revitalization of Soviet society and the economy, but without jeopardizing the system guaranteeing the Communist Party's and, hence, his own monopoly of power. Internally his initial boost to the economy proved fleeting, and the inherent contradictions and resistance of the system have pushed him toward ever-thinner ice in regard to safeguarding the position of the Party. The external answer to achieving his dual goals (reconciling the irreconcilable in the political and economic systems) was to gain access to foreign investment, trade, and technology, and to limit or reduce his own military costs by removing the threat of the Reagan military buildup and SDI. But just as with the internal component of his strategy for making his mark in history, the external corollary had met with no visible success. In the first scenario for Reykjavik, there was an opportunity to put an "exclamation point" on Gorbachev's search for policy successes that would guarantee his personal survival at the top. In the second scenario the opportunity was for a "comma" marking the transition to success via political pressure that would at least abort the U.S. military buildup, and might do so at virtually no cost to the Soviet military machine.

For these purposes, probably Gorbachev's main personal priority, stopping SDI and reducing nuclear arsenals would be a bird in hand, giving his economic program a boost and greatly adding to his prestige and personal security. Discrediting Reagan and SDI might well eventually bring an equal success at less cost, but it was both uncertain of succeeding in its ultimate goal and it delayed achievement of the kind of success that he needed to prevent opposition from arising at home. Either way, it is a reasonable assumption that without the U.S. intention to deploy SDI and without the need for economic reform in the USSR, Gorbachev would not have insisted with such haste on the Reykjavik summit.

In our earlier examination of Gorbachev's foreign policy in regard to the West, we concluded that his preferred goal was a temporary, tactical detente with the United States, temporary and tactical because nothing indicates a willingness to abandon the historic, global struggle. An agreement at Reykjavik would have given Gorbachev his U.S.-Soviet detente in one fell swoop. Moreover, there would be no real need to follow a dramatic arms control agreement, including the aborting of SDI, with the implied concessions on human rights and other issues around the world. Western public opinion and political realities could be counted upon to guarantee that the United States would go ahead with such an arms control deal once it was announced regardless of these other issues. Further, experience had demonstrated that given an arms control detente, Western publics and parliamentarians have tended blissfully and thankfully to turn to other, internal issues, and their support for military buildups or global activism has faded. In such an environment Western business could also be counted upon to demand effectively a dramatic reduction in the barriers against trade and technology transfer. All Moscow would have to do would be to avoid initiating some new aggression on the order of Afghanistan.

The second Soviet scenario for Reykjavik would not give this result, but it would not preclude it for the future. However, our previous analysis also identified a parallel, fallback strategy of splitting the West and achieving selective detente with U.S. industrial allies. The second Reykjavik strategy was made to order for this. Moreover, both Reykjavik scenarios contained one component that, as it turned out, was sure to put a new strain on the NATO alliance: the zero-option in INF. Western European governments had accepted it and in some cases encouraged it to satisfy domestic politics, but they had never wanted to see it accepted. The U.S. INF deployments in Europe had been in response to West European requests. In the eyes of Washington's principal allies these weapons were the guarantee of the linkage to the U.S. strategic nuclear umbrella. An actual zero-option agreement would terrify Western European governments, who would feel themselves at the mercy of a perceived irresistible Soviet conventional military superiority. NATO strategy and the comfortable absence of the necessity to jeopardize their economies by massive military buildups were both based on the U.S. nuclear guarantee. Even the realization that the United States was ready to agree to a zero-option put all of this at risk. With or without an agreement's being put into effect, an additional strain would be placed between Washington and its major European allies.

Finally, we earlier identified a last-ditch fallback strategy of total confrontation. Agreement at Reykjavik would avoid this undesirable alternative while putting the blame on Reagan and the United States for failure, would facilitate justification of the kind of siege mentality in the Soviet and Eastern European populations that such an option would have to include.

As noted above, either way it came out, the meeting in Iceland would not affect Soviet policy in the Third World because it would not really be necessary to follow a comprehensive nuclear arms agreement with agreements and changes of policy toward various regional sources of tension. Actually, however, the second Iceland scenario could give an additional boost to Soviet propaganda aimed at increasing anti-Americanism and mobilizing Third World support for declared Soviet nuclear policies. It would reinforce Moscow's favorite thesis that U.S. imperialism and aggressive ambitions were blocking the freeing of resources to support Third World economic concerns.

In fact, had Gorbachev really been interested in arms control as a means to real guarantees of peace and detente, he should have taken a very different approach: giving greater priority to the other differences between the superpowers. According to Leninist ideology as well as any realistic analysis of history, it is not weapons levels that create tensions and conflicts, although they can certainly add to fears. Rather, it is political, economic, and ideological rivalries and conflicts of interests that lead to weapons buildups. Arms reductions only scale down the parameters involved; they do not affect the basic roots of rivalry and competition. Moreover, they limit the forms of potential warfare only if they are truly equitable and *observed*. As long as the fundamental causes of conflict remain, there is an almost irresistible temptation on the part of the rivals to cheat on agreed arms limitations. Further, this temptation is much easier for a totalitarian society to succumb to than it is for a pluralistic society with a free press.

Resolution of more fundamental rivalries—particularly Soviet aggressive expansionism and the attempt to change the status quo by revolution rather than evolution, especially in the Third World—would greatly reduce the need for massive military arsenals. Similarly, if the USSR would act at home more in accord with Western values in human rights and in a more open and tolerant way, it would greatly reduce Western suspicions and have the same results. In the face of economic costs and inordinate nuclear overkill, arms reductions could easily follow from such changes but would be relatively meaningless without them. Not only would more than enough terrifying weaponry remain as long as virtually total nuclear disarmament did not occur but modern conventional weaponry is fully sufficient to wreak far more havoc on a global scale than World War II did in Central Europe. Actually, the danger of war could increase from any hypothetical elimination of nuclear weapons not accompanied by other, far more fundamental changes in behavior and policy. This is the case because the inhibiting factor of mutual assured destruction, which it can be argued is precisely what kept the fragile peace in Europe for the past forty years, would be removed and Soviet conventional military superiorities would be more meaningful.

The evidence shows that SDI is terribly frightening to the Soviet military establishment, and that stopping SDI and slowing down the whole U.S. military modernization are crucial to continued defense establishment support of the rest of Gorbachev's policies. Some of the reasons for this are worth elaboration.

SDI threatens to nullify all the gains the Soviet military has made in shifting the strategic nuclear correlation of forces and to deprive it of the prescriptive possibility of a war-winning deterrence and means of exerting political pressure. It does not even have to succeed in providing an impervious shield protecting the U.S. population and economy to do this. Even a partial SDI would make Soviet war-fighting so uncertain and the possibility of achieving the necessary goals of preemptive, or deliberate surprise, attack so problematical that any Soviet rational-actor decision making would have much greater hesitation in considering it. Deterrence, and hence the inhibitions against U.S. active response to more limited Soviet aggressive activities or political pressure would be increased.

Probably better than anyone else in the USSR, the military establishment knows that Soviet technology and the current economic capabilities cannot keep up with a concerted and sustained U.S. effort to develop a real SDI. At the same time the incontrovertible evidence of a long-extant, if of necessity more measured, Soviet program to develop the same kinds of SDI technologies and the abundant body of theoretical writings appearing before SDI was announced and before Moscow's political line changed to stress nuclear disarmament both clearly indicate that the Soviets believe that SDI is technologically possible and/or that it encompasses capabilities that can be decisive in a strategic offensive role. (In fact, Soviet military writing before the political line changed frequently noted that space was the new high ground in military affairs, and that exotic e.g. beam weapons, and the like were the next offensive stage beyond nuclear missiles.)

Further, the Soviet military is very conscious of the fact that SDI has implications that go far beyond strategic nuclear defenses or offenses. SDI programs involve and require major advances in microelectronics and in computers for battle management and weapons accuracy. Lasers and other exotic weapons have direct applications on the terrestrial battlefield, whether it is nuclear or purely conventional. A majority of theoreticians in the Soviet military have for several years been stressing the high-technology, high-speed, deep-penetration warfare of the future. Soviet military writing exhibits great concern over similar Western trends, epitomized in long-distance remote-controlled precision weapons and in the U.S. air-land battle doctrine. Because these technologies represent the greatest area of comparative U.S. advantage, they are precisely the ones in which the Soviets would be least able to keep up with a concerted and sustained Western program.

Finally, the Soviet defense leadership seems to have accepted the Ogarkov argument that Soviet industry and its research and development structure need to be reconstructed in order to provide the high-technology weapons of the future battlefield, a battlefield regarding which Soviet doctrine has been shifting to try to find a non-nuclear answer to assured victory. Because of this, the senior military leadership has largely accepted the argument that overall revitalization and upgrading of the economy are the best way to ensure that its capabilities meet these needs.

Gorbachev's first Reykjavik scenario—a full agreement—would provide the respite from the U.S. SDI that would be needed for the Soviets to hope to catch up. Also, it could have distinct advantages in military terms, advantages for which the Soviet defense establishment undoubtedly hoped. At Reykjavik the two national leaders were talking about the basic, general outlines of a full agreement. It would still remain for many fine and very critical details to be worked out on precise numbers, sublimits, definitions of what new or modernized weapons were allowable, and so on. Once Western publics were told that such dramatic agreements had been achieved, it would be much harder for U.S. negotiators to stand firm on all of these details. Unlike their Soviet counterparts, they would be concerned about risking the expectations of the voters, upon whom the fortunes of the political leadership depend. The Soviet military would have a good reason to believe that the final outcome would not be nearly as equitable and balanced as the original agreement suggested. Further, once SDI was offered up as a sacrifice to a nuclear weapons reduction, still to be fully worked out, U.S. budgetary concerns would be likely to ensure that funding was greatly reduced. Finally, even if the agreement eventually proved short-lived, the Soviet defense research programs would have gained valuable time to close existing and potential gaps. For all of these reasons Gorbachev's first Iceland scenario was acceptable to the military and the wider defense establishment.

The same rationale would attract the military to the second scenario. However, even though the final outcome would remain uncertain, many if not most of the defense leaders can be assumed to have preferred this second scenario over the first. To start with, it represented a more traditional Soviet tactic, and military leaderships are normally more conservative than are other policymakers in regard to such activities. More important, if psychological and political pressure alone could emasculate the U.S. threat, the impact on Soviet vested defense interests would be minimized and military planners would be spared the agonizing reappraisals required by major shifts in available weaponry. If anything, Reykjavik demonstrated that SDI looms even larger in Soviet calculations than previously indicated. In addition, it confirmed that for all his fine words, Gorbachev—just as much as any previous Soviet leader—is fully committed to waging the "historic struggle" and to unrelenting pursuit of Soviet relative advantage in the perceived East-West contest for global predominance.

In terms of the question as to which of the two scenarios was preferred or expected by the Soviets, the answer is still uncertain. Our conclusion is that *either* outcome was acceptable and worth the effort. As to preferences, they probably varied among the different policymakers who put the Reykjavik gambit together. For reasons explained, Gorbachev himself may have hoped more for an agreement on his terms. Others, particularly the defense establishment could accept that but probably felt more comfortable with the second scenario. What Moscow expected can be argued either way, but there can be no doubt that the careful buildup, the fostering of exaggerated Western expectations, and the obviously well prepared propaganda blitz following the summit meeting conform to a carefully thought out disinformation plan and its subsequent exploitation. Moreover, the fact that Gorbachev suddenly went back on his earlier clear indications that an INF agreement would not depend upon any SDI linkage seems to fit a trap scenario designed to put blame on the United States better than it fits a scenario designed to force the American president into a corner where he would have to trade away his SDI.

In regard to this question, the reader will have to draw his or her own conclusions. Throughout this book the coauthors have had little or no difficulty in agreeing on the judgments expressed. This is the one real exception. One author believes that the primary goal was to force Reagan to give Gorbachev the agreement he proposed, with the placing of blame for failure on Reagan and SDI as a fallback, a highly acceptable but still the secondary goal. The other author believes that the whole thing was first and foremost a tactical gambit in a longer game, with the possibility of an actual agreement only an acceptable alternative that had to be taken into account.

What else did Reykjavik mean? Was there really a winner and a loser? Here the answer has to be that at least initially Gorbachev won more in Iceland than he lost, even if his main hope was to conclude an agreement. However, the extent, significance, and durability of his gains are debatable.

By manipulating the meeting so that arms control hugely overshadowed all other possible issues, Gorbachev gained an important edge. He also scored a gain for the image of the USSR. Whenever the West agrees to negotiate with Moscow on disarmament without insisting on a clear linkage to other issues that really divide East and West, it inevitably obfuscates the real differences between the two sides. It reinforces the idea that the qualitative, social, and political differences are irrelevant, that what counts is some kind of abstract commonality: They both have similar quantities of lethal weapons that must be diminished so that peace and prosperity can reign over the earth. This eclipses the aggressive nature of Soviet policy, the Soviet drive to change the global status quo and correlations—a drive that has brought the world to the brink of global war at least once and that constantly exacerbates regional tensions and encourages local wars. Few intellectual concepts are either so erroneous or so dangerous to freedom as the idea that the superpowers are mere mirror images, equally rapacious and equally to blame for humankind's many troubles. For all the faults and self-serving or misguided interventions of the West, the differences are fundamental.

Second, Gorbachev and his carefully rehearsed associates certainly had some success in furthering the part of their propaganda and public relations strategy that seeks to convince world opinion that the USSR is really changing, that its new leaders are normal civilized statesmen and quite possibly liberalizers. There is far too great a tendency on the part of far too large a proportion of Western publics and, sad to say, some otherwise hardheaded politicians—who more than anyone should know better—to equate good manners and surface gloss or charm with good intentions and with nonaggressive motivations.

On balance, too, the Soviets demonstrated that the new leadership may be more effective diplomatically than its main rivals in the West. Gorbachev clearly maneuvered Reagan into largely dancing to his tune. Further, the consistent way in which Gorbachev presented to the world his implied willingness to redress human rights and trade greater emigration from the USSR for an agreement but carefully avoided giving any hints of these possibilities to domestic audiences in the USSR stood in sharp contrast to the all too frequent contradictions and confusions in Western accounts of the meeting.

In terms of the agreements reached and then, of course, nullified, the picture is more complex. The most militarily and politically significant of these was the sweeping zero-option for INF. Certainly, Reagan appeared to have made a mistake in saying yes to it. At least for a while this "agreement" frightened West European governments and strategists and put strains upon NATO. The dismay it generated among many of the president's own politico-military advisers predictably led to an apparent subsequent U.S. disavowal of it. The turnabout could only damage the U.S. administration's image of competency. As undoubtedly a large majority of strategists in the West see it, without a clear linkage to the U.S. strategic nuclear umbrella and without a nuclear basis for NATO strategy, overwhelming Soviet conventional superiorities in Europe would be decisive in allowing political pressure and blackmail to be applied. They even might well tempt the USSR to embark upon a military conquest. According to this line of thinking, Gorbachev blundered by insisting on the linkage between an INF agreement and SDI, a step that may reinforce the argument that his primary strategy at Reykjavik was to embarrass Reagan, not reach the agreement package he proposed.

On the other hand, in spite of the very real quantitative Warsaw Pact superiorities in hardware and in ready divisions, it is not at all certain that Soviet military planners would share the confidence that they really could win a conventional war. Quality is also a real factor. NSWP forces may well be distrusted. Although NATO force comparisons routinely leave out the French, the Soviet General Staff is not likely to do so, nor is it likely to ignore the very sizeable mobilization potential of such forces as the large West German territorial troops. Moreover, without a quick and total victory, heavily dependent upon the uncertainties of achieving real surprise, the incomparably greater industrial mobilization potential of Western Europe and the United States would come into play. The real ability of the Kremlin to exploit conventional superiority politically may be more in the eyes of the West than in those of the Soviets. Unfortunately, perceptions could be more important than realities in this regard.

Further, given the existence of the French and British forces, and particularly the huge short-range, "tactical" nuclear capabilities of both sides, even an INF zero-option would not lead to a non-nuclear European equation. Military strategists of all stripes in Western Europe and the United States have long given verbal support to the idea that NATO must dramatically improve its conventional balance vis-à-vis the Warsaw Pact, a capability that the West certainly has if it can ever muster the political will. By making it clear that an INF *missile* zero-option (it was missiles, not deep-strike aircraft, that Reagan agreed to zero out) could be a real possibility, the United States may in the long run have added some impetus to the forces seeking to improve NATO's conventional deterrence. At a minimum, the possibility of such an agreement forces Western strategists and decision makers out of comfortable ruts and into more creative thinking—which has to be a good thing.

Finally, it must be recognized that whatever its impact in Europe, Reagan's agreement on INF was not inconsistent with one aspect of U.S. self-interest. For Washington, as long as deterrence can be maintained in some other way, any *automatic* linkage between aggression in Europe and the nuclear destruction of the United States is hardly desirable.

Nor is it at all clear, other than in public image, who won or lost by the failure to conclude an agreement for deep cuts in strategic offensive forces. Even much deeper cuts than those foreseen for the first phase would not affect either side's ability effectively to destroy the other's society and perhaps even civilization itself. All the fine words about totally eliminating superpower nuclear weapons really cannot be taken very seriously as long as more basic sources of rivalry and conflict exist and as long as other states possess or potentially possess such weapons. Much more water would have to flow over the dam before negotiations and implementation of such an idealistic (and naive) hope could be actually realized. Meanwhile, through reductions both sides would undoubtedly save some money, although it is not really clear that the amounts would be truly significant. Strategic weaponry other than SDI represents a mere drop in the bucket of overall military expenditures. Further, the transferability to the civilian economy of expertise and production capabilities associated with strategic ballistic missiles is undoubtedly much less than that of tanks to tractors or the effects of releasing large numbers of conventional forces troops to the civilian work force. Finally, there is an inescapable logic to the proposition that SDI would be much easier to develop and deploy if accompanied by real limitations on the offensive forces it is designed to counter.

Rather than practical or concrete, the real danger to the West of dramatic nuclear arms reductions and agreements is psychological. Lulled by such agreements, even relatively meaningless ones, Western publics and legislatures have demonstrated a disconcerting tendency to cut off financial support for needed military programs permitted by the treaties. Needless to say, the USSR operates under no such constraints. Effective leadership can theoretically limit this kind of damage in the West, but the precedents are not encouraging.

All of this aside, the real question in terms of who won or lost at Reykjavik, and what was won or lost, relates to the success of the second Soviet scenario. Because the meeting did not produce any agreements, what remains to be asked is whether Gorbachev was succcessful in placing the blame on Reagan, whether any such success is translatable into future gains, and how great those gains might be.

To some degree Gorbachev did apparently succeed in scapegoating the president, although in the United States at least the initial public opinion polls supported by a large majority Reagan's refusal to agree to the whole package. Nor is it likely that Reykjavik really contributed to Democratic gains in the November elections. It is possible that a dramatic agreement would have saved some Republican seats, but the converse, that failure to reach agreement lost seats that would have been won, is much less likely to have been true. Off-year elections are normally decided by local issues, and this seems to have been the case in 1986. On the other hand, Reagan preserved SDI and military modernization, even if they are in some potential budgetary dangers. Moreover, in future negotiations, having agreed to sweeping reductions, Gorbachev and the Soviet leadership will be hard put to take them back. If his priority goal was the package of agreements, this may not be a loss for Gorbachev. But if his main intent was simply to discredit the United States and to increase future pressure for unilateral disarmament measures, Gorbachev may have made a move that he may come to regret.

More to the point, Reykjavik rather quickly disappeared from Western political consciousness in wake of the Iran imbroglio. As adroit as Gorbachev's tactics have been, self-inflicted wounds such as Iran and the unfortunate disclosure of a disinformation campaign against Libya, plus the continuing U.S. budget deficit, are much more likely to undermine Western unity, resolve, and willingness to persevere.

Gorbachev's trap at Reykjavik was very well laid and played; but these other factors, along with the buildup to the 1988 US presidential elections and a resurgent Democratic Party seeking to increase the gains they made at the congressional level in 1986, were probably at least equally responsible for what followed.

Reykjavik was followed by a relative hiatus in arms control. By the beginning of 1987, as the various negotiating forums reconvened on schedule, Gorbachev and the Soviets had prepared themselves to move ahead with maximum public pressure on the US and the West.

First, Gorbachev announced that the USSR would, "reluctantly," have to resume nuclear testing when the US next conducted a weapons test; but he kept his eye on image and public opinion by stating that Moscow was still prepared to stop when the US did. An interesting sidelight had to say something about the seriousness of earlier Soviet affirmations of their willingness to allow open, more effective test monitoring. When, in February, the USSR did conduct its first nuclear test since the moratorium, the American academics who had been allowed with such fanfare to set up their seismic monitoring equipment at Semiplatinsk were told to turn off their devices during the test.

Then, in February, Gorbachev announced "another" concession. Once again he indicated that an INF treaty could be acceptable without linkage to SDI and strategic defenses; returning in this aspect to his announced pre-Reykjavik position. With this barrier removed, both sides evidently concentrated on INF at Geneva. The scheduled session of the three-part strategic arms talks was extended for two days in early March and a special INF session was held later in the month.

In April, Gorbachev made another concession, one hinted at in Iceland. During his Prague visit Gorbachev announced that Moscow was prepared to negotiate reductions or elimination of shorter-range nuclear missiles in Europe simultaneously with the intermediate missiles. This was important for more than one reason. West European governments and a significant number of American strategists had faulted the US willingness to agree to an INF-missile zero option on the basis that such a step would leave the Soviets with unanswered superiorities in shorter range nuclear weapons and in conventional forces in Europe. A partial answer to these charges had been made by the US administration when it began to much more firmly tie its Reykjavik willingness to agree on INF missiles to a simultaneous balancing or elimination of the shorter range missiles. If any in the West had thought that the latter weapons would prove a bar to an INF agreement perceived as dangerous, Gorbachev had cut some of the ground out from under them. At the same time, he had strengthened the hand of those Western advisors who felt that an INF agreement, even by itself, was nevertheless in the West's interest.

This step also gave Moscow another issue with which to pressure the West Germans and possibly increase NATO alliance strains. Negotiating shorter range missiles allowed Moscow to more credibly raise the issue of the West German Pershing-Is whose nuclear warheads were retained in US hands. For a while it looked as if this would be a real sticking point; but Bonn eventually announced its willingness to refrain from modernizing these weapons and to eventually eliminate them when, and if, the US and Soviets agreed to and implemented an elimination of both intermediate and shorter range nuclear missiles in Europe.

The West German and several other NATO governments, especially the British and French, had expressed grave reservations over an INF zeroing in isolation from other adjustments in force balance levels. However, these governments, the French less than the others, were under strong domestic public pressure to agree to the deal; and it is evident that they were being heavily lobbied by the US administration to endorse it. What is not entirely clear is which of these twin pressures was decisive in their all coming to accept the radical removal of a whole class of weapons, with all of the real implications for NATO's strategy of flexible response, controlled escalation and linkage of the US strategic nuclear umbrella to the defense of Europe. On balance, the most likely answer is that both pressures played an important role with US lobbying being decisive and with Gorbachev's willingness to include shorter range missiles being a critical additional inducement. To the extent that US administration pressure played a role, it seems likely that it left many West European leaders with a bad taste. European conservatives and most European military strategists had fought a long battle against usually large anti-nuclear, anti-American and pacifist elements of their publics. Now they had the ground cut out from under them and could no longer blame the Americans for their unwillingness to accommodate these parts of their political constituencies. Such feelings could only add to underlying tensions within the Western alliance and would undoubtedly make the Europeans more vulnerable to increased future pacifist and accommodationist public pressure in regard to other aspects of military strength. In turn this could be expected to increase European pressure on Washington to come to agreements on additional arms control, including measures that would stop or slow the SDI. It would take an unusual degree of leadership resolve and exceptional political skills for West European governments to convince their populaces that a resultant removal of nuclear missiles from the theater equation required a commensurate increase in conventional forces and capabilities at the expense of various popular social and economic programs.

By late summer 1987 it was evident that a zero-option INF treaty was almost sure to be completed before the end of the year; unless, of course, Gorbachev repeated his last minute reversal by demanding a linkage to the SDI. Whatever the objective merits for the US and the West of a treaty eliminating intermediate and shorter range missiles in Europe without it being accompanied by treaties adjusting the strategic nuclear and conventional balances (and there are many who argue for and many who oppose this,) the likelihood of such an outcome and the ways in which it had been facilitated undoubtedly advanced many of Mikhail Gorbachev's avowed goals and the traditional objectives of Soviet foreign policy, objectives which were hardly intended to eliminate rivalry between East and West or to hamper Soviet abilities to apply political-military pressure on the West.

Meanwhile, the US and Soviets announced in May that their negotiators had come to agreement on a new treaty to establish nuclear crisis control centers (NCC). This modest agreement was hailed as a major event since it was the first bilateral arms-related agreement reached since Reagan and Gorbachev had come to office. This treaty undoubtedly provided some improved modalities for superpower consultation and cooperation in minor crises between them and for such worrisome possibilities as third-party nuclear actions and nuclear terrorism; or at least it would *if* the parties were really prepared to utilize the NCCs. But it was liable to prove irrelevant to any full-blown US-Soviet or East-West military crisis. What it did was to provide the Americans with some claim to progress and partial success with the Soviets. More importantly, for Gorbachev it added to the general atmosphere of inexorably rising pressure and support for detente and arms control.

On the other hand, there was virtually no sign of any substantive progress in conventional arms control. The Soviets continued to express their readiness for major reductions in conventional forces and, undoubtedly with Moscow's blessing, Polish leader Jaruzelsky floated yet another conventional arms option. The Polish proposal called for deep reductions by both sides, not only in numbers of personnel, but also in various categories of equipment. This resuscitated a long-standing Soviet demand to include weapons in MBFR. More realistically, however, it only served to cloud the issues since an additional proliferation of possible and competing forums and formulas for conventional arms reductions could well result in all being stalemated.

Over the same time frame, to fall 1987, US and Soviet negotiators and experts continued to meet on chemical weapons and nuclear testing. In the latter area, there was little real sign of progress toward any agreement that would end all nuclear weapons testing. However, by the end of summer Moscow seemed clearly more willing to begin with partial measures that would improve verification and allow the US government to ratify the TTBT and the US seemed to be edging toward a clearer commitment to eventually seek a total nuclear test ban.

Progress in CW was also claimed as the Soviets apparently partially acquiesced to a more complete program of OSI than they had previously agreed to. This, OSI, brings us to the final development in the drama leading to an apparently imminent INF treaty. Moreover, it was a development that seemed to turn the two sides' positions topsy turvy.

Washington had long insisted on rigid and comprehensive provisions for almost unrestricted on-demand OSI, both in CW and INF as well as, in large measure, in other negotiations. Except for the limited agreement in CSCBMDE, Moscow had not backed up its generalized public assertions of willingness with any concrete actions. By summer, this situation seemed to change. The first indication of a real Soviet willingness to contemplate wide-ranging, hard-toothed OSI apparently came in CW. Strangely—but not really surprisingly if one had really thought about it—this generated second thoughts in the US. It was one thing to demand unrestricted, on-demand access to Soviet state facilities, but it was another to give the same access to Soviet inspectors. It was not simply, or even in the case of CW, necessarily a matter of American insincerity. In the West, potential chemical agent producers are largely private industries operating on contracts from the government, not state industries. Unrestricted access by foreigners, including actual or potential commercial rivals, would run into many potential difficulties involving commercial law, property rights, and industrial secrets.

At the same time, the looming possibility of really agreeing to unrestricted OSI began to generate expressions of concern in other quarters by intelligence officials and hard-line anti-Communists who feared that such rights would allow espionage fishing expeditions into areas not included in a CW or other arms control agreement. This concern soon was expressed in regard to INF OSI. Apparently the first public expression came from a West German official who indicated reservations about giving Soviet arms control inspectors too free access to NATO military facilities, but it soon became a matter of discussion in the US as well. By fall it was Washington which, in fact, seemed to be backing off from and compromising on its earlier demands for comprehensive and wide-ranging OSI. Some justified this by the argument that a treaty totally banning weapons systems did not require as strict a set of verification measures as a deep reductions treaty would; but the nuances of such an argument were unlikely to impress skeptics. By accepting, and possibly even exceeding, Western demands publically, Gorbachev had apparently succeeded in preventing their actually being fully implemented. One cannot know for certain whether he was ever really serious about opening up the USSR to real OSI except in a very carefully controlled and limited way, or whether the whole episode represented a highly sophisticated propaganda tactic. Both answers are possible. Considering all things, Soviet history and internal political ramifications, it is very likely that the latter was the case. Mikhail Gorbachev had already demonstrated at Reykjavik that such machiavellian reverse tactics were not beyond him.

Finally, one has to ask whether an imminent INF treaty in the absence of any linkage to SDI represents a victory or a loss for Gorbachev. (One could ask the same question for Ronald Reagan, but this is after all a book about Gorbachev.) Certainly in Iceland the Soviet leader had firmly tied the two together. Here it is worth noting that, although Soviet rhetoric against SDI, and their efforts to hamstring it via such things as a space agreement and monitoring agency in the CD (which was proposed again in March 1987), had remained strong; its extent, and particularly the degree to which the SDI was tied to all other arms control arenas, somewhat lessened during 1987. Did this mean that stopping the SDI was no longer the central aim of Soviet maneuvering? Hardly. What had to be increasingly clear and encouraging to Gorbachev was that the overall arms control atmosphere, combined with US budget problems and domestic politics, was making it increasingly uncertain whether the Reagan administration could continue with the SDI. Whatever else its implications in the East-West struggle and balance, an INF treaty seemed certain to increase the probability that the challenge of the SDI and indeed of the whole Reagan military buildup would self-destruct.

In sum, by spring of 1987 it was the Soviets and Gorbachev who seemed to be standing firm in arms control while the US, beset with political and budgetary difficulties, gave the impression of being the side ready to compromise on previous demands, a condition reminiscent of the early and mid-1970s. It is not entirely certain that this judgement is a fair one. After all, it remains possible that the US can extract something fairly tangible out of Moscow in terms of its behavior in the Third World, human rights, etc. It is also possible that an INF agreement will either set the stage for more meaningful treaties in conventional force reductions, or will lead to the US and West Europe actually taking the hard steps necessary to rectify perceived imbalances in other systems and forces, and that the SDI will not be unilaterally gutted in Washington. If so, the Reagan strategy will be justified. If not, however, it is likely that Gorbachev will have achieved a very great victory, at least psychologically and perhaps also in real military terms.

In any event, the post-Reykjavik period seems to indicate that Gorbachev has gained the upper hand. At a minimum, he has again demonstrated that he is very skillful at maneuvering in the international political arena. Whether his policies on arms control also indicate that he is seeking to fundamentally change the USSR's approach to foreign policy and to the "historical struggle" is a much more dubious proposition. Before we can assess this latter possibility, we need to look at the rest of Gorbachev's foreign policy and, particularly, at his military policies.

Selected Arms Control Chronology

(In addition to entries in this chronology, arms control issues featured prominently in almost all of the political and economic meetings between Gorbachev and visitors, as well as in many involving other senior Soviet leaders (see other chronologies). There were also frequent, regular arms control press briefings by senior officials).

March 1985

11	Mikhail Gorbachev was elected general secretary, CPSU.
12	The first round of U.S.-Soviet strategic weapons negotiations opened on schedule in Geneva and continued until 23 April with little indication of progress. Thereafter, a pattern of three such sessions a year was maintained, one early in the year, one from late spring or early summer to mid summer and one in the fall. Except where significant developments occurred, these subsequent sessions are not specifically identified in this chronology.
25	A Foreign Ministry delegation held working-level talks with the Australians, in Canberra, on space arms control, nuclear testing, and so on. Throughout the next two and one-half years such consultations with US allies were very common, particularly just prior to and just after major negotiating sessions, summits and the like. While most US allies were given this treatment, the greatest emphasis was on the Germans, British and French. Only the more significant of these meetings and consultations are listed in the rest of this chronology.

April 1985

8	In a *Pravda* interview, Gorbachev announced a moratorium on further SS-20 deployments until November (when the Dutch government was to decide whether to accept stationing of U.S. INF systems in the Netherlands).
12	U.S.-Soviet Standing Consultative Commission (SCC) opened its regular spring round of discussions on SALT I and ABM treaty issues. The sides clarified two ABM treaty "common understandings" and agreed on limited measures to reduce the risk of accidental nuclear war due to terrorist action. The round closed 14 June after a longer session than

194

usual. The SCC regularly meets twice a year, usually for a few days to two weeks, once in the spring and once in the fall. This continued through the period of this chronology and except for unusually significant meetings SCC sessions are not further listed.

15-19   Foreign Ministry and U.S. Department of State officials held regular NPT (nuclear nonproliferation treaty) consultations in Helsinki.

May 1985

5   The defense minister, Marshal Sokolov, in an official speech denied the existence of any Soviet space weapons programs whatsoever, asserting that the only military programs connected with space were for early warning, reconnaissance, communications, and navigation. With a few notable exceptions, this claim would be regularly repeated in speeches and articles by Soviet civilian and military officials.

14   In speech honoring the thirtieth anniversary of the Warsaw Pact, First deputy commander in chief, General of the Army Gribkov reiterated the Soviet unilateral policy declaration of no first use of nuclear weapons and called for nuclear-free zones in Europe. This standard theme would be repeated in all such speeches throughout the year.

The sixth round of the Conference on Security and Confidence Building Measures and Disarmament in Europe (CSCBMDE) opened in Stockholm and continued until 5 July with little or no real progress reported. The previous round has been from January to late March. CSCBMDE would reconvene on schedule twice more in 1985 (September–October and November–December) and three times in 1986 (January–March, April–July with a short recess in late May to early June, and August–September). Except for major developments the individual sessions are not further listed.

23   The thirty-sixth round of the talks on mutual and balanced force reductions in Europe (MBFR) opened in Vienna and continued until 11 July with little or no progress reported. In the earlier 1985 round, which had run from January to late March, the Soviets had put on the table a "new" proposal remarkably similar to earlier ones. As had been the case for years, MBFR continued to meet three times a year: January to mid-March; a relatively short break, April or May to July; and in the fall from mid-September to about mid-December. Except for major developments these are not further specifically listed.

June 1985

10   The Supreme Soviet ratified earlier announced agreement to open some Soviet nuclear energy plants to IAEC inspection (related to the NPT).

11	The forty-nation Conference on Disarmament (CD) opened its summer round in Geneva and continued until 24 August with no signs of significant progress. A committee for limiting the militarization of space was formed to add to previous ones on chemical weapons, nuclear tests, and so on. The previous session had been from 5 February to 24 March with little signs of anything but atmospherics. The CD regularly meets twice a year at about these same times and, except for major developments, its sessions will not be further listed.
11	A Soviet General Staff spokesman, in a press conference in Moscow, admitted that the USSR had tested an ASAT system (In contrast to the minister of defense's categorical denial of any space-related weapons; see above). The admission was doubly unusual because the text was carried in the Soviet press. Such more candid statements, when they do appear, are usually made verbally to only foreign audiences.
19	GDR and SPD (FRG) representatives jointly called for a chemical-weapons-free zone in Central Europe.
24–25	Italian and Soviet Foreign Ministry representatives met in Moscow to discuss disarmament.

July 1985

5	The Soviet press featured a Gorbachev public letter in response to one received from the Union of Concerned Scientists about nuclear arms control. This is the first of a series of such forums used by Gorbachev to present his views to the world.
16	At the press conference at the end of the second round of US-Soviet strategic nuclear weapons talks (30 May to 16 July), the Soviets claimed that they had made many concrete proposals but the US had made none. The American statement and, even more, subsequent US official reports indicated that the Soviets had begun to address specifics rather than general statements of principle. The Americans also claimed that the Soviets had made an "informal" (i.e. unofficial) proposal for a 30% cut in strategic weapons in return for a ban on the SDI.
25	In connection with another of the regular, major press conferences on arms control issues, the Soviets issued a slick public affairs booklet, "Star Wars: Illusion and Dangers." In October the United States "responded" with its own, "Soviet Strategic Defense Programs," thus continuing the public relations and propaganda war of glossy publications that had been escalating ever since publication of the first issue of *Soviet Military Power* by the U.S. Department of Defense in 1981.

29   Gorbachev announced a unilateral moratorium on nuclear
weapons testing to extend from the anniversary of
Hiroshima (6 August) until the end of the year. The United
States and other nuclear weapons states were urged to join
in it and to make it permanent.

August 1985

13   The Soviets published a three-quarter-page advertisement
in the *New York Times* attacking U.S. obstinacy in regard
to nuclear arms control and on SDI.
14   A major press interview by Gorbachev was published on
nuclear test issues.
17   The Soviet press published the letter from Foreign Minister
Shevardnadze to the United Nations proposing an international conference to develop a treaty banning militarization
of space and to establish a worldwide organization for cooperation in the peaceful development of outer space.
27   The NPT review conference opened in Geneva. It closed a
day late, on 21 September, after all-night negotiations
avoided condemnation of both superpowers in the final
communique.

September 1985

30   At the third round of US-Soviet strategic arms talks (19
September to 7 November) the Soviets began tabling (completed on 1 October) a major "new proposal" (it was given
wide publicity) calling for 50 percent reductions in strategic
offensive arms if SDI were banned. The proposal, however,
counted U.S. FBS aircraft in these totals. At the end of the
round, the United States made a counterproposal.

October 1985

2–5   The Gorbachev-Mitterand summit in Paris. Gorbachev
heavily stressed arms control in his speeches and proposed
direct INF talks with France and the United Kingdom,
both of which rejected the idea. A proposal for a chemical
weapons nonproliferation treaty was also put forth by Gorbachev.
18–23   A regular meeting of Soviet and U.S. officials was held in
Washington to discuss nuclear nonproliferation issues.
22–23   Gorbachev led the Soviet delegation to the meeting of the
Warsaw Pact Political Consultative Committee in Sofia (at
heads-of-state level). The main focus of the communique
was on arms control, with all participants fully endorsing
all Soviet positions.

23   At a press conference following the meeting, the Soviets indicated that an agreement on INF, separate from and regardless of the outcome of talks on strategic offensive and defensive arms, could be possible.

26   The text of the new draft Party Program was published; it emphasized the necessity for arms control and eliminating nuclear weapons.

November 1985

18–20   The Gorbachev-Reagan summit in Geneva. A heavy focus was on arms control, with both sides indicating optimism for the future.

27   Gorbachev made an optimistic speech, reporting on the Geneva summit to the Supreme Soviet.

December 1985

5   The fall round of MBFR (26 September–5 December) closed with NATO tabling a new proposal designed to avoid the data discrepancy issue, but strengthening verification measures.

18   Gorbachev met with the U.S. and Soviet cochairmen of the organization of physicians against nuclear war in another public relations event to support Soviet arms control proposals.

19   The Soviet press featured an offer by Gorbachev to allow "certain measures" of OSI as part of an international verification system for a nuclear test ban if the United States joined. The issue was addressed in terms of an earlier proposal for a nuclear test ban regime made by the heads of six nonaligned states.

27   Gorbachev addressed the foreign diplomatic corps in Moscow, stressing arms control proposals.

31   The SALT II treaty officially expired. Both sides indicated an intent to continue to observe its provisions, dependent upon the other's continued compliance.

January 1986

3   The Soviet press featured Gorbachev's answer to a letter from a leftist member of the Greater London City Council. This was another media event used to present arms control proposals.

13   U.S. and Soviet representatives met in Geneva for informal talks on chemical weapons arms control.

15   Gorbachev made a speech (published 16 January) outlining a proposed three-stage reduction to complete elimination

of nuclear weapons by the year 2000. The proposal would have required U.S. abandonment of SDI and no modernization or increase in French or U.K. nuclear forces. At the same time the Soviet unilateral moratorium on nuclear weapons testing was extended to March. The speech also addressed chemical weapons, and MBFR and CSCBMDE proposals, and called arms control too important to depend on first resolving regional tensions.

February 1986

10   The U.S. and Soviet CD delegations met separately for additional informal bilateral CW talks.
20   At the MBFR session (30 January–20 March), the Soviets tabled a "new" proposal which was described by Western spokesmen as basically the same as earlier ones.
25 February–6 March   XXVII Congress of the CPSU. The foreign policy speeches all stressed arms control.

March 1986

5–6   U.S. and Soviet delegations met in Bern for chemical weapons nonproliferation discussions.
12   The Soviets announced a further extension of the nuclear test moratorium until the United States tested again.
20   The Soviet press published a direct appeal by the Supreme Soviet to the U.S. Congress to stop nuclear testing.
30   Gorbachev made a national television speech addressing nuclear testing. He stated, regretfully, that Soviets could not continue risking their own security in the face of U.S. continued testing, but offered to stop if the United States did. He also called for a nuclear test summit meeting in any European capital at the first opportunity.

April 1986

8   In Sofia all Western (NATO) and nonaligned European ambassadors were called together and presented with a Warsaw Pact proposal for a nuclear-free Europe (or for any of the various subregional nuclear-free-zone proposals previously offered).
12   An official Soviet government communique reiterated Gorbachev's statement that the USSR must resume nuclear testing for its own security, but added that the Soviet Union would stop immediately if the United States did.
17   The Soviet press announced that Ambassador Kvitsinskiy, currently chairman of the offensive strategic arms talks delegation and former Soviet INF negotiator, would become

the new ambassador to the FRG. Subsequent announcements indicated that Ambassador Karpov, the overall head of the Soviet delegation to the three-part Geneva negotiations, would also head this part of the talks rather than having a replacement named for Kvitsinskiy. This was reported in March in the Western press.

18   At the East German Party Congress, Gorbachev made a major speech in which he offered extensive conventional force reductions from the Atlantic to the Urals, accompanied "where necessary" by OSI. He reversed himself somewhat by expressing a linkage between arms control and U.S. regional policies in regard to Nicaragua and Libya. He also attacked French and U.K. nuclear arms programs and the European Defense Initiative (EDI) as bars to agreements. In June it was indicated that the formal proposal, which was to be made at a Warsaw Pact summit meeting, would call for reductions of around 150,000 personnel on each side.

22   At the CD round (4 February–25 April), the Soviets tabled a new CW proposal which accepted some aspects of Western demands. At the end of the round many observers were expressing optimism.

28   U.S.-Soviet representatives completed another round of bilateral talks on chemical weapons in Geneva. Reportedly, the sides were closer to an agreement but there were still difficulties over adequate verification procedures.

May 1986

3   The Soviet press published Gorbachev's official answer to the nuclear test ban proposal of six nonaligned nations in which he reiterated Soviet willingness not to test if the United States did not.

5–6   U.S. and Soviet officials held preliminary talks on establishing nuclear crisis centers to reduce the risk of accidental nuclear war.

15   Gorbachev addressed the Chernobyl nuclear energy plant accident on Soviet television, turning the issue to the question of nuclear testing and arms control. Further, he announced another extension of the unilateral nuclear weapons test moratorium until 6 August (the anniversary of Hiroshima).

26   Gorbachev met with visiting U.K. parliamentarians and "offered" equivalent Soviet reductions if the United Kingdom scrapped its nuclear arsenal.

26 May–2 June   A Supreme Soviet delegation attended the VI Interparliamentary Conference on Cooperation and Security in Europe, in Bonn, pushing Soviet positions.

June 1986

10–11   The Warsaw Pact Political Consultative Committee (at heads-of-state level) met in Budapest. The communique focused on arms control, especially Gorbachev's January comprehensive nuclear disarmament program, his Berlin proposal for major reductions in conventional forces from the Atlantic to the Urals, and the need for a nuclear test ban. The communique spelled out additional details of the Berlin proposal and closed on an appeal to all Europeans states to support these goals.

12   Chairman of the Council of Ministers Ryzhkov's letter to UN Secretary General Peres de Cuellar, essentially reiterating Shevardnadze's August 1985 letter on a program for peaceful development of space, was published.

16   In the communique and speeches of the plenum of the CPSU Gorbachev revealed some of the elements of the "new" Soviet strategic weapons proposals put on the table earlier in the month in Geneva (ABM treaty to be strengthened and guaranteed for fifteen years, with SDI limited to the laboratory and no new programs; major reductions taken equally in ICBMs, SLBMs, and heavy bombers; treat INF and cruise missiles separately, with possibility to eliminate Soviet and U.S. INF missiles in Europe if French and British forces not increased).

20   A joint session of the Foreign Affairs Commissions of both houses of the Supreme Soviet listed the priorities of Soviet foreign policy as (1) an international nuclear weapons test ban; (2) Gorbachev's proposal to eliminate all nuclear weapons by the year 2000; (3) elimination of U.S. and Soviet INF weapons in Europe; (4) elimination by the year 2000 of all chemical weapons and the industrial base for their production; (5) conventional force reductions from the Atlantic to the Urals; (6) international cooperation for peaceful exploitation of outer space; (7) achievement of all means to verify arms control, including OSI. All other national foreign policy aims were described as subordinate to this list in the ballyhooed propaganda statement.

23   The Central Committee published a message and appeal for support to Soviet arms control objectives sent to the XVII Socialist International in Lima, Peru.

July 1986

1   In a speech at the Polish Party Congress in Warsaw, Gorbachev accused the U.S. administration and Reagan of "open obstruction" in arms control.

1–18	U.S. and Soviet representatives held discussions on CW verification issues in Geneva.
7–9	French President Mitterand's visit to the USSR, Gorbachev's reported comments stressed arms control, particularly in the European context.
9	The Soviet press published Foreign Minister Shevardnadze's lettter to the UN formally proposing a nuclear-free Mediterranean and the mutual withdrawal of U.S. and Soviet fleets from that sea.
14	The Soviet press played up Gorbachev's meeting and discussions with visiting scientists attending a nuclear test ban symposium.
14	In a press conference it was announced that a private U.S. arms control group had been permitted to set up nuclear test monitoring devices at the Soviet test site at Semiplatinsk and that a group of Soviet scientists would go to the United States in October to do the same in Nevada.
22	At the IAEC meeting on nuclear safety that opened in Vienna the Soviet representative made a rather candid report of the Chernobyl accident, but again focused on the lesson that a nuclear test ban was needed.
22–30	An extraordinary session of the SCC was held in Geneva at Soviet request to discuss the U.S.-announced plans to exceed SALT II aggregate limits in the fall. In early August the Soviets presented an unusually detailed press conference about these ostensibly confidential talks in which they strongly criticized the United States.
25	President Reagan sent a letter to Gorbachev reportedly offering to abide by the ABM treaty for some seven years in the context of a strategic arms agreement permitting continued research and developmental testing of SDI.
25 July–1 August	U.S. and Soviet representatives met in Geneva to discuss nuclear test issues.
28 July–1 August	U.S. and Soviet representatives met in Moscow to discuss nuclear nonproliferation and nuclear safety.
29	The Soviet press published Gorbachev's major speech in Vladivostok in which he stressed, among other arms control related issues, an Asian and Pacific security system similar to CSCE, reductions in forces in Asia and the Pacific (including Soviet and U.S. forces, and starting with Soviet-Chinese measures), and the possibility of reductions in Soviet forces in Mongolia. He also announced a partial withdrawal, actually a token, from Afghanistan.

August 1986

4	Both Washington and Moscow announced that Foreign Minister Shevardnadze would meet with U.S. Secretary of State Schultz in Washington on 19 and 20 September to

discuss arms control and other matters having to do with U.S.-Soviet relations.

11-12 A senior U.S. arms control team headed by Paul Nitze and including the U.S. Geneva negotiators met in Moscow with Soviet counterparts. Tight secrecy on specifics was maintained except that the meeting was indicated as without positive results. This meeting was not reported in the main Soviet domestic press.

14-15 U.S. and Soviet CSCBMDE delegations held advanced bilateral discussions in Stockholm.

18-20 U.S. and Soviet representatives held CW talks in Geneva.

19 On nationwide television Gorbachev again extended the unilateral Soviet nuclear test moratorium, this time to 1 January 1987. *As before,* he characterized the extension as "one last chance" for the United States to reciprocate.

19 The CSCBMDE resumed in Stockholm for what was scheduled to be the final round to develop an agreed regimen of CBMs. At the opening session the Soviets, for the first time in their history, agreed to a small number of mandatory on-site-inspections. This was expanded later in the month to include aerial inspections when First Deputy Minister of Defense Marshal Akhromeev made an unprecedented visit to address the conference.

22 The Soviet press published yet another Gorbachev reply to the six nations' proposal for a CTB.

25 U.S. and Soviet representatives held the second meeting in Geneva to discuss nuclear crisis centers.

September 1986

4-5 Another round of U.S.-Soviet talks was held on CW non-proliferation in Bern.

5-6 U.S. and Soviet senior representatives held another meeting on strategic arms, this one in Washington as a follow-on to the August talks in Moscow. This time the Soviet press did report the meeting and identified it as the second one (which must have confused some readers). Afterward the chief Soviet delegate Karpov gave another negative characterization of the meeting to the Western press.

5-18 U.S. and Soviet representatives held a second round of talks in Geneva on nuclear test issues.

9 The Soviet press published the text of a Gorbachev interview in the Czech paper *Rude Pravo*; he blamed the problems in reaching arms control agreements on those around President Reagan but expressed hopes that things would be turned around by the growing "forces for peace," including those in the U.S. Congress.

9-27 A BW treaty review conference was held in Geneva. Little of substance other than charges and countercharges and denials of charges was reported.

19–20	Foreign Minister Shevardnadze held extensive talks in Washington with U.S. Secretary of State Schultz and met also with President Reagan on the nineteenth. In his 21 September press conference Shevardnadze presented a mostly negative assessment.
22	The CSCBMDE closed with an agreement on an expanded set of military confidence building measures (CBMs) which included a number of annual mandatory on-site-inspections as well as increased access for foreign observers at large field exercises and an exchange of exercise schedules. Although the agreement did not represent arms control per se, it marked a major precedent for other negotiations in regard to OSI.
27	The Soviets took foreign press correspondents on a tour of their Semiplatinsk nuclear test site, emphasizing the message that their test site was closed while the US was continuing testing and the arms race.
30	Shevardnadze and Schultz met again in New York and then announced the forthcoming Reykjavik meeting between Gorbachev and Reagan.

October 1986

6	The Western press quoted foreign ministry spokesman Gerasimov and other unnamed Soviet officials as indicating that a separate agreement on INF was the most likely outcome of the Reykjavik summit.
10–12	The Reykjavik summit was held in Iceland amid great fanfare and high expectations which were dashed at the last minute by sudden Soviet demands that everything which had been agreed depended upon US abandonment of the SDI. During the summit, the Geneva strategic arms talks, which had resumed on 18 September, were recessed but resumed on 15 October. The rest of the round reportedly was featured by continuing Soviet recriminations over US refusal to agree to their demands at Reykjavik.
14	Gorbachev addressed the Soviet Union and the world at length on television about Reykjavik, blaming the US for the failure to agree.
23	Gorbachev again appeared on Soviet television for a major address about Reykjavik. As before the message included a strong element of regret, along with heavy condemnation of the Americans and appeals for the US to come to its senses. The speech was printed in the Soviet press the next day.
28–18 November	US and Soviet representatives met on CW in New York.

November 1986

5–6	Foreign Minister Shevardnadze met with US Secretary of State Shultz at the opening of the CSCE human rights re-

	view conference in Vienna. Strong criticisms were exchanged, including over arms control.
13–25	Soviet and US nuclear test experts held consultations in Geneva.
24–17 December	CD chemical weapons committee chairmen met in an extraordinary session in Geneva.

December 1986

2–5	US and Soviet strategic weapons negotiators met in a special meeting in Geneva. This was a follow-up to the August and September meetings in Moscow and Washington; the regular negotiating round had closed 13 November.
12	The South Pacific Nuclear-Free-Zone went into effect when the eighth nation, Australia, ratified the treaty. From the beginning the Soviet Union had vigorously supported the idea and became the first, and only, nuclear weapons state to agree to abide by its provisions.
15–18	US and Soviet specialists met in Washington for another of the regular consultations on nuclear nonproliferation.

January 1987

6	Foreign ministry spokesman Gerasimov, at a press conference, stated that "a US request" for a new summit was under consideration but would be dependent upon American realism over SDI. Such statements were repeated throughout the early months of the year.
14	Another round, billed as the first round of formal discussions, of US-Soviet talks on nuclear crisis centers opened in Geneva.
15	When the strategic nuclear arms talks reconvened in Geneva, as announced earlier First Deputy Foreign Minister Vorontsev had replaced Ambassador Karpov and the head of the Soviet delegations in a move clearly intended to demonstrate Moscow's seriousness in contrast with the US. Throughout the year Vorontsev spent about as much time giving special briefings to West European officials before and after the negotiating rounds as he did in Geneva.
16	Moscow formally announced a partial withdrawal of troops, one division plus several separate units, from Mongolia to take place in April and May. The occasion was used to again promote proposals for Asian/Pacific arms control and security conferences.
22–11 February	US and Soviet nuclear test experts met again.
30	A featured article in the Soviet press strongly attacked chief US strategic arms negotiator Kampelman for "anti-Soviet bias" and "obstructionism."

February 1987

5   The Soviets announced that they would have to resume nuclear testing but expressed a willingness to stop if the US did.

14-16   A huge, gala anti-nuclear conference and media event was held in Moscow with large numbers of Western politicians, scientists, businessmen and show-business and literary figures in attendance. The majority were well known for their pro-arms control and anti-nuclear stances but more conservative hard-liners were also present.

17   At the CD, which had reconvened the 3rd, the Soviets for the first time agreed to full declaration of all CW stockpiles once a treaty would be signed and to OSI of suspected CW production facilities: but with the caveat "except in cases of supreme national interest." Subsequently in the same round, the CD agreed to form a committee to prevent an arms race in space, a longtime Soviet goal.

17   NATO and Warsaw Pact representatives met at the French Embassy in Vienna for informal talks on setting up a new forum to discuss conventional arms control "from the Atlantic to the Urals." Such meetings, exploring Gorbachev's Berlin proposals of the previous spring, thereafter became a regular occurance, but without any noticeable signs of progress.

18   US and Soviet CW verification experts met bilaterally in Geneva. They had also met separately prior to the opening of the CD.

26   The Soviets conducted their first nuclear test since the unilateral moratorium began in August 1985. The explosion was said to be a non-weapons research test.

March 1987

1   *Pravda* announced that Gorbachev had offered to negotiate and INF treaty separate from strategic defenses, was also prepared to eliminate all INF missiles from Europe and all but 100 from Asia, and would be ready to commence separate and parallel talks of shorter range missiles.

4-6   The US-Soviet strategic arms talks were extended two days beyond their scheduled recess to address INF. The US tabled a proposed (draft) treaty.

10-26   A special INF negotiating session was held in Geneva. The US tabled a detailed verification program including a rigorous OSI regimen. The Soviet spokesmen described the session as not very productive.

12   The Soviets conducted their second nuclear test since the end of the moratorium, this one described as weapons-related. Fairly regular testing would continue thereafter.

16–20   US and Soviet nuclear test experts met again. Afterwards, the Soviets castigated the American attitude as unproductive and designed to prevent any agreement on a test ban.

17   In the CD the Soviet Ambassador formally proposed an international arms monitoring agency specifically aimed at preventing "the militarization of space."

24–28   A regional conference of Pacific states was held in Beijing. The Soviet delegation stressed Asian and Pacific arms control proposals and the Soviet press described the conference as being for "security and disarmament."

April 1987

10   In a speech in Prague, Gorbachev announced agreement to simultaneous and connected talks on shorter range missiles in the INF context and stated that the USSR was willing to remove its SS-12 and SS-22 missiles from the CSSR and the GDR in conjunction with an INF treaty.

13–15   US Secretary of State Shultz, with a large entourage, made an official visit to Moscow. Arms control issues were one main item on the discussions agenda. Subsequently, Soviet press commentary on the visit was quite negative.

23   US-Soviet INF negotiations resumed almost two weeks before the rest of the strategic arms talks in Geneva. The new Soviet chief INF negotiator was a military man, General V. Medvedev, suggesting greater seriousness about details. On the 27th the Soviets tabled their own new draft INF treaty.

May 1987

5   The US and USSR announced agreement on a treaty for nuclear crisis centers; the first arms control related treaty concluded bilaterally since either Reagan or Gorbachev had come to office.

8   At the strategic arms talks, which had reconvened fully on 5 May, the US tabled another "new" proposal.

8   Polish leader Jaruzelski proposed a new conventional arms reductions forum which would involve all thirty five European states plus the US and Canada and would negotiate both force and weapons reductions from the Atlantic to the Urals. This proposal, which was undoubtedly approved in advance by Moscow, expanded upon Gorbachev's earlier proposal (made in 1986) by including weapons, but it further clouded the issue of who would negotiate what in conventional arms reductions.

18–29   US and Soviet nuclear test experts again met in Geneva.

19   At a speech at a reception for the visiting Vietnamese Party leader, Gorbachev proposed complete elimination of all Soviet Asian-based INF missiles if the US would remove nu-

clear weapons from the Western Pacific and the Philippines. Although clearly purely propaganda, the formula was interesting since the Soviets had traditionally defended their need for Asian-based INF missiles on the basis of third-party, i.e., the PRC, nuclear missiles as well as on the "US threat."

20   The Soviet press featured a Gorbachev interview for the Italian Communist paper *L'Unita* which again heavily emphasized arms control, including the European role in promoting it.

28–29   The meeting of the Warsaw Pact Political Consultative Committee in Warsaw failed to produce any major new arms control proposals, as had been predicted by many in the West. However, Gorbachev expounded extensively on the "purely defensive" nature of Soviet military doctrine and made a highly propagandistic appeal for NATO and WP representatives to meet for discussions designed to ensure that both sides' military doctrine and strategy would be purely defensive.

June 1987

There were no particularly significant developments reported. Regular sessions of scheduled negotiations were held and the Soviet press and spokesmen reiterated the same arguments and proposals that they had presented earlier.

9

The Burdens and Benefits of Empire: Relations with Eastern Europe

> *Have we reached communism yet, or is it going to get worse?*
>
> —Eastern European saying

Upon coming to power Gorbachev inherited a troubled empire in Eastern Europe. All of the states had very serious economic problems. Eastern European products, with a few exceptions, were not very competitive in the West and in the Third World. The Non-Soviet Warsaw Pact (NSWP) countries—Poland, East Germany (the GDR), Czechoslovakia (the CSSR), Hungary, Romania, and Bulgaria—had accumulated tremendous foreign debts, and Western governments and banks were very reluctant to extend new credits or even reschedule old ones without good prospects of economic improvement. Moreover, the six Eastern European states were tied to the Soviet Union in an inefficiently managed, sometimes divisive economic union, the Council for Economic Mutual Assistance (CEMA), that included such poorly or unevenly developed economic debtor nations as Mongolia, Cuba, and Vietnam. Yugoslavia, a nonaligned communist state that also currently faces serious economic problems, has in CEMA the status of "observer" (but a very involved observer).

Eastern Europe was economically tied to the USSR in another significant way. Paradoxical as it may seem, the Soviet Union has functioned as an underdeveloped economy in relation to Eastern Europe, which it has mostly supplied with raw materials at artificially low prices in return for industrial and finished products. The situations had ramifications beyond the purely economic, for Soviet citizens could not escape the realization that their politically subordinate allies had generally and sometimes dramatically higher standards of living, and in most cases enjoyed much greater political freedom. Similarly, the Soviet defense establishment, under mounting pressure from competing domestic economic priorities, most probably viewed with dissatisfaction the much lower percentages of gross national product and of the budget devoted to defense in Eastern Europe than in the USSR.

There were other problems in Eastern Europe. Although greatly quieted since the early 1980s, the volcano of social, political, and economic unrest continued to rumble in Poland and could always erupt again with suddenness. A parallel situation existed to one degree or another in the other five satellite states. A small but bono fide pacifist movement had been allowed to develop in East Germany. Access to "subversive" Western media was widespread, especially in East Germany and Czechoslovakia, which both bordered on the West. A few Eastern European Communist governments had increasingly adopted semi-independent foreign policy positions and attitudes. Both Berlin and Prague had with open reluctance accepted deployment of new Soviet tactical missiles announced as a response to NATO INF deployments. Romania had long gone its own way in a number of foreign policy areas and had even implicitly criticized Soviet arms control proposals by calling for much more impartial policies of mutual actions by *both* East and West.

In sum, CEMA was a hollow imitation of the Western European Economic Community (EEC), and the Warsaw Pact's military strength was much more overwhelmingly dependent upon the USSR than NATO's was on the United States. The West European states provided far more significant military inputs to NATO than the East Europeans did to the WP; and Soviet political control over their allies, although still tight (and undoubtedly ultimately decisive on any issue deemed vital by Moscow) had progressively lost much of its pervasiveness, especially in regard to many routine matters.

During Gorbachev's two and a half years there was a great deal of interaction between USSR and Eastern European delegations, representatives, and individuals from nearly all walks of life: frequent visits in both directions by economic officials (from the level of chairman of the Council of Ministers, through ministers and further down to executive-level functionaries and even enterprise representatives); Foreign Ministry officials of all levels; cultural, media, academic, and scientific officials; Party officials and delegations; military and defense officials, and many others. In addition, Gorbachev himself met face to face with every Eastern European national leader several times, both alone and in groups, and the USSR signed a host of economic, cultural, and scientific agreements with each of the states. None of this, of course, was really unusual. Such interchange had been the norm ever since Soviet domination over Eastern Europe was established after World War II. In the cases of some of these states, though, the frequency of visits was perhaps higher than in many of the past years.

In a broad sense, there were two aspects of the relationship between the USSR and Eastern Europe that were new in content and degree; they were the distinctive features of Gorbachev's policy toward the troubled Eastern European empire he inherited. The first was one of style and form, designed both to improve attitudes within the socialist community and to present a better image of that community for foreign consumption. Basically, it can be summed up as the appearance of a greater degree of give and take in consultations. Thus, great stress was placed on Gorbachev's traveling for special "consultative" meetings, in Sofia before the summit with Reagan and in Prague after the summit. As presented to the public inside and outside the Communist bloc, these were meetings between true equals at which the Eastern Europeans were given real opportunities to influence the Soviet leader's policies. This, in fact, seems very doubtful. In the days prior to the presummit Warsaw Pact meeting, the first deputy minister of defense and commander in chief of the Warsaw Pact forces, Marshal Kulikov, made special trips to each of the Eastern European states except Romania, whose participation in the pact, and therefore its say, is less complete than the others. It is a safe conclusion that Kulikov was a "point man" laying down the parameters of what Gorbachev intended.

The second significant feature of Gorbachev's Eastern European policy was primarily economic but had political and social implications. It provided the major thrust of his regional policy, one that has the potential for profoundly affecting the future of the USSR's six "partners." This point requires presentation in some detail. Ever since CEMA was created in the 1950s, one of its underlying purposes, from Moscow's perspective, has been to integrate the "socialist commonwealth" in order to ensure both its unity and its dependence upon the Soviet Union. There have been many ups and downs, many fits and starts in the progress toward these goals. Integration has indeed often been more facade than reality. For all the compelling economic logic behind specialization and division of labor, the goals have primarily served as means of ensuring Eastern European dependency and Soviet control, and as such have been resisted in various ways at various times by each of the governments.

Both the thrust and details of Gorbachev's policies since he became general secretary clearly indicate that the new Soviet leadership team intends to put real teeth into a comprehensively conceived integration of the region. The implication of Moscow's policies is that the corollary to integration is to be the subordination of Eastern European economies to the Soviet economy. In other words, Eastern Europe's role will be to assist in the implementation of Gorbachev's vision of economic revitalization in the Soviet Union.

At each of the senior CEMA meetings, including the extraordinary

CEMA meeting called in December 1985, the message was plain. Each CEMA state was to adopt a comprehensive economic and social plan, extending to the year 2000, that directly paralleled the Gorbachev team's plan for the USSR. At almost every one of the many regular CEMA meetings dealing with particular sectors of the economy or an industry, the same agenda predominated: how effectively to incorporate the principles of the USSR's "complex" economic program into the planning and operations of each economic sector of the respective CEMA member states. The same was true of the vast majority of the bilateral ministry and enterprise-to-enterprise consultations between Eastern Europeans and Soviet representatives. "Coordination" of national economic plans was not new. What was new was the kind of purposeful integration demanded. It encompassed the same organizational reforms, vertical cartelization in essence, that the Soviets had made and that had been earlier pursued in East Germany; the same economic strategies (more modernization and retooling with the same modern technologies rather than investment in new construction); wider use of bonuses, incentives, and disciplinary measures; and the same emphasis on quality over quantity and on direct, long-term coordination between, and integration of, individual enterprises and enterprise conglomerates. Particular elements of such reforms might have been designed or implemented before, but these reforms were unaccustomedly comprehensive.

Given the habitual Soviet methods of control and accountability and of democratic centralism, and given the reforms' imposition upon and replication within each Eastern European state, the most likely outcome of the reforms will be to subordinate the Eastern European economies much more thoroughly to that of the USSR and to force the states to pattern their methods of management and organization after those of the Soviets. Further, the new trade agreements signed between the Eastern European states and the USSR projected major increases in bilateral turnover marked by a much larger diversion to the USSR of precisely the products that had been most competitive in the nonsocialist world markets. At the same time the Eastern European states were repeatedly cautioned to reduce significantly their economic dependence on the capitalist West, and were directed to assume a greater share of the burden of assisting the economies of weaker (non-European) CEMA members and Soviet client states, such as Nicaragua, Angola, and Mozambique. Eastern European governments also signed agreements to help underwrite the costs of Soviet infrastructure (such as gas pipelines, energy and transportation lines) and to assist in the reconstruction and modernization of Soviet factories. They also signed contracts as well to provide the Soviets with significantly greater amounts of specified modern production technologies, contracts that further extend the pattern of increased specialization within the Eastern bloc. Western reports also indicate that the Eastern Europeans have committed themselves in writing to specialized contributions in research fields applicable to the Soviet variety of SDI. With the notable but apparently only initial and partial, exception of Romania, each of the Eastern European governments has apparently fully complied in undertaking to meet the required burdens. Virtually all Soviet reports of every political or economic meeting, and absolutely all of the military and arms control meetings reports, have featured the code words "complete unity of views." There were only two common exceptions. In a few communiques regarding Soviet-Polish meetings, primarily political rather than economic, "complete unity" was replaced by "mutual understanding"—an indication of the persistence of some real differences. The second exception was Romania. In this case, code words for even greater differences appeared, including the loaded phrase at the extraordinary CEMA meeting convened to adopt the integrated long-term plan of "realistically" taking into account each state's own program. On the other hand, communiques of subsequent consultations in the spring and summer of 1986 suggested that the Romanians were also beginning to fall in line.

The policy of establishing joint enterprises, given greater impetus after the fall of 1986, seemed in particular to be designed to increase the subservience and integration of the Eastern Europeans—whatever its corollary goals in regard to rationalization or improvement of Soviet managerial efficiency, or as a means of gaining greater Western investment and technology access. Moreover, once again the initial reports of such joint firms suggested that they would be concentrated in precisely those sectors of the Eastern European economies that were most efficient. In other words, the thrust was clearly toward benefiting the Soviets at whatever costs their allies might have to bear. Given their financial difficulties in regard to the West and their almost universal dependence upon the Soviets for energy resources and raw materials (to say nothing of political realities), the Eastern Europeans were in a very poor position to resist such programs.

In respects other than the foregoing, the patterns under Gorbachev varied little from those under his predecessors. East Germany, Poland, and Czechoslovakia led the list of apparent economic priority in Soviet attentions. Hungary remained a special case: it retained a bit of economic freedom as an experimental laboratory but was increasingly drawn into entangling economic relationships that threatened to make that country more of a carbon copy of the USSR. The East German military apparently continued to receive the greatest attention, because of East Germany's relatively greater military reliability and because it both stood on the front lines and for a variety of reasons had to remain under firm control. Gor-

bachev seemed to have relatively greater patience with the Jaruzelski regime in Poland because the Polish leader gave evidence of having overcome
at least partially the worst of his difficulties and because of Poland's absolutely critical position astride the lines of communication to any theater of
confrontation with NATO. It seems significant that Gorbachev used the
Polish Party Congress to reaffirm in effect the Brezhnev doctrine of the
Soviet right to interfere to preclude any slippage from the socialist camp.

One other point—already alluded to in the discussions of Soviet domestic affairs—may be relevant to Gorbachev's intentions in the USSR. As
noted, there is a suggestion being circulated that Gorbachev forced the
political amnesty on Jaruzelski in Poland. What is far less certain, assuming this scenario is accurate, is what it really means. The "optimistic"
interpretation is that Gorbachev yearned to liberalize, and used the Poles
as a laboratory to test the outcome of such a step. This cannot be con-
clusively disproven, but far too many other explanations and considerations argue for very different conclusions, even if we start by accepting the
uncertain claim that the Soviet leader forced the Polish marshal and secretary general to take this step against his will. Economically, Moscow has
almost as much to gain from an easing of Polish debt payment and new
loan conditions from the West as does Warsaw. Second, as noted, freeing a
few, or even quite a few, political prisoners for a while does not equate with
granting and guaranteeing civil liberties on a meaningful scale. A great
amount of additional proof needs to be put into that pudding. Nevertheless, even releasing any significant number of such individuals upsets
and worries quite a few important people in a communist police state. The
conclusion that Gorbachev wanted to use Poland as a testing ground for
true social and political liberalization simply runs counter to too many
things in the system and in his own personal background. But this does not
mean that he could not well have envisioned Poland as a laboratory to test
whether a limited and controlled "liberalization"—one intended as a facade for both domestic and (primarily) foreign audiences—could not
achieve its propaganda purposes while still being kept under sufficient
control to avoid real domestic difficulties.

The point about the perceived utility, in Soviet eyes, of Eastern European
political and economic experiments should be kept in mind by all who seek
to predict Soviet intentions on the basis of those relationships. However,
there is a second possible point to this whole line of reasoning. The precise
illiberal and machiavellian approach we have suggested for Gorbachev
could further impel him unwittingly along the kind of slippery slope upon
which we have earlier indicated he may have embarked. The ability of a
communist regime to retain power and limit the effects of various social,
political, and economic liberalizations is unlikely to be the same in Eastern

Europe as it might be in the USSR. In Eastern Europe there is always the watchful Communist big brother in Moscow to bail out a regime that has risked too much. The USSR has no such guardian angel of its totalitarian system.

Whatever the real goals, and whatever the dangers in the long term, the very example of a comparative liberalization and of glasnost in the USSR had to reverberate in East Europe. East Europeans of many stripes, intellectuals, ordinary citizens, economic rationalists, reform-minded members of the state and party bureaucracies and the like, could be expected to become emboldened and to step up their efforts to modify their own political, cultural and economic mileaus. Not only has this happened, but Gorbachev and his cohorts have clearly encouraged movement in this direction.

In much of East Europe, however, there are additional factors at play, factors which go beyond those applicable to the USSR itself. To start with, the existing levels of contact and exposure to much more free-wheeling Western liberties and diversity have long been much higher than in the USSR, particularly in some of these states. This had already resulted in somewhat greater freedom of expression and certainly of greater access to other ideas in almost all of the East European nations, and much higher in a few. This different starting point inevitably has meant that a further relaxation of the norms of Communist totalitarianism would be easier for some; but it also meant that controlling rising expectations is likely to be much more difficult.

Second, in most of these states there is a long history of distrust or even active dislike of Russia affecting large portions of the populace. Most of the East European nations' histories have been characterized by endless or recurring struggles to avoid or shake off Russian domination. Basically, the history of Eastern Europe has been a struggle for precarious independence between Russia and Germany, with for most Germany being the lesser of evils (at least until Hitler) because she was more modern and could be partially balanced by leapfrogging ties to France or England. Possibly the only real exception to this has been Bulgaria, and to a lesser extent the Slovak part of Czechoslovakia. Against this backdrop, liberalization within Eastern Europe always carries the danger of encouraging anti-Russian nationalism. This, of course, is precisely what happened in 1953 in the GDR, in 1956 in Hungary, and in 1968 in the CSSR; and the latent strength of anti-Russian feelings in Poland has repeatedly been a factor in impelling Soviet caution and an effort to find ways other than brute force to defuse dangerous crises there.

Third, basically speaking, none of the Communist governments of the six NSWP states came to power on their own. They were imposed by the

Red Army and for most of the post-war period their continuing rule was only ensured by Soviet power. Predictably, the corollary has been a number of East European regimes which have relied on being "more Catholic than the Pope" in copying traditional Soviet norms. Romania, for all its foreign policy deviations, has cónsistently been ruled in a very Stalinist style. The East Germans have been almost as rigorous in regard to their population. After 1968 the frightened Czech leaders joined these models. The several Polish leaderships have repeatedly swung pendulum-like between the boundaries of partial social freedom and somewhat less-onorous restrictions than in the USSR. Even Hungary, where Kadar allowed probably the greatest degree of economic and cultural freedom, has walked a very careful line. Bulgaria, of course, with its long history of Russian orientation, has simply tended to copy whatever existed in the USSR; but even here, domestic liberalization tended toward caution and moved more slowly than in the USSR during Khrushchev's "thaw" or under Gorbachev. As a result, incipient reformers within most of the East European states have faced strong opposition from fearful traditionalist leaders at the top of the national Communist parties.

Poland's Jaruzelsky seems to have been the most enthusiastic in casting his lot with Gorbachev. Faced with economic disaster and with the complications of a strong, partially independent Catholic Church and the stubborn Solidarity movement, Jaruzelsky needed a new strategy and probably couldn't afford total repression unless Gorbachev would completely back him. But this would undermine the carefully built image the Soviet leader was cultivating in the West.

Logically, Hungary could have been expected to be the one most enthusiastically following, or even building on, Gorbachev's example; and in some ways she has been. But Hungary faced a different problem than the others. Her existing economic liberalization had lost some of its glow. Problems were accumulating in large measure because of the inherent contradictions between a partially free and a partially command economy and there were real internal pressures on the leadership to retrench. For most of Gorbachev's first two years, the Kadar leadership seemed cautious, content to let the Soviets move to catch up with the limited freedoms of the Hungarian system and see if that didn't provide beneficial rationalities in the wider CEMA economy. Certainly, the Hungarians were among the leaders in trying joint ventures and direct enterprise-to-enterprise cooperation with the Soviets. By summer of 1987 it appeared that a more vigorous reform group under the new prime minister was becoming more assertive and that Party leader Kadar was becoming less active.

For some time the Czechs almost totally resisted allowing even the limited openings that Gorbachev was instituting in the USSR; but after a series of high level Soviet visits and Gorbachev's 1987 visit, seemed to be reluctantly falling into line. Whether Husak can control a new mini "Prague spring" or even maintain himself in power with a partial relaxation remains to be seen. Honecker and the East Germans have been similar. However with the strongest East European economy, and one whose feature of vertical cartellization was an attractive model to Moscow, the pressures on East Berlin were less in many ways than on the other East European capitals. Moreover, given Soviet appreciation of the strong pull West Germany exercises on the East Germans and Soviet recognition of the relative strength of the East German economy, Soviet pressure on East Berlin to follow Moscow's social and economic lead was undoubtedly less than on the other NSWP governments. For Gorbachev the most compelling reasons for pressuring the East Europeans to copy his methods had to be basically the same as his main purposes at home, to galvanize and revitalize a stagnant economy and to facilitate the images that he desired to create abroad. Nevertheless, by late summer 1987, even Honecker seemed to be gradually loosening some of his controls at home. Further, he was moving to improve ties with the FRG. This latter policy carried great dangers, but it could also greatly facilitate Moscow's efforts to influence Bonn in favorable directions.

The Bulgarians, as might easily have been expected, were fairly enthusiastically following the Soviet lead economically while being a bit more cautious socially and in the intellectual spheres.

Only Causescu in Romania seemed to be totally resisting copying the major aspects of Soviet liberalization. Still, Bucharest was step-by-step bowing to Soviet pressure in some economic aspects. After initially resisting the CEMA long term economic program, the Romanians began to fall into line—but more by agreeing on goals and accepting greater economic integration in contracts and joint ventures than by decentralizing. Meanwhile, under pressure socially, politically and economically from Moscow, the Romanians were muting their celebrated foreign policy deviances.

In sum, Gorbachev's policies toward Eastern Europe have the clear goal of exploiting the Eastern Europeans to serve his domestic economic goals. His success in this venture would also entail more effectively integrating the bloc, enhancing long-term Soviet domination over its allies, and (possibly) relieving the economic burden increasingly imposed on the USSR by Eastern Europe. The "consultations of equals" provided a facade but does not seem to have done much more that that. In pursuing the above goals, Gorbachev simultaneously is paving the way for possible socialist autarky, i.e. for a last-ditch fallback strategy of independence and isolation in the struggle with the West. The danger is that, as before, partial liberalization in East Europe will get out of hand, threatening the Communist regimes and the unity of the bloc. If that happens, Gorbachev's potential rivals at home will have a strong issue to wield against him. Whether the Gorbachev approach succeeds will have important ramifications not only for the general secretary and the USSR but even more so for the Eastern Europeans.

Selected Soviet-Eastern European Chronology

(Because of the extreme frequency of visits to and from Eastern European states, this chronology is slightly less detailed than the others. None of the many middle- and low-level Party, parliamentary, government, or military visits are listed; rather, only a few of the more significant visits by Party secretaries or full government ministers are listed. The regular sessions of joint Soviet-East European commissions for economic or scientific-technical cooperation, which exist and meet regularly at deputy chairman, council of ministers level for each NSWP state, are also not included. The same holds true for the vast majority of CEMA commissions or committees. These exist for almost every sector of the economies of these states and they meet once or twice a year, usually in one of the national capitals and often on a rotating basis (although several of the most important always meet in Moscow). On the other hand activities and meetings with the Yugoslavs are reported in somewhat greater detail since Yugoslavia, although Communist, is not as closely aligned. Yugoslavia does participate in most CEMA commissions as a semi-observer and the reader should bear that in mind.)

March 1985

11	Mikhail Gorbachev was elected general secretary, C.P.S.U.
13–14	Gorbachev met with the heads of state of all six *NSWP states* and *Yugoslavia,* who were in Moscow for the Chernenko funeral. Most of the Eastern European delegations to the funeral included other major government leaders and ministers, who met separately with Soviet counterparts.
17	Chairman Dascelescu, Council of Ministers of *Romania,* and the foreign minister and chairman of the State Planning Commission met with Soviet counterparts and signed documents expanding trade and economic cooperation, 1986–90.
19	Chairman Filipov, Council of Ministers of *Bulgaria,* and the chairman of the State Planning Committee, the minister of foreign trade, and the minister of finance held official talks with Soviet counterparts in Moscow.
26	CC Secretary and Politburo member Romanov led the Soviet delegation to the *Hungarian Party Congress.*

April 1985

1	Chairman Lazar, Council of Ministers of Hungary, met with Gorbachev in Moscow.

9–13	Defense Minister Sokolov visited Poland for consultations.
26–27	Warsaw Pact Political Consultative Committee meeting in Warsaw. Gorbachev led the Soviet delegation. All state delegations included heads of state, chairmen of the Councils of Ministers, ministers of foreign affairs and of defense, and some other officials. The Warsaw Pact Treaty was extended twenty years.

May 1985

4–5	G.D.R. leader Honecker made an official visit to Supreme Soviet of the U.S.S.R.; met with Gorbachev on 5 May.
8	World War II victory celebration in Moscow. The WP states were represented variously: Hungary by the minister of defense, the others by deputy minister, chief of General Staff, or chief of a main political directorate. On the civilian side all except Bulgaria were represented by midlevel officials; Bulgaria was represented by Chairman of the Peoples Assembly Todorov.
14–17	Politburo member Grishin led a delegation on an official visit to the G.D.R. and met with East German leader Honecker.
15–18	One hundred fourteenth meeting of the Executive Committee, CEMA (deputy-chairman-of-the-Council-of-Ministers level), in Moscow. The agenda focused on plan coordination for 1986–90 and to the year 2000, and preparations for the CEMA meeting at heads-of-state level.
21	Gorbachev met with heads of delegations to a CEMA CP secretaries meeting ongoing in Moscow.
20–23	The Warsaw Pact Military Council meeting in Budapast, chaired by the commander in chief of the Warsaw Pact, Marshal Kulikov, who stayed over for Ministry of defense consultations.
30–31	Czech leader Husak visited Moscow and met with Gorbachev on 31 May. He was accompanied by two deputy chairmen of the Council of Ministers.

June 1985

7	Bulgarian leader Zhivkov, accompanied by a first deputy chairman and a deputy chairman of the Council of Ministers, made a one-day official visit. Zhivkov met with Gorbachev and an agreement for economic and scientific-technical cooperation, 1986–90 and to the year 2000 was signed.
25–27	The fortieth meeting of CEMA (chairman-of-the-Council-of-Ministers level) was held in Warsaw. Chairman Tikhonov led the Soviet delegation, which also included CC Secretary and Politburo member Ryzhkov, GOSPLAN

Chairman Baybakov, and Deputy Chairmen of the Council of Ministers Martynov and Talyzin. Observers were present from seven Third World client states. The emphasis was on planning coordination, introduction, and application of modern technology, and assistance to less-developed CEMA states (Cuba, Mongolia, Vietnam). GOSPLAN Chairman Baybakov stayed on until the end of the month.

July 1985

4   Gorbachev met with Yugoslav leader Planinc, who was in the U.S.S.R.

August 1985

2   Chairman Stoph, Council of Ministers of the G.D.R. met with Tikhonov in Moscow.

9   Chairman Filipov, Council of Ministers of Bulgaria (accompanied by the minister of machine construction and electronics, the minister of foreign trade, and the chairman of the State Planning Commission) met with Soviet counterparts in Moscow. A trade agreement was signed.

September 1985

9–13   CC Secretary Zaykov led a delegation to the G.D.R. and met with East German leader Honecker.

23–28   CC Secretary Nikonov led an agricultural delegation to Hungary and met with Hungarian leader Kadar on 26 September.

24–25   Hungarian leader Kadar made an official visit. On 25 September he met with Gorbachev and most of the top Soviet leadership.

27   Foreign Minister Shevardnadze, in New York for the opening of the UNGA, met with Polish leader Jaruzelski and with each of the Eastern European foreign ministers separately.

October 1985

22–23   The *Warsaw Pact* Political Consultative Committee met in Sofia. Gorbachev led the Soviet delegation, which included Gromyko, Ryzhkov, Sokolov, Rusakov, Aristov, and Marshal Kulikov. The NSWP states were similarly represented. Focus was on arms control and "support" to Third World struggles against imperialism.

24–25   Gorbachev stayed over in Bulgaria and met with Zhivkov.

26   The published text of the draft CPSU Party Program called

for increased cooperation and economic integration of CEMA states along the same lines as the Soviet economic program.

November 1985

4

Deputy Chairman Antonov, Council of Ministers, was confirmed as the replacement for Talyzin as USSR permanent representative to CEMA (Talyzin was previously promoted to first deputy chairman, Council of Ministers, and chairman, GOSPLAN).

12–14

The *Warsaw Pact* Military Council met in Berlin; Marshal Kulikov chaired.

18–19

The one hundred seventeenth CEMA Executive Committee meeting was held in Moscow (deputy-chairman-of-the-Council-of-Ministers level). The focus was on science and technology. The deputy chairmen of the Councils of Ministers of Bulgaria and Romania were reported to have held separate bilateral meetings with Soviet counterparts.

20–22

Politboro member Grishin went to Prague for a Moscow City Day celebration and met with Husak on 22 November.

21

Gorbachev met with the other East European leaders in Prague to report on the summit with Reagan. He also met separately with Czech leader Husak.

December 1985

2–5

A meeting of *Warsaw Pact* ministers of defense in Berlin; Marshal Sokolov stayed over until 7 December for private discussions.

9–13

CC Secretary Nikonov (agriculture) to Yugoslavia.

17–18

An extraordinary 41st CEMA meeting at chairman-of-Council-of-Ministers level was held in Moscow. The delegations all also included numerous other ministers (chairmen, state planning committees; ministers of foreign trade, and others), many of whom stayed for additional bilateral meetings with Soviet counterparts. Gorbachev addressed the chairmen on 17 December; Ryzhkov made the other main speech. All but Romania agreed to a comprehensive program for economic development to the year 2000 that very closely paralleled the Soviet domestic program in every way. The C.S.S.R. and Hungary also signed 1986–90 trade agreements with the USSR; and Bulgaria signed an agreement coordinating state plans for 1986–90.

19–21

CC Secretaries Ponomarev and Zimyanin led the Soviet delegation to a Party secretaries meeting in Budapest.

Other Agreements and Treaties Reported, March–December 1985

With Bulgaria:

To establish joint scientific-production enterprises in machine tool industries. (October)

1986–1990 cooperation in light industries. (November)
1986–1990 cultural and scientific exchange. (December)

With the CSSR: Cooperation in construction of an industrial robots factory complex. (March)
Protocol for coordination of state plans, 1986–1990 and to 2000. (October)
1986–1990 cultural and scientific exchange. (December)

With the GDR: Scientific-technical cooperation, 1986–1990 and to 2000. (June)
Cooperation in tourism. (June)
Protocol for coordination of state plans, 1986–1990. (October)
Cooperation in expanding a metallurgical factory. (November)
1986–1990 trade and payments. (December)

With Hungary: Program to develop economic and scientific-technical cooperation, 1986–1990 and to 2000. (April)
Cooperation in culture. (June)

With Poland: Economic and scientific-technical cooperation, 1986–1990 and to 2000. (June)
Long term scientific and technical cooperation. (September)
Protocol to coordinate state plans, 1986–1990. (October)

With Romania: 1986–1990 trade. (December)
Protocol to coordinate state plans, 1986–1990. (December)
Romanian assistance in constructing the Yamburg pipeline. (December)

With Yugoslavia: Economic and scientific-technical cooperation, 1986–1990 and to 2000. (June)
Protocol for trade and economic development cooperation, 1986–1990. (December)

CEMA: Economic cooperation with Mozambique. (May)
Protocol of trade, 1986–1990. (June)
Protocol to increase developmental assistance to Nicaragua. (October)

January 1986

8–12   The Yugoslav foreign minister visited, met with Shevardnadze and Gromyko and signed a 1986–1987 cultural cooperation agreement.

21–23   A CEMA Executive Committee meeting, in Moscow (deputy-chairman-of-the-Council-of-Ministers level).

February 1986

18–19   Chairman Messner, Council of Ministers of Poland, accompanied by two deputy chairmen one of whom was the chairman of the State Committee for Scientific and Technological Progress, the minister of foreign trade, and deputies from the Foreign Ministry and the State Planning Commission, met with counterparts in Moscow and "signed a number of joint agreements." Messner met separately with Gorbachev on 19 February.

26 February–6 March   The XXVII *CPSU Congress*. All six NSWP leaders arrived one to two days early, and all met separately with Gorbachev. The NSWP delegations also included some government ministers.

March 1986

17–18   Foreign Minister Shevardnadze went to Poland for private discussions in advance of the WP meeting. He met with Jaruzelski on 18 March.

19–20   A meeting of Warsaw Pact foreign ministers was held in Warsaw.

23–28   Politburo member Solomentsev and CC Secretary Nikonov led the delegation to the Czech Party Congress in Prague.

April 1986

1–6   Politburo member and Chairman of the Council of Ministers Ryzhkov and CC Secretary Razumovskiy led the delegation to the Bulgarian Party Congress in Sofia. Ryzhkov met separately with Zhivkov.

16–22   Gorbachev, accompanied by CC Secretary Medvedev, led the delegation to the East German Party Congress. Gorbachev held private meetings with Honeker and visited factories.

23–25   Politburo member and KGB Chief Chebrikov visited Budapest and met with Kadar.

23–25   A Warsaw Pact Military Council meeting was held in Warsaw; Marshal Kulikov chaired.

May 1986

5–11   CC Secretary Zimyanin led a Party and Supreme Soviet delegation to Poland. He met with Jaruzelsky on 10 May.

16   Romanian leader Ceausescu (accompanied by a deputy chairman of the Council of Ministers and the foreign minister) came to Moscow, where he met with Gorbachev and signed a long-term program of economic and scientific-technical cooperation to the year 2000. The program paralleled the earlier CEMA program and heavily stressed specialization and so on, but also retained references to that which was deemed "mutually beneficial" and to each state's own needs and programs—indicating some differences still

	existed even though Romania was falling into line with the rest of the CEMA states.
20–22	The 119th CEMA Executive Committee meeting was held in Moscow (deputy-Chairman-of-the-Council-of-Ministers level).

June 1986

2	The chairman of the state committee for science and technology, Yugoslavia, visited and met with his Soviet counterpart, Marchuk.
8–9	Gorbachev, accompanied by CC Secretary Medvedev, visited Hungary and met with Kadar and other leaders. Gorbachev toured and spoke at a factory.
9–11	The chief of the Yugoslavian armed forces General Staff made an official visit and met with the military leadership.
10–11	The WP Political Consultative Committee met in Budapest. Gromyko, Ryzhkov, Shevardnadze, and Marshal Sokolov joined Gorbachev, who was already there. The communique stressed arms control and formally reiterated Gorbachev's Berlin proposal for reductions from the Atlantic to the Urals. Gorbachev held separate meetings with each NSWP leader.
12–16	The Bulgarian minister of defense made an official visit and met with the military leadership.
24–29	Politburo Member Aliev led the delegation to the Yugoslav Party Congress.
28–4/7	Gorbachev, accompanied by Shevardnadze and CC Secretary Yakovlev, led the delegation to the Polish Party Congress. His speech stressed support to Jaruzelski, arms control, and Soviet and CEMA economic programs. He returned to Moscow on 1 July; the others stayed on.

September 1986

22–26	Politburo member and Chairman of the Party Control Committee Solomentsev and a delegation visited Hungary.
22–27	Candidate Politburo member Slyunkov led a Supreme Soviet delegation in a visit to the C.S.S.R.
30	Gorbachev met with Polish leader Jaruzelsky on the latter's return from a visit to Mongolia, North Korea, and the PRC. During his trip Jaruzelsky also visited the Irkutsk region.

October 1986

5	Gorbachev met with East German leader Honecker who was there for a short visit. Both this and the meeting with

Jaruzelsky undoubtedly included discussion of plans for the upcoming US-Soviet summit in Reykjavik.

November 1986

5	The 42nd CEMA executive council meeting, in Bucharest, addressed the strategy of acceleration of the economies. The Party leaders met on the 11th.

December 1986

1–3	Warsaw Pact ministers of defense met in Warsaw to discuss the outcome and the implications of the Reykjavik summit.
11–13	The chairman of the presidium of the Yugoslav League of Communists and a senior delegation made an official visit.

Other Agreements and Treaties Reported in 1986:

With Bulgaria: 1986–90 Trade Agreement (Jan).
Cooperation in reconstructing and modernizing several enterprises (Jan).
Construction of a nuclear energy plant in Bulgaria (Jan).
Joint development and production of automotive electronics (Jan).
Bulgarian assistance in construction of the Yamburg pipeline (Mar).
Merchant Fleet cooperation, 1986–90 and to 2000 (May).
Branch cooperation in machine construction and electrotechnical industries (May).
Program of cooperation and joint research in "several" industrial sectors to 2000 (July).

With the CSSR: Cooperation and coordination in nuclear energy (Jan).
1986–90 Trade Protocol (Jan).
Cooperation in construction of a robotics plant in the U.S.S.R. (Mar).
Construction of a rapid transit system in Bratislava (Mar).
Construction of a mining combine in the Krivoi Rog with Soviet payment in iron ore (Sept).

With the GDR: 1986–90 Trade Protocol (Jan).
German assistance in construction of the Yamburg pipeline (Jan).
Cooperation in nuclear and thermo-energy (Jan).
Protocol to establish a commission for cultural cooperation (Jan).
Otherwise unidentified agreements for priority cooperation in "selected" scientific and technological areas suggested as military in *Western* commentary (Jun).

With Hungary: A series of enterprise-to-enterprise cooperation agreements, 1986–90 (Feb).
Assistance to Hungary in nuclear energy (Feb).

Joint research in tapping and utilizing heat discharges from electric power stations (Jun).
Construction in Hungary of two nuclear power plants (Aug).

With Poland: Cooperation in branches of the machine construction industry (Jan).
1986 cultural agreement (Apr).
Cooperation in biocybernetics and biomedical engineering (May).
Cooperation protocol in material-technical supply (May).
For Joint Enterprises (JVs) in machine construction, light industry and chemical industry (May).

With Romania: 1986–90 Scientific and Technical Cooperation (Jan).
Protocol of cooperation between Soviet Aviation Industry and the Romanian Ministry of Machine Construction Industries (Jun).
1986–87 Ideological Cooperation (Jul).
1986–90 tools and equipment sales agreement and cooperation in industrial enterprise construction (Aug).

With Yugoslavia: 1986–90 sales agreement (Jan).
Protocol to update a 1981 agreement for cooperation in reconstruction of industrial and "other" facilities (Apr).

CEMA: Cooperation in Soviet industrial robotics plant construction (Mar).
Cooperation in introduction of new materials, new technology, and new biotechnology (Mar).
Protocol of cooperation between coal industries (Apr).
Agreement to develop and introduce an automated construction system for nuclear power stations with Yugoslavia (Jun).
Nuclear power station safety (Jun).

January 1987

19–20 CC Secretary Dobrynin visited the G.D.R. and met with Honecker.
20–21 The one hundred twenty-second session of the CEMA Executive Committee met in Moscow at Deputy Chairman, Council of Ministers level.

February 1987

2–5 Foreign Minister Shevardnadze visited the C.S.S.R. and G.D.R. meeting with the top leadership.
2–4 The Chairman, Bulgarian Council of Ministers Atanasov, with a senior delegation, made an official visit but he fell ill and the meeting was curtailed.
9–13 Defense Minister Sokolov, accompanied by MPA Chief

11

General Lizichev visited the CSSR, met with civil and military leaders and toured installations and factories.

Gorbachev met with visiting East European party secretaries for agriculture who were there for a conference which emphasized agricultural applications of biotechnology.

March 1987

2-5

CC Secretary and Politburo Member Zaikov, who has Secretariat responsibility for military industries, visited the CSSR and met with Husak and other leaders. He also toured several factories. Taken together, Zaikov's and Sokolov's visits to the CSSR in March and February probably were in part designed to lay groundwork for Gorbachev's visit and the clear pressures he put on Husak to fall more in line with Soviet style reorganization and style of leadership.

21

Deputy Chairman, Council of Ministers for military industries Maslyukov visited Poland and met with Chairman Messner, Polish Council of Ministers.

24

The Minister of defense, Hungary, visited and met with top military leadership.

25

Gorbachev met with Warsaw Pact Foreign Ministers who were there for a conference. Predictably they all fully endorsed Soviet foreign policy lines.

30

A senior Yugoslav Party delegation visited.

April 1987

9-11

Gorbachev, accompanied by CC Secretary Medvedev and Raisa Gorbachev, visited the C.S.S.R. He met twice with Husak and with other Czech leaders and toured factories and mixed with citizens who cheered his style and references to the perestroika and glasnost.

16-18

The Warsaw Pact Military Council at the Ministers of defense level met in Minsk.

21-22

Polish leader Jaruzelski made an official visit and met with Gorbachev.

22-26

CC Secretary and Politburo Member Ligachev visited Hungary, met with Kadar, and toured installations and factories.

27-28

Bulgarian Chairman Council of Ministers Atanasov, in better health, made an official visit which was a continuation of the one cut short in February and met with Ryzhkov and others.

May 1987

5

The Commander of the Yugoslav Air Forces and Air Defense Forces made a visit.

11	Gorbachev met with Bulgarian leader Zhivkov who stopped in Moscow for two days enroute home from a visit to the PRC.
18	The Chief of Staff of Polish Armed Forces met with top military leaders and then toured installations.
19-22	Defense Minister Sokolov, accompanied by MPA Chief General Lizichev, Air Force CinC, Deputy Defense Minister Marshal Yefimov, and Deputy Defense Minister of armaments, General Shabanov visited Hungary, met military leaders, toured installations and factories, and also met with Kadar.
25-27	Gorbachev, accompanied by CC Secretary Medvedev and Raisa Gorbachev, visited Romania, touring, meeting citizens, and holding extensive talks with Ceauseseu.
28-29	Gorbachev led the delegation to the Warsaw Pact Political Consultative Committee meeting in Berlin, where he also met separately with Honecker. Others in the delegation included Gromyko, Ryzhkov, Shevardnadze, Sokolov, and Medvedev.

June 1987

3-4	A conference of the heads of main political administrations of Warsaw Pact armed forces was held to address political and ideological work in accord with the new directions taken by the U.S.S.R. and the Pact in regard to arms control and military doctrine.
4-5	The one-hundred-twenty-third session of the CEMA executive committee took place in Moscow.
15-19	Foreign Minister Shevardnadze made successive official visits to Bulgaria, Hungary, and Yugoslavia where he met with top leaders. In Bulgaria and Hungary the meetings' communiques stressed arms control and a Balkan Nuclear Free Zone proposal. In Yugoslavia, the communique stressed future economic and political cooperation.

Other Agreements and Treaties Reported in 1987, through June:

With Bulgaria:	1987 Trade Protocol (Jan).
	5-year sales agreement for ships and ship equipment (Jan).
	1987 Protocol of cooperation between Ministries of Culture (Jan).
	Plan of Cooperation between Writers' Unions (Apr).
	Agreement to form a joint machinebuilding trust (Apr).
	1987-90 Cooperation Agreement between GOSNAB, The State Committee for Material Supply, and Bulgarian counterpart (May).
With the CSSR:	1986-90 Protocol of Cooperation in civil aviation (Feb).
With the GDR:	Working plan of cooperation between film industries (Feb).
	Protocol of Cultural Cooperation (Apr).
With Hungary:	Various cooperation agreements between enterprises in en-

ergy, chemical and machine construction and in mechanization of materials-handling equipment (Mar).

Announced opening of the first Soviet-Hungarian JV, Micromed, to produce cardiographic and other medical equipment (Apr).

Sale of 1.4 million tons of petroleum products from the U.S.S.R. (Apr).

Agreement for a microelectronics JV to open in Budapest in the third quarter of the year; plus contracts for two more JVs—one in Budapest and one in Vilnius, as well as a joint design office (Apr).

With Poland: Protocol to establish a commission for cultural and scientific cooperation (Jan).

1987 friendship society protocol of cooperation (Apr).

Protocol of cooperation in technical servicing of machines and equipment (Apr).

With Romania: Protocol of cooperation in development of border water resources (Mar).

Friendship societies cooperation plan (May).

With Yugoslavia: Working Protocol of Cooperation between State Television and Radio Committees (May).

1988–90 program of basic directions of cooperation with Montenegran Yugoslav Republic (May).

CEMA: Future cooperation in storage equipment, utilization of wastage and dry batteries production (Mar).

Cooperation in production of passenger aircraft, ships, metal cutting presses, and various instruments in Vietnamese enterprises (Mar).

Agreement in principle to create a CEMA Center for Informatics and Electronics (Apr).

To form a CEMA multinational enterprise for deep seabed mining. Active participants to be the U.S.S.R., Bulgaria, C.S.S.R., Cuba, G.D.R., Poland, and Vietnam (Apr).

10

The "Mongol Hordes": Relations with the People's Republic of China

An old joke was told in varying versions about both Khrushchev and Brezhnev. The Soviet leader kept having dreams that awoke him in the middle of the night. He consulted his psychiatrist and explained that his dreams always started out wonderfully but then turned so frightening that he woke up and could not go back to sleep. The doctor asked him to describe the dreams. The red-eyed general secretary recounted the sequence of his recurring nightmare: He was called to the television to see the marvelous news that in all Western European capitals the workers were rioting and demonstrating against their governments, which were falling, one by one. Then, just as he was at the peak of his exultation, he would notice that the placards the workers carried were all written in Chinese!

Well before Gorbachev became general secretary, the "nightmare" challenge that Mao had mounted on the ideological front for the leadership of the world's communist and revolutionary movements had abated. Mao's successors had turned inward and, in fact, had begun a dramatic economic and social restructuring of their society. By the standards of Marxist ideology the Chinese comrades appeared revisionist, almost "capitalist-roaders," to the point of vindicating Stalin's derogatory remark that the Chinese were "radish communists": red on the outside but white on the inside.

Nevertheless, the challenges posed by the People's Republic of China (PRC) to Soviet foreign policy did not go away. In some ways they were even more disturbing. For if the PRC no longer was seriously competing with the Soviets in support of revolutionary liberation movements, it was still posing problems for Moscow in the Third World by preaching self-development and stigmatizing the Soviets as being just as imperialist as the West. Chinese maps showing great areas of Soviet Asia as properly part of the PRC were no longer being widely circulated and publicized, but the claims to this territory were still not settled and remained a potential time

bomb. The great masses of China were living side by side with underpopu-
lated expanses of Soviet territory. The PRC continued to pressure
Moscow's valued client Vietnam, actively supported Hanoi's enemies in
Southeast Asia, and provided arms to the Afghanistan rebels fighting the
Soviet army. An even more disturbing feature was the fact that the new
Chinese leadership had turned significantly toward the West, not only for
economic cooperation but for possible military assistance and political ties
as well. The historic Russian nightmare of facing allied enemy powers both
on the Western borders and in Asia had become a growing possibility.

Once in power, Gorbachev, like his predecessors, set out to improve
relations with Beijing, and indeed he has apparently achieved some tangible successes in expanding economic and cultural ties. These ties, although
never completely severed, had for long years been a mere shadow of what
they once were. Politically and strategically, however, Gorbachev's gains
have so far amounted at best to only incremental progress over what had
been achieved by preceding Soviet leaders. Yet, if his successes thus far have
been limited, it certainly was not for lack of trying. From the start, the
Gorbachev Kremlin treated the Chinese with kid gloves. Official messages
were markedly conciliatory. Economic, cultural, and parliamentary delegations were dispatched and received; and the most senior Chinese officials
in many a year were invited, and came, to Moscow, where Gorbachev
himself received Chinese Deputy Premier Li Peng in March and in December 1985.

Gorbachev's greatest accomplishments in this field have been in renewing economic and cultural ties. Significant successes were achieved at two
major rounds of negotiations in which First Deputy Chairman of the
Council of Ministers Arkhipov led the Soviet delegation. The first was in
Moscow in July 1985; the second in Beijing in March 1986. As a result,
trade, economic, and cultural cooperation agreements were signed, providing for a notable increase of bilateral trade over the next five years and for
sending Soviet technicians back to China for the first time since they had
been withdrawn by Khrushchev. Their task was to renovate industrial facilities originally built with Soviet help and to assist in building new ones. It
has even been rumored, though not fully confirmed, that the Soviets have
offered to assist the Chinese nuclear energy program. In addition, the
number of Chinese students receiving training in the U.S.S.R. was to be
increased. All of this was definitely a good beginning.

It was a beginning upon which the Soviets were clearly determined to
build. Gorbachev's Vladivostok speech in July 1986 included strong emphasis on cooperative economic projects that would involve the Chinese.
Practical economic and commercial measures were agreed to in a fairly
large number of arenas (sales contracts, customs streamlining, transporta-

tion, port arrangements, water utilization, and so on), especially during 1986 and the first half of 1987. The Talyzin visit to Beijing in September marked a definite stepping up of these efforts. Arkhipov had also been a first deputy chairman of the Council of Ministers, but he was more a holdover from the past; Talyzin was a candidate Politburo member and someone who had been promoted and given greater prestige and authority by Gorbachev—in other words, one of the members of Gorbachev's inner circle. Moreover, the fact that Talyzin had come to what had once been the "forbidden city" of the "middle kingdom" at the "center of the earth" to confer with his Chinese counterparts and, presumably, familiarize himself with their planning reforms and tour agricultural and industrial regions where the reforms had been put into effect had to be gratifying to his hosts. It did not matter whether or not any aspects of the reforms was being considered for adoption by the USSR.

On the other hand, in spite of all the efforts, Gorbachev has so far made much less progress on the political level. After both Arkhipov visits the Soviet press attempted to paint a picture of warmer political relations, but each time the reports coming out of the PRC were categorical in indicating that no real progress had been made in this regard. Beijing continued to insist adamantly that a true political rapprochement would require (1) removal and/or a major reduction of the very large Soviet military presence along the shared border; (2) full withdrawal from Afghanistan; and (3) cessation of Soviet support for Vietnamese interference in Kampuchea.

In July 1986 and subsequently, Moscow stepped up its political efforts to woo Beijing. At Vladivostok Gorbachev offered the possibility of mutual troop reductions, including a unilateral removal of some of the Soviet forces in Mongolia. He announced the imminent withdrawal of some Soviet troops from Afghanistan; and he urged the Chinese and Vietnamese to get together to resolve their differences. In the latter regard, this tepid response to the Chinese position on Southeast Asia was possibly formulated in a way so as not to offend the Vietnamese, for there were a number of concurrent indications, even if tenuous and circumstantial, that behind the scenes the Soviets were pressuring Hanoi to be more responsive. Then too, Moscow apparently followed up Gorbachev's words with some small but nonetheless real deeds. For example, the Kremlin evidently conceded to Beijing on defining the border between the two countries as running along the main channel of boundary rivers instead of at the Chinese shores. Although this does not sound like much of a concession (the Chinese position has reflected the more common norms of international law), it did mean ceding several small disputed islands; the ceding of territory, no matter how small and insignificant, is not something that Moscow has been known to do easily. Further, Gorbachev appointed a new head of the Soviet delegation to the regular political consultations that had been for so many years at a virtual impasse. The removal of the eighty-year-old Ilichev from the post that he had occupied during the long years of Soviet intransigence to be replaced by Deputy Foreign Minister Rogachev could only suggest the possibility of a more forthcoming Soviet attitude in the future.

Beijing's reaction to all this was cautious. Deng Xiaoping belittled the token force reduction in Afghanistan and repeated the Chinese demand for a complete and total Soviet withdrawal. He did note, however, that Gorbachev's speech had contained some positive elements: evidently the proposal for troop reductions along the border and the possibility of removal of some forces from Mongolia. It was plain that both Moscow and Beijing had no desire to make an issue of the border clash that evidently occurred in mid-July, which would not have been the case only a few short years ago. In fact, a September statement by Deng suggested that among the three Chinese conditions for better political ties, Kampuchea was the really critical one. According to Western reports, the Chinese leader said that he would be willing to meet with Gorbachev when solid steps had been taken to get the Vietnamese out of Kampuchea. Even if this did indicate an easing of Beijing's demands, it may not be of practical help because it is very unlikely that Gorbachev could or would pressure Hanoi to withdraw, given the strategic importance of the ties with Vietnam and the military bases the Soviets have acquired there.

Chinese relations with the United States and with other NATO countries meanwhile continued to improve. For Moscow, the only consolation here was the fact that Beijing remained at odds with Washington in regard to a number of significant Third World issues. In fact, all of Gorbachev's efforts to build bridges to the Chinese are likely to have much less influence upon Beijing's response to Soviet advances than are Chinese relations with the West and Chinese perceptions of U.S. attitudes. As long as Deng believes that he has more to gain in terms of economic and possibly military relationships with the West by appearing to be as at odds with Moscow, he is unlikely to allow the Moscow-Beijing thaw to proceed too far. Much more than Washington's or Moscow's (now or someday) playing the "China card," it is the astute Chinese who have been playing the superpowers like a well-tuned violin and are likely to keep on doing so.

Still, Gorbachev has kept trying. In September 1986 Polish leader Jaruzelski traveled to the P.R.C., and Honecker of the G.D.R. was due in October; others followed in 1987. The Eastern European diplomatic rumor mill was indicating that the NSWP states expected to reestablish direct party-to-party ties with the Chinese soon (except for Romania, which never broke them). One hardly needs to say that these things would not happen except with Soviet approval; it is more probable, in fact, that they are occurring at Soviet instigation.

While trying to improve relations with the P.R.C., Gorbachev has simultaneously pursued other policies aimed at undermining Chinese regional influence. For example, throughout 1986 the Gorbachev team made major efforts to upset North Korea's traditional balancing act between the two communist giants and to draw Pyongyang closer to Moscow. The U.S.S.R. has also continued to support vigorously its strategically located client in Hanoi. In regard to both countries Gorbachev achieved tangible successes: Korean-Soviet cooperation noticeably increased, and Hanoi remained at bitter odds with the PRC. Gorbachev also revived the Soviet diplomatic campaign for an Asian security conference, but so far with no signs of success. Although this policy initiative was essentially intended as an adjunct to his global arms control policies vis-à-vis the West, in Beijing it inevitably evokes memories of Brezhnev's encirclement policy against the PRC.

By the middle of 1987 Gorbachev had made a fair beginning in what would in any case have to be a long-term program to restore closer ties with the PRC and, it was hoped, reduce the degree of Beijing's cooperation with the West. Yet it was only a beginning. Although economic cooperation and trade between the two countries were on the upswing, these were areas where the USSR would have difficulty in competing with the West. Economic ties alone are likely to accomplish little beyond contributing to a favorable atmosphere for political rapprochement. In the political sphere Gorbachev has made a better beginning than any Soviet leader since the Sino-Soviet split. Yet despite his success in improving the atmosphere between the USSR and the PRC, fundamental strategic and political differences between them remain. It would not be reasonable to expect the differences to disappear in the forseeable future.

Selected Sino-Soviet Chronology

(Because of the low level at which Sino-Soviet relations started when Gorbachev came to power and because of the relative importance of even small efforts to improve ties, this chronology is in greater detail than the others)

March 1985

3–14	A P.R.C. parliamentary delagation was visiting the U.S.S.R. Gorbachev met with PRC Vice Premier Li Peng on 14 March.
11	Gorbachev elected general secretary, CPSU.

April 1985

1	A PRC delegation, headed by a deputy chairman of the State Economic Commission, held talks in Moscow with Ministry of Foreign Trade officials and signed a protocol relating to transport of trade goods between the two countries.
9	The regular round of political consultations at the level of deputy foreign minister began in Moscow.
15	The Union of Soviet Friendship Societies (SSOD) and PRC counterparts met to discuss the 1985 plan for cooperation under auspices of the Soviet-Chinese Friendship Society.

May 1985
Nothing reported.

June 1985

4	Deputy Minister of Foreign Trade Toluveyev was reported in Beijing. The same day an informal cooperation agreement was reported signed between the Soviet telegraph agency and the Sinkiang Information Agency.
22	The Commission of Automotive Transportation and Highways of the Organization of Rail Cooperation (PRC, USSR, Eastern European states, and North Korea) met in Beijing.

July 1985

9–16   PRC Deputy Prime Minister Yao Yilin was in Moscow and met with First Deputy Chairman Arkhipov, Council of Ministers, and others. He signed a trade agreement for 1986–90 calling for doubling 1985 trade turnover by 1990, plus Soviet assistance in modernizing older industrial facilities and in building new ones in the PRC. He met with Tikhonov on 11 July and later traveled in U.S.S.R.

August 1985

10   A Soviet trade union delegation was reported visiting the PRC, the first to do so in 20 years.

September 1985

2–3   The chairman of PRC Council for Promotion of Trade was in Moscow for a trade exposition. He met with First Deputy Chairman Arkhipov, Council of Ministers, and signed an agreement of cooperation with the Industrial Trade Chamber of the U.S.S.R.

27   Foreign Minister Shevandnadze held talks with the Chinese foreign minister in New York at the UNGA.

October 1985

4–18   Deputy Minister of Foreign Affairs Ilichev (also the regular representative to the Soviet—PRC Political Consultative Committee) met with Chinese officials in the seventh round of consultations. The discussions were described as "frank, calm and business like" (meaning: extensive disagreement calmly discussed).

9–14   A Supreme Soviet delegation visited the PRC.

6–14   The Head of PRC State Statistical Directorate, and a delegation, visited Moscow.

24   A Soviet Women's Committee delegation was reported in the PRC.

November 1985

11–26   PRC Foreign Ministry representatives were in Moscow and signed a consular agreement.

18   A writers delegation from the PRC was reported in Moscow.

18 November–   Delegation of PRC economists from the Institute of Plan-

| 17 December | ned Economy (under the State Planning Committee) in the U.S.S.R. as guests of the Academy of Sciences. |
| 21 | Chairman of the State Committee for Cinematography Ermash was reported in the PRC with a Soviet film industry delegation. |

December 1985

| 7–13 | Deputy Foreign Minister Kapitsa, with delegation, was in Beijing for consultations. |
| 23 | PRC Vice Premier Li Peng made an official visit to the U.S.S.R. He met with Gorbachev, and separately with GOSPLAN Chairman Talyzin (who is also the first deputy chairman of the Council of Ministers). |

January 1986

| 23 | A Soviet-PRC Protocol of Trade and Payments for 1986 was signed. Soviet exports were listed as machines, tools, transportation equipment, ferrous metals, fertilizers, cement, and finished wood products. The Chinese exports listed included raw materials and light industry, textile and cultural products, and agricultural products. |

February 1986

Again, there was no PRC delegation at the CPSU Congress.

March 1986

| 14–21 | First Deputy Chairman Arkhipov, Council of Ministers, led the most senior delegation in many years to the PRC for the first meeting of the new Soviet-Chinese Commission for Economic, Trade, and Scientific-Technical Cooperation. A protocol was signed involving Soviet assistance in reconstruction of older industrial facitities and help with new ones (this part was evidently a formalization of elements of the agreement signed in July 1985 in Moscow [see above]), cooperation in planning, educational exchanges, and so on. Contrary to suggestions in the Soviet press, the Chinese stated that political issues remained without improvement. |
| 31 | A Foreign Minstry representative went to Beijing for consultations related to the UNGA. |

April 1986

| 7–14 | The eighth round of Soviet-PRC Political consultations (at deputy-foreign-minister level) were held in Moscow. The |

talks were described as "quiet, open and businesslike" (indicating only a trace less disagreement than in the October round). Afterward the Chinese deputy foreign minister met with Shevardnadze.

24   A large mobile Soviet industrial exposition opened in Beijing. It was scheduled to travel to many parts of the PRC.

25   A protocol was signed to improve and facilitate the movement of goods between Soviet and Chinese Amur River ports.

May 1986

11 May–2 June   A delegation from the PRC Academy of Social Sciences visited the USSR.

20   A PRC delegation was reported in Moscow. Its members met with Minister of Culture (and candidate Politburo member) Demichev and signed a cultural agreement for 1986–87.

31   An agreement was signed with the PRC to facilitate port procedures for Soviet vessels in China.

June 1986

3–19   A PRC women's delegation visited.

18   The Soviet SSOD signed a cooperation plan with PRC counterparts for 1986–87.

Exact dates not given   An Academy of Science delegation spent a week in the PRC and signed an agreement for literature and science exchanges.

29 June–21 July   The deputy chairman of the PRC State Planning Commission was in the USSR. He visited nuclear power plants and held meeting with GKES Chairman Katuschev.

July 1986

7   A working plan of cooperation for 1986–87 was signed between the Soviet State Film Committee and the PRC Ministry of Radio, Cinematography, and Television.

12   A border incident involving shooting took place, according to Japanese press reports; in August both Chinese and Soviet spokesmen admitted this but played down its seriousness.

13   A delegation of the PRC Trade Union of Workers in Machine Construction and Metallurgy was reported in the U.S.S.R.

25   The chairman of the PRC Committee to Assist Development of International Trade opened a trade fair in Moscow. Twenty-seven Chinese ministries and trade companies were

represented in the fair, which lasted until 10 August. This was the first purely PRC trade fair in the U.S.S.R. since 1953.

29   In his Vladivostok speech Gorbachev called for several lines of developing better relations with the PRC, including economic cooperation, resolution of border disagreements, force reductions along the borders, and so on. Other parts of the speech were also clearly aimed at the PRC as much as at other audiences or even more so (e.g. the announced withdrawal of some forces from Afghanistan, the willingness to reduce Soviet forces in Mongolia, and the like). He also urged the PRC and Vietnam to settle their differences. Initially, the Chinese response was mostly non-committal, stating that the Chinese were studying the speech. On 30 July, Deng Xiaoping was quoted as saying that there were some "positive aspects," but he called unequivocally for a "complete and total" Soviet withdrawal from Afghanistan.

31   The Soviet-PRC Border Railroad Commission met in Harbin and signed a protocol to facilitate cross-border rail traffic.

August 1986

9   First Deputy Chairman Arkhipov, Council of Ministers, went to Beijing for acupuncture treatment.
Although the trip was "unofficial" he was reported to have met with PRC officials while there.

15   A Soviet friendship society delegation was in Beijing for World War II victory celebrations.

17 August–
1 September   The mayor of Beijing and a delegation were in the U.S.S.R. On 1 September he met with Yeltsin.

19   Discussions in Alma Alta were completed between representatives of the Export-Import Company of Sinkiang and the Soviet Central Asian and Kazakhstan Foreign Trade Trust ("Vostokintorg"); a number of contracts relating to regional products sales were signed.

20 August–
5 September   A PRC Friendship Society delegation was reported traveling in the U.S.S.R.

22–29   A Supreme Soviet delegation from the Planning and Budget Commission visited the PRC.

September 1986

3–15   A delegation of Chinese international relations academics was hosted by the Soviet Academy of Sciences.

5   A large Soviet delegation attended a book fair in Beijing.

8–15   First Deputy Chairman Talyzin, Council of Ministers (who is also chairman of GOSPLAN), accompanied by GKES

Chairman Katushev, Minister of the Lumber, Celloulose-Paper and Woodworking Industries Busygin, and Foreign Ministry representatives, made a major visit to the PRC. Numerous group and individual discussions were held with Chinese officials including Premier Zhao Ziyang, Deputy Premiers Yao Yilin and Li Peng, the head of the Chinese Planning Commission, and others. The Soviets also toured agricultural and industrial regions in which the Chinese had instituted economic liberalization reforms. Agreements for cooperation between state planning committees; a consular agreement; and several documents adding products to the trade agreement, as well as relating to transportation questions, were signed.

12–19   The deputy chairman of the PRC State Committee for Education and a delegation visited the U.S.S.R.

17   Foreign Ministry representatives opened border discussions with the PRC in Beijing. Earlier a Soviet deputy foreign minister had stated that Moscow was prepared to accept PRC demands that the border be delineated along the main channels of the Amur and Issuri rivers (instead of on the Chinese banks). This would result in the transfer of several disputed islands to the PRC.

25   Soviet and Chinese experts meeting in Beijing reached agreement on cooperation in joint usage of the waters of the Amur and Argun rivers.

25   Foreign Minister Shevardnadze met in New York with PRC Foreign Minister Wu Xuegian.

October 1986

5   Special emissary of the Soviet government Deputy Minister of Foreign Affairs Rogachev arrived in Beijing for the ninth round of Sino-Soviet talks.

11–20   Delegation of Chinese historians visited the U.S.S.R.

15   Rogachev and O. Troyanovskiy, Soviet Ambassador to the PRC, met in Beijing with the Chinese Deputy Minister of Foreign Affairs to inform him about the Iceland summit.

15   Chairman of State Committee for Scientific and Technological Ties Marchuk received his Chinese counterpart.

23   Sino-Soviet agreement was signed in Moscow on the establishment of a joint commission to work out a plan for rights to use the border areas of the Argun and Amur Rivers.

November 1986

25   The fourth All-Union Conference of Soviet-Chinese Friendship Societies met in Moscow.

30   A delegation of the Finance and Economic Commission of

the Chinese parliament began an official visit to the U.S.S.R.

December 1986

5
First Deputy Chairman Demichev, Presidium of the Supreme Soviet received the visiting Chinese parliamentary delegation.

11
Chinese consulate opened in Leningrad.

12
Soviet delegation of the Union of Journalists of the U.S.S.R. headed by General Secretary of TASS, S. Losev, visited Beijing as guests of the Chinese Association of Journalists.

13
Ryzhkov sent greetings to the visitors to the Soviet trade and industrial exhibition in China, the largest of its kind in thirty years.

January 1987

15
The Soviet press made a formal announcement that one motorized rifle division and several independent units would be withdrawn from Mongolia in April and June. This was the confirmation of Gorbachev's announcement the previous July and was obviously aimed at influencing the Chinese who were not overly impressed since a full four divisions, plus support troops remained.

16
A press article reported that about 200 Soviets were studying or teaching in the PRC.

9-10
Foreign Ministry colleague Polyakov visited the PRC for consultations on the Middle East.

February 1987

7
It was announced that a contract for the sale of railroad freight wagons to the Chinese had been signed by a Soviet trust.

9-23
Soviet-PRC bordr talks were held in Moscow at the Deputy Foreign Minister level.

March 1987

2-16
Soviet and Chinese experts met to work out a specific plan to utilize the water resources of the Amur and Argun rivers.

16
The 1987 Soviet-PRC Trade protocol was signed in Beijing. Reportedly, the terms envisaged a significant increase over 1986 levels.

24-28
The fourteenth regional conference of Pacific states was held in Beijing. The Soviet delegation, led by Deputy For-

eign Minister Petrovskiy, stressed regional security proposals. Petrovskiy also held private consultations with
Chinese counterparts.

April 1987

14–20   Soviet-PRC Political talks were held in Moscow. Deputy
Foreign Minister Qian Qichen led the PRC delegation; the
talks were described as "businesslike and open"—indicating remaining differences.

May 1987

1   The education working group of the Soviet-PRC Commission for Economic and Scientific-Technical Cooperation
met in Beijing.

11–14   The second session of the Soviet-PRC Commission for Economic and Scientific-Technical Cooperation met in
Moscow. Deputy Premier Yao Yilin led the Chinese delegation and also met separately with Ryzhkov and several economic ministers.

21   A 1987–89 Academies of Sciences cooperation plan was
signed in Beijing by the vice president of the Soviet Academy of Sciences.

21   A 1987–89 cooperation agreement between State Committees for television and radio was signed.

28   A 1988–89 protocol of working relations between State
Committees for Publication, Polygraphics and Book Trade
was signed in Beijing.

29   The fifteenth session of the Conference of Ministers' Organization for Railroad Cooperation (PRC, U.S.S.R., East Europe and North Korea) opened in Beijing.

June 1987

No date given   A P.R.C. Department of Tourism delegation visited and
signed a memmorandum to increase tourism between
U.S.S.R. and the P.R.C.

11

Winning the Hearts and Minds: Relations with the Third World

"When you're wounded and left on Afghanistan's plains, And the women come out to cut up what remains; Jest roll to your rifle and blow out your brains, An' go to your Gawd like a soldier!"

—Rudyard Kipling

In early 1985, whenever the new general secretary and his advisers took stock of Soviet international positions, they undoubtedly were concerned with many uncertainties and problems in the Third World. At the same time they could be quite pleased about opportunities there.

Most of the USSR's uncertainties, problems, and opportunities in the Third World are either well known or have been mentioned in earlier chapters and need not be repeated in detail here. Some, however, are worth reiterating or elaborating upon. Throughout the Third World the Soviets had succeeded in maintaining their predominant influence and/or close ties with most of the states that had become Soviet clients during or even before the heady days of detente. These relationships had brought the USSR many strategic assets in the global East-West competition. States like Vietnam, Afghanistan, Ethiopia, South Yemen (the PDRY), Mozambique, Angola, Syria, Iraq, Libya, Cuba, and Nicaragua are strategically located astride or adjacent to major international lines of communication and commerce, or they provide convenient access to trouble spots that pose tempting targets for expanding Soviet influence at the expense of the West. A few of these states possess valuable natural resources, and all are potentially very important locations for military bases or access that could play a key role in any armed conflict. Some, Cuba in particular, provided surrogate military forces that were instrumental in maintaining or expanding the scope of Soviet influence. Other states in which Soviet influence was much less but still significant, such as India, Algeria, and Guinea, offered other or similar potential benefits.

On the other hand, virtually all of Moscow's clients, to say nothing of the rest of the Third World, were demonstrating a disconcerting tendency to increasingly turn to the West for closer economic and, in some cases, even military ties. Most of the Third World clients represented economic burdens; some, such as Cuba and Vietnam, very heavy ones. Soviet control over almost all of them was imperfect; several, particularly Libya and Syria, posed the constant danger of embroiling the USSR in unwanted or unprofitable regional adventures. Iraq had already put Moscow in a predicament by forcing it to balance its existing stake in Baghdad against its desires to control strategically much more valuable Iran. Association with some of these states (e.g. Vietnam, Ethiopia, Libya) was costly in terms of negative impact on neighboring nations, which, if not threatened by a Soviet client, could potentially be promising targets for increased Soviet influence. In one case, that of Iraq and Syria, two clients were almost as much at odds with one another as they were with their more Western-aligned neighbors. Several client states were engaged in difficult, protracted civil or regional conflicts, and the USSR itself had been drawn into a costly and seemingly endless war in Afghanistan. Finally, after a period of retreat and disengagement, the United States was once again mounting a major, if only partially successful, challenge to the relatively free hand that Moscow had enjoyed in the Third World for several years. Moreover, Washington continued to proclaim a linkage between Soviet and Soviet-client activity in the Third World and any improvement in U.S.-Soviet relations—and sometimes the Americans acted accordingly.

Gradually, the outlines of Gorbachev's policies toward the Third World in general, and toward various regions in particular, have begun to emerge and then to take on a fuller shape. Although fully consistent with previously pursued Soviet policies, Gorbachev's have included some significant shifts in emphasis. The record strongly indicates that in large measure his was a process of trial-and-error learning and of the gradual fashioning of choices rather than a case of following a comprehensive concept or blueprint from the beginning. Gorbachev acted early on to cement and reinforce ties with important Third World leaders such as Gandhi and Ortega. As the year progressed, virtually every leader of every client state was either entertained in Moscow or called there for consultations. Similar efforts were made in regard to less closely aligned but still Soviet-leaning countries and to more pro-Western and even anti-Soviet ones. Wherever heads-of-state visits were not practical, major economic, cultural, and parliamentary delegations were dispatched and hosted. The number, frequency, and scope of these exchanges began to assume a scale exceeding that of previous years, reaching out to nations that formerly had had almost no contacts with Moscow.

Gorbachev has continued the traditional Soviet verbal support for issues dear to Third World hearts, but he has done it in a way suggestive of a firmer, more articulate, and more specific Soviet interest and commitment than previously. He has sought simultaneously to marshal greater international support for distinctly Soviet objectives by emphasizing that renunciation of SDI and the reduction of the arms race by the United States and the West is a prerequisite to realization of Third World aspirations and tangible levels of Soviet support for them.

Although Soviet military assistance to Third World states and revolutionary causes under Gorbachev has probably not been markedly reduced and in some cases may have expanded, both the rhetoric and at least some of the realities of Soviet assistance have been increasingly focused on economic, technical, diplomatic, and cultural arrangements. (Levels of actual miliary assistance, especially current or recent levels, are hard to determine accurately from open sources, a problem discussed at the end of the chronology accompanying this chapter. One estimate published in late 1986 indicated that Soviet arms exports to the noncommunist Third World were 25 percent less in 1985 than in 1984. Such a figure cannot really be evaluated until one knows what is being compared—credits, agreements for future sales, cash sales, deliveries, or the like—and what definitions are used. In this chapter we are referring to Soviet military assistance to all Third World states and causes, communist or noncommunist. It is worth noting that other reports stated that the Soviets sold far more arms in 1985 than did the United States, 30.4 percent of the global total compared to 17.8 percent, and that several very large arms deals in 1986 have come to light; see chronology.) A series of agreements and discussions in 1985 and 1986 ended with proclamations of either concrete plans for, or intentions of, increased trade. Agreements on direct assistance in economic projects have been concluded with a number of Third World states, and apparently proposed to many more.

Moscow has loudly proclaimed its willingness, and even eagerness, to participate in and support regional agreements aimed at reducing tensions and conflicts through "mutual accommodation." The Soviets have put forth proposals for such regional agreements or indicated their support for those put forth by their clients. Unfortunately, a closer look at the proposals tends to reveal some flies in the ointment. For example, the proposals coming from Moscow, Kabul, Luanda, Managua, and Hanoi all imply the settlement of regional or civil strife on the basis of the complete cessation of outside interference and foreign support of rebel causes, and guarantees for the preservation of the incumbent pro-Moscow governments. Yet, along with outpouring of Soviet rhetoric in the cause of reduction of conflicts, the actual pace and intensity of Soviet or client-state military operations in Afghanistan, Kampuchea, and Angola has dramatically escalated. The rhetoric is reasonable and accommodationist but the reality seems to reflect more attempts to "solve" the problems by increasing the costs to the West and by creating military facts on the ground. Furthermore, although Gorbachev's new Party Program was significantly less bellicose and much more ambiguous than previous official formulations on the subject of supporting wars of national liberation and revolutionary movements, it is hard to find concrete cases where such support is actually on the wane.

Gorbachev has also heavily indulged in the traditional Soviet excoriation of U.S. and Western imperialism as the cause of virtually all the ills plaguing the Third World. Even in the propagandistically more "subdued" period directly preceding and following the Geneva summit, it was impossible to detect any change in the Soviet press. There was a steady regurgitation of charges of covert U.S. involvement in various nefarious pursuits, including such farfetched concoctions as the production and use by South Africa of chemical or biological weapons supposed to affect only the blacks. Predictably, the Gorbachev regime attempted to reap the maximal propaganda payoffs from such developments as the U.S. strikes against Libya, South African incursions into neighboring states, Israeli actions in southern Lebanon, and the numerous instances of repression or civil disturbances in El Salvador, Chile, the Philippines, South Africa, South Korea, the Israeli-occupied West Bank (Judea and Samaria), and so on. If anything, such rhetoric has increased. On the other hand, Soviet actions have been far milder than Soviet words, for example, in the aftermath of the Libyan strikes, when there was also circumstantial evidence that the Soviets were pressuring Libya and Syria to tone down their rhetoric and to diminish or disguise their support for international terror.

Several basic conclusions seem to be warranted.

First, Gorbachev and his associates have no intention of abandoning the long and traditional struggle to extend Soviet influence throughout the Third World at the expense of that of the West in general and the United States in particular. Although Moscow has some purely regional interests in specific parts of the Third World and also a more diffuse long-term aspiration to see its brand of "socialism" spread throughout the globe, the main and normally overriding focus of Soviet Third World policy relates to the struggle with the West. The conduct of this policy by and large follows recognizable geopolitical and "pragmatic" great power patterns. And despite ideological rationalizations, it has long been evident that the fortunes of local Communist parties always take a back seat when they stand in the way of the foreign policies of the USSR.

The second conclusion: as long as the central goals of Soviet foreign policy are focused on restoration of East-West detente and reduction through arms control of the U.S. strategic military challenge, it is recognizably in Gorbachev's interest to reduce the overall incidence of visible confrontation and adventurism in the Third World—especially military confrontation. Because of its continued commitment to the long-term struggle, the Gorbachev regime seems just as determined as any of its predecessors to use all the means at its disposal to prevent losses or setbacks in the existing network of its client states and positions of influence.

As long as major losses can be avoided, Gorbachev seems perfectly prepared to make modest accommodations and, where needed, to put a damper on some of his clients. In places these two imperatives appear to clash, clear cases in point being Afghanistan and Angola, the apparent pattern is to press for local military victory as quickly as possible. Moreover, Soviet domestic economic needs create strong incentives for Gorbachev to seek ways to reduce the costs of maintaining far-flung positions. Averting military confrontations is one direct means. Pressuring Eastern European allies to assume a greater share of the burden of the bloc's overall military and economic assistance to Third World clients is another. It is an advantageous one, for it would also boost integration of the Soviet bloc and contribute to the reduction of Eastern European reliance on Western economic ties. Seeking mutually beneficial economic relationships with Third World states is still another means, albeit in many cases a less promising one, given economic realities on both end of such relationships.

The third conclusion: Gorbachev has obviously sought to mobilize as much of the Third World as possible in his campaign to bring international pressure on the United States to halt SDI and to yield to Soviet demands regarding nuclear arms control. This aspect of Gorbachev's policy is not without its ironic side. Although Gorbachev himself has with one exception consistently followed his predecessors' policy of denying the validity of any linkage between Soviet behavior in the Third World and arms control or U.S.-Soviet economic relations, his rhetoric about the need to settle regional conflicts peacefully and his presentation of Third World issues as first requiring an end to SDI and the nuclear arms race undermine his own arguments against such linkage. Even more ironically, under Gorbachev the Soviet press has featured a number of articles that argue the Soviet case against U.S. behavior and policies in Nicaragua, Angola, Kampuchea, and Afghanistan precisely in terms of such a linkage.

The fourth conclusion: Gorbachev's policies in a number of Third World regions indicate a pattern of preparing the groundwork for optimal exploitation of future opportunities, even when those policies run counter to the objective of avoiding U.S.-Soviet confrontation. The clearest example of this is in southern Africa, where conditions are favorable for continuing recruitment of allies under the banner of anti-Americanism and where a collapse of the South African regime must be considered as a possibility. A critical question is whether Gorbachev and company would see such opportunities as tempting enough to engage in some provocations and adventurism, even if this would mean sacrificing his current policy objectives toward the United States. The answer probably would depend on many factors—regional, domestic (economic), and global (U.S.-Soviet relationships)—at the time such a dilemma arose. Like any good chess player, Gorbachev wants to keep his options open.

The final conclusion: Soviet behavior has shown recently that the Gorbachev leadership remains just as wary as its predecessors of getting involved in any situation that could inadvertently escalate into an uncontrollable military confrontation with the United States. This, of course, is a function of both U.S. actions and Soviet perceptions of U.S. resolve and inclination to take risks. Where the United States seems to be willing and able to take firm military measures—especially in instances like the Libyan strikes, in which Congress and public opinion do not inhibit the administration—the Soviet Union under Gorbachev has so far shown clear restraint in regard to direct miliary response. Of course, waves of indignant and condemnatory rhetoric have invariably followed all instances of U.S. resort to arms. When an activist U.S. administration appears to operate under considerable domestic and international pressure against its preferred policies, for example in Nicaragua, Gorbachev appears quite willing to continue levels of support that could potentially lead to a confrontation—even at a distance or in a location where all of the local military advantages would be in the hands of the Americans.

These are the general patterns detectable in Gorbachev's policies toward the Third World. Let us examine the actual steps he has undertaken in regard to individual Third World regions and subregions.

East Asia and the Pacific

For a little over a year, Gorbachev's policy approach to East Asia and the Pacific, and in fact to the whole of Asia, was not noticeably different from that of his recent predecessors. There were some differences in nuance and priorities in regard to particular states, and the Soviets became more active in doing the things they had always done, but that was really all. Then at the end of July 1986, Gorbachev unveiled a fairly dramatic emphasis upon Asia and the Pacific, upon all of Asia except the Middle East rather than just the subregion discussed here. At Vladivostok he again put an Asian version of CSCE up front in Soviet policy proposals. He stressed Asian and Pacific economic cooperation and integration, asserted that the USSR was also a major Asian nation (a truism), and seemed to promise a future Soviet focus on Asia and the Pacific that would rival the traditional Russian and Soviet preoccupation with Europe and the West.

The USSR has, of course, become much more of an Asian power than before. The Pacific fleet is now the largest of the four Soviet fleets, and Soviet operational bases are located in Vietnam, at least rivaling if still a long way from equaling those the United States maintains in the Philippines. The very large ground forces in the East are largely composed of lower-category motorized infantry divisions, not the combat-ready, tank-division-heavy forces opposite NATO and Europe, but they are backed up by a very sizeable bomber and SS-20 nuclear strike force. In spite of the inadequacies of the trans-Siberian railroad and the Baikal-Amur Magistral (BAM) that has been built to parallel and supplement it, and in spite of the distances, in miliary terms the USSR is very much an Asian and Pacific power.

The Soviet Far East and Siberia are richly endowed with natural resources, and every Soviet leader has called for a greater effort to develop and exploit those resources. Japan is courted not only because it is the world's second economic power, and because of what it could conceivably provide to assist the development of Soviet Asia, but also because of fears over what its technology could add to the U.S. SDI; what its economy could add to Chinese growth and to overall regional development, hampering Soviet opportunities for expansion; and what its potential military rearmament could do to alter both the regional and global correlation of forces. China, of course, with all its great potential is also both an object of Soviet courtship and a traditional object of Soviet fear.

Other Asian and Pacific states are also important to Moscow. Vietnam provides a geostrategic treasure astride a major global maritime chokepoint. Together, the nations of Southeast Asia and the Indonesian archipelago possess vast natural resources and potentially serve the same geostrategic function as Hanoi. Australia has been an important source of Soviet grain purchases and it and all the island states of the Central, Southern, and Western Pacific are critical elements in the U.S. ability to challenge the USSR for regional dominance. Indeed, by all logic Asia and the Pacific should be of major interest and high priority to the Kremlin. Nevertheless, there are many reasons to take Gorbachev's words at Vladivostok with a heavy dose of salt.

Soviet leaders have always talked about developing Siberia, but distances, climate, lack of infrastructure, inadequate population, preoccupation with both Eastern and Western Europe, the relatively much greater influence of political and economic elites in other regions, and other factors have always combined to insure that priorities are not changed. To

develop eastern Siberia's full potential would require inordinate investment and, probably, technology not yet available to the Soviets. Gorbachev's economic program cannot spare limited investment funds from
reconstruction in the more western parts of the country. Moreover, if he
were to shift funds significantly in favor of the East he would be taking great
political risks. Although Gorbachev may be riding tall in the saddle now, he
needs to achieve real success in either his main domestic economic or his
foreign policy lines, or both. Concentrating investment in the Soviet Far
East and Siberia is too long term a proposition to yield results in time.
Hence, it hardly seems insignificant that the emphasis was placed on regional self-sufficiency and initiative, or that Gorbachev called upon the
inhabitants of the Soviet East to take their destinies into their own hands.
Certainly, Moscow will continue to develop the region gradually; funds
that can be spared will undoubtedly be provided. But this will not be at the
expense of other, more traditional centers. Internal economic dynamics
will insure the predominance of the Soviet West over the Soviet East in
USSR foreign policy.

When one looks at the foreign policy content of Gorbachev's
Vladivostok speech in a wider context, the judgment that it does not mark
any real shift in Soviet foreign policy is reinforced. Certainly, the speech
was designed to support Soviet objectives in regard to Japan and the PRC,
but it should be seen primarily as another component of an overall strategy
aimed at the West in general and the United States in particular. It marks at
most a broadening of that central competition and relationship, not a shift
away from it. Within this context, let us now consider Gorbachev's policies
toward the other states in the region.

We have noted Gorbachev's relative success in strengthening relations
with North Korea. In addition to disrupting Pyongyang's traditional balancing act between Moscow and Beijing, this may have been designed to
ensure firmer Soviet control over potential developments on the Korean
Peninsula in the event of civil unrest or any attempt to pursue Korean
reunification, and to avoid any unfavorable developments arising from a
succession crisis in North Korea when Kim Il-Sung dies. In this, the Gorbachev Politburo was simply pursuing long-standing Soviet policy goals,
but evidently with greater success than ever before, due in no small measure to Pyongyang's disapaproval of the PRC's rapprochement with the
United States.

The USSR has three additional considerations in regard to North Korea.
First, North Korean military advisers and pilots have for some years
formed a useful, if relatively small, adjunct to the surrogates that the
Soviets have used as part of their overall Third World military involvement. Closer ties with Moscow and greater reliance on Soviet economic

and military support both enhance the North Korean role in the Third World and guarantee that North Korean performance there will conform to Soviet wishes and produce no adverse effects for the USSR.

The second consideration is longer term and relates to Japan. Tokyo commands the second-mightiest economy in the world and has the potential of becoming a military power of considerable significance. Should present Soviet attempts to establish closer ties with the Japanese fail and should Japan begin to seriously rearm, the traditional Soviet method of simultaneously applying both political and military pressure on Japan would be facilitated by Soviet retention of firm control over North Korea.

The third consideration relates to the PRC. Gorbachev may have reversed the Khrushchev-Brezhnev policy of encircling and isolating China by recruiting allies and forming a "security community" in Asia, and may now be thinking more in terms of pushing back the United States in Asia and the Pacific. Still, the Khrushchev-Brezhnev policy pattern remains a likely fallback option should relations with Beijing take a significant turn for the worse. In that case North Korea would be slated to be part of an anti-Chinese ring of alliances and relationships, along with the rest of the Asian nations extending south and then west around the PRC.

Gorbachev stepped up Soviet efforts in the Pacific to improve ties with the many tiny island states that have emerged there. Three objectives are indicated by the tenor and content of Soviet press commentary. One is military and is aimed at pushing back U.S. bases and control of the Western Pacific while expanding the reach and access of the Soviet Pacific fleet. The second is economic; it involves fishing access and has been the ostensible purpose of direct negotiations with these ministates. The third objective is diplomatic: to increase the number of nations supporting Soviet positions in the UN.

Southeast Asia

The Gorbachev team has worked hard to strengthen close Soviet relationships with Vietnam, Laos, and Kampuchea. Economic and military contacts have predominated, although cultural and educational programs have not been neglected. The bases and access for the Soviet navy and air force in Vietnam are so strategically valuable for Moscow that it has no option but to provide full support to Hanoi. At the same time Vietnamese determination to dominate Laos and Kampuchea places a major obstacle in the path of improving Soviet ties with the PRC and with other regional states that feel threatened by Hanoi. In the long run Indonesia and Malaysia, with their equally strategic locations and much greater wealth of natural resources, are more valuable prizes. The policy solution that Gorbachev seems to have adopted for the present is to continue to provide full-scale support to the Vietnamese military effort in Kampuchea in the hope of bringing it quickly to a successful conclusion. The expectation is that the fears of the neighboring states could eventually be somehow dissipated.

The same approach also appears to be the main one that Moscow is taking to sidestep the PRC's condition that Vietnam must be forced to withdraw from Kampuchea before Soviet-Chinese ties can be fully normalized. Hanoi is simply too important to Moscow for Gorbachev to comply with Beijing's demand, assuming that the Vietnamese would actually bend to Soviet pressure on this, which is not at all certain. Moreover, it is almost inevitable that Beijing and Moscow be rivals for influence in Hanoi, unless the communist world were somehow to unite under one banner and one central leadership, which hardly seems possible. Gorbachev's only realistic hope seems to be that once Hanoi is fully victorious in Kampuchea, this obstacle to better relations with the PRC will simply disappear, even though Beijing will not be pleased with the result.

Gorbachev's policy has also assigned high priority to developing closer economic relationships with the three Indo-Chinese states. Vietnam was already a member of CEMA when Gorbachev came to power, and economic ties with Laos and Kampuchea were already quite close. Under Gorbachev they have been strengthened to the extent that the Laotians and Kampucheans have coordinated state plans and signed agreements for increasing trade with the USSR to virtually the same levels as formal members of CEMA. In addition to the direct benefits such links provide, they also tend to promote the integration of the economies of the three Indo-Chinese nations in a way serving Soviet interests.

Economically, Vietnam and its satellites also pose a problem for Moscow. With its own economic problems and priorities, the Soviet Union is hardly in a position to increase the already considerable economic burden of supporting three virtually "basket-case" Southeast Asian national economies. If other considerations did not stand in the way, Moscow would undoubtedly prefer to reduce these expenses. In concrete actions so far, Gorbachev's answer to this dilemma has been to encourage or, more accurately, to demand that the Eastern Europeans step up their economic assistance to Hanoi (this on top of all the other demands Gorbachev has placed on them). Economic costs are also a factor of Soviet determination to see the Kampuchean war terminated as quickly as possible. In all these things, Gorbachev has been simply continuing his predecessors' policies, but apparently with a greater sense of urgency.

In mid-1986, there were indications that Gorbachev and company were adding a new element to their strategy for reducing the Vietnam problem. After Le Duan's death, and possibly beginning even before, it appeared that

Moscow was pressuring Hanoi to "get its act together"—especially eco-nomically, and perhaps in regard to behaving with a bit more sensitivity toward Beijing. The large delegation that Ryzhkov led to Le Duan's funeral engaged in extensive talks with the new Vietnamese leader, Truong Chinh. This was followed by a meeting the next month in Moscow between Gor-bachev and Truong Chinh. About that time reports began to circulate that Hanoi had been told in strong terms to straighten out its economy along the same lines that Gorbachev was instituting in the USSR. Subsequently, at the Vietnamese Party meetings in the fall, there was a great emphasis on economic reform and indications of the beginnings of a major personnel shakeup. Near the end of the year the shakeup took place, with even Truong Chinh falling after only a half-year at the top. The winners were apparently the "reformers"; a Soviet hand in these developments seems likely.

Gorbachev has also taken steps to try to improve relations with other states of the region, including sending senior economic delegations to Mal-aysia and Indonesia, and parliamentary groups to Thailand and the Philip-pines. Representatives from each of these nations were also received in Moscow in 1986. These efforts were aimed primarily at Jakarta and Kuala Lumpur, but in spite of the seniority of the Soviet delegations (headed by then Deputy Chairman Ryabov of the Council of Ministers) and repor-tedly attractive trade and assistance offers, the degree of success achieved has apparently not yet been very high.

In regard to the Philippines, Gorbachev's foreign policy advisers seem to have led him astray. Removal of the U.S. military bases in the Philippines has long been a Soviet goal, and Moscow had long attempted to cultivate the Marcos family. The existence of a sizeable homegrown communist insurgency did not help these policies, even though evidence of direct Soviet support to the rebels has been very limited and ambiguous. At the very height of Marcos's difficulties Moscow blundered by being the first to congratulate him warmly on his fraudulent and fleeting electoral "victory." It took the Kremlin several long days to readjust and begin to try to patch things up with the new Aquino government.

South Asia

Right from the beginning the Gorbachev Politburo moved to buttress relations with India, with the aim of encouraging Prime Minister Gandhi to continue his mother's anti-American, pro-Moscow orientation. Gandhi himself was repeatedly entertained royally, and it was hardly accidental that India became the first Third World state visited by Gorbachev. Strong support was voiced for traditional Indian policy goals and a steady stream of high-level economic, political, and military delegations traveled both ways between Moscow and New Delhi. Gorbachev continued previous policies of emphasizing technological and the most modern military assistance, as well as trade subsidies. The facts that India, first among the nations that are not Soviet satellites, has received production rights for some very modern Soviet military hardware (including the MiG-29 in summer 1986) and that is the steady recipient of the most advanced military weaponry exported by the USSR underscore the importance Moscow attaches to its relations with New Delhi. With a new, U.S.-educated leader in New Delhi and with Washington attempting to improve its relations through more modern technological assistance to India, Gorbachev faced a challenge that he quickly attempted to meet. He has apparently succeeded so far in preventing any real loss of Soviet influence. Indicative of this success in India's continued policy of reacting to the Soviet involvement in Afghanistan more evasively than most nonaligned states. At the same time the Soviets apparently have not been able to totally block some limited rapprochement between Washington and New Delhi. The contest between the USSR and the West for influence in India remains very much alive.

As noted, Gorbachev's policy in Afghanistan has been to step up the pace of the war in an effort to bring it to a successful conclusion and concurrently to mollify the outside world with talk about a withdrawal. In the second half of 1986 the talk about withdrawal was backed up by some deeds, at least ostensibly. At Vladivostok in July Gorbachev announced the intent to pull out some 6,000 to 9,000 troops (in six regiments). The withdrawal took place in the fall amid great fanfare, but it appears to have been little more than a token or sham. The numbers represented only a very small proportion of the total Soviet occupation force, which most Western estimates placed at 115,000 to 120,000, not counting troops immediately available in adjacent Soviet territory that have often been used in brief cross-border operations. Half of the forces taken out were in air defense units that were not really involved in the war. The whole affair is reminiscent of a similar highly publicized withdrawal of 20,000 troops (in a full division and several separate brigades) from East Germany several years earlier. The announced withdrawal was made on schedule but there was no reduction in force. A concurrent reorganization of the Group of Soviet Forces in Germany (GSFG) was adding elements (artillery, motorized-infantry subunits, and others) to existing units so as to improve actual combat capabilities. The result was either no change in total Soviet strength in East Germany or possibly even some increase. The same thing seems to have taken place in Afghanistan; at least U.S. intelligence—repeated or conceivably supplemented by the Pakistanis—subsequently claimed that the withdrawal had been more than compensated for by the unannounced introduction of 15,000 new troops. In fact, in an even more blunt charge of Soviet deception, the US Department of Defense later published an analysis (in spring, 1987) revealing that the two motorized rifle regiments and major portions of the tank regiment withdrawn had actually been introduced, into Afghanistan just before their withdrawal solely for the purpose of carrying out the visible "reduction" in forces!

Everything the Soviets have done so far, including the change in the Kabul leadership in spring 1986, which was obviously engineered by Moscow, points to their continuing determination to ensure the survival of the Communist regime there. Meanwhile, according to Western reports, the buildup of military infrastructure has continued at a rapid pace, indicating both Soviet determination to stay the course and Soviet appreciation of the potential strategic value of Afghanistan as a launching pad for extending political and military influence in the direction of the Indian Ocean and Persian Gulf.

The Afghan war remains a running sore that poisons Soviet relations not only with the West but also with many parts of the Third World, particularly the Islamic nations. In addition, in spite of the fabled Russian capacity for endurance and public passivity, the costs of the war appear to be beginning to haunt the men in the Kremlin. Awareness of casualties has spread, and the continued financial burden cannot be a happy prospect during a major domestic economic reconstruction. For these reasons, Gorbachev's expressions of a desire to resolve the conflict may well be sincere.

If Gorbachev fails to win the war in Afghanistan fairly quickly, he will undoubtedly find himself under even stronger pressures. Whether the pressures will be sufficient to persuade him to accept what would amount to a Soviet defeat is uncertain. On balance, the answer seems to be negative unless the costs escalate very sharply. Afghanistan remains a significant regional strategic prize. The price of allowing a proclaimed Marxist-Leninist state to revert to a "less-advanced" social and political structure in what would amount to a reversal of the "inevitable laws of history" would not be insignificant for a regime whose legitimacy rests largely on ideology. Possibly even more important, a fundamentalist Islamic state, the stated goal of most of the rebels, on the borders of Soviet Central Asia—where, as even the Soviet press admits, Islam is on the rise—would not be a desirable outcome.

In consideration of all of the pros and cons, it seems probable that the Western optimists who believe that Gorbachev wants a face-saving exit out of the Afghan problem may be right. Their error is in not recognizing that the face he is offering to save is not his own but that of the states who have opposed Soviet involvement in Afghanistan. Meanwhile, he has intensified the appeals to Soviet citizenry to stand by Communist internationalism and to keep up the war. In the longer run Gorbachev must find a safe path between the present alternatives of an unpalatable defeat or a protracted war, both of which could provide his potential rivals with an issue to use against him.

The Middle East

Gorbachev inherited a painful foreign policy dilemma in regard to the Iran-Iraq war. Iran is the real strategic prize in the region, and has been a traditional target of every ruler in Moscow since the Russian Empire expanded into Central Asia. On the other hand, Iraq was a Soviet client bound by a treaty of friendship and cooperation. To complicate matters, two other key Soviet Middle Eastern clients, Syria and Libya, were aiding Iran. An Iraqi victory, an unlikely outcome at the time when Gorbachev came to power, could destroy Soviet hopes of gaining influence with Tehran or controlling whatever regime emerged in there if Moscow was perceived as having had to open a hand in assisting Baghdad; an Iranian victory could solidify the anti-Soviet fundamentalist regime in Iran and drive the frightened Gulf states into the arms of the United States.

Gorbachev's predecessors had waffled on the Iran-Iraq war, trying to avoid totally alienating either belligerent. The result was diminished Soviet influence in both camps. For a long time Gorbachev seemed to be able to find no better solution. Then, in spring 1986 he appeared to make a choice. After a visit to Tehran by First Deputy Foreign Minister Kornienko apparently failed to achieve anything, the already high pace of consultations at all levels with the Iraqis was stepped up. Meanwhile, there were Western reports that additional Soviet military advisers had been sent to Iraq and that the Soviets were even putting some pressure on Damascus to mitigate its antagonism toward the rival Baathist regime in Baghdad, a development that could assist Soviet policies in other areas of the Middle East.

Subsequently, it became evident that Moscow was still hedging its bets. Consular talks were held with Tehran in June; in August a senior Iranian foreign affairs and economic delegation visited Moscow, and in September a Soviet trade delegation went to Iran. In 1987, the Iranian Foreign Minister visited Moscow for extensive discussions (in February), which although reported as characterized by "frank discussions" and disagreements on both the war with Iraq and Afghanistan, showed Moscow's determination not to close all doors to Tehran. Similarly, Soviet Foreign Ministry officials made several trips to Tehran in the first half of 1987. Moreover, although Soviet military support to Iraq (including a rescheduling of Iraq's arms debt) was reported to have been increased after the Iraqi Foreign Minisiter visited Moscow the same month as the Iranian one, there were continuing

Western and regional reports claiming Soviet arms offers to Iran and the continuation of laundered Soviet military equipment deliveries. In addition, new economic agreements have evidently been reached with Iran. Finally, the Soviets have evidently continued to allow North Korea and others to transit Soviet airspace to deliver arms to Khomeini; and alleged pressure from Moscow has so far been inadequate (if it has taken place) to dissuade Syria and Libya from continuing their support to Tehran.

In the spring of 1987 a new twist to the Gulf situation took place when the Soviets leased three oil tankers to Kuwait. Predictably, this contributed to the subsequent US decision to follow suit and the buildup of US naval forces in the Gulf. Although one Soviet-flag tanker was atacked by an Iranian small boat and another struck a mine evidently laid by Iran, Soviet reaction against Tehran was rather proforma and, in fact, it was the US which became the central figure in military confrontations between outsiders and the Gulf belligerents. Meanwhile, Moscow could claim to be assisting the smaller Gulf states fearful of the war spreading to encompass them, while the US became the focus of Khomeini's reaction and those parts of Western public opinion which feared that Washington's policy would drag America into a real war in the region could be counted upon to focus their rhetoric and political pressures on the Reagan administration. The only real danger for Moscow in this was the outside chance that US Gulf assertiveness would somehow bring the conflict under control in such a way that Iran became both less radical and belligerent but also emerged with a stable government. On the other hand if, once embarked on an activist role in the region, Washington either proved impotent in protecting the Arabs or allowed casualties or other political pressures to force a withdrawal (as had happened earlier in Lebanon), Moscow would be ideally positioned to gain credit with the rest of the states in the region.

Although tilting towards Iraq and exhibiting concern for the fears of the smaller Arab Gulf states, Moscow clearly was continuing to keep lines open to Iran and to at least partially play both ends against the middle. The long range goal was obviously to be in a position to influence a post-Khomeini Iranian regime or to step in if Iran collapsed into civil strife—always a possibility in such an ethnically diverse country if the central regime were to fall apart.

In the longer run, both Iran and the greater Gulf region (including the Arabian peninsula) remained the real prizes. Iraq has always been merely a stepping stone to this and to the Western levant area. The worse outcomes of the present war for Moscow would be those which reinforced and expanded US influence in the gulf, in Bagdad, or even in Tehran at the expense of Moscow—or a sequence of events which resulted in direct US-Soviet military confrontation of a nature which would trigger a global war.

This means that unless local developments and US firmnesss combine to end the war in ways which lead to Soviet exclusion and an increase in US influence, Moscow is not really interested in seeing the war terminated except on its own terms. For the Soviets a continuing conflict in which the US loses credit and Gulf states have to turn to Moscow or one leading to a collapse of unity in Iran and an opportunity for Moscow to pick up the pieces there is preferable—all public posturing and rhetoric notwithstanding.

Elsewhere in the Middle East, Soviet performance under Gorbachev has shown no signs of major deviation from patterns established in the past. As before, Soviet policies are guided by the goal of forging a united Arab front that would drive the United States out of the region and turn it into a Soviet zone of influence.

The situation that the new Kremlin leadership had inherited, however, was far from encouraging after earlier setbacks that put the Soviets generally on the defensive. The Iran-Iraq war had exacerbated the never good relations between Syria, Moscow's most useful Arab ally, and Iraq, which also had a friendship treaty with Moscow. And it added to the disarray in the Arab front against Israel, a nation that the Soviets have always used as a central issue to win influence with the Arabs. The Egyptian government remained pro-American. Contrary to Soviet bluster and in spite of the fairly rapid increase in modern arms transfers to Syria, the reputation of Soviet military hardware and of Soviet reliability as an Arab ally had not fully recovered from the damage wrought by Moscow's dithering during Israel's invasion of Lebanon. The Palestinians were in greater disorder than ever, and Jordanian policies were creating problems for Moscow. Hussein was talking moderation, as he does whenever he wants more aid from Washington; in the process he appeared to be strengthening Arafat's hand in Arafat's struggles against the Syrian-backed Palestinian factions, and further decreasing Arab unity vis-à-vis Israel and the United States. Also, both Assad and Qaddafi in Libya (the other most important Soviet source for obtaining much-needed hand currency for arms and in its effort to drive the United States out of the region) were persisting in their disconcerting tendency to act on their own with little concern for the preferences of Moscow. Qaddafi, in particular, could only be described as a "loose cannon."

Gorbachev's initial moves were predictable if unimaginative. Arms supplies to Syria and Libya were stepped up. Arabs of all political stripes were invited to Moscow to be feted and "consulted," and a host of Soviet functionaries were dispatched to pro-Western as well pro-Soviet Middle Eastern countries. For example, Gorbachev's Foreign Ministry increased its efforts to establish better relations with the anti-Soviet Arab Gulf states. A particular attempt was made to encourage some new form of Palestinian unity, to tempt Hussein with promises of weapon deliveries as a substitute for those he could not obtain from the United States, and to promote a rapprochement between Amman and Damascus. Economic delegations were sent to, and invited from, Egypt. The propaganda mill regularly churned out provocative and horrifying anti-American and anti-Israeli stories and accusations. At the same time the indispensability and advantages of Soviet participation in any international conference dealing with an Arab-Israel settlement was heavily stressed.

The results of all of these activities were rather problematic and in many cases disappointing. The potential propaganda benefits of the U.S. strikes against Libya were not fully exploited because of the lack of concrete Soviet reaction; Qaddafi's rather bad odor in much of the Arab world, verbal support of all Arab states for Qaddafi in the wake of the bombings notwithstanding; and the emerging consensus of both regional and outside states that something indeed needed to be done to reduce international terrorism. Gorbachev's restraint in the aftermath of the U.S. strikes served notice that the USSR would behave cautiously in cases with a potential for direct confrontation with the United States, and that its relations with the West had priority over those with its Third World clients. At least in the short term, however, this hardly seemed likely to advance the Soviet cause in the Arab world significantly. Disclosure of the U.S. disinformation campaign against Libya affected these outcomes, but it was not clear to what degree.

In regard to terrorism the Soviets, who previously had viewed this phenomenon as a useful means of engaging in relatively safe "low-intensity" conflict, now obviously felt the need to adopt a more internationally acceptable profile. The Soviet effort to defuse the issue of terrorism appeared to strengthen as evidence in trials in England and West Germany increasingly confirmed the direct role of Syria. Moscow could ill afford to have its most valuable Middle Eastern ally ostracized and discredited, or to have Syrian actions drag the USSR into either a direct confrontation with the West or a position where Moscow's client would be humiliated. The irony in all this, of course, is that there has been absolutely no indication that the Gorbachev regime was in any way reducing the long extant but more carefully laundered Soviet direct and indirect suport to terrorist and nongovernmental "liberation" movements. According to the press, the U.S. CIA has estimated such support (including the USSR's own covert activities) to cost annually, on average, about $4 billion.

As 1986 drew to a close, the necessity for Moscow to constrain its allies' open use of terror appeared to have been greatly reduced. Revelations of dealings with Iran by the United States and other countries, and French appeasement of terror via deals with Damascus, greatly undermined the earlier growing international consensus against this adjunct of indirect warfare.

Hussein's joint peace initiative with the PLO, which Moscow strongly opposed, came a cropper, but hardly because of any action by the Soviets. Moreover, although the Jordanians finally did make a substantial arms deal with Moscow, it did not seem to greatly affect the Hashemite kingdom's basically pro-Western and anti-Soviet alignment, initially at least. In spite of ongoing Soviet efforts to promote Palestinian reconciliation, crowned by some meetings between representatives of at least some of the warring Palestinian factions, their splits seem as intractable as ever. Relations between Syria and Jordan were ostensibly improved for a while, but because of the self-interest of their respective rulers rather than any help from Moscow—although Gorbachev may have exerted some influence on Assad when he called him to Moscow in 1985.

Then, in spring of 1987, faced with the spector of a peace conference in which they might be either excluded or have to participate while still split, the Palestinians achieved a degree of reunification in Algiers—a reunification which favored Arafat over the Syrian supported or controlled factions even if its true extent or durability was uncertain. Soviet representatives and delegations were very active throughout the region both before and after the Palestinian reunification conference in Algiers and the fact that Damascus eventually seemed to more or less accept the pro-Arafat outcome had to be at least be partially attributed to Soviet pressure.

Syria remains the single most important Soviet ally in the region, but one that often appears to be the tail wagging the Soviet dog and threatening to drag Moscow in directions it does not wish to go. Like his predecessors, Gorbachev always seeks to support Syria in its confrontations with Israel and the United States. Moscow has never wanted a settlement of the Arab-Israeli conflict except in the context of a totally Soviet dominated region. At the same time the Soviets do not want the conflict to get out of hand and put them toe to toe with the United States. This is especially true during periods when detente with the West is the order of the day. The Soviets seek Arab unity against Israel and the West, but they have no interest in a more fundamental Arab unity; a unified Arab world would be less interested in Soviet relations and goals and certainly much harder to influence or control. Assad's involvement in Lebanon both threatens to trigger direct confrontation with the West and detracts from his focus on Israel and anti-Americanism. The Soviets have long opposed Damascus's policies in Lebanon yet been unable to prevent them.

Moscow similarly opposes Syrian efforts to bring the disparate elements of the PLO under total Syrian control. In fact, it is questionable whether

Moscow really desires to see the PLO united unless that unification would make the Palestinians totally subservient to the Kremlin. It is sufficient for Soviet purposes that the Palestinians continue to oppose Israel. A united PLO not under effective Soviet control would be a wild card, far too likely to upset the pattern of the continuous but at least partially controlled hatreds and instability that so well serves Soviet interests. Meanwhile, to manipulate events, and as an insurance policy against someone else's uniting and controlling the PLO, Moscow plays the game of furthering Palestinian unity and promoting its choices for leadership within the rival factions.

Gorbachev's policies in regard to Syria, the Palestinians, and Lebanon have built upon the tactics of his predecessors. In the process, however, he has been increasingly dragged toward a position that could greatly add to the risk that a new regional conflict would escalate out of control and bring the USSR face to face with the possibility of a World War III with the United States. Step by step, to maintain both Assad's and its own position, Moscow has felt compelled to provide Syria with additional weaponry and capabilities that threaten to change fundamentally the nature of any future Arab-Israeli war. In the past neither side, especially the Arabs, could hope for an immediate total victory. Victory could be won on the battlefield, but there would be time for the superpowers to prevent a complete conquest and avoid the need for the kind of direct armed intervention that could spark a superpower war. Soviet provision of longer-range, accurate missiles—which, while tactical in the superpower arsenal or in the European context, become strategic weapons in the narrow confines of the region—and similar aircraft, to say nothing of the delivery means and "defensive" equipment for chemical warfare, have begun to give Damascus the capability to try for a war-winning deep surprise attack against Israel. (In summer 1986 there were increasingly credible reports that Syria had acquired or was acquiring a significant battlefield and strategic advanced chemical weapons capability. The actual means of production evidently had been obtained from West European business firms, but the means of delivery were of Soviet origin, as was the "defensive" equipment allowing operation on a chemical battlefield. There was nothing to indicate that Moscow had attempted to block Syria from acquiring these capabilities.) The result of such an attack would be the great likelihood of an Israeli deep preemption or retaliation, possibly even with the nuclear weapons that most of the world believes to be in Jerusalem's arsenal. The qualitatively new kind of Arab-Israeli war would be certain to inflict immediate significant casualties on Soviet advisory and support elements in Syria, and would virtually force at least a regional superpower armed confrontation.

In August 1986 the Gorbachev leadership appeared to be exploring a new tactic that would reverse a long-standing Soviet policy line. After several weeks of unofficial hints and rumors, and some more concrete steps by one or two of Moscow's NSWP allies, it looked as if the Kremlin was moving toward restoration of diplomatic relations with Israel, which had been broken after the 1967 Middle East war. At Soviet request a midlevel Foreign Ministry meeting was held in Helsinki to discuss consular relations. Many thought that this was only the first stage to full diplomatic ties, although Moscow's ostensible reasons for the meeting were only to deal with Soviet church property affairs and to represent Soviet citizens in Israel. The talks were scheduled for two days but were broken off after just ninety minutes when the Israelis focused on full reciprocity and Jewish emigration from the USSR as preconditions. The main Soviet press did not even report the talks.

It is not beyond belief that the Soviets were mostly interested in precisely the reasons they gave for holding the talks, but it is far more likely that other tactical considerations were at play. One was probably to test the waters. If some sort of peace conference were to somehow emerge for the Middle East, Moscow would be at a disadvantage in controlling the outcome without diplomatic relations with both sides. This motive alone, however, would not have sufficed for holding an official and publicized meeting. More likely, Moscow considered such a step to be useful for its peace propaganda campaign in the West. At the same time limited consular relations could serve the purposes related to a peace conference almost as well as full diplomatic relations, with the advantage that they would generate a less negative reaction from the Arabs.

Two other considerations might also have had some bearing on the scheduling of the talks. Israeli participation in the U.S. SDI makes Israel a higher priority target for Soviet espionage, an activity greatly facilitated by a Soviet diplomatic base there. Second, a Soviet consulate in East Jerusalem would be ready-made for enhancing Soviet support for any eventual Palestinian state and ensuring that it would be heavily influenced by Moscow. Meanwhile, the extent of any price that the Israelis might be willing to pay for diplomatic ties with Moscow could be put to a practical test. As it turned out, the price demanded by Jerusalem was too high, and the attempt by Gorbachev to initiate something new in the region came to naught. Moreover, the reaction of most Arab states had been quite negative, and it was probably at least partly due to this that a first deputy and a deputy foreign minister were dispatched almost immediately afterward on visits to most of the major Arab capitals.

The Soviet assault on the "Israeli front" did not cease. During 1987 on several occasions Soviet diplomats in the United States and Western Europe met with Israeli representatives to discuss the nature of, and preconditions for, an international conference on the Middle East. Aware of the divisions on this issue within the Israeli government, Moscow played to the ambitions of the leaders of the Labor Party Alignment by encouraging them to believe that in return for appropriate concessions on their part, that party would gain the credit for renewing ties with Moscow. In summer 1987 Moscow was openly mooting the possibility of inviting a member of the Israeli government to visit the USSR. Its choice fell upon a minister in the National Unity Government representing the Labor Party, Ezer Weizman. Although the choice of Weizman was contemplated in the Labor Party as well, it was made by Moscow. This is clear from the hints of the Soviet press recurring for several months, starting with the fall of 1986, to the effect that Weizman was the only Israeli politician the Soviets could deal with. Unlike other top Israeli statesmen, Weizman at that time was never criticized in the Soviet press, even in the mildest terms.

Meanwhile, the Soviet stance on a peace conference underwent minor perturbations within a consistant demand that it would have to include full Soviet participation, and Palestinian representation, and would have to be aimed at satisfying the "just demands" of the Palestinian people—meaning a Palestinian state. Whenever it appeared that some conference might possibly be convened under other than these terms, the Soviet approach was to denounce it vigorously as a sellout to U.S. and Israeli "imperialism," while fostering the idea that only full Soviet participation could lead to a meaningful conference. When this latter idea gained in prominence and popularity, Moscow became more vigorous in supporting a conference. During a period of pushing for East-West detente, the Soviets seek to dampen any possibilities of a new outbreak of war in the Middle East and to appear to be actively seeking to resolve the regional tensions. Nevertheless, the long term conflict-model approach to expanding Soviet influence and reducing that of the US has remained the underlying basis of Soviet regional strategy. Any peace conference has to be organized so as to ensure an outcome favorable to Moscow and any Palestinian state which might someday emerge in the West Bank (or even in Jordan) has to be one in which Soviet influence will predominate. The tactics shift a bit under Gorbachev, but so far the strategy shows no signs of change.

Gorbachev achieved a modest success in September 1985 by opening diplomatic relations with Oman, the first such opening to a Gulf state other than Kuwait. This was followed by a similar diplomatic opening to the United Arab Emirates, and was expected to pave the way for diplomatic relations and thereby a limited presence throughout the Gulf subregion. However, after the bloody coup in South Yemen (the PDRY), continuing Soviet overtures apparently fell on deaf ears in the remaining shiekdoms and ministates.

Although the evidence concerning the 1986 coup in the PDRY is contra-dictory, it appears that Moscow was taken by surprise by the speed of events. It reacted quickly by bringing the leaders of the prospective winning side to Moscow, consulting with them, and then taking a direct part in the fighting until its termination. The possibility that Soviet involvement dated from the very beginning cannot be precluded. In any event, even if the developments in Aden hindered Soviet efforts to improve relations with nearby conservative Arab states at least temporarily, the coup brought to power an even more pro-Moscow regime, one that seemed even less inter-ested than its predecessors in developing relationships with the West. Elsewhere in the region, in spite of Gorbachev's overtures, Soviet-Egyptian relations have improved only modestly. Then, in the wake of the dis-closures of the US efforts in Iran, Moscow's efforts among the Gulf and Arabian peninsula states both gained new impetus and showed signs of greater potential success. In January, the Saudi Minister of Oil made an unprecedented visit to Moscow. While the direct results were inconclusive or minimal (except in terms of possibly influencing Soviet oil pricing and export policy), the visit marked a real breakthrough for Moscow.

Elsewhere in the immediate region, steady and patient Soviet efforts to improve relations with Egypt showed at best only modest success until 1987 when some limited gains were made. In January a two year cultural and scientific cooperation agreement was signed and several mid-to-low-level Soviet delegations visited Egypt in February. Then in April, the Egyp-tian opposition press reported that a high-level miliary delegation had made a secret visit to Moscow. For some time, the Soviets had stated that increased economic aid and military parts and supplies for the Egyptian armed forces (which still had extensive stocks of aging Soviet hardware) depended upon resolving issues related to Egypt's outstanding debts to the USSR. If, as seems probable, this visit did take place it had to be seen both in this context and in that of Mubarak's tight-rope act in trying to amelio-rate domestic disatisfaction, regain a place in the Arab mainstream and pressure the US to be even more forthcoming in aid than it had been. Moscow, of course, was only too willing to take advantage of any oppor-tunities this might present and in fact it was reported in March that the Egyptian debt to the USSR had been resolved. The Mubarak government remained strongly pro-Western, but inch-by-inch Egyptian problems and Gorbachev's policies (along with US vacillations) were gradually leading to a very partial restoration of Soviet influence in Cairo. By late 1987, this restoration remained very limited, but clearly held the potential for greater success should Mubarak choose to try to play the superpowers off against one another or if domestic and/or foreign policy frustrations lead to a change in the Egyptian government.

In North Africa Gorbachev's policies have been mostly reactive. Arms deliveries to Libya, including SA-5 long-range air defense missiles continued. Soviet warships made demonstration visits to Libyan ports and waters both prior to and after the U.S. strikes, but the same warships were hardly in sight during the actual combat. Economic ties have continued, and in spring 1986 it was reported that Moscow was prepared to assist Libya in the construction of a nuclear power plant; Soviet assistance to a Libyan nuclear research institute had been provided long beforehand. It also appeared that Gorbachev had turned down Qadaffi's requests for more formal military treaty ties and for a rescheduling of payments for Soviet assistance; Libya had previously paid Moscow sizeable amounts either in hard currency or in oil, which the Soviets then resold for hard currency. Throughout the year Gorbachev worked hard to show his support for the Tripoli regime but, like his predecessors, he combined that support with noticeable restraint and circumspection in his treatment of this volatile and least controllable of his clients. Late in the spring of 1986 the Libyan number-two leader, Jalloud, and Syrian Vice President Khaddam were individually but almost simultaneously called to Moscow for discussions. All indications were that Gorbachev was exorting pressure on Libya and Syria to lower their profiles in regard to international terrorism.

In 1987, various delegations travelled both ways between Tripoli and Moscow with the Libyan Foreign minister visiting the USSR in both April and May and senior Soviets travelling to Tripoli and signing scientific cooperation and (largely unspecified) economic and technical agreements. Many of the Foreign Ministry consultations were evidently aimed at coordinating positions on the Palestinian issue and probably also the Iran-Iraq issue as well with Moscow's evident preference for the increasingly embattled Qadaffi to keep on at least temporarily lower profile. At the same time the Soviet press tried hard to support Qadaffi in regard to developments in Chad. For a long time Soviet "glasnost" in reportage of the fighting there would have left the reader with the impression that Libya was totally uninvolved in fighting which was solely instigated by the French and Americans. Finally, after Tripoli admitted involvement, this fact came out in the pages of *Pravda* and *Izvestiya*—but still in a way that painted a very different picture than audiences in other countries were receiving.

Moscow reacted to the coup in the Sudan quickly with a bid to improve relationships. Senior Sudanese officials were invited to Moscow and new trade and assistance programs werre offered. However, in spite of the anti-American stance of the new regime in Khartoum, and in spite of the visit by Prime Minister Al Mahdi in August 1986, it was not clear how much progress had been made.

In the Maghreb, the Soviets have continued to make special efforts to improve ties with Algeria (which have been generally quite good) and with Tunisia. Ultimately, however, this has amounted to little more than a continuation of long term policies and it is not evident that any changes, either for the better or for the worse, have occurred in Soviet relations with these two states.

In sum, in spite of a considerable increase in activity, Gorbachev has so far stuck to basically the same tried-and-true patterns of Soviet policy in the Middle East. Reacting, rather than acting, he seems still unable to capture the initiative. Nor has he achieved any major breakthroughs. The most that can be said is that the new Soviet leadership may have succeeded in laying a more solid groundwork for more effective future policy options.

Sub-Saharan Africa

Gorbachev's policy has in Sub-Saharan Africa focused mostly on Ethiopia and the southern African states bordering South Africa, although other regions, particularly on the West coast, are not neglected. Moscow's principal African clients continue to receive the heaviest attention. Mengistu (Ethiopia), Machel (Mozambique), and Dos Santos (Angola) all led major delegations to Moscow and engaged in direct talks with Gorbachev. Senior delegations moved in both directions between the USSR and these states, as well as between Moscow and other clients, semiclients, and allies (e.g. Congo, Mali, Guinea-Bissau, Benin, Equatorial Guinea, Tanzania, and others), but the most noticeable policy initiatives and reactions to developments related to the South of the continent.

Throughout Gorbachev's rule to date, but especially during 1985 and 1986, there have been sizeable arms deliveries to Angola. Soviet transportation, logistical, and reportedly even air-firepower support and tactical combat advisers down to regimental or possibly battalion level have assisted Angolan and Cuban offensives against the UNITA rebels. As in Afghanistan, the Gorbachev regime seems to be opting for a more intensive effort to win this conflict on the ground before UNITA leader Savimbi can obtain substantial arms deliveries from the United States.

Gorbachev did achieve a major success in improving relations with Zimbabwe, which had been rather coldly correct ever since Mugabe came to power by defeating not only the white regimes but his Soviet-backed black rivals. Mugabe visited Moscow twice, once on a stopover and once on a formal state visit. A promising Soviet beginning was cut short in tiny Lesotho when South African pressure resulted in overthrowing the government, which had been expanding its relations with the Soviets and allowing an increased Soviet and North Korean presence in that country. Likewise, the Gorbachev leadership has made efforts to improve its already rather good relationships with Zambia and with the major black guerrilla and opposition movements, the South West African People's Organization (SWAPO) and the African National Congress (ANC). In all of this the Cubans have remained quite active and out in front of Moscow. In January 1986 and March 1987 major trilateral consulations were held in Moscow among high-level military and foreign policy delegations from Cuba, Angola, and the USSR. It can be presumed that the war in Angola was discussed in detail, but it also seems almost certain that prospects in Namibia and contingency planning for the event of the collapse of the Pretoria regime were also on the agenda.

Everything in the Soviet performance under Gorbachev has indicated a major Soviet interest in maintaining and consolidating relationships and positions of influence in Africa. Special efforts have been directed at improving relations with southern African states that previously had not been Soviet clients, with the aim of forging a more united pro-Soviet bloc among the African confrontation states. For the moment, except for stepping up efforts to defeat UNITA in Angola, Gorbachev appears to be playing a waiting game. Nevertheless, he is certainly watching developments in South Africa very closely, with the purpose of laying groundwork for taking maximum advantage of any emerging opportunities. Whether he would be willing to jeopardize relations with Washington and the West by engaging in a major African adventure if opportunity arises cannot now be predicted with any certainty. The temptation would obviously be great. In the meantime Moscow clearly wants to keep all the options open.

Latin America

The new Soviet leadership has basically followed the same patterns of policy in Latin America as in other parts of the Third World. Long-standing policy lines have been maintained, the primary difference being only that of increased activism and tempo. Gorbachev has stepped up the level and seniority of exchange visits with the Cubans and has fully kept up the enormous Soviet military and economic support, all the while pressuring the Eastern Europeans to assume a greater share. By spring 1986 he had apparently repaired the somewhat cooler than normal attitude Castro had developed toward his immediate predecessors.

As elsewhere, efforts to improve relationships with selected nonclient states have been given increased emphasis. A modicum of success has been achieved in improving economic and diplomatic relations with several key South American states. Important visiting delegations have been hosted from Argentina, Mexico, Brazil, and Uruguay, and senior Soviet delegations have visited those states plus Peru, Colombia, Bolivia, Venezuela,

Ecuador, and Mexico. Lower-level visits either to or from most of the other regional states except Chile also have taken place.

Nicaragua remains the most crucial of all current issues in Latin America. It has direct impact on U.S.-Soviet relations and a potential for major communist successes in troubled Central America. Gorbachev and the Soviet apparatus have given strong propaganda and diplomatic support to the Sandinistas, and generous promises of economic aid have been accompanied by pressure on Eastern Europeans to increase their shares of support. Militarily, Moscow has continued is own comparatively modest military deliveries, but the Eastern Europeans were again pressed to increase theirs. In spite of the lofty rhetoric and quite substantial overall levels of military and economic aid to Managua, Gorbachev has behaved with considerable circumspection. Much of the military aid is funneled through Cuba, and the foreign military and security adviser forces in Nicaragua remain primarily Cuban, Eastern European, or even Palestinian, North Korean, and so on rather than Soviet. Moreover, early in the fall of 1985, when U.S. military pressure on Managua was at a peak and when the U.S. Congress seemed to rally behind the administration's policies, Soviet behavior became even more cautious and suggestive of readiness for a tacit accommodation. Later, when the Reagan administration encountered growing congressional opposition to its policies, the Soviets apparently believed that they could afford to support Managua more openly and assertively—and did so in the spring of 1986. When Congress authorized selective support to the U.S.-backed Contras but continued to constrain more direct U.S. involvement, Moscow took a middle position. As 1986 drew to a close, it remained to be seen whether the revelations of the Reagan administration's illegal diversion of funds obtained from the ill-fated Iranian arms affair would result in withdrawal of even this limited congressional support for action against Managua, and whether—as the earlier pattern suggested—this would lead to an increase in overt Soviet assistance to the Sandinistas.

As 1987 unfolded, it appeared that Moscow had again chosen a middle course. Soviet and Soviet-inspired assistance continued, with the military component maintained but kept as low key and unobtrusive as possible while economic help from the USSR and its allies was given greater visibility. Meanwhile, it also appeared that Moscow was encouraging the Sandinistas to project a more reasonable image designed to increase pressures both within the region and from US domestic audiences upon the American-administration and those regional states supporting the contras.

The weight of the evidence indicates that under Gorbachev Moscow is unlikely to risk a major confrontation with Washington, even if the Sandinista regime's survival is at stake, but that as long as things do not get out of hand, Soviet support for Nicaragua will continue. The long-term Soviet expectation seems to be that a pragmatic policy involving tactical advances and retreats and temporary accommodations might well succeed in turning Nicaragua into another Cuba, a Moscow-aligned outpost in the U.S. backyard. It goes without saying that if the United States fails to overturn or change the government of Nicaragua, Moscow and Havana will receive a tremendous boon. But even if the United States succeeds in overthrowing the Sandinistas, whether by overt or covert interference, the USSR will find itself in a position to rally significant forces in other parts of the Third World and in the Western Left under the banners of militant anti-Americanism.

Latin America's endemic economic and social problems seem to guarantee that regardless of what happens in Nicaragua, new opportunities are bound to arise. As in southern Africa, Moscow's current preferred policy line seems to be a waiting game, accompanied by a steady effort to improve relations with selective target and client states on the economic, cultural, and—more selectively—military levels so as to be in a position to reap profits whenever opportunities arise.

In sum, our survey of Gorbachev's specific policies toward various Third World regions reveals a considerable continuity with previous Soviet behavior. In diplomacy and economic relations his performance is more extensive and flexible than that of his recent predecessors, but military support levels have remained roughly comparable to before. He has generally moved cautiously and in a manner basically designed to consolidate existing positions of influence rather than precipitate confrontations. The exceptions to this pattern have been the almost desperate efforts to achieve quick military victories in Afghanistan, Angola, and more measuredly, in Kampuchea. Although Gorbachev seems willing to have his country continue to bear quite considerable economic burdens to pursue Soviet Third World goals, he has implied that he will be selective in the dispensation of aid and that he expects his allies to make ever-increasing contributions. Meanwhile, he is keeping all options open for more adventuristic and aggressive policies in the event that sufficiently attractive opportunities arise, especially in southern Africa and the Middle East.

Thus far, Gorbachev has mostly reacted, but he has kept an eye peeled for opportunities for seizing the initiative in the future. Without doubt he intends to continue the struggle for "the minds and the hearts" of the Third World. For the time being, however, he has more important priorities and cannot afford to jeopardize domestic economic reconstruction and a managed detente with the United States except for very major gains. As in other areas on his agenda, the evidence reflects Gorbachev's desires and efforts to improve Soviet performance in the Third World by making it more sophisticated and flexible. In his domestic programs and his strategy for East-West relations, Gorbachev clearly started and followed a well-elaborated set of guidelines but has had to adjust as he went along—particularly domestically, where he has had to incrementally add ever more controversial reforms. In the Third World, he began on a trial and error basis, tentatively threading his way through the mazes of the developing world while seeking the most promising policy courses. Moreover, as the process evolved and he settled into a more coherent approach to Third World policy, a general pattern has emerged. The evident features of this pattern are: (1) operations "on all fronts"—Soviet emissaries are busy and activities widespread throughout every region, including increasing efforts to influence such previously lower priority regions as South America; (2) flexibility in the form of promoting ties and a greater willingness to deal with an increasing number of regimes and political parties which have often previously been shunned; (3) a "counterpuncher" strategy which seeks to be as pervasively positioned as possible to take maximum advantage of developments or to exploit difficulties afflicting rivals while simultaneously laying the groundwork for possible policy initiatives at some point in the future; (4) playing a longterm game which seeks to avoid any major short term losses, e.g., to lessen the cost of Afghanistan by seeking ways to "resolve" the problem, but only in ways which will ensure the survival of a Soviet dominated regime; and (5) bipolarity, continuing to subordinate regional policy to the demands of the central East-West competition—currently requiring a balancing act between the twin imperatives of promoting detente and the continuing drive to reduce or replace Western influence and eventually isolate the US and the West.

Selected Soviet-Third World Chronology, from March 1985*

Section I (Monthly Developments)**
March 1985

11	Gorbachev was elected General Secretary, CPSU.
13-14	Gorbachev was reported to have met with Third World leaders (or their deputies, present for Chernenko's funeral), including those from: The PDRY, India, Afghanistan, Pakistan, Mongolia, Vietnam, Laos, Philippines, Nicaragua, Ethiopia, Angola and Mozambique. Representatives from Lebanon, North Korea, Kampuchea and Mexico were reported to have met with Tikhonov; while those from Syria and Algeria were reported to have met with CC secretary Ponomarev.
16	The Soviet press reported a new Ambassador to Jordan. Through June, 1987 there would be 63 other notices of new or changed Ambassadorial appointments in the Third World (12 in the Middle East, 15 in the rest of Asia or the Pacific; 28 (in 26 states) in Sub-Saharan Africa; and 8 in Latin America).
20	Gorbachev met with Cuban number two leader (and Minis-

*This chronology contains less detail for contacts and activities involving those states very closely aligned with the USSR (Afghanistan, Angola, Congo, Cuba, Ethiopia, Kampuchea, Laos, Mongolia, Mozambique and North Korea) than for others. For the former, only a more selected listing is included and the reader should be aware that various Party, state and military visits to and from these states are frequent occurences. Some Soviet aligned states (e.g. Nicaragua) are reported in the same detail as more non-aligned nations because of the importance of the extent and kinds of ties. In addition, it should be kept in mind that Cuba, Mongolia and Vietnam are full members of CEMA attending all of the multudinous CEMA commission meetings along with the USSR and the NSWP states. Further, other Third World states associated with the USSR (e.g. the PDRY, Laos, etc) often attend CEMA meetings as observers.
**Due to the difficulty in timely identification of arms agreements in the open press, these are not included in this part of the chronology. A partial summary of such information is included in Section II.

ter of Defense), Raul Castro Rus who was in Moscow for a two-week visit mostly with the Ministry of Defense.

30–4/4   The Minister of Defense of India made an official visit; meetings were reported with Foreign Minister Gromyko, the Chairman of the State Committee for Economic Ties and with the Minister of Defense, Chief of the General Staff and other military officials.

Other senior Third World visits in March:

Middle East:***   Foreign Minister, Iraq.

Lebanese Druse Chieftain, Jumblatt

Asia: Minister of Defense, Laos.

Africa:****   Minister of Foreign Affairs, Burundi.

Other senior Soviet visits to the Third World in March:

To Asia: A Deputy Foreign Minister to Thailand.

To Africa: Meeting of the Soviet-Angolan Commission for Economic, Technical and Trade Cooperation was held in Luanda. A protocol was signed for scientific and cultural cooperation, 1985–1986.

A CPSU delegation to Mali.

A Supreme Soviet delegation to the 73rd Interparliamentary Conference in Togo.

To Latin America: Supreme Soviet delegations to Venezuela and Brazil.

Other agreements reported in March:

—An agreement to widen trade with Venezuela.

April 1985

18   Gorbachev met with the Minister of Foreign Affairs of North Korea who was in Moscow for a one week official visit.

29   Gorbachev met with Nicaraguan President Ortega, who was in Moscow with a political and economic delegation from 28–30 April. The communique indicated that Moscow had pledged further economic and diplomatic support. The Western press later reported pledges of $400 million in economic assistance to Nicaragua from the USSR, the NSWP States and Yugoslavia. An agreement was signed to establish a commission for Economic, Trade and Scientific-Technical Cooperation.

Other senior Third World visits in April:

Middle East: The Soviet-Algerian Commission for Economic and Scientific-Technical Cooperation met in Moscow. An agreement was signed to expand economic and technical cooperation. Minister of Urban Construction and Housing, Algeria.

***Includes from Morocco to Iran and south through Sudan and the entire Arabian Peninsula.
****Includes all of Africa south of the "Middle East."

A deputy Minister of Foreign Affairs, Iran (met with Gromyko).

Asia: A Deputy Foreign Minister, Malaysia.

Africa: The Soviet-Mozambique commission for Economic, Scientific-Technical and Trade Cooperation met in Moscow. A protocol for assistance in mining, industry, transportation and fishing was signed.

The General Secretary of SWAPO.

Party delegations from Madagascar and Ghana.

Latin America: The First Vice President of the Central Bank of Nicaragua.

Other senior Soviet visits to the Third World in April:

To the Middle East: A Ministry of Foreign Affairs and CC International Department delegation to the PDRY.

CPSU delegations to Algeria and Syria.

To Africa: CPSU delegations to Cape Verde, Mozambique and Tanzania.

To Latin America: The Soviet-Cuban Commission for Economic and Scientific-Technical Cooperation met in Havana. First Deputy Chairman, Council of Ministers Arkhipov led the Soviet delegation.

Other agreements reported in April:

—A 1985 protocol of cultural cooperation with Iraq.

—An agreement for economic and technical cooperation, 1985–1990, with Syria. New credits extended.

—A 1985–1986 program of cultural and scientific cooperation with Tunisia.

—A 1985 protocol of cultural cooperation with Laos.

—An agreement for cooperation in rubber production in Vietnam.

Other: The Western press reported heavy Soviet-Afghan offensives in Afghanistan. The Soviet Press reported a cross border raid into Pakistan allegedly to rescue prisoners held in a rebel camp.

May 1985

9 Celebrations of WW II victory took place in Moscow. Senior political delegations (some with economic ministers included) were reported from Afghanistan, Laos, Mongolia, North Korea, Congo and Cuba. Senior military delegations (most of which stayed several days) were reported from Syria (Minister of Defense), Laos, Mongolia, North Korea (Chief of the General Staff), Vietnam (Chief of the General Staff), Ethiopia (Commander of Ground Forces), Mozambique (Minister of Defense) and Cuba.

13–17 Politburo Member Solomentsev led a delegation to Cuba for the Cuban Party celebrations.

21–27 Indian Prime Minister Gandhi was in the USSR on a state visit (accompanied by the Ministers of Finance and of Energy plus other political officials). He met with most of the top Soviet leaders (including the Minister of Defense) on the 21st and again privately with Gorbachev on the 22nd. An agreement for Trade, Economic and Scientific-Technical Cooperation to 2000 was signed.

26–27   Representatives of the League of Arab States attended a meeting in Moscow, ostensibly focussed on the Iran-Iraq war. Separate meetings were held with the Foreign Ministers of Jordan, Iraq and the PDRY.

Other senior Third World visits in May:

Middle East: Minister of Water, Forestry and the Environment, Algeria. Minister of Transportation and Communications, Tunisia. A delegation from the Palestinian CP.

Asia: Minister of Foreign Affairs, Malaysia.

Africa: Minister of Foreign Affairs, Cape Verde.

Other senior Soviet visits to the Third World in May:

To the Middle East: A naval port call of the aircraft carrier, "Kiev," and two other combatants took place in Algeria.

To Asia: Deputy Minister of Defense, CinC Air Force, Marshal Yefimov to India.

To Africa: A CPSU delegation to Madagascar.

Other agreements reported in May:

—A cultural and scientific exchange with Peru.

—A trade agreement with Cuba.

—An agreement for cooperation between CEMA and Mozambique.

—Agreement to increase the number of students from North Korea studying in the USSR

Other: The Western Press again reported major Soviet-Afghan offensives in Afghanistan (along the border with Pakistan).

June 1985

19–22   Syrian President Assad (accompanied by a senior economic, political and military delegation) was in Moscow for an official visit. He met with Gorbachev on the 19th. The indications were that Assad was called to Moscow by the Soviets, who stressed the need for Palestinian unity in the communique.

25–1/7   Vietnamese leader Le Duan (accompanied by two deputy chairmen, Council of Ministers and senior Party officials) was in the USSR. He met with Gorbachev on the 28th. The communique indicated that a new or updated agreement to increase economic credits to Vietnam, 1986–1990, had been signed.

Other senior Third World visits in June:

Middle East: Minister of Industry and Mineral Resources, Iraq, for the Soviet-Iraqi Commission for Economic and Scientific-Technical Cooperation. He signed a protocol for increased economic cooperation.

	Commander, of the Navy, Tunisia.
	A parliamentary delegation, Tunisia.
	A Party delegation, Syria.
Asia:	A Foreign Ministry delegation, India.
Africa:	Party delegations from Sao Tome et Principe and Tanzania.
Latin America:	Deputy Foreign Minister, Bolivia.
	Parliamentary delegations, Nicaragua, Peru.
	A Party delegation from Bolivia.

Other senior Soviet visits to the Third World in June:

To Africa:	A Supreme Soviet delegation to Togo.
To Latin America:	A Supreme Soviet delegation to Argentina.
	A CPSU delegation to Bolivia.

Other agreements reported in June:

—Cooperation and assistance in nuclear energy, with Cuba.

—A protocol of TV and Radio cooperation with Iraq.

—An agreement for regular exchange of information between CEMA and the Latin American "Cartagena" economic community.

July 1985

18	Liberia broke diplomatic relations with the USSR.

Other senior Third World visits in July:

Middle East:	Deputy Minister of Foreign Affairs, Egypt, who signed a 1985–86 cultural and scientific exchange agreement.
	A trade and economic delegation, Iran.
	A parliamentary delegation, PDRY.
Asia:	A parliamentary delegation from Indonesia.
	A Party delegation from Sri Lanka.
Africa:	A parliamentary delegation, Guinea-Bissau.
	A Party delegation, Mali.
Latin America:	Minister of Foreign Affairs, Argentina.
	State Secretary for Economic Cooperation, Argentina.

Other senior Soviet visitors to the Third World in July:

To the Middle East:	GOSBANK Director, Alkhimov, and an economic delegation to Egypt.
To Africa:	Women's delegation to UN women's conference in Kenya.
To Latin America:	Supreme Soviet delegations to Peru and Nicaragua.

Other agreements reported in July:

—A 1985–86 cultural and scientific exchange agreement with Rwanda.

Other:	Western press reports indicated that renewed Soviet-Afghan offensives in Afghanistan began late in July after heavy rebel counter offensives earlier in the month.

August 1985

13–20	Politburo Member Aliev led a large Party-state delegation to the North Korean independence day celebrations and

met with Kim Il Sung. In addition, a major (separate) military delegation headed by Deputy Minister of Defense Marshal Petrov, was in N. Korea from 11 to 20 August; the First Deputy Commander of the Pacific Fleet brought a naval port call to Wonsan; and regional state/Party delegations from the Soviet Far East also visited North Korea. Taken all together, this was a massive show of interest in and solidarity with Pyongyang.

25–28   Laotian leader Phomvihane made an official visit to the USSR and met with Gorbachev on the 27th.

29   Mongolian leader Batmunkh met with Gorbachev and signed a long term agreement for economic and scientific-technical cooperation to 2000.

30–4/9   Politburo Member, Vorotnikov, led the Soviet delegation to Vietnamese independence celebrations. He met with Le Duan on the 30th. Although large, the Soviet delegation was nowhere nearly as impressive as the combined ones to North Korea.

Other senior Third World visits in August:

Middle East: Prime Minister, Algeria met with Tikhonov and Ryzhkov.
Commander of the Air Force, Algeria.
Port call by a naval combatant from Algeria, in Odessa.
A parliamentary delegation, Egypt.
Minister of Irrigation, Iraq.
A PFLP delegation headed by Habash.

Asia: Chief of Staff, Indian Army.
Minister of Foreign Affairs, Pakistan.

Africa: Zimbabwe leader, Mugabe on a stop-over, not an official state visit, met with First Deputy Chairman, Council of Ministers Arkhipov and Foreign Ministry officials.
Parliamentary delegations from Congo and Senegal.
ANC General Secretary, Tambo.

Latin America: Minister of Culture, Nicaragua.
A Party delegation, Ecuador.

Other senior Soviet visits to the Third World in August:

To the Middle East: Naval port call by 2 major surface combatants, to Tunisia.
CPSU delegation to Syria.

To Asia: Supreme Soviet delegations to India and the Philippines.

To Africa: Foreign Ministry delegations to Ethiopia and Zambia.

To Latin America: A Supreme Soviet delegation to Guiana.
CPSU delegations to Guiana (two separate) and Uruguay.

Other agreements reported in August:

        —Cultural and scientific exchange with Ecuador.
        —A fishing access agreement with Kiribati.

Other: —The Western press reported very heavy Soviet-Afghan offensives continuing throughout the month in Afghanistan.
—A major Cuban-Angolan offensive, with Soviet advisor and pilot participation, was reported (by Western sources) against UNITA in Angola.

September 1985

14–21	The Chief of Staff, Jordanian Army, LTG Taleb, made an official visit, meeting with most of the senior Soviet military leadership.
22–27	Foreign Minister Shevardnadze (in New York for UNGA) held a series of group and separate meetings with Third world foreign ministers, including all CEMA states, Laos, North Korea, Angola, PDRY, Ethiopia, Nicaragua, Syria, Algeria, Argentina, Brazil, Mexico, Pakistan, India and the representatives of the League of Arab States.
26	An agreement to open diplomatic relations with Oman was announced.
27–1/10	President Ratsiraka, Madagascar, made an official visit to the USSR. He met with Gromyko on the 30th.

Other senior Third World visits in September:

Middle East:	General Director of Economic Affairs, Foreign Ministry, Iran.
	General Secretary, Foreign Ministry, Morocco.
	A program of cultural and scientific cooperation was signed.
	Minister of Oil and Mineral Resources, Syria.
Asia:	Minister of Science and Technology, India.
	A meeting of the Soviet-Kampuchean Commission for Trade, Economic and Scientific-Technical Cooperation was held in Moscow.
Africa:	A military political officers' delegation from Guinea-Bissau.
Latin America:	A parliamentary delegation, Surinam.

Other senior visits to the Third World in September.

To Africa:	A Foreign ministry delegation to Ghana.
To Latin America:	A CPSU delegation to Jamaica.
Other:	The Western press reported that a Soviet-Afghan August offensive in Afghanistan continued until mid month; and that a new large-scale offensive began late in September. The heavy attacks reported against UNITA in August in Angola were reported to have continued during the first part of September.

October 1985

10–14	Libyan leader Qaddafi, with a large economic and military delegation, made an official visit. The Libyans met with Gorbachev and most of the senior Soviet leadership on the 10th; Qadaffi met separately with Gorbachev on the 11th; and Qaddafi with his Foreign Minister and armed forces chief held long talks with Shevardnadze and Marshal Sokolov on the 12th. A long-term agreement for trade, economic and scientific-technical cooperation was signed. The

	Western press initially reported that Qaddafi failed to get what he sought militarily; however later deliveries of SA-5 SAMS suggests this may not be fully true.
24-26	Foreign Minister Shevardnadze (in New York for UN anniverary celebrations) held private talks with the North Korean Vice-President and the Foreign Ministers of India and Nicaragua.
26	The Soviet press published the draft text of the new CPSU Program. The sections on relations with Third World states and national liberation movements expressed solidarity with their struggles, but placed most emphasis on economic and political support in contrast to the 1961 Program's pointed rhetoric about direct support to armed struggle and "wars of national liberation."
26-27	Indian Prime Minister Gandhi was again in Moscow and met with Gorbachev on the 26th.
28-29	Foreign Minister Shevardnadze was in Cuba and met with Castro.

Other senior Third World visits in October:

Middle East:	A Deputy Minister of Trade, Algeria.
	Minister of Construction, Tunisia.
	A political officers' delegation, PDRY.
	General Secretary, SAIQA.
Asia:	A parliamentary delegation, India.
	A meeting of the Soviet-Laotian Commission for Scientific-Technical and Economic Cooperation was held in Moscow.
	Imelda Marcos (wife of the Philippines' President and a cabinet minister) met with Gromyko and Shevardnadze.
Africa:	A combined Party-parliamentary delegation, Cape Verde.
	Minister of Planning and Natural Resources, Guinea.
	A Party delegation from Burundi.
	A political officers' delegation from Tanzania.
Latin America:	State Secretary for Culture, Argentina.
	A meeting of the Soviet-Argentine Commission for Trade, Economic and Scientific-Technical Cooperations was held in Moscow.

Other senior Soviet visits to the Third World in October:

To the Middle East:	Deputy Chief of the CC International Department, Brutents, to Syria; met with Vice President Khaddam and stayed over until mid-November (see November).
	A Supreme Soviet delegation to Algeria.
To Asia:	First Deputy CinC of the Navy, Fleet Admiral Chernavin to India (visit began 30 September)
	Deputy Chairman, Council of Ministers Ryabov, to Indonesia. He signed an agreement to establish a Soviet-Indonesian Commission for Trade and Economic Cooperation.
	A Supreme Soviet delegations to Thailand.
To Africa:	A meeting of the Soviet-Ethiopian Commission for Economic, Scientific-Technical and Trade Cooperation was held in Addis Ababa.

To Latin America: A CPSU delegation to Venezuela.
Other agreements reported in October:
—A 1986–1990 trade agreement with Mozambique.
—A 1986–1990 cultural and scientific cooperation agreement with Togo.
—Agreement for increased developmental assistance between CEMA and Nicaragua.

Other: —Heavy fighting and extensive Soviet bombing was reported in Afghanistan by the Western press late in October.
—A report of a fairly large scale mutiny by Soviet Central Asian soldiers was also circulated in the West.
—Of possible Soviet-related significance, the leaders of Angola, Zimbabwe and Zambia all visited Cuba during October and held extensive discussions with Castro.

November 1985

1–9   Ethiopian leader Mengistu, with a senior political, foreign affairs and economic delegation, made an official visit. Members met with Gorbachev and most of the top Soviet leadership (including military) on the 1st. Separate group meetings were held between Mengistu and the economic leadership and with Shevardnadze and foreign affairs officials. Counterpart meetings were also held by individual members of the Ethiopian delegation. A 1986 trade protocol was signed.

6   Gorbachev met with the Foreign Minister of Mozambique who was on a five-day official visit with a senior political, economic and military delegation.

15   The opening of diplomatic relations with the United Arab Emirates (effective the 20th) was announced.

30–5/12   Politburo Member Aliev led a Soviet delegation to the MPLA Congress in Angola.

Other senior Third World visits in November:
Middle East: Minister of Oil, Iraq.
A Party delegation, Syria.
An economic and trade delegation, UAE.
DFLP General Secretary, Hawatmeh.
Asia: Vice President, India.
Minister of Education and Culture, India.
A parliamentary delegation, Thailand.
A meeting of the Soviet-Vietnamese Commission for Economic and Scientific-Technical Cooperation was held in Moscow. An agreement for economic and scientific cooperation and coordinating state plans for 1986–1990 was signed.
Africa: A parliamentary delegation, Zimbabwe.
An ANC delegation led by a member of the executive committee, Mbeki.

Latin America:	A parliamentary delegation, Argentina.
	A Party delegation, Uruguay.

Other senior Soviet visits to the Third World in November:

To the Middle East:	A deputy Minister of Foreign Trade to Kuwait.

A senior foreign ministry official to various (unnamed) Gulf states (almost all month), reported to have met with PLO leader Arafat.

Deputy head of the CC International Department, Brutents, to Jordan (met with King Hussein) and Syria (met with Assad). This was a long extension of his October trip (see above).

To Asia: A first deputy foreign minister to India (met with Gandhi). Deputy Chairman, Council of Ministers, Ryabov, to Malaysia, signed an agreement for regular political consultations.

A Supreme Soviet delegation to the Philippines.

Other agreements reported in November:

—1986–1990 scientific and cultural cooperation with Mongolia.

Other: The Western press reported very heavy shelling and air strikes in Afghanistan most of the month.

December 1985

2–4	Zimbabwe leader, Mugabe (with a senior foreign affairs, economic and military delegation) made an official visit. Mugabe met with Gorbachev on the 3rd. Full delegation and counterpart talks were also held with other Soviet leaders. An economic and technical cooperation agreement was signed.
11	Gorbachev (with Ponomarev) met with senior member of the Algerian leadership, Politburo and Secretariat member, Messadia, who was on a 5 day official visit during which a protocol of party to party cooperation was signed.
16–17	Iraqi leader Saddam Hussein (with a senior economic, foreign affairs and military delegation) made an official visit. Hussain and his Foreign Minister met with Gorbachev and Shevardnadze on the 16th and with full delegations with Gromyko, Shevardnadze, Sokolov and Soviet economic ministers separately the same day. Counterpart meetings were held the 17th. The communique described the talks as "open, friendly and businesslike" and "protracted" (indicating some real differences).
24–27	North Korean Premier, Kan Sen San (with a foreign affairs and economic delegation) made an official visit. Meetings were held with Ryzhkov and other top Soviet leaders. A 1986–1990 trade protocol was signed, as well as agreement for Soviet assistance in building a nuclear power station.

Other senior Third World visits in December:

Middle East:	State Secretary to the Foreign Minister, Tunisia.
	A Party delegation, PDRY, for foreign ministry discussions.
Asia:	Minister of Trade, India, signed a 1986–1990 trade agreement.
Africa:	State Information Secretary, Guinea-Bissau.
	Foreign Minister, Lesotho (two week visit), signed a cultural and scientific cooperation agreement and an economic cooperation agreement.
	A Party delegation, Tanzania.
Latin America:	Foreign Minister, Brazil. He met with Gromyko and Shevardnadze and signed a memorandum for political consultations.
	A Party delegation and a senator from Peru.

Other senior Soviet visits to the Third World in December:

To the Middle East:	Deputy Minister of Defense and CinC of Ground Forces, General of the Army Ivanovskiy, to Algeria.
	Deputy Head, CC International Department, Brutents, to Kuwait.
	Deputy Minister of Defense and CinC of the Navy, Fleet Admiral Chernavin (newly promoted to the position), to Tunisia.
	A low level CPSU delegation to Israel for CP Conference.
To Asia:	Deputy Minister of Defense and CinC of Ground Forces, General of the Army Ivanovskiy, to India.
	A CPSU delegation to India.
To Africa:	A foreign ministry delegation to Togo.
To Latin America:	A meeting of the Soviet-Mexican Commission for Ocean Navigation. A protocol of cooperation was signed.
	The first meeting of the Soviet-Nicaraguan Commission for Economic, Trade and Scientific-Technical Cooperation. A 1986–1987 trade agreement and a 1986–1987 economic and technical cooperation agreement were signed.

Other agreements reported in December:

—A 1986–1990 cultural and scientific cooperation agreement with Afghanistan.

—A 1985–1987 interparty cooperation agreement with Zambia.

Other:	Western sources reported heavy military operations in Afghanistan; and by Cubans and Angolans with Soviet support in Angola.

January 1986

8–15	Candidate Politburo Member, First Deputy Chairman Council of Ministers and Chairman GOSPLAN Talyzin led a delegation to Vietnam, Laos and Kampuchea. In Vietnam at a CEMA meeting, he signed an agreement coordinating State plans, 1986–1990. He signed similar agreements with Laos and Kampuchea plus a 1986–1990

trade and economic cooperation agreement with Kampuchea.

15–24   Then prime minister, but future PDRY leader, Abu Bakr al Attas (with the PDRY Foreign Minister and Minister of Trade and Supply) held extensive consultations including those reported with Aliev, Ligachev and Ponomarev. The South Yemenis had rushed to Moscow from India when news of the coup in Aden broke. During the several days of heavy fighting there, the Soviets helped evacuate foreign nationals (including their own) and, on the 27th, began providing food and medical aid. Subsequent Western and Gulf state reports indicated that sometime during the fighting Soviet pilots and Cubans began actively assisting the rebels.

27   A tripartite meeting of senior foreign affairs, but especially military officials, was held in Moscow between the USSR, Cuba and Angola. In addition to references to internal struggles in Angola, the communique mentioned wider southern African issues and support for SWAPO, the ANC and anti-apartheid forces in South Africa.

28   The Soviet press published Foreign Minister Shevardnadze's letter to the UN on "the Economic Security of States," which, among other things, stressed Soviet support for Third World issues such as the "New International Economic Order" and the problem of Third World debts.

Other senior Third World visits in January:

Middle East: Minister of Development, Yemen Arab Republic, for the first meeting of the Soviet-North Yemeni Commission for Economic and Technical Cooperation.

Chief of the PLO Political Directorate, Khaddoumi, who held "friendly, businesslike" discussions with Foreign Minister Shevardnadze.

A foreign ministry delegation from Lebanon.

Africa: The Minister of Trade, Madagascar, accompanied by the Minister of Culture and the Arts.

A senior Party delegation, Mali.

Latin America: Foreign Minister, Argentina. He signed a 1986–1990 grain sales agreement, a cultural and scientific cooperation agreement, and a protocol for regular political consultations.

Minister of Economic Development, Colombia, for a meeting of the Soviet-Colombian Commission for Trade, Economic and Scientific-Technical Cooperation.

Other senior Soviet visits to the Third World in January:

To the Middle East: A Union of Journalists delegation to Jordan.

Deputy Minister of Defense, General of the Army Govorov, to Kuwait.

A Deputy Minister of Culture to Tunisia.

To Asia: A Supreme Soviet delegation, headed by Candidate Politburo Member Kuznetsov, to India.

First Deputy Chairman, Council of Ministers

Murakhovskiy, to Mongolia for a meeting of the Soviet-Mongolian Commission for Economic and Scientific-Technical Cooperation.

To Africa: A Supreme Soviet delegation to Sierra Leone.
To Latin America: A CPSU delegation to Panama.

Other agreements reported in January:

—A 1986–1990 economic and scientific-technical cooperation agreement with Mongolia.

—A 1986–1987 cultural and scientific cooperation agreement with Sudan.

—A 1986–1990 Trade agreement, a 1986 Trade Protocol and a 1986–1990 Economic and Technical Cooperation agreement, all with Vietnam.

—An agricultural assistance agreement, with Angola.

—A 1986–1987 TV and Radio cooperation protocol with Cuba.

Other: —The Western press reported heavy fighting and new Soviet/Afghan offensives in Afghanistan.

—A scheduled visit to Moscow by the Deputy Chairman of the ruling Transitional Military Council, Sudan, was cancelled, reportedly by Soviet request.

February 1986

3–8   Politburo Member, CC Secretary Ligachev led the delegation to the Cuban Party congress.

20   The opening of diplomatic relations with the Ivory Coast was announced.

26–6/3   XXVII Congress of the CPSU. Majority of Third World states which are closely aligned to Moscow were represented by the actual heads of state (Afghanistan, Mongolia, Laos, Kampuchea, Vietnam, Ethiopia, Angola, Cuba), accompanied in most cases by other senior government officials (political economic or defense). Other close clients, such as Libya, Syria, North Korea, Mozambique, Nicaragua, sent the number two man in the government or a very senior official (e.g. Foreign Minister). Government ministers or senior state officials were also sent by PDRY, Benin, Burundi, Burkina Faso, Cape Verde, Ghana, Guinea, Guinea-Bissau, Madagascar, Mali, Saô Tomé and Principe, Seychelles, Zimbabwe, and Guiana. All told some 94 Third World delegations from 72 sovereign states (15 Middle Eastern, 13 Asian, 20 African and 24 Latin American) were represented. One notable absence from the list of client state leaders (or deputies) who were reported to have held private talks with Gorbachev (or others of the very top Soviet leadership) was Karmal of Afghanistan—possibly foreshadowing his subsequent downgrading and replacement as head of state.

Other senior Third World visits in February:

Middle East: Foreign Minister, Iraq.
Minister of Oil and Industry, Kuwait, signed a protocol of economic, trade, financial and scientific cooperation.

Asia: Special representatives of Fiji, Papau-New Guinea, Solomon Islands, and Cook Islands as part of a group representing the forum of Pacific nations declaring a nuclear-free zone.

Other senior Soviet visitors to the Third World in February:

To the Middle East: First Deputy Foreign Minister, Kornienko, to Iran.

To Africa: A naval port call by one major surface combatant to Guinea-Bissau.

Other agreements reported in February:

—A 1986–1990 Trade agreement with North Korea.

—A 1986–1990 Trade agreement and a 1986 Trade protocol, with Afghanistan.

March 1986 (other than Congress related)

11–12 Cuban leader Castro was back in Moscow (he had gone to North Korea after the Soviet Congress). He met with Shevardnadze and Yeltsin on the 11th and with Gorbachev on the 12th.

14 Vietnamese leader Le Duan (who had stayed in the USSR on vacation after the Congress) met with Gorbachev.

15 In Stockholm for the Palme funeral, Chairman of the Council of Ministers Ryzhkov was reported to have had private talks with Indian Prime Minister Gandhi and Nicaraguan President Ortega.

24–25 U.S. strikes in Libya were made in response to armed reaction to U.S. presence in the Gulf of Sidra (claimed by Libya). The Soviet reaction was heavy on words, but noticeably lacking in concrete actions.

25–28 Algerian President Benjedid (with a senior political and economic delegation) made a state visit. On both the 26th and 27th he and his delegation met with Gorbachev and other senior Soviet counterparts (but also including the Soviet Minister of Defense). Algerian ministers also met separately with Soviet counterparts. An agreement and a program for long-term trade, economic, and scientific-technical cooperation was signed, as was a protocol for regular political consultations.

30–1/4 Mozambiquan leader Machel (with a senior foreign affairs, economic and military delegation) made a state visit. On the 31st the Mozambiquans met with Ryzhkov and other top Soviet counterparts. On the 1st of April, Machel met with Gorbachev alone except for interpreters. Counterpart meetings were also reported.

Other senior Third World visits in March:

Middle East:	Minister of Economics and Foreign Trade, Egypt.
	A parliamentary delegation, Iraq.
Africa:	A parliamentary delegation, Sierra Leone.
	Prime Minister, Equatorial Guinea.

Other senior Soviet visits to the Third World in March:

To the Middle East:	Minister of Energy and Electrification, Maiorets, with a Supreme Soviet delegation, to Egypt.
To Asia:	Candidate Politburo Member and Minister of Culture, Demichev, with a delegation, to the Indian CP congress. While there Demichev met with Prime Minister Gandhi. A foreign ministry delegation to India.
	Deputy Chairman, Council of Ministers, Ryabov to the meeting of the Soviet-North Korean Commission for Economic and Scientific-Technical Cooperation. He met with Kim Il Sung while there.
To Latin America:	A Supreme Soviet delegation to (in turn) Peru, Ecuador, Venezuela and Mexico.

Other agreements reported in March:

—A 1986 trade protocol with North Korea.

—A 1986 cultural and scientific cooperation agreement with Sri Lanka.

—A 1986–1987 interparty cooperation program with Tanzania.

—A 1986–1990 Trade agreement and a 1986 Trade protocol with Kampuchea.

Other:

—Western reports indicated preparations for a major offensive against UNITA in Angola.

—Western reports also said that on 30 March Afghanistan leader Karmal made a sudden trip to the USSR.

April 1986

14–15   U.S. strikes were made against Libya in response to Libyan involvement in international terrorism. Soviet reaction was very loud, but other than cancelling a scheduled meeting (in May) of the Foreign Minister and the U.S. Secretary of State, was restrained in actions. On the 15th, Gorbachev sent a telegram of support to Qaddafi stating that Moscow would "firmly fulfill the agreed programs to strengthen (Libyan) defenses"; but the wording gave no indication of any willingness to increase such support. Persistent Western and Gulf Arab press reports indicated that Washington had warned the Soviets in advance. Notably, Soviet ships which had been in the area moved out just before the attack; a Soviet economic delegation (see below) left (quickly?) on the 14th; and the Kuwaiti press even claimed that hundreds of Soviet military technicians were pulled out of the SA-5 bases on the 13th. Moscow denied all such allegations. The UAE press also reported that subsequently (on the 25th)

| | Qaddafi requested to join the Warsaw Pact, but was turned down. |

17-19   First Deputy Prime Minister, Ramadan, of Iraq led a senior economic and military delegation to Moscow for discussions with Ryzhkov, other Soviet economic ministers and the Minister of Defense.

18   According to Western press reports, Gorbachev met with PLO Chairman Arafat at the East German Party congress. These reports also claimed Gorbachev and Arafat met "secretly" earlier in February.

Other senior Third world visits in April:

Middle East: Minister of the Economy and Foreign Trade, Egypt.
A Party delegation, Syria.

Asia: President Karmal of Afghanistan was in the USSR all month, reportedly for medical treatment. (This was not mentioned in the central Soviet press).

Africa: General Director of the Foreign Ministry, Benin.
A Party delegations from Benin.

Latin America: Minister of Agricultural Development and Agrarian Reform, Nicaragua.

Other senior Soviet visits to the Third World in April:

To the Middle East: A senior Foreign Ministry official (Head of the Middle-East Department), to Syria where he met with Assad and with Palestinian faction leaders, Habash and Hawatmeh.
Chairman, State Committee for Economic Ties, Katushev, to Libya (he left just before the U.S. strikes after five days), met with Qaddafi.
Naval port call (late in the month) by one major surface combatant to Tripoli. (The Libyan news agency reported 4 combatants rather than the one in the Soviet report).
A Supreme Soviet delegation to Tunisia.
A political officers' delegation from YAR.

To Asia: First Deputy Chairman, Council of Ministers, Arkhipov attended a meeting of the Soviet-Indian Commission for Economic and Scientific-Technical Cooperation in Delhi, where it was agreed to rework and expand the 1986–1990 program of economic cooperation.
A deputy foreign minister to the Philippines, met with President Aquino. The visit was timed to precede U.S. President Reagan's arrival.

To Latin America: A meeting of the Soviet-Brazilian Commission, for Economic, Trade and Scientific-Technical Cooperation was held in Rio de Janeiro.
First Deputy Chairman, Council of Ministers, Arkhipov attended a meeting of the Soviet-Cuban Commission for Economic and Scientific-Technical Cooperation in Havana. A 1986–1990 trade and payments agreement and a 1986 trade protocol were signed, as was a protocol summary of results so far of measures to implement the agreement to coordinate state plans for 1986–1990.

A supreme Soviet delegation attended the 75th Interparliamentary Union conference in Mexico.
A CPSU delegation to Bolivia.

Other agreements reported in April:

—A ,1986–1987 plan for interparty ties with Congo.

—A plan for interparty cooperation with Saô Tomé and Principe.

—Agreement on "the Basic Directions of 1986–1990 Economic Cooperation" with Afghanistan.

—1986–1990 Trade and Payments agreement and a 1986 Trade Protocol with Mongolia.

Other: The Western press reported a very large scale Soviet-Afghan offensive beginning early in April and lasting all month in SE Afghanistan. Uncharacteristically, the Soviet press also carried partial coverage, claiming great victories by the Afghan army.

May 1986

5   In Kabul, Karmal was replaced as the real Afghan leader by the former head of the security services, Nadjibullah (the Soviet press report did not mention Nadjibullah's security background), who promised to "crush the rebels." Western reports indicated that Soviet troops ringed the city and the site of the Afghan Party plenum during the meeting which replaced Karmal (indicating Soviet involvement).

6–8   Angolan leader Dos Santos (with a large, senior economic, foreign affairs and military delegation) made a state visit. On the 6th he and his foreign minister met with Gorbachev and Shevardnadze. On the 7th the entire delegation met with Gorbachev and Soviet counterparts and again with Gromyko, Shevardnadze, Dobrynin and Marshal Sokolov. A 1986–1988 Party cooperation agreement was signed. The joint communique, besides mentioning internal Angolan matters, pledged full support for SWAPO and for the anti-apartheid struggle in South Africa.

23–24   A major foreign policy meeting was held in Moscow. See East-West chronology.

26–30   Libyan number two leader Jalloud (with a senior foreign affairs and economic delegation) made an official visit. The delegation included the head of the Libyan nuclear energy directorate, confirming the earlier indications (by the Soviet Ambassador in Libya) that the Soviets will help build a nuclear power plant in Libya. Jalloud met with Gorbachev on the 27th and with Marshal Sokolov on the 28th. The meeting with Gorbachev was described as "friendly and businesslike" and that with Sokolov as "friendly and with mutual understanding" (both indicating differences, but less so in the latter case). Separate counterpart meetings were also held. The Soviet wording of their opposition to international terrorism suggested that the Libyans were told to lower their profile.

27–29 Syrian Vice President Khaddam (with a senior economic, military and foreign affairs delegation) made an official visit. He met with Gorbachev on the 28th and also separately with Gromyko, Shevardnadze and Marshal Sokolov the same day. There were also counterpart meetings. In contrast to the Libyan visit, this one was described as "warm and friendly" with full pledges of continued Soviet support.

Other senior Third World visits in May:

Middle East: The Secretary General of the League of Arab States, met with Gromyko and Shevardnadze.
Minister of Culture, Syria.
Commander of the Navy, Syria.
Chief of the General Staff, YAR.

Asia: An Indian naval combatant made a port call to Sevastopol.

Latin America: A Senior parliamentary delegation, Argentina.

Other senior Soviet visits to the Third World in May:

To the Middle East: A meeting with the Soviet-Iraqi Commission for Economic, Scientific-Technical and Trade Cooperation was held in Bagdad. An agreement for 1986–1990 economic and scientific-technical cooperation was signed. Contracts were also signed for Soviet assistance in construction of a pipeline, a canal and "other projects." GKES chairman Katushev, who led the Soviet delegation, also met with Iraqi leader Hussain.
Chief of the MPA, Army General Lizichev visited Syria and met with Assad.

To Asia: A Supreme Soviet delegation to Indonesia.
A CPSU delegations to Sri Lanka.

To Latin America: A Supreme Soviet delegation to Costa Rica and then to Nicaragua where they met with President Ortega.

Other agreements reported in May:

—A 1986–1990 cultural protocol with the PDRY.
—A 1986–1987 trade agreement with Indonesia.
—A 1986–1987 interparty cooperation plan with Mali.
—A 1986–1988 cultural, education and social sciences exchange agreement, with Mexico.
—A 1986–1988 cultural and scientific cooperation agreement with Venezuela.
—A number or otherwise unspecified trade and economic agreements with Cuba.

June 1986

3–5 PDRY Prime Minister Naoman (with a large economic, foreign affairs and defense delegation) visited and met with

Ryzhkov, Talyzin and Aristov on the 4th. Counterpart meetings were held and economic protocols (not further identified) were signed.

29   The opening of diplomatic relations with the Pacific island nation of Vanuatu was announced.

Other senior Third World visits in June:

Middle East: Chief of Staff of the Army, Algeria.

Minister of Foreign Affairs, Egypt (there for an academic conference, but met with Shevardnadze).

A Foreign Ministry delegation, Iran, for consular discussions.

Minister of Trade, Iraq. A 1986–1990 trade turnover agreement was signed.

A parliamentary delegation, Lebanon.

Asia: A parliamentary delegation, Thailand.

Africa: Minister of Information, Ideological Orientation and Co-operation, Madagascar. A telegraph agency agreement was signed.

A parliamentary delegation, Togo.

The General Secretary, United Independence Party, Zambia (on a stopover from North Korea).

A separate Party delegation, Zambia.

Latin America: State Secretary for Science and Technology, Argentina.

Other senior Soviet visits to the Third World in June:

To the Middle East: The Soviet-Algerian Commission for Economic and Scientific-Technical Cooperation met in Algiers. A protocol to widen cooperation in metallurgy, mining, geology, electric energy and the petro-gas industry, plus a credit agreement between the Soviet Export Bank and the Algerian National Bank were signed.

A cultural delegation, to Libya.

Chairman, GKES Katushev, to Syria, met with Assad.

A low-level CPSU delegation to Tunisia.

To Asia: First Deputy Chairman, Council of Ministers Arkhipov, to India (for the opening of the Soviet-Indian Chamber of Commerce and Industry).

A Supreme Soviet delegation (the same that was in Indonesia in May), to Singapore, Malaysia and Thailand (in turn).

Other agreements reported in June:

—A 1987–1988 protocol of cooperation in radio and TV, with Afghanistan.

—A 1986–1987 Cultural and Scientific Cooperation Plan, with Jordan.

Other: In Afghanistan, the Soviets repeated several Kabul claims of tactical victories; and the Western press contained analyses stating that a combination of improved tactics (heavy use of SPETSNAZ troops and commandos and more effective air firepower) were turning the battlefield tide there. Western sources also reported two Soviet diplomats had been executed in Kabul for aiding the rebels.

In an Angolan port, two Soviet merchant vessels were badly damaged (and a Cuban ship sunk) by South African commandos on 5 June.

July 1986

4–8	Candidate Politburo Member Solovyev led a large delegation to North Korea to celebrate the 25th anniversary of the Treaty of Friendship and Cooperation. He met with Kim Il Sung on the 7th. There was also a large military delegation including a three-vessel naval port call with the Commander of the Pacific Fleet ADM Sidorov and an air force detachment. This continued the pattern of very large delegations to Korean celebrations.
13–15	Chairman, Council of Ministers Ryzhkov and CC Secretary Dobrynin led a large delegation to Vietnam for the funeral of Le Duan who died on the 10th. They held meetings with the new Vietnamese leader Troung Chinh.
14–19	President Traore of Mali (with an economic and foreign affairs delegation) made an official visit. He met with Gorbachev on 10 July. Counterpart meetings were held and documents for economic and scientific cooperation, an agreement on inter-party cooperation and a declaration to further develop friendship were signed.
19–27	Chairman, Central Revision Commission, CPSU, Kapitonov led a foreign affairs delegation to the PDRY (19–23 July), Ethiopia (23–25 July) and the YAR (25–27 July). Extensive talks were held with the top leadership of each country. Those with the PDRY were described as "comradely with full mutual understanding and complete unity of views of major international policies," while those in Sana (YAR) were characterized as "businesslike and friendly."
21	Diplomatic relations (broken in July, 1985 by Monrovia) were reestablished with Liberia.
29	Gorbachev proposed various Asian and Pacific economic and security cooperation programs and announced a partial (6,000 to 9,000 man) troop withdrawal from Afghanistan (in his speech at Vladivostok).

Other Third World visits to the USSR in July:

Middle East:	Unidentified government minister, Iraq, leading a friendship society delegation.
	Lebanese Druse leader Jumblatt, met with Dobrynin.
	A mid-level Baath Party delegation, Syria.
Asia:	Minister of Trade, Burma.
Africa:	A party delegation, Cape Verde.
	The CP General Secretary, Martinique, for an award.
	Chief of the General Staff, Nigeria leading an "economic" delegation. He met with Ryzhkov, Gromyko and Arkhipov.

| | Chief of the General Staff, Tanzania. |
| Latin America: | A parliamentary delegation, Argentina. |

Minister of Foreign Affairs, Uruguay. A Cultural and Scientific Cooperation agreement and a protocol for political consultations were signed.

Other senior Soviet visits to the Third World in July:

| To the Middle East: | GKES Chairman Katushev, to Kuwait. |

A mid-level CPSU delegation, to Libya.

| To Latin America: | A mid-level CPSU delegation, to Mexico. |

Communications Minister Shamshin, to Nicaragua for the opening of a space tracking station. He met with Ortega.

Other agreements reported in July:

—A fishing cooperation agreement with Argentina, apparently including permission for Soviet fishing in waters claimed by the UK.

—A consular agreement with Seychelles.

—The sale of 50 trolleys to Uruguay.

—A 1986–1990 Trade Turnover agreement, a 1986 Trade protocol and a 1986–1990 Economic and Scientific-Technical Cooperation agreement with Laos.

Other: The Soviet press carried several small articles reporting Afghan claims of tactical victories over the rebels. The Western press carried similar articles (especially later in the month) claiming successful rebel operations against Soviet and Afghan regime troops. It also reported fresh major Soviet/Afghan offensives in the South and Southeast late in the month.

In Angola the same pattern was repeated with the Soviets repeating several Luanda claims of sizeable tactical successes, while Western reports focussed on UNITA claims of similar successes, including shooting down a MiG-23. Western reports also indicated that UNITA had stepped up operation in the North and East (they are usually more active in the South and Southeast)—especially against economic targets.

August 1986

11–15 Prime Minister Al Mahdi, Sudan (with an economic, political and military delegation), made an official visit. He met alone with Ryzhkov on the 11th and with him and a large group of deputy economic ministers on the 12th. Counterpart meetings were held and the Sudanese spent three days travelling in the USSR.

12 Gorbachev held talks with the new Vietnamese leader Troung Chinh who had been vacationing in the USSR. These talks were evidently more substantive than the more pro forma ones described below.

Gorbachev also met with Mongolian leader Batmunkh who had been vacationing in the USSR.

18	Mid-level Foreign Ministry officials held the first formal discussions with Israel (in Helsinki) since the breaking of relations by the USSR in 1967. The talks, which were supposed to last 2 days, were broken off by the Soviets after 90 minutes. They were not reported in the main Soviet press.
19	The Iranian Minister of Oil met (separately) with Ryzhkov and Ministry of Foreign Trade officials in Moscow. Later, the Iranians (but not the main Soviet press) announced that the Soviets had agreed to support OPEC pricing efforts by cutting oil deliveries to West Europe and that an agreement had been signed to resume Soviet import of Iranian natural gas, as well as its transportation across the USSR for delivery to Europe.
30–3/9	First Deputy Chairman, Presidium of the Supreme Soviet Demichev led a delegation, which included the Chief of Staff of Air Defense Troops, to Libya. The Soviets met with both Qaddafi and Jalloud (separately).

Other Third World visits to the USSR in August:

Middle East:	Party Secretary and Politburo member Messadia, Algeria, made a visit, met with Ligachev.
	Representatives of 31 state and private firms, Algeria, for a trade exposition.
	A Deputy Foreign Minister, Iran.
	A parliamentary delegation, Libya.
Asia:	Delegations and officials from several of the USSR's major Asian client states, but also including Indian Prime Minister Gandhi, stopped over for short meetings enroute to and from other meetings. Gandhi's visit was apparently unexpected, met with Aliev.
	A delegation from the National People's Party, Pakistan.
Africa:	A political officers' delegation, Benin.
	A parliamentary delegation, Senegal.
Latin America:	A Foreign Ministry delegation, Ecuador (for UNGA talks).
	Party delegations from Mexico (United Socialist Party) and Venezuela (Party for Direct Action).

Other Soviet visits to the Third World in August:

To the Middle East:	Deputy Foreign Minister Petrovskiy in turn to Tunisia, Egypt and Iraq.
	First Deputy Foreign Minister Vorontsev, first to Syria and then to Jordan. He met with Assad in Syria and Hussein in Jordan.
	(Both of the above trips took place in the last ten days of the month and were clearly connected).
To Asia:	A Supreme Soviet delegation, to India.
To Africa:	CPSU delegations to Ghana and Madagascar.
	A Deputy Foreign Minister, to Zambia. A protocol of scientific and technical cooperation was signed.
To Latin America:	Foreign Ministry delegations to Argentina, and to Trinidad and Tobago, for talks related to the UNGA.
	A Supreme Soviet delegation, to Colombia (for the presidential inauguration).

Other agreements reported in August:

—A protocol of assistance in agronomy and agrotechnology, with Afghanistan.

—A 1986–1987 protocol on students in the USSR, with Afghanistan.

—A protocol on economic, technical and trade cooperation, 1986–1990, with Angola.

Other: The Soviet press continued to carry small articles repeating Kabul's claims of tactical successes against the Afghan rebels. One claimed that a rebel group was intercepted with chemical weapons that they had intended to use.

In Angola, both the government and the UNITA forces claimed tactical successes.

September 1986

22–30 Foreign Minister Shevardnadze was reported to have held meetings in New York with the Foreign Ministers of 27 Third World states (and in a few cases heads of states) present for the UNGA. The only Soviet allies and clients not listed among these meetings were: Congo, Kampuchea and Mozambique. Other meetings listed included: Bangladesh, India, Indonesia, Brazil, Mexico, Kuwait, Egypt, Pakistan, Israel and Zimbabwe. The Israeli meeting was with Prime Minister Peres; the Soviet press, which claimed the meeting was held at Peres' request, published an account solely limited to describing Soviet general Middle East positions with no mention of anything the Israelis had brought up. Shevardnadze also met with PLO representative Khaddoumi. After the UNGA and a trip to Ottawa, Shevardnadze was due in Mexico and Cuba in early October.

24–2/10 President Ratsiraka of Madagascar, with a political and a very large economic delegation, made an official visit. He met with Gromyko and economic officials on the 24th and with Gorbachev on the 26th. Counterpart meetings were also held. Agreements were signed, including: a declaration of mutual friendship, a party cooperation plan, and a 1986–2000 long-term program of trade and economic and scientific-technical cooperation.

Other Third World visits to the USSR in September:

Middle East: A trade union delegation, Iraq, signed a cooperation agreement with Soviet counterparts.

Minister of Internal Affairs, PDRY.

A deputy secretary general of the Baath party, Syria.

Asia: Minister of Energy, India.

A First Deputy Minister of Trade and Industry, Maldives.

A CP delegation from Sri Lanka.

The exiled Dalai Lama, Tibet.

Africa: Party delegations from Kenya and Mali.

A veterans' delegation, Nigeria.

Latin America: Minister of Urban Construction, Brazil.

Other Soviet visits to the Third World in September:

To the Middle East: First Deputy Foreign Minister Vorontsev, to Algeria. This was a continuation of the same official's trip to Syria and Jordan in late August.

A Trade and Industry Chamber delegation, to Iran.

First Deputy CinC, Navy ADM Smirnov, to PDRY.

To Africa: A Supreme Soviet delegation, to Botswana.

To Latin America: A Foreign Ministery delegation (UNGA talks) and (separately) a mid-level CPSU delegation, to Jamaica.

An otherwise unidentified group of economic experts, to Nicaragua, where a "number" of unidentified economic documents were signed.

A CPSU delegation headed by Deputy Head, CC International Department Brutents (normally strictly associated with the Middle East) to (in turn) Uruguay, Argentina and (in early October) to Panama.

Other: The Western press reported sizeable rebel offensives North and East of Kabul (and a car bomb in the city as well as two rocket attacks on the Soviet compound) in Afghanistan. Kabul reported a large Soviet-Afghan counterattack and claimed full success.

Luanda continued to report tactical successes against UNITA in Angola.

In early September, the Kuwaiti press reported that Syrian leader Assad had made a secret trip to Moscow in late August; but there was no other confirmation.

October 1986

4 Foreign Minister Shevardnadze, who visited Mexico after Canada, held talks with the Mexican foreign minister. While there he also met with President de la Madrid. An agreement on future regular political consultations was reached.

6 Zimbabwean Prime Minister Mugabe and his foreign minister stopped over in the USSR enroute on a trip. The foreign minister met with Shevardnadze on the 8th.

8 Gorbachev met with the Burkina Faso leader, Sankar, who was there on an official visit. A 1987–88 plan for interParty ties was signed.

13–17 Argentinian President Alfonsin made a state visit. He met with Gorbachev on the 15th and the communique on the talks stated that various forms of cooperation had been agreed upon.

26 Gorbachev met with North Korean leader Kim Il Sung who was on an official visit with a senior delegation.

28–29 Politburo member and First Deputy Chairman, Council of

Ministers Aliev headed a party-state delegation to Angola to discuss broad cooperation. He met with Angolan leader Dos Santos who expressed full support for Soviet policies.

Other Third World visits to the USSR in October:

Asia:	A parliamentary delegation and a state official identified as a first deputy minister, India.
	A deputy foreign minister, Philippines.
	A foreign ministry delegation, Singapore.
Africa:	President Ratsiraka, Madagascar on a stopover.
	Parliamentary delegations from Guinea and Sierra Leone.
Latin America:	Minister of Urban Affairs and the Environment, Brazil; met with Katushev.
	A deputy foreign minister, Colombia.
	The Minister of Trade and Industry, Mexico, for the fourth session of the Soviet-Mexican commission on trade and economic cooperation.
	A Socialist party delegation, Uraguay.

Other Soviet visits to the Third World in October:

To Asia:	GKES Chairman Katushev to India and Bangladesh.
To Africa:	A Supreme Soviet delegation to Botswana.
To Latin America:	A Supreme Soviet delegation to Argentina.

Other agreements reported in October:

—An accord on further economic and technical cooperation with the PDRY.

November 1986

4	Gorbachev met with the visiting Indian foreign minister who had met with state economic officials the day before.
4	Gorbachev met with the President of the ANC, Tambo.
21	Gorbachev met with President Kereku, Benin, who was on an official visit lasting until the 27th when a declaration of Soviet-Benin friendship and cooperation was signed.
24–29	Gorbachev, with a senior entourage made an official visit to India where he made speeches, toured and met citizens and held extensive consultations with Gandhi and other Indian leaders. A joint declaration on a world free of nuclear weapons and the imposition of force was signed.

Other Third World visits to the USSR in November:

Africa:	A foreign ministry delegation, Somalia, for consultations on bilateral relations and on Afghanistan.
	The Minister of Mining, Zambia; met with Katushev.
Latin America:	The vice president, Guyana.

Other Soviet visits to the Third World in November:

To Latin America:	Delegation to the third session of the Soviet-Cuban commission on cultural cooperation.

Other agreements reported in November:

—Cooperation between TASS and the Benin information agency.

—1986–1987 cultural and scientific cooperation with Kampuchea.

December 1986

12	Gorbachev met with Afghan leader Nadjibullah who was on an official visit with a senior delegation. It is likely that the Afghan government's January 1987 declaration of a ceasefire and an amnesty was discussed and finalized.
29	An official government communique in TASS accused the US of instigating the conflict in Chad.

Other Third World visits to the USSR in December:

Middle East:	The Libyan foreign minister who met with Shevardnadze.
Asia:	A first deputy foreign minister, Pakistan.
Africa:	A party delegation, Guinea.
Latin America:	The Minister of Foreign Economic Cooperation, Nicaragua.

Other Soviet visits to the Third World in December:

To the Middle East:	An economic delegation to Egypt for discussions on financial credits.
To Asia:	Chief of the MPA, General Lizichev to North Korea where he met with Kim Il Sung as well as military officials.
To Africa:	A Supreme Soviet delegation to Mali.

Other agreements reported in December:

—1987 trade protocol with Egypt.
—Protocol of cooperation in education and culture with Nigeria.
—1987–1990 cooperation in geological exploration, with the PDRY.

January 1987

1	Afghan leader Nadjibullah announced a cease fire effective 15 January and offered a "government of national unity" along with amnesty for "thousands" of political prisoners. The Soviet press reported this on the 2nd and thereafter played it up greatly. The government of national unity proposed bore a striking resemblance to those in East Europe after WWII during the interim before the communists moved openly to take over.
5–7	Foreign Minister Shevardnadze and CC Secretary Dobrynin visited Afghanistan, holding extensive discussions with the leadership and undoubtedly further coordinating the "ceasefire."
20–22	The Saudi Minister of Oil and Mineral Resources made a visit, meeting with Ryzhkov and other officials. This was the first official government visit by a Saudi official.

Other Third World visits to the USSR in January:

Middle East:	A mid-level Party delegation, Algeria.

Asia: Deputy Prime Minister Arora and State Minister for For-
                               eign Affairs Singh, India.
                               A friendship society delegation led by a member of parlia-
                               ment, India.
                               A Deputy Chairman, Council of Ministers, Vietnam for the
                               XII session of the Soviet-Vietnamese Commission for Eco-
                               nomic and Scientific-Technical Cooperation in Moscow.
Africa: A member of the ANC Executive Committee.
                               A parliamentary delegation, Zimbabwe.

Other Soviet visits to the Third World in January:

To the Middle East: An Academy of Sciences group to Libya where they signed
                               a cooperation agreement with counterparts.
                               Chairman of the Religious Affairs Council of the Council
                               of Ministers to Syria, where he met with Assad.
                               Deputy Head of the CC International Department, Bru-
                               tents, to Syria.
To Asia: The Minister of Energy and Electrification to India where
                               he signed a protocol to explore the feasibility of Soviet con-
                               struction of coal energy plants.
                               A deputy Foreign Minister to Pakistan where he met with
                               President Zia.
To Africa: A Supreme Soviet delegation to Togo.

Other agreements reported in January:

                               —A 1987–1988 Cultural and Scientific Cooperation plan,
                               with Egypt.
                               —An agreement for cooperation in irrigation, agriculture,
                               housing, energy and transportation assistance, with
                               Afghanistan.
                               —A 1987 trade agreement with Bangladesh.
                               —A 1987 working plan of cooperation between the Minis-
                               try of Cinematography and the North Korean Ministry of
                               Culture.
                               —A Foreign Ministry cooperation plan, with Mongolia.
                               —A Fishing Rights and Access agreement with Vanuatu.
                               —A 1987 Trade protocol with Cuba (for over 8 billion ru-
                               bles).
                               —A working agreement between TASS and counterparts in
                               Djibouti.

Other: Western press reports claimed that there were indications
                               of a new Soviet offensive in Afghanistan near the end of the
                               month in spite of the cease fire. The Soviets had reported
                               several rebel "violations" of the ceasefire (which the rebels
                               had not accepted).
                               The Soviet press gave extensive reportage of the fighting in
                               Chad, but most reports made no mention of Libyan in-
                               volvement.
                               In the West it was reported that Communist rebels in the
                               Philippines had rejected Soviet offers of assistance because
                               of "strings" attached. The Soviets denied the reports.

February 1987

9-11	PDRY leader and Party General Secretary Al-Bayd visited with a large military, economic and political delegation. He met with Gorbachev on the 10th, extensive counterpart meetings were held and a 1987–1988 Cultural and Scientific Cooperation agreement and a protocol of foreign ministry cooperation were signed.
13-14	The Iranian Foreign Minister visited and met with Gromyko, Shevardnadze, Ryzhkov and others. The meetings were described as "frank" with "disagreements" on the Iran-Iraq war and Iranian support for Afghan rebels.
17-18	Chairman, Council of Ministers Keshtmand, Afghanistan, with a large economic delegation, visited. A protocol for Soviet construction of industrial and "other" facilities was signed.

Other Third World visits to the USSR in February:

Middle East:	The General Secretary, Organization of Islamic Conferences.
	A Foreign Ministry delegation from Algeria.
	The Iraqi Foreign Minister, who met with Gromyko, Shevardnadze and Ryzhkov (the same main ones who met with the Iranian foreign minister) in talks described as "unconstrained and friendly."
	The Chief of the General Staff, Syria who met with Deputy Chairman, Council of Ministers Kamentsev for talks on "economic" cooperation.
Asia:	The Foreign Minister, Pakistan (twice) meeting with Shevardnadze enroute to and from talks on the Afghan war in Geneva.
	A friendship society delegation, Sri Lanka.
	The Chairman of the Foreign Affairs Commission, Parliament of Thailand.
	The Crown Prince, Tonga (also the Foreign and Defense Minister).
Africa:	The Minister of Culture, Youth and Sport, Benin.
Latin America:	The General Secretary of the CP Argentina, who stayed over into March when he met with Gorbachev on the 3rd.
	A parliamentary delegation, Panama.

Other Soviet visits to the Third World in February:

To the Middle East:	An Academy of Sciences delegation, a delegation of the Soviet Society for Assistance to the UN, and a friendship society delegation, to Egypt.
	Deputy Head, CC International Department Brutents from Syria to Lebanon and back to Syria where he met with Assad.
Asia:	The Minister of Aviation Industry to India to discuss Mig-29 coproduction.
	A CPSU delegation to Sri Lanka.

	A Supreme Soviet delegation to Thailand.
To Africa:	A Supreme Soviet delegation to Sudan.
	A mid-level Party delegation to Tanzania.
To Latin America:	Deputy Foreign Minister Komplektov to Brazil, Uruguay and Mexico.

Other agreements reported in February:

—A $150 million loan from a consortium of Kuwaiti banks.

—Radio and TV cooperation with North Korea.

Other: Afghan and Soviet sources claimed several thousand rebels returning to government control; but the number of "ceasefire violations" reported (504 by mid-month), and articles describing the need for strong protective forces to secure refugee "return" camps near the borders, suggested that the fighting was continuing unabated and seemed to be laying the basis for a renewal of Soviet-Afghan offensives. In fact Western sources indicated that just such an offensive was in preparation late in the month. Pakistani sources reported heavy fighting near Kabul, Kandahar and Herat.

March 1987

1–4	Candidate Politburo Member Solovyev led a delegation to Libya and met with Qaddafi.
1–13	Foreign Minister Shevardnadze made a tour of SE Asia, to Thailand, Australia, Indonesia, Laos, Kampuchea and Vietnam in turn. He preached Gorbachev's policies to mixed reactions including egg-throwing in Australia and a bomb in Laos.
3–5	Candidate Politburo Member Yeltsin led a delegation to Nicaragua, meeting with Ortega. Enroute home he met with Castro in Cuba.
10–11	Military and political delegations from Angola and Cuba met with Soviet counterparts for the annual meeting on Angolan war and South African policies, in Moscow.
20–27	The Soviet-Angolan Commission for Economic and Scientific-Technical Cooperation met in Moscow and signed a 1986–1990 (and to 2000) Program of Economic and Technical Cooperation, plus unspecified "intragovernmental" agreements.
24–28	At an Asian and Pacific regional security conference in Beijing, Deputy Foreign Minister Petrovskiy emphasized Asian and Pacific security issues and disarmament.
28–2/4	Candidate Politburo Member and GOSPLAN head Talyzin led an economic, military and political delegation to Mozambique where he held extensive talks with new leader Chissano. Enroute and on his return, Talysin stopped in the PDRY where he met with the leadership. Earlier the Soviet-Mozambiquan Commission for Economic and Technical Cooperation and Trade had met in Maputo.

Other Third World visits to the USSR in March:
Middle East: A delegation of the Palestinian CP.
Africa: A Party delegation, Cape Verde.
Latin America: The Minister of Foreign Trade, Nicaragua.
Other Soviet visits to the Third World in March:
To the Middle East: A Foreign Ministry delegation led by ministry colleague Mendelevich to Syria and then Iran.
                      A first Deputy Minister of the Merchant Fleet to Kuwait (not reported in the Soviet press).
                      A delegation to a Joint Fishing Commission meeting in the PDRY.
                      Ambassador at large Sytenko and (separately) a Supreme Soviet delegation to Jordan. Both met with King Hussein.
To Asia: Deputy Defense Minister and CinC, Navy, Fleet Adm Chernavin to India.
                      President, Academy of Sciences Marchuk to India.
                      A solidarity committee to Mauritius.
                      A low-level CPSU delegation to Sri Lanka.
To Africa: A Supreme Soviet delegation (in turn) to Angola, Zambia, Botswana, Zimbabwe and Tanzania.
                      Another Supreme Soviet delegation to Ghana.
                      A low-level CPSU delegation to Mali.
To Latin America: A Supreme Soviet delegation to Colombia and Peru.
                      A low-level CPSU delegation to Mexico.
                      First MPA Chief GEN Lizichev and then KGB Chief/Politburo Member Chebrikov, who met with Castro, to Cuba.
Other agreements reported in March:
                      —A 1987–1988 plan of cultural and scientific cooperation with Iraq.
                      —A program of cultural cooperation with Kuwait.
                      —A 1986–1990 (and to 2000) Program of Economic and Technical Cooperation, plus unspecified "intergovernmental" agreements, with Angola.
                      —A 1987–1989 plan of Party cooperation with Frelimo (Mozambique).
                      —A cooperation agreement between TASS and the Brazilian Information Agency.
Other: On 8 March, Afghan rebels rocketed a Soviet village across the border. This was not reported in the Soviet press until April, when *Krasnaya zvezda* ran a highly indignant article. Throughout the month, the Soviet press gave extensive coverage of fighting in Chad, but the picture painted was of a mix of tactical victories by both sides, only occasional mention of the Libyans and extensive castigation of US and French "interference."

April 1987

10   Deputy Chairman, Council of Ministers Kamentsev, who was heading the delegation to the Soviet-Indian Commis-

	sion for Economic and Scientific-Technical Cooperation in Delhi, met with Premier Gandhi.
17	Gorbachev met with Ethiopian leader Mengistu who was there on a stopover enroute home from North Korea.
23–25	Syrian President Assad, with a senior political, military and economic delegation, held talks with Gorbachev privately and with the leadership groups. Extensive counterpart talks were held by other members of the delegation.
29	Gorbachev (and later Shevardnadze) met with Foreign Ministers of the African "confrontation states" (Angola, Mozambique, Tanzania, Zambia and Zimbabwe) who were there for a conference.
29–30	The XVII Soviet-Cuban Commission for Economic and Scientific-Technical Cooperation met in Moscow at Deputy Chairman, Council of Minister level. An agreement in principle for the creation of Joint Ventures was signed.

Other Third World visits to the USSR in April:

Middle East:	The Minister of Internal Affairs, the Chief of the Army Political Administration and a delegation, and the General Secretary of the Defense Ministry, Algeria (all separately). A high ranking military delegation, Egypt (not reported officially, but leaked or claimed) by Egyptian press sources. A delegation of the League of Arab States including the Foreign Ministers of Iraq and Morocco and a ministry official from Kuwait. Lebanese Druze leader Jumblatt and two CP representatives. The Foreign Minister, Libya. A friendship society, PDRY. Representatives of the DFLP, Fatah and the Palestinian CP.
Asia:	A friendship society delegation, India.
Africa:	The President of Guinea, President Ratsiraka of Madagascar and a Deputy Chairman, Council of Ministers of Guinea-Bissau all while enroute to North Korea. The Prime Minister of Zambia who met with Ryzhkov and others on cooperation in chemical fertilizers and paper-cellulose. Party delegations from Burkina Faso and Madagascar.
Latin America:	The Prime Minister, Guyana and a parliamentary delegation, Venezuela, enroute to North Korea. The head of the Mexican CD delegation to receive an honorary degree.

Other Soviet visits to Third World in April:

To the Middle East:	Deputy Defense Minister and CinC, Air Forces Marshal Yefimov to Algeria where he met with President Benjedid. A delegation from the Kirghiz Republic and the General Director of TASS to Algeria (during the Palestinian Congress). First Deputy Foreign Minister Vorontsev to Libya and Algeria.

First Deputy, Presidium of the Supreme Soviet (and Candidate Politburo Member) Demichev with an economic delegation to Iraq where he met with Hussain.

Deputy Foreign Minister Petrovskiy to (in turn) Kuwait, UAE, Oman and Iraq.

Delegations of the Committee of Solidarity with the States of Asia and Africa to Libya, Syria and the YAR:

Deputy Defense Minister and CinC, Ground Forces, GEN Ivanovskiy to the PDRY where he met with Al Bayd.

Ambassador at Large Sytenko as Gorbachev's personal representative to the YAR.

To Asia: A friendship society delegation to India.

A mid-level CPSU delegation to Bangladesh.

To Africa: A Supreme Soviet delegation (the same that toured "frontline" states in March) to Kenya.

A low-level CPSU delegation to Saô Tomé and Principe (also visited Congo).

To Latin America: A Supreme Soviet delegation to Nicaragua for an Interparliamentary Conference. While there they met separately with President Ortega.

Low-level CPSU delegations to Bolivia and Colombia.

Other agreements reported in April:

—A 1987-Trade protocol and sales agreements for several products, 1987–1990 with the PDRY.

—A 1987–1988 Sports Cooperation agreement with Tunisia.

—Cooperation agreement between TASS and Algerian counterparts.

Other: On the 8th Afghan rebel crossborder raiders engaged in a fire fight with Soviet border guards. Western reports claimed massive retaliation in the border regions of Afghanistan by Soviet forces. Late in the month KGB Chief Chebrikov and the Commander of KGB Border Troops toured the region and reportedly levied heavy disciplinary punishments. Afghan sources claimed some 35,000 rebels or refugees had accepted the ceasefire, but reports of heavy fighting, complaints about "violations" and the shootdown of an Afghan plane over Pakistan indicated that the process was not working as well as indicated.

May 1987

6 Gorbachev met with the Foreign Minister of Mexico who was on an official visit.

11–17 The Agricultural Working Group of the Soviet-Nicaraguan Commission for Economic, Trade and Scientific-Technical Cooperation held its first meeting in Managua.

17–21 New Vietnamese leader Van Linh, with a foreign affairs and economic delegation, made an official visit, meeting with Gorbachev and others.

19–22	The Soviet-Mongolian Commission for Economic and Scientific-Technical Cooperation met in Moscow.
21–27	CC Secretary Dobrynin made an official visit to India meeting with Ghandi and the political, economic and military leadership.
23	CEMA representatives met with Latin American Economic System officials about closer direct ties.
27–3/6	The XXI session of the Soviet-North Korean Commission for Economic and Scientific-Technical Questions met in Moscow. An agreement in principle and of procedures for Joint Ventures was signed.
28–29	The II session of the Soviet-Ecuadorian Commission (Economics and Trade) was held and an agreement for the sale of machines and equipment to Ecuador was signed.

Other Third World visits to the USSR in May:

Middle East:	The Foreign Minister, Libya.
	The Minister of Defense, the PDRY.
Asia:	The General Secretary of the CP, India.
	The Foreign Minister, Thailand who met with Shevardnadze and signed a protocol to form a trade commission.
Africa:	The Deputy Chairman of the ruling junta, Ghana.
	Party delegations from Madagascar and Zimbabwe.
Latin America:	A parliamentary delegation, Uruguay.
	A Deputy Foreign Minister, Venezuela.

Other Soviet visits to the Third World in May:

To the Middle East:	A low-level and small friendship society delegation to Israel.
	Special Ambassador Sytenko to Syria where he met with Assad.
To Asia:	Deputy Foreign Minister Rogachev to (in turn) Bangladesh, Nepal, and Burma.
To Africa:	A Low-level CPSU delegations to Cape Verde.
	A naval port call (one combatant) to Saô Tomé et Principe.
To Latin America:	A mid-level CPSU delegation to Peru.

Other agreements reported in May:

—Otherwise unidentified "economic and technical cooperation documents" with Libya.

—An agreement for long-term cooperation in fishing with North Korea.

—1987–1990 (and to 2000) cooperation agreement on light industries, with Vietnam.

—General cooperation agreement on tea growing and processing, an agreement for cooperation in the production of coconut oil, a cooperation agreement for production of electro-technical equipment and "other documents" (unspecified), all with Vietnam.

—A protocol of cooperation between TASS and Nigerian counterparts.

—A 1987–1988 working protocol on TV and radio with Peru.

Other: Western sources reported 29 Soviet made aircraft and heli-
                              copters were shot down by Afghan rebels in May alone.
                              Meanwhile, the Soviet press seemed to carry a greater
                              number of articles about heroism by Soviet forces in
                              Afghanistan.
                              Western sources also indicated extensive preparations for
                              an offensive against UNITA in Angola.

June 1987

17   A Supreme Soviet delegation visiting Egypt met with Presi-
                              dent Mubarak and discussed expansion of economic ties.
                              Earlier the delegation had been in Libya and Algeria, and
                              afterwards it flew to Damascus and met with Syrian Presi-
                              dent Assad.
19   First Deputy Foreign Minister Vorontsov met with Iranian
                              President Khameni in Tehran for discussions on Iran-Iraq
                              war.
27   Gorbachev met with visiting PM Mugabe of Zimbabwe.
Other Third World visits to the USSR in June:
Asia: The Foreign Minister, India, as part of the delegation to a
                              meeting of the Soviet-Indian Commission for Economic
                              and Scientific-Technical Cooperation.
Latin America: A parliamentary delegation, Bolivia, which discussed a pro-
                              posal to create a Soviet-Bolivian Commission for Trade and
                              Economic Cooperation.
Other Soviet visits to the Third World in June:
To the Middle East: A delegation to a meeting of the Soviet-Syrian Commission
                              for Economic and Scientific-Technical Cooperation in
                              Damascus and GKES Chairman Katushev, who met with
                              Syrian ministers and signed an agreement for Soviet con-
                              struction of a hydroelectric station on the Euphrates River.
                              Supreme Soviet delegations to Algeria and Morocco.
Asia: Deputy Chairman, Presidium of the Supreme Soviet Tar-
                              azevich to Indonesia where he met with President Suharto.
Africa: A Supreme Soviet delegation to Ruanda.
                              Deputy Foreign Minister Adamshin to Ghana where agree-
                              ment was reached to begin consultations on the creation of
                              an institutional structure for closer political consultation
                              and cooperation.
Other agreements reported in June:
                              —An agreement for participation of Indian specialists in
                              construction of a hotel in Soviet Central Asia.
                              —An agreement on the expansion of political and eco-
                              nomic ties with Burma.
                              —A Fisheries Cooperation agreement with Angola.
                              —A Cooperation agreement between TASS and the press
                              agency Prensa Latina.
Other: Western sources reported that major Soviet-Afghan offen-

sives were underway in Afghanistan in the East and South since the latter days of May.

Section II
Military Assistance to the Third World

Open press reporting does not allow a very confident assessment of Soviet military assistance levels—especially of such assistance provided by the Gorbachev-led USSR. U.S. ACDA and other organizations do publish yearly values of arms transfers to various individual states and regions. However, these are usually 1 to 2 years behind the current year and are expressed in $ value based on varying formulae and according to varying interpretations of the value of infrastructure and training assistance vice actual hardware. Open source U.S. government figures are generally expressed similarly and cover actual deliveries of selected items and total estimated $ value most often for a five to six year period. It is difficult to extract from such material specific yearly figures, since any given year's publication of data may reflect corrections to previous yearly totals based on new information or revised analysis. Press reporting is sporadic, often quite incomplete, of less certain accuracy, and often fails to differentiate clearly between deliveries and agreements for the future. Moreover, in many cases actual deliveries over the period of an agreement do not equal the original sales or credit agreement. The Soviet press simply does not provide any meaningful data on this subject.

Nevertheless, the overall open source data do provide a good indication of the general scale and trends involved. Unfortunately for the purposes of this book, the information available does not clearly reflect how much of 1985 and 1986 deliveries of Soviet military assistance are the results of decisions by the Gorbachev team, rather than the simple fulfillment of early agreements—nor does the information allow us to differentiate with any degree of certainty between deliveries in 1985 before and after Gorbachev assumed power. The following data and statements are culled from Western sources, and should give the reader at least a sense of the scale of this activity by the Gorbachev-led USSR.

(1) 1985 Soviet deliveries of major items of military hardware to Third World regions reflect *up to* the following quantities:

Exhibit I
Selected Soviet Military Equipment Deliveries in 1985*

	Middle East & South Asia	Sub-Saharan Africa	Latin America	East Asia & the Pacific
Tanks/self propelled guns	460	130	100	unclear**
Light armor	1,925	330	85	20
Artillery	220	185	120	80
Major Surface Combatants	5	—	—	2
Minor Surface Combatants	4	4	11	7
Submarines	2	0	—	0
Supersonic Aircraft	—	35	—	65
Subsonic Aircraft	15	—	—	—
Helicopters	110	50	—	—
Surface to Air Missiles	2,920	1,345	380	80

*Data derived from U.S. Department of Defense figures in *Soviet Military Power 1985 and 1986* editions. However, these figures, which reflect the differences in the two editions for the period 1980–1984 and 1980–1985, cannot be fully taken at face value. The 1980–1985 totals reflect current revised information. This means that the totals may reflect both a reevaluation of 1980–1984 totals and/or incomplete 1985 data. They do, however, provide one indication of delivery scales.

**This statement indicates identical or smaller figures provided for the 1980–1985 period compared with those for 1980–1984. The uncertainties reflect both the above described conditions *and/or* conflicting other reports.

Another way to look at military aid is in terms of the value of arms exports and military assistance. US ACDA published data indicates the following comparisons between Soviet and NSWP arms deliveries to the Third World in 1984 and 1985—showing a slightly less than 25% decrease in 1985 in deliveries and in Soviet agreements, but an increase in NSWP 1985 agreements. How much this apparent decrease means, however, is far from clear since similar fluctuations occured in many years before Gorbachev came to power. ACDA data broken down by Third World region reflects the combined totals for 1982–1985 and therefore does not help in estimating 1985 figures.

Exhibit II
Total Value of Military Aid to the Third World

	1984		1985	
	USSR	NSWP	USSR	NSWP
Arms delivery value (in current $US billion)	9.8	2.3	7.6	1.6
Arms Agreement value (in current $US billion)	12.9	1.7	9.5	2.6

(2) U.S. government sources also identify the following types of hardware delivered in 1985 to selected countries: (Only a partial listing extracted from a text, meant to be illustrative rather than definitive)

SYRIA: SA-5s, Patrol boats, STYX and SEPAL anti-ship missiles, T-72s

IRAQ: Su-25s (the first such state to receive these attack aircraft), SA-13s

LIBYA: SA-5s

Y.A.R.: T-62s

INDIA: IL-76s, AN-32s, KILO Class submarines

NORTH KOREA: MIG-23s, SA-13s

ANGOLA: Mi-24s, Mi-17s, SU-22s, MIG-23s, SA-13s

ETHIOPIA: APCs, T-55s, MIG-23s

MOZAMBIQUE: Mi-24s, PT-76s, APCs, Artillery, BM-24s, SA-3s, Patrol Boats, YEVGENY class minesweepers.

CUBA: Sa-13s, SA-14s, Fast Patrol Boats (received a total of 5% of all Soviet 1985 military assistance)

(3) The US DoD published only cumulative totals of hardware delivery for 1981–1986 (a new base line different from that used the previous two years when 1980–1984 and 1980–1985 totals were printed) and ACDA publications had not included 1986 when this analysis was made. Nevertheless US Dod did give some textual statements on the type of equipment and some value levels for Soviet military aid in 1986 to some Third World states. These include:

—FLOGGER aircraft, HIP H helicopters, SA-3 and SA-8 air defense missiles and BMP combat personnel carriers to Angola.

—FULCRUM (Mig-29) aircraft, CANDID and CLINE air transports, a KILO submarine and SS-N2 missiles to India.

—SA-5 air defense missiles and the SENEZH air defense command and control system, a KONI class frigate and a NATYA minesweeper to Libya.

—FLOGGER aircraft, HIP helicopters, T-62 and T-54/55 tanks, and BM-21 rocket artillery launchers to Cuba.

—HIND and HIP helicopters, CURL air transports, ZHUK patrol boats and some 1200 military vehicles to Nicaragua in deliveries amounting to $600 million in value and 23,000 metric tons from the USSR and the NSWP states (significant increases over 1985 when 13,000 metric tons of equipment worth $115 million were provided).

—During 1985 and 1986 Iraq received $3.5 billion in military aid and a recent arms aid agreement with Algeria is estimated at $2 billion.

(4) Press reporting, often based on government provided data has included the following partial information:

—In 1985, the USSR had 30.4% of the world's arms sales market, down from 37.4% in 1984 and second to Western Europe (well ahead of the U.S.).

—Soviet hard currency earnings from arms sales in 1985 dropped 30%

from 1984 (this figure has little meaning in terms of arms volume since it does not clarify how much this was related to a change in the mix of sales versus low credits or direct grants. It does, however, indicate an international economic problem similar to the loss of earnings from the drop in oil prices).

—In 1985 arms deliveries increased to Nicaragua, Afghanistan, Ethiopia, Syria, Vietnam, and Angola.

—1984–1985 military assistance to Angola was over $2 billion.

—In May, 1985, MIG-23s were reported delivered to North Korea with more reported in November.

—In July, 1985, it was reported that the Soviets had agreed to provide 3.1 billion in additional assistance to Iraq, including long range fighter-bombers, surface to surface missiles, T-72 tanks.

—In July, 1985, it was reported that a $327 million arms deal had been signed with Kuwait, including surface to air missiles and other equipment.

—In August, 1985, MIG-23s were reported delivered to Vietnam.

—In October, 1985, Soviet arms were reported being transferred to Nicaraguan freighters in a minor Cuban harbor. In November, these deliveries were reported as including T-54 tanks and military trucks. The same report stated that there had previously been such deliveries in the early Fall.

—In November, 1985, it was reported that over the previous six months Nicaraguan inventories of Soviet built howitzers had tripled and that the Sandinistas had received a dozen new aircraft.

—In November, 1985, SA-5 deliveries to Libya were first reported. These reportedly sped up in early January along with the reported arrival of up to 2000 new Soviet military and other technicians to support the new air defenses.

—In December, 1985, Syria was reported to have received four missile boats (believed to have been ordered in 1981).

—A March, 1986 report indicated that Nicaragua was expected to receive additional Soviet helicopters and transport aircraft plus Czech jet trainer aircraft during the summer.

—In May, 1986, the press cited a CIA estimate that the USSR spends $4 billion a year on its own *covert actions* and direct support to various *terrorist organizations*.

—In May, 1986 reports indicated Soviet cargo ships making the first direct delivery of arms to Nicaragua since 1984. The same report stated that 1986 Soviet arms deliveries to Nicaragua (including those transshipped through Cuba) had alrady exceeded the total for 1985 by 2,000 tons.

—June, 1986 reporting indicated: that additional Soviety military technicians had arrived in Nicaragua: that India had received a license to build MIG-29 aircraft and would shortly receive their first direct shipments of these aircraft; that Syria was expected to receive MIG-29s and SS-23 missiles; and that 250 tons of Soviet arms had been intercepted in Panama onboard a Danish vessel headed for Peru where they were to be provided to "Shining Path" rebels. The Libyan press was also reported to have stated that a large Soviet military delegation was expected later in the month to negotiate a major new arms sale. This was never confirmed as having taken place.

—In July, 1986 it was announced in Delhi that an agreement had been reached to purchase two squadrons of the MIG-29s from the USSR and to establish an Indian factory with production rights for this aircraft (confirming unofficial June reports).

—In August, 1986, Jordanian officials confirmed that a $1.6 billion purchase of SA-8s and SA-13s had been concluded. Unofficial Arab press reports indicated that the first of these missiles had already arrived and that negotiations for APCs and other equipment were underway.

—Throughout the summer of 1986 there were conflicting reports as to whether Syria had, in fact, completed a deal or had already received MIG 29s, MIG 31s, and SS-23 missiles. These continued into 1987 without confirmation. However, one would have expected the US DoD to note these deliveries in the 1987 edition of *Soviet Military Power* if they were true. What this publication said was that the Syrians were expected to soon receive MIG-29s. What seems evident is that Moscow, while providing large quanitites of new equipment to Syria, was delaying on some modern systems—evidently in an attempt to influence Assad's policies.

—In January, 1987, the Indian press reported a Soviet offer to sell India the IL-76 MAINSTAY AWACS type system.

—In March, 1987, Jordanian sources stated that the Soviets had agreed to provide Iraq with MIG-29s and other weapons.

—In April 1987, reports began circulating that Zimbabwe had purchased MIG-29s (for later delivery) and that pilots were already training in the USSR on this aircraft. The Zimbabwean government denied the story, but it kept reappearing with additional details about visits by military delegations and pilots training in the USSR.

—Also in April, a report that the Soviets had offered Iran some 200 SCUD missiles for the rights to use former US intelligence SIGINT facilities in Iran was circulated, but denied by all. It is likely that this rumor was either a garble or disinformation. However, French claims that in 1986 the Soviets had funneled $18 million in arms to Iran through middlemen were more persuasive.

—Thai sources in April claimed that Kampuchea was being provided some 40 MIG-21s

—US press reports the same month stated that Angola received an estimated $1 billion in military assistance in 1986 (a 50% increase over 1985).
—Arab sources in May claimed that Syria would soon receive SS-23 missiles, T-80 tanks, MIG-29s and SA-11, -13 and 14 air defense missiles.
—May US press reports stated that in the first three months of 1987, Nicaragua had received 5,700 tons of military equipment worth $140 million. This would be a rate equivalent to that of 1986.

Part III

Military Policies

How many divisions does the Pope have?
—Attributed to Josef Stalin

12

The Metal Eaters: The Armed Forces and Soviet Military Doctrine

> *In determining the correlation of forces of the states, all factors of nuclear might require first priority evaluation. . . . First and foremost, account should be taken of the fact that the established correlation of forces determines the actual capabilities of the sides to exert influence on one another at a given moment with a determined degree of the probability of success. In the process the advantage in principle accrues to that side which significantly surpasses the other in strength in the aggregate or in individual and the more essential elements of combat might.*
>
> —S. Tyushkevich, in a major *classified* Soviet journal

When Gorbachev came to power he inherited a military machine and a military-industrial-Party complex of awesome proportions. Its sheer size, capabilities, and central position in the Soviet structure have profound implications for the economy, foreign policy and according to some, even for the very supremacy of the Party. To understand Gorbachev's problems, to assess his intentions, and to anticipate his future actions, one must examine these relationships in some detail.

Defense, in the widest possible meaning of the term, has dominated and warped the Soviet economy. It is not an exaggeration to say that defense has shaped and directed the entire Soviet economy, one correctly described by many Western observers as a "mobilization economy." Military requirements eat up a disproportionate share of Soviet resources. According to the commonly accepted Western estimates, between 14 and 20 percent of the GNP goes directly into defense. And it has not been too many years since a Soviet dissident economist, using somewhat wider definitions, declared that the figure is really closer to 44 percent. There are other, very serious, hidden costs not included in the Western figures. Defense industries receive the lion's share of high-quality raw and processed materials. Defense research institutes and industries siphon off a disproportionate share of the best scientific and engineering minds. In times of production or extraction shortfalls, defense priorities are met while civilian needs wait their turn. Perhaps even more important, such a scale of priorities is bound to have adverse side effects upon the economy in general and upon the process of technological advancement in particular. This is because the protection of "state secrets" requires severe limitations on, and compartmentalization of, access to them. In the Soviet Union, where secrecy is an ingrained way of life and where the definition of *state secret* is extremely broad, this amounts to a virtual preemption of free and critical communication among scientists, engineers, and technicians. In the absence of the unfettered exchange of ideas, scientific and applied technical progress is bound to be impeded severely, with the effect of permanently handicapping the USSR in its rivalry with other, particularly Western, industrial nations. Gorbachev's economic revitalization program, with its demand for shifts in investment priorities and the widest possible application of high technology in areas with military applications, is bound to be seriously hampered if not totally undermined if these direct and indirect defense costs cannot be reduced, and unless scientific and technical knowledge and ingenuity are shared much more broadly.

The defense industrial sector has also provided the new general secretary with a model for reforms for much of the remainder of the Soviet economy. Western analysts have long held that Soviet defense industries were significantly more efficient than the rest of the economy. Although some recent studies have called the exact extent of this difference into question, its very existence is not in doubt, if for no other reasons than the size, diversity, and technological quality of Soviet military production and the relative speed with which advanced technology is introduced into serial production of military hardware. To a significant degree, the Ministry of Defense and the defense industries have been structured along the lines of the vertical cartelization that has produced relative successes in a few earlier Soviet regional experiments and in East Germany, and that now seems to serve as a basic model of industrial structure in Gorbachev's economic reform program. Ministry of Defense quality-control procedures—the presence at every stage of industrial production of what amounts to consumer quality control involving officials with wide authority to reject the products—are likewise an obvious model for other industries to follow. In fact, the formation of on-site quality-control inspection teams drawn from a much wider range of bodies outside the enterprises than ever before has been explicitly stated as one of Gorbachev's reforms.

The prerequisites of any meaningful revitalization of Soviet economy pose two painful dilemmas. The first relates to foreign policy. The main criterion—according to some outside observers, the only criterion—for defining the USSR as a superpower is its military might. Military capabilities and military assistance are the primary source of the Soviet Union's foreign influence and a sine qua non for the Kremlin's ability to compete in the world arena. This means that under any circumstances there are very definite limits to the extent that any Soviet leader can reduce the USSR's commitment to building and maintaining military strength. In the face of strongly active Western or regional competition backed by a vigorous Western military modernization, the question becomes not how much Soviet military costs can be reduced but how much increase in those costs can be afforded. (As noted, the U.S. SDI could force Moscow into the predicament of an endless cost escalation.) Of course, the Soviets could compete with the West in fields other than military, but this is purely a theoretical prospect. Whatever its residual strength at home, Soviet ideology has lost most of its appeal abroad. What remains is some appeal of some sort of socialism, preferably in versions other than the Soviet one, and the attraction the model of the Leninist party has for many ruling elites anxious either to seize power or to retain it as long as possible. Other than that, the Soviet civilian economy, without changes going far beyond Gorbachev's currently proclaimed short-term plans, is simply incapable of competing with the West except on rare and very special occasions. This is why Gorbachev's economic program stresses the prospect of some form of a detente that would reduce the military challenge from abroad. This is also why Gorbachev's preferred strategy must be to seek a detente with the United States.

The second painful dilemma has to do with the implications of the powerful defense establishment for the CPSU and for Party politics in the USSR. Some Western observers frequently uphold the hypothesis that the Party and the armed forces are distinct power centers with inevitably conflicting interests, and that therefore the army might one day supplant the Party. This idea seems to have been at least in part influenced by the early Bolshevik fear of "Bonapartism" of the kind that followed the French Revolution as a potential outome of all revolutions. In the early period after the 1917 Revolution, when the Party, new and unsafe in power, had to rely heavily on nonrevolutionary military professionals from the ancien régime to stave off enemies in the Civil War and during the Western interventions, the concern about "Bonapartism" was realistic enough. Today, it is not.

But the theory of the Party and the army as copretenders to power also draws heavily upon Western "pluralist" models of interest group politics and separate bureaucracies and institutions that retain their cohesiveness and pursue their distinct interests in competition with rivals. When applied to the USSR, this notion is mistaken. Once the Bolsheviks survived the Civil War and built a new army in their own image, and especially when they imposed the complex web of surveillance, management, and control that characterizes the mature Leninist party in power—this is probably their most significant contribution to political theory and practice—the prospects of development toward either "Bonapartism" or "pluralism" existed no more.

It does not follow that there are no interest groups in the Soviet Union. Rather, those that do exist operate in setting and in ways very different from those Western models assume. Each of the institutional structures identified in Western literature as separate interest groups in the USSR have been both coopted and isolated, placed under strict Party control, and spiked by Party and KGB agents from top to bottom. As a result, any interest group politics in which these institutions can possibly engage as cohesive structures is very much bounded within parameters of ideological acceptability and therefore carried on in the inner corridors of the Party. The interest groups that actually crop up on the Soviet scene tend to be shifting, fluid, temporary coalitions often formed on a regional basis or across formal institutional lines. They are additionally weakened by the absence of legitimacy accruing to their counterparts in the West, for by the ideological standards of the "leading role of the Party" and "democratic centralism" they are not supposed to exist. Far from functioning as institutionally based elites or coalitions of such, they function as power bases for one or another power contender within the top leadership. In other words, it is the struggles for power within the Party officialdom that enable the interest groups to mount challenges to, or put pressures on, policy decision makers.

Within the Soviet setting, the armed forces have been coopted, infiltrated, and subjected to political socialization to a greater extent and with a higher intensity than any other sector in Soviet society, precisely *because* they possess the armed wherewithal to impose and enforce their will. The KGB (formally a part of the armed forces but actually independent from them) and other security organs are in a similar situation, except that the army is infiltrated by both the Party and the KGB, and the KGB is by necessity infiltrated by the Party alone. The result is that although both the military and the police structures do have ways to influence Party decisions, they are executive extensions of the Party's will, not its rivals for power. Due to shifting configurations of factional forces within top Party leadership, the competing institutions can temporarily acquire an elevated status of seemingly independent loci of power, but as soon as factional struggles within the top Party leadership are resolved, they revert to the humbler role of the "swords and shields" of the Party.

If all this is so, then why, how, and to what degree can the Soviet armed forces exert an influence and constrain Gorbachev's policies? To begin with, the professional military is a part of a much wider grouping with shared interests. *This is the key point.* The defense "interest group" that Gorbachev must take into account is a much larger and somewhat more amorphous body encompassing not only the professional military but also the Party and state managers of defense-related industries. And it includes individuals from within Gorbachev's own circle of close associates within the Party leadership. It is a military-defense industry-Party complex rather than a mere defense interest group. This complex can attract wide support from the Party leaders of nondefense bureaucracies ranging from the foreign policy establishment to Party and state bureaucrats in distinctly non-military sectors of the economy, to say nothing of the security organs. This phenomenon, which in itself is a product of the Soviet Communist Party structure and of Soviet political socialization, is usually not adequately recognized by outsiders used to drawing sharp distinctions between the civilian and the military.

The CPSU, the professional military, and to a certain extent the entire Soviet political elite and body politic share concepts and beliefs that go beyond simple political consensus on goals and basic means. The mind-set of the CPSU leadership includes some dominant characteristics of what in the West is usually described as the "military mind." Such characteristics are shaped by the Party structure, the heritage of Lenin, (including the *kto-kogo* principle), the ideology, and the entire political socialization with its constant regurgitation of the themes of struggle and militancy. The Party organization, professional "elitism," internal social mobility, and the principle of democratic centralism bear direct resemblance to military organizational structures and their lines of command. Lenin's approach to strategy and tactics and his conscious application of Clausewitzean principles to politics are almost exactly the same as the contents of the training of senior military officers everywhere. The analytic methodology implicit in the "correlation of forces" concept is identical to any sound military decision making. The belief in the "historically objective" and "inevitable" nature of the struggle between socialism, led by the USSR, and capitalism provides validation for the understanding of realities in military terms and thus reinforces this mind-set enormously. In fact, the entire structure of management of the Soviet economy and society, with its focus on directed, centralized mobilization of human and material resources and its penchant for concrete target setting, is also closely analogous to a military management structure.

Not only is there an extensive symbiosis among the Party, the economy, and the military, but the far-reaching congruencies in perceptions, ways of thinking, and organizational structures combine to ensure a high degree of cohesiveness. The cohesiveness in its own right serves as a powerful incentive for the civilian leadership to embark on its own on policies that in other societies would be attributed to influence or pressures on the part of a military interest group.

There is a second way by which the defense establishment and more particularly the Ministry of Defense and the General Staff can influence Soviet policy making. It consists of their "monopoly" of information about military strength and capabilities and their being the "sole" source of military technical expertise. Undoubtedly, some amount of influence is exerted by the military through this medium, but its extent tends to be grossly overstated in the West. It is true that data on military structure, capabilities, and the like are not shared with foreign policy operators in the Ministry of Foreign Affairs or with academic policy advisers, at least not routinely nor in any great detail. But this circumstance would have real significance only if these experts participated in making policy decisions rather than just carrying out the decisions of the Politburo—*which does have full access to such data.* The question of military monopoly of the expertise for technical analysis is a little more meaningful, but not to the extent to which it may appear. In part this is because of the congruencies in mind-set and ways of thinking. More important, even if the U.S.S.R. does not have a visible civilian strategist layer overseeing the military, as is common in the West (e.g. in the U.S. Department of Defense), the reality is not nearly so different as believed by many Western civilian analysts, whose assessments tend to be biased by exaggerated notions of their own importance and irreplaceability. Can anyone really doubt that Ustinov, for example, who despite his military rank and some quasi-military training was essentially a civilian Party and industrial manager, was not fully conversant with military-technical data?

Given these realities, what has been the impact of the military on Gorbachev's decisions during his first two and a half years in power? The record is fairly clear as far as the relations between the Party and the military are concerned, almost as clear for foreign policy, and a bit murky in regard to the economy.

In Party-military relations, Gorbachev has shown a firm and adroit hand. He quickly elevated his colorless minister of defense, Marshal Sokolov, to candidate membership in the Politburo. By virtue of refusing to promote him to full membership, he clearly underscored the principle of Party supremacy, which in effect meant putting Sokolov, and thereby the entire uniformed defense establishment on probation, which Sokolov ultimately did not pass. He was replaced in early June 1987. At the same time Gorbachev mollified Sokolov and his coterie within the military by lavishing prestigious appointments and promotions on generals who had been associated with Sokolov when he was first deputy minister of defense and in charge of setting up the Southern Theater of Military Operations (TVD) and preparing for the Afghanistan operation. For example, Army General Lushev, who in 1979 had been commander of the Central Asian Military District (MD) and in late 1980 had become commander of the Moscow MD, in the summer of 1985 became the commander in chief (*Glavnokommanduyushchiy*) of the absolute prize field command, the Group of Soviet Forces in Germany (GSFG). In summer 1986 Lushev was promoted to first deputy minister of defense. To take another example, Col. General Maksimov, who had in 1979 commanded the Turkestan MD and had been promoted to army general in 1982, became in the summer of 1985 the commander in chief of the Strategic Rocket Forces.

By contrast, such long-time top military figures as Fleet Admiral Gorshkov, Marshal Tolubko, and Marshal Yepishev, the head of the key Military Political Administration (MPA), who could be expected to argue more vigorously against changes in politico-military strategy or in defense investment allocations, were during 1985 moved to the sidelines through either retirement (Yepishev) or reassignment to the honorific Ministry of Defense Inspectorate group (Tolubko and Gorshkov). Gorbachev also showed his adroitness here by allowing those old warhorses to retain their Central Committee membership and thus their high prestige, thereby reducing the potential for resentment on the part of their uniformed protégés.

In late summer 1986 there were new changes at the very top of the Ministry of Defense structure that also may have been related to discontent about the directions being taken in either economic or foreign policy, actually arms control, or both. Marshal Petrov, who had been first deputy minister of defense for only some eighteen months, was apparently retired in connection with Lushev's second position promotion in a year; his replacement was Army General Tretyak, previously the commander in chief of the Far Eastern theater of military operations (TVD). In January, 1987 another replacement in Deputy Defense Minister slot was made. This time Army General Dmitri Yazov was brought from his position as Military District Commander in the Far East to become Deputy Minister of Defense for Cadres. Although it was not realized at the time, this was a highly significant move. Reportedly, Yazov had greatly impressed Gorbachev with his candor and honesty when the General Secretary made his visit to the Far East in late summer, 1986. According to unofficial reports, Yazov told Gorbachev that discipline was not up to snuff and had even slipped in some regards in his district. What wasn't realized until later was that Yazov evidently owed his elevation to deputy ministership to Gorbachev who already at that time apparently had the idea of purging armed forces cadres. About the same time, and continuing into the spring, there were a fairly large number of changes of command in the top military positions.

Meanwhile, during the winter of 1986–87 and into the spring of 1987 there were more personnel changes than usual throughout the military command structure just below the Ministry of Defense. From the end of summer 1986 (when GEN Tretyak moved up to be a Deputy Defense Minister), at least seven of sixteen military district commanders, one of four groups-of-force commanders and one of four fleet commanders were changed. Interestingly in connection with the previous discussion about Yazov and Tretyak, two of the new MD commanders (Odessa and the Far East) were formerly Yazov's deputies.

Concurrently, in a bow to glasnost, the military press began featuring an almost constant stream of articles in which junior officers wrote letters exposing corruption, favoritism and sheer inefficiency on the part of various unit and school commanders and staffs. Each month *Krasnaya zvezda* would publish quite a few of these letters. A few weeks (or a couple of months) later, a follow-up article would report that the complaints were justified and that disciplinary action had been taken against the culprits. Such "features" in *Krasnaya zvezda* were not unheard of formerly, but their number and the scale of the picture of corruption, inefficiency and disregard for the rights of subordinates was almost unprecedented for the armed forces. In a few cases, deputy commanders (invariably for administrative or logistical functions) were punished but the named culprits were mostly mid-level staff officers or relatively junior commanders—not the senior leadership at the military district or fleet level. This is not to say that the malfeasance of subordinates did not necessarily reflect on their superiors—after all, some of the commanders who were replaced during the period had presided over districts in which many complaints had been aired and one could suspect that there was a connection. Nevertheless, the opposite seems to have been true. In the one case where the most inferential information was available from the Soviet press, the district commander who was replaced actually received a promotion to a more prestigious position. Accounts of problems in the Central Asian MD abounded—especially after the previous commander, Colonel General Lobov was replaced at the end of January, 1987 shortly after the political leadership of the same region was shaken up with the removal of Kunaev and his cronies. But Lobov became a First Deputy Chief of the General Staff—a promotion by any criteria.

Then, at the end of May, when Matthais Rust evaded Soviet air defenses and succeeded in reaching Moscow, the Minister of Defense, Marshal Sokolov, and a Deputy Minister, the CinC of Air Defense Forces (PVO strany, one of the five combat services in the Soviet armed forces) were sacked. In June there were clear indications that senior leadership was no longer to be exempt from by-name criticism for problems within their command. In fact, the events of late May and June gave the distinct impression that a new era may have dawned in the saga of Gorbachev and his military establishment. This could be very important and needs to be looked at closely and in perspective.

We have noted that Gorbachev had handled his military leadership with a certain amount of circumspection and a definite adroitness. Marshal Sokolov had been made a Candidate Member of the Politburo and his presumed favorites in the command structure had prospered. Crusty warhorses, who may have opposed shifts in foreign policy in regard to arms control or in doctrine stressing nuclear war and the preeminence of the Strategic Rocket Forces (SRF) like Fleet Admiral Gorshkov and Marshal Tolubko were replaced, but allowed to retain their honors and place on the Central Committee. Moreover, at the 27th Party Congress Gorbachev seemed to confirm earlier signals that the military was not out of favor—as long as it supported his programs and policies. The military was very well represented in the new lineup of the Party's senior and honorific ranks. Twenty three serving military officers were full members of the Central Committee (eight fresh or promoted from Candidate Membership) and a twenty fourth military man, Marshal of Aviation Bugayev was on the CC as Minister of Civil Aviation (in June 1987 another (Yazov) was made full member). Thirteen more were named candidate members (eight for the first time) and four more were members of the Central Revision Committee (two new). Such numbers were not indicative of any reduction in uniformed representation in the CC as compared with previous slates. On the other hand, throughout the period that Gorbachev has been General Secretary the number of senior military reassignments has apparently been much higher than normal for the Soviet Union where command positions usually turn over much less frequently than in the West. If one counts the 44 most senior defense slots (Minister, First Deputy and Deputy Ministers of Defense, Head of the Main Political Administration (MPA), 4 theater CinCs, Commanders of 4 Groups of Forces, the 4 main fleets and the 16 military districts (MDs), at least 27 incumbents as of mid-1987 had been named during this period. Actually the number may have been higher since identification of such transfers, and particularly their exact timing is very uncertain. Soviet open source materials do not normally report such things. Rather, the outside analyst not privy to classified intelligence data must often rely on unconfirmed second hand reports and such indications as the identification in an article or article byline of a new officer in a position of command or a senior staff position—which often happens long after the actual reassignment took place. The table at the end of the chapter lists the most important of these identified changes.

The changes under Gorbachev, which seemed to step up in 1987, reflected a continuation of a pattern set during the second half of 1984 and early 1985 when Gorbachev was the "second General Secretary" in charge of cadres, Uniformed military cadres were then under his purview since virtually all officers—certainly all senior ones—are Party members. If one counts this period also, the number of the 44 senior military positions turned over under Gorbachev rises to a whopping 39. Of course, many of the identified changes below the levels of Minister, First Deputy and Deputy Minister can be presumed to have been more-or-less "normal," routine military personnel decisions. Even in such cases, however, senior positions and promotions require Party approval. Moreover, it is a safe conclusion that some of these reassignments stemmed from Party preferences expressed through the medium of the Ministry of Defense or the MPA.

Obviously, then, the "Gorbachevshchina"—or personnel purge—had been extending to the military all along, even if it was being done much more quietly and with far less public criticism than in the civilian state and Party ranks. After Rust flew to Red Square, the purge of the military apparently began to take on the same characteristics as its civilian counterpart. To assess this conclusion and to explain it one must consider these developments more closely.

It goes without saying that with Gorbachev's ascent to power the status of the armed forces changed from what was before simply because Soviet society, of which the army is an integral part, had also changed. For no less than the past thirty years, the army has been an important, and at times the most important, locus of power. The degree of the army's support determined the degree of influence and the range of choices of Soviet rulers. Twice in Soviet history Kremlin rulers had made use of the armed forces in their struggle for power: in 1957 the armed forces helped Khrushchev defeat his opponents; in 1964 they brought an end to his rule by supporting Brezhnev. From that time on all Soviet rulers, Brezhnev, Andropov, and Chernenko, courted the army's favor and mobilized its support. During the period of Chernenko's deteriorating health, the armed forces became increasingly deeply involved in domestic as well as foreign affairs. At that time it was Minister of Defense Ustinov who jointly with Gromyko and Gorbachev determined the process of reaching decisions in the Politburo and the nature of its rulings.

All this explains why, when Gorbachev became general secretary, he continued to court the favor of the armed forces, even if not quite as zealously as did Andropov and Chernenko. Gorbachev could afford to be less zealous because, unlike his two predecessors, he did not owe his position to the army and because the powerful Ustinov was no longer alive and Ustinov's successor Sokolov was old and infirm. Still, Gorbachev considered it advisable to raise the minister of defense whom he had "inherited" to the rank of candidate member of the Politburo. He did so not out of free choice (Sokolov was not his man) but because of the logic of the pursuit of his personal power. This logic dictated the need to keep the army loyal as a precondition of proceeding with his far-reaching and risk-entailing reforms. If it had depended on Gorbachev alone, he would have preferred a younger and more dynamic figure, more closely attuned to him in spirit than Sokolov who had to be mollified by favors and benefits.

By some quirk of fate, fortune blessed Gorbachev in the person of Mathias Rust, the German youth who landed a small plane right in the heart of the Soviet capital near the Kremlin wall. Rust's success suggested that the Soviet armed forces were incapable of defending Soviet air space from penetration and thereby revealed serious problems in their organization and structure. "What if the plane had been carrying a bomb?" must have been the natural reaction of many in Moscow. It could have been quite conceivable if the plane had been piloted by a terrorist. This was no academic contemplation of some hypothetical Third World War, but was perceived on the gut-level as a threat to both the Soviet regime and the very lives of the Kremlin leaders. Consequently the entire Politburo was furious and the decision to fire Sokolov was reached without opposition. At the same time, Marshal Koldunov, the Deputy Defense Minister and CinC of Air Defense Forces was fired openly without the transparent pretext of attributing his departure to health as had been done with Sokolov.

This not only gave Gorbachev his long-awaited opportunity to replace his inherited Defense Minister, but it also provided an opening to bring his quiet purge of the military into the open and to decisively preempt any significant military opposition to his reforms. Even more significantly for the broader domestic picture, Gorbachev was possibly also preparing the ground for diverting massive resources from military to civilian needs. He had made repeated statements of precisely such intention. If this is his intention indeed, a neutralization of military opposition was almost certainly a precondition for his acting upon it.

Up to summer of 1987 the majority of the military leadership had evidently gone along with Gorbachev's domestic reforms and his foreign policy shifts, but there had been clear indications of concern on at least the levels below the top—and possibly among the ostensibly supportive senior leaders as well. If nothing else, the frequency and extent to which the military press and periodicals had contained articles by senior military spokesmen explaining why reforms and arms control concessions were really in the best interest of the armed forces demonstrated the existence of doubts in the ranks—doubts which could easily have grown into full-fledged opposition.

One of the thrusts of Gorbachev's policies has been to limit the growth rate of military spending and investment while the overall economy is being restructured and revitalized. As further discussed later, the evidence indicates that the senior military leadership had accepted this as a necessary step to ensuring that Soviet industry and technology would be able to provide the high technology hardware needed for the future battlefield. At the same time, however, the uniformed military and those sharing their views in the wider defense-related sphere (both Party and state officials) would undoubtedly like increased allocations. Even more unsettling from their point of view, Gorbachev had been increasingly talking (only talking so far) of the desirability of diverting real, significant resources to civilian needs.

More to the point, Gorbachev had consistently espoused and progressively moved toward arms control agreements which would result in very deep cuts in military force structures and possibly foreclose future growth opportunities and perceived security needs in some technologies. For reasons also discussed later, the senior military and defense leadership had also gone along with this. Still, the concessions offered by Gorbachev in arms control had increasingly cut closer to the bone without yet guaranteeing the primary result (prerequisite in the eyes of defense strategists) of stopping the US SDI and aborting the Western military modernization.

Consequently, by the time the opportunity came to remove Sokolov, military patience may well have already begun to run thin and, out of public view, the military leadership may have begun to directly question their political masters. Moreover, this condition may well have coincided with a point where Gorbachev, increasingly frustrated by the failure of his existing reforms to really galvanize the Soviet economy, was ready to risk some more fundamental changes in resource allocation. As outlined in previous chapters, Gorbachev's economic reforms had not really shifted the priority of investment in heavy industries and modern technology over consumer satisfaction and needs. What they had done was to temporarily divert investment in those branches of the economy which supported military power from ever more massive production lines to retooling and modernization for a more effective and higher quality of production in the future—something that far-sighted military figures could accept. Meanwhile, he had tried to improve and galvanize light industry and consumer services by means of exhortation, management reforms, etc—but not by any really significant diversion of resources. By summer of 1987 it was growing increasingly obvious that this approach was not providing the incentives needed to fundamentally change the attitudes or living conditions of the workers who were supposed to make the new approaches work successfully. Along with his stepped-up attacks on bureaucratic immobilism and refusal to change, Gorbachev may well have reached the point where the alternative of actually shifting real resources would be the logical next step. If so, military opposition could be expected to become real.

As already explained, Gorbachev does not have to fear a military "revolt" over his policies. What he does have to fear is that a potential rival from within the top Party leadership will utilize the military and defense constituencies within the Party as a vehicle to replace him. Through mid-1987, those in the Politburo and Secretariat who would have any realistic chance of doing this were all part of his team; but history and the nature of the political system show that each of his current allies and followers is a potential future rival. Gorbachev knows this and all of the others know that their peers among Gorbachev's current team of followers are their own competitors in the jockeying for relative power and position under Gorbachev and for the leading spot as his potential replacement.

Furthermore, all of the state and Party bureaucrats (at all levels) who wished to oppose other elements of Gorbachev's reforms (because they were in danger of losing their accustomed powers and perquisites—or even for "ideological" reasons (if any remain who are really motivated by such) would find ready allies among the military.

In any case, an appropriate psychological climate for reassigning a segment of the military budget to civilian production had arisen and, judging from the civilian press, Gorbachev resolved to take advantage of the dissatisfaction of Soviet citizens who were sick and tired of the constant exhortations to make sacrifices in favor of the country's defense. Questions which the General Secretary encouraged people to think about were in the following vein: why should the Soviet people make all kinds of sacrifices for the military if a foreign pilot, an amateur at that, can get through Soviet defenses unharmed and land in Red Square? Gorbachev aroused concern about a decline in the Soviet armed forces not only on the street but in the press as well. *Literaturnaya gazeta* was permitted to question the utility of universal military service, and *Pravda* and *Izvestiya* printed articles criticizing the military academies and calling for a review of current military doctrine.

Thus cleverly and subtly manipulating public opinion and playing on feelings of national pride, Gorbachev launched his "restructuring" of the armed forces. The purge that he prepared and carried through in the Ministry of Defense was unmatched in its scale and in the publicity it was given since the purges of 1937–38.

What happened in the purge? The commander of the Air Defense District had been removed. Lt. General Yu. Brazhnikov, Lt. General N. Markov, Major General V. Reznichenko, and a number of other high-ranking antiaircraft defense officers of the District were deprived of their Party memberships, and consequently of their posts and privileges. The style and character of army performance became the subjects of sharp criticism. The chief of staff of the same military district, Col. General Yu. Gorkov, was accused of crude behavior and intimidation of subordinates. It was further revealed that the command of the district had deceived the public with a flow of inflated and even simply false reports of its military preparedness.

As is usual in the USSR, the purge entailed the rituals of public humiliation of its victims. In mid-June 1987 a meeting was convened of the most active Party members of the Air Defense District. Young officers were encouraged to speak out against their illustrious, long-serving commanders. The officers were charged with the task of "bringing to light and exposing, without respect to person, the failures of the district." This offered them an opportunity to win favor and promotion, and the Party leadership had the responsibility of translating such criticism into concrete punishments.

The purge began by affecting only one military district but will undoubtedly soon encompass others as well. Confirmation of this was provided by the speech of B. Yeltsin, the first secretary of the Moscow city Party committee at the meeting of Party activists. Yeltsin warned that there was a danger of minimizing criticism of the military and ascribing its serious failures merely to negligence or thoughtlessness. He urged the top officials of the Ministry of Defense to look the Soviet working people square in the eye and "answer for their irresponsibility, incompetence, and lack of organization."

Yeltsin attributed the crisis to several faults in the nature of the administration of the armed forces. Among these were the practices of claiming nonexistent achievements, and harming morale by humiliating subordinates. From Yeltsin's speech one gathered that there had developed a pervasive state of self-satisfaction, boasting, and complacency in the armed forces. It appeared that Soviet officers neither understood nor respected their soldiers. Favoritism and nepotism had become rife. Yeltsin assigned primary responsibility for the decline in the armed forces to the loss of authority of the Party organization; commanders, for example, were not taking into consideration its views in regard to new postings and promotions. Yeltsin also spoke of what for many years had only been whispered about in the armed forces: veteran military personnel often harassed new recruits.

The armed forces were also criticized from a political perspective: they acted "as if the resolutions of congresses and Central Committee plenums did not concern them." Further, in accord with the principle of *glasnost,* of the frank criticism touted by Gorbachev, the head of the Moscow Party organization noted, "Responsibility for the failures are borne by all members of the Military Council, the whole command and political staff and all Party members." He specified: "The style of work of the staff of the region headed by Yu. Gorkov is dominated by bureaucratism, useless busywork, and rapid turnover of personnel"; the leadership "avoids solving problems" and "has made it a practice of falsifying its reports to enhance its accomplishments." P. Khotylev, deputy commander of the district, was accused of incompetence, as was the commander of the Soviet radar troops, A. Gukov, and aviation commander O. Lengarov was charged with having failed to organize flight units properly. Yeltsin did not leave unassailed even personnel appointed by Gorbachev himself; V. Tsarkov, the new commander of the region, was reprimanded for "not realizing the seriousness of the situation and not undertaking measures to improve the operations of the command."

This was the first time that the Gorbachev administration directed such a sharp attack against the armed forces, but one expects it will not be the last. Other military districts will come in for their share of attention as Gorbachev's restructuring moves on to encompass the rest of the armed forces.

The foregoing is not intended to mean that the Soviet military establishment has been destroyed. On the contrary, it remains in existence and is bound to retain an influence on foreign policy. What is this influence likely to be?

The reasons for the defense establishment's probable support or denial of support for Gorbachev's detente strategy have been discussed in previous chapters. Our conclusion was that most of the defense establishment can go along with, and may even fully support, a detente policy that is really no more than another temporary tactical shift designed to reap advantages in the future or avoid losses during a period of domestic economic reconstruction. The support would in likelihood be all the stronger if the military industry and the military educational system were also believed to be in need of a major overhaul.

Significantly, just before he was sacked as first deputy minister of defense and chief of the General Staff in fall 1984, Marshall Ogarkov—perhaps the single most competent and dynamic of all the USSR's marshals and generals—spoke out very strongly on the demands of new technologies and quite sharply questioned the capability of Soviet industry to provide the military with the quantity and quality of the new military hardware it needed. In effect he was calling for a restructuring and retooling of the defense industry with and for advanced technology, a program quite analogous to what Gorbachev has proclaimed for the entire economy. Meanwhile, in books and articles, including those published both before and *after* his dismissal, Ogarkov pressed for what would amount to a comprehensive reassessment of official Soviet military doctrine. This is no small matter. Ogarkov's ideas are replete with implications that deserve a closer examination—all the more so because his ideas appear to have been shared by a substantial number of the leading theoretical writers in recent years, such as Colonel General Gareev and others.

There have been two periods when the Soviets apparently energetically sought to shift economic priorities toward consumer needs, when they made significant reductions in the size of the armed forces, and when they insistently avowed their desire for "peaceful coexistence" with the West. The first period was in the 1920s with the New Economic Program (NEP); the second was in the late 1950s and early 1960s under Khruschev. Each time these developments were preceded and accompanied by a major reassessment of the implications of new military technologies and by calls and then programs (1) to (re)educate a new generation of military commanders and personnel in order to be capable of effectively employing the new technologies and doctrines, *and* (2) to restructure the economy so as to enable it to provide the new equipment in the quantity and quality needed. This ostensible pattern appears to be repeating itself.

New technologies (including microcircuitry, directed energy, genetic engineering, and the real foreseeable possibility of a full-fledged new combat dimension involving systems and forces based in space) require new doctrinal and strategic precepts, new industrial and research capabilities, and much better educated military personnel. Once again the USSR faces a need to revitalize and reconstruct its economic base; once again there is a renewal of a detente-promotion, or peaceful coexistence, policy; and once again there are good reasons to believe that a third comprehensive review of military doctrine—the third military revolution, in effect—may be well under way. Notably, each of the two earlier periods marked temporary stages in Soviet economic and foreign policy that were followed by a reversion to strong emphasis on heavy industry and military growth. True, there exist other perfectly good reasons for each of the economic and foreign policy programs undertaken by Gorbachev. Nevertheless, the similarities with the two earlier periods are striking and force us to consider whether the outcome is likely to be much different this time, and whether the policies normally interpreted as having quite "peaceful" purposes are not in fact dictated by military exigencies.

As noted earlier, the record of Gorbachev in power is not as clear in regard to the current, let alone the future, effects of his economic programs on the defense establishment and defense industries. After reading Gorbachev's arms control proposals and pondering the implications of his declared economic plans, many foreign observers took it for granted that defense expenditure was cut or was meant to be cut. So far, however, almost all evidence in support of this assumption can at the very best be described as highly circumstantial. It is true that the announced 1986 state budget shows a tiny projected decrease of defense expenditure in real terms, but Soviet published defense budget figures have long been consensually recognized as grossly deceptive and fragmentary. Omitting, therefore, the announced military budget figures, there is some intriguing *inferential* evidence that must be considered.

From the latter half of 1985 through 1986 the military press indeed featured more than the usual quantity of articles demanding reductions in operating costs, especially in consumption of petroleum products, by means of an increase in training on simulators and in the classroom in place of hands-on field and flying operations. Not surprisingly, the Soviets have not had any difficulty in finding more than enough military professionals to espouse this view. However, because the commonly held conventional military view, particularly among field commanders and line officers, is that there is no substitute for hands-on training, one can conjecture that training budgets (which could conceivably mean the entire military budget) were being debated. This, of course, could very easily be a reflection only of the need to save on one part of the defense budget in order to expand others (e.g. the operational costs of Afghanistan). This "debate" seemed to quiet down in the first half of 1987.

The second set of evidence is the demand of the new leadership that defense industry enterprises increasingly undertake some simultaneous increased production of civilian consumer goods. It is hardly clear how much of such production is being contemplated, but it is manifest that any nontoken change in this respect would inevitably entail a reduction of military production unless the total production and investment in defense industries is expanded accordingly. This is analogous to the apparently continuing demand that the uniformed military devote more time and personnel resources to assisting Soviet agriculture. This policy received impetus in Brezhnev's later years and led to some tensions in regard to military budgetary allocations.

Both of the above sets of evidence—drawn from tracking discussion in the press that did not ostensibly directly address military expenditure allocations but could have had them in mind—are extremely circumstantial and could very easily have no meaning in regard to overall military spending. On 15 August 1986, however, there was an extremely significant article, signed by a deputy minister of defense, that *may* have provided some rather more concrete, if still inferential, indications of a real intent to reduce military spending. The article also contained indications of shifts in military thinking that would be highly significant for arms control. We will return to these arms control and doctrinal aspects at the end of this chapter. Here, we need to see what was said that may have implications for military spending in the aggregate.

The article was written by Army General Shabanov, the deputy minister of defense for material-technical supply of the armed forces (the chief of armaments), and appeared in *Krasnaya zvezda* (Red star). *Krasnaya zvezda* is the official newspaper of the Ministry of Defense and the armed forces, and is used—in the case of such articles—to disseminate "the word" to the uniformed services. Shabanov opened with the usual statements to the effect that Soviet military strength is critical to the security and defense of the homeland and, as could be expected considering his duties, stated the centrality of the material-technical supply base of the armed forces. He then stressed very strongly, however, that the surest and by far the best way to insure that the military's needs are met is through the Party's (i.e. Gorbachev's) program of economic and technical revitalization. He went on to devote much of the article to the theme that professional mastery of equipment and tactics is much more important than quantities of the latest military hardware. To reemphasize this point, he more than once stressed that if used properly, older equipment is quite satisfactory. One could hardly imagine finding a more pointed indication that military procurement was not going to grow as fast as the military might like; in fact, the implied message was either that it was going to slow down or that it was already doing so.

A major reduction in the growth of military procurement could obviously suggest a shift in the military's overall share of the economic pie— but not necessarily so. It could also be the result of shifts in the spending pattern within a still predominant defense share of the total. A defense industrial sector that still commanded the lion's share of Soviet economic resources but that was also entering a period of technological restructuring and retooling of the means of production (the overall Gorbachev strategy for the economy) would perforce have to temporarily reduce its current output, either in absolute terms or in growth rate. This, of course, is precisely what the formulas implied by Ogarkov and others, described earlier, called for.

Similarly, a defense establishment whose budget growth was constrained, but that had to meet ever-growing operational costs in Afghanistan and elsewhere and that found it necessary to maintain or even increase training outlays so as to master real combat skills with ever-more-complex equipment and ever-more sophisticated battlefield doctrine would also have to limit direct procurement.

Finally, procurement for Soviet forces could be affected by foreign military assistance. As noted in the previous chapter, Soviet military deliveries to the Third World remain high. Perhaps they are not as high quantitatively as they have sometimes been, but they increasingly involve some of the newest hardware, hardware upon which one would expect the Soviet armed forces normally to have first call. A case in point. The MiG-29 is one of the newest and most sophisticated Soviet aircraft, and is obviously in high demand for Soviet air force units. According to a normally reliable Western press source, the total number in service in the Soviet air force is only some 150. At the same time it has been confirmed that some 40 are to be provided to India (the first deliveries took place in summer 1986) and as many as 80 were expected to be provided to Syria, although by summer 1987 there was still some uncertainty in open-source reporting whether the Syrian deliveries had commenced.

Shabanov's clearly indicated reduction in procurement could reflect any, all, or a combination of the above factors, not a reduction in overall military spending. For a more confident assessment of which is the case, other indications have to be compared.

One other such body of evidence in regard to Soviet military spending is Western assessments of such spending and of production. These data indicate that during 1986 military production continued to receive as disproportionately high allocations as in the past. The most widely accepted and authoritative Western data on Soviet military expenditures and production all point to this conclusion. Analysts may hold different views about the precise percentage of Soviet GNP being spent on the military, about the value in dollar equivalents or in rubles of these costs, or about rates of growth, but almost all estimates that can be considered reliable fall within a fairly narrow range and indicate roughly the same trends. Thus, it can be confidently presumed that after a period from the 1960s through the mid-to-late 1970s in which Soviet defense expenditures *grew* annually at the impressive rate of 4 to 6 percent in real terms, they leveled off to about 2 percent. This coincided roughly with a similar drop in the overall growth rate of the Soviet economy, but throughout the period the growth of defense expenditures either exceeded or was roughly equal to overall economic growth. Accordingly, U.S. intelligence and other Western sources estimated the percentage of the Soviet GNP absorbed by defense as rising from about 11 percent in the early 1970s to between 15 and 17 percent in 1985. Furthermore, most Western estimates of the defense expenditure growth rate for 1985 point to a slight increase over preceding years (2 to 2.5 percent), and 1986 data suggest a 3 percent growth rate.

In regard to military production outputs there is virtually no disagreement among Western experts. Their estimates of major Soviet military hardware production not only show no decrease from previous years but point to slight increases in several high-cost systems. These same estimates show a 1985 increase in total floor space, an indication of ongoing investment and expansion in production facilities for virtually all major military hardware. Evidently, as the high rate of growth in military spending slowed to come more in line with that of the overall economy, procurement was relatively the most affected. What this meant was not a reduction in military procurement but a slowing of its rate of increase. For a country with an inventory of some 45,000 tanks and an annual production rate of between 2,500 and 3,000 new tanks, one cannot make much of a case out of this for reductions in defense.

Of course, the data cited above refers to 1985 and 1986 and could reflect the momentum of the past. It does not prove that Gorbachev does not intend to alter the priorities assigned to the military, or that he has not already begun to do so in 1987. To be absolutely sure either way, we must await data for future years. It does not follow, however, that we lack any clues to make reasonable assessments of what his present intentions are.

An unconfirmed report circulated in diplomatic circles can be considered one such clue. According to this report, in late summer of 1985 Gorbachev promised the military a 3 percent growth rate in defense expenditures. This is hardly the reduction that his overall domestic economic program seemed to call for. A more persuasive case to the same effect can be built by reference to the fact that investment in retooling and modernizing heavy industry, particularly those sectors that are critical to defense, continues to be accorded priority. Theoretically, such investment can be intended to meet solely or primarily civilian needs, but in the absence of more definitive evidence to the contrary, it has to be assessed as aimed at revitalizing both the defense and the civilian economy, not as a shift from the former to the latter. Considering the needs of adapting the defense economy to today's modern technologies, the real purpose behind it could as well be an increase in the USSR's raw military power over the long term. In the face of these uncertainties we have to seek additional clues. Fortunately, there is a fairly unique feature of Soviet reality that provides some such clues. This is Soviet military doctrine.

Military doctrine in the USSR is not simply a subjective and amorphous body of changing ideas. It is defined by the Soviets themselves as a formal body of official state policy that comprises a political component and military-technical component. The political component consists of the formal guidelines issued by the top Party leadership on the basis of the inputs received from uniformed military and the wider defense establishment as to what is militarily feasible or realistic. As such, it is no less the "law of the land" than a Politburo resolution or any act of legislation.

The military-technical component can be divided into two categories. One consists of broad military strategy; it contains definitions, such as the nature of modern armed conflict, the kinds of strategic military challenges the USSR must be prepared to meet, and the policies or strategies prerequisite to preparedness to meet these challenges or to seize opportunities as they arise. This part is apparently authored by the top political and the senior military leaderships working in tandem. (The locus of this activity may well be solely or primarily the Defense Council, a body chaired by Gorbachev). The more purely military an aspect of it is, the more likely the military is to have a greater voice in its formulation, but all of formal military doctrine is subject to explicit approval by the Politburo and Secretariat. Consequently, it too amounts to an authoritative statement of official policy, and it too has the binding force of a law. In other words, Soviet military doctrine on the one hand provides guidance for the military and on the other hand draws upon the data and assessments of Soviet military science, derived from the multidisciplinary examination of all the various "nuts and bolts" of military training, weapons requirements, field operations, and so on that fall under the military's sphere of competence.

What this implies is that the content of the Soviet military doctrine in the form adopted by the Gorbachev leadership provides probably the second most important body of evidence—after that provided by concrete actions, not rhetoric and fine-sounding generalities—pertinent to the intended thrust of economic programs, arms policies, and foreign policies. Although evidence derived from this source remains somewhat ambiguous, it is hardly reassuring for those who perceive the Gorbachev leadership as seeking to move the USSR away from an ultimate reliance on military strength and from the pursuit of the global struggle for world domination.

Since the end of the 1950s and very first years of the 1960s (i.e. since what the Soviets call "the second revolution in military affairs"), Soviet Military doctrine has been remarkably stable and consistent. It has adhered rigorously to the notions of the East-West struggle as inevitable, and of war as a definite possibility for which the USSR had to be prepared. It has posited that nuclear weapons would be decisive in any such war, by virtue of either their actual use or the impact of their existence upon the conduct of conventional operations. It has further posited that victory is possible in a nuclear war and has defined victory as the only conceivable goal of such a war. On these assumptions, Soviet military doctrine defined the reliability of any deterrence of war, or of escalation control in a war, as dependent upon the extent of across-the-board military superiority, particularly in nuclear capabilities. The doctrine also stressed the importance of strategic surprise (achievable first and foremost by deceiving the enemy about one's political intentions), of preemption in case enemy attack or escalation is believed imminent, and the utility of both overall and local relative military superiorities in achieving political objectives.

The doctrine underwent modifications, shifting from its earlier focus on short, all-out nuclear war and deterrence to a more flexible scheme envisioning conventional war phases and limited conventional wars with ever-increasing degrees of escalation control. Throughout these modifications the doctrine's fundamental assumptions of nuclear war winnability and of military superiority as the decisive element of political domination, war deterrence, escalation control, and victory remained unchanged. Because the doctrine's purpose has been to provide the basic framework within which all Soviet policy had to be fit, the consequences have been that (1) the buildup of military power continued to be the overriding orientation of the Soviet economy; (2) foreign policy was aimed at securing potentially useful forward military positions and retaining those already obtained; (3) arms control policies were prompted by the search for advantages; (4) detente with the West was seen as a means to encourage Western restraint and gain access to trade and strategic technology.

Even prior to Gorbachev's rise to power and certainly subsequently, there have appeared indications of major changes in this body of authoritative ideas. Starting in the latter 1970s, high-level statements were recurringly made that at face value indicated a process of fundamental change in some of the central elements of the doctrine, including the concept of the winnability of a nuclear war and of strategic nuclear superiority as the formula for deterrence. The first solid hint came in a speech by Brezhnev in 1977; he clearly expressed the view that in the foreseeable future neither side could achieve first-strike superiority. Following this, there began to appear a number of articles by apparently newly rehabilitated authors who had been previously castigated for arguing that nuclear war had become unthinkable because it was unwinnable. At the 26th Party Congress in 1981 Brezhnev stated that "to expect victory in nuclear war is dangerous insanity." An elaborate "doctrine" of no first use contained in statements of such authoritative defense establishment figures as Marshal Ustinov who was the minister of defense, and even Marshal Ogarkov followed suit. Ogarkov was quoted as denying the possibility of victory in a nuclear war barely a year after he had forcefully argued the opposite. His later statement, which some have interpreted as a forced recantation of his previous views (he was sacked shortly thereafter), suggests that a vigorous debate was going on within the Soviet leadership.

The pronouncements of the new Gorbachev leadership in the same vein have been even more forceful. The following excerpts from Gorbachev's main speech at the 27th Party Congress this year can serve as good examples:

The nature of present weapons does not allow any state the hope of defending itself only by military-technical means . . . [even]by the most powerful defense.

Security cannot endlessly be based on the fear of retaliation, that is on the doctrine of "restraint" or "intimidation" . . . [This is] absurdness and immorality.

These doctrines stimulate the arms race, which sooner or later can break loose out of control.

Security, if [we] speak of relations between the USSR and the USA, can only be mutual.

To win the arms race, as [to win] a nuclear war, is already impossible . . . the struggle for military superiority objectively cannot bring political gains to anyone.

At first glance, such formulations appear to reverse fundamental earlier assumptions of the doctrine; they can be even interpreted as the adoption of a deterrence policy based on a combination of victory denial, mutual assured destruction, and true parity rather than superiority. A closer look at just what was said and what was not said calls this interpretation into question. If mutual assured destruction is accepted as a fact of life that cannot be changed for the foreseeable future, it is still rejected—even in the quoted passages—as a basis for stable and enduring security. It is also noteworthy that in his speech at the same Party congress in which no first use of nuclear weapons was repeatedly affirmed, Defense Minister Sokolov reiterated the traditional slogan about "rebuffing" any aggression. (In the Soviet lexicon, "rebuffing," "repelling," or "countering" the enemy's aggression is by definition "defensive," never "preemptive" and certainly never aggressive in its own right.)

Subsequent Soviet statements by both political and military figures spoke even more forcefully of nuclear war no longer being a rational means to political goals, and seemed to put into question the basic Leninist dictum that wars are created and fought, and their strategies determined, by political objectives. In fact, if one looks closely at what has been said, one finds no change in the view that wars are started for political goals or as result of political and class conflicts, and there is nothing whatsoever that changes the dictum that the actual strategies used to wage a war must be determined in accord with accomplishing the political objectives. What was being stressed was that nuclear war was not a rational way to achieve political objectives. At the same time military and political writings continued to indicate that the USSR must and would remain prepared to conduct nuclear war as effectively as possible if it were thrust upon it.

In the May 1987 Warsaw Pact Political Consultative Committee meeting, a generalized proposal was floated for NATO and the Warsaw Pact to convene discussions designed to ensure that both sides make any necessary adjustments in their military doctrines and strategies to assure the other that these are strictly defensive. Some Western observers immediately seized upon this and equally generalized proposals for wide-ranging reductions in conventional-force components as indicating a new willingness to abandon the traditional Soviet emphasis on offensive operations. Certainly, Gorbachev has made it clear that he wants to find ways to reduce his military costs—at least until he can successfully revitalize the Soviet economy—but the words about a defensive doctrine are all too glib by far.

The fact that at the strategic and operational levels the best way to conduct a defense has invariably been seen as vigorous and comprehensive offensive action has always been proclaimed to be "only" a military-technical detail that in no way contradicts the supposed basic doctrinal description as defensive. Similarly, the "minor" detail that not only are preemption and surprise best and necessary as means to conduct a war with modern weapons but they do not equate to "offensive war" would have to be discounted to accept that Soviet doctrine has changed or will change. This is particularly true because it is a fundamental ideological concept that socialism is by nature peace loving and defensive, and that capitalism is aggressive and imperialistic. This "truth"—which has not been modified in the least—allows the Soviets to claim that any war, no matter what the sequence of the first shots or the strategic objectives of either side, or whether the "defensive" side preempted because of "objective" political and military conditions, is by nature defensive if waged by the USSR. From the ideological view, a view that is critical to Gorbachev's own legitimacy within the Soviet system, any significant force capabilities and any responsive doctrine such as the U.S. air-land-battle deep-strike tactics are inherently offensive; any Soviet doctrine of preemption, offensive operations, or any Soviet and Warsaw Pact military force structure and capabilities are inherently defensive. This definitional standard can only mean that the call for "defensive military doctrines" is a one-sided farce designed for foreign policy and arms control atmospherics.

Given all of this, do these statements really mean what they have been interpreted by some to mean, and do they mark any fundamental shift in nuclear doctrine and strategy? The answer to the first of these two questions is that they probably do mean what they literally state, but with two provisions: (1) that their meaning is conditioned by the standard Soviet meanings of the terms used (e.g. preemption when faced by "imminent or even probable" enemy first use of nuclear weapons is not really "first use," and a socialist offensive military operation is really a defensive action); and (2) that one should not read into them anything more than what they expressly say.

The Soviets have always have always recognized the great uncertainties and undesirabilities of engaging in a nuclear war. Their emphasis upon victory has at all times been a question of which posture provides the best deterrent, and of how to be best prepared to meet an unwanted but likely contingency. It is very doubtful whether the title of Richard Pipe's famous article, "Why the Soviet Union Thinks It Can Fight and Win a Nuclear War," ever expressed a current, confidently held operational viewpoint. The more recent pronouncements suggest that the Soviets probably genuinely perceive a war-surviving, war-winning capability as extremely problematic. On the other hand, it is well worth bearing in mind that these statements have conveniently appeared at a time when the Soviets have been engaged in intensive diplomatic and propaganda campaigns aimed at undermining NATO INF deployments, derailing the Reagan programs for U.S. nuclear and conventional modernization, stopping the U.S. SDI, limiting French and U.K. nuclear modernizations, and generally promoting detente with the West.

Whether these Soviet statements mark a fundamental shift in nuclear strategy and doctrine has to be answered in the negative, with the proviso that they may indicate a move toward a modification in detail if not in nature. What many things suggest is undergoing or has undergone change is the content of military science, a separate body of theory subordinate to and influencing military doctrine in Soviet terminology but encompassing many things that in less formal Western usage are described as doctrine. This is where the Soviets include such things, among others, as employing offensive operations and preemption in defense; and it is here that methods of escalation control, necessary-force ratios, and so on, are found. On the face of it, some of the potential arms control agreements being proposed would impose adjustments on military science, but this is not so certain. To start with, Soviet military leaders have long called for capabilities and flexibilities to conduct operations at any level of weaponry, nuclear or nonnuclear. Increasingly, their calls have stressed the apparent conviction that war should be kept non-nuclear, if possible. Moreover, to take one example, even a full-zero INF missile treaty would not really eliminate the USSR's ability to wage a resolutely nuclear theater war. Not only are there plenty of other intermediate-range and shorter-range nuclear delivery systems in the Soviet arsenal but the newer "strategic" systems are quite employable against theater targets.

Needless to say, there have been no such indications of fundamental change in terms of actual Soviet weapons and force programs as far as they are known in the West. Deployment of the new, mobile SS-25 fourth-generation ICBM is proceeding apace, and that of the larger, rail-mobile SS-X-24 is either about to begin or already has begun. New TYPHOON missile submarines are being produced at a steady rate. A 3,000km-range air-launched cruise missile (ALCM) has been operational since 1984, and both ground- and sea-launched versions were reported in the later stages of development in the end of 1986. A stategic bomber comparable to the U.S. B-1 is being tested. Moreover, follow-ons for these and other older systems are known to be in the development stage. When one adds to this in-complete listing of new Soviet strategic nuclear hardware all of the sim-ilarly new and advanced weapons and equipment for theater or battlefield nuclear operations, for conventional (i.e. non-nuclear) military warfare, for chemical operations, for strategic air and antimissile defense, the exten-sive military space program, and the long-standing major research effort in exotic new weaponry (lasers, directed energy beams, and so on)—to say nothing of genetic engineering research and the evidence of a bac-teriological warfare program involving mycotoxins ("yellow rain")—one is forced to recognize a continuing commitment to improving real war-fight-ing capabilities and, particularly when considered all together, nuclear war-fighting capabilities.

There are, however, definite indications of important shifts within the same war-fighting, war-winning military doctrine. These indications do not change the basic approach of seeking military superiorities for deterrence, for the underpinning of political and psychological pressure, or for war winning in the event conflict is necessary. But they do have major implica-tions in regard to arms control and, potentially, in regard to the nuclear aspects of military affairs.

Once again, a major proponent of these shifts has been Marshal Ogarkov. Ogarkov has for some years been associated with the argument that a major East-West war could well be fought from beginning to end without the use of nuclear weapons. He has called for a restructuring and reequipping of Soviet general-purpose forces and their operational employment doctrine to allow a rapid, continuous and decisive theater victory that would over-run NATO in weeks without the need for nuclear weapons should war occur. In addition, he has increasingly categorically proclaimed not only that a nuclear war might be unnecessary but that it would be such an unmitigated disaster that it cannot be rationally contemplated. Signifi-cantly, this line of thought is not just one of Ogarkov's conceptual theoriz-ings. Its central thrust of restructuring general-purpose forces for an integrated, high-technology blitzkrieg concept of warfare in Europe—ei-ther in a purely conventional or in a nuclear environment—is precisely what many Western observers have concluded they are seeing in the ongo-ing force improvements in the Soviet armed forces. Moreover, its the-oretical basis has been the predominant theme of most other Soviet military theoretical writings for several years now.

Such a doctrinal shift fits far better within the framework of an overall national doctrine that seeks ways effectively to employ military power or its threat even in the nuclear age than it does within one seeking only deter-rence against potential enemy aggression. It is a war-winning, correlation-of-power-shifting doctrine that at a minimum seeks to add a new dimension and new options to the ones existing with nuclear weapons, but that is also potentially the substitute for nuclear weapons for a state that wishes to retain the option of military aggression and expansion. To the extent to which this doctrinal shift seeks to do the latter (substitute for nuclear warfare), it logically shifts the burden placed on nuclear strike forces more toward deterrence and to being more a type of insurance of the last resort. Significantly, there is some striking inferential evidence in this regard, and it is found, among other places, in the article by General Shabanov that was discussed earlier.

In his article, Shabanov used formulations and made statements that would be fully consistent with such a shift in the thrust of nuclear doctrine, and the formulations were particularly significant because they were new for the Soviets. He abandoned the usual phraseology stating that the most important part of the USSR's strategic deterrence was the ICBM forces of the Strategic Rocket Forces (SRF). Instead, he very pointedly spoke of the nuclear capabilities of the Soviet "triad." He was not only saying that future Soviet strategic nuclear force development would be much more balanced, with the long-range bomber force and the navy's missile submarines (the other two parts of a triad) no longer the stepchildren of the SRF, but apparently implying something quite important about the central thrust of strategic nuclear doctrine. (One may even logically speculate that Marshal Tolubko's surprise retirement as commander in chief of the SRF in summer 1985 may have been due to his entrenched protectionism of the primacy of the SRF and his opposition to such a doctrinal shift.)

A balanced triad is not simply a more diverse structure for waging offensive nuclear war; it is even more a structure whose essential rationale lies in ensuring traditional deterrence by enhancing the survivability of retaliatory forces. Moreover, strategic bombers are recallable; unlike ballistic missiles, after launching they can up to the last minute be recalled to halt their strikes if crisis management has forestalled armageddon. In addition, they take much more time to reach their targets. Strategic bombers are essentially second-strike retaliatory or follow-on weapons, not preemptive or surprise-attack counterforce systems. And submarine-launched ballistic missiles (SLBMs), in spite of the steady improvements being made in their accuracy, are also much more of a second-strike type system because of their relative survivability and flexible deployability in the vast reaches of the ocean depths. Over and above its greater focus on survival of retaliatory forces, a balanced triad provides much greater possibilities for the kinds of flexibilities that are essential to escalation control. It does not necessarily detract from the kind of destabilizing offensive first-strike counterforce capabilities needed for a nuclear war-winning strategy, but it does allow the kind of shift in emphasis that would be required to adopt a different course.

Through Gorbachev's first two and a quarter years, the Soviets made many atypical, concessional-type moves in arms control. High-flown rhetoric about complete nuclear disarmament is nothing new, but Gorbachev has added a wholly new degree of actual content to those essentially propagandistic and unrealistic formulas. The specific figures offered for deep cuts in existing forces go far beyond anything Moscow has ever before put into formal proposals in actual negotiations; if implemented, they would have major effects upon Soviet force structures. Even more significant in this regard, Gorbachev has step by step adjusted and sweetened his proposals in ways that both added to their potential in these regards and brought them closer to U.S. demands. Nevertheless, this process by mid 1987 had still fallen short of amounting to the kind of total package of limitations, reductions, bans and effective verification measures that would confirm any real intention to abandon war-fighting, war-winning and war-survival as the central feature of nuclear strategy.

In sum, the evidence through mid-summer, 1987 was not sufficient to indicate that Moscow had abandoned nuclear war-winning as the basic prescriptive goal for military force structure and capabilities. It did suggest that within that doctrinal goal the emphasis was shifting toward a purely conventional war-winning capability with nuclear weapons serving primarily as a deterrent against escalation by the foe or as a means of last resort. Such a shift would be a logical corollary of the desire to continue to base the pursuit of the historic struggle upon military power and the threat or actuality of armed aggression in a world where such things as the destruction of civilization might be the very real outcome of a nuclear war-fighting approach.

On balance, the most logical—in fact the only safe—conclusion about Gorbachev's new approach to nuclear realities and his doctrinal statements is that they are the logical and predictable verbal props for current Soviet policies and strategies aimed at decoupling Europe from the U.S. strategic deterrent and achieving a position to be able to win a theater war without recourse to nuclear weapons. Moreover, even if Gorbachev's version of Soviet military doctrine does imply a reorientation of Soviet military programs and conduct of foreign affairs in a non-nuclear direction, there is nothing in it that would indicate his renunciation of the concept of total struggle against the West or of his reliance on superior military power. Because conventional forces consume the bulk of defense expenditures, the prospect for any substantial reduction in the Soviet defense burden is hardly auspicious.

Nevertheless, if a meaningful shift in Soviet military doctrine really occurs, or has occurred, it would be a major development with enormous significance for the entire world. It would undoubtedly spell much better prospects for a degree of relatively meaningful nuclear arms control. This would be almost certain to have spillover effects, conceivably quite favorable, on other aspects of East-West relations. In the USSR, it would quite possibly give Gorbachev room for the flexibility that he needs to succeed in his program of accelerating the introduction of modern technology into the Soviet economy, regardless of whether the defense sector is ultimately reduced in size or simply reconstructed and modernized along with the rest.

One last and very important point needs to be made in this analysis of Gorbachev's military policies: it would be very premature to conclude that he does not have the support and backing of that wide-based defense establishment that we have described. Certainly there are potential or implied elements of the new leadership's policies and strategies that could worry the military leadership, but the evidence indicates that it is with him so far. Most of these have already been discussed and do not need to be reiterated here; the actual state of the defense establishment's concern over the implications of Gorbachev's policies is, once again, best expressed in the Shabanov article to which we have twice before referred.

As noted, Shabanov—clearly speaking for the military to the leadership—said that Gorbachev's economic strategy, even if it temporarily cost the military some of its priority position for the distribution of resources, was acceptable and in fact the best way to proceed. In regard to arms control and the basic thrust of foreign policy, Shabanov was saying something quite similar, but he placed a highly meaningful caveat upon the support he expressed. He discussed at length factors in the strategic balance and in Soviet security as well as, in general but highly revealing terms, the kinds of responses that the USSR would have to make if current policies failed to achieve their goals. The general emphasized the necessity of a different approach if the United States persisted in nuclear testing, and with SDI and its other military (especially strategic) modernizations. "In these circumstances, the CPSU, the Soviet government, must undertake the inescapable, and I directly say, the necessary measures to strengthen the defensive capabilities of the country, not allowing the United States and NATO to gain superiority over the Soviet Union and the Warsaw Pact." Here, beyond any doubt, was a pointed warning that Gorbachev absolutely must succeed in stopping the U.S. programs if he wants the continued support of the military for the policies he has proclaimed.

Shabanov was also speaking for the military leadership to its subordinates. He was telling them not to worry about the changes and the implications of current policy lines. The fact that it was believed necessary to do this confirms that such worry and some *incipient* opposition to the new policies already existed. Moreover, Shabanov indicated that even further departures from traditional Soviet arms control policies and the resultant effects upon force structure could be acceptable if the goal of stopping the United States programs were to be achieved. The reference to the full adequacy of a triad implied that one should not fear even deeper cuts in the ICBM force than military thinking had ever before accepted. In addition, the deputy defense minister went on to apply the triad to the theater nuclear balance, stating that it (the *strategic* triad) was fully adequate to counter any surprise attack, even by Pershing 2s stationed in Europe. Previously, the Soviets had harped upon the destabilizing capabilities of the Pershing 2s and defended their SS-20 force in large part as a counter to them. Now Shabanov was saying that the senior military leadership could accept deep cuts in theater (INF) missiles even if some of the U.S. INF missiles remained. These statements presaged positions Gorbachev was to take in 1987, and they indicate that what he offered then had the backing of the leadership of the Soviet defense complex. On the other hand, if Gorbachev does (or already has) come to the conclusion that a real substantive shift in resources away from the heavy industry that supports military power is needed, then the military would be very likely to object. If they do object, Gorbachev must be able to ensure that the armed forces are in no position to throw their weight behind any political rivals who arise within the Party—and hence the purge he has carried out, first quietly and then more pointedly and openly, in the military leadership.

Partial and Illustrative List of Senior Military Reassignments

1984–early 1985 (when Gorbachev was in charge of Party cadres)

Marshal Sokolov appointed minister of defense, 12/84.
Marshal Akhromeyev appointed first deputy minister of defense, chief of the General Staff, 9/84. Raised to full Central Committee member, 3/86, as was Army General Shabanov, deputy minister of defense since 1980.
Marshall Petrov named first deputy minister of defense, 1/85.
Army General Ivanovskiy named deputy minister of defense, commander in chief, Ground Forces, 2/85.
Marshal of Aviation Yefimov named deputy minister of defense, commander in chief of Air Forces, 12/84. Raised to full Central Committee membership, 3/86.
Army General Govorov named deputy minister of defense, chief inspector, 6/84.
Marshal Ogarkov named commander in chief of Western Theater of Military Operations, 9/84.
Army General Gerasimov named commander in chief of Southwest The-

ater of Military Operations, ?/84. Raised to full Central Committee membership, 3/86.

Army General Tretyak named commander in chief of Far Eastern Theater of Military Operations, 6/84.

Col. General Kovtunov named commander, Northern Group of Forces, ?/84.

Col. General Yermakov named commander, Central Group of Forces, ?/84.

Army General Yazov named commander, Far Eastern Military District, 6/84.

Col. General Postnikov named commander, TransBaikal Military District, ?/84.

Col. General Popov named commander, Turkestan Military District, ?/84.

Col. General Osipov* named commander, Kiev Military District, 9/84.

Col. General Shuralev* named commander, Byelorussian Military District, 2/85.

1985-1986 (after Gorbachev became general secretary, CPSU)

Col. General (later promoted to Army General) Lizichev named chief, main political directorate of the Armed Forces, 7/85. Raised to full Central Committee membership, 3/86.

Army General Maksimov named deputy minister of defense, commander in chief of Strategic Rocket Forces, 7/85. Raised to full Central Committee membership, 3/86.

Fleet Admiral Chernavin named deputy minister of defense, commander in chief of Naval Forces, 12/85. Raised to full Central Committee membership, 3/86.

Army General Zaitsev named commander in chief of Southern Theater of Military Operations, 7/85.

Army General Lushev named commander in chief of Group of Soviet Forces in Germany, 8/85.

Admiral Kapitanets* named commander, Northern Fleet, summer/85.

Admiral Makarov named commander, Baltic Fleet, ?/85.

Lt. General Denidov named commander, Southern Group of Forces, ?/85.

Col. General Arkhipov named commander, Moscow Military District, 7/85. Raised to full Central Committee membership, 3/86.

Col. General Patrikeyev named commander, Volga Military District, 11/85.

Army General Lushev promoted to first deputy minister of defense (his second reassignment under Gorbachev), apparently replacing Marshal Petrov, 7/86.

Vice Admiral Ivanov named commander, Baltic Fleet (replacing Gorbachev appointee Admiral Makarov after about one year), summer ?/86.

Army General Tretyak named deputy minister of defense (his second reassignment during the period Gorbachev was either in charge of cadres or in power), 8/86.

Army General Belikov* named commander in chief of Group of Soviet Forces in Germany, 8/86.

Vice Admiral G. Khvatov identified as commander, Pacific Fleet, 1/87.

Col. General A. Kovtunov named commander, Central Asian Military District, 2/87. His predecessor, Col. General V. Lobov, was subsequently identified as first deputy chief of the General Staff, possibly replacing General V.I. Varennikov, but this is not certain.

General D.T. Yazov was identified as deputy minister of defense for cadres, 2/87.

Lt. General M.A. Moiseev was identified as the new commander, Far East Military District, 2/87.

Lt. General I.S. Morozov was identified as commander, Odessa Military District, 2/87.

Col. General V. Skokov was identified as commander, Carpathian Military District, 2/87, but probably assigned earlier, when his predecessor was reassigned in 8/86.

Lt. General L.S. Shustko was identified as commander, North Caucasus Military District 2/87, but probably assigned earlier, when his predecessor, Col. General Skokov, was probably reassigned. (see above).

General S.I. Postnikov (previously commander, Transbaikal Military District, and promoted to general 11/86) was identified as first deputy commander in chief of Ground Forces (possibly replacing General A. Mairov, not mentioned in the press since 11/87), 2/87.

Lt. General V. Grishin was identified as commander, Baltic Military District, 5/87.

Marshal A.U. Konstantinov was reported by the Western press, but not in Soviet publications, as having been replaced as commander, Moscow Air Defense District, 5/87. The sacking reportedly took place prior to the Rust air penetration incident.

Marshal A.I. Koldunov was relieved as deputy defense minister, commander in chief of Air Defense Forces, 5/87, in connection with the Rust incident.

General D.T. Yazov named minister of defense, replacing retired, Marshal Sokolov, 5/87. Yazov was promoted from candidate CC member to full CC member and candidate Politburo member, 6/87.

General I.M. Tretyak was named commander in chief of Air Defense Forces (he was already a deputy defense minister as chief inspector, a position for which the replacement had not yet been identified), 6/87.

In addition, there were a large number of deputy commanders and senior staff officer positions identified as changed. However, it may be very significant that there were comparatively far fewer political deputy commander positions changed throughout the periods when Gorbachev was general secretary or even the "second general secretary" in charge of cadres.

Note: See text of chapter 12 for considerations on accurate identification of names and dates. Note also that many dates are less than certain.

*Raised to candidate CC member, 3/86. (Among others promoted within the Party hierarchy in this way: Army General Belikov, commander, Carpathian Military District since 1979; Army General Varennikov, first deputy chief of the General Staff since 1979; Marshal of Aviation Konstantinov, commander, Moscow Air Defense District since 1980; Col. General Rodin, chief, Political Directorate, Strategic Rocket Forces since 1986; Col. General Snetkov in May promoted to army general commander, Leningrad Military District since 1981; Admiral Sorokin, first deputy chief, Main Political Administration since 1981.)

Part IV
Conclusions

For now we see through a glass, darkly.
—1 Cor. 13:12

13

The Emperor's New Clothes:
What the Record Reveals

Plus ca change, plus c'est la meme chose,
but
Things are often not what they seem to be.

Throughout the preceding chapters there is one central unifying theme: comparative power. Power can fairly be said to be what Soviet politics, economics, social mechanisms, and foreign policy are essentially all about. It begins with power relations within the Kremlin, which are a fundamental part of every aspect of Gorbachev's policies and furture prospects.

In a dramatically short period, really in his first year, Gorbachev and his associates have moved faster and more decisively than any of their predecessors in consolidating their position and power within the USSR. In the process they have demonstrated an activist, dynamic style and a sense of purpose that holds promise of ending the long period of drift and rudderless leadership. Whatever the intent or longer-term effects of their programs, the period of sweeping accumulating problems under the rug has been replaced by one in which problems are recognized and solutions to them are sought. This, by itself, is no mean achievement in a system wherein perfection and infallibility are deemed to be inherent in the correct application of "scientific" Marxist-Leninist principles. The Gorbachev leadership has introduced a number of changes in organizational structure and standard procedures that even if palliative, can have significant ramifications. At the same time the leadership has embarked on foreign policies clearly intended to facilitate solutions to domestic problems. Yet, however motivated, such foreign policies contain the potential for significant changes in international relationships around the world.

Any consideration of Gorbachev's personnel appointments, economic reform program, or foreign policies in terms of how his potential rivals and various interest groups behind them are likely to respond leads to one inescapable conclusion. In a little over a year, Gorbachev had succeeded in solidly taking charge—more so than Khrushvhev or Brezhnev managed to do in far longer periods, and much more so than Andropov, who had barely begun the job (Chernenko does not even deserve to be considered in such a comparison). In fact, Gorbachev took charge far faster than Stalin; however, this comparison is of limited value because Stalin had to deal with a very different political and social environment and to contend with rivals of incomparably greater prestige and abilities.

When between April and the beginning of July 1985 Gorbachev brought four new faces to full membership in the Politburo, plus one new candidate member, and selected three new CC secretaries, all while eliminating his erstwhile principal rival Romanov and moving Gromyko out of foreign policy management, he had already gone a long way in making the transition from "first among equals" to "first above equals." Then when he retired Tikhonov and Grishin in the fall and winter and quite radically changed the composition of the Politburo and Secretariat at the Party Congress in the spring, he completed the process. By his wholesale replacement of ministers and chairmen of state committees and his numerous personnel appointments further down the Party and state chains of command, he not only served notice that his policy preferences were not to be opposed but, more importantly, ensured that for the time being at least neither any of the few remaining holdovers from the old guard nor any would-be rival from among his supporters or protégés could find a base of support to challenge him. By spring 1986 at the latest, Gorbachev was without question firmly in control of the commanding heights of the central leadership. Short of major policy failures or setbacks, he was immune to challenge.

Although Gorbachev has reached the pinnacle of power and made himself into the undisputable first above equals, he has not yet succeeded in becoming the supreme *vozhd* (leader). Yet, the latter status is, as Soviet history suggests, the natural corollary of the pyramidal power structure of the Party and state and of the principle of democratic centralism. The problem for Gorbachev in becoming a true *vozhd* is that it is far from clear whether he can achieve this without terror, without making the KGB and police security organs into his own personal tool rather than that of the Party. In any event, this would require the permanent implementation of "cadres policy" down to the lowest level of the apparatus. Gorbachev has made some beginnings toward this end, apparently as yet modest ones, as indicated by the numbers of middle- and lower-echelon *nomenklatura* members who have hung onto their jobs, and by the evidence, clearly detectable in the Soviet press, of widescale resistance to changes in management methods and in attitudes toward work. The latter phenomenon may well reflect nothing more than the momentum of immobilism and the fear of losing acquired perquisites and privileges, but it jeopardizes Gorbachev's chances of success and makes the job easier for his potential rivals.

The immobilism and resistance to change of the entire interlocking Soviet system may in fact, well be the critical factor for the success or failure of either Gorbachev's current reform efforts or of any wider, more fundamental efforts that may eventually be called for. To borrow a metaphor from biology, the multiple mechanisms of interpenetrating controls and the brunt of Soviet and Russian history—including purges, gulags, ubiquitous propoganda reiteration, social "atomization," sacrifices, pervasive bureaucracies, and carefully allocated privileges and rewards—have created an organism with a remarkably effective immunological system. Significant reforms in this context are like invading foreign organisms. Either the system swallows them up and nullifies them or they fully infect and overcome the existing organism. The smaller and less fundamental the reforms are the more likely they are to be defeated by the system's ingrained defenses. In contrast, major reforms, like more serious diseases, carry risks of a fatal infection—or, in the political context, of disruption and breakdown of the CPSU dictatorship.

Eventually, of course, Gorbachev's currently loyal supporters will probably seek to unseat him. This seems to be a pattern in Soviet history. But Soviet history also provides Gorbachev with three models for surviving such challenges. Stalin relied on "cadres policy" and on terror, surveillance, and purges of even his closest associates in the leadership. Khrushchev borrowed Stalin's "cadres policy" but found no way of guaranteeing the lasting loyalty of his own people. Brezhnev, having apprenticed under both Stalin and Khrushchev, continually reshuffled his top cadres, establishing one clique only to replace it after a while with another.

Gorbachev will have to find his own solution to the problem of surviving in power. Thus far he has proceeded in combining the pace and scale of Stalin with Khrushchev's abstention from using police terror against the leadership. Eventually, he may yet turn to the Brezhnev pattern and begin to gradually replace all or most of those he has installed at the top echelons of power. But he may also make an original contribution to the art of achieving longevity of rule in the USSR. One rather new thing for contemporary Soviet society that he gives the appearance of trying to do is to generate mass, popular support. It is possible to interpret his carefully staged sessions of mixing with workers and ordinary citizens in this way. Such a conclusion, however, is probably mistaken. Rather, such actions are more likely a combination of Gorbachev's own style and vanity, and of the usual Soviet desire to instill mass enthusiasm for policies. It may, however, also include an element of Gorbachev's propensity for more fully assessing the problems and limits involved in implementing decisions. Unlike most Soviet leaders, he seems to value some input from below and from academia.

If a fourth alternative exists, it seems to have to be one that would give Gorbachev an aura of indispensability comparable to that once enjoyed by Lenin. True, he can in no way match Lenin's intellectual prowess; but within a leadership no longer deeply committed to an increasingly amorphous and less relevant ideology, the intellectual qualities of Lenin could probably be compensated for by a chain of relatively unbroken successes in implementing policies clearly identifiable with his name. So far, however, Gorbachev has not been able to do this. His main policy drives—to revitalize the economy and to defuse the challenges, especially military, from an activist U.S. administration—have not met with real success, and he has been forced progressively to institute new economic and social measures and to make new arms control concessions so as to overcome obstacles to his chosen paths. The process appears to be carrying him further than he had any intention of going, and it definitely increases the risks that he will provoke real opposition from among his present associates.

Gorbachev's efforts to insure his grip on power by achieving policy successes can in a sense also be characterized as the attempt to make his mark on history. Here it is not a question of ambition or vanity. Rather, it is a social necessity inherent in the Soviet system. Consolidation of power and consolidation of a place for oneself in history are interconnected in the Communist society. Power is the basis and precondition for entering history, which is written anew with each new general secretary, and the mantle of history (hence of infallibility) serves to facilitate the accumulation and retention of power. What a general secretary requires in order to make his mark on history is a certain degree of political originality. He cannot be a carbon copy of his predecessors. He need not be totally original; it is quite adequate to present a mélange of the methods or programs of previous leaders. Still, at least something novel or something borrowed from the forgotten past, from the time of Lenin or Stalin, is required.

Thus, Gorbachev faced the problem, at least initially, of getting the society moving. Even if he could not really generate movement in the system, he had to generate its appearance, to make the society feel that a new boss was in charge—a new boss with new slogans or exhortations. The question was, what should these slogans or exhortations be?

To call for a major campaign of terror in the name of some pressing problem would be dangerous, for terror would have to be virtually total in order to succeed. The Partocracy would be opposed, out of fear of itself being swallowed up by this method introduced by Lenin and perfected by Stalin. To focus on patriotism and external threat to temporarily unite the people would be extremely risky in the nuclear age. Stalin had succeeded this way, but his parallel foreign policies had probably been a factor in precipitating World War II. More importantly there was no guarantee that the Soviets could win a new world war or even survive one if "victory" was theirs—and defeat in even a limited war would certainly undermine the current leadership and perhaps the entire regime. Finally, not only did the Soviet economy need access to foreign technology and investment but a period of harsh and unmitigated international confrontation would simply increase the West's determination to persevere in its threatening military buildup and anti-Soviet political activism. Nevertheless, in Soviet propaganda under Gorbachev and in the "reluctant" formulas referring to largely unspecified steps that would have to be taken if the West, mostly the United States, continued its "irresponsible and imperialist" ways, the seeds of just such a fallback policy of a return to intense "cold war" have been evident.

To leave everything as it was (the Brezhnev approach), to limit himself to mere discussions about new departures might have been possible and would certainly have made life easy and ruling uncomplicated if the general secretary had been older. But not to change anything for twenty-five years, the period in office that Gorbachev could hope for, hardly seemed realistic. More critical to his position, the economic and social problems facing the country were not imaginary. Unchecked, they could lead to such serious and irreversible consequences as the disintegration of Soviet social structure and the decline of Soviet military might—the main, if not the only, basis for Soviet world power.

Only one politically realistic choice remained: to effect a revitalization, the slogan word used is *acceleration,* of the economy and society while preserving the existing politial ruling structure. The problem was how to do both of these things at once. The kind of labor-intensive, capital-extensive industry building that Stalin had used, and that ever since had been the basic economic strategy of the USSR, was no longer applicable. But the capital-intensive, high-technology, and modern decentralized management methods now required would undermine CPSU control if carried too far. It seems certain that Gorbachev understood this, but he did not know how many or how far bureaucratic centralized controls could be loosened without jeopardizing his and the Party's position.

Consequently, Gorbachev embarked on the path of social and economic reform, at first cautiously without fully committing himself, then more coherently and fully. Yet, when he plunged more wholeheartedly into change, he kept to reforms that were in the interest of the ruling oligarchy and that were therefore limited, incomplete, or truncated. Herein lies the crux of the problem, the reason Gorbachev has so far failed to galvanize and transform the Soviet economy. He has tried to achieve the impossible: to engender initiative and dynamism down to the lowest levels via government direction, centralized planning, total control, and routine ways of thinking. Rather than attempting profound changes, he resorted to half-measures like the antialcohol campaign, the tightening of labor discipline, and the reorganization of management structures more than methods, and so on.

As could have been expected, given the amount of slack in the system and the abundance of inefficient, lacadaisical, and corrupt work practices, these tinkerings at peripheries of the system initially produced some apparent improvement. But after only a few months, in the spring of 1986, his widely propagandized transformation of the Soviet Union, with which he was to make his mark on history, lost steam and slowed dramatically. Because Gorbachev could not abandon his self-proclaimed program, he had to try something else to salvage his chosen path for economic revitalization and to ensure his own prestige and power.

The rescue effort inexorably pushed the Gorbachev leadership ever further down the path of reform and change. The result was the wider innovations, described in chapter 3, that began to accumulate in late summer and fall of 1986. These still limited reforms have not yet changed the system, but several of them (the "family-brigade" contractor system, small-scale individual private enterprise in over thirty types of trades and service industries, greater industrial decentralization, the attempt to introduce computers and information networks, "independent" enterprise operations in foreign markets, and so on), do open the door to systemic change. In effect, Gorbachev moved out onto a slippery slope without apparently realizing the extent to which many of his partial reforms are incompatible with the very essence of the Soviet system and hence might lead to unexpected outcomes.

It is doubtful that these further innovations will achieve their goals, and the leadership seemed to realize it. Casting about for ways out of this dilemma, the Soviets began in the second half of 1986 to look more closely at economic reforms put into effect in other Communist states. One such laboratory is Hungary. Indeed, all through 1986 but especially in June, August, and September, the main Soviet theoretical economic journal was replete with articles examining the Hungarian approach, one that both Gorbachev and Ligachev had reportedly expressly rejected earlier for the USSR. But Hungary is not the USSR. Its fairly successful blend of economic liberalization and continued Party control has been possible precisely because there is a Communist big brother in Moscow to insure the Party's monopoly of real power. There is no such big brother available to a Soviet leadership that had abandoned some of its centralized control.

Moreover, not only has the Hungarian economic boom been fading but the whole thrust of Gorbachev's Eastern European policy has been to force the CEMA economies into greater integration, greater dependence, and a closer copy of Moscow's programs and economic strategies.

A second model would be the PRC, and indeed the Talyzin visit in September 1986 seemed directed at least in part to examining Chinese reforms. Here, too, the prospects would be daunting. Gorbachev and company are well aware of the social and politial prices Beijing is paying for partial reform. The Soviet press has noted the financial and social dislocations taking place in China—albeit guardedly, for better political relations with the PRC are a major Soviet goal. Moreover, the demonstrations and rioting in favor of electoral democracy that erupted in the PRC in December 1986 must be frightening to the oligarchs in the Kremlin.

During the first half of 1987, Gorbachev moved further in the direction of real reform—but he still held back from taking the bull by the horns and moving all the way in an integrated and comprehensive manner. The new law on state enterprises and the extension of earlier management and planning reforms (e.g., self-financing, profit criteria for success, etc.) from a select few to a much wider number of economic branches marked another major step in the direction of market rationality. This was reinforced by the decree establishing cooperative societies for food production and by the new law on Joint Ventures (which although evidently aimed at acquisition of foreign technology and investment was bound to create pressures for greater market rationality if very many Western firms undertook the plunge and set up such operations).

Nevertheless, these further steps were still only half-measures. For them to achieve the desired results the actual extent of manager independence (not just its acclamation in words) would have to be far greater than the history of the system suggested it would ever really be; and the provisions for closing unprofitable enterprises would have to be utilized in a way which would truly shake the images and traditions of the system by allowing extensive unemployment and severe dislocation to occur. Even more important, for both real managerial independence and for profit to be a meaningful measure of enterprise success or failure, a rational pricing system would be needed. But allowing real costs and (even more important) market supply and demand to determine prices would carry two rather significant consequences for the men in the Kremlin. Artificial prices (both for end products for the consumer and for raw materials and component parts for the producer) have been an integral part of the system of centralized control for the Party and state leadership. Along with allocation of investment and the setting of production goals by fiat, the centralized pricing system was critical in the consolidation of top leadership control over the Soviet political-economy. Consequently changing it could only be seen as a very difficult step to take. Secondly, rational pricing would inescapably result in much greater hardship for the ordinary citizen who has long received his housing, food and many services (as poor as they might be) at a fraction of his income. In turn, without a combination of probably unaffordably higher wages and a real increase in adequate consumer goods the withdrawal of subsidies would easily destroy whatever credibility Gorbachev's appeal to self-interest had as a means to raise productivity and efficiency.

By the middle of 1987, this dilemma was apparently becoming more evident to the Kremlin and there were hints that pricing reform was at least under consideration. Mostly this was confined to few academic articles by economic theorists, but there were even a few passages in Gorbachev's speeches which suggested at least frustration with artificial prices. Nevertheless, and in spite of the fact that the economic results in the first half of the year were still incommensurate with the goals being proclaimed, there was very little concrete evidence that the leadership was yet prepared to risk removal of the price pillar of centralized power.

Of course, in theory the Soviet leadership could achieve fairly significant economic improvements even without allowing market mechanisms to operate. It could do this by dramatically shifting its priorities, as reflected in real relative investment levels, from group A (heavy industry) to group B (light industry and consumer goods and services), and particularly from military to civilian production. In fact, even in the later Brezhnev years there was a slight shift in that the rate of planned growth in investment in Group B was raised to slightly higher than that for Group A. But given the great disparity between the two, this meant little or nothing in absolute terms and would take many, many years to produce a significant real shift. Even in a highly centralized command economy this should result in providing the workers with much greater incentives, and thus lead to better overall economic performance even if the systemic obstacles to economic rationality were left largely intact. The shift, however, would mark a radical departure from the official legitimizing ideology, from Soviet global aspirations, and from the pattern to which all of Soviet history conforms. Needless to say, there have been no signs of real moves in that direction. The bulk of investment money has been designated for group A industries and for high technology in areas that serve those industries and that have military applications; management reform, exhortation, self-sufficient innovation, and much less money have been prescribed for group B.

Nevertheless, late in 1986 some real indications of possible reductions in the military's share of the economic pie appeared, although as noted in chapter 12, these could be indications of shifts *within* the defense budget, not its overall size. Assuming that such reductions are contemplated, they have been imposed in part, by the drop in oil prices. Gorbachev's economic experts can perform the same calculations that have been reported in the West. They know that to carry out the program of retooling with modern technology, Moscow has either to find the funds to purchase Western machinery or increase greatly the civilian share of the USSRs own output. Without the hard currency revenues from oil and gas, this simply requires taking on unacceptable levels of debt. Moreover, without a detente, which would lower the barriers to Western investment and technology acquisition, it might not be possible even if the resultant international debt were acceptable. More to the point, defense reductions cannot be contemplated seriously as long as the U.S. military modernization and SDI cannot be halted. The Soviet defense establishment has gone along with Gorbachev's detente and the arms control program precisely on the condition that these goals are achieved—and achieved in such a way as to retain potential Soviet advantages in the overall military correlation of forces.

During his two and one-half years, Gorbachev's efforts to revitalize the Soviet economy reflected a clear pattern. Minimal but highly touted "reforms" were progressively deepened and expanded as the economy continued to fail to respond in the manner desired. Partial organizational changes intended to avoid the need for real systemic reform were deepened. Meanwhile, half-measures in the real workings of the economic system were gradually introduced and expanded in their application. But neither full systemic reform allowing rational market economics nor a fundamental shift in investment priorities were yet dared. Nevertheless, by the second half of 1987 Gorbachev seemed to be approaching a major decision point. Clearly he had started out trying to preserve the system while improving it, and just as clearly something more seemed needed. Now he apparently faced three alternatives. Via one, he could truly decentralize the economy—including prices—but this would inevitably threaten total CPSU control and thereby Gorbachev himself. A second alternative was to dramatically shift investment away from heavy industry and the military. This could only be done if the perceived external challenges were significantly reduced and if no major foreign policy setbacks affected Soviet global influence and power—yet such an environment would inevitably encourage potential opponents to argue that there was now too great an opportunity to decisively shift the global correlation of forces to waste by shifting investment from the sources of national power for an uncertain future. The third apparent alternative would be for Gorbachev to essentially stop where he was in meaningful economic reform and, as had been the case with past Soviet economic tinkering, let words and appearances substitute for real long-term progress. Initially, this would reduce the danger of internal Party opposition and opportunism; but in the longer term unless the economy somehow improved without going any further and or the Western challenges self-destructed, this would probably not be an approach that could sustain Gorbachev in power without a reversion to more absolutist, more Stalinistic, controls. If the West did not hand him successes on a silver platter or if, against all odds, the economy somehow took off the way he wanted it to, the pattern of his first two and a half years would seem to be likely to impel Gorbachev further on the slippery slope of systemic reform ever more threatening to the power structure and to himself. The evidence of his efforts to reach an arms agreement with the West and of the June attacks on the military and defense allocation of resources suggested that Gorbachev was leaning towards the second alternative of shifting some of the investment priorities. However, it was still not really clear whether this was truly the case; what remained certain was that without success in his foreign policies he would be hard put to go very far in this direction.

The Gorbachev leadership has also tried to reeducate society: to inculcate discipline, enthusiasm, and *glasnost* and to overcome corruption and alcoholism. Very little in the way it has gone about this, however, suggests any intent to create the kind of open society found in the West. If anything, for most of Gorbachev's reign, dissidence, or "anti-Soviet tendencies" (as very broadly defined in the USSR), was even less tolerated than before. Then, in the closing days of 1986, the release of Sakharov and rumors of a large-scale political amnesty suggested that a change could be under way. Without a great deal more taking place, this has to be assessed as an attempt to kindle enthusiasm and promote the Soviet image abroad, as a sophisticated version of Khrushchev's thaw. *Glasnost* is a part of this, intended (1) to reduce the lying in official reports that impedes effective decision making; (2) to boost the economy by encouraging people to work harder and more productively; and (3) to provide a pretext for selective personnel dismissals to get rid of current and potential political rivals and their supporters. All along there was relatively little to suggest that the campaigns have had the intended effect on the populace. Reports coming out of the USSR via visitors and diplomats, as well as indications gleaned between the lines of the Soviet press—in which the usual outpourings of articles featuring happy, enthusiastic workers are juxtaposed with denunciations of continuing apathy and resistance to change—suggest that the population remains by and large stubbornly apathetic and cynical or at best highly skeptical. Only in the ranks of the political and intellectual elite have these campaigns seemed to arouse some (far from universal) hope and enthusiasm, but the true extent of this enthusiasm must be suspect due to the self-interest involved. The failure so far of the campaign to "catch fire" in the attitude of the masses may be a major reason Gorbachev has risked pushing it even further. If so, it is another example of the ways in which his chosen strategies are putting him ever further out on an uncertain and almost unintended limb.

Gorbachev may well have generated a process admittedly quite germinal so far, that eventually he will not be able to control. In an earlier chapter we described the dramatic speech by Yevgeny Yevtushenko at a writers congress in December 1985. In June 1986 he made an even sharper speech, and he was not alone. As before, there was undoubtedly a degree of staging in this. Both instances are also probably a part of internal writers union politics wherein the younger luminaries seek to displace the older, longtime incumbent leadership that blocks their advance. But there is another, potentially more meaningful implication. Selective, highly controlled *glasnost*—which is what the Gorbachev regime has clearly sought—is for the intellectual like salted peanuts: it only whets the appetite for more. Combined with modest but limited improvements in the availability of consumer goods and services, it has the potential of generating a revolution of rising expectations rather than zealous compliance, as intended. And last but not least, Gorbachev's emphasis on discipline, elimination of corruption, cracking down on anti-Soviet behavior, and so on has inevitably resulted in a greater role for, and visibility of, the KGB and other security organizations. It is a process that is likely to continue.

All told, this somewhat zig-zag path of ever-new innovations and reforms, of testing the limits of the control system and yet pushing the regime further down a slippery slope cannot have failed to arouse concern in the Politburo. One cannot say that there is yet senior opposition to Gorbachev; the top leadership figures are almost all his men. At the most to this point, they can but cautiously express the worry that things might be going too far in the direction of weakening the general secretary's and hence their own power. The holdovers from Gorbachev's predecessors know well enough to refrain from even cautious criticism; they are too vulnerable to being made the scapegoats if the reforms fail to achieve their objectives.

It is difficult to define the nature of the relationships in the Politburo; the kaleidoscope constantly changes, with no single stable pattern of either total support for, or total lack of confidence in, the general secretary. To establish one way of thinking in the Politburo, as in the country as a whole, the dictatorship of the Partocracy requires its own dictator so as to function effectively. At the same time it does not want a dictator. Therefore, it endeavors to reserve a dictatorship without a dictator. This inherent contradiction is resolvable either by the victory of the Politburo as a corporate group, in which case the power and authority of the general secretary would be weakened, or by the victory of the general secretary, in which case the

Politburo would be weakened. Through 1986 and 1987 Gorbachev still had good chances to become an autocratic general secretary, for the most important members of the Politburo and Secretariat owe their positions to him and he, in turn, is not obligated to anyone in the present Politburo. But to reach this goal—probably the only basis for political equilibrium in the CPSU—he must succeed in his economic and foreign policy programs.

Gorbachev's foreign policies have clearly been related to his economic revitalization program. Nothing in them has indicated any slackening of the "historic struggle" against capitalism, a struggle that in practice is tantamount to Soviet state expansionism, ultimately aiming at establishing a pax Sovietica over the entire globe. The current strategic line and tactical approaches have shifted, in some aspects significantly, in others only slightly. However, considering Soviet actions (e.g., increased offensives in Afghanistan, Angola, and Kampuchea; the continuing military production programs; foreign military assistance levels; the specific content of arms control proposals; the preservation of the core of earlier proclaimed state military doctrine, and so on) and the unchanged form and continuing virulence of anti-Western and anti-imperialist propaganda, the ultimate objectives cannot be assumed to have changed, detente rhetoric notwithstanding. What Gorbachev has attempted to do so far has been to change the parameters of the struggle, not abandon it.

There can be no doubt that the central motivation behind Gorbachev's deeds and words in the area of foreign policy has thus far been to facilitate his economic programs. Only through detente can Gorbachev hope to obtain access to Western trade investment, credits, and technology in the amounts needed. Only through detente can he hope to lessen even temporarily the burdens that the defense sector imposes on the rest of the economy, and only thus can he modernize and retool the defense industry itself instead of further expanding current weapons and equipment production. Only through detente can he have any confidence that perceptions of the Soviets' falling behind in the arms race with the West will not serve the purposes of potential rivals. Only through detente can he hope that the West may halt its current military modernization and expansions, particularly programs such as the U.S. SDI, which have potentially open-ended competitive costs. Finally, only through detente can he hope that the current U.S. military activism in the Third World may ease up. At the same time detente rhetoric helps undermine Western governments and promote a favorable image of the USSR during any period when detente is very limited or virtually nonexistent.

We have indicated that the chief target of Gorbachev's detente policies has been the United States, their primary objectives being stopping the SDI, derailing Reagan's military modernization and expansion programs, and dampening U.S. activism in the Third World. Almost without exception every Soviet foreign policy measure outside Eastern Europe, and some even there, can be explained either directly or indirectly in these terms, as a means of mounting pressures on Washington. Gorbachev's new rhetoric stressing the futility of seeking advantages in nuclear weaponry and the inherent unwinnability of a nuclear war has therefore to remain suspect in view of its obvious utility for achieving these objectives, and in view of the absence of real changes in industrial investment priorities, in military programs, and so on.

We also noted that Gorbachev's actions indicated a second priority fallback strategy of selective detente with Western Europe and Japan in the event of failure to achieve the desired relationships with the United States. Such an outcome would have to be a second choice during any period of economic reconstruction because of the scale of benefit opportunities that the U.S. economy alone can provide and because only a detente with the United States can reduce the military challenges (and hence demands placed on the Soviet economy) either strategically or in various regions of the world. Moreover, although in Europe and in Japan Soviet peace rhetoric has found a resonant echo, the history of the post-World War II period cannot generate high optimism in the Kremlin over the prospects of fundamentally splitting the West. Nevertheless, Soviet behavior clearly indicates that the fallback option of seeking detente with Europe and Japan is already being pursued parallel to the search for a detente with the United States.

Finally, any Soviet leader embarking on the two policies Gorbachev has so evidently pursued would have to be prepared for a contingency of failure in both and have a less attractive alternative or line of retreat. Some of Gorbachev's actions already point in the direction of such a worst-case scenario. Strengthening the KGB, stepping up the pace of Eastern European political and economic integration, preparing the population psychologically for the efforts that would be required if the Western "imperialists" do not listen to reason, and even economic reconstruction (even if it can serve other purposes as well) all bespeak a resolve to hold onto power in the event that both Gorbachev's detente policies end in failure.

Throughout his term in office so far Gorbachev has sought to renew Soviet activism in regard to the rest of the world. In Eastern Europe, he has set in motion a program to assist his own domestic economic plans and to enhance and ensure Soviet domination over his Warsaw Pact allies through a markedly more comprehensive economic integration, through coordination of the Eastern European economies with the Soviet economy, and through setting up the Soviet economic reforms as a model for the East Europeans to follow. To all appearances, he had had greater success in this than in his other foreign policies.

In the Third World, he has sought first and foremost to consolidate existing Soviet positions of influence in ways conducive to his detente objectives, either by disguising Soviet combativeness and lowering the intensity of confrontations or else by trying to eliminate the most visible running sores (such as Afghanistan) through quick military victory. While trying not to allow Third World confrontations to become a barrier to detente with the West, Gorbachev has been careful to both avoid any unnecessary losses and to prepare the USSR to exploit any and all opportunities to reap gains (especially for example in Southern Africa). After a period of trial and error, a possibly dominant motif of Gorbachev's approach to Third World strategy appears to have emerged in the Middle East. By a careful tilt towards Iraq while maintaining openings to Iran, and by much more limited openings towards Israel and a stepped up wooing of moderate Arab regimes, the USSR has been positioning itself as a powerbroker able to deal with both sides in the endemic regional conflicts precisely at a time when Washington has managed to lose credibility in its claim to a monopoly on being the only mediator able to address both sides in these issues (especially in the Gulf region).

This clearly indicates that he means to continue the struggle for predominance and to adhere to the ultimate goal of defeating the West by outflanking it, especially by establishing footholds in those regions of the world in which Soviet anti-imperialist rhetoric, the legacy of Western colonialism, and perceptions of continuing economic exploitation by the West could give Moscow an advantage. In this regard, it is worth noting that one function the pursuit of struggles in the Third World has long had is legitimizing the ideology. Every past Soviet setback in the Third World has been followed by an agonizing reappraisal of events and policies couched in terms of "correct" applications of Marxism-Leninism to the objective local circumstances. This means that a total renunciation of Soviet support for Third World causes would be seen as betrayal, and is therefore unthinkable. It means further that any major Soviet defeat in the Third World could be seized upon by Gorbachev's potential domestic rivals to build up support against him within the Party. Temporary setbacks, especially in regions where all the concrete, material military advantages belong to the United States, such as in Nicaragua, are more amenable to a face-saving escape rationale for withdrawal. But even in such cases, the most likely conclusion to be arrived at by the Soviet leadership would be the need to increase Soviet military capabilities and reach. Like his stategy toward the West, Gorbachev's Third World strategy has sought to change temporarily the terms of reference, not the basic thrust and goals.

Finally, with his characteristic sense of urgency, Gorbachev has undertaken a concerted effort to mend relations with the PRC, a policy undoubtedly impelled by the growing Chinese-Western rapprochement. So far, aside from some progress in economic relations that may eventually improve the atmosphere in Sino-Soviet relationships, he seems to have made little headway with Beijing.

In the military realm Gorbachev's policies and actions to date—his arms control rhetoric, apparent concessions, and professed desire to reduce military expenditure notwithstanding—indicate little meaningful change from the past. Investment in the defense sector and military hardware production levels cannot yet be said to be all lower than they were when he came to power and, in some cases, are probably higher. No military weapons development program is known to have been cut or even significantly slowed. Arms deliveries to Soviet Third World clients have apparently continued at close to previous levels, with qualitative increases reported. The military evidently has been given more latitude in devising ways to win the war in Afghanistan and to assist the Cubans and Angolans against UNITA.

The economic reconstruction program accords top priority to the industries that sustain military strength, and efforts to introduce modern technology are concentrated in sectors in which the technologies have millitary applications. In fact, the entire economic program can be assessed as being at least as conducive to a modernization of the defense-industrial sector through introduction of new technologies as to any other goals.

Although the ministers of defense, Marshal Sokolov and his successor General Yazov, here has remained only a candidate member of the Politburo, the military brass is strongly represented in the Central Committee, and many of Gorbachev's appointees to the Council of Ministers and in the Central Committee and Secretariat have backgrounds in the defense-industrial sector. But even if one assumes that the anti-nuclear tenets of the new leadership's pronouncements are genuine new aspects of Soviet military doctrine, they may still be intended to give Moscow a better chance to exploit conventional superiorities in a world in which conventional conflicts would no longer carry the threat of escalating into nuclear ones. This non-nuclear war-fighting goal has been clearly indicated in much military theoretical writing for several years. Ultimately, therefore, the antinuclear creed of Gorbachev's time does little to lower the intensity of global competition, and in the absence of meaningful nuclear deterrents may even increase the danger of outbreaks of conventional warfare.

Much of what Gorbachev has accomplished can be attributed to such favorable circumstances or inescapable realities as the old age, debility, and malperformance of most of his rivals; the growing recognition that things could not be allowed to continue to drift, and that any change was better than no change; the shifts in alliances and in the relative influence of various Soviet institutions acting as interest groups that had occurred under his predecessors; and changes in the international environment caused by factors both impersonal and personal, the dynamic activism of the new U.S. president prominent among the latter. But such circumstances do not account for the whole story. Something must be attributed to Gorbachev the man.

Gorbachev is clearly a dynamic, highly competent, and energetic leader—conceivably the most capable at least since Stalin. Moreover, in spite of the rough, almost comic-opera unpredictability of Khrushchev and in spite of the obvious malperformance of the subsequent Soviet leaders since about 1976 at least, it must be kept in mind that not one of Gorbachev's predecessors, including even the hapless Chernenko, got to the top by being an incompetent or a fool. The skills that got Gorbachev where he is now can be expected to help him to stay there, barring an unlikely sudden health problem or major policy failures. And even the latter, if they stop short of being downright disastrous, might be something that this resourceful Soviet politician would be able to weather. So far, his foreign policy ventures have produced mostly atmospherics and a sense of movement. Concrete achievements are few. But he has laid the groundwork for a much more active and adroit Soviet foreign policy. This man, who will probably remain general secretary for some time to come, may well develop into the cleverest strategist of them all, the most capable adversary the West has yet to face in the "historic struggle."

In discussing Gorbachev the man, we cannot ignore his ultimate intentions. It cannot be entirely precluded that he is a type of Soviet "closet liberal," at least in economics and foreign policy. Human history abounds in oddities, and Gorbachev's "closet liberalism" could conceivably be one of them. Still, it would be an oddity indeed: His whole background, entire political socialization, personal (as part of the CPSU) dependence on the legitimizing aspects of the struggle to defeat capitalism, and—on top of all this—everything he has done to date argue against the "closet liberalism" hypothesis. It is far more certain that Gorbachev is committed to the Soviet brand of socialism, to maintaining and increasing the relative strength of the Soviet state compared to the West, to the pursuit of the "historic struggle," and to transforming the world in Moscow's image. What we have seen thus far is most probably what we are likely to get in the future. Gorbachev is a problem solver, a tenacious competitor, and in the Soviet context, a pragmatist. In fact, as we shall argue in the final chapter, it is probably irrelevant to the course of global politics and even to the future of the USSR, if, contrary to all the evidence, Gorbachev is a closet liberal.

One truly striking thing about the policy structure that Gorbachev and his associates have thus far erected is the way in which all components of that structure interact. Like a house of cards, each policy reinforces every other policy. But also like a house of cards, the entire edifice appears to depend to a large extent on almost each policy component upon which it rests. This mutually supportive and mutually interdependent nature of Gorbachev's policies is readily detectable no matter from which angle one looks at them.

Societal discipline, economic restructuring, and foreign policies all call for and prop up a cadres policy devised to consolidate Gorbachev's personal power. Success, or at least absence of serious setbacks, in each of the three policy areas is essential to prevent the emergence of a support base for Gorbachev's potential rivals. Preservation of power, societal discipline, a period of East-West detente, and deceleration of the arms race are all crucial for the success of his economic program. Economic improvement and all its prerequisites are a key element in sweetening the imposition of harsh societal discipline by offering material rewards and incentives. At the same time unchallenged personal control, a more disciplined society, a more sophisticated foreign policy, and especially an economic infrastructure advanced enough to absorb new high technologies to maximum benefit are sine qua nons of successful competition in the global struggle, whether pursued by armed force or by any other means. In addition, the inner coherence of this policy complex provides a strong argument for the hypothesis that within the present leadership Gorbachev enjoys a wide consensus for most, if not all, of his policies. This would in turn indicate that the clear evidence of resistance to the implementation of his policies is more a matter of systemic inertia than of principled opposition.

Some analysts have reached different conclusions about Gorbachev and his policy intentions than we have. By examining the word and actions relative to one or two of Gorbachev's policy arenas it is possible to see him as a true liberal, or as a man struggling to change his Neanderthal compatriots, or as hedged in by the KGB or the military. By projecting one's own values and hopes and by focusing on words rather than all the related specifics, it is easy to acclaim him as a peacemaker or as a nuclear disarmer. But when one considers all the various materials that we have examined in this book, it is difficult to bring such conclusions into consonance with the evidence from all of the separate areas examined. Taken together, the separate strands of evidence related to different aspects of Gorbachev's policies provide a strikingly coherent, mutually reinforcing set of conclusions.

Once one looks behind the new style, the dynamism and the edifice of ostensible major reforms, most of which are hardly major as yet—in effect when one looks at the reality under the emperor's new clothes—Mikhail Gorbachev is revealed as but one more variant in a consistent train of Soviet leaders, and the Soviet Union remains basically what it has been all along. At the same time Gorbachev has set in motion trends that may well transform aspects of Soviet reality. In this regard the things that he has tried to do to revitalize the system while retaining its basic nature may well not be what they seem to him to be. Whether he realizes it or not, Gorbachev has opened a pandora's box of new pressures on the system he wishes to maintain.

14

The Past Is but Prologue:
Projections for the Future

To prophesy is extremely difficult—especially with regard to the future.

—A Chinese proverb

It is difficult and even problematic to attempt to sketch Gorbachev's future course: where his interlocking policies will take him, the USSR, and inevitably, the world that must live with the Soviet Union. Not even the time-honored easy way out—the staid straight-line projection—is really useful very far into the future.

The Gorbachev leadership may well have set out only to revitalize the economy and society, to make them work, without changing the basic system supporting the Party monopoly of power and centralized control. It may also have set out simply to find better tactics with which to pursue just as ardently the expansion of Soviet power, the "historic" global struggle, and inevitably, the long-term generalized objective of Soviet global predominance. But in each case the strategies chosen, and in many ways forced upon the Gorbachev leadership by internal conditions and external forces, have inexorably led to domestic measures and foreign policy activities that seem certain to carry Gorbachev and the USSR to major forks in the road.

Only for the near-term future is a straight-line projection both reasonable and fully justified by the evidence we have examined. But that same evidence indicates that the trend consists of incrementally adding new reforms, new concessions and new initiatives that strain the existing systemic and foreign policy fabric, all in the effort to make the chosen but so far basically unsuccessful strategy succeed.

The dilemma is that the chosen strategy seeks two contradictory goals. The first is to preserve the system of power, of *kto-kogo*, and represents the direct continuation of the aggressive, totalitarian Soviet state as well as

369

Gorbachev's personal struggle in the pattern of every Soviet contender for political power to become the traditional *vozhd*. The second goal is to take an ossified, declining socioeconomic system that has reached close to its limits and inject into it the vitality, dynamism, and adaptability necessary to face current and future challenges. The root of the contradiction between these two goals is that the very features of the socioeconomic system that have caused it to become ossified and go into decline, the features that inhibit vitality, dynamism, and adaptability, are precisely the ones that support and maintain the power structure system. Gorbachev is trying to square the circle, and it is not at all certain that he can find a workable balance between these conflicting imperatives.

The current trends of Gorbachev's policies can be expected to continue for a while, but then they will inevitably reach the point at which they may well proceed in varying directions. In other words, using decision-tree analogy, choices will either have to be made or events will take things along in new directions. This latter possibility is the slippery slope to which we have several times alluded in earlier chapters.

The trends in Gorbachev's policies can potentially develop in several radically different directions. It is not difficult to identify the alternatives, but the prediction of the actual choices that will be made, or that will come about regardless of the conscious intentions of the leadership, is problematical at best. Nevertheless, we will attempt to suggest the outcome of these forks in the road ahead.

The primary keys are the interaction of personal power and consensus building, and the success or failure of economic programs. These are central and they will determine much of the foreign policy approach. Nevertheless, foreign policy, particularly as it interacts with internal power considerations, is also important. It has the potential to substitute for domestic economic failure in building and maintaining Gorbachev's personal authority. In addition, it is a major ingredient in the chosen strategy of socioeconomic revitalization. In other words, there is a definite and very important feedback effect. Inevitably, then, the definition of the forks in the road—the decision points—is in part determined by the actions and choices of external actors in the international arena.

Initially, the dominant trend of Gorbachev's policies was fully consistent with the Soviet past. The only real difference was the almost unprecedented pace. His early economic reforms, up to the Party Congress in March 1986, were intended to generate new movement in the economy, but they were far more the vehicle by which Gorbachev was to achieve his place in history and through which he was able to consolidate personal power by purging the old elite. The principle of *glasnost* did not entail the free expression of people's views. It was strictly confined to the bounds of permitted frankness against acceptable or designated targets. *Glasnost* was not a moral imperative, although it may in part have reflected Gorbachev's own confidence in the system's capabilities and his belief in the utility of a somewhat greater amount of subordinate feedback in implementing policy. *Glasnost* is basically a utilitarian device that the regime, and particularly Gorbachev himself, can exploit in order to criticize undesirable social phenomena and Party leaders whose replacement is desired. It is another in a long line of Soviet psychological tactics to mobilize the populace without giving it any real voice.

By the XXVII Party Congress, Gorbachev had basically succeeded in consolidating power at the top, although there were a few loose ends remaining, and the combination of very limited reform and the psychological impact of a more dynamic, newer, and younger leadership had produced some favorable improvements in economic performance. This relatively successful beginning lasted only a short while; it quickly became apparent that massive resistance to change, potentially leading to the emergence of serious political opposition, still existed at middle and lower levels and that the economy was sliding back toward decline. The very limited reforms had succeeded only in temporarily taking up some of the slack in the existing economic structure.

Gorbachev and his associates had placed their personal prestige, and hence their futures, on achieving successes in the policy lines they had chosen and that had become identified with them. The logical—and perhaps inevitable—step was to test the limits further, to introduce new, slightly more radical reforms in the economy, and to increase the effort to mobilize the population by stretching the boundaries of *glasnost*. In turn this also required the resumption of the personnel shakeups and purges, including in December of 1986, a purge of one of the few loose ends in restructuring the senior leadership: Dinmukhamed Kunaev, Brezhnev's old crony and protégé in Kazakhstan. Then another holdover, Zimyanin, was removed from the Politburo in January and in both January and June 1987 Gorbachev pushed through major additions and promotions for his proteges.

Shakeups and purges were all the more necessary because Gorbachev had not yet achieved the kind of foreign policy success that could temporarily substitute for continued frustrations in the economy at home. At the same time that he expanded his socioeconomic reforms and purges at home, Gorbachev (as noted in the preceding chapter) threw the dice in a dramatic and well thought out and prepared gamble to achieve just such a foreign policy coup: to break down the barriers against increased access to Western investment and technology and to boost his economic program by presumably justifying a greater shift in share of the economic pie from the military to the civilian sector.

The reforms introduced in the latter part of 1986 and the first half of

1987 are similar to the earlier ones in that they also mostly operate at the periphery of the centralized, totalitarian system. However, they differ in that they more truly stretch the fabric of that system, or at least would do so if they were really allowed to operate as depicted. Moreover, they threaten the comfortable positions of a larger number of bureaucrats within the Party and state *nomenklatura*. Like the earlier more limited reforms they are also likely to produce some initial improvements; but just as with the previous phase, the improvements are likely to be ephemeral. Eventually, Gorbachev will have to face the inherent dilemma of the economy. Either we will have to keep extending his reforms further into the heart of the system, challenging the principles of centralization, production planning, and government monopoly on prices and property and thereby undermine the totalitarian foundations of the regime, or in effect he will have to return or attempt to return the economy to the situation that obtained when he came to power. A third alternative, that of significantly shifting resources away from heavy and defense industries would help the economy, but probably only temporarily since it would still not fully address the systemic barriers to efficiency. Moreover, as long as the US military challenge retains vitality and without continuing Soviet foreign policy successes, this would almost certainly generate major opposition within the Party leadership and from the defense establishment—something it might do under any circumstances.

The later reforms can meanwhile be expected to give him a measure of time before he has to push the limits further. The outcome of his arms control strategy and the actions of other actors in the international arena may help extend this period of respite, but they have also introduced elements that could add to the internal strains and bring the day of reckoning closer.

Reykjavik did not mark a clear foreign policy breakthrough providing Gorbachev with the kind of dramatic success that would insure his place in Soviet history and lead to the kind of tactical detente by which he has sought to boost his domestic economic program without risking his and the Party's power. But it did result in what may prove to be a highly significant tactical success that could lead to such results in the future. The Reykjavik gambit of seeking to place on the U.S. administration all blame for the lack of progress in arms control inevitably strikes a resonant chord with a wide body of Western European and even U.S. public opinion. Moreover, it could have similar, if lesser, effects as a corollary to Moscow's efforts to focus Third World opinion on the West and the United States as the source of all ills. Even if Reykjavik did not produce enough pressure on the Reagan administration to force it to hand Gorbachev a major foreign policy success, it seemed sure both to buy him time and to guarantee that he will continue further along the foreign policy paths he has chosen.

Other foreign developments, particularly in the United States, could serve Gorbachev's purposes just as well and more painlessly. The combination of the blunders of the Reagan team (e.g. Iran) and the U.S. budget dilemma threaten either to lead to unilaterally emasculation of SDI, the Reagan military buildup, and U.S. international activism or to force Washington to accede to Gorbachev's arms control package without linking it to Soviet human rights or Third World behavior. This prospect—of which Moscow is well aware and for which it is hoping—also serves both to reduce the urgency for further dangerous domestic economic reform and to discourage Gorbachev's would-be rivals from challenging him on the basis of foreign or military policy. Gorbachev can do relatively little to promote this possibility actively except to avoid the kind of egregious foreign adventure or massive domestic repression that would frighten accommodationists in the West.

Nevertheless, the logic of the post-Reykjavik situation seems to have pushed Gorbachev toward another kind of domestic risk. The situation and possibilities resulting from the meeting in Iceland, and U.S. domestic politics, have to be seen as a primary impetus to Gorbachev's further pushing *glasnost* in the USSR and making such dramatic gestures as the release of Andrei Sakharov from internal exile.

Glasnost poses a real danger in that it might get out of control. It could gather a momentum of its own and become criticism of phenomena and people that the regime does not want criticized, including the regime itself. Even if it does not go that far, it seems almost certain to encourage potential political rivals to seek other, more promising vehicles with which to mount effective opposition. Already it has to be upsetting to traditionalists among the Soviet elite. If *glasnost* does go too far, one alternative for Gorbachev would be to broaden it until it truly became freedom of opinion. This would almost certainly clash with the basic system and with the requirement to protect the primacy of the Party. The other alternative would be to close *glasnost* off after the carefully controlled doses currently being administered have served their purposes.

So far the freeing of Sakharov, like the careful dribble of gestures involving other prominent refuseniks and dissidents, is still clearly only a tactic to impress the West. The basic, broader system of repression and human rights violations continues. Nevertheless, by freeing Sakharov to resume his activity *in the USSR* as Sakharov has done (and not, for example, expelling him, as was done to Solzhenitsyn), Gorbachev has in effect admitted that the regime itself had committed a grave injustice and given credence to other internal, "subversive" critics of the system. He has also opened wider a partially closed window through which foreign observers may be reminded of the nature of the Soviet tyranny by future words from Sakharov himself. Why, then, this move? The obvious answer appears to be that it was intended to build on all of Gorbachev's careful efforts to influence foreign opinion. Moreover, it suggests that Gorbachev believes that he is sufficiently strong at home to risk the potential discomfort to the system and to himself. One other possibility must be considered, one that could not be fully confirmed yet when these words were written. Sakharov was a powerful proponent of arms control in the past, but one who simultaneously supported the U.S. buildup and SDI as the best way to force the USSR to agree to real arms control and modify its aggressive foreign and domestic policies. Already Sakharov has said that he does not think SDI is militarily viable, but also that the Soviet position that the United States drop its research into the program as a condition for any arms control agreement is "illegal and improper." It may be that Gorbachev expects Sakharov's future statements to support Moscow's arms control policies even more fully.

Given all of the above circumstances, it can be expected that the basic thrust and pattern of Gorbachev's policy lines will persist in the relatively near-term future.

Personnel turnover should continue, especially at the middle and lower echelons as Gorbachev attempts to extend his consolidation of power, find scapegoats for continued economic failures, and goad the bureaucrats to improve their performance. He can also be expected to seek to free himself from the remaining holdovers from the past among the top leadership. Shcherbitskiy, because of his age and long affiliation with the old guard, is the most likely candidate to be next to go. Aliev's long term future is also quite problematical. Others are not so much in full jeopardy, but now that Yakovlev, Slyunkov and Nikonov (all Gorbachev proteges) have joined the list of CC Secretaries who are concurrently full Politburo Members, Ligachev's importance can be expected to steadily decrease. In regard to the senior state (as opposed to Party) leadership where the eighty year old First Deputy Chairman of the Council of Ministers, Arkhipov was retired (in October, 1986), the same factors—as expected—led to the replacement of the seventy-four year old Antonov as Deputy Chairman, Council of Ministers in summer 1987. One other council of Ministers Deputy Chairman was also removed; although he was younger than Arkhipov and Antonov, Shcherbina was a Ukrainian with presumable ties to Shcherbitskiy and the old Brezhnev clique. Similarly the shift of another Ukrainian, Marchuk, from Deputy Chairman, Council of Ministers to the more honorific post of President of the Academy of Sciences (in fall, 1986) was also quite possibly related to his ties with Shcherbitskiy.

Shcherbitskiy's ouster may take a bit longer. His position is stronger than Kunaev's was and the preliminary groundwork within the local Party structure has apparently not proceeded as far in the Ukraine as in Kazakhstan.

Moreover, the justification for Kunaev's removal was bolstered by the fact that the Kazakh agricultural harvest was a particular disaster. Further, the Ukraine, as the only one of the two non-Great-Russian Slavic republics with a bonafide nationalistic history is perhaps the one Union Republic in which the central authorities have always moved the most cautiously since the time of Stalin. Still, the Chernobyl disaster (which faciliated criticism and replacements in the Ukrainian Party nomenklatura), the direct personal criticism of Brezhnev which appeared in December, 1986, and the exposure of corruption in an office of the KGB (!) in the Ukraine in January, 1987, all seemed to mark a major political offensive against Shcherbitskiy—an offensive which was reportedly intended to culminate in his removal at the delayed January CC Plenum. The very careful and adaptable Shcherbitskiy survived this challenge and was still in place after June, 1987 (possibly with the help of others who saw their own power being diluted by Gorbachev's packing of the Secretariat and Politburo with his own proteges), but clearly his days are numbered.

Sooner or later, it is also very likely that we shall see the Minister of Defense promoted to full membership in the Politburo now that Gorbachev has replaced Sokolov with his own choice as head of the defense establishment. The defense leadership has so far supported Gorbachev's policies, but there is probably a limit to that support if he fails to succeed in his chosen tactics to eliminate the threats of the SDI (or if he really chooses to significantly shift resources and investment from heavy to light industry). If he is to avoid defense establishment opposition to his policies, Gorbachev must continue to either coopt this important constituency or he must bring it under full personal control—something which he appeared ready to attempt after the Rust incident gave him the opportunity to sack Marshal Sokolov and turn loose a protege (Yeltsin) to openly criticize the military in general (as discussed in chapter 12).

Meanwhile, Gromyko—already partially removed from real power—has his days numbered if by nothing else than age and health. In fact, Demichev (who is also vulnerable due to his long association with the Brezhnev reign) has increasingly substituted for Gromyko in many official meetings.

Likewise, the discipline-strengthening and anti-corruption campaigns can be expected to continue—and to be as selectively applied as before. In this regard, the treatment of dissidents is of special interest. Some have been released and allowed to resume limited agitation and a number of Jewish "refuseniks" have been allowed to emigrate as part of the modest increase (modest by previous highs and in relation to what would likely happen if all bars were removed) in overall Jewish emigration. On the other hand, there have been many indications of an increased crack-down on other manifestations of dissidence and one can only estimate the (undoubtedly large) numbers of dissidents and would-be emigrants who are still repressed. In fact the record strongly suggests a conscious strategy of accomodating highly visible dissidents and would-be emigrants in order to impress the West while making sure that the real situation in human rights does not change. For any really full freedom for Jews and others to emigrate two other things would be required. First, there could not be any clearly stated legal obligation imposed on the Kremlin (at least no more legal obligation that already extant in signed—and ignored—treaties dealing with human rights in generalized terms). Soviet "face" would have to be preserved. Second Moscow would have to be seeking continued additional concessions from the West. Once Gorbachev obtains all the concessions he seeks, he will no longer need to make further Soviet accomodations. It follows that further Soviet concessions on emigration and human rights in general are most likely to come about as a result of steadfast pressure, by "holding Gorbachev's feet to the fire," by the West not signing accords on arms control and regional issues in isolation (as the Soviets wish) without insisting on meaningful linkages—unless such agreements are clearly in the West's interest on their own merits. Meanwhile, emigration barriers are unlikely to be loosened much more than they already have in 1987. Concurrently, the most likely thing to happen would be the continuation of the sporadic release of prominent dissidents to satisfy the West while the great mass of unknown political prisoners continue to languish in obscurity. Crackdowns on any new or expanded anti-regime (or dissident) activities may even intensify since one of Gorbachev's main purposes is most probably the reduction of the numbers and the visibility of the applicants for emigration in order to minimize the price that may have to be paid for detente on his terms.

In foreign policy, Gorbachev is also likely to continue his current course, but his policies in regard to the US and arms control will probably reach critical decision points sooner than his domestic policies. After what he agreed to at Reykjavik there could not be very many more concessions Gorbachev could make. In spring of 1987 he made perhaps the last he could by agreeing to an INF treaty without tying it to SDI and in further agreeing to simultaneous negotiating of agreement on shorter range nuclear weapons. Of course, by the end of summer it still remained to be seen whether he would stick to this or once again revert to the SDI-related linkage. Moreover, the decision to resume nuclear testing strongly suggested that these limits had been reached.

Undoubtedly, the Kremlin will continue to carefully evaluate the extent to which West European and US political opinion buys the idea that Reagan and the SDI are to blame for the failure to reach a dramatic arms control agreement and the degree to which budgetary and election-year political fallout will destroy the basic defense and foreign policies of the Reagan administration. If either of these trends shows real promise of a victory "on the cheap," Gorbachev may up the ante by another dramatic unilateral concession such as resumption of the nuclear test moratorium after enough tests have been conducted to mollify his own defense planners.

European developments could also affect these considerations. The conservative Kohl government in the FRG seems safe, but the English elections (expected in 1987) may be up for grabs. An anti-Washington, anti-nuclear victory in a major European country could well tip the scales in favor of Gorbachev's fallback strategy of selective dentente with Europe even if the signs in Washington pointed toward a continued Reagan-type military buildup and no agreement had been reached with the Americans.

Without other factors and developments interfering, this approach to the central issues with the United States seems likely to continue at least until after the 1988 presidential elections—although, all things being equal, Gorbachev may well try another public relations gambit (concessions or something similar to Reykjavik) to achieve his goals by trying to exploit or influence the U.S. political scene.

Domestically, Gorbachev is likely initially to let his most recent economic reforms run their course. If, as seems almost certain, their result is again a very temporary improvement in Soviet economic performance, he will then and perhaps fairly soon, either have to cut them short or go further along that slippery slope. Considering the main (U.S.-related) foreign policy orientation, he may not have to reach more fundamental decision points on how far to push domestic reform until after 1988.

All such speculations, however, assume the absence of a new major opportunity or confrontation in the Third World. As long as Gorbachev sticks to his current policies, he is unlikely to initiate developments in this direction. However, such developments may occur without Gorbachev's being able to control them. Another limited U.S. military action, similar to that in Libya in 1986, would probably turn out to be nothing more than another "hiccup" in the process of seeking detente with the United States, but this would depend upon the scale and circumstances of such action, and especially upon whether the action would be another one-time affair or whether it became a recurrent policy. If U.S. actions of this sort do continue, Gorbachev would probably in the end be driven toward one of his fallback policies.

A more serious development would be a major Third World conflict, such as another Middle East war between superpower clients. This would undoubtedly considerably cool U.S.-Soviet relations for some time. On the other hand, if the superpowers succeed in visibly cooperating in terminat-

ing the war and if neither is driven out of the region entirely by its oppo-
nent, a Middle East war could even be a catalyst for subsequently drawing
Moscow and Washington closer to agreement on other issues.

A truly major opportunity, such as the collapse of the Pretoria regime
and a civil war in South Africa, particularly a multisided civil war in which
the blacks were divided into pro-Moscow forces (say, the ANC) and pro-
Western forces (say, Chief Buthelezi and his Zulus), would probably be too
much of a temptation for Moscow to resist. This particularly could be the
case if Gorbachev were not in too much economic trouble at home and if
detente were still not either well under way or highly promising. In the
longer term the shape of the Soviet economy would probably turn out to be
the more critical of the two factors. The Kremlin could well find the temptation sufficiently irresistible to risk upsetting any detente as long as the
economy was functioning even only more or less satisfactorily. On the
other hand, if current efforts to find a way to win militarily continue to fail
in Afghanistan, Gorbachev may try harder to find a diplomatic solution to
Soviet problems there. This could include an offer to withdraw the Soviet
forces back behind the border in return for a complete cessation of all
external support to the Afghan rebels (including that from Pakistan, from
the West and even from the PRC). Needless to say, such a formula would do
nothing to stop Soviet military assistance and supply to the Kabul regime.
Under such circumstances and with the extensive infrastructure the Soviets
have built in Afghanistan and with the Soviet army remaining just across
the border, this would almost certainly be a ploy to appear to exit with
grace while doing the maximum to ensure the survival of a fully client
regime in Kabul.

One other potential development, not very likely but possible, could
have a quite forceful impact upon Soviet policies. This would be a global
economic collapse that would particularly hit the Western economies. In
such a case the Soviet economy might well be much less affected, with the
result that the men in the Kremlin would probably be irresistibly tempted
to play political and political-military "hardball" with the West.

In the longer term Gorbachev faces still more fundamental problems.
They mostly stem from internal conditions but can be greatly accelerated
or decelerated by external factors. The central problem is the Soviet economy. In the absence of a more significant systemic reform of the economic
structure, there is probably a very definite limit to the improvements his
programs can achieve. After this point is reached, the Soviet economy is
quite likely to succumb to another, more permanent, decline. This is likely
to happen even if the USSR succeeds through detente in obtaining increased access to Western trade, credits, and technology. Such access, even
on the scale reached in the mid-1970s (and how much more can real-

istically be expected?) would probably suffice only to postpone Moscow's economic day of reckoning, not prevent it. Importing technology is not enough. The critical factor is the Soviet ability, thus far quite problematic, to absorb this technology in the production of anything other than a few serially produced items of military hardware. A major rise in world oil prices, which would improve the Soviet balance of payments and hurt the Western economies, would also help postpone the day of reckoning. But sooner or later that day will probably arrive. The men in the Kremlin will be faced with some tough choices at that point.

The exact nature of those choices depends upon several circumstances. The choices would be very much affected by the extent of any discontent within the Soviet population. There would also be a significant difference whether economic collapse would occur suddenly or, as is far more likely, would come as a result of a protracted period of slow but inexorable decline. Finally, economic decline would appear more tolerable for the Soviet leadership if the West were simultaneously in economic trouble for one reason or another. For Soviet decision making, the "correlation of forces" is more critical than its own situation in isolation.

Basically, then, we are saying that the key to Soviet foreign policy lies in domestic politics, which in turn is inextricably tied up with Soviet economic structure and progress. Foreign policy results—and, equally, foreign policy developments outside direct Soviet influence and control—do impact domestic politics in a type of feedback loop and can occasionally substitute for domestic successes, but they are generally secondary to the internal scene.

In the final analysis even the Soviet Communist regime has to demonstrate to its citizens that it is socially and economically of value to them and that it is able to compete with Western societies. Unless eventual major reforms and a basic transformation of Soviet society take place, or unless the West either self-destructs or unilaterally gives up on maintaining the means to compete—which amounts to the same thing—the Soviet regime would have to accept failure of its domestic policies and seek confirmation of its power and survivability in an aggressive foreign policy.

Gorbachev has introduced factors into this complex equation that could significantly change Soviet political dynamics and thus the outcome. For the first time since the brief "romantic" period of the Revolution, Gorbachev is bringing the popular masses into the active political scene. He appeals to the people, meets with them, calls for their support, and even "consults" with them. Of course, one should not exaggerate this trend. The popular masses still play very much a supporting role; they are still "extras" in the social drama being staged. Moreover, Gorbachev is not the first Soviet leader to nudge political activity out of the exclusive precincts of the

Party sphere. For the first thirty-five years or so, during the time of Lenin and Stalin, policy was set exclusively in the corridors of the Party or, more precisely, of the Party apparat. (In fact, in the latter part of this early period, policy was basically set by one man alone, Stalin, although the apparat could influence its implementation.) It was there that economic plans were made, social norms set, leaders removed from power, and others who won their way into grace were allowed to make successful careers. In brief, for more than three decades Soviet history was made by the Party apparat with practically no involvement by other social groups.

It was Khrushchev who, in his struggle to retain power, was the first to turn to an outside, non-Party, institution: the armed forces. After introducing the army into the political arena, he later fell victim to it when he was overthrown by his Party opponents with the support of the military. Brezhnev largely restored the primacy of the Party, but either by choice or necessity (more likely the latter) he kept the military in the picture. He tried to balance it by slightly increasing the roles of the security police and the foreign policy apparatus.

Then Andropov, in his struggle to attain power, again directly used an outside-the-Party institution: the state security organ, the KGB. Gorbachev, in turn, followed his mentor's model and also used the KGB to smooth his way to the top.

One should not overstate a trend, but trend it is. As we have noted before, the Party has remained supreme; other institutional forces have been used by Party rivals or themselves have directly influenced political developments only when the power struggles within the Party have allowed them to do so. Nevertheless, once given an entrance into the real political arena, these other forces have resisted subsequent exclusion and have not stayed passive. As a result, although the Party remains supreme, it is no longer fully exclusive; a power triangle (albeit a very unequal triangle) of the Party, the armed forces, and the KGB exists. Still, basically, the USSR remained a Partocracy, neither a military-Party complex or a military-Party-police complex.

Wittingly or not, Gorbachev may have carried this trend further. The additional factor that he has begun to introduce into the power equation, the popular masses, may not remain totally under the control of the CPSU leadership. If so, either under Gorbachev or his successors the existing triangle might come apart. Either it could be restructured as a quadrangle or other additional institutional or national groups might arise, adding to the complexity of the "geometry" characterizing the power model of Soviet politics. Needless to say, such an outcome would have profound effects upon the nature of the Soviet system. The growing influence of the armed forces and KGB as even factors in Soviet politics has not significantly affected the basically power-oriented and defensively aggressive or expansionistic nature of the system. On the other hand, new "players" arising out of the broader masses of the population are likely to have somewhat different values and objectives.

Such a political development is all the more possible because for really the first time in Soviet history Gorbachev has broken a sacred taboo: the principle of the inviolability and infallibility of the Party. Before Gorbachev, individual Party leaders might be subject to judgment, but the Partocracy itself, the ruling center, was unassailable. Khrushchev came close to breaking this rule, but he carefully attempted to restrict the blame to one leader, Stalin, and only in regard to the latter part of Stalin's long rule. Nevertheless, the inevitable implications of Party or systemic complicity set into motion immediate forces that convulsed the Soviet empire and brought into being the longer-term forces and dissidence with which Khrushchev's successors are still grappling.

In his campaign against corruption Gorbachev has for the first time attacked the Secretariat of the Party and the ministerial elite, and thereby cast doubt on the principle that the Party is above any reproach. Gorbachev initially attempted to restrict his campaign of discreditation to the lower and middle levels of the elite, but such a process may prove very difficult to limit. Unless it is halted or controlled, it could well reach into the higher levels of the elite as well. That this danger is not unrecognized is suggested by the fact that in December 1986 very specific personal criticism was directed against Brezhnev. This is comparable to Khrushchev's tactic of blaming Party failures and shortcomings of the system on one flawed individual and the "cult of the personality."

In all of this Gorbachev—even though he apparently is much more adroit and not vulnerable to criticism on account of his "comic," embarrassing style of behavior—could be in a position analogous to that of Khrushchev. His policies, like those of Khrushchev, have also jeopardized many a privileged member of the elite, and he too has cracked open the door to unsettling criticisms of Soviet perfection. Should he suffer a truly major foreign policy reverse, as Khrushchev did in Cuba, or as is more probable, should he suffer a string of foreign setbacks without succeeding in galvanizing the economy at home, his rule might be just as suddenly and surprisingly cut short. Such a development would probably mean a return to an essentially "conservative" leadership in the Brezhnev mold that would try to maintain the existing system at all costs.

Looking to the longer term and assuming (as we do) that Gorbachev's current economic program proves inadequate (a rather high-confidence assumption), we believe he will have to choose between two basic options. One would be to hang tough on maintaining the centralized command economy with all its shortcomings. This would almost certainly require a great increase in repression and control, possibly short of a full-scale reversion to arbitrary Stalinist terror over the Party but almost certainly a no less arbitrary rule by a possibly more sophisticated terror over the general population. If the economic slide is gradual, the tightening of the police screws can also be gradual. In such a situation Gorbachev would then also need to undertake another major turnover of the top leadership—both to provide himself with scapegoats and to forestall the rivals who would then be sure to emerge.

The hard-line domestic option would also probably have to be accompanied with a much harder international policy line, simply because the safest way for a Soviet leader to crack down at home is to exaggerate the foreign threat and thus appeal to Soviet patriotism and to the self-interest of Soviet hard-liners, particularly in the KGB and military establishments. In this way the Kremlin could conceivably be pushed to embark on very risky foreign adventures as a distraction from and as a justification for domestic repression. But unless the domestic temperature had risen very high indeed, the more likely course would be increased cold war rhetoric accompanied, as usual, by a quite cautious foreign policy performance. The most likely long-term outcome in such a case would be the slow slide of the USSR into irrelevance, which may even portend a day in the distant future when the dictatorship of the CPSU collapses.

As a problem solver and Soviet-type pragmatist, Gorbachev is quite likely to anticipate such long-term consequences. This is what may well predispose him toward the second basic option: major systemic reforms of the economy and, possibly, of the body politic. (One must not confuse the rationalization of the economy with political democracy and/or an absence of an aggressive, expansionistic foreign policy. Nazi Germany stands as a premier example of the fact that the latter two characteristics do not necessarily accompany economic efficiency.) This option is bound to threaten significantly the legitimacy of the CPSU's rule, and thereby the power, privileges, and perquisites of the present Soviet elite. Consequently, systemic reform would probably have to be carried out incrementally—but like a snowball rolling down a long hill, it could accumulate momentum and weight with surprising rapidity.

Although internal politics and economics are central to all Soviet policies, including foreign policy, external relations could significantly tip the scales in the direction of either the first or the second basic option. Success in removing the challenge of the U.S. military buildup and in obtaining foreign investment, trade, and technology would put off the day of reckoning. If accompanied or followed by further dramatic successes in splitting the West or in major areas of the Third World, the result would probably be a strengthening of the totalitarian system at home and a stepped-up aggressiveness abroad. Serious foreign setbacks, not just the continuation of the present standoff, could work either way. If not too dramatic and regime threatening, such setbacks could well accelerate the process of serious reform at home. If the setbacks were too severe, the more likely outcome would be to so frighten the men in the Kremlin that they would harshly crack down at home and might even strike out in a desperate attempt to save themselves. The clear implication of the latter probability is that the Western world is best served by continued vigilance, a strong defense, determination to contain further Soviet aggressive advances, and by not giving Moscow any economic or military balance-of-power gains without demanding an accompanying shift in Soviet internal policies and/or Soviet actions in Third World arenas of competition and instability. A concomitant implication is that the West must very carefully consider the possible outcomes before attempting *to intiate* any major efforts to break up the Soviet empire or destroy the regime in Moscow. Meanwhile, either as a result of the combination of Gorbachev's adroit tactics and Western hopes and/or naivete, or as a corollary to real internal reform in the USSR, a period of detente might be reestablished.

What would then be the meaning of a new detente if Gorbachev succeeds in achieving one? The point is that no East-West detente can end the "historical struggle" for global predominance—except if, rather inconceivably, an outside threat appears, compelling enough to unite the United States and USSR. The internalized contents of Soviet ideology and, even more so, the imperative of providing constant legitimization for that ideology guarantee that the "struggle" will persist. Still, regardless of all ideology, the mere existence of two separate national power centers whose overall military and economic strength is disproportionate to that of the rest of the world inevitably spells conflicts of interest and competition. Should the international system really change from an essentially bipolar to a genuinely multipolar model, the competition between the contenders might well shift to a more fluid pattern involving variable alliances. But for better or worse, both the Communist ideology and the bipolarity in the world's international system are still with us and are unlikely to suddenly vanish into thin air. Western European unity is still unconsummated; Japan is still a very one-dimensional (i.e., economic) superpower; and both Western Europe and Japan are still closely tied to the United States. Potential future superpowers, such as China and conceivably India or Brazil, still have a very long and perilous distance to traverse. It follows that any conceivable detente can only be incomplete and partial, with recurring strains appearing as new confrontations and opportunities for either side arise around the world. The terms of reference would change but the end result would very likely be another period similar to the first half of the 1970s, when Western restraint permitted the USSR to seek vigorously greater latitude for its actions in the Third World.

Significantly, these prospects are unrelated to Gorbachev the man. Should he fall from power or die suddenly, any of his rivals or successors will have to face essentially the same constraints and make choices within the same ranges of options. This is also a reason to perceive Gorbachev's intentions as irrelevant. Even if Gorbachev were a closet liberal, a man who because of his principles secretly yearns to transform the Soviet system rather than just to make it work more effectively, he would be limited by the constraints of the system of which he is a part. Stalin did not face similar constraints because his control over every part of the system precluded any limitations upon free exercise of his will. Short of a return to full-scale Stalinism, Gorbachev cannot just impose his own will without considering what the rest of the leadership is prepared to do or forced to do and what imposing his will would mean for his own personal power. Moreover, the kind of total Stalinist control Gorbachev would need in order to impose his will freely on the rest of the leadership, power elite, and institutional bureaucracies would require a heavy reliance on the loyalty of the KGB and security organs, i.e. on the least likely source of support for systemic political or economic change.

On the other hand, once the combination of internal and external conditions brings the day of reckoning that we have anticipated, Gorbachev or any other Soviet leader might be forced to make systemic reforms. Among those currently identifiable on the Soviet political scene, Gorbachev, the pragmatic problem solver, seems to be the one then most likely to prefer systemic reforms to the return to Stalinism or to just "hanging on." Nevertheless, it does not follow that others, under the same conditions, would necessarily make a different choice.

Some final points must be stressed rather forcefully. One should not expect the day of reckoning to come either very soon or painlessly. Accelerating economic and social reforms could bring about fairly sudden changes in the USSR; but an excess of rising popular expectations which got out of hand would certainly lead to an internal political convulsion in which the winners are most likely to be a different group of hard liners. The kind of change which avoids a modern, Soviet thermidor will probably have to be slow and evolutionary—in fits and starts—rather than sudden and dramatic. A real day of reckoning is much more likely to come as a consequence of major international confrontations yet to unfold than in any way which would spare us from the dangers of such confrontations. History does show that major political changes can occasionally happen with suddenness—but almost only when they are triggered by cataclysmic wars or economic collapse. The Soviet Union is a vast, rich and resilent country and the mechanisms of control exercised by the CPSU remain pervasive and tight. Furthermore, quite independent of the East-West rivalry, continuing global conflicts of interest such as the so-called North-South issues and the self-containment of nation states guarantee multiple and recurring conflicts. We live in a world marked by growing interdependence, the eventual depletion of at least some natural resources vital to basic needs, and the dislocations inherent in the transition of the advanced states from the industrial to the post-industrial age while many states are still trying to reach the industrial age. In this period of multiple conflicts, both the East and the West and some others possess cataclysmic weaponry and huge military arsenals. Taken all together, this virtually guarantees that the relative strengths and preponderence compared to other constellations of power of the East and West blocs are unlikely to change dramatically or quickly. If the preponderence in national or bloc power does not change, history teaches us that the superpowers (the U.S. and the U.S.S.R.) will continue to be rivals no matter what changes occur in their forms of government. On the other hand, those who look forward to the imminent collapse of the Soviet economy or to the USSR becoming irrelevant in global power struggles would be well advised to recall an old Russian proverb: "A year is but a day!"

Appendix I
Changes in the Council of Ministers, Ministers, and Chairman of State Committees

Announced since Gorbachev Became General Secretary

March 1985

Minister of energy and electrification   *A.I. Maiorets* (former minister of electrotechnical industry) appointed. P.S. Neporozhniy *retired*; health.

Note: Retirements ascribed to health reasons are in accord with reports in the Soviet press. In some cases, perhaps most, this is probably at least only partly true and may be only a gesture.

May 1985

Deputy chairman, Council of Ministers   I.I. Bodyula *retired*; health.
Minister of transport construction   *V.A. Brezhnev* appointed.
      I.D. Sosnov *retired*; health.
Minister of electrotechnical industry   *G.P. Voronovskiy* appointed.
      A.I. Maiorets previously reassigned (see above).

July 1985

Minister of foreign affairs   *E.A. Shevardnadze* appointed.
      A.A. Gromyko named chairman, Presidium of the Supreme Soviet.
Minister of ferrous metallurgical industry   *S.V. Kolpakov* appointed.
      I.P. Kazanets *retired*; health.
Minister of light industry   *V.G. Klyuev* appointed.
      N.N. Tarasov *retired*.
Minister of industrial construction   *A.N. Shchepetilnikov* appointed.
      Yu.F. Solovev reassigned.
Minister of industrial construction materials   *S.F. Voyenushkin* appointed.
      A.I. Yashin *retired*.

| Minister of higher and intermediate specialized education | G.A. Yagodin appointed. V.P. Yelyutin retired. |

August 1985

| Minister of machine building for construction, urban and interurban roads | E.A. Varnachev appointed. V.I. Chudin retired; health. |

September 1985

| Chairman, Council of Ministers | N.Z. Ryzhkov appointed. N.A. Tikhonov retired; health. |

October 1986

Chairman, State Planning Committee, and Deputy chairman, Council of Ministers	N.V. Talyzin appointed; named first deputy chairman, Council of Ministers (former deputy chairman, Council of Ministers). N.K. Baybakov retired (later identified as economic adviser of The Council of Ministers).
Minister of oil refining and petro-chemical industry	N.V. Lemayev appointed. V.S. Federov retired.
Minister of foreign trade	B.I. Aristov appointed. N.S. Patolichev retired; health.

November 1985

First deputy chairman, Council of Ministers	V.S. Murakhovskiy appointed. Z.N. Nuriyev (who was deputy chairman, Council of Ministers) retired.
Minister of aviation industry	A.S. Systsov appointed. I.S. Silayev promoted (see below).
Deputy chairman, Council of Ministers	I.S. Silayev (former minister of aviation industry) appointed.
Minister of finance	V.F. Garbuzov died.
Deputy chairman, Council of Ministers, and chairman, State Committee for Material and Technical Supply	L.A. Voronin appointed. N.V. Martynov retired.
Minister of electronic industry	V.G. Kolesnikov appointed. A.I. Shokin retired.
Minister of agriculture	V.K. Mesyats reassigned (became first secretary, Moscow Obkom, CPSU).

Deputy Chairman, Council of
Ministers (for military industries)
Ministry of Medical Industry and
Ministry of Microbiological Industry

Ministry of Agriculture
Ministry of Fruit and Vegetable
Industries
Ministry of Meat and Dairy Industries
Ministry of Food Industries
Ministry of Agriculture Industries
State Committee for Material and
Technical Supply for Agriculture
Chairman, GOSAGROPROM
Chairman, State Committee for
Foreign Economic Ties (GKES)
"Minister of the USSR"

Yu.D. Maslyukov appointed.
L.V. Smirnov *retired.*
Combined into one Minister of
Medical and Microbiological
Industry
All combined into new State
Committee for Agricultural
Industries (GOSAGROPROM),
which also incorporated branch
functions of several other ministries
and state committees (see below).

V.S. Murakhovskiy appointed.
K.F. Katushev appointed.
M.A. Sergeychik *retired.*
Ye.l. Sizenko, first deputy chairman,
GOSAGROPROM, so designated.

December 1985

Minister of (the new) medical and
micro-biological industry
Chairman, Central Statistical
Directorate
Chairman, State Committee for
Petroleum Product Supply
Minister of grain production

Minister of finance
Named as addition member of The
Council of Ministers
Minister of coal industry

Chairman, State Committee for
Television and Radio
"Minister of the USSR"

Deputy chairman, Council of Ministers

V.A. Bykov appointed.

M.A. Korolev appointed.
L.M. Volodarskiy *retired*; health.
T.Z. Khuramshin *relieved; dropped
from CPSU.*
G.S. Zolotukhin appointed.
Previous incumbent not mentioned.
B.I. Gostev appointed (see above).
A.A. Reut, first deputy chairman,
GOSPLAN, for general questions.
M.I. Shchadov appointed.
B.F. Bratchenko *retired*; health.
A.N. Aksenov appointed.
S.G. Lapin *retired.*
I.A. Iyevlev, first deputy chairman,
GOSAGROPROM, so designated.
Yu.P. Batalin appointed.
V.E. Dymshits *retired.*

January 1986

Minister of chemical and petroleum
machine construction
Chairman, State Bank (GOSBANK)

Chairman, State Committee for Labor
and Social Issues

V.M. Lukyanenko appointed.
K.I. Brekhov *retired*; health.
V.V. Dementsev appointed.
V.S. Alkhimov *retired.*
I.I. Gladkiy appointed.
Previous incumbent not mentioned.

Chairman, State Committee for Professional-Technical Education	*A.P. Dumachev* appointed. N.A. Petrovichev *retired.*
Minister of machine construction for animal husbandry and food production	*L.I. Khitrun* appointed. K.N. Belyak *retired.*
Minister of Construction	*V.I. Reshetilov* appointed. G.A. Karavayev *retired.*
Minister of construction of heavy industry enterprises	*S.V. Bashilov* appointed. N.V. Goldin *retired.*
Minister of internal affairs (MVD)	*A.V. Vlasov* appointed. V.V. Fedorchuk reassigned.

February 1986

Chairman, State Committee for Publishing, Typography, and Book Trade	*M.F. Nenashev* appointed. V.N. Pastukhov reassigned (ambassador to Denmark).

March 1986

No new appointments.
Announced creation of State Committee for Electronic Computer Technology and Information Science

April 1986

Chairman, State Committee for Electronic Computer Technology and Information Science (see above)	*V.N. Gorshkov* appointed.
New State Committee for Physical Culture and Sport created from same, older Council of Ministers committee	*M.V. Gramov* appointed (he was also chairman of the older committee).
Chairman, State Committee for Material Reserves	A.V. Kovalenko *retired.*

June 1986

Minister of culture	*P.N. Demichev* released, named first deputy chairman, Presidum of the Supreme Soviet.
Deputy chairman, Council of Ministers	*V.K. Gusev* appointed. *G.G. Vedernikov* appointed. Ya.P. Ryabov reassigned and named ambassador to France.
Chairman, State Committee for Material Reserves	*F.I. Loshchenko* appointed. (position vacant since April)

July 1986

Minister of machine tool and instrument industry	N.A. Panichev appointed. B.V. Balmont retired
Minister of electrotechnical industry	O.G. Anfimov appointed. G.P. Voronovskiy retired.
Minister of nuclear energy (a new ministry)	N.F. Lukonin appointed.

August 1986

Minister of culture	V.G. Zakharov appointed. (position vacant since June)
Minister of chemical industry	Yu.A. Bespalov appointed. V.V. Listov reassigned.
Chairman, State Committee of Prices	V.S. Pavlov appointed. N.T. Glushkov retired.
Chairman, State Committee for Construction (new union-republic committee on the basis of older State Committee for Construction Affairs, the chairmanship of which was vacant)	Deputy Chairman Yu.P. Balatin, Council of Ministers, appointed.
"Minister of the USSR"	L.A. Bibin, named first deputy chairman, State Committee for Construction and so designated.
Minister of construction in Northern and Eastern Regions (new ministry)	V.I. Reshetilov appointed (previously was minister of construction).
Minister of construction in the Southern Region (new ministry)	A.N. Shchetelnikov appointed (previously was minister of industrial construction).
Minister of construction for the Urals and West Siberian Regions (new ministry)	S.V. Bashilov appointed (previouslly was minister of construction for enterprises of heavy industry).

(These three new regional ministries were evidently created on the basis of three previous ministries—Construction; Industrial construction; and Construction of Enterprises of Heavy Industry—the functions of which were apparently divided up among these three and an existing regional ministry.)

Minister of production of mineral fertilizer	A.G. Petrishchev died.

September 1986

Deputy chairman, Council of Ministers	V.M. Kamentsev appointed.
Minister of fishing industries	V.M. Kamentsev reassigned (see above).

Chairman, State Committee for
Nuclear Energy Safety
V.M. Malishev appointed.

(The Soviet press identified this as a new state committee. No mention was made of what, if any, change occurred in the previously existing State Committee for Oversight of Safety in Work related to Nuclear Energy, Gosatomenergonadzor.)

Minister of production of mineral
fertilizer
N.M. Olshanskiy appointed
(incumbent died in August).

Minister of the merchant fleet
T.B. Guzhenko *retired.*

October 1986

First deputy chairman, Council of
Ministers
I.V. Arkhipov retired; health.

Minister of automotive industry
N.A. Pygin appointed.
V.N. Polyakov *retired.*

Minister of the merchant fleet
Yu.M. Volmer appointed (incumbent
retired in September).

Deputy chairman, Council of
Ministers, and chairman, State
Committee for Science and
Technology
G.I. Marchuk reassigned as president,
Academy of Sciences.

November 1986

Minister of ferrous metallurgy
V.A. Durasov appointed.
P.F. Lomako *retired.*

Minister of medium machine-
construction industries
L.D. Ryabev appointed.
E.P. Slavskiy *retired*; health.

December 1986

Minister of trade
K. Gerekh appointed.
G.I. Vashchenko *retired.*

Chairman, State Committee for
Cinematography
A. Kamshalov appointed.
F.T. Yermash *retired.*

January 1987

Minister of fishing industry
N.I. Kotlyar appointed (position vacant
since September 1986).

Chairman, State Committee for
Petroleum Products Supply
L.M. Smagin appointed (position
vacant since December 1985).

Chairman, State Committee for
Women
Z.P. Pukhova appointed.
V.V. Tereshkov reassigned as chairman,
SSOD.

February 1987

Deputy Chairman, Council of Ministers, and chairman, State Committee for Science and Technology	*B.L. Tolstoi* appointed (position vacant since October, 1986).
Minister of public health	*E.I. Chazov* appointed (press did not report what had happened to the incumbent, S.P. Byrenkov).
People's Control Committee	*S.I. Manyakin* appointed.
	A.M. Shkolnikov *retired.*

March 1987

Chief state arbiter	*V.V. Naidenov* appointed (a new position).

April 1987

Minister of grain products	*A.D. Budyka* appointed.
	G.S. Zolotukhin *retired.*

May 1987

Minister of civil aviation	*Col. General A.N. Volkov* appointed.
	Marshall B.P. Bugayev reassigned.
Minister of defense	*General D.T. Yazov* appointed.
	Marshal S.L. Sokolov, *retired.*

June 1987

Chief State Arbitrator	N.P. Malshakov appointed, replacing Naidenov (*see* March).

Other and Summary

In addition, during the same period seven of the chairmen of Union-Republic Councils of Ministers (also members of the USSR Council of Ministers) were replaced: Byelorussia, Georgia, Kirghizia, Lithuania, Moldavia, Tadzhikistan, and Turkmenistan).

All told, of the 61 ministers heading ministries and included in the Council of Ministers, 38 were appointed between Gorbachev's election as general secretary and June of 1987. In the same time frame: two newly appointed first deputy ministers of GOSAGROPROM and one of GOSTROI were named "Ministers of the USSR" and included in the Council of

Ministers; 19 of 28 state committees included in the Council of Ministers were appointed; and one first deputy chairman of GOSPLAN was appointed and made a member of the Council of Ministers. This means that of some 118 formal members of the Council of Ministers, 82 have been appointed since Gorbachev became general secretary.

In the Presidium of the Council of Ministers, the chairman, two of three first deputy chairmen, and eight of ten deputies have been appointed by Gorbachev.

Twelve previous ministries or state committees were combined into six new ones; two completely new state committees and two new ministries were created; and a Council of Ministers committee was elevated to a state committee.

Gorbachev has sacked and replaced two ministers whom he appointed.

Appendix II
Politburo and Central Committee Meetings since Gorbachev Became General Secretary

through June 1987

March 1985

22 March: *Politburo meeting*
Agenda: Mobilization of Party, state, and social organizations to intensify economic development.
Gorbachev's and other senior leaders' meetings with attendees at the Chernenko funeral.
Agricultural and agroindustrial issues in Rostov Province.
Preparations for celebrations of the fortieth anniversary of the World War II victory.
Vorotnikov's visit to Yugoslavia.
Consultations with the foreign minister of France.
Shcherbitskiy's visit to the United States.
Other questions related to internal and foreign policy.

22 March: *Central Committee meeting*
Agenda: The capital construction plan for 1985 and stimulation of the construction industry.

29 March: *Politburo meeting*
Agenda: 1986–90 retooling and reconstruction of electric-power-generating stations of the Ministry of Energy and Electrification.

Note: Dates are *either* as appearing in the Soviet press or as reported. For most of the period, the Soviet press did not give the actual date of the meetings, which were presumably held the day before the communiques first appeared in the central press. Later in the period, the actual meeting dates often began to appear.

For Politburo meetings, the agenda as reported is fully summarized; for central Committee meetings, only the main issue is identified in the appendix.

Almost all Soviet reports of Politburo meetings end with "other questions related to internal and foreign policy" or some similar catchall phrase; in this appendix the flavor of the wording has been retained as a guide to the reader. Other catchall phrases at the end of reports of Politburo meetings often refer to state, economic, or social "construction"; Western readers who find this normal Soviet terminology to be strange should mentally substitute the word *development*.

Reforms and adaptation of automatic data processing and computers in general schools and professional-education schools.

Improving public medical care.

Raul Castro's visit.

Disarmament and arms control.

Visits by the prime minister of Romania, the chairman of the Council of Ministers of Bulgaria, and the foreign minister of the GDR.

Economic relations with the PRC.

Other internal questions and the promotion of the Party's peace-loving foreign policy.

April 1985

2 April: Publication of *Central Committee and Council of Ministers decree* on increasing pensions for World War II veterans and families of deceased veterans.

5 April: *Politburo meeting*

Agenda: May Day celebration.

Preparations for the XXVII Party Congress.

Struggle against alcoholism.

Romanov's visit to Hungary.

Visit of the president of the FRG Bundesrat.

Other economic and social issues.

Cooperation with brotherly socialist parties and the achievement of global peace and security.

8 April: *Central committee meeting*, with industrial and agricultural ministers and managers in attendance.

Agenda: Measures to fulfill the 1985 plan.

12 April: *Politburo meeting*

Agenda: Spring planting.

Cooperation and coordination among ministries, enterprises, and farms in agriculture and agroindustry.

Material-technical support to agriculture, especially the introduction and utilization of new technology.

Speeding up the economic development of the Tuva ASSR.

Visits by U.S. Speaker of the House O'Neill, Foreign Minister Clark of Canada, and the Netherlands foreign minister.

Other questions of internal and foreign policy.

14 April: Publication of 7 March *Central Committee and Council of Ministers decree* on measures to improve services for repair and construction for gardeners, garages, and other activities.

19 April: *Politburo meeting*

Agenda: Agricultural improvements.

Enterprise shortfalls in metal products.

Modernization and retooling of enterprises of the oil and gas industries.

	Improving local industries, 1986–90 and to the year 2000. Cooperation with various CEMA bodies for construction of a mining (ore) enrichment combine in Krivoy Rog. Other questions of state, economic, and sociocultural construction and foreign policy.
21 April:	*Central Committee meeting*, with Union-Republic Party secretaries in attendance. Agenda: Meeting the 1985 plan.
23 April:	*Plenum of the Central Committee* (see internal chronology).
30 April:	Publication of 18 April *Central Committee and Council of Ministers decree* on further development of local industries in 1986–90 and to the year 2000.

May 1985

6 May:	*Central Committee and Politburo meeting*, with war and labor veterans.
7 May:	*Politburo meeting* Agenda: Warsaw pact summit meeting in April. Retooling of automotive enterprises. Extension of oil and gas resource exploration. Strengthening the observance of norms in the expenditures of grain and other agricultural products. Development of collective gardening. Recent North Korean visits and relations with North Korea. Visit by Nicaraguan President Ortega. Other economic and social questions, and cooperation with friendly states in the struggle for peace.
15 May:	*Politburo meeting* Agenda: The All-Union Communist "Subbotnik" ("voluntary" extra day of work). Improved pay for scientific workers, builders, and technical workers. Increased construction of homes for invalid care. Increased aid to families with children and to single mothers. Raises in age and disability pensions. Other questions related to economic and social policies, and relations with brotherly socialist states.
16 May:	Publication of *Central Committee and Council of Ministers decree* thanking the workers for the 4 May Communist "Subbotnik."
17 May:	Publication of *Central Committee resolution* on overcoming drunkenness and alcoholism.
21 May:	Publication of *Central Committee and Council of Ministers* decree on measures to improve the material condition of low-income pensioners, families as well as solitary citizens.

25 May: *Politburo meeting*
Agenda: 1986–90 economic and social development through technological improvements and better planning.
CEMA Executive Committee meeting.
Indian Prime Minister Gandhi's visit.
Gromyko's visit to Austria (particularly his meeting with U.S. Secretary of State Shultz).
Solomentsev's visit to Cuba.
Other questions of internal and foreign policy.

31 May: *Politburo meeting*
Agenda: 1986–90 improvements in agriculture in the RSFSR.
Improvements in radio broadcasting.
Improving the Moscow subway.
Visits by former FRG Chancellor Brandt and Italian Prime Minister Craxi.
Other questions of internal and foreign policy.

June 1985

7 June: *Politburo meeting*
Agenda: Increased labor productivity.
Measures to prepare for harvesting season.
1986–90 plan for development in Leningrad and Leningrad Province.
Visit by Czech leader Husak.
Improvements in physical culture and sport.
Vorotnikov's visit to Canada.

11–12 June: Joint *meeting of Central Committee and Council of Ministers* and other top and middle leadership.
Agenda: Restructuring and improving the economy. Major Gorbachev speech.

16 June: Publication of *Central Committee resolution* of 12 June on improving the utilization of club and sports facilities.

18 June: *Central Committee meeting* with heads of information services.
Agenda: Publicizing the Party's policies.

21 June: *Politburo meeting*
Agenda: Acceleration of introduction of advanced technology into the economy.
Republic and regional Party work and attitudes toward the reforms.
Fuel and electric supply for the winter.
Visits by Bulgarian leader Zhivkov and President Koivisto of Finland.
Information obtained from citizens' letters to the Central Committee about alcoholism and the fight against it.
Other questions of internal and foreign policy.

30 June: *Politburo meeting*
Agenda: Preparation of the draft Party Program.
Confirmation of Gorbachev as head of the editorial commission for the new Party Program.
Visit by Syrian President Assad.
Other issues of Party and state construction.

July 1985

1 July: *Plenum of the Central Committee* (see internal chronology).
5 July: *Central Committee meeting*
Agenda: Work of the Kharkov city committee of the Ukrainian Communist Party.
7 July: *Politburo meeting*
Agenda: Economic development in machine construction, and in light and consumer goods industries, 1986–90 and to the year 2000.
Improving living conditions for young families.
Improving health services.
Visit by Vietnamese leader Le Duan.
CEMA meeting in Warsaw.
Other questions of foreign policy.
7 July: Publication of 19 June *Central Committee resolution* on measures taken in the RSFSR to improve living conditions.
13 July: *Politburo meeting*
Agenda: Economic progress in the first half of 1985.
New management procedures for the economy.
Results and success of economic experiments in certain branches and enterprises in 1984.
Measures to increase the number of ministries that will shift to operations that accord with the guidelines of the April and July CC plenums.
The Baikal-Amur railway.
Alternative uses for grapes and fruit formerly used to produce wine and spirits.
Visit by Yugoslavian leader Planinc.
Shevardnadze's meeting with the Hungarian foreign minister.
Other Party, state, and economic questions.
16 July: Publication of *Central Committee and Council of Ministers decree* on improving the wage of scientists and technical workers in industry.
19 July: *Politburo meeting*
Agenda: Consumer goods production, 1986–90 and to the year 2000.
Material-technical support to the publishing industry.
Initiatives tried by the Volga light automobile production enterprises.

Tourism.
Issues raised in letters to lower Party organizations and how they are handled at the local levels.
Visit by Yao Yilin of the PRC.
Preparations for the XXVII Party Congress.
Other questions of foreign policy and the development of the economy.

20 July: Publication of *Central Committee and Council of Ministers decree* on measures to improve the winter harvest.

26 July: *Central Committee* meeting with second secretaries and heads of departments for Party organizational work at republic, territory, and province levels.
Agenda: Party elections.

26 July: *Politburo meeting*
Agenda: Agroindustrial experiments in the RSFSR.
Moscow youth festival.
Improving the material-technical base for production and commerce of consumer goods.
Strengthening observance of the law in matters related to protecting the environment.
Ties with socialist and other friendly states in promoting the "struggle for peace and security."

August 1985

2 August: *Politburo meeting*
Agenda: Improved introduction of new technology through closer cooperation with CEMA states in the machine construction industries.
Closer, more effective coordination between ministries, enterprises, and workers' collectives.
Improving the highways in the RSFSR.
Other questions of economic and social development and foreign policy.

4 August: Publication of *Central Committee and Council of Ministers decree* on disseminating new methods of management and accelerating scientific-technical progress.

9 August: *Politburo meeting*
Agenda: Measures to incorporate the recommendations of a July Novosibirsk academic conference into the basic program for economic development, 1986–90 and to the year 2000.
1986–90 development of West Siberian oil and gas.
Measures to improve production of chemical fibers and synthetics for consumer goods, 1986–90.
Animal husbandry activities during the winter.
The role of local Soviets in resolving municipal issues.
Shevardnadze's meeting in Helsinki.
Increasing the material well-being of workers.

	Workers related to individual branches of industry.
	Other foreign policy issues.
10 August:	Publication of *Central Committee resolution* on Party work in supporting reforms in general and professional schools in Gorkiy Province.
16 August:	*Politburo meeting*
	Agenda: Improving industrial construction.
	Improving the development and utilization of new biotechnology.
	New methods of evaluating worker performance.
	Responses to letters to the Central Committee on the introduction and utilization of new technology.
	Improving the integration of CEMA economies, especially in high technology fields.
	Visit by the chairman of the Bulgarian Council of Ministers.
	Other questions related to the economy, cultural issues, and foreign policy.
21 August:	*Combined Central Committee and Council of Ministers meeting*
	Agenda: Livestock production.
23 August:	*Central Committee conference* with economic managers and ministers.
	Agenda: Economic and social portions of the 1986–90 five-year plan.
23 August:	*Politburo meeting*
	Agenda: Grain harvest and distribution.
	Further development of Caspian Sea oil.
	Moscow Youth festival.
	Aliev's visit to North Korea.
	Upcoming session of the UNGA.
	Other questions of internal and foreign policy.
30 August:	*Politburo meeting*
	Agenda: Aspects of the 1986 economic plan and 1986–90 five-year plans related to work organization, discipline, and the introduction of high technology.
	Stepping up of measures to fulfill the 1985 plan.
	Improving the chemical fertilizer industry.
	Efforts in the Ukraine to introduce new technology and materials and to reduce waste.
	Home and cultural facilities construction in Astrakhan.
	Visit by Laotian leader Phomivane.
	Other questions of economic and social policy, and of relations with brotherly socialist states.
31 August:	Publication of *Central Committee and Council of Ministers decree* on raising labor productivity in industrial construction activities.

September 1985

12 September:	*Politburo meeting*

Agenda: Improving oil and gas production.
Gorbachev's visit to Tyumen Province and Tselinograd.
Measures to improve agriculture.
Progress in the campaign against alcoholism.
Improving Yalta resorts.
Visits by Mongolian leater Batmunkh and the head of the French Communist Party, Marchais.
Other internal and foreign policy questions.

16 September: *Central Committee meeting*, with party secretaries and directors of ministries and departments down to regional levels.
Agenda: Economic measures for the fall and winter, 1985–86.

19 September: *Politburo meeting*
Agenda: Implementation of measures against alcoholism.

20 September: *Politburo meeting*
Agenda: The Complex Program for production of consumer goods and the provision of services, 1986–90 and to the year 2000.
Visit by the delegation of the Socialist Party of Japan.
Zaykov's visit to the GDR.
Other questions of economic and cultural development and of strengthening ties with brotherly socialist states.

21 September: *Central Committee meeting*, with veterans of the Stakhanovite movement.
Agenda: Honoring the veterans of the Stakhanovite movement and increasing workers' efforts.

27 September: *Central Committee meeting*, with secretaries of republic, regional, and city Party committees and ministers.
Agenda: Development of the West Siberian oil and gas complex, 1986–90.

27 September: *Politburo meeting*
Agenda: Preparation of the new Party program.
Changes in Party regulations.
Long-range economic and social program for 1986–90 and to the year 2000.
Visits by Hungarian leader Kadar and Finnish President Koivisto.
Other Party and state questions.

October 1985

1 October: *Central Committee meeting*
Agenda: Complex Program for development of consumer goods and services to the year 2000.

3 October: *Central Committee meeting*
Agenda: Improving discipline at production facilities, based on letters from workers.

11 October: *Politburo meeting*
Agenda: Program for development of chemical industries to the year 2000, with emphasis on mineral fertilizers,

insecticides, plastics, and chemical fibers, as well as the living conditions of chemical industry workers.
Improving ferrous metal production, 1986–90.
Priorities for the development of natural resources and the technological base, 1986–90.
Living conditions of workers in the Far East.
Gorbachev's trip to France.
Visit by President Ratsiraka of Medagascar.
Shevardnadze's visit to the UNGA and his meeting with U.S. President Reagan.
Other questions of internal and foreign policy.

15 October: *Plenum of the Central Committee*
Agenda: New Party Program and Regulations.
Economic and social development strategy.

18 October: *Politburo meeting*
Agenda: Publicity and discussion procedures for the new Party Program and Regulations.
Measures to increase the accountability of ministers, enterprises, and branches for the fulfillment of the 1985 plan.
Establishing a permanent bureau of the Council of Ministers to organize and guide the machine construction industries, plus other measures to improve those industries.
The development of agricultural activities at industrial enterprises.
Visits by Libyan leader Qaddafi and by Japanese and Luxemburg parliamentary delegations.
Other questions of economic relations with bordering states.

22 October: *Central Committee meeting*, with heads of mass information organizations and of ideological institutes.
Agenda: Publicizing the new Party Program and Regulations.

November 1985

1 November: Publication of *Central Committee and Council of Ministers decree* on socialist competition in animal husbandry.

1 November: *Politburo meeting*
Agenda: Warsaw Pact Political Consultative Committee meeting.
Gorbachev's visit to Bulgaria.
Gorbachev's meeting with Gandhi.
Visit of the Yugoslavian parliamentary delegation.
Ponomarev's visit to the Socialist International meeting in Vienna.
1985 state awards.
Economic plans for the city of Baku for 1986–90.
Other internal and foreign policy questions.

6 November: Publication of *Central Committee and Council of Ministers decree* on the 1985 state awards.

15 November:	*Politburo meeting*
	Agenda: The 1986 state plan and budget, especially as related to increasing wages and improving living conditions.
	Development of agroindustrial complexes.
	Visit by Ethiopian leader Mengistu.
	Shevardnadze's trip to Cuba.
	The visits by U.S. Secretary of State Shultz and the foreign minister of Mozambique.
	Other questions related to life in the USSR and the party's "peace-loving" foreign policy.
23 November:	Publication of *Central Committee and Council of Ministers decree* establishing the State Committee for Agroindustries (GOSAGROPROM).
26 November:	*Politburo meeting*
	Agenda: Results of the Geneva summit.
	Gorbachev's meeting with Warsaw Pact leaders after the summit.
28 November:	*Central Committee meeting* with Union-Republic and regional party secretaries.
	Agenda: party organization and elections.
30 November:	*Politburo meeting*
	Agenda: Increasing the role of sections and shops in enterprises in the organization of industrial production.
	The need for a 1989 census.
	Increasing living-space allocations for armed forces personnel.
	Improving the completeness and accuracy of information in government and state organization.
	Lower-level Party organization and preparations for elections for the XXVII Congress.
	Other questions related to the internal life of the country and achieving the foreign policy goals of the Party and state for peace and security.

December 1985

6–7 December:	*Central Committee meeting,* with Republic and regional Party secretaries, Republic Councils of Ministers, and regional executive committees.
	Agenda: Supply of food products and stimulation of light industry.
13 December:	Publication of *Central Committee resolution* on increasing the role of Party activists in machine tool and instrument industries.
13 December:	*Politburo meeting*
	Agenda: Party elections and insurance that local Party members fully take criticisms of candidates' records into account.

Creation of interbranch scientific-technical complexes.
Plan for economic development in Irkutsk Province.
Further development of tractor machine construction.
Visit by Zimbabwe leader Mugabe.
Aliev's trip to Angola.
Enhancing scientific-technical cooperation in CEMA.
Other internal and foreign policy issues.

20 December: *Politburo meeting*
Agenda: Accelerating the reconstruction and modernization of agroindustry.
Visit by Algerian Party officials.
Preparations for the XXVII Party Congress.
Other internal and foreign policy questions.

27 December: *Politburo meeting*
Agenda: Results of the extraordinary 41st CEMA meeting
Production of consumer goods.
Upgrading and modernization of the "Don" family of grain combines.
Ponomarev's and Zimyanin's trip to Bucharest for the meeting of secretaries of Communist and workers' parties of socialist states.
Visit by Iraqi leader Hussain.
Other questions related to internal policies and the economic and social development of the country.

January 1986

4 January: *Politburo meeting*
Agenda: New Party Program.
Communist "Subbotnik."
Strengthening cadres in the clothing industry.
Visit by Korean Premier Kan Sen San.
Extent of success in implementing previous CC and Council of Ministers decrees.
Other internal and foreign policy issues.

10 January: Publication of *Central Committee resolution* on adapting new management methods in service ministries in the RSFSR.

10 January: *Politburo meeting*
Agenda: Improving the quality of marketing of goods.
Improving the material-technical base for rural organizations.
Far East pay scales.
Political organs in civil aviation.
Increasing the size of allowances for children of armed forces personnel.
Preparations for the Party Congress.
Activities of Soviet representatives in international organizations.
Fuller implementation of the Party's cadres policy.

15 January: *Central Committee meeting*
Agenda: Health care in various industries.
18 January: *Central Committee meeting*, with republic secretaries and ministers of technical education.
Agenda: Improving technical education.
24 January: *Politburo meeting*
Agenda: 1985 socialist competition results.
Improving labor discipline and combating alcoholism.
Increasing the production of computers and videos.
1986–90 plan for development of the city of Tbilisi.
Preparations for the Party Congress.
Other questions of economic, social, and foreign policy.
25 January: Publication of *Central Committee and Council of Ministers decree* on the results of 1985 socialist competition and winners.
31 January: *Politburo meeting*
Agenda: Problems in the Moscow city Party organization.
Preparations for spring planting.
Construction of agricultural complexes.
Shevardnadze's trip to Japan, Mongolia, and North Korea.
Visit by the head of the Italian Communist Party, Natta.
Party issues.
Cooperation with socialist and developing states.

February 1986

1 February: Publication of *Central Committee and Council of Ministers decree* on the further development of cooperative organizations to meet the needs of the populace.
7 February: *Politburo meeting*
Agenda: Preparations for the Party Congress.
1985 work of the Party Control Commission.
Kuznetsov's visit to India.
Other internal and foreign policy questions.
11 February: *Central Committee meeting*
Agenda: "Unpartylike" attacks on newspaper editors who expose inefficiency.
18 February: *Politburo meeting*
Agenda: Preparations for the Party Congress.
Party organizational and work issues.
Results of the Communist "Subbotnik."
Work of the Supreme Soviet in 1985.
Ligachev's visit to Cuba.
Other questions of the internal life of the country and of foreign policy.
18 February: *Plenum of Central Committee* (see internal chronology)

25 February: XXVII Congress of the CPSU opened.

March 1986

6 March: XXVII Congress of the CPSU closed.
13 March: *Politburo meeting*
Agenda: Follow-up actions to the Congress, including the recommendations from foreign Party and state delegations that attended.
Improving the management of fuel-energy branches of the economy, with emphasis on greater CEMA cooperation.
Introduction of new technology, particularly electronic technology and microprocessing.
Capital construction measures.
Improving measures to implement the Congress decisions related to internal and foreign policy.

15 March: *Central Committee meeting*, with the heads of mass information and propaganda organs.
Agenda: Tasks from the Congress; Ligachev and Yakovlev made addresses.

20 March: *Politburo meeting*
Agenda: The need for the CC and Council of Ministers to enact specific measures and legal acts without delay in order to fulfill the tasks set by the Congress.
Wider utilization of computers.
Developing a stable plan for financial support to agroindustry enterprises and organizations, and for the purchase of grain and other agricultural products.
More effective implementation of new management, planning and incentive mechanisms.
Improving rural "House of Culture."
Funding of mass organizations.
Venera spaceship mission to Halley's Comet.
Other questions of the social and economic development of the country and of foreign policy.

27 March: *Politburo meeting*
Agenda: Changeover of certain enterprises, ministries (especially in light industry) to material supply support on the basis of wholesale trade.
Measures to cut down on illegal earnings and improper utilization of state property (coupled with some legitimization of some limited practices).
Animal fodder production.
Trips by Shevardnadze and Demichev (to Poland for Warsaw Pact foreign ministers meeting and to India, respectively).
Other foreign policy and arms control issues.

29 March: Publication of *Central committee and Council of Ministers decree* on improving the management of agroindustrial complexes.

April 1986

3 April: *Politburo meeting*
Agenda: Plans for May Day celebrations.
Improving the availability of apartments and increasing housing space for citizens.
Measures to encourage and improve the work of rationalizers and inventors.
Visit by Algerian leader Benjedid.
Solomentsev's trip to Czech Party congress.
Other questions of socialist cooperation, European and international security, and of peaceful coexistence in relations between states with different social systems.

6 April: *Central Committee meeting* with Party, soviet ("legislative") and economic managers.
Agenda: Tasks from the Congress in the field of agriculture.

10 April: *Politburo meeting*
Agenda: Gorbachev's trip to Kuibyshev and Togliatti.
Tasks from the Congress to improve higher and intermediate education and to increase research levels.
Increasing the number of concerts and the quality of musical training.
Visits by Mozambique leader Machel and Austrian Chancellor Sinovatz.
Ryzhkov's trip to the Bulgarian Party congress.
The results of the first meeting of the Soviet-PRC economic cooperation commission.
Other internal and foreign policy issues.

22 April: Publication of *Central Committee and Council of Ministers decree* on the new Lenin prizes in science and technology, and in literature, the arts, and architecture.

24 April: Publication of *Central Committee resolution* of 17 April to speed up solutions to housing problems.

24 April: *Politburo meeting*
Agenda: The All-Union "Subbotnik" in honor of Lenin's birthday.
Progress in fulfilling the tasks set by the Congress in regard to Party organizational work.
Reorganization of Party, state, and economic organizations to meet the tasks set by the Congress.
Planning, economic stimulation, and improved management of consumer goods production and a more rational coordination between all elements of light industry.
Creation of a multibranch complex for microsurgery of the eye.
Gorbachev's trip to the GDR Party congress.
Zaykov's trip to the Italian Party congress.
Visit by Swedish Prime Minister Carlsson.
Other internal and foreign policy questions.

27 April: Publication of *Central Committee and Council of Ministers decree* on the 19 April "Subbotnik."

May 1986

6 May: Publication of *Central Committee and Council of Ministers decree* on improving planning, economic stimulation, and perfecting the management of production of consumer goods in light industry.

8 May: *Politburo meeting*

Agenda: Measures to improve the quality of production, especially through faster introduction of modern equipment and the creation of multiple-manned quality-control inspectorates from outside enterprises and ministries, and through increasing the accountability of ministries, economic enterprise managers, and workers' collectives for their results.

Greater utilization of rotary assembly lines, especially in all aspects of machine construction.

Review of Leningrad Obkom proposal relative to priorities for technological retooling (in effect, they were told to use existing means and to divert capital funding from new projects and construction to retooling).

Chernobyl accident.

Other domestic and foreign policy questions

15 May: *Politburo meeting*

Agenda: Better utilization and reduced waste of raw materials, fuel energy, and other material resources.

Measures to further the development of family and enterprise collective gardening.

Increasing the rights of organization and enterprise directors to allocate funds.

Yeltsin's visit to the West German CP congress.

Zimyanin's visit to Poland.

Other internal and foreign policy questions.

18 May: Publication of *Central Committee resolution* regarding a 20 April *Pravda* expose of improper Party and state behavior in sacking an individual who had complained of his superiors' malfeasance.

21 May: *Central Committee meeting* with Gorbachev, Ryzhkov, and other senior economic and Party officials in attendance.

Agenda: Improvement of the machine construction industries.

22 May: *Politburo meeting*

Agenda: Socialist competition during 1986–90.

Creation of a special center for information sciences and electronics (from research through application) in cooperation with CEMA partners.

Reduction of unneeded statistical reports.

	Visits by Romanian leader Ceausescu, Portuguese Communist Party leader Cunhal, and Spanish Prime Minister Gonzales.

Other questions of developing the economy and of implementing Soviet foreign policy.

28 May: Publication of *decrees by the Central Committee and by the Council of Ministers* to strengthen the struggle against unearned income.

31 May: *Politburo meeting*

Agenda: Chernobyl cleanup and investigation.

Preparations for conservation of coal, oil, gas, and electricity during the coming fall and winter.

Plans to improve railroad transportation.

Improving the work of Party revision commissions at the union-republic and regional level.

Vistis by Libyan number-two leader Jalloud and Syrian Vice-president Khaddam.

Other internal and foreign policy issues.

June 1986

3 June: Report of *Central Committee meeting*

Agenda: Failures and shortcomings by managers and the Party Committee of an enterprise of the Ministry of Radio Industry.

5 June: *Politburo meeting*

Agenda: Report on Chernobyl cleanup.

Measures to ensure a timely and quality harvest.

Discipline in planning and meeting sales contracts, especially in regard to consumer goods.

Preparation of youth for military service.

May Foreign Ministry meeting in which Gorbachev participated.

Meetings in Moscow with Japanese Foreign Minister Shintaro Abe and with PDRY Prime Minister Naoman's delegation.

Vorotnikov's visit to Mongolia.

Other internal and foreign policy questions.

6 June: *Central Committee Meeting*, with Party secretaries of union-republic and regional committees.

Agenda: Electric energy programs.

6 June: Report of *Central Committee meeting* with participants of the plenum of the Union of Journalists.

Agenda: Information policy.

9 June: Report of *Central Committee meeting* with Labor Union Council, officials from the KOMSOMOL and other mass organizations. Ligachev spoke.

Agenda: Discipline, productivity, and the antialcohol campaign.

13 June: *Politburo meeting*

Agenda: 1986–90 economic plan, with emphasis on the expected slowdown in the growth of material and labor resources.

U.S imperialism and failure to adhere to the spirit of Geneva.

Gorbachev's meeting with Hungarian leader Kadar.

Other questions of Party and state policy and of implementing Soviet foreign policy.

16 June: *Plenum of the Central Committee* (see internal chronology).

19 June: *Central Committee meeting*, with writers who are Supreme Soviet deputies and Moscow literary figures. Gorbachev spoke and Ligachev participated.

Agenda: Role of literature in the USSR.

20 June: *Politburo meeting*

Agenda: Steps to carry out the decisions of the Plenum.

Increasing the role of local soviets (councils).

Consumer goods production.

Increased production and availability of computers (especially in regard to CEMA projects).

Other questions of the socioeconomic development of the country and of foreign policy.

26 June: *Politburo meeting*

Agenda: Political education of Party cadres.

Additional privileges and rights for metallurgical workers.

Gorbachev's meeting with Indian Foreign Minister Shankar.

Report by the delegation to CSCBMDE.

Other questions of economic and cultural development and foreign policy.

30 June: *Central Committee meeting*, with secretaries of union republic and regional Party committees, deputy chairmen of the Council of Ministers, and representatives of educational ministries and organizations. Aliev, Ligachev, Demichev, and others participated.

Agenda: Professional-education improvement.

July 1986

2 July: Publication of *Central Committee and Council of Ministers decree* on measures to improve the quality of production (aimed at scientific and technical workers).

4 July: Report of *Central Committee meeting*

Agenda: Faults in the organizational and political work of the Nizhnevartovsk City Party Committee.

11 July: *Politburo meeting*

Agenda: Economic results of the first six months of 1986.

Gorbachev's visit to the Polish Party congress and Aliev's to the Yugoslav Party congress.

	Visit by French President Mitterand.
	Other questions related to decisions of the Party Congress in the socioeconomic and foreign policy spheres.
17 July:	Publication of *Central Committee Communique* on the economic results of the first six months of 1986.
17 July:	*Politburo meeting*
	Agenda: Improvements (including going to self-financing in 1987) in the Ministry of Chemical and Oil Machine Construction.
	Improving planning through self-financing.
	Ratification of Council of Ministers decree on improving planning and economic stimulation in production of consumer goods
	Report of the director of a joint Soviet-Bulgarian enterprise as an encouragement of other such efforts in CEMA.
	Fuel supply for the population and for enterprises.
	CPSU assistance and guidance to local Soviets.
	Reports of visits by Ryzhkov to Vietnam, Solovyev to North Korea, and Shevardnadze to the United Kingdom.
	Several other internal and external issues.
20 July:	Report published of special Politburo meeting.
	Agenda: Chernobyl investigation of fault.
24 July:	*Politburo meeting*
	Agenda: Work of the journal *Kommunist.*
	Improving the quality and repair service of radios, television sets, and phonographs.
	Visits by President Traore of Mali and Foreign Minister Genscher of the FRG.
	Marshal Sokolov's visit to Finland.
	Other internal and external questions.
30 July:	Publication of *decree by the Central Committee, Councils of Ministers, and Supreme Soviet* on increasing the role of local soviets in social and economic activities.
30 July:	Report of *Central Committee meeting*
	Agenda: Increasing the role of the Party in guiding the local Soviets.

August 1986

5 August:	Publication of *decree by the Central Committee and Council of Ministers* on improving planning, economic stimulation, and management in state trade and consumer cooperative societies.
6 August:	Publication of *decree by the Central Committee and Council of Ministers* on measures to improve the stability of the grain economy and increase fodder production in the twelfth Five Year Plan.
6 August:	*Central Committee meeting*, with ministers and regional Party secretaries from the RSFSR.

	Agenda: Agricultural production and the harvest.
8 August:	*Central Committee meeting*, with Party secretaries of union republics and regional committees, ministry representatives.
	Agenda: Technical quality and competitiveness of machines and equipment for export.
12 August:	Publication of *Central Committee and Council of Ministers decree* on increasing the accountability of trusts, enterprises, and organizations in fulfilling sales contracts.
12 August:	Publication of *Central Committee and Council of Ministers decree* on measures to improve the provision of fuel to the population during the Five Year Plan.
14 August:	Report of *Central Committee meeting*
	Agenda: Organization of political and economic education of workers in the 1986–87 academic year.
15 August:	Report of *Central Committee meeting*
	Agenda: Improper activities in Leningrad housing construction (as earlier reported in *Pravda*).
16 August:	Communique of *Politburo meeting*
	Agenda: Gorbachev's trip to the Soviet Far East.
	Stopping the project to divert waters from Siberian rivers.
	Reorganization of construction ministries and state committees.
	Service and consumer cooperatives.
	Rights of ministries, trusts, and enterprises to engage independently in foreign trade activities.
	Shifting the Ministry of Instrument and Automatic Production Control Industries and the Ministry of Chemical Industry to full self-financing in 1987.
	Competition for a World War II victory monument.
	Gorbachev's meetings with the new Vietnamese leader Truong Chinh and with Mongolian leader Batmunkh.
	The visit by Prime Minister Ozal of Turkey.
	Kapitanov's trip to the PDRY, Ethiopia, and the YAR.
	Other questions of socioeconomic development and of ties with foreign states.
20 August:	Publication of *Central Committee and Council of Ministers decree* on stopping the project to divert waters from Siberian rivers.
21 August:	*Politburo meeting*
	Agenda: Energy preparations for the coming winter.
	Measures to increase the supply of potatoes and vegetables to Moscow and Leningrad.
	Measures to improve propaganda in the fine arts.
	The visit by the minister of defense of Sudan.
	Other questions of internal and external policy (noted that decisions were taken).
24 August:	Publication of *decree by the Central Committee, Council of Ministers, KOMSOMOL, and Trade Union Central Committee* on socialist competition in livestock production, 1985–86.

28 August:	Report of *Central Committee meeting* Agenda: Inadequate work of Party, local soviet, and economic organizations in Kazakhstan in agricultural production and animal husbandry.
28 August:	*Politburo meeting* Agenda: Improving higher and intermediate specialized education. Measures to improve the effectiveness of bonus payments. Efforts to substitute natural gas for gasoline as an automotive fuel. Improving law enforcement. Ligachev and Medvedev's meeting with World Trade Union Federation representatives. Several questions of economic construction, the preparation of juridical cadres, and the Party's foreign policy.
29 August:	*Central Committee meeting*, with Party secretaries of union republics and regional committees of oil- and gas-producing regions and representatives of related ministries, trusts, and enterprises. Agenda: Inadequate introduction and utilization of new technology.
30 August:	Report of *Central Committee meeting* Agenda: The outstanding success of three West Siberian enterprises and the failure of ministries to take this into account and propagate the example shown.
31 August:	Report of *Central Committee meeting* Agenda: Inadequate work by communications and housing construction ministries of the RSFSR in preparing for the winter.

September 1986

3 September:	*Central Committee meeting*, with representatives of ministries and state committees of the RSFSR. Agenda: Economic education of workers.
4 September:	*Politburo meeting* Agenda: Remaining tasks for the fall planting and preparations of collective and state farms for the winter. Increasing technical equipment for producing prepared and packaged food products. Switching the Ministry of the Merchant Fleet to full self-financing in 1987. Plans to produce a "world-standard" light automobile at the Volga automotive plant. The visits by Chairman Sodnom, Mongolian Council of Ministers, and Algerian Party Secretary Messadia. Several questions of economic and social development and of foreign policy.
11 September:	Publication of *Central Committee and Council of Ministers decree* on improving the fine arts and their contribution to the Communist education of workers.

11 September: *Politburo meeting*
Agenda: Efforts by the Gorkiy automotive enterprise to provide all workers with their own apartments.
Need for a new pension law.
Increasing the technical level of means of communication.
Upcoming IAEC safety meeting.
Visit by the Swiss foreign minister.
Demichev's visit to Finland.
Several other questions of economic relations with foreign states and strengthening international cooperation.

13 September: Publication of *Central Committee and Council of Ministers decree* on organization of the national construction complex.

16 September: *Central Committee meeting*, with heads of construction departments of the Central Committees of Union Republics and regional committees.

17 September: Report of *Central Committee meeting*, with heads of higher educational institutes; Ligachev spoke.
Agenda: Better meeting the demands of the Party Congress.

18 September: *Politburo meeting*
Agenda: Improved payment of bonuses in collectives.
Increased payments to veterans and dependents of World War II.
Letters from the citizens to the Central Committee in regard to the Party Congress.
Talyzin's visit to the PRC.
Other issues from the party Congress relating to economic and social development and foreign policy.

20 September: *Central Committee meeting*, with ministers and secretaries of union republics and regional committees involved in construction activities; Batalin spoke.
Agenda: Implementing the reorganization of construction.

24 September: Report of *Central Committee meeting*.
Agenda: Successes achieved by certain enterprises of the coal industry.

24 September: Publication of *Central Committee and Council of Ministers decree* on improving foreign economic ties.

25 September: *Politburo meeting*
Agenda: Gorbachev's visit to Krasnodar and Stavropol regions.
Completing the fall harvest.
Long-term plan to develop the city of Moscow.
Measures to help poor families with more than three children.
Formation of an all-union society combining military and labor force pensioner organizations.
Conference of nonaligned states in Zimbabwe.
Also examined and took decisions of other questions of social and economic development, of perfecting Soviet democracy, and strengthening the union of socialist states.

| 25 September: | Publication of *Central Committee decree* on the results and lessons from Gorbachev's visit to Krasnodar and Stavropol. |

October 1986

1 October:	*Central Committee Meeting* Agenda: Gorbachev's trip and meetings in Stavropol and Krasnodar.
5 October:	*Central Committee Conference* with Ministers and Party secretaries. Agenda: Inadequate preparations and unfulfilled tasks to get ready for Winter.
14 October:	*Politburo meeting* Agenda: Gorbachev's report on the Reykjavik summit.
16 October:	*Politburo meeting* Agenda: Economic results the first nine months of 1986.
22 October:	*Central Committee Conference* Agenda: Progress in fulfilling CC and Council of Ministers' decree on improving concert activities and the material-technical base of concert organizations.
23 October:	*Central Committee meeting* Agenda: Inadequacies in eradicating falsification (eyewash).
23 October:	*Politburo meeting* Agenda: Training and retraining of cadres in new technology.
30 October:	*Politburo meeting* Agenda: The draft state economic and social plan for 1987.

November 1986

12 November:	*Central Committee conference* with responsible CC officials, heads of ministries and offices. Agenda: Progress in increasing labor discipline. The struggle to eradicate alcoholism. The struggle against unearned income.
13 November:	*Politburo meeting* Agenda: Report on the meeting of the heads of fraternal Parties of CEMA states.
20 November:	*Politburo meeting* Agenda: Introduction of government production manuals into industrial enterprises and trusts.
23 November:	*Central Committee meeting* Agenda: Results of the annual economic plan and inadequacies in many industries and branches.
30 November:	*Central Committee meeting* Agenda: Further strengthening Socialist legality and law enforcement, strengthening the rights and legal interests of citizens.

December 1986

4 December:	*Politburo meeting* Agenda: Gorbachev's trip to India.
11 December:	*Politburo meeting* Agenda: Progress in preparation of the new law on state enterprises. The Chernobyl cleanup. CC and Council of Ministers decree on measures to improve livestock breeding (approved).
18 December:	*Central Committee decree* on "Urgent measures to Improve Labor Productivity in Agriculture on the basis of Introducing Rational Forms of Organization and Self-financing."
24 December:	*Central Committee conference* with the heads of Union Ministries and offices (Gorbachev chaired). Agenda: Economic results in 1986 and the tasks ahead.
25 December:	*Politburo meeting* Agenda: Formation of Joint Ventures in the USSR with foreign firms.

January 1987

5 January:	*Central Committee conference* with heads of several ministries, several Party Secretaries, Chairman GOSPLAN and Deputy Chairman, Council of Ministers. Agenda: Relations with Vietnam.
6 January:	*Politburo meeting* Agenda: Reconstruction of higher and intermediate specialized education. Improving pay and support to workers in schools, aspirants and students. Proposals to carry out the program developed at the working meeting of the heads of CEMA Parties. Other issues of economic construction, ideological work and international cooperation between states.
12 January:	*Central Committee meeting* Agenda: Problems (many) in preparations for spring planting.
14 January:	Report of *Central Committee meeting* Agenda: Irresponsible preparations for winter in Gorkii and Murmansk.
17 January:	Report of *Central Committee meeting* Agenda: Problems in Krasnoyarsk Territorial Committee in improving the social living conditions of workers.
20 January:	Report of *Central Committee meeting* Agenda: Problems in improving telephone and other public communications.

22 January:	*Politburo meeting*
	Agenda: Improvements in the Machine Construction Industry.
	Improving state arbitration organs and increasing their authority.
	Improving conditions for the aged, the invalid, children and orphans.
	New rules for intermediate general education schools.
	Visits by Ryzhkov to Finland, Shevardnadze and Dobrynin to Afghanistan.
	Other question of internal politics, Party construction and cooperation with fraternal parties.
23 January:	*Central Committee meeting* with Party Secretaries (CC, republic and regional levels), Chairman Council of Ministers of Republics, Agricultural chairmen at all levels. (Gorbachev chaired and spoke, as did Ligachev and Nikonov).
	Agenda: Party tasks in improving labor productivity in agriculture.
27 January:	Published *Council of Ministers decrees* on Joint Ventures (1) with CEMA states, and (2) with other foreign states and firms.
27–28 January:	*Plenum of the Central Committee* (see internal chronology).
29 January:	*Politburo meeting*
	Agenda: High priority issues from the CC Plenum.
	Draft new rules for the All-Union Council of Trade Unions.
	Results of the 1986 socialist competitions.
	Trips to Poland by Yakovlev, Dobrynin and Medvedev.

February 1987

5 February:	*Politburo meeting*
	Agenda: Consumer goods cooperatives.
	Improving the work of literary and artistic creative unions.
	Improving support to clubs, etc. engaged in technical creativity (inventions).
	1986 Party Control Commission work.
	Other questions of Party organizational work and foreign policy activities for peace and security.
12 February:	Published *Councils of Ministers decree* on establishing cooperatives for food production.
13 February:	*Central Committee conference* with heads of the means of mass information and propaganda (Gorbachev chaired and spoke).
	Agenda: Carrying out the tasks set by the January Party plenum.
20–21 February:	*Central Committee meeting* with national, republic and regional heads of Party Control Commissions.

	Agenda: Tasks and problem in light of the January CC Plenum.
24 February:	Published report of *Central Committee meeting.*
	Agenda: Results and work of the Tadzhik Party, Soviets and Economic organs in 1986 (commended in agriculture).
24 February	Published *Central Committee and Council of Ministers decree* on "Improving the Conditions and Activities of Creative Unions."
27 February:	*Politburo meeting*
	Agenda: Gorbachev's trip to Latvia and Estonia.
	Preparations for the 70th anniversary of the Revolution.
	Measures to improve collective farm markets.
	Several other internal and foreign policy questions.
27 February:	Published *Central Committee and Council of Ministers decrees* on (1) Measures to Further Develop Independent Technical Creativity" (jointly with the KOMSOMOL and All-Union Council of Trade Unions), and (2) "Measures to Improve the Condition of the Aged and Infirm" (jointly with the Council of Trade Unions).
28 February:	Published *Central Committee and Council of Ministers decree* on "Further Perfecting the Organs of State Arbitration and Increasing Their Role in Strengthening Legality and Contract Discipline in the Economy."

March 1987

3–4 March:	*Central Committee conference* with central press workers, TASS officials, etc. (Medvedev spoke).
	Agenda: Tasks in developing cooperation with Socialist states.
5 March:	Press report of *Central Committee and Council of Ministers meeting.*
	Agenda: Review of 1986 socialist competition, due to failures to adapt, several regions and the RSFSR did not receive award winners.
5 March:	*Politburo meeting*
	Agenda: Accelerating agriculture development (emphasis on technology and supply).
	Personnel attestations.
	Transferring the State Committee for Tourism to full self-financing.
	Gorbachev's meetings with President Fanfani and Foreign Minister Andreotti (Italy) and with the Secretary General of the Argentinian CP.
	Slyunkov's visit to Portugal.
	Other questions of economic construction, organizational-Party work, ideological work and cooperation with foreign states.
12 March:	*Politburo meeting*
	Agenda: Improving shortfalls in communal living construction.

Trips by Zaykov to the CSSR, Yeltsin to Nicaragua, Solovyev to Libya and Kapitanov to the Swiss Labor Party congress.

Other internal and foreign policy issues.

14 March: Published the *Central Committee decree* on preparations for the 70th anniversary (Jubilee) of the Revolution.

19 March: *Politburo meeting*

Agenda: Improving and restructuring workers' political and economic studies (serious faults noted).

Yakovlev's visit to Spain.

Other regional Party issues and relations with foreign states.

21 March: Published *Central Committee and Council of Ministers decree* on "Basic Directions of the Reconstruction of Higher and Intermediate Specialized Education in the Country."

25 March: Published *Central Committee and Council of Ministers decree* on "Measures to Fundamentally Improve the Quality of Preparation of Specialists with Higher Education in the National Economy."

26 March: Published *Central Committee and Council of Ministers decree* on "Measures to Improve Preparation and Utilization of Scientific Teaching and Scientific Cadres."

26 March: *Politburo meeting*

Agenda: Achieving goals of the 5-year plan in developing the material-technical base in the Socio-Cultural field.

Scientific support to agroindustry.

Visits by Shevardnadze to SE Asia and Biryukova to Vietnam.

Other questions in implementing the January CC Plenum decisions in foreign and domestic areas.

27 March: Published *Central Committee and Council of Ministers decree* on "Increasing the Role of Scientific Educational Institutes in Accelerating Scientific-Technical Progress and Improving the Preparation of Specialists."

28 March: Published *Central Committee and Council of Ministers decree* on "Increasing the Pay in Higher School Institutions."

29 March: Published *Central Committee and Council of Ministers decree* on "Measures to Increase Material and Living Conditions of Aspirants and Students in Higher and Intermediate Specialized Schools." (Jointly with the KOMSOMOL and Trade Union Council.)

31 March: *Central Committee conference* with the heads of means of mass information. (Yakovlev spoke).

Agenda: Tasks to support the reconstruction.

April 1987

2 April: *Politburo meeting*

Agenda: The Chernobyl cleanup.

Rationalizing statistical reporting requirements.

Rational utilization of the resources of Lake Baikal and protection of its environment.

Laws to allow citizens to appeal the acts of officials.

Warsaw Pact Foreign Ministers' meeting in Moscow.

British Prime Minister Thatcher's visit.

Trips by Solomentsev to Bulgaria and Lukyanov to Denmark.

Other questions of state construction, cadres policies and relations with developing states.

3 April: *Central Committee conference* with Secretaries of republics territories and regions and heads of higher Party schools, other school faculty heads, press workers and representatives of several ministries. (Zaykov opened the conference).

Agenda: Tasks in accord with the January CC Plenum in political education.

14 April: Published *Central Committee and Council of Ministers decree* on "Measures to Further Improve the Work of the Communal-Housing Economy of the Country."

15 April: Published *Central Committee project* on "Basic Directions to Reconstruct the System of Political and Economic Training of Workers."

18 April: Communique of *Politburo meeting*

Agenda: May Day as day of worker's solidarity.

Economic results during the first 3 months of 1987.

Measures to meet state demands in vegetable oils production.

Approved a new (spring) tax law.

Environmental protection problems around Lake Ladoga.

A new higher education institute in Moscow.

Gorbachev's visit to the CSSR.

U.S. Secretary of State Shultz's visit.

Visits by Chebrikov to Cuba and Talyzin to Mozambique and the PDRY.

Other foreign and domestic problems.

21 April: Published *Central Committee decree* on serious problems in the Altai territorial Party committee.

23 April: *Politburo meeting*

Agenda: Reconstructing the finance credit system to meet the needs of the new law on state entreprises.

Price formation.

Gorbachev's meetings with Polish leader Jaruzelsky and Ethiopian leader Mengistu.

Demichev's trip to Iraq.

Other issues related to meeting the goals of the January CC Plenum.

25 April: *Central Committee Conference* with representatives of all branches of energy production and supply and with several State Committee heads.

Agenda: Raising the technical level and capabilities to meet future energy demands.

30 April: *Politburo meeting*
Agenda: Results of the 18 April All-Union "Subbotnik." Proposals to reconstruct planning and material-technical supply.
Increasing the role of the State Committee for Science and Technology in scientific and technical progress.
Visits by Syrian leader Assad, Bulgarian Chairman, Council of Ministers Atanasev and the head of the Luxemburg CP.
Ligachev's visit to Hungary.
Other internal and external policy questions.

May 1987

4 May: Report of *Central Committee meeting*
Agenda: The Movement for a Collective Guarantee of Labor and Societal Discipline.

5 May: Published *Central Committee and Council of Ministers decree* on "Measures to Fulfill the Demands of the 12th Five Year Plan for the Development of the Material-Technical Basis of the Socio-Cultural Area.

9 May: Communique of *Politburo meeting*
Agenda: Letters from citizens on the tasks of the January CC Plenum.
Problems in meeting the consumer goods production plan.
Improving future work with youth.
Progress in CEMA economic relations (emphasis on JVs).
Gorbachev's meeting with French CP leader Marchais and with the Mexican Foreign Minister.
Other internal and foreign policy issues.

16 May: Report of *Central Committee meeting.*
Agenda: Serious problems in environmental protection of Lake Baikal and the surrounding region (many ministries harshly criticized).

16 May: Report of *Central Committee meeting.*
Agenda: Shortcomings in Party, local Soviet and agricultural organs of several republics and regions in regard to animal husbandry.

22 May: *Central Committee conference* with most of the top leaders below Gorbachev, Party secretaries Republics and regions, several ministers, and local organs. (Ligachev opened and closed the conference).
Agenda: Increasing the production of consumer goods.

23 May: Communique of *Politburo meeting.*
Agenda: Perfecting the work of the Council of Ministers.
Proposal to create a micro-electronics and automatization center in Ulyanovsk for the machine construction industries.

The campaign against alcohol.

Gorbachev's meetings with Vietnamese leader Van Linh and with French Premier Chirac.

Visits by Solomenstev to Greece, Demichev to Bulgaria, Dolgikh to North Korea, Medvedev to Berlin and Razumovskiy's meeting with Secretaries of Socialist states.

Other internal and foreign policy issues.

25 May: *Central Committee Conference* with many of the top leadership below Gorbachev, Party secretaries of Republics and regions, several ministries and representatives of republic councils of ministers. (Ligachev opened and closed the conference.)

Agenda: Processing branches in storage bases for material-technical supply and agricultural storage (severe problems noted).

29 May: Report of *Central Committee meeting*.

Agenda: Citizens complaints about environmental problems around Lake Ladoga.

30 May: Report of *Central Committee meeting*.

Agenda: Serious inadequacies in animal fodder production in Lithuania and a large number of regions.

30 May: *"Emergency" meeting of Politburo*.

Agenda: The Rust violation of Soviet airspace and landing in Moscow. (see internal chronology and Chapter 12)

June 1987

2 June: *Central Committee conference*.

Agenda: The campaign against alcoholism.

4 June: Published *Central Committee decree* on "Measures for Increasing the Role of Procuratorial Oversight in Strengthening Socialist Legality and Law and Order."

8–9 June: *Central Committee conference* (Slyunkov chaired).

Agenda: Radical reconstruction of the administration of the economy.

11 June: Communique of *Politburo meeting*.

Agenda: Gradual transfer of trusts, enterprises and economic organizations to full self-finance in 1988–89.

Internationalist and patriotic education in Kazakhstan.

20 June: *Central Committee meeting*.

Agenda: Unsatisfactory utilization of economic resources in agroindustry in the Uzbek, Tadzhik and Turkmen Republics.

25–26 June: *Central Committee Plenum* (see internal chronology).

Appendix III
Announced Changes in the Diplomatic Corps and Foreign Ministry as Reported in the Soviet Press

Note: Soviet press reports normally do not indicate to where replaced ambassadors are reassigned; such information has been added when later reports provide the answer. In spring of 1986, evidently in the new spirit of *glasnost*, the Soviet Press began to publish more complete biographies of some new appointments. This adds to information but still does not fully solve the above problem.

A. Soviet Ambassadorial Changes

Month and State	New Appointee	Incumbent
March 1985:		
Jordan	A. I. Zinchuk	R. N. Nishanov Reasigned
Netherlands	A. I. Blatov (a former assistant to Brezhnev)	V. N. Beletskiy Reassigned
April 1985:		
Ethiopia	G. N. Andreyev (died February 1986)	K. E. Fomichenko Reassigned to Mongolia
Mongolia	K. E. Fomichenko (from Ethiopia)	S. P. Pavlov Reassigned later to Burma
May 1985:		
Lesotho	V. I. Gavryushkin	Y. F. Sepelev Was also ambassador to Mozambique; stayed in that post
Botswana	V. G. Krivda	M. N. Petrov Reassigned
Pakistan	K. Vezirov (from Nepal)	V. S. Smirnov Reassigned

423

A. Soviet Ambassadorial Changes (Continued)

Month and State	New Appointee	Incumbent
June 1985:		
Nepal	G. K. Shcheglov	K. Vezirov Previously reassigned to Pakistan
July 1985:		
Kenya	V. L. Ostashenko	A. D. Chikvaidze Reassigned
Hungary	B. I. Stukalin	V. N. Bazovskiy Reassigned
Burma	S. P. Pavlov (from Mongolia)	*Retired*
August 1985:		
Tanzania	S. I. Illarionov	Yu. A. Yukalov Reassigned
September 1985:		
Benin	V. V. Pavlov	V. I. Agapov Reassigned
Zambia	V. A. Likhachev	V. I. Cherednik Reassigned
Burkina Faso	F. P. Bogdanov	*Retired*
October 1985:		
Nigeria	Yu. V. Kuplyakov	V. V. Snegirov Reassigned
November 1985:		
Sri Lanka	K. N. Kylmatov	*Retired*
December 1985:		
Philippines	V. I. Shabalin	Yu. A. Sholmov Reassigned

January 1986:		
Somalia	B. A. Abdurazokov	B. I. Ilichev Reassigned
Poland	V. I. Brovikov	A. N. Aksenov Reassigned previously to chairman, State Committee for Television and Radio
Zaire	V. V. Soldatov	V. G. Filatov Reassigned
Cuba	A. S. Kapto	K. F. Katushev Reassigned
Maldive Islands	K. N. Kylmatov (also ambassador to Sri Lanka)	Retired (see November 1985; he was also ambassador to Sri Lanka)
February 1986:		
Greece	V. P. Stukalin (formerly deputy foreign minister)	I. Yu Andropov Reassigned
Oman	A. I. Zinchuk (also ambassador to Jordan)	(New diplomatic posting)
March 1986:		
United Nations	Yu. V. Dubinin (from Spain; later transferred to United States)	O. A. Troyanovskiy Reassigned to the PRC
April 1986:		
Denmark	B. N. Pastukhov (from chairman, State Committee for Publishing, Typography, and Book Trade)	L. I. Mendelevich Reassigned (later identified as MFA "Colleague")
PRC	O. A. Troyanovskiy (from the UN)	Retired
Spain	S. K. Romanovskiy	Yu. V. Dubinin Reassigned to the UN

A. Soviet Ambassadorial Changes (Continued)

Month and State	New Appointee	Incumbent
United Kingdom	L. M. Zamyatin (from International Information Department, CC)	Retired
FRG	Yu. A. Kvitsinskiy (from arms control negotiations)	Retired
May 1986:		
Nicaragua	V. I. Vyalyas (from Venezuela)	G. E. Shlyapnikov Reassigned
Lebanon	V. I. Kolotusha	Retired
Japan	N. N. Solovev	Retired (after just over one year on post)
Papua-New Guinea	E. M. Somateikin (ambassador to Australia given double posting)	
United States	Yu. V. Dubinin (from the UN)	A. F. Dobrynin Reassigned (promoted) to CC secretary
Burundi	V. V. Tsybukov (was identified as MFA "Colleague")	Retired
June 1986:		
France	Ya. P. Ryabov (former deputy chairman, Council of Ministers)	Yu. M. Vorontsev Reassigned (promoted) to first deputy foreign minister earlier
Yugoslavia	V. F. Maltsev (former first deputy foreign minister)	Retired
July 1986:		
PDRY	A. I. Rachov (was second secretary, Turkman CP)	Y. P. Zhukov Reassigned
Ethiopia	V. I. Dmitriev (was second secretary, Latvian CP)	G. N. Andreyev died February 1986

August 1986:

Post	New appointee	Former / Status
São Tomé and Príncipe		
Vietnam	V. N. Kuznetsov	*Retired*
	D. I. Kachin	B. N. Chaplin Reassigned previously as deputy foreign minister
United Nations	A. M. Belonogov (from Egypt)	Yu. V. Dubinin Reassigned earlier to United States
Afghanistan	P. P. Mozhayev (was second secretary, Leningrad Obkom)	F. A. Tabayev Reassigned
Cameroon	V. I. Fedorov (formerly director, 2d African Department, MFA)	*Retired*
United Nations, Geneva, and International Organizations	Ye. N. Makeek	*Retired*
Djibouti	V. L. Zhuravlev (was a sector chief, 1st African Department, MFA)	*Retired*

September 1986:

Post	New appointee	Former / Status
Ecuador	V. G. Chekmazov (was deputy director, 2d Latin American Department, MFA)	F. N. Kovalev Reassigned
Cyprus	Yu. E. Fokin (was general secretary, MFA)	*Retired*
Madagascar	P. P. Petrik	*Retired*
Vanuatu	Ye. M. Samoteikin (also ambassador to Australia and Papua-New Guinea)	(new diplomatic post)
Venezuela	V. M. Goncharenko (was deputy director, 1st Latin America Department, MFA)	V. I. Vyalyas Reassigned to Nicaragua earlier
Egypt	G. K. Zhuravlev (was first deputy minister of foreign trade)	A. M. Belonogov Reassigned to UN earlier

A. Soviet Ambassadorial Changes (Continued)

Month and State	New Appointee	Incumbent
Guinea	V. N. Raevskiy (was an Obkom secretary, Ukrainian CP)	V. S. Kitaev Reassigned
Syria	A. S. Dzasokhov (was first deputy chairman, Soviet Committee for Solidarity with the Nations of Africa and Asia)	F. N. Fedotov Reassigned to UAE in October
October 1986:		
Uganda	S. N. Semenenko (was a senior assistant to a first deputy foreign minister)	*Retired*
Brazil	V. F. Isakov (was a consulate advisor in Soviet Embassy in the United States)	V. I. Chernyshev Reassigned
Guinea Bissau	V. V. Aldoshin (was deputy director, 1st African Department, MFA)	*Retired*
Sierra Leone	V. S. Novotseltsev (was an Omsk Obkom secretary who then attended the Diplomatic Academy)	*Retired*
Laos	Yu Ya Mikheev (previously a "Southeast Asia Specialist" in the MFA)	V. F. Sobchenko
United Arab Emirates	F. N. Fedotov (previously ambassador to Syria)	Reassigned as ambassador to Tunisia New post
Libya	P. S. Akopov (had been ambassador to Kuwait)	O. G. Peresypkin Reassigned
Austria	G. S. Shikin (was deputy head of General Secretariat, MFA)	*Retired*
November 1986:		
Mozambique	N. K. Dubenko (previously a 2d secretary, Lithuanian CP)	Yu. F. Sepelev Reassigned

Tunisia	V. F. Sobchenko (previously ambassador to Laos)	V. L. Kizinchenko Reassigned
Mauritania	L. M. Komogorov (previously a consul general in Oman, Algeria)	*Retired*
Ireland	G. V. Uranov (previously a secretary assigned to the Soviet UNESCO Commission)	*Retired*
Mauritius	Yu. A. Kirichenko	N. A. Pankov Reassigned
Kuwait	E.N. Zverev	P. S. Akopov Reassigned as ambassador to Libya
Ivory Coast	B. I. Minakov	New post
December 1986:		
Iceland	I. N. Krasavin (previously deputy head, 2d European Department, MFA)	*Retired*
January 1987:		
None		
February 1987:		
None		
March 1987:		
Uruguay	I. K. Laptev	*Retired*
Zimbabwe	A. M. Glukhov (previously ambassador to Bolivia)	G. A. Ter-Gazaryants Reassigned
Indonesia	V. M. Semenov (previously ambassador to Singapore)	S. I. Semivolos Reassigned
April 1987:		
Cape Verde	P. M. Shmelkov	*Retired*
Norway	A. V. Teterin	*Retired*
Jamaica	V. A. Romanchenko	*Retired*

A. Soviet Ambassadorial Changes (Continued)

Month and State	New Appointee	Incumbent
May 1987:		
Sudan	V. Ya. Sukhin	*Retired*
Seychelles	V. V. Anisomov	M. G. Orlov Reassigned
Zambia	O. S. Miroshkin	*Retired*
June 1987:		
Bolivia	T. Dudyrev	A. M. Glukhov had been reassigned as Ambassador to Zimbabwe in March.
Y. A. R.	V. Popov	A. I. Filev was reassigned.
Togo	K. Kotov	S. D. Shaverdyan was reassigned

B. Recapitulation: Ambassadors, March 1985–June 1987

1. Eighty-three new ambassadorial appointments were announced for 72 different posts; one ambassadorship (Singapore) was vacant. Of these 12 were transfers from previous ambassadorships (two of which involved the same man, who was reassigned twice in a two-month period) and 4 were additional (double) postings for incumbent ambassadors to other states.

2. Four outgoing ambassadors were promoted to more senior identified government posts (two in the Foreign Ministry), and a fifth was later identified as a ministry "colleague." Thirty were retired. The remainder were reassigned, most without indication of particular post.

3. Two incoming ambassadors were "demoted" from senior Foreign Ministry positions (1 first deputy minister, and 1 deputy minister); 1 from deputy minister of foreign trade; 1 from deputy chairman, Council of Ministers; 1 from chairman of a state committee; and 1 from head of a reorganized CC department.

4. Geographic distribution of appointments
   - Industrial world (West Europe, North America, Japan and United Nations): Seventeen appointments to 16 posts (one man appointed to two posts in succession).
   - Asia (less the Middle East) including Pacific states:
   Fifteen appointments (one double and one triple posting). One post, Singapore was vacant at the end of June 1987.
   - Middle East and North Africa:
   Twelve appointments (one double posting).
   - Sub-Saharan Africa (including the Sahel states):

Twenty-eight appointments to 25 posts (one incumbent new appointee died in office and one was retired after twenty months in position)
- Latin America:
  Eight appointments.
- Eastern Europe:
  Three appointments.

C. Senior Foreign Ministry Changes: Minister, First Deputy, and Deputy Ministers

July 1985
Foreign minister — Eduard Shevardnadze (formerly first secretary, Georgian Communist Party (and made Politburo member)
A. A. Gromyko was made chairman, Presidium off the Supreme Soviet

October 1985
Deputy minister — B. I. Aristov transferred to become minister of foreign trade

December 1985
Deputy minister — V.M. Nikiforov (formerly deputy head, Organizational-Party Work Department, Central Committee)
V. P. Loginov (formerly director, 5th European Department, MFA)

February 1986
Deputy minister — V. P. Stukalin transferred to be ambassador to Greece

May 1986
First deputy ministers — Yu. M. Vorontsev (formerly ambassador to France)
A. G. Kovalev (formerly deputy minister)
G. N. Kornienko transferred to be first deputy, International Department, CC.

Deputy ministers — A. A. Bessmertnykh (formerly director, USA Department, MFA)
B. N. Chaplin (formerly ambassador to Vietnam)
A. L. Adamshin (formerly director, 1st European Department, MFA)
V. F. Petrovskiy (formerly director, International Organizations Department, MFA)

June 1986
First deputy minister — V. F. Maltsev transferred to be ambassador to Yugoslavia

C. Senior Foreign Ministry Changes: Minister, First Deputy, and Deputy Ministers (Continued)

August 1986

Deputy minister   I. A. Rogachev (formerly chairman, Directorate of Asian Socialist States, MFA)

Unknown date

Deputy minister   N. S. Ryzhkov either retired or reassigned sometime after January 1986 with no announcement

D. Recapitulation: Ministers and Deputies

As of June 1987, the foreign minister, both first deputy ministers, and seven of ten deputy ministers had been appointed since Gorbachev was elected general secretary. One of the two first deputies had, however, been promoted from the position of deputy minister, which he held when Gorbachev was elected.

Bibliography

I. Primary Soviet Sources

Research for this book was primarily based on a *complete review* of every issue for 1985 through June 1987 of the following Soviet newspapers and periodicals:

Aviatsiva i Kosmonavtika
Bakinakiy rabochiy
Izvestiya
Kommunist
Kommunist vooruzhennykh Sil
Komsomolskaya pravda
Krasnaya zvezda
Literaturnaya gazeta
Mezhdunarodnaya zhizn
Nedelya
Novoye vremya
Ogonek
Partinynaya zhizn
Pravda
Sotsialisticheskaya industriya
Sovetskoye voyennoye obozreniye
Voprooy ekononiiki
Voyenny vestnik

II. Supplementary Western Press Sources

In addition, the following Western publications were researched on a more selective basis (except where noted):
Baltimore Sun
Boston Globe
Business Week
Chicago Tribune
Defense Week
Detroit News

Forbes
Frankfurter Allegemeine Zeitung
International Herald Tribune
Jane's Defense Weekly (every issued, 1985 through May 1987)
Jerusalem Post (every issue, 1985 through June 1987)
Journal of Commerce
London Observer
Los Angeles Times
New York News
New York Post
New York Times
Newsweek (every issue, 1985 through June 1987)
Novoye russkoye slovo
Radio avoboda issledovutelskiy byulletin (every issue, 1985 through May 1986)
Soviet Nationality Survey (every issue, 1985 through January 1986)
Soviet Union and the Middle East (each issue, January through October 1986)
Time (every issue, 1985 through June 1986)
U.S. News and World Report
USSR Overview (every issue, May 1985 through May 1987)
Wall Street Journal
Washington Inquirer
Washington Post
Washington Times

III. Material was also obtained from commentary and newscasts from the Voice of America and the British Broadcasting Corporation.

IV. *Books and Articles* (including recent background material)

Note: The reader will notice that, with a few exceptions, this bibliography includes publications only from 1984 through 1987. The authors, of course, drew on their familiarity with many fine earlier works but did not specifically refer to them in their research for this study.

Adelman, Jonathan R. "The Soviet Use of Force: Four Cases of Soviet Crisis Decisionmaking." *Crossroads*, no. 19 (1985): 47-81.
Adomeit, Hannes. "Soviet Crisis Prevention and Management: Why and When Do the Soviet Leaders Take Risks?" *Orbis* 30 (Spring 1986): 42-64.
Alexeyeva, Ludmilla. *Soviet Dissent: Contemporary Movements for National, Religious, and Human Rights.* Middletown, Conn.: Wesleyan University Press, 1985.

Alexiev, Alex R. "Soviet Strategy and the Mujahidin." *Orbis* 29 (Spring 1985): 31-40.
_____. "The Soviet Campaign Against INF: Strategy, Tactics and Means." *Orbis* 29 (Summer, 1985): 319-50.
Alford, Jonathan, ed. *The Soviet Union: Security Policies and Constraints.* New York: St. Martins' Press, 1985.
Alsudiary, Abdulaziz bin Khalid, Yehuda Bar, Lee Suk Bok, Ahmed M Abdel-Halim and Zia Ullah Khan. *Five War Zones: The Views of Local Military Commanders,* Washington, D.C.: Pergammon-Brassey's International Defense Publishers, 1986.
Anderson, Lisa. "Qadhdhafi and the Kremlin." *Problems of Communism* 34 (September-October, 1985): 29-44.
Atherton, Alfred L., Jr. "The Soviet Role in the Middle East: An American View." *Middle East Journal* 39 (Autumn 1985): 688-715.
Baxter, William P. *Soviet Airland Battle Tactics.* Novato, Calif.: Presidio Press, 1985.
Beissinger, Mark R. "In Search of Generations in Soviet Politics." *World Politics* 38 (January 1986) 288-314.
Bennett, Alexander J. "Arms Transfers as an Instrument of Soviet Policy in the Middle East." *The Middle East Journal* 39, (Autumn 1985): 745-74.
Bennigsen, Alexander. "Islam in the Soviet Union." *Journal of South Asian and Middle Eastern Studies,* 8 (Summer, 1985): 115-33.
Berliner, Joseph. *The Innovation Decision in Soviet Industry.* Cambridge: MIT Press, 1978.
_____. "Prospects for Technological Progress." In *Soviet Economy in a New Perspective,* compiled by Joint Economic Committee, U.S. Congress. Washington, D.C.: Government Printing Office, 1976.
Bialer, Seweryn. *The Soviet Paradox: External Expansion, Internal Decline.* New York: Knopf, 1986.
Birman, Igor. *Ekonomika Nedostach* (The scarcity economy). New York: Chalidze Publications, 1983.
Bittman, Ladislav. *The KGB and Soviet Disinformation: An Insider's View* New York: Pergammon-Brassey's, 1985.
Bodansky, Yossef. "The Initial Period of War—Surprise and Special Operations." *Global Affairs* 1 (Spring, 1986): 123-35.
Bond, Daniel L., and Herbert S. Levine. "The 11th Five-Year Plan, 1981-1985." In *Russia at the Crossroads: The 26th Congress of the CPSU,* edited by Seweryn Bialer and Thane Gustafson. London: Allen & Unwin, 1982.
Bornstein, Morris. "Improving the Soviet Economic Mechanism." *Soviet Studies* 37 (January 1985): 1-30.
Brown, Archie. "Gorbachev: New Man in the Kremlin." *Problems of Communism* 34 (May-June 1985) 1-23.
Brzezinski, Zbigniew. *Game Plan: How to Conduct the US-Soviet Contest.* Boston: Atlantic Monthly Press, 1986.

_____. "National Strategy and Arms Control." *The Washington Quarterly* (Winter 1987) 5-10.

Bush, Keith. "Major Decree on Private Plots and Livestock Holdings." *Radio Liberty Research Bulletin* 38/81, 26 January 1981.

Butson, Thomas G. *Gorbachev: A Biography.* New York: Stein & Day, 1985.

Chadwick, Michael Loyd. "The Strategy Defense Initiative: Meeting the Soviet Military Challenge in the 21st Century" *Global Affairs* 1 (Spring 1986) 136-48.

Cigar, Norman. "South Yemen and the U.S.S.R.: Prospects for the Relationship." *The Middle East Journal* 39 (Autumn 1985) 775-95.

Clement, Peter. "Moscow and Southern Africa." *Problems of Communism* 34 (March-April 1985): 29-50.

Cohen, Stephen. *Sovieticus: American Perceptions and Soviet Realities.* New York: Norton, 1985.

Coker, Christopher. *NATO, the Warsaw Pact and Africa.* New York: St. Martin's Press, 1985.

Colton, Timothy J. *The Dilemma of Reform in the Soviet Union* New York: Council on Foreign Relations, 1984.

Conner, Walter D. "Social Policy under Gorbachev." *Problems of Communism* 35 (July-August 1986): 31-46.

Csaba, Laslo. *Problems of Intra-CMEA Cooperation After the Moscow Summit* (Köln: Berichte des Bundesinstituts für ostwissenschaftliche und internationale Studien, 34-1986).

Daniels, Robert V. *Russia: The Roots of Confrontation.* Cambridge, Massachusetts: Harvard University Press, 1985.

Davis, M. Scott and Sloss, Leon. *A Game For High Stakes: Lessons Learned in Negotiating with the Soviet Union.* Cambridge: Ballinger, 1986.

D'Encausse, Helene Carrere. *Ni paix, ni guerre. Le nouvel empire soviétique ou du bon usage de la detente* (Neither Peace nor War. The New Soviet Empire, or Putting Detente to Good Use) Paris: Flammarion, 1986.

Diamond, Douglas B. "Soviet Agricultural Plans for 1981-1985." In *Russia at the Crossroads: The 26th Congress of the CPSU,* edited by Seweryn Bialer and Thane Gustafson. London: Allen & Unwin, 1982.

Douglas, Joseph D., Jr. "The Expanding Threat of Chemical-Biological Warfare: A Case of US Tunnel-Vision." *Strategic Review* (Fall, 1986): 37-45.

Duncan, W. Raymond. "Castro and Gorbachev: Politics of Accommodation." *Problems of Communism* 35 (March-April 1986): 45-57.

Elad, Shlomi, and Ariel Merari. *The Soviet Bloc and World Terrorism.* Tel Aviv: Tel Aviv University, Jaffe Center for Strategic Studies, 1984.

Ellison, Herbert J. "United Front Strategy and Soviet Foreign Policy." *Problems of Communism* 34 (September-October 1985): 45-64.

_____. "Changing Sino-Soviet Relations." *Problems of Communism* (May-June 1987): 17-29.

Ellison, Herbert J., and Jiri Valenta eds. *Grenada and Soviet Cuban Policy.* Boulder, Colo.: Westview Press, 1986.

Erisman, H. Michael. *Cuba's International Relations: The Anatomy of a Nationalistic Foreign Policy.* Boulder, Colo.: Westview, 1985.

Falk, Pamela. *Cuban Foreign Policy: Caribbean Tempest.* Lexington, Mass.: Lexington Books, 1985.

Farrar, John H. "Soviet Strategic Nuclear Thought." *Crossroads* no. 21 (1986): 31-57.

Fitzgerald, Mary C. "Marshall Ogarkov on the Modern Theater Operation." *Naval War College Review* 39 (Autumn 1986): 6-25.

Foreign Agricultural Circular, "Grains: USSR Grain Situation and Outlook," US Department of Agriculture, May 1985.

Freedman, Robert O. "Moscow and a Middle East Peace Settlement." *Washington Quarterly* (Summer 1985): 143-60.

Fremeaux, Philippe, and Christine Durand. *Comprendre l'Economie Sovietique* (Understanding the Soviet economy). Paris: Syros, 1985.

Fukuyama, Francis. *Moscow's Post-Brezhnev Reassessment of the Third World* (Santa Monica, Ca.: Rand Corporation, 1986).

Gaddis, John Lewis. "The Long Peace: Elements of Stability in the Postwar International System." *International Security* 10 (Spring 1986): 99-142.

Garfinkle, Adam M. "Obstacles and Optimism at Geneva." *Orbis* 29 (Summer 1985): 268-80.

Gati, Charles. "The Soviet Empire: Alive But Not Well." *Problems of Communism* 34 (March-April 1985).

Gelman, Harry. "Rise and Fall of Detente." *Problems of Communism* 34 (March-April 1985): 51-72.

Golan,, Galia. "The Soviet Union and the PLO since the War in Lebanon." *Middle East Journal* 40 (Spring 1986): 285-305.

Gonzalez, Edward. "The Cuban and Soviet Challenge in the Caribbean Basin." *Orbis* 29 (Spring 1985): 73-94.

Griffith, William E. "Superpower Problems in Europe: A Comparative Assessment.: *Orbis* 29 (Winter 1986): 735-52.

Grossman, Gregory. "The Brezhnev Era: An Economy at Middle Age." *Problems of Communism,* March-April 1976.

_____. "Notes for a Theory of the Command Economy." *Soviet Studies,* October 1963.

Gustafson, Thane. *Reform in Soviet Politics.* New York: Cambridge University Press, 1981.

Gustafson, Thane and Mann, Dawn. "Gorbachev at the Helm: Building Power and Authority." *Problems of Communism* 35 (May-June 1986): 1-19.

Ha, Joseph M. "The Soviet Policy Toward East Asia: Its Perception on the

Korean Unification." *Asian Perspective* 10 (Spring-Summer 1986) 113-41.

Hamburg, Roger. "Soviet Perspectives on the Cuban, Chilean, and Nicaraguan Revolutions." *Crossroads* 24, 1987 65-76.

Hamm, Manfred K. "The Umbrella Talks." *Washington Quarterly* 8 (Spring 1985): 133-45.

Hardenbergh, Chalmers. "The Other Negotiations." *Bulletin of the Atomic Scientists* (March 1987): 48-9.

Harris, William R. "Arms Control Treaties: How Do They Restrain Soviet Strategic Defense Programs?" *Orbis* 29 (Winter 1986): 701-8.

Hasselkorn, Avigdor. "The Soviet Union and the Radical Entente." *Global Affairs* 1 (Spring 1986): 100-22.

Hasewega, Tsuypshi. "Soviets on Nuclear-War-Fighting." *Problems of Communism* 35 (July-August 1986) 68-79.

Hauner, Milan. "Seizing the Third Parallel: Geopolitics and the Soviet Advance into Central Asia." *Orbis* 29 (Spring 1985): 5-31.

Hewett, Ed A. "Gorbachev's Economic Strategy: A Preliminary Assessment." *Soviet Economy* 1 (October-December 1985): 285-305.

Hoffman, Eric P., and Laird, Robin F. *Technocratic Socialism: The Soviet Union in the Advanced Industrial Era* Durham: Duke University Press, 1985.

———. *The Politics of Economic Modernization in the Soviet Union.* Ithaca, Cornell University Press, 1984.

Hühmann, Hans-Hermann. *Strukturen, Probleme und Perspektiven sowjetischer Wirtschaftspolitik nach dem XXVII Parteitag der KPdSU* (Structures, Problems and Prospects of Soviet Economic Policy following the XXVII Party Congress of the CPSU) (Köln: Berichte des Bundesinstituts für ostwissenschaftliche und internationale Studien 22, 1986).

Holloway, David. *The Soviet Union and the Arms Race.* 2 ed. New Haven: Yale University Press, 1984.

Horelick, Arnold. "U.S.—Soviet Relations: The Return of Arms Control." *Foreign Affairs* 63, 511-37.

Hutchings, Raymond. *The Soviet Budget.* Albany: State University of New York Press, 1983.

Mough, Jerry F. *The Struggle for the Third World: Soviet Debates and American Options.* Washington: Brookings Institution, 1986.

International Institute for Strategic Studies. *The Military Balance, 1985-1986.* London: I.I.S.S., 1985.

———. *The Military Balance, 1986-1987* London: I.I.S.S., 1986.

———. *Strategic Survey, 1984-1985* London: I.I.S.S., 1985.

———. *Strategic Survey, 1985-1986* London: I.I.S.S., 1986.

Ioffe, Olimpiad S. *Soviet Law and Soviet Reality* Dordrecht: Martinus Nijhoff, 1985.

Jamgotch, Niah, Jr., ed. *Sectors of Mutual Benefit in U.S.-Soviet Relations.* Durham: Duke University Press, 1985.

Jokay, Charles Z. "A Lion in Chains" the CPSU and the Soviet Military," *Crossroads* 24 (1987): 51-64.

Johnson, D. Gale, and Karen McConnell Brooks. *Prospects for Soviet Agriculture in the 1980s.* Bloomington: Indiana University Press, 1984.

Johnson, Paul G. "Arms Control and Managing Linkage" *Survival,* 28 (September-October 1986): 431-44.

Jones, Ellen. *Red Army and Society* London and Boston: Allen and Unwin, 1985.

Jones, Ellen and Benjamin L. Woodbury "Chernobyl and Glasnost" *Problems of Communism* 35 (November-Decemaber 1986): 28-39.

Jönsson, Christer. "The Superpower Factor in Soviet Foreign Policy-Making" *Crossroads* 24 (1987): 17-28.

Kanet, Roger E. and Ganguly, Sumit. "Soviet Strategy in Southwest Asia and the Persian Gulf Region." *Crossroads* no. 20 (1986): 1-20.

Kass, Ilana and Burger, Ethan A. "Soviet Responses to the U.S. Strategic Defense Initiative: The ABM Gambit Revisited." *Air University Review* (March-April 1985): 55-64.

Katsenelinboigen, Aron. *Soviet Economic Thought and Political Power in the USSR.* New York: Pergamon Press, 1980.

Katz, Mark N. *Russia and Arabia: Soviet Foreign Policy Toward the Arabian Peninsula* Baltimore: Johns Hopkins University Press, 1986.

Khalidi, Rashid. "Arab Views of the Soviet Role in the Middle East." *The Middle East Journal* 39 (Autumn 1985): 716-32.

Khalilzad, Zalmay. "Moscow's Afghan War." *Problems of Communism* 35 (January-February 1986): 1-20.

Kimura, Hiroshi. "Soviet Focus on the Pacific." *Problems of Communism* 36 (May-June 1987): 1-16.

Kirby, Stuart. "Siberia and the Soviet Far East: Resources for the Future.: Special Report, no. 117. London: The Economist Intelligence Unit, October 1984.

Kitrinos, Robert W. "International Department of the CPSU." *Problems of Communism* 33 (September-October 1984): 47-75.

Klinghoffer, Arthur Jay. "The Angolan War: A Study in Regional Insecurity." *The Jerusalem Journal of International Relations* 8 (June 1986): 142-59.

———. "Soviet-Israeli Relations and a Middle East Settlement." *Crossroads* 23 (1987): 1-13.

Kontorovich, Vladimir. "Discipline and Growth in the Soviet Economy.: *Problems of Communism* 34 (November-December 1985): 18-31.

Kramer, John M. "Soviet-CEMA Energy Ties." *Problems of Communism* 34 (July-August 1985): 32-47.

Kruzel, Joseph. "From Rush-Bagot to START: The Lessons of Arms Control." *Orbis* 30 (Spring 1986): 193-216.

Kushnirsky, Fyodor I. "The Limits of Soviet Economic Reform." *Problems of Communism* 33 (July-August 1984): 33-43.

Kusin, Vladimir V. "Gorbachev and East Europe." *Problems of Communism* 35 (January-February 1986): 39-53.
Leonhard, Wolfgang. *The Kremlin and the West: A Realistic Approach.* (Translated by Houchang Chehabi) New York: Norton, 1986.
Lewis, William H., and Stephen C. Moss. "The Soviet Arms Transfer Program." *Journal of Northeast Asian Studies* (Fall 1984): 3-15.
Linde, Gerd *Libyan—Terroristenbasis und sowjetischer Klient* (Libya—a Base for terrorists and a Soviet client) Köln: Berichte des Bundesinstituts für ostwissenschaftliche und internationale Studien, 25-1986.
Litwack, Robert S, and S. Neil Macfarlane. "Soviet Activism in the Third World." *Survival* 29 (January-February 1987): 21-39.
Luttwak, Edward W. "Delusions of Soviet Weakness." *Commentary* (January 1985): 32-38.
MacFarlane, S. Neil. *Superpower Rivalry and Third World Radicalism: The Idea of National Liberation.* Baltimore: Johns Hopkins University Press, 1985.
_____. "The Soviet Conception of Regional Security." *World Politics* 37 (April 1985): 235-316.
Mackintosh, Malcolm. "The Russian Attitude to Defense and Disarmament." *International Affairs* 61 (Summer 1985): 385-94.
Mastanduno, Michael. "Strategies of Economic Containment: U.S. Trade Relations with the Soviet Union." *World Politics* 37 (July 1985): 503-31.
May, Michael M. "The U.S.-Soviet Approach to Nuclear Weapons." *International Security* (Spring 1985): 140-53.
MccGwire, Michael, "Why the Soviets Want Arms Control," *Technology Review*, Feb/March, 1987, pp 85-94.
_____. *Military Objectives in Soviet Foreign Policy.* Washington, D.C.: The Brookings Institution, 1987.
McConnell, James M.. "Shifts in Soviet Views on the Proper Focus of Military Development." *World Politics* 37 (April 1985): 317-43.
Medvedev, Zhores A. *Gorbachev.* New York and London: Norton, 1986.
Meier, Christian. *Der RGW: Wirtschaftsgemeinschaft oder Instrument sowjetischer Hegemonialpolitik?* Koln: Berichte des Bundesinstituts fur ostwissenschaftliche und internationale Studien, 24-1986.
Miller, Robert F. "The Politics of Policy Implementation in the USSR: Soviet Policies on Agricultural Integration under Brezhnev." *Soviet Studies,* April 1980.
Mitchell, R. Judson and Teresa Gee. "The Soviet Succession Crisis and Its Aftermatth."*Orbis* 29 (Summer 1985): 293-317.
Mitchell, R. Judson. "The CPSU Politburo in 1990: A Projection." *Crossroads* no. 19 (1986): 21-44.
Moreton, Edwina, and Gerald Segal. eds., *Soviet Strategy toward Western Europe* London: Allen & Unwin, 1984.

Murphy, Patrick. "Soviet Shabashniki: Material Incentives at Work." *Problems of Communism* 34 (November-December 1985): 48-57.

Napper, Larry C. "The Arab Autumn of 1984: A Case Study of Soviet Middle East Policy." *The Middle East Journal* 39 (Autumn 1985): 733-44.

Nation, R. Craig and Mark V. Kauppi. eds. *The Soviet Impact on Africa* Lexington, Mass.: Lexington Books, 1984.

Nimitz, Nancy. "Reform and Technological Innovation in the Eleventh Five-Year Plan." In *Russia at the Crossroads: The 26th Congress of the CPSU,* edited by Seweryn Bialer and Thane Gustafson. London: Allen & Unwin, 1982.

Noorzoy, M. Siddieq. "Soviet Economic Interests in Afghanistan," *Problems of Communism* 36 (May-June 1987): 43-54.

Nove, Alec. *The Economics of Feasible Socialism.* London: Allen & Unwin, 1983.

Odom, William E. "Soviet Force Posture: Dilemmas and Directions." *Problems of Communism* 34 (July-August 1985): 1-14.

Ogarkov, N.V. *Istoriya uchit bditelnosti* (History teaches vigilence). Moscow: Voyenizdat, 1985.

Paarlberg, R. L. *Food Trade and Foreign Policy.* Ithaca and London: Cornell University Press, 1985.

Page, Stephen. *The Soviet Union and the Yemens: Influence in Assymetrical Relationships.* New York: Praeger, 1985.

Papp, Daniel S. *Soviet Perceptions of the Developing World in the 1980s: The Ideological Basis.* Lexington, Mass.: Heath, 1985.

Payne, Keith B. "The Soviet Union and Strategic Defense: The Failure and Future of Arms Control." *Orbis* 29 (Winter 1986): 673-88.

Payne, Keith B. *Strategic Defense: "Star Wars" in Perspective.* Lanham, Md.: Hamilton Press, 1986.

Pipes, Richard. *Survival Is Not Enough: Soviet Realities and America's Future.* New York: Simon & Schuster, 1984.

Platt, Alan. "Soviet-West European Relations." Report. Santa Monica; Calif.: Rand Corporation, March 1986.

Poljanski, Nikolai and Alexander Rahr. *Gorbatschjow: Der Neue Mann* (Gorbachev: The new man. Munich: Verlag Universitas, 1986.

Pollock, David. Moscow and Aden: Coping with a Coup." *Problems of Communism* 35 (May-June 1986) 50-70.

Porket, J. L. "Unemployment in the Midst of Labour Waste." *Survey* 29, 1 (Spring 1985): 19-28.

Prybyla, Jann S. "The Dawn of Real Communism: Problems of COMECON." *Orbis* 29 (Summer 1985): 387-402.

Ramet, Pedro. "The Soviet-Syrian Relationship." *Problems of Communism* 35 (September-October 1986): 35-46.

Rivkin, David B., Jr. "What Does Moscow Think? *Foreign Policy,* no. 59, (Summer 1985): 85-105.

Rostow, Eugene V. "Why the Soviets Want an Arms Control Agreement and Why They Want it Now." *Commentary* (February 1987): 19-26.

Rubinstein, Alvin Z. "The Changing Strategic Balance and Soviet Third World Risk-Taking." *Naval War College Review* 38 (March-April 1985): 5-17.

Rubenstein, Joshua. *Soviet Dissidents: Their Struggle for Human Rights*, 2 ed. Boston: Beacon Press, 1985.

Rumer, Boris. "Realities of Gorbachev's Economic Program." *Problems of Communism* 35 (May-June 1986): 20-31.

_____. "Structural Imbalance in the Soviet Economy." *Problems of Communism* 43 (July-August 1984): 24-32.

Ryavec, Karl. *Implementation of Soviet Economic Reforms*. New York: Praeger, 1976.

Rywkin, Michael. "Reading Soviet Signals." *American Foreign Policy Newsletter* 8 (April 1985): 1-7.

Schlesinger, James. "The Eagle and the Bear: Ruminatimons on Forty Years of Superpower Relations." *Foreign Affairs* (Summer 1985): 937-61.

Schmidt-Häuer, Christian. *Gorbachev: The Path to Power*. London: I. B. Tauris, 1986.

Schroeder, Gertrude E. "The Slowdown in Soviet Industry, 1976-1982." *Soviet Economy* 1 (January-March 1985): 42-74.

Shevchenko, Arkady N. *Breaking With Moscow*. New York: Knopf, 1985.

Shultz, Richard H., and Roy Godson. *Dezinformatsia: Active Measures in Soviet Strategy*. Washington: Pergammon-Brassey's, 1984.

Simes, Dimitrik. "Are the Soviets Interested in Arms Control?" *Washington Quarterly* 8 (Spring 1985): 147-56.

Skaggs, David C. "MR Update: MBFR." *Military Review* (February 1987): 85-94.

Smits, William H., Jr. "Significance of the Question of High-Technology Transfer to the Soviet Union and Soviet-Bloc States." *Technology in Society* 8, (1986): 157-170.

Spaulding, Wallace. "Communist Fronts in 1985." *Problems of Communism* 35 (March-April 1986): 72-78.

_____. "Shifts in CPSU ID." *Problems of Communism* 35 (July-August 1986): 80-86.

Steinbrunner, John. "Arms Control or Compromise." *Foreign Affairs* (Summer 1985): 1036-47.

Stent, Angela E., ed. *Economic Relations with the Soviet Union: American and West German Perspectives*. Boulder, Colo.: Westview Press, 1985.

Stevens, Sayre. "The Soviet Factor in SDI". *Orbis* 29 (Winter 1986): 689-700.

Strode, Rebecca. "The Soviet Armed Forces: Adaptation to Resource Scarcity." *The Washington Quarterly* 9 (Spring 1986): 55-69.

Stubbs, Eric. "Soviet Strategic Defense Technology." *Bulletin of the Atomic Scientists* (April 1987): 14-19.

Thomas, John R. *Natural Resources in Soviet Foreign Policy* New York: National Strategy Information Center, 1985.

Thornton, Richard C. "Is Detente Inevitable?" East Asia Forum Series. Washington; D.C.: The Washington Institute for Values in Public Policy, 1985.

Thornton, Judith. "'Chernobyl' and Soviet Energy." *Problems of Communism* 35 (November-December 1986): 1-16.

Timmermann, Heinz. *Gorbatschows aussenpolitische Leitlinien: Die internationalen Beziehungen Moskaus auf dem 27 Parteitag der KPdSU* (Gorbachev's foreign policy program: Moscow's international relations at the 27th Party Congress of the CPSU). Koln: Berichte des Bundesinstituts fur ostwissenschaftliche und internationale Studien, 13-1986.

Trump, Thomas M. "The Membership Dilemma of the CPSU: Impact on the Party Congress." *Crossroads* 24 (1987): 1-16

U.S. Arms Control and Disarmament Agency. *World Military Expenditures and Arms Transfers 1986.* Washington, DC: U.S. Government Printing Office, 1987.

U.S. Department of Agriculture. "Grains: USSR Grain Situation and Outlook." Foreign Agriculture Circular. Washington, D.C., May 1985.

U.S. Department of Defense. *Soviet Military Power, 1986.* Washington: U.S. Govenment Printing Office, 1986.

_____. *Soviet Military Power, 1987* Washington: U.S. Government Printing Office, 1987.

Urban, Joan Barth, *Moscow and the Italian Communist Party* Ithaca: Cornell University Press, 1986.

Valenta, Jiri. "Nicaragua: Soviet-Cuban Pawn or Non-Aligned Country?" *Journal of Interamerican Studies and World Affairs* (Fall, 1985).

Valenta, Jiri and William Potters, eds. *Soviet Decisionmaking for National Security.* London and Boston: Allen and Unwin, 1984.

Valenta, Jiri and Virginia Valenta. "Soviet Strategy and Politics in the Caribbean Basin." in Howard J. Wiarda, ed. *Rift and revolution: The Central American Imbroglio.* Washington and London: The American Enterprise Institute for Public Policy Research, 1984, 197-252.

_____. "Sandinistas in Power." *Problems of Communism* 34 (September-October 1985) 1-28.

Valkenier, Elizabeth K. "Revolutionary Change in the Third World: Recent Soviet Reassessments." *World Politics* (April 1986): 415-434.

van der Kroef, Justus M. "The East-West Conflict and the Cambodian Problem. *Crossroads* 18 (1985) 1-21.

Vigor, Peter. "The Soviet View of Geopolitics." in C. E. Zappo and C. Zorgibe, eds. *On Geopolitics: Classical and Nuclear.* Dordrecht: M. N. Nijhoff, 1985. 131-38.

Voslenskiy, Mikhail. *Nomenklatura: gospodstvuyushchiy klass sovetskogo soyusa* (The Nomenclature: ruling class of the Soviet Union). London: Overseas Publication Interchange, 1985.

Weinstein, John M. "Nonmilitary Threats to Soviet National Security." *Naval War College Review* 38 (July-August 1985): 28-40.

Wettig, Gerhard. *"Friedliche Koexistenz" und "Gemeinsame Sicherheit" in Sowjetischer Darstellung* (Peaceful Coexistence and Mutual Security from the Soviet Viewpoint). Koln: Berichte des Bundesinstituts fur ostwissenachaftliche und internationale Studien, 34, 1986..

Wettig, Gerhard. *A New Soviet Approach to Arms Control.* Koln: Berichte des Bundesinstituts fųr ostwissenschaftliche und internationale Studien, 2, 1987.

White, Stephan. "Propagating Communist Values in the USSR." *Problems of Communism* 34 (November-December 1985): 1-17.

Willis, David K. *Klass: How the Russians Really Live.* New York: St. Martins, 1985.

Wohlstetter, Alfred. "Between an Un Free World and None: Increasing ouf Choices." *Foreign Affairs* (Summer 1985) 962-94.

Yost, David S. "Soviet Ballistic Missile Defense and NATO." *Orbis* 29 (Summer 1985): 281-292.

Zemtsov, Ilya. *Policy Dilemmas and the Struggle for Power in the Kremlin, I. The Andropov Period.* Fairfax: Hero Books, 1985.

_____. *Lexicon of Soviet Political Terms.* Fairfax: Hero Books, 1985.

Glossary of Abbreviations, Acronyms, and Soviet Terms

ABM	Anti-Ballistic-Missile (Adjective, as in ABM Treaty, ABM defense).
ACDA	Arms Control and Disarmament Agency (US Cabinet level agency).
ACTIV	(Russian). The most active members, as in "partianiy aktiv" the more active members of the Party organization.
ADD	Air Defense District (from the English translation of Okrug protivovozdushnoi oboroni). The U.S.S.R. is divided into five air defense districts for air defense command and control.
ADP	Automatic Data Processing.
ALCM	Air Launched Cruise Missile.
ANC	African National Congress (Black nationalist political movement in South Africa—outlawed by the government).
Apparat	(Russian). Meaning the State machinery, the organization and the people in official positions, the bureaucracy.
ASAT	Anti-Satellite (Adjective as in ASAT weapon, ASAT treaty, ASAT negotiations).
ASSR	(Russian) Avtonomnaya Sovetskaya Sotsialisticheskaya Respublika (Autonomous Soviet Socialist Republic).
BAM	(Russian). Baikal-Amur-Magistral. The railline built parallel to, and north of, the Trans-Siberian railway.
BENELUX	Belgium, Netherlands and Luxemburg (Adjective, as in BENELUX nations).
CBM	Confidence Building Measure. A treaty provision designed to increase mutual confidence or provide information rather than reduce or limit forces.
CC	Central Committee (from English translation of Russian Tsentralny Komitet) (Theoretically the top Party organization, the CC elects a Politburo and a Secretariat to act for it when not in full session—they are the top political organizations in the U.S.S.R.).
CD	Committee on Disarmament (40 nation permanent committee under UN auspices which meets twice a year in Geneva)
CDU	Christian Democratic Union. West German right-center party.
CEMA	Council for Economic Mutual Assistance (from English

Translation of Russian Sovyet Ekonomicheskoi Vzaimopomoshchly). (Soviet-Eastern European economic union, which also includes Cuba, Mongolia and Vietnam as full members, and several other states as observers. Yugoslavia is a special observer case in that it participates in virtually all of the CEMA commissions. Often called CMEA or COMECON.

CinC
Commander in Chief. Used in military terminology for the commanders of very major formations or commands, usually above army group or front level (although the commander of GSFG is a CinC). In the U.S.S.R. the service chiefs are CinCs, such as CinC Navy; in the United States they are chiefs of staff of the army and air force of the chief of naval operations for the navy.

COCOM
Coordinating Committee. Committee established by the United States and NATO, plus Japan, to regulate the transfer of strategic technology to the U.S.S.R.

COL GEN
Abbreviation for colonel general. In the Soviet army and air forces a colonel general ranks between a lieutenant general and a general; Equivalent to a U.S. lieutenant general.

CP
Communist Party.

CPSU
Communist Party of the Soviet Union.

CSCBMDE
Conference on Security and Confidence Building Measures and Disarmament in Europe. (Military and security follow-on to CSCE that has been meeting in Stockholm. European nations (NATO, Warsaw Pact and nonaligned) plus the United States and Canada participate.

CSCE
Conference for Security and Cooperation in Europe. Originally convened in Helsinki with the participation of all European states plus the United States and Canada, the CSCE agreed to a treaty addressing European borders and security and cooperation measure relating to human rights; economic, cultural, and scientific cooperation; and the notification of large military exercises. The CSCE holds regular review conferences. The CSCBMDE is an outgrowth of CSCE.

CSSR
Czechoslovak Socialist Republic.

CTB
Comprehensive Test Ban. Properly an adjective, as in CBT treaty or CTB negotiations, but sometimes used in place of CTBT; refers to nuclear weapons testing.

CTBT
Comprehensive Test Ban Treaty (see above).

CW
Chemical Weapons or Chemical Warfare.

DFLP
Democratic Front for the Liberation of Palestine. One of the several Palestinian liberation organizations ostensibly under the PLO but actually competing for leadership.

EDI
European Defense Initiative. West European independent equivalent of the U.S. Strategic Defense Initiative. Proposed by France; wider advanced technology goals than simply missile defense but also including such defense.

EEC
European Economic Community. Economic union of Western European states.

FBS	Forward Based Systems. Refers to U.S. theater aircraft and missile systems based in Europe or elsewhere on the periphery of the USSR that could deliver nuclear weapons to targets on Soviet territory.
FDP	Free Democratic Party. West German right-of-center (liberal) political party.
FRG	Federal Republic of Germany; West Germany.
GATT	General Agreement on Tariffs and Trade.
GDR	German Democratic Republic. East Germany; DDR in German abbreviations.
GKES	Russian. Gosudarstyenniy Komitet po Vneshnim Ekonomicheskim Svyazam. State Committee for (Foreign) Economic Relations.
glasnost	Russian. Openness; the slogan of Gorbachev's campaign for frankness and truthfulness in reporting.
glavnokoman-duyushchiy	Russian. Chief of main commander, i.e. CinC.
GLCM	Ground-launched cruise missile.
GNP	Gross national product. A measure of the total value of a nation's economy, including production and service.
GOSAGROPROM	Russian. Gosudarstvenniy Komitet Agro-Promyshlennosti. State Committee for Agrocultural Industry.
GOSPLAN	Russian. Gosudarstvenniy Planoviy Komitet. State Planning Committee.
GOSSTROI	Russian. Gosudarstvenniy Komitet po delam Stroitelstva. State Committee for Construction.
GS	General Staff.
GSFG	Group of Soviet Force in Germany.
IAEC	International Atomic Energy Commission.
ICBM	Intercontinental ballistic missile.
INF	Intermediate nuclear forces. Theater-range nuclear weapons, usually considered as having less than intercontinental range but over 1,000kkm range. Normally used as an adjective, as in INF weapon, INF negotiation, INF Treaty.
IO	Indian Ocean. During the Carter administration, the United States and USSR engaged in negotiations to restrict military force levels in the Indian Ocean.
KGB	Russian. Komitet Gosudarstvennoy Bezopasnosti. Committee of State Security; the Soviet secret police.
Khozraschet	Russian. Self-supporting; operating on a profit-and-loss basis; not financed by the stae.
kolkhoz	Russian. Collective farm.
kolkhoznik	Russian. A worker (member) in a collective farm.
KOMSOMOL	Russian. Kommunisticheskiy Soyuz Molodezhi. Young Communist League; youth organization of the Party.
Kraikom	Russian. Krayevoy komitet. Territorial committee of the CP.
kto kogo	Russian. Who-whom. Originally coined by Lenin in regard to the question of who would win a Party struggle; it has become commonly used to refer to the idea of who has power over whom.

LTBT	Limited Test Ban Treaty. Nuclear testing limitation treaty between the United States and USSR that prohibited nuclear weapons tests in the atmosphere.
LTG	Abbreviation for lieutenant general. A U.S. lt. general is equivalent to a Soviet col. general; a Soviet lt. general is the same as a U.S. major general.
MBFR	Mutual and Balanced Force Reductions. Negotiation about conventional-force reductions in the so-called NATO guidelines area of Europe (West Germany and the Benelux, Poland, the GDR, and Czechoslovakia) that has been under way since the early 1970s between NATO (less France) and the Warsaw Pact.
MD	Military district. From English translation of Russian Voyenniy Okrog. The USSR is divided administratively into sixteen MDs, each of which controls all mobilization and other military activities within a geographical region, and many of which would form "fronts" (army groups) during wartime.
MFA	Ministry of Foreign Affairs.
MG	Abbreviation for major general; general major, in Russian. A U.S. major general is equivalent to a Soviet lt. general; a Soviet major general is the same as a U.S. brigadier general.
MIRV	Multiple independent reentry vehicle. A MIRVed ballistic missile splits en route into separate missiles, each following its own path to its own target.
MPA	Main political administration of the Soviet armed forces. (From English translation of Russian *Glavnove Politicheskoye Upravleniye.*
MPLA	From Portuguese. In English, the Popular Movement for the Liberation of Angola. The MPLA is the ruling party in the country.
NATO	North Atlantic Treaty Organization. Political and military organization of fourteen European states, the United States, and Canada. France belongs to NATO politically but is not part of the unified military structure.
NEP	Russian. Novaya Ekonomicheskaya Politika (New Economic Policy). Temporary economic liberalization instituted by Lenin in the 1920s to salvage a collapsed economy. The NEP allowed a considerable amount of small capitalism and market economics, retaining only the "commanding heights" as state or socialist economy.
nomenklatura	Russian. A table of ranks that defines precisely the place of an official in Soviet society. Also used—as here—as the body of individuals on that listing. In effect, the wider Soviet political elite.
NPT	Non-Proliferation Treaty. Treaty signed by most of the states of the world to prevent the spread of nuclear weapons. Currently, the idea of a chemical nonproliferation treaty to prevent the spread of chemical weapons is under consideration.

NSA	Negative security assurances. The idea that a nuclear weapons state will guarantee a non-nuclear weapons state that it will not attack it with nuclear weapons in return for certain conditions, e.g. nonalignment or not allowing nuclear weapons of a third state to be deployed on its territory. The Soviets have pushed this idea.
NSWP	Non-Soviet Warsaw Pact. Adjective, as in NSWP states, i.e. the six Eastern European states belonging to the Warsaw Pact along with the Soviet Union.
NTM	National technical means. The technical intelligence collection means owned by one state in an arms control treaty whereby that state verifies compliance by the other party to the treaty. Usually implied to mean satellite collectors of photographic, electronic, and other intelligence data.
NWS	Nuclear weapons state(s). A nation possessing nuclear weapons, as opposed to a non-nuclear weapons state.
Obkom	Russian. *Oblastnoy komitet.* Province committee of the CP.
ochkovtiratelstvo	Russian. Eyewash; a facade or phony characterization of reality.
OPEC	Organization of Petroleum Exporting Countries. A cartel formed by several major oil-exporting nations to control (and maximize) prices for both political and economic purposes. The USSR does not belong to OPEC. However, the USSR generally supports OPEC verbally while normally undercutting its prices slightly in order to insure its own market. The Soviet Union is the world's largest producer of petroleum products.
OSI	On-site-inspection. The right of one party in an arms control or security treaty to conduct verification inspections "on-site" in the other's territory. A mandatory OSI is one that the inspected or challenged state cannot refuse without violating the treaty.
P2	Pershing 2. A U.S. intermediate-range ballistic missile system.
PDRY	Peoples' Democratic Republic of Yemen. South Yemen.
PFLP	Popular Front for the Liberation of Palestine. One of several Palestinian liberation organizations; see also DFLP.
PLO	Palestine Liberation Organaization. In theory, and formally, the unbrella organization uniting almost all the various Palestinian liberation groups. In fact, the major such group currently headed by Yasir Arafat.
PNET	Peaceful Nuclear Explosions Treaty. Treaty between the United States and USSR (the United States never ratified it) regulating and limiting the size of nuclear explosions for nonmilitary purposes.
PRC	Peoples' Republic of China. Communist, or mainland, China.
PVO	Russian. *Protivo-Vozdushnaya Oborona* Antiair defense. Usually refers to PVO troops or PVO of the country. PVO *strany* is the national air defense command, a separate serv-

ice that is one of five Soviet armed forces. It can also refer to PVO *voisk* (troops), meaning the tactical air defense elements of ground formations. PVO *strany* includes aircraft interceptor units, surface-to-air missiles, and radar means. It also includes the ABM and space defense forces.

RSFSR   Russian. Rossiskaya Sovetskaya Federativnaya Sotsialisticheskay Respublika (Russian Soviet Federated Socialist Republic). The largest of the union republics making up the Soviet Union, consisting of the Great Russian homeland territories plus much of Siberia.

SA-   Surface-to-air (missile), as in SA-5 or SA-8. Various models of Soviet surface-to-air defensive missiles.

SAIQA   Another of the Palestinian liberation groups. *Saiqa* was formed and is controlled by Syria.

SALT   Strategic Arms Limitation Treaty. Usually an adjective, as in SALT talks or SALT negotiations, but can be a noun. SALT I was signed and ratified between the United States and USSR. SALT II was signed but never ratified; it has technically expired.

SAM   Surface-to-air missile.

SCC   Standing Consultative Commission. Soviet-U.S. commission established by the ABM/SALT I treaty; meets twice a year to address questions arising from the strategic arms agreements.

SDI   Strategic Defense Initiative. U.S. program of strategic missile and space defenses, referred to popularly and by detractors as "star wars."

spetsnaz   Russian. *Voiska Spetsialnogo Naznacheniya* (troops of special designation). Forces trained to operate behind enemy lines in raids, sabotage, communications, and so on. Often confused with either commandos or U.S.-type special forces, *spetsnaz* troops combine some of the functions of both, plus that of long-range reconnaisance elements similar to those of the U.S. Marine Corps.

SDP   Social Democrat Party. British centrist political party formed as a break-away party from the Labour Party in protest over its leftward radicalization.

SLBM   Submarine-launched ballistic missile.

SLCM   Submarine- (or sea-) launched cruise missile.

socialist realism   Artistic style fostered in the USSR, especially under Stalin, to accentuate only positive political values—applies to art such as painting, sculpture, and so on, as well as to creative writing.

SPD   Socialist Party (of) Democrats or Social Democrat Party. West German leftist political party.

SRF   Strategic Rocket Forces. (From English translation of Russian, *Raketniye Voiska Strategicheskogo Naznacheniya.* One of five services in the Soviet armed forces, consisting of strategic and intermediate-range missile forces.

SS-   Surface-to-surface (missile), as in SS-20 or SS-18, variants of Soviet surface-to-surface ballistic missiles.

SSBN	Subsurface Ballistic Missile. Adjective or acronym for the class of nuclear-powered submarines armed with ballistic missiles.
SSM	Surface-to-surface missile (see above).
SSOD	Russian. Soyuz Sovetskikh Obshestv Druzhby (Union of Soviet Societies of Friendship).
SS-X-	Surface-to-surface experimental (missile). (See above.) A surface-to-surface missile still in development and test process and not yet operationally deployed. The same nomenclature system (-X-) is used the same way for surface-to-air missiles and so on.
stakhanovite	Russian. One who works extra diligently for ideological or patriotic reasons. Coined after the name of Stakhanov, a worker-hero of the Stalin era who became the state-designated model for other workers to overachieve.
START	Strategic Arms Reductions Treaty. Adjective, as in START negotiations. Coined by the Reagan administrataion to differentiate its strategic arms negotiations from past "flawed" ones, i.e. SALT.
SWAPO	Southwest African Peoples' Organization. Liberation organization seeking independence in Namibia.
subbotnik	Russian. A day given freely to the state for extra work without any pay. *Subbotniki* have become a state-inspired Soviet tradition.
TTBT	Threshold Test Ban Treaty. Treaty between the United States and USSR banning nuclear weapons tests in excess of 150kt equivalent explosive power.
TVD	Russian. *Teatr Voennykh Deistviy* (theater of military operations). An integrated geographical area of military operations combined into a senior command and consisting of several "fronts" (army groups) and/or fleets.
UAE	United Arab Emirates.
UK	United Kingdom (England, Scotland, Wales, and Northern Ireland).
UN	United Nations.
UNGA	United Nations General Assembly.
UNITA	From Portuguese. In English, the National Union for the Total Independence of Angola. UNITA is the antigovernment rebel movement led by Jonas Savimbi.
VADM	Abbreviation for vice-admiral.
vozhd	Russian. Leader, chief. Often, and in this book, used in the connotation of the supreme national leader.
WP	Warsaw Pact. The unified military alliance headed by the USSR, and including also Bulgaria, the CSSR, the GDR, Hungary, Romania, and Poland.
YAR	Yemen Arab Republic (North Yemen).

Index

Abe, Shintaro, 117, 133
Adamshin, Anatoliy, 305, also Appendix III
Afanasyev, Viktor, 11
Afghanistan war: and arms control, 143; conduct of, 245, 246-47, 248, 274-306 (Third World chronology); and foreign policy, 108, 118, 256, 270-71, 364; future prospects of, 256-57, 378; and the military, 110, 365; 1986 partial troop withdrawal, 202, 255-56. *See also* Military assistance
agriculture: major Gorbachev speech, 27; state of, 13, 29, 54, 57-9; workers' living conditions, 16. *See also* Economy, reforms of; GOSAGROPROM; Politburo and Central Committee decrees and meetings (Appendix II)
Akhromeev, Sergei, General, 134, 157, 174, 203, 344
alcoholism, 13, 86, 87; Campaign against, 21, 32, 51, 85-7, 93-4, 356; as rationale for purges, 86-7. *See also* drugs; Glasnost; personnel changes (purges); Politburo and Central Committeee meeetings (Appendix II); social reforms
Alfonsin, Raul, 295
Aliev, Gaider, 12, 29, 37, 40, 41, 46; and East-European relations, 127, 255; future prospects, 374; and Third World relations, 276, 280, 283, 293, 296
Alkhimov, V.S., 276, also Appendix I
Andreotti, Guilio, 127, 137
Andropov, Yuriy, x, 1; and the armed forces, 324; as Gorbachev's patron and model, 7, 8, 9, 10, 12, 32, 34, 86, 93, 380
Angola civil war: conduct of, 246-57, 267, 268, 277, 278, 282, 286, 291, 292, 294, 295, 305; coordination of efforts, 283, 300; and foreign policy, 248, 280. *See also* Foreign policy, sub-Saharan Africa; military assistance

annual state plan, see economy, performance of
Antonov, Aleksei, 41, 222, 374
Aquino, Corazon, 254, 287
Arafat, Yasser, 261, 281, 287
Arbatov, Georgiy, 111, 178
Aristov, Boris, 42, 137, 221, 290, also Appendices I and III
Arkhipov, Vladimir, 41, 374; and PRC relations, 232, 233, 237, 238, 240; and Third World relations, 274, 277, 287, 290, 291
armed forces: and glasnost, 322; and Gorbachev's policies, 38, 114, 164, 172, 181-83, 325-27, 329-30, 332, 343-44, 359, 375; political influence and relationship with the CPSU, 47, 317-20, 324-35, 334-35, 380; representation on the Central Committee, 323; restructuring of, 329-30. *See also* Afghanistan war; Angola civil war; arms control; Defense Council; Defense expenditures; East-West military balance; Military assistance; Military doctrine; Military science; personnel changes (purges), and the armed forces; Space, militarization of; space program, Soviet; Strategic Defense Initiative (SDI); Warsaw Pact
arms control, 111-112, 118, 119, 123-24, 129, 131, 142-208, 348; and the armed forces, 114, 164, 172, 181-83, 326-27, 343-44, 359; chemical weapons negotiations, 143, 160-61, 162, 191; Conference on Disarmament, 143, 160; conventional forces negotiations, 143, 156-60, 162, 190-91; intermediate nuclear forces negotiations (INF), 124, 138, 143, 144-45, 150, 151-52, 162, 165, 167, 168-69, 176, 185-86, 188-90, 192; nuclear crisis centers, 138, 162, 190; nuclear test negotiations, 143, 154-56, 162, 175, 191; policymaking structure, 148; short-range

Council for Economic Mutual Assistance (CEMA): long-term integration of, 51, 54, 124, 211-13, 216, 217, 220-21, 222, 223, 224-25, 227, 229, 357; multilateral agreements, 223, 227, 230; with non-members, 212, 219, 221, 223; relations with the EEC, 62, 127, 134, 137; structure and functioning, 209, 210, 219, 222, 253, 272. *See also* economy, reforms of; foreign economic relations; foreign policy, East Europe; Warsaw Pact

Council of Ministers: decrees and meetings, 21-30 (internal chronology), also Appendix II; membership, 41. *See also* personnel changes (purges)

CPSU (Communist Party of the Soviet Union): XXVII Congress, 24, 36-7, 41, 54, 55, 95-6, 131, 199, 224, 238, 284, 323; general composition of 36; role in economic management, 51, 73, 81. *See also* armed forces, political influence and relationship with the CPSU; Central Committee of the CPSU; KGB, political influence and relationship with the CPSU; Party Control Commission; Party Program; Party Regulations (ustav); personnel changes (purges); Politburo; political dynamics

Craxi, Bettino, 127, 132

Cunhal, Alvaro, 128, 132, 135

Cuellar, Perez De, 139, 201

Danilof, Nicholas, 122, 134, 135, 162, 171, 172. *See also* Reykjavik summit

Dascelescu, Konstantin, 219

Defense Council: function of 335; Gorbachev as chairman, 22

defense expenditures, 71, 317, 326, 329-34, 358-59, 365. *See also* armed forces; defense industry; economy, reforms of; military assistance; military doctrine; Strategic Defense Initiative (SDI)

defense industry: described, 14, 71-2, 315-16, 326, 365; management of, 29, 33-4, 319; need to reform, 71, 113, 182-83, 329. *See also* armed forces, political influence and relationship with the CPSU; defense expenditures; economy, reforms of; military doctrine; political dynamics; science

and technology; space program, Soviet; Strategic Defense Initiative (SDI)

Demichev, Pyotr, 25, 40, 375; and PRC relations, 239, 242; and Third World relations, 286, 293, 303, also Appendix I

Democratic centralism, 44, 65, 75, 318, 319. *See also* political dynamics

Deng Xiaoping, 234, 240

dissidents and emigration, 89-91, 123, 172, 360, 373-74, 375-76. *See also* Glasnost; legal system; nationalities policies; social reforms

Dobrynin, Anatoly, 24, 37, 39, 40, 41-2, 94; and East-West relations, 111, 133, 137, 174, 178; and East-European relations, 227; and Third World relations, 288, 291, 297, 304. *See also* foreign policy formulation and decisionmaking

Dolgikh, Vladimir, 29, 40

Dos Santos, Jose Eduardo, 267, 288, 296

drugs, 87. *See also* alcoholism; corruption in the USSR; Glasnost; social reforms

Dumas, Roland, 128

East-West military balance, 106, 157, 182, 185-86, 210. *See also* arms control; correlation of forces; military doctrine; Strategic Defense Initiative; Warsaw Pact

economy, 13-14, 16, 49-84, 353, 355-60, 370-72, 377-82; management of, 14, 44-5, 50, 75; performance of, 13-4, 16, 23, 25, 27, 29, 54-5, 57-8, 59-61, 66-7, 76-9; reforms of: compared to GDR, 52, 73; compared to Hungary, 52, 81, 356-7; compared to NEP, 67-8; described 49-70; evaluated, 70-81, 353, 355-60, 365, 370, 371-72; projections for, 377, 378-79, 381-82; Politburo and Central Committee discussions of and decrees on, 21-30 (Internal Chronology), also Appendix II. *See also* agriculture; central planning system; Council for Economic Mutual Assistance (CEMA); Council of Ministers; CPSU, role in economic management; defense expenditures, defense industry; foreign economic relations; GOSAGROPROM; GOSSTROI; New Economic Policy (NEP); personnel changes, in the state bureaucracy; resistance to Gorbachev

USSR; Council of Ministers; CPSU; Defense Council; Democratic centralism; economy, management of; election reforms; foreign policy, formulation and decisionmaking, KGB, political influence and relationship with the CPSU; localism (mestnichestvo); local Soviets; nationalities policy; personnel changes (purges); resistance to Gorbachev and his policies; Supreme Soviet
Polyakov, Vladimir, 242
Ponomarev, Boris, 15, 24, 37, 39, 40, 41-2, 129, 222, 272, 281, 283
Pope John Paul, 108

Qaddafi, Muammar, 118, 259, 260, 266, 278, 279, 286, 287, 293, 300
Qian Qichen, 242

Ramadan, Taha Yasin, 287
Ratsiraka, Didier, 278, 294, 296, 302
Ratushinskaya, Irina, 172
Rau, Johannes, 129, 133
Razumovskiy, Georgiy, 24, 37, 40, 224
Reagan, Ronald: and general US-Soviet relations, 14, 108-09, 110, 163, 172, 179; and Geneva summit, 113, 128, 129, 198, 211, 222; and Reykjavik summit, 122, 123-24, 134-35, 161, 164, 165, 166-68, 170-71, 172-73, 175, 177-78, 184, 185, 186, 187, 204, 372-73; Soviet press coverage of, 121-22, 131, 162, 170-71, 201, 203; trip to the Philippines, 287. *See also* foreign policy, East-West relations; Reykjavik; Strategic Defense Initiative (SDI)
resistance to Gorbachev and his policies: bureaucratic, 25, 26, 28, 29, 30, 38, 55, 56, 67, 70, 83-4, 327; false reporting and "eye wash," 26, 66-7, 97; Intelligentsia, 360-61; leadership, 28, 39, 46, 82-3, 114, 120, 165, 172, 360, 361-62, 373, 375; popular, 28, 361; systemic, 367. *See also* armed forces, and Gorbachev; dissidents and emigration; Glasnost; KGB, and Gorbachev; localism (mestnichestvo); personnel changes (purges); political dynamics
Rykjavik summit, 94, 122, 123, 135, 158, 161, 162, 164-65, 166-88, 192, 204, 226,

372-3, 376. *See also* Arms control; Foreign policy, East-West relations; Reagan, Ronald; Strategic Defense Initiative (SDI)
Reznichenko, V., Major General: criticized, 327
Rogachev, Igor, 234, 241, 304, also Appendix III
Romanov, Grigoriy, 7, 12-3, 22, 32-3, 40, 148, 219, 352
Rusakov, Konstantin, 24, 36, 40, 221
Rust, Mathias, 47, 323, 324, 325
Ryabov, Yacov, 41, 126, 254, 279, 281, 286, also Appendix I, III
Ryzhkov, Nikolai: and East-West relations, 115, 131, 132, 133, 134, 135, 137, 138; and East-European relations, 220, 221, 222, 224, 225, 228, 229; and internal politics and economic affairs, 22, 23, 25, 28, 30, 40, 53, 54, 55; and PRC relations, 242, 243; and Third World relations, 254, 277, 281, 285, 287, 290, 291, 292, 293, 297, 299, 302, also Appendix I

Sakharov, Andrei, 89, 360, 373, 374
SALT I/ABM Treaties, 149, 150
Sankar, Thomas, 295
Savimbi, Jonas, 267
Schmidt, H., 127
science and technology, 24, 26, 59, 182. *See also* defense industry, need to reform; economy, reforms of; space program, Soviet; Strategic Defense Initiative (SDI), Soviet equivalent of; technology acquisition and transfer
Shabanov, Vitaliy, General, 171, 176, 229, 332-33, 341, 343-44
Shamshin, Vasiliy, 292, also Appendix I
Shcharansky, Anatoliy, 89
Shcherbitskiy, Vladimir, 12, 29, 37, 40, 46, 82, 92, 374-75
Shcherbina, Boris, 41, 374
Shevardnadze, Eduard: appointed Foreign Minister, 22, 39, also Appendix I and III; background, 33, 82, compared to Litvinov, 94; and East-West relations, 117, 122, 128, 129, 131, 133, 134, 138, 148, 161, 170, 175, 197, 202, 204; and East-European relations, 221, 223, 224, 225, 227, 229; and PRC relations, 237, 239,

This index has been prepared only for the body of the book. Names and subjects appearing only in the appendices have not been indexed, nor have specific page references in the appendices been listed for names and subjects found in the body of the book. Similarly, names in the tables in chapters 2 and 12 have only been indexed if they appear elsewhere in the text. Names appearing in the several chronologies have been indexed by page; but, for the most part, subject references index entries simply refer the reader to one or more chronologies as appropriate.